ASHEVILLE-BUNCOMBE TECHNICAL INSTITUTE NORTH CAROLINA
STATE BOARD OF EDUCATION
DEPT. OF COMMUNITY COLLEGE

Y0-CUH-505

DISCARDED

AUG 6 2025

GOD'S GOLD

God's Gold

THE STORY OF ROCKEFELLER AND HIS TIMES

BY JOHN T. FLYNN

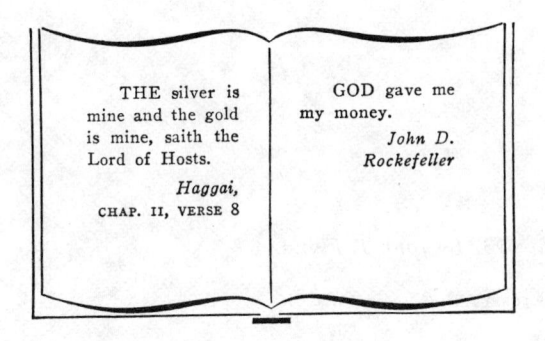

> THE silver is mine and the gold is mine, saith the Lord of Hosts.
> *Haggai,* CHAP. II, VERSE 8

> GOD gave me my money.
> *John D. Rockefeller*

GREENWOOD PRESS, PUBLISHERS
WESTPORT, CONNECTICUT

Copyright 1932 by John T. Flynn

All rights reserved

Originally published in 1932
by Harcourt, Brace and Company, New York

Reprinted with permission

First Greenwood Reprinting 1971

Library of Congress Catalogue Card Number 78-138231

ISBN 0-8371-5588-6

Printed in the United States of America

PREFACE

SOMETHING *is due, before we plunge into this story, to the curiosity of the reader who wishes to know*

First, why the author chose to write the history of a man who still lives and whose history, therefore, has not yet been fully made up, and

Second, what were the sources of this narrative and how far the Rockefeller family has participated in its preparation.

The answer to the first is that the career of John D. Rockefeller, so far as history is concerned, is quite finished and has been for more than fifteen years. When Mr. Rockefeller has made an end of the business of living, some sympathetic biographer, enjoying the confidence of his family, will be able to add many unimportant personal incidents in the life of a retired country gentleman during the last score of years. These doubtless will be interesting, but will hardly add anything to the picture about which history is concerned, the materials for which are already available.

The answer to the second question is that the materials have been gathered from the vast records of the age in which Mr. Rockefeller lived, as made up in innumerable legislative and congressional investigations and countless court decisions, all of which have been carefully read; in an endless array of pamphlets, articles, addresses and letters and in the records of the daily press from the time of Rockefeller's birth to date, all of which, including the newspapers of Owego, Auburn in New York, of Cleveland and of New York City, Oil City and Titusville in Pennsylvania, have been read and compared for the whole period which this volume covers. I have, of course, talked with a very large number of persons who took part in the events described or who found themselves in a position to observe them.

For reasons which seem sufficient to the author no application was made to the Rockefeller family for information until the work

PREFACE

of collection had been completed and the results assembled in a tentative draft. I then submitted to Mr. Ivy Lee, the representative of the Rockefeller family, a list of forty-two questions covering obscure or disputed points. These questions were, with a few exceptions, answered quite fully and frankly. After this, the completed manuscript was turned over to Mr. William O. Inglis, a writer and journalist of ability and experience, who spent ten years working with the elder John D. Rockefeller collecting materials for an official biography. Mr. Inglis was commissioned by Mr. Lee to examine my manuscript and to note such statements of fact and opinion as he believed to be at variance with the accepted Rockefeller version. Mr. Inglis spent many weeks in this work and submitted to me one hundred and eighty suggested corrections or criticisms. I discussed these criticisms at length with him in a number of very pleasant conferences. In the end I adopted sixty-four of these corrections. As for the others, I felt constrained to adhere to my own findings and views. Mr. Inglis also supplied me with a large number of interesting and important personal details and was good enough to put at my disposal a very considerable mass of his own notes on certain highly controversial points.

This course was adopted in an effort to be quite just to the subject of this history and to his family by making it possible for them to call attention to inaccuracies before, rather than after, this book is published. Where the Rockefeller version of the incidents described has been rejected a note has been carried, wherever possible, giving the other side of the case. This, of course, must be understood along with the further statement that in certain important, major episodes, the records and the opinions of the Rockefeller family are so at variance with the interpretations of the author that it has seemed unnecessary to call attention to the difference.

It is worth noting, in justification of this work, that no life of Mr. Rockefeller has yet appeared. Miss Ida Tarbell's brilliant account of the Standard Oil Company's affairs between 1872 and 1898 as well as Henry Demarest Lloyd's earlier volume, were not biographies. They were attacks; and though they deserve to rank among the most important documents in our industrial history, they did not pretend to be biographies. Since the writer began work on this volume nearly four years ago, two books have appeared about Mr. Rockefeller, one a brief journalistic sketch, the other a

PREFACE

rambling and incoherent attack, chiefly upon his philanthropies. Countless articles have appeared in magazines and newspapers about the man, most of them violent attacks called forth by the events of the time, some of them, especially in recent years, fulsome panegyrics. No one has made an effort to examine, impartially, the whole record of this extraordinary man's life and to relate his character and achievements to his times.

For the story itself I can claim but one virtue; that I have tried honestly to disengage the character of the subject from the features with which both hatred and affection have invested it and to make a true picture of him and the times in which he moved.

J. T. F.

Bayside, Long Island
June 3, 1932

CONTENTS

PART ONE: THE QUIET YEARS

HORNS AND HALO	3
I. MICHIGAN HILL	6
II. THE LAND OF SUPERIOR CUNNING	31
III. "HE WHO SEEKS THE WAMPUM BELT"	40

PART TWO: BUSINESS AND RELIGION

I. NEW CONNECTICUT	50
II. TWO MEDICINE MEN	53
III. THE CHAIN COLLEGE	57
IV. A BOY WHOLESALER	63

PART THREE: OIL DORADO

I. DRAKE HITS OIL	75
II. A VISITOR AT THE CREEK	89
III. VEGETABLES AND WAR	98
IV. ROCKEFELLER GOES INTO OIL	105
V. TWO DECISIONS	114

PART FOUR: WAR AT THE CREEK

I. THE MAGIC CITY	117
II. THE HOSTILE CAMPS	124

III. A NEW WEAPON	135
IV. THE DREAM OF MONOPOLY	143

PART FIVE: THE GREAT CONSUMMATION

I. MR. ROCKEFELLER LOOKS ABOUT	171
II. THE COMBINATION OF BRAINS	175
III. BUILDING STANDARD OIL	183
IV. THE GRAND DESIGN	187
V. THE BATTLE WITH THE EMPIRE	190

PART SIX: GATHERING STORMS

I. THE VOICE OF SCANDAL	199
II. SIGNS OF REVOLT	205
III. THE STORM SPREADS	208
IV. AT THE BAR	215
V. THE HEPBURN INVESTIGATION	218
VI. ROCKEFELLER TRIUMPHS	220
VII. CRUSHING THE TIDEWATER	224

PART SEVEN: THE FINAL FLIGHT

I. MOMENTS AT HOME	231
II. THE GREAT STRUCTURE	236
III. THE TRUST IS BORN	248
IV. THE STORY OF RICE	257
V. AN EXPLOSION IN BUFFALO	269
VI. WAR ON THE TRUSTS	277
VII. WAR WEARY	288

VIII. DISSOLVING THE TRUST	297
IX. THE GREAT BAPTIST DREAM	303
X. IRON MEN AND WAXEN LAWS	312
XI. OLD ENEMIES ON THE MARCH	320
XII. LEAVING THE STAGE	325

PART EIGHT: MOUNTAINS OF HATE

I. THE NEW LEADERS	334
II. THE STANDARD OIL GANG	344
III. IN THE LABORATORY OF A CORRUPTIONIST	352
IV. LIGHTING THE WORLD	361
V. SENATORS IN HARNESS	363
VI. MICE AND MEN	374
VII. THE MUCKRAKERS	385
VIII. GOD'S GOLD	394
IX. ENEMIES CLOSE IN	405
X. THE BIG STICK STRIKES	422
XI. MURDER WILL OUT	433
XII. THE LUDLOW MASSACRE	453
XIII. MRS. ROCKEFELLER'S DEATH	462
XIV. THE LAIRD OF KIJKUIT	465
SOURCES	489
INDEX	509

ILLUSTRATIONS

OLD ROCKEFELLER MILL	14
JOHN D. ROCKEFELLER'S BIRTHPLACE AT RICHFORD, N. Y.	14
WILLIAM ROCKEFELLER AT THE AGE OF 11	15
JOHN D. ROCKEFELLER AT THE AGE OF 13	15
CARY, THE FIRST OIL MAN	22
VIEW OF THE ROCKEFELLER COUNTRY	46
OWEGO ACADEMY	47
"DR." WILLIAM ROCKEFELLER	47
ELIZA DAVISON ROCKEFELLER	47
FACSIMILE REPRODUCTION OF CIRCULAR ISSUED BY SAMUEL M. KIER IN 1850	56
BRINE WELLS IN TARENTUM, PENNSYLVANIA	76
ERIE STREET BAPTIST MISSION	78
DEACON ALEXANDER SKED	78
SAMUEL KIER	78
ROCKEFELLER FAMILY GROUP ABOUT 1859	79
COLONEL A. C. FERRIS	79
KIER'S $400 ROCK OIL NOTE	80
COLONEL EDWIN L. DRAKE'S FIRST WELL NEAR TITUSVILLE	82
KICKING DOWN AN EARLY WELL	87
OIL CREEK A FEW YEARS AFTER DRAKE'S DISCOVERY	90

TITUSVILLE, THE NEW OIL CENTER, SHORTLY AFTER DISCOVERY OF PETROLEUM	94
TEAMING IN THE OIL REGIONS	96
MAP OF EARLY OIL REGIONS IN PENNSYLVANIA	99
"POMEROY'S EXPRESS"	106
"COLONEL" EDWIN L. DRAKE	110
BILLY SMITH	110
HENRY M. FLAGLER	111
S. V. HARKNESS	111
HENRY H. ROGERS	111
JOHN D. ARCHBOLD	111
STREET SCENE IN TITUSVILLE	112
ADVENTURERS RUSHING TO THE CARS STARTING FOR OIL CREEK	113
NIGHT SCENES IN OIL REGION HOTEL LOBBY	119
OIL SEEKERS	121
THE DRAKE MONUMENT ON THE SITE OF THE OLD WELL	142
PRIMITIVE METHOD OF FILLING BARRELS	150
THE BLACK LIST PUBLISHED BY THE OIL CITY "DERRICK"	166
STAGES IN THE VARYING FORTUNES OF THE OIL PRODUCERS	180
THE BY-PRODUCTS OF PETROLEUM	240
FACSIMILE OF LETTER FROM CHESS, CARLEY & CO. TO RAILROAD FREIGHT AGENT	258
JOHN D. ROCKEFELLER AT 18 YEARS OF AGE	302
JOHN D. ROCKEFELLER IN 1865	302
JOHN D. ROCKEFELLER IN 1867	302
JOHN D. ROCKEFELLER IN 1870	302

WILLIAM A. ROCKEFELLER	303
ELIZA DAVISON ROCKEFELLER	303
CARTOON FROM "THE MINNEAPOLIS JOURNAL"	304
MR. JOHN D. ROCKEFELLER IN 1888	334
JOHN D. ROCKEFELLER IN 1900	335
CARTOON FROM CLEVELAND "PLAIN DEALER"	338
CARTOON FROM "THE PHILADELPHIA NORTH AMERICAN"	348
CARTOON FROM THE "NEW YORK JOURNAL"	350
PART OF LETTER TO ARCHBOLD, WHILE SIBLEY WAS A MEMBER OF CONGRESS	354
LETTER FROM ARCHBOLD TO GOVERNOR HASTINGS	356
LETTER FROM ARCHBOLD TO THOS. A. MORRISON	357
LETTER FROM ARCHBOLD TO SENATOR JOSEPH B. FORAKER	359
CARTOON FROM "THE ROCKY MOUNTAIN NEWS"	364
NOTE MADE BY SENATOR BAILEY TO HENRY CLAY PIERCE	368
LETTERS FROM ARCHBOLD TO QUAY	369, 370
LETTERS FROM ARCHBOLD TO PENROSE	371, 373
CARTOON FROM THE "SATURDAY GLOBE"	410
CARTOON FROM THE "EVENING MAIL"	425
CARTOON FROM "MINNEAPOLIS TRIBUNE"	426
CARTOON FROM THE "DAILY EAGLE"	430
JOHN D. ROCKEFELLER IN 1904	430
MRS. JOHN D. ROCKEFELLER IN 1904	430
IDA TARBELL	431
FRANK S. MONNETT	431
GEORGE RICE	431

HENRY D. LLOYD	431
LETTER FROM ARCHBOLD TO PROF. GEORGE GUNTON	440
CARTOON FROM THE "POST-DISPATCH"	446
JOHN D. ROCKEFELLER, ABOUT 1907	462
JOHN D. ROCKEFELLER AT THE AGE OF 93	463
CHART: EXPENDITURES OF ROCKEFELLER FOUNDATION	476

GOD'S GOLD

PART ONE

THE QUIET YEARS

HORNS AND HALO

For forty years—from 1872 to 1914—the name of John D. Rockefeller was the most execrated name in American life. It was associated with greed, rapacity, cruelty, hypocrisy, and corruption. Upon it was showered such odium as has stained the name of no other American. Theodore Roosevelt denounced Rockefeller as a law-breaker. William J. Bryan, his fellow Christian, went up and down the land demanding that he be put in jail. The attorney-generals of half a dozen states clamored for his imprisonment. LaFollette called him the greatest criminal of the age. Tolstoi said no honest man should work for him. Ministers of the gospel called the money he showered upon churches and colleges tainted. For years no man spoke a good word for John D. Rockefeller, save the sycophant and the time-server.

Then somehow a kind of languor fell upon the man's traducers. As the years passed there came a mitigation of the old hatreds. In some way the once hated Rockefeller emerged into a kind of genial sainthood. A newspaper poll voted him one of the greatest Americans. John Singer Sargent, who made his portrait, said that when painting him he felt himself to be in the presence of a medieval saint—compared him to St. Francis of Assisi. His birthday has become a kind of annual newspaper event. One may wonder if the redemption has not been quite as excessive as the damnation.

The beatification of Rockefeller in this second phase of his career may well reveal to the practiced eye all the mechanism of patient and sustained propaganda. What is not so clear to the casual observer is that the earlier proscription was equally the work of propaganda. It was propaganda even more intense and sustained, but not so obviously propaganda, because it proceeded, not from a centrally organized bureau, but from the outraged interests of thousands of little, wasteful, inefficient, selfish business men who at the time clung to the unworkable methods of the old school and were in possession of the favor of press, political leaders, and all the agencies of opinion. The implements for making and spreading opinion have changed hands. The result has been to shear Mr. Rockefeller of his horns and fasten a halo where they grew. Perhaps the truth about Mr. Rockefeller lies somewhere between the extravagant abuse of the politically-owned press of the last century and the extravagant approval of the business-owned press of this one.

The story of Rockefeller is not just a tale of piling up a vast fortune. The chronicles of American fortune building are not very noble ones. The first great American millionaires like Astor and his contemporaries came from the land. Astor himself laid the foundations of his fortune trading with the Indians and swindling them by the generous use of rum. The millions he later amassed were got in land grants, many of which were acquired by sheer corruption. The ultimate value in the land was expanded by just holding on and doing nothing. Most of these early aristocratic fortunes were built by sitting idly upon their acres while the great cities grew around them through the energies of other men.

The fortunes of the next generation were for the most part acquired through downright frauds or stock-jobbing operations closely bordering upon fraud. Russell Sage laid the cornerstone of his by stealing a small railroad from a city of which he was an official. Upon that foundation he built through a series of land swindles and railroad adventures of amazing audacity. The Gould fortune was reared through a career of almost unparalleled security frauds in which one episode was the looting of the Erie Railroad in an adventure which still stands as a masterpiece of knavery. The great railroad fortunes of the West—of Huntington, Leland Stanford, Crocker, and Mark Hopkins—were chiefly the fruit of gigantic frauds upon the government, upon the public through stock issues and upon stockholders through schemes directed against their own companies. The Elkins fortune began in land grabbing in the Southwest and ended in widespread utility promotions in the East. Most of the fortunes of Rockefeller's wealthiest contemporaries were made through stock promotions, including those of Morgan and Harriman. And if all of these were not utterly dishonest they were certainly parasitic, collected without the performance of any important or necessary service to society.

Singularly, no one of these men has come in for the robust hatred which was expended on Rockefeller. And yet Rockefeller's great fortune was not only the most honestly acquired but was amassed in the building of a great constructive producing business and in the development of a new system in industry. His wealth was made up of profits taken out of a productive industry, not out of stock schemes or land and franchise raids.

It is therefore not merely the least tainted of all the great fortunes of his day, but is easily the most important and significant. To tell the manner of its making is to tell the story of the development of American business as we now know it. It is to trace the evolution of the economic system under which American business now flourishes. For this reason the career of this man cannot be told by limiting it to his own immediate surroundings. His portrait must be painted upon a canvas large enough to include, not merely his figure and those of his immediate collaborators, but a background of the forces in our whole economic life. The story of Rockefeller and his "crimes" which the last generation relished was the story of a brutal big business man projected against a background drawn to include a lot of things which that generation loved much, but which we have come to know were not so desirable and are no longer possible. It was dramatized as the story of the lion and the mouse. It was rather the story of a large, powerful, intelligent lion who knew what he was doing in a vastly altered jungle and a whole race of mice, disordered, disorganized, running about in circles without any notion of the changes that had taken place in the forest. We know a good deal more about that background now and by correcting its outlines, its colors, and composition to conform to the facts, the whole picture of Rockefeller and his contemporaries becomes different. This is the reason why this volume must be a history of Rockefeller *and his times*.

Was he an honest man? Was he a great man? What was his chief contribution to the world? What was the chief injury which he inflicted on it? Did he give to the world more than he took from it? What were the chief elements behind his success? Indeed was his life a success at all? Could such a career be duplicated now? The answer lies of course in the simple facts of his life and times. The answer begins in 1839 when Martin Van Buren was President of the United States.

CHAPTER I. MICHIGAN HILL

On a summer's night a horseman galloped up to a small house on the edge of the village of Richford in New York. Without dismounting he knocked clamorously above the door. A nightcapped head was pushed out of the upper window.

"What's all the noise?" it asked in a sleepy voice.

"Tell Mrs. Thompson," the horseman replied breathlessly, "to come over to our house at once. Mrs. Rockefeller is goin' to have a baby."

The man in the window saw that the rider held by the bridle another horse to carry Mrs. Thompson to the Rockefeller house on Michigan Hill. In a dozen minutes a woman climbed into the saddle and, through the darkness and over the uncertain roads, the two picked their way up the hill. Across the twin brooks and through the circle of apple trees and they were on the crest of Michigan Hill and before the cottage of Bill Rockefeller.

Inside Mrs. Thompson found Eliza Rockefeller in the small room at the front and to the right of the house on her bed of pain. The room was little bigger than the bed and almost bare. In a cradle at the left of the bed another child only 18 months old slept undisturbed by the groans of the mother. A sperm candle filled the room with a dim yellow glow and with dimmer moving shadows. And in the shadows, near the head of the bed, stood a tall, broad-shouldered young man, handsome, a little frightened and looking down with a troubled eye upon his frail wife, rigid and white with pain, her teeth set as she fought the surging agony.

Before the night was over the baby came. It was a boy. Then the broad-shouldered man went out and walked hurriedly across the top of the hill to the house of his father, Godfrey Rockefeller.

But not to his father. He was going to his strong-minded mother to tell her that Eliza had been delivered of a son. Very soon the pair were walking back through the early dawn to Bill Rockefeller's own cottage.

"What are you going to call him?" the mother asked.

"Well, we haven't had much talk about it yet. But I know Eliza will want to call him after her father, John Davison. John's a good name for a Rockefeller. There's always been a John in every generation of Rockefellers."

And so they called the boy John Davison Rockefeller.

II

ALL DAY that big man gazed down upon the indefinite infant with a puzzled look. Now, at the end of more than ninety years, the world looks no less puzzled at the old man, who was that infant, hidden away amid his five thousand acres of more than regal park, surrounded by a thousand servants, concealed in the depths of the most magnificent estate in the world. No man has been so much scrutinized; about no man does the world know less. Newspapers have printed more about him than about any American president. For years certain editors kept men continuously on his trail. In a dozen sensational lawsuits he has been pilloried and examined and searched. Twenty times the United States Congress and the legislatures of various states have investigated him, searching out all the acts of his life. Enemies—thousands of them—have followed every minute suggestion of wrong-doing and scandal. He has been grilled, exposed, turned inside out. Yet he has remained actually one of the most completely unknown men in American public life.

III

THE SCENE we have described took place in the little village of Richford on July 8, 1839—a small village of New York about one hundred and twenty-five miles from New York City.

Some years before this a powerfully built young man, astride an excellent horse, galloped one morning into the village square of Richford. The square looked then much as it does today. There was the broad, triangular green, with its high grass and the roads meeting in a fork. On the west side was the store of Chauncey Rich. There was an old hotel at one end of the Green and another store on the left, opposite Rich's. The hotel and both stores are standing today. There were a good many lumbermen coming into Richford all the time and farmers bringing in their produce and occasionally wagons of travelers—immigrants on the move and striking north for the lakes and across to Ohio. There were always a goodly number in little groups in that busy village plaza.

Into this square rode the big man on the horse. He was a striking figure. His clothes were good. He wore a broad-brimmed hat and long black coat. His horse too was a good one and he rode it like a true horseman. He reined up in front of a small group near Rich's store and saluted them. Then he drew from under his coat a small slate with a pencil tied to it. He wrote on the slate:

"Where is the house of Godfrey Rockefeller?"

He exhibited the slate to the group and made signs to indicate that he was deaf and dumb. One of the men who could write scribbled a direction under the question and pointed to the narrow wagon tracks leading off to the east and up the hill. That was where Godfrey Rockefeller lived. The big man wheeled his horse about and galloped briskly up the hill.

Thus William Avery Rockefeller, the father of John D. Rockefeller, arrived in Richford.[1] When he got to his mother's home he continued to use his slate to the great distress of the whole family. When his joke had gone far enough he broke into a loud laugh and announced that he intended to live in Richford.

For many weeks young Bill Rockefeller remained under the family roof on Michigan Hill. And for most of this time, when around the village square, he carried on his pretense of dumbness. Then he suddenly recovered his speech and spent many hours every day near the village green. He wore good clothes, seemed to have nothing to do and no plans aside from amusing himself in conversation.

Now he made up for his recent dumbness, for he became known as a glib talker, a little given to speech-making. He was but twenty-six years old, but he had traveled about a good deal and this gave him a marked advantage over the yokels who haunted the little common, most of whom had never been outside of Tioga County.

In a few weeks Big Bill, as he came to be known, was seen no

[1] The Rockefeller family insists that the elder William Rockefeller went to Richford with his family and that the story given here is not true.

more about the public square. But he had remained long enough to make an impression and to be the subject of talk. What did Bill Rockefeller do for a living? That's what the village busy-bodies wanted to know. He seemed to have plenty of money in his pocket. But he said nothing about his business. They put their heads together and allowed it was very strange. But Bill was gone now and in a few more weeks was out of people's minds.

IV

GODFREY ROCKEFELLER—Big Bill's father—a thriftless, shiftless fellow, fond of his tipple, liked to talk about his grandfather, Johann Peter, who planted the Rockefeller seed in America. More than a hundred years before this—in 1722—Johann Peter Rockefeller had come over from the village of Sagendorf in Germany, bringing with him his second wife and a goodly progeny by his first wife. He settled in Somerville, New Jersey, where other children were born. He was a farmer there, though he had been a miller in Germany, and in 1729 we find him purchasing some land in Amwell, New Jersey, where he was to spend the remainder of his life. He died in 1765, the year an English parliament imposed the Stamp Tax.

Johann Peter had five children by his first wife, all born in Germany. Two were boys and both were called Johann. Big Bill was right when he said there was always a John in every generation of Rockefellers. In this one there were two—Johann William and Johann Peter. They were brought with the other children to Somerville and later to Amwell.

This second Johann Peter married twice. His first wife presented him with nine children. There was a John among them. But we are concerned with the fifth, William Rockefeller. This William, born in 1750 in Amwell, married another Rockefeller, Christina, the granddaughter of Diell Rockefeller, in Germantown, New York. There are two Rockefeller strains in America. One flows from that Johann Peter, who settled in Amwell. The other flows from Diell, who settled in Germantown. The William whom we have now reached united both strains by his marriage to Christina.

To this union were born many children. One of them was Godfrey Rockefeller, who was born in Germantown just two years after the surrender at Yorktown. Godfrey married Lucy Avery of

Great Barrington and promptly settled there. This pair had ten children, the third oldest being that huge fellow named William who appeared on his horse and in his fine clothes and pretended to dumbness on the Richford common sometime in 1836 or 1837. This William Rockefeller, who was born at Granger, New York, November 30, 1810, was the father of John D. Rockefeller.

These Rockefellers were a fecund and long-lived strain. The original Johann Peter lived to be eighty-four. His son, Johann Peter, died at the age of three score and fifteen. His son William's age is not known. But Godfrey Rockefeller, in spite of a generous disregard of the laws of health, lived to be seventy-four. William Avery—Big Bill—lived to be at least ninety-six.

This is, perhaps, all that is known with certainty of the Rockefeller line. But a richly embroidered tapestry of noble and near-royal progenitors has been woven by the inevitable genealogists of the millionaire American.

There is in existence an organization known as the Rockefeller Family Association—one of those numerous confederations of miscellaneous kinsmen which are preserving the virtues of clan life in America. The Rockefeller Association, whose members become more numerous with each year, now has more than 800. It meets annually. It has regional branches which hold their own conclaves and in many states there are chapters which foregather more frequently. The proceedings of the national body are preserved each year in printed reports. And in the last few years they have set up a magazine published quarterly called the *Rockefeller Family News*. Thus all the doings of the far-flung clan, the trivial performances of all the aunts and uncles, their small visitations to other members of the family, are recorded in verse and in prose, which sometimes rises to lofty altitudes.

There is no record that John D. Rockefeller, in whose reflected glory the association has its being, has ever joined it. Neither is the name of John D., Jr., found on its rolls. When the family meets in New York, a visit to Pocantico Hills is always the high spot of the meeting. The great herd of cousins go to the magnificent barony of its most illustrious scion. But John D. is never there when they arrive. The flag is flown—a favorite Rockefeller gesture. But the honors are extended by the superintendent.

In 1906 the family, through the munificence of John D., erected at Somerville, New Jersey, a modest monument to the first American Rockefeller—Johann Peter of Sagendorf. There were speeches and the story got into the newspapers. In some way it drifted over to Germany. There a modest little minister, the pastor of a church at Rheinbrohl, read the accounts. He sat down at once and wrote to John D. Rockefeller. There were still Rockenfellers at Sagendorf, he announced, and what was more, the old stone mill where Johann Peter had ground his rye flour was still standing. And moreover these Rockenfellers at Sagendorf and all about that part of Germany had always believed they were of the same blood as the great American Oil King. John handed the letter to his brother William and William handed it to Mr. Aaron R. Lewis, the genealogist who had traced the American lineage. Mr. Lewis went to Germany and investigated. And in October, 1907, he stood before the assembled kinsmen at their annual convention and revealed to them the result of his researches and the secret of their existence. It was a story which made them swell with family pride. He carried the line back to 940 A.D. The family had been delighted at the simple Rockefeller origins in Sagendorf. But Mr. Lewis had a more impressive tale to tell. "There is no doubt," he said, "that your family originated in France, down in the Southern part, in that old province known as Languedoc, near the old cities of Montpellier, Nîmes, Toulouse, and Beziers.

"I have been able to trace your name back as far as the year 949 in the old town of Lodève near where they owned a château."

This was a precious morsel. It drew additional flavor from the discovery that the name was originally Roquefeuille and that there was a Latin rendition of it—Rocafolio. And then the whole clan leaned forward breathlessly as the speaker assured them:

"They were titled people (these Roquefeuilles) and married and inter-married with the nobility and associated with the best people of their day and generation.

"Away back in the money age," he proceeded, "they had money —coins—bearing their name."

Money called after Rockefeller 900 years ago! The kinsmen smiled knowingly at that. Then Mr. Lewis begged them to read the history of France from 1640 and 1690 and then to go back still further and read especially the story of that grim slaughter of Protestants at St. Bartholomew in 1572. On that dark night the assassins murdered that great Admiral and Huguenot leader, Gaspard Coligny.

"Read how he was murdered," ended Mr. Lewis, "while sitting wounded in his room, his body thrown from a window to the street, the head severed from it and then the headless trunk hung up in a public square for days to be scoffed at."

Then, as these gruesome incidents sank in, Mr. Lewis uttered his climax:

"It was his grandson, Gaspard Coligny 3rd, who married one of your kindred."

These German Rockenfellers at Sagendorf then were old French Huguenots who had fled from persecution. The dramatic fitness of all this must have fallen with a thrill upon the souls of the Rockefeller clansmen, for at the moment of its telling—1907—the hue and cry was raised all over America after their celebrated kinsman, John D. Rockefeller, and with an intensity which must have seemed hardly less furious than the hatred which did for the unhappy Admiral so many centuries before.

A Cleveland genealogist named Avery has traced the ancestry of Rockefeller's grandmother back to John Humphrey of Massachusetts, exiled sword bearer of the parliament which beheaded Charles I and beyond that to the Plantagenets, including 16 English kings, one king of Scotland, a king of France and a German emperor.

This history does not vouch for the authenticity of this imposing Avery record—which has been questioned—nor for the somewhat fanciful generations of Roquefeuilles unearthed by Mr. Lewis. Providing American millionaires with aristocratic and even regal ancestries has become a recognized industry. Perhaps no genealogist has disinterred and laid down in his client's drawing room a more extensive quantity-delivery of kings and princes than Mr. Avery did for Mr. Rockefeller.

V

THIS chronicle has now arrived at what might be called the confluence of the royal blood of the Plantagenets and the noble corpuscles of the Roquefeuilles, which rush together in the veins of William Avery Rockefeller, the father of John D. This was achieved through the union of Godfrey Rockefeller with Lucy

Avery at Great Barrington in 1786. The Averys were thrifty farmers and neighbors wagged their heads mournfully when Lucy Avery joined fortunes with this careless, restless, tippling man. But Lucy was more than a match for him. Under her strong hand Godfrey settled down to make something of himself. He became Sheriff of Great Barrington, but lingered not long in this eminence, for before his second child was born he had changed his base again and was at Granger, New York. Lucy bore him ten children, one at Great Barrington, three at Granger, three more at Ancram, and finally three more at Great Barrington to which they had returned. The third of these children was William Avery Rockefeller. He was born at Granger in 1810.

After all these moves, Godfrey Rockefeller at fifty was ready for another change of base. He settled in Richford. What brought him to Richford is not known. It is a little village in Tioga County, New York, on Owego Creek and about seventeen miles north of Owego, the county seat. It is near the southern boundary of New York State and a little northwest of New York City. It lies about fifty miles south of Lake Ontario and reposes in the soft, fertile, undulating country just off the lovely Susquehanna River and just beyond the reach of those beautiful Finger Lakes which, like the fingers of a giant hand, reach down from Lake Ontario to grasp it.

When Godfrey Rockefeller entered the village it was a prosperous settlement of fifteen hundred souls. Land was going up in price. Lumbering was the chief occupation along Owego Creek, but the village had all the little shops which went to form the self-contained community of that day. There was a sawmill, two general stores, a millinery shop, tin shop, harness, wagon, and blacksmith shops, two grist mills, a small whiskey still, and a church, a hotel, a post office, and a schoolhouse.

Godfrey bought a farm on Michigan Hill, located about two miles from the center of the village. The houses on the hill were rude farmer homes. Godfrey's, which still stands, was the best of the lot. But he was known here as a thriftless man, a poor farmer, a source of endless trouble to his wife. She more than he managed the farm and the home. There is still standing, a score of yards from the house, a heap of field stones—the remnant of a stone fence which Lucy Rockefeller built. This rugged woman marked out the line and bossed the job and while two men under her put the heavier rocks in place she carried some of the smaller ones in her own apron.

The Rockefellers worked the farm and some of the boys helped. But Big Bill was never seen there until the day he made his curious entry into the village with the mockery of dumbness. Nor did he ever do any work on the farm. He would be gone for months at a time. Then he would come home, always unheralded and either astride a good horse or driving a decent-looking rig. At such times he spent most of his days around the grass common. He was full of tales of Indians. He had stories to tell of trips through New England and all over Northern New York. He used no liquor. He could grow eloquent against the rum mill of the town. But his companions observed that no pretty girl passed without a complete scrutiny by Bill. He was a handsome fellow, with a fine figure, a kind of virile and obvious strength which made him seem bigger than he really was. Women looked at him with an approving eye. He had a strong jaw and a commanding glance. He was jovial and a good story teller. He liked to tell tales of his own smartness—to laugh at the work of suckers he seemed to meet everywhere. There was just a little bluster and swagger about the fellow. He kept his business to himself, however. But he was a man of huge animal spirits and a quick mind who apparently found his fun along with his business as he traveled about.

Whatever Bill Rockefeller did for a living, it was plain that all his expeditions did not take him great distances from Richford. He was often seen up around Auburn, the prison city, in Cayuga County and frequently roved about the country that skirted Owasco Lake. He had a way of captivating the younger people and filling the older heads with suspicion. And so there was much talk when the neighbors around Niles noticed the swaggering big fellow who drove up in such a good-looking rig so often to the home of farmer Davison. John Davison was one of the most prosperous farmers around Niles. These Davisons were a mixture of Scotch and English, a little dour—stern Baptists, the kind of people who are fond of using the word "righteous." Bill would sit for long hours talking to Eliza Davison. In some way she had met him as he roamed the country-side. She had been brought up in an austere atmosphere by a stern father. But she was not so austere herself. She loved a good laugh and a jolly prank and it was plain to sol-

Upper, OLD ROCKEFELLER MILL OPERATED BY JOHANN ROCKEFELLER IN ARINHELLER, GERMANY, DURING THE LATTER PART OF THE 17TH CENTURY. *Lower*, JOHN D. ROCKEFELLER'S BIRTHPLACE AT RICHFORD, N. Y. PHOTOGRAPH TAKEN IN 1873

Right, JOHN D. ROCKEFELLER AT THE AGE OF 13. *Left*, HIS BROTHER, WILLIAM ROCKEFELLER, AT THE AGE OF 11

emn old John Davison that this righteous Baptist daughter of his had fallen in love with this unknown adventurer. As in Richford there was much curiosity as to what Bill Rockefeller did. Well, he was a salesman—or so he said—and he sold medicines and traveled about to do it. In any event, he satisfied Eliza Davison, though he did not satisfy her father. And when Bill proposed marriage John Davison held out against it. So one day in February, 1837, Bill drove up to John Davison's home in broad daylight in a good rig and Eliza drove away with him to the house of a friend to be married. It was not an elopement. It was a quiet marriage but without the blessing of the bride's father. A little later Bill and his wife drove up before Godfrey Rockefeller's home on Michigan Hill.

VI

On the road leading over Michigan Hill to Godfrey Rockefeller's farm was a new house. It had been built two years before by a man named Avery Rockhill, perhaps a relative of Bill Rockefeller's mother. It was strongly made, though a simple cottage. It stood on the very crest of the hill and commanded a beautiful view of the surrounding country and the soft green hills to the West. Just below the last rise of the hill are two brooks which meet there and flow off toward Harford Mills. Bill Rockefeller's sportsman's eye quickly observed that there were trout in these brooks. The house itself was surrounded by apple trees. The trees—very old and gnarled—are there yet, for this is a country of old trees. The house was small, the lower floor being divided into three rooms—one main chamber and two quite small ones. To the left—a kind of separate annex—was a kitchen and a woodshed, both of which have been removed.[1] The second floor is just a half-story attic in which one must stoop to walk about. There were then and still are two very large barns. One of these barns has been cut into in its upper

---

[1] The remainder of the house still stands. It was purchased three years ago from Mrs. Carrie Rockefeller, a cousin who owned and had lived in it, by Mrs. Sarah S. Dennen of Brooklyn, to be moved to Coney Island and set up there as a Rockefeller museum and exhibit. The plan was opposed by the members of the Rockefeller Family Association and ultimately abandoned. It is a cherished hope of the people in this region to have the old Rockefeller farm and adjacent country developed into a "Rockefeller Park" with the house as a central attraction. A generous Rockefeller contribution to this end is eagerly hoped for as the basis of this dream.

wall for ventilation and decoration with three small openings. On close inspection it is seen that this is a godless bit of art—a decanter and two glasses—on the barn of the rum-hating Bill and Eliza Rockefeller. A farm of sixty acres stretched back from the house. Here Bill Rockefeller established his young wife. And here just one year after their marriage the first child was born—Lucy Rockefeller, called after her grandmother. Then eighteen months later the boy was born whose arrival is chronicled in the opening paragraphs of this story. Two years later another boy, William, appeared.

Bill Rockefeller, the father, did no farming. He had a hired hand who worked a patch of ground and helped around the place. Bill himself was away most of the time, coming home at intervals, always a welcome arrival to his wife and his small brood.

VII

IN THE year 1840, the country was, as Henry Clay said, like an "ocean convulsed by a terrible storm." William Henry Harrison, the hero of Tippecanoe, was the Whig candidate for president. Against him was pitted Martin Van Buren. Up in Tioga County the wide circling waves of this turbulent battle were rolling in upon the forest towns. Around the village common of Richford the yokel statesmen talked about the panic of 1837. Down in Owego the county leaders were preparing a great meeting.

On the morning of this great event the people of Tioga County were pouring in from every road—on horseback, in farm carts, on foot, their wives and children and hired hands with them, their blankets and copper pots and dishes of wood and victuals for a stay of a day or more.

That morning the population of Richford was on the move. It was a good twelve miles' journey down to Owego and the quiet village of lumbermen and farmers were aboard their carts and rumbling down to the county seat at an early hour. The air was filled with a festival odor. There was a jug of whiskey and a larger jug of cider on every wagon. Richford, as well as all Tioga County, was a drinking community. The remains of the old whiskey still not far from the green still stand. Everywhere liquor was as free as water. The village merchants sold liquor and at low prices so that the poorest man was able to buy all he could carry. In most of the

MICHIGAN HILL

stores there stood upon the counter a pail of whiskey and a tin cup so that the customer was able to dip out a stout drink for himself. Liquor was kept in every home. "The children were helped moderately in their infancy and helped themselves abundantly in later life," says an old chronicler. "The house was but indifferently furnished which had not a jug of black strap in its cupboard."

But there was one house where there was no black strap. And as the farmers moved into Owego that morning there was one wagon in which reposed no jug of cider or whiskey. That was the wagon of Bill Rockefeller. Bill was back for the big meeting at Owego. And this morning, with his wife and little Lucy, then two years old and the infant John held close in his mother's arms, he was on his way with all the residents of Richford.

Into the famous county seat upon the Susquehanna, Rockefeller's wagon, drawn by two excellent horses, moved amid an uproar. Tioga was Whig. Everybody said New York State would surely go for Harrison and Tyler if it were not for that wicked Tammany Hall in the big city down state. Around the Awaga Hotel idle crowds were gathered looking up at the place where the great men of the county were housed for the moment. Important-looking gentlemen in high hats and bottle-green coats went in and out. The streets were filled with a talking, laughing, noisy people, hailing each other from a distance, hucksters selling corn and cider and baubles and flags. Down beyond the public square and across the bridge over the Susquehanna in the open fields the wagons were camped and women were making ready for the noon-day meal over the camp spits.

Big Bill saw more than one face he knew. He hailed acquaintances with a broad laugh. But Eliza Rockefeller looked with dismay upon the almost riotous merriment of this crowd. Everywhere were men well-steeped in whiskey or sinking rapidly into that condition. There were some Rockefellers there no better than the rest. The air had the odor of wickedness for Eliza. She was not any more the merry girl of Niles. A young mother of two small children living in a lonely farmhouse from which her adventurous husband was almost always absent, she had become a little sad-faced and a little stern. Now she was a troubled woman. She wished she had not come.

This was a Whig crowd, filled with enthusiasm for its candidates

—Tippecanoe and Tyler Too. But there were a few whose enthusiasm was a trifle dampened as Eliza Rockefeller's was. There was more than one strait-laced, God-fearing, rum-hating farmer who was disturbed at what seemed the bungling of the Harrison managers. Harrison to be sure was a cider drinker. But so was everybody else. Yet somehow there had been so much talk of the General's cider drinking that one might suppose he did nothing else. The Whigs had played up the fact that General Harrison had been born in a log cabin. Down in Baltimore an editor with a caustic pen had replied that Harrison seemed more in his element in his log cabin with his cider barrel than he would in the White House. Everybody had read that in the little weekly Democratic paper of Owego—the *Gazette*. The Whigs had replied by making the cider barrel along with the log cabin the emblem of the Whig campaign. The log cabin was all right. But the cider barrel—to some that was a godless symbol. And the Democrats were making much of it. But the vast majority of the crowd this day seemed to like it as they seemed also to like their own cider barrels.

Bill Rockefeller has parked his wagon under a broad elm near the river within view of the speakers' stand. And now, just after noon, there is a general movement toward the courthouse square. The big parade is getting under way. The crowd is forming around the speakers' stand. On the outskirts of the square men and women are standing in their carts to get a better view. The sound of drums and fifes comes from the direction of Front Street and the Awaga Hotel. The rattle of the drums and the squeal of the fifes grow louder and suddenly the parade emerges upon the square. There are Whigs on horseback made up like Indians and others, in their coonskin caps, dressed as frontiersmen. Then come the big Whigs on horseback. Now a great shout—the float is in sight. There is a broad wagon and on it a small log cabin. In front of the cabin is a cider barrel. Men in buskins stand about ostentatiously dipping out of the barrel with cups and drinking with a flourish to the health of the crowd. A shout goes up from the godless rabble. There is something more than mock cider in those dancing men on the float. The crowd is delighted. Shouts and wild laughter vie with the screaming fifes. Most of the crowd have had their cider and whiskey for their dinner. Many dance up and down and emit yells like Indians and squeal for joy.

Here and there a few grim-visaged men and women look with disgust and horror upon the spectacle. Big Bill Rockefeller stands at the back of his wagon supporting with his powerful arms the woman in front of him, her shawl wrapped about her and sheltering the infant in her arms. She sees this unholy joy with horror. The undying hatred of her life is rum. She remembers all the liquor guzzling she has seen about her, especially since she has come to Richford. Why does a just God permit such an evil in the world? When will He drive it forth? She feels a twinge of fear for the boy at her breast. She presses him closer to her heart. How little she knows—this strong, resolute, pious woman—she holds in her arms Nemesis—the boy who will be a man and whose gold will smite the cider barrel and the rum bottle. She holds in her arms the instrument of God.

VIII

HARRISON and Tyler were elected. Perhaps never again was a man to be elected President who could get votes with a cider barrel. He was inaugurated March 4, 1841. A month later Harrison died. The news reached Richford about the middle of April. Then Eliza Davison was looking forward to the coming of another child. Big Bill was home, as usual, to be by his wife's side. And a month later the child arrived. This boy was called after his father—William. He was born May 31, 1841. After this Bill remained around, making only a few, brief, swift journeys on his mysterious adventures, until the summer. Then one day he went down to the store of Mr. Rich and announced that he was going away on a long journey.

"Look after my family's wants, Mr. Rich," he said. "Give them whatever they require. I'll be gone longer than usual. When I return I will settle as always." A day or two later he drove away leaving Eliza with three small children in the small house on Michigan Hill. This was a lonely home for this woman. Bears were still in the forests. Occasionally a panther ventured to the edge of the clearings. Sometimes an Iroquois Indian roamed up from the Susquehanna.

There is little doubt that at this time the Rockefellers were in straitened circumstances. Bill Rockefeller found himself moving through occasional patches of mild prosperity. At such times he would return to look after his family. But when he went away again the family quickly consumed the money he left. The credit at Rich's store was their sole support. Sometimes it was a grim battle to keep the wolf from the door. Young John, all through these early years, must have seen his mother practice economy that extended to every little item. The house itself was a poor place. It was one of the humblest in the neighborhood. It stands today a witness of this fact. From its roof emerged a brick chimney. Every well-to-do house had a fireplace, broad and comfortable. The Rockefeller house had a chimney, but no fireplace. The chimney was just an humble piece of outward show. It can be seen today where it begins, just under the roof of the attic, resting on a wooden platform and then pushing up through the shingles, making a brave show outside.

Here, in this small cottage, looking out upon a glorious landscape of soft green hills and luxuriant foliage, this boy spent his first years. Here he lived until he was four years old and his sister Lucy and brother William were respectively six and two. There were plenty of Rockefellers just over the hill where Godfrey and his numerous family lived, and, apparently, in no great state of peace. This little John was a strong, quiet, grave-faced child, with a habit of looking intently at people and things, and a fondness for playing by himself. Eliza Rockefeller had little occasion to be merry and slowly grew to be a serious-faced woman. There was no great religious activity around Richford. As for Eliza there was no church for her to attend. She was not an active church member yet and her husband was in no sense a religious man. A few rods from the house was a little one-room schoolhouse. There is such a one standing there today. It is pointed out to visitors as the first one John D. attended. He never attended school there. Moreover the small frame structure now standing is not the one which stood there in those days. But the presence of the school and the teacher helped to fill up some of the lonely days of Eliza Rockefeller while her husband was away on his mysterious jaunts. Bill was never away for any fixed period. Usually the first notice of his return was the sight of his spanking rig and team coming up the slope of Michigan Hill. Whenever Eliza looked down the hill; when the children looked that way, always there was the thought that perhaps the big, jovial, laughing, handsome father might suddenly appear around the bend of the road. All through the year 1843, Richford folks whose business brought them across that trail, became accustomed to the occasional sight of Eliza Rockefeller standing at her door, looking through the apple trees, across the twin brooks and down Michigan Hill.

IX

THESE were the quiet years. A candle burning in a cottage. The sound of horses' hoofs upon a dirt road. The muffled thump of the water wheel at the side of the little mill. These represented the light, the power, and the transportation of the America of that early day.

When night came down upon the Rockefeller cottage a candle of sperm or tallow furnished the light for the brief period after dark before bedtime. This was the age of the candle.

Though the small boy of 1843, playing under the apple trees and in the twin brooks of Michigan Hill, gave it no thought, America was at this moment looking with busy eyes for light. Larger factories, railroad trains traveling at night, steamboats on the rivers—all these things needed light. The farthest advance made was in the use of coal gas. Twenty years before Boston streets were lit by gas. A little later New York, Philadelphia, New Orleans, and other smaller cities had gas-lit streets. The gas was made from coal, but a few companies made it from resin and tar. Even natural gas had been used to light a few villages. But the country as a whole depended on a few lamps and its candles. Down at Owego in the beautiful home of Mr. Hewitt there were lamps with their Argand burners and glass chimneys which burned whale oil. Some of the better homes in the West burned lard oil made in Cincinnati. A few fine old mansions in the South burned cottonseed oil made at Petersburg, Virginia, and along the Gulf coast resin and turpentine were distilled for camphine, a dangerous illuminant. But the candle, made from fats or sperm or spermaceti lit almost all the homes in America. The biggest oil industry was on the New England coast. Its headquarters were at New Bedford. The oil men went out to sea in ships to fetch their oil from the whale. And the great man of that industry was Mr. Gideon Howland, Jr., the grandfather of Hetty Green.

There was another oil man, far more obscure, but interesting in the light of all that has followed. His name was Cary. Far from New Bedford and from Richford, in Crawford County, Pennsylvania, Cary had settled on that crazy little trickle of grease and water called Oil Creek. A queer ill-smelling oil called petroleum floated on the surface of this creek. The Indians used it as a medicine and the settlers about rubbed their joints with it for pain.

CARY, THE FIRST OIL MAN.
(From Leslie's *Illustrated Newspaper*, 1865)

Cary skimmed the oil from the creek, put it into kegs, hung one on each side of his horse and rode 150 miles along the Allegheny River to Pittsburgh. There he traded his five-gallon kegs for commodities, which he packed back to Crawford. In value he got about ten dollars. At Pittsburgh the petroleum was sold in small quantities to apothecaries who used it for medicine.

Cary was the first oil producer. He was producer and transporter. Occasionally some river man would gather a barrel of oil and deliver it to Pittsburgh. If he got there before Cary that gentleman found the market glutted on his arrival. He was the first to suffer from that monster, over-production of oil.

X

"THE SPONGE OF MONOPOLY has absorbed the whole wealth of the nation." Thus the Alabama legislature fulminated against the tiny octopus whose feeble tentacles wriggled a little a few years before John D. Rockefeller was born. This feverish sentence seems a little absurd to describe the simple economic life of that remote day. More than any other place in the world the northern states, at least, were committed to the system of individualism which had grown increasingly popular since the Physiocrats and later Adam Smith had proclaimed it in the preceding century. These states were quite settled that the main business of the state is to keep order. In the industrial and economic world the great regulating force is self-love. *Laissez faire, laissez passer.* Economic life will develop best when it is wholly unhampered. Free competition— that was the stimulating and regulating power. Each man following his own special advantage, driven forward by the desire of living and for riches, will develop his own forces to the limit to the general advantage of all. Each man does the thing he likes best and can do best. For the next one hundred years this word "competition" will be heard again and again until men will yield to it a kind of religious worship. Into such a world John D. Rockefeller was born like a germ. He would learn quickly enough to despise competition. But he would cling to the other word, "individualism," after the meaning had gone out of it. His entry into business and his career after that would be in large measure the story of American economic development and the war on *laissez faire.*

The life of that day was so different from our own that it is difficult for us to picture it. A line drawn along the western boundary of New York State, across the northern line of Ohio, Indiana, Illinois, and then southward along the western frontier of Missouri, Arkansas, Louisiana, marked the western frontier of all the states. Beyond Missouri were no states. Michigan, Wisconsin, Kansas, Iowa, were not yet states. Texas, Arizona, Idaho, Oregon, Washington, California, belonged to Mexico. There were just thirty states and the population of all of them was not as great as that of New York and Ohio today. Boston, Baltimore, and Philadelphia all had less than 100,000 people. The bulk of the population was gathered along the Atlantic coast, save in Ohio where over a million people had already settled. But from the Atlantic to the Mississippi there was a thin layer of population everywhere. This population was almost wholly agricultural and those who did not live on farms lived in small villages, and these villages were of the old-fashioned, self-sustaining type. The government was in the hands of men sympathetic to the agricultural population. The conditions of life did not favor the growth of large cities. There were some good-sized factories; there was steam and there were railroads. But these things were new and exceptional. They did not give to the country its special character.

One might find, traveling about, every stage of development—the primitive, economically independent farm, the self-sustaining village, the small water-driven mill of the merchant-manufacturer, the large corporation-owned factory. In or near Richford all of these periods were represented. In the Valley of the Susquehanna were farms where the householders raised their own cattle and swine and sheep. The itinerant butchers slaughtered their meat and the hides were taken to the village tanner and then to the currier. The wool from their sheep they had worked into yarn and cloth by the village wool carder. Cotton cloth they bought at the village store but they made their own clothes, save the fine gentlemen who lived in Owego and went up to Auburn or even across to New Haven for tailors. They got good iron plows from the factory set up by Jethro Wood, the first man to make a metal plow in interchangeable parts, for Wood lived close by. But most of their other farm tools were made by the village blacksmith. The saddler and harness maker, the joiner and cabinet maker, the blacksmith and the gunsmith, the shoemaker, these supplied the industrial wants of the village and the open country about it. There was a gristmill, a sawmill, and a whiskey still, and, of course, a barber.

But factories were coming. There were even some large plants—large at least for that day. At Waltham and particularly at Lowell huge textile mills employed each many hundreds, chiefly women. William Morris made locomotives in Philadelphia and even exported them. The Great Western Iron Works, later the Brady's Bend Iron Co., had an investment of a million dollars and housed 537 families on its property. A single clock firm sold 40,000 clocks abroad. There was about $50,000,000 invested in cotton mills and $250,000,000 in factories of all sorts.

MICHIGAN HILL

But even the large factories were not very big measured by later standards. Thus the Ames Works made shovels, and people gasped at the output of 480 shovels a day. But most of the factories were hardly that at all. They were mills or shops where some machinery was used. They were small affairs run by merchant-producers, men who made their small supply of products and sold them directly. The tin manufacturer put his pack on his back or mounted his wagon and peddled his wares from house to house. Others sold their output chiefly in the villages and surrounding country. Others filled their wagons and carted them to the nearest city. The iron-mill producer loaded his output into a flat boat, moved it up the canals and rivers and sold directly from the barge. But however small, they were beginning to find themselves and they were also beginning to cluster around given points. Danbury was a hat town, Gloversville a glove town. Lynn was known for its shoe factories, Lancaster for its metal workers, Germantown for its knitted stockings, Wilmington and Rochester for their flour.

But chiefly these little plants were found around water-power sites. There were steam factories, particularly in Pennsylvania. But in New York and New England the water wheel was the power machine. Along the valley of the Blackstone, for instance, between Worcester and Providence in 1840 there was a continuous string of factories—ninety-four cotton mills, twenty-two woolen mills, thirty-four machine shops and iron works. Steam had been used as far back as 1803 for pumping out mines and twenty years before steam engines were being manufactured in Pittsburgh. Now in Pennsylvania perhaps half the factories were run by steam. But in New York, New England, and New Jersey water was king.

The railroads had come but as yet they performed no very important service in freight transportation. The farm cart and stagecoach were as yet the chief means of travel and for heavy freight the barge and steamboat on the canals and rivers and lakes. This steamboat and canal development had greatly enlarged the life of the people and expanded their trading areas. But now the railroads were to influence the course of business and life. It is easy to see why men lived in small neighborhoods and limited their business to local markets when it cost four dollars to send a barrel of flour overland from Pittsburgh to Philadelphia. With the horse, overland freight cost twenty to sixty cents a ton mile. Early railroad charges soon fell to three cents a ton mile.

Now these forces—machinery and railroads—were to set the young nation upon a new course. The year of Rockefeller's birth marks the end of the old era and the beginning of a new one. The country, without being aware of it, was under the dominion of new forces which were gathering. Everything was in motion. Always since the end of the Revolution the endless migrations west were under way. The wagons were on the move first beyond the Alleghenies, then beyond the Mississippi, then on beyond to Oregon. From New York and Connecticut the caravans moved to Ohio and every day the carts and covered wagons rumbled along the road past the square of Richford, up to Lake Erie. Everything was in ferment. New peoples were pouring into the country—a half million in the ten years before Rockefeller's birth, three times that many in the next ten. Now, added to the migrations, there was a further movement—just moving and shifting about. Girls were leaving the farms to go to the textile mills in the near-by towns. The new things were making changes in the lives of the people. The grain fields were moving west. New cities were springing up in remote Ohio and Missouri and Indiana. The rule of old aristocrats was over and new men, men of the soil, men of the log cabins, had taken hold. The rustle of life was in the air; the invisible winds that sweep through peoples, stir them, and hurry them forward were blowing over the land.

The older people shook their heads. Factories were breaking up the American home, they moaned. Senator Isaac Hill, of Vermont, addressing the conscript fathers, spoke feelingly of the good old times when every family raised and spun and wove materials for its own clothing. "Now large factories supported by overgrown and unscrupulously managed capital had annihilated the household industry." Over in the House, Representative Christopher Rankin of Mississippi, bewailed the "death of so many small establishments which might separately and silently work their way into honorable existences." "Now," he moaned, "one great establishment rises on the ruins of all the surrounding ones."

Thus they looked with fear upon these little corporations and their plants employing five hundred or a thousand people, capitalized at half a million or more and engaging the activities of only a very small percentage of the population. How little they supposed that a boy was then playing barefooted in a home-made muslin suit on a village farm who would before another half century passed, amass a fortune sufficient to buy out with a fifth of his capital every factory great and small that affrighted the souls of the America of 1840.

XI

It is true that one generation always nurtures the germs of the forces which will dominate the next one; one social system breeds the things which control the one which succeeds it. In 1840 there was present, even in that scarcely launched small factory age, almost all of the devices which Rockefeller and his contemporaries would use to build the era of mass production. At that very moment England was repealing some thirty or more old regulatory laws to make way for the golden age of unregulated competition. But at the same time all of the tools which Rockefeller would use to rear his industrial empire and undertake privately to supply the regulation of trade where the government had abdicated were in use. Not only was the corporation being developed, but the widespread sale of stock to provide the funds, while at the same time a few gentlemen at the center usurped the control, was already understood by a few. By 1840, the fifteen original owners of a Massachusetts corporation called the Merrimac Company had been expanded to 390 stockholders all over New England. Already it was charged that a clique of Boston stockholders had learned how to perpetuate their control by having the stockholders sign proxies in their favor. They held stockholders' meetings in small rooms and called many meetings of various companies at the same hour to divide the opposition of the independent stockholders who owned shares in various companies. In this way the affairs of most of the manufacturing companies in Massachusetts were under the dominion of less than a score of Boston capitalists. One man is said to have been a director in twenty-three companies. These financial magnates also controlled a Massachusetts life insurance company with a capital of $500,000 and with that they dominated nearly ten times that amount of investment funds.

They had already carried out a corporate merger and invented a holding company. Lowell, Moody, Appleton, Kirk Booth, and others brought about a merger of the Boston Manufacturing Company, the Merrimac Company, and the Pawtucket Canal Company in order to combine the processes of the first, the capital of the second, and the water power of the third. Developing more water power than they needed and controlling the process patents, they proceeded to sell the excess power and rent out the patents. They manufactured textile machinery and set up as a subsidiary a building concern to erect textile plants. Thus they would help finance the formation of a new company, put up the building, supply it with machinery, sell it a site, and furnish the water power. All this in addition to their own business which was thus a perfect example of an integrated industry. Moreover, in the process they built the first tailor-made industrial city—Lowell, Massachusetts—and to unite their various holdings the principle of the holding company was introduced. In addition to all this they formed a patent pool.

Lowell and Moody and others continued to carry on experiments in perfecting textile and power machinery, thus establishing the first industrial research. They introduced company hospitals, libraries, improvement circles, night schools, clinics, and an extensive housing program and a very remarkable magazine edited by the girl employees which brought high praise from Charles Dickens and was the parent of the long line of house organs and company journals now so numerous.

One thing had not yet appeared. Along with machinery and the railroads and the development of corporation finance it was to be the most powerful factor in the magic development of the next fifty years. This was the uncovering of the vast natural resources of America. Perhaps no one thing, economically, makes such a difference between the America after the Civil War and the America of 1839 as this. It is a common notion that this immense continent and its riches lay here almost like an open paradise of natural treasures. But when the Rockefellers lived at Richford our natural riches were almost unknown. American blacksmiths made shoes from iron gotten mostly from Great Britain. Our first textile mills used cotton which they imported. It was the presence of the mills which encouraged Southerners to plant cotton. Such copper and other metals as we required came from abroad. The tin makers of Connecticut got their sheets from Europe. Our rum makers imported molasses from Great Britain. And our tanners had to get most of their hides from other countries. Even wood—strange as it may seem in a land of primeval forests—began to be scarce. For the little steam engines burned all that was in the neighborhood and transportation was far too costly to permit of the carriage of wood. Our chief wealth was in grain and this was located along the Atlantic seaboard though now the grain fields were moving west. The making of flour and whiskey was the chief manufacturing supported by our own produce. We had a little iron and some coal—indeed a little of everything but not much of anything. Men had not yet begun to scratch under the surface of our mountains and valleys. But they were to begin this soon. And that was to mark the next great change in the lives and industry of the people.

XII

THE NEW nation had already harvested its first crop of millionaires. There were no less than twenty-five of them. The most important of them were land barons. John Jacob Astor led the list with a fortune of $25,000,000. His son, William, was reputed to have $5,000,000. Next was Stephen Van Rensselaer with $10,000,000. The well-known names of Henry Brevoort, Gouverneur Morris, Peter G. Stuyvesant, Peter Schermerhorn, James B. Lennox, and William Crosby follow, each worth from one to four million and all immortalized in the names of New York streets. There were two bankers—Isaac Bronson and John Mason—worth around a million each. There were some traders—merchant-adventurers of the old school in New York, Philadelphia, and Boston—Stephen Hunt, John Bohlen, Samuel Appleton, Peter C. Brooks, John Bryant, John P. Cushing, Thomas H. Perkins, and Robert G. Shaw. The richest of these—Stephen Girard—had died the year before in Philadelphia leaving about $7,500,000.

The industrialists were few—Amos and Abbot Lawrence, textile manufacturers worth together $5,000,000. David Sears in Boston was something quite new—a millionaire stockholder in many enterprises. Equally new was Jacob Little, the first professional security speculator, the first bear, and possessor of the dubious glory of inventing the short sale. August Belmont had just arrived from Cuba, the agent of the Rothschilds, the first of that line of bankers to handle the flood into America of foreign funds into our railroad and utility investments. There is not a single descendant of this list of twenty-seven millionaires of 1839 who qualifies for a place on the roll of the nation's business leaders today.

Some of the names on the list are familiar. The descendants of most of these men are still among our wealthiest families. But this only serves to emphasize that while they may retain much of the wealth piled up by thrifty ancestors, they do not continue to exercise a control over our industrial or financial affairs. The wealth may remain, but it is no longer dynamic. Its fecundity is enormously diminished. Its possessors are merely rich men; they are not powerful men. Still less are they dominant leaders.

XIII

THE WEEKS following Bill Rockefeller's departure wore on into months. The winter of 1843 came down with all its rigors—and this was a cruel winter. Eliza Rockefeller looked across the apple trees and down the trail toward the village many days. But Big Bill Rockefeller never appeared. Lucy was a handsome child of five, John an active, large boy of four, the baby, William, was almost 18 months old. And in this little group the endless question was when will the father come home. Across the hill the other Rockefellers would ask if there was news from Bill. Apparently there was no great bond of affection between Eliza and her husband's family. They were a different breed from herself. They were a hard, restless, worldly lot. There was plenty of liquor drunk among them. Occasionally she would see one of them go reeling over the hill past her door to Godfrey's home. Jacob Rockefeller, Bill's youngest brother, was the most persistent tippler. In old man Pierce's store in Richford today is preserved an old ledger from Rich's store where the Rockefellers traded. One day Rich said to Jacob Rockefeller that he would give him five dollars if he would come into the store sober once. Jacob owed a bill and went into Rich's store to pay it. He was sober and Mr. Rich, true to his promise, gave him a credit of five dollars on his bill. And there is the entry to this day on Rich's ledger—"Allowed Jacob Rockefeller, for not drinking, five dollars."

Amid these neighbors much of Eliza's merriness was leaving her. The cares of motherhood, the loneliness, the long winter days and nights waiting for her husband's return had sobered her face and written some lines in it. She had lapsed into the religious mood of her serious forebears. She disliked Richford. It was a godless place. Many years later John D., when he was a great figure, told his fashionable Cleveland minister, Dr. Eaton, that he was glad he had not grown up in Richford, that it was an irreligious and godless town, and the daughter of that same storekeeper Chauncey Rich publicly took him to task for the statement. But his mother was weary of Richford and her in-laws down the road. And she grew impatient of Bill and his long absences. Then one day in November a black figure patterned itself against the powdery snow down the road to Richford. There was a hurrying and scampering among the children. In a few minutes Bill was driving a handsome rig into his dooryard. He wore better clothes than he had ever had on. He had plenty of money in his wallet—a great wad of it. He had already stopped at Rich's store and paid his whole bill—nearly a thousand dollars. The children clambered over his giant figure. Eliza wept and later poured out her woes. She wanted to be nearer her own people. Bill agreed to make the change and before long the Rockefellers were on the move for their next home in Moravia, about forty miles northward toward Lake Ontario. Eliza had been angry with him. And yet she must have loved him. Beyond a doubt this man who had taken her against her father's wishes and in spite of her trim, puritanical training and his own roving, adventurous, mysterious ways, exercised a powerful influence over her mind. As he came home now, full of news and of money, with his fine horses, settling up all his accounts and looking like a figure of fashion and romance, her heart melted. This was November. Nine months later, when they were in Moravia, another child was born. Bill had been forgiven.

CHAPTER II. THE LAND OF SUPERIOR CUNNING

THE HOUSE which William Rockefeller provided for the family was about three miles north of the village of Moravia. Moravia was at the time a small settlement of perhaps not more than five hundred inhabitants. It had a cotton mill run by water power that employed a hundred people. The Moravia Hotel which still stands was its chief ornament. Built in 1831, it is a huge, box-like structure with a great porch running about its whole length. These large early hotels, out of proportion to their villages, are explained by the heavy traffic by horseback and river boat and stagecoaches in those days. Men broke their journeys by night in hotels, as they do now in automobile travel.

The town is built on an expanse of rolling upland broken by the deep and narrow valleys of Owasco Inlet and its tributaries. Rockefeller's house was on the Lake Road. On a sloping terrace it looked out over Lake Owasco, the smallest and loveliest of the celebrated Finger Lakes. It was a country of abundance with many good farms raising grain and truck and cattle and hay. The woods were filled with game and in Lake Owasco were pike and pickerel and bass and trout. This lovely country, filled with glens and falls and gorges, was the home of the famous Six Nations—the Mohawks, Oneidas, Onondagas, Senecas, Tuscaroras, and Cayugas. Here near Owasco the Cayugas made their home. The county was called Cayuga County. Cayuga means "Land of Superior Cunning." Here, then, William Rockefeller proceeded in his odd moments to sharpen the wits of his boys and chiefly that silent, searching lad named John.

The house was a much better one than the cottage they had left at Richford. Moreover this one Bill Rockefeller bought. There were a hundred acres of farm land behind it. It was a better place for Mrs. Rockefeller because her father's home was on the other side of the Lake and near by were neighbors on each side of her home. On one side was the Rosekrans family, on the other side the Hewetts. Their descendants still occupy those houses. The Rockefeller house is no longer to be seen. It was destroyed in 1926 by fire when being used as a convict camp.

Big Bill went on with his old business—selling medicines—and his old ways, his long absences, though he spent more time with his family now. He mingled more freely with his neighbors. Turkey shoots were a favorite sport of the day and Bill, who loved a good rifle, never missed a turkey shoot when he was home and he never failed to delight his boys with his great skill as a shot. He took some part in local affairs. He was an advocate of building a new school and somehow was charged with the commission to locate it. The dispute over the site Bill settled by declaring it should be located in the precise center of the district. And this he proceeded to ascertain by an original method. He drove his rig from north to south and then from east to west, counting the revolutions of the wagon wheels. Then he repeated the process, driving only half the number of revolutions north to south and east to west. This gave him the center. It turned out to be near his own home, a fact which he observed with a twinkle in his eye.

There was a hired man on the farm but not a great deal of farming was done. Bill's chief occupation was his selling. But, he allowed, he turned a penny now and then trading horses. And he bought up some timber rights and hired a gang of men to cut the trees and haul them down to Lake Owasco, where they were rafted to Prison City as Auburn was called. This was just a flyer in lumber, not a regular business. He still was a little mysterious. His neighbors were never quite sure what his business was and they wagged their heads about it.

But for all his swaggering, wandering, extravagant ways, and his long absences, this odd, fun-loving man, given a little to brawling and with a ready eye for a good-looking woman, loved his family in his strange way. He knew how to play with the children and he had a special weakness at first for his son John. He took the boys down to Owasco Lake, taught them how to swim and row a boat. He showed them how to drive a horse, to ride in the saddle and to hold a gun. He supported his family, though in a manner uncertain and harrowing to his poor wife. He was by turns flush with money and in want. Always he came home with plenty of money and with a new team of horses. Moreover he brought with him great tales of the Indians he had met and the great figures of the day he had seen and of the wonders of the railroads and steamboats and huge water wheels. But gradually there accumulated on his head a weight of suspicion which filled the whole countryside.

II

ON A chest in the living room stood a little blue bowl. Here, when John was seven years old, went two York shillings—the first money he had ever earned. Precocity in finance is as common as in literature. The man who founded the House of Rothschild began to be interested in coins at the age of ten. Hetty Green opened her first bank account when she was eight and at ten could name offhand the prices of most New York Stock Exchange securities. Russell Sage was a successful wholesale merchant at twenty-four. John D. Rockefeller picked up stones on a neighbor's farm and was paid two shillings. His first real business venture was to come later.

One day, as he stood near the house, the boy saw a turkey peering cautiously about her, sniffing the wind, pushing her long neck in different directions with great stealth. The country boy did not have to be told what this meant. He knew the turkey was preparing to "steal her nest." He ran at top speed to his mother with the news. Eliza told her excited son that if he would follow the turkey and find her brood he might have them and raise them for himself. This was not such an easy task. It meant stalking the mother turkey. She eluded the boy for two days. But she little knew the spirit of the patient mind that shadowed her. She was perhaps the first victim of that relentless, ruthless patience with which this boy would pursue greater objectives in the years to come. In the end the young turkey fancier entered the woodshed with a huge basket and in it his cargo of young turkeys.

Among the pursuits of that primitive region was driving wild turkeys to market. Men came through at intervals like drovers, pushing ahead of them huge flocks of the birds. The flocks scampered ahead of their drivers, by day filling the countryside with their clamor. At night they darkened the trees near the farmhouse where the turkey drover roosted for the night. Thus John, the young turkey man, had a ready market for his turkeys when the next drover came through. He continued to manage his flock, selling off some of them and building on the foundation of York shillings in the blue bowl on his mother's mantel.

III

THESE were troubled, difficult days for Eliza Rockefeller. Not long after the family settled in Moravia a fourth child—Mary Ann—was born. Two years later Eliza bore twins. One of these twins was Frank, who was to play so strange a part in the life of his famous brother. The other was called Francis, a frail child demanding incessant care. With six children to care for—the oldest little over seven—Mrs. Rockefeller's cares were many. For some reason she mixed very little with her neighbors. They were a strange crowd.

THE LAND OF SUPERIOR CUNNING

But the children—all save Francis—grew amazingly. They were growing to be large-boned and powerful. John was not robust and deep-chested like William, but he had a large frame though there was little flesh on it. This Finger Lake region is a land of big men and big trees and of long-lived men and trees. All through the region one is shown ancient trees—the great giant elm at Waterloo believed to be 350 years old, the Patriarch Elm beside the Old Indian Trail, another veteran of 350 years, and a famous tree at Naples which local authorities believe, perhaps without sufficient data, to be the oldest tree in the world. As for men, the crumbling tombstones at Harford Mills tell of its hardy octogenarians. And as for strength and size, they used to tell in Moravia of old John Sabin, who could lift two cider barrels filled with cider by holding them with his fingers in the bungholes. The boys went swimming in Owasco Lake and brought trout and bass home to their mother to cook. William and Frank were given to waywardness. They were hard to control. People said they were like their father. But John was like his mother. He was quiet, reserved, shy, serious. He had a narrow, long, lean face, lacking in mobility of expression and small bright eyes that looked with great intentness at one. And as he grew older he grew closer and closer to his mother. The children went to school in the little near-by schoolhouse which Bill had planted so conveniently. But the schooling was very slight. The teacher was there for but a few months in the year. The source of their scholarship was those old Peter Parley books then as much in use as McGuffey's books were at a later day.

IV

STRANGE stories were going about Moravia about horse stealing. Eliza Rockefeller had liked very little the godless neighborhood of Richford. She now found that she liked less the even more godless neighborhood in which she lived. A stranger collection of neighbors was never gathered together in a quiet rural setting. Before long stories began to connect the names of these neighbors with the horse thefts. Rockefeller's hired man, Scott Brower, was under suspicion and people whispered the name of Big Bill himself as implicated in the conspiracy. Some said he acted as the fence, receiving the horses in his large barn and then running them across the country through a deep gully still to be seen near the ruined foundations of the old Rockefeller cottage. These rumors were not long in blossoming into definite indictments. Several of the neighbors were arrested. No charge was made against Bill himself and he returned home in the midst of the scandal with something of the air of a man who was not afraid. The men arrested were convicted and sent to State's prison. And to this day there are people in Moravia who will tell you that Bill escaped because he knew how to cover his tracks. This is doubtless unfair to Rockefeller. There is no evidence of any sort connecting him with these horse stealings. But the whole episode left a stain on his name and made life in Moravia difficult and painful for his wife.

To deepen the shadows about her the youngest child—Francis—died about this time. And the sorrow of Eliza Rockefeller was intensified and complicated by a new group of rumors which went around about her husband's relations with women. She was now, under the weight of many cares, turning more and more toward religion and to the stern morality of her forebears. She was a proud woman and as the shadows gathered about her she exhibited a strength of character which commanded the respect of her neighbors. But she clung to her wayward husband and there are no stories in the neighborhood of any serious trouble between them.

V

THE LAKE ROAD which passed the Rockefeller home led to Prison City—Auburn. On the other side of the lake was the Plank Road along which the endless caravans of pioneers moved toward Lake Erie and across to Ohio and further West. But when the weather was good those who wished to save the toll fees traveled by the Lake Road. Young John could see the wagons moving, scores of them every day, in that ceaseless westward migration which had begun thirty years before. By this road the silent boy would sit in the long summer evenings. To get down to Lake Owasco he had to cross the road. And always, like his mother, and his older sister, as he sat there or wandered across the road he cast a glance toward Auburn hoping perhaps his father's horse might come swinging around the sharp curve.

Big Bill came home in May. He arrived in great good humor and with his pockets full. At the moment Moravia was in great excitement over the wonderful thing which had happened in California. A man had found gold on his ranch—General Sutter. The wagons began to pass in greater numbers—great Conestoga wagons now. Men were flocking across the mountains and on horseback. The fever for gold was in the air. Politics, rum, riches, and religion—these were the favorite topics of American cracker-barrel debaters. Now riches outranked them all. Only a little while before Mr. Meade—G. L. Meade of Moravia—a farmer, with his gun strapped to his back and a sea-chest on his shoulder, had started for Auburn. There he joined the expedition of the Cayuga Joint Stock Company—seventy-nine hardy gold hunters who had put in five hundred dollars apiece and chartered the barque *Belvidere* and were making ready to sail around the Horn to San Francisco. Each man took his chest, his arms, supplies for three years, and medicines and mining tools. Here was an adventure to stir the imagination of a small boy. The barque *Belvidere* actually sailed in February. Three months later Bill came home full of stories about the gold rush. John listened to all this, looked wistfully at the little blue bowl that held his fortune and put all this wisdom away in his head.

VI

THE NAME of Johann August Sutter—and gold—was on every tongue. But there was another name, which we have forgotten now, but which came in for a little mention then—and another article more precious than gold. Dr. Abraham Gessner and coal oil. Up in Prince Edward Island, Dr. Gessner, an able engineer, successfully distilled oil from coalshale. He called it kerosene. This was in 1846. But in a few years it was introduced into the United States. The North American Gas Light Company set up its refineries at Hunters Point on Long Island and soon became rich making coal oil. Coal-oil lamps appeared in the Moravia Hotel. The lamp was a wonderful thing. And men said this new form of lighting would soon sweep the world. Refineries sprang up everywhere. The whale-oil business of New England saw its days numbered.

VII

BILL ROCKEFELLER remained about Moravia for a while—longer indeed, as we shall see, than was good for him. His reputation was now seriously tarnished. But he was a great talker, a pleasant companion, a man of the world. He did not drink but he spent much time on the old Moravia Hotel porch and in the bar where there was plenty of talk about the gold in Cal-a-for-ny-ae and the coming election and the fact that Millard Fillmore, who lived a little way up the road, was going to run for Vice-President.

About this time a great agitation swept over the country for temperance. The Washington Society was organized to fight liquor and a branch of it was set up in Moravia. Bill was always ready to hold forth eloquently against liquor and to illustrate his talk with horrific examples from his own family. If he didn't drink, however, he had other ways of regaling himself. There was a girl working in the Rockefeller home named Anne. She was young and comely. Among the neighbors it was whispered Bill made love to her violently, an alleged transgression which was to have a powerful influence on the subsequent history of his family. It was May—Spring—when a man's fancy lightly turns to thoughts of love. Bill's fancy, said his unfriendly neighbors, turned in that direction now—but not lightly. A little later he left Moravia on one of his trips.

After he had gone the story got about. His enemies were anxious to see him out of Moravia. How long he was gone we do not know, but in July of the following year the Grand Jury of Cayuga County returned to the Court of Oyer and Terminer an indictment against him for ravishing Anne.

Rockefeller was warned in advance. He went to Niles, the home of John Davison, his father-in-law, and begged him to sign his bail bond. Davison said he was too old to go bail for any man. As a matter of fact, he hated Rockefeller and now had an additional grievance against him. Bill owed him money.

The hotly pressed man went at night to his home near Owasco Lake. The sheriff was notified of his presence and hurried down from Auburn. But Bill got wind of his coming, bade good-by to his family and left Moravia forever.[1]

---

[1] This simple statement of facts hardly tells the whole story. If Rockefeller was innocent why did he run away? Unable to obtain bail the prospect of remaining for a long siege in jail awaiting trial may have been a sufficient reason to a man who lived as much on the fringes of organized society as the elder Rockefeller. Besides he may have felt in great peril from the presence of many very industrious enemies. The whole incident is a little lighted up by a curious volume which appeared in print for private circulation in Moravia only three years ago. This

THE LAND OF SUPERIOR CUNNING 39

A few days later John Davison brought suit on two notes made in 1845 and 1846 by William Rockefeller for nearly a thousand dollars. A few days after that the sheriff returned to Moravia, and added to the shame and grief of Eliza Rockefeller by appraising and seizing the farm and its personal effects upon the application of her father. The following year after the family had left Moravia it was all sold for $4,173.

VIII

AFTER the indictment life in Moravia any longer was insupportable for the family. A little later William Rockefeller sent word to his wife that he had rented a house near Owego, the county seat of Tioga County, the county where John D. was born. That was only about forty miles away, but was separated by a wilderness. It was far enough away for Bill's safety and the peace of his family. And so in 1850 the remnants of the household effects not taken in the attachment were piled upon a wagon. Lucy sat beside her mother holding the infant Frank. John, now tall and angular, dangled his long legs over the back of the poorly stocked wagon, with chubby little William beside him. The Rockefeller family, bankrupt save for the courage of their Spartan mother, was on the move again.

extraordinary literary production was called "Joshua, a Man of the Finger Lakes." It was the product of a literary grocer of Syracuse, who was inspired and commissioned by a descendant of one of Bill Rockefeller's Moravia neighbors. Joshua, the man of the Finger Lakes, was Joshua Rosekrans who was indicted for horse stealing at the time. The belief persists among his descendants that this indictment was the work of Bill Rockefeller. The book, after all these years, was produced to prove that Joshua was as innocent as the driven snow, the real culprit being William Rockefeller. The author has sufficiently examined the facts surrounding the writing of this astonishing volume to know that much of it is pure fiction. The book reveals, however, what the Rockefellers in the district have always believed: that there was a deep-seated enmity toward the elder Rockefeller among his immediate neighbors. They have always believed that this enmity was responsible for the charges made against him at Auburn. In any case, it is worth observing that the indictment made in July, 1849, was based on an alleged offense committed in April, 1848, nearly fifteen months earlier.

CHAPTER III. "HE WHO SEEKS THE WAMPUM BELT"

MRS. ROCKEFELLER now found herself with her brood of five small children secluded in a small house off a remote road about three miles outside of Owego. Her husband was gone. She was among strangers. Moravia had been a complete disaster. The world had come down about her ears and she faced the future filled with many misgivings and forebodings.

The house was well away from the beaten road. That, doubtless, was why it was chosen. It was not so good as the place they had lost and left in Moravia. It is by no means certain that the house still standing and visited by many people as the boyhood home of John D. Rockefeller is the one to which Bill had brought his family. The house now in existence belonged to Buffington Montaigne, whereas their first refuge in Owego belonged to the LaMonte family. It is likely the first house was destroyed by fire after which Bill went to Montaigne and rented the second one. Fire has seemed to pursue John D. Rockefeller. The Moravia house was burned to the ground. This Owego asylum went the same way. The house they lived in at Strongville, Ohio, was destroyed by fire. The fine home at Forest Hill was razed to the ground by fire. The original home at Pocantico was also destroyed by fire. And in the early days of the oil business Rockefeller himself said they lived in perpetual fear of the fire alarm bell. Many fires wiped out hundreds of thousands of dollars. One almost wrecked his business.

The house where the family finally settled was and still is near the banks of the Susquehanna River and opposite an island then called Big Island but now known as Hiawatha Island. This island was the favorite playground of the young Rockefeller boys. And some one has called attention to the fact that it now bears a name (Hiawatha) which means "He Who Seeks the Wampum Belt."

Eliza Rockefeller was now thirty-six years old. Her full, well-rounded face had now grown thin, her eyes wide, her forehead streaked with care. But there was a certain delicacy about her features, a certain keenness mixed with wistfulness, which led Ida Tarbell to observe later, very justly, her resemblance to Letitia

Romolina, the mother of Napoleon. Managing her three sons, alive with the energy of robust boyhood, drew heavily upon her strength. But she was a stern disciplinarian. Believing in the rod, she was forced to brandish it over the heads of her turbulent colony many times. One day the whole flock broke into a kind of general riot. The mother hailed them into the house, stood them in a row and went for her rod. This she flourished over their heads in a manner which left no room for doubt that she was prepared to use it. When complete silence fell upon the shuffling row of rebels she said:

"Now do you think you can play without fighting?" She compelled each child in turn to answer that question and then dismissed them all amid silence.

Once John was summoned for a switching. In the midst of it he attempted a panicky and explanatory defense.

"Never mind," she interrupted. "This will do for the next time."

John and William loved to skate on the Susquehanna near Big Island. Once their mother, fearing the ice was too fragile, forbade them to go on the river. But they crept away and were in full career on their skates when they were startled by a cry for help. Another boy skating alone had broken through the ice and plunged into the water. John and William raced to his rescue, pulled him through the ice and then, forgetting their own transgression in the wave of heroism that engulfed them, went proudly home with the news of their achievement. Their mother greeted them with her switch, praised them for their bravery and then whipped them for disobeying her.

But the river beckoned to John. Somehow he has always contrived to keep himself rooted close by the water. His last home looked out on Owasco Lake. Here at Owego he could gaze wistfully for hours at the Susquehanna. In Cleveland his first job planted him on the very banks of the Cuyahoga and his first business was on River Street beside that same stream. In New York his office has always looked out upon the Hudson and today, from his home upon a hill at Tarrytown, he has expended endless money and attention upon the views of the glorious river which open to him there. "He shall be like a tree planted by the rivers of water, that bringeth forth his fruit in season; his leaf also shall not wither and whatsoever he doeth shall prosper."

II

This year—1849—when America was aflame over the discovery of gold, young John Rockefeller, just ten, made an equally famous discovery for himself. He discovered interest. Through all the family trials John had held fast to his little blue bowl and its growing fortune. One day he was told a farmer near by wished to borrow $50. The farmer was willing to pay seven per cent interest. This boy, wise in money beyond his years, wanted to know all about interest. What is it? What is seven per cent? How much is that on $50? And so out of his blue bowl he counted fifty dollars and the small boy, only a little over ten, loaned the grown man the desired sum. This was the first act in that adventure. A year later the farmer went to the Rockefeller house and handed John his fifty dollars and the three dollars and fifty cents interest along with it. Then the quiet, solemn-visaged boy went aside and looked with intentness at that interest. He had been hoeing potatoes for another man and had just been paid for the work. It amounted to thirty-seven and a half cents a day, which was very good pay for a boy. As he looked at his interest money an illuminating thought broke in his mind. This $3.50 interest was as much as ten days' pay. This fifty dollars had been working for him all through that year, night and day, and had earned for him as much as he could earn himself working hard all day for ten full days. What if he had another fifty dollars at work and many of them? The discovery fascinated him. In later years he said: "From that time onward I determined to make money work for me."

III

Eliza Rockefeller, as she grew more religious, had been compelled to manage along without a church. In Owego, however, her neighbor, Mr. LaMonte, would take the Rockefeller family along with his own in his wagon to the village on Sunday for services.

Mary Curtis was the schoolmistress. A brisk young woman, she got eight dollars a month and board in the homes of the various scholars. Mary Curtis's daughter still lives in Owego and retains many memories of her mother's early friendship with the Rockefellers.

The Rockefeller children did not do so well in school. Mrs. Rockefeller was unable to preserve in their small front room at night that calm required for study. William and Frank were disturbing elements. Down the road lived the LaMonte family. The LaMonte children were rated the best students in the school and Susan, sixteen years old, the eldest, was the prize scholar. Mrs. Rockefeller wondered why her children were so backward and the LaMontes so advanced. She adopted the most direct means of resolving the point. She went one night to Mrs. LaMonte and asked. She was told that the LaMonte children sat quietly and studied every night under the direction of Susan.

"Well," said Mrs. Rockefeller, "that's what my children need and I don't seem to be able to help them. I wonder if mine couldn't come down here in the evening and study with your children?"

"They can if Susan says so," replied Mrs. LaMonte. "Susan's the head of this school."

Susan assured Mrs. Rockefeller her children might come on one condition—that they remain quiet, that they study and do not distract the others.

Without further delay Lucy, John, William, Frank, and Mary went each evening after supper to the LaMonte study hour. Susan soon noticed that John was in earnest but that his brothers were chiefly bent on knocking some fun out of the session. They kicked each other under the table, made faces, snickered and had a good time generally. When their fun-making became too troublesome good Mrs. LaMonte led them into the next room where they would distract no one. And while they played, their sober-faced brother bent over his book in the next room.

These details are worth recording for this was the beginning of one of the most notable careers of any American woman in the field of education. Susan LaMonte, now ninety-seven years of age and known as Mrs. Susan Life, is still living in Owego, after a long and brilliant career as the founder and mistress of the Rye Select Academy for Girls, where many of the most widely known women in America were reared under her hands. John D. Rockefeller himself has never visited these old boyhood haunts without calling on both Susan Life and Mary Curtis, the daughter of the little schoolmistress.

IV

AFTER a year in Mary Curtis's school John, William, and Lucy were sent to Owego Academy. Owego was the home of many prosperous families whose fine houses are yet to be seen on Front Street almost facing the Susquehanna River. The young men of these families were sent to Yale University. It was not uncommon to see the wealthier ones being driven after holidays to college in fine carriages attended by their servants. But there was no preparatory school. And so the citizens established Owego Academy, "for males and females." Dr. William Smythe, who had his Bachelor's Degree from Edinburgh, was brought over to be the master. He remained for many years, later establishing a weekly paper which still flourishes under the editorship of his son. A substantial brick building was put up for the Academy and this may be found standing opposite the courthouse. It is used now as an office building. The sons and daughters of Owego's best families went to the Academy. The tuition was for Reading, Writing, Orthography, Elocution, Mental Algebra, Geography, and use of the globes and was three dollars per term. More advanced students had to pay five dollars for Latin, Greek, Hebrew, French, Moral Science, Political Economy, Botany, Mineralogy, Geology, and other natural sciences. To this was added a charge of twenty-five cents for fuel in the Fall term and thirty cents in the Winter.

This curious course cost little enough if we understand the fees in the money of our own day. But it was considerable for that period when dollars were very scarce. How much a dollar was worth may be seen from another entry in the catalogue which announces that board with a respectable family could be had for from 14 to 16 shillings a week—the shilling at the time being worth 12½ cents.

With three pupils in the Academy it will be seen the Rockefeller family was spending $10.50 a quarter for tuition and another 75 cents for fuel. They did not board in the town but lived at home and walked the three miles back and forth each day.

V

THERE were other boys in Owego Academy at the time who would be heard from in after years. One of them was to become United

States Senator, to be known as the "easy boss" of New York State and one of the leaders of the Republican party in the Senate—Tom Platt. Another—Ben Tracy—with the title of General—would become Secretary of the Navy under Hayes. Still another was Frederick Hewett, to become a man of vast wealth and the munificent donor of $2,500,000 to the New York Post Graduate Hospital and $250,000 to Yale. There was another potential general among them—General Isaac C. Catlin—and George Worthington, to become Bishop of Nebraska.

VI

ONE DAY a photographer arrived at the school to take group pictures of the class. When John's and William's classes were lined up to be photographed, the two boys remained apart. That picture hangs today in the home of Dr. Smythe's son. A few years ago John D. Rockefeller and a grand-nephew visited Mr. Smythe. The nephew scanned the picture looking for the boyhood countenance of his famous uncle.

"Uncle John," he said, "I don't see your picture."

"No," answered the great man, "William and I had to remain out of it. We didn't have good enough suits."

Much has been made of the children's attendance at this school to prove that Rockefeller was brought up in a well-to-do family. As a matter of fact, they were poor—not poor in the meaning of that word today, for then no one was in actual want. But they were not so well off as most of their neighbors. The charges at the school were a heavy burden. But this proves no more than that Bill Rockefeller, for all his faults, looked after his family. They were not so poor that they had to invade John's blue bowl. He was permitted to keep that intact.

This boy, now in his teens, was at least among better people than he had known before, though it was by no means an atmosphere of culture. His preference, as always, was for arithmetic. He had a fondness for calculation and particularly for mental arithmetic, though in later life he insisted even arithmetic did not come easy to him. When he had grown to manhood he was never given to laying out plans on paper. One day after his rise to fame he called his secretary, reeled off some figures and asked for the answer. The secretary worked it quickly in his head. That pleased Rockefeller very much. He knew the answer and smilingly told his assistant he had given him the problem just to see if he could manage it. There were no books in the house. Poetry, pictures, art, the well-known literary classics—these things he heard little of. But he did hear a good deal about figures from both his father and mother.

Money was much on his mind at the time. To go to school he had to pass the handsome home of Mr. Hewett, Owego's richest citizen. There were other rich men's homes on the way. One day as he was walking home from school he said to his boy companion:

"Charlie, what do you want to do when you grow up?"

Charlie extended his arm in a sweeping gesture.

"I want to own all the land," he confessed, "from here down to the schoolhouse. And you—what do you want to do?"

"Charlie," he replied with the air of one whose decision had been deliberately taken, "you know what I want to do? When I grow up I want to be worth $100,000. And I'm going to be too."

He liked to play checkers. Once when playing his companion became a little impatient at John's deliberation. He took plenty of time over every move. Finally the boy said:

"Hurry up and move. What do you take so long for?"

John looked up gravely.

"I'll move as soon as I know what move to make."

He pondered a moment longer. Then he commented:

"What do you think I'm playing for—to let you beat me?"

When released at recess if John was in the mood to play at all, he invariably had his own idea of the game to be played. If the others were satisfied to play his game he went along with them full tilt. But if he suggested a game and some other were adopted, he would remain out of the play. An old schoolfellow of his, telling of this, said: "He would not get mad. He would stand on the side and watch the game. But he wouldn't play." The game had to be his or none.

Another schoolfellow told an odd story of him, the meaning of which was wholly lost on the teller. "John," he said, "seemed a lazy boy. William was brisk and energetic. If he had something to do he would pitch right in and do it. But not John. If he was told to do something he would sit around and start figuring out the easiest way. He was lazy."

It was impossible for Rockefeller to begin any job in a haphazard

VIEW OF THE ROCKEFELLER COUNTRY

In the foreground, Owego, about the middle of the last century. Rockefeller's home was opposite Big Island, which is seen in the Susquehanna River. Richford, Rockefeller's birthplace, nestles among the hills in the background to the right. Citizens of Owego cherish a hope that the Rockefeller family may acquire and make into a state park, to be known as Rockefeller Park, the hilly country stretching northward from Owego.

Top, OWEGO ACADEMY, WHERE ROCKEFELLER ATTENDED SCHOOL. *Bottom*, "DR." WILLIAM ROCKEFELLER AND ELIZA DAVISON ROCKEFELLER, FATHER AND MOTHER OF JOHN D.

way. The oil world was to learn one day that whenever John D. Rockefeller moved it was after he had sat around and figured out the way. The key to this man's life is that everything in it has been carried out in accordance with a carefully considered plan. His life has been as completely devoid of accident as that of any other human being who ever lived. He has lived a planned life in everything—in his work and his play.

VII

THE SMALL house across the bay from Big Island is in darkness. The children are in bed. The hired man has retired and Eliza Rockefeller sits alone. By the fire in the front room she sits mending the boys' clothes, thinking of her fugitive husband and smoking her pipe. She has taken to that now to beguile her loneliness. Presently she is done with her work and taking her candle she goes, accompanied by huge bobbing shadows, to her room upstairs. She is soon in bed but not asleep. Always she lays awake and listens—thinks and listens. For what?

Along the road out of the darkness emerges the shadowy figure of a man on horseback. He puts his horse quietly in the barn and then goes cautiously to the side of the house. There is a ladder lying on the ground. It is always there. He raises the ladder to the side window of the attic, well-concealed behind the trees. This big man cautiously mounts the ladder. At the window he takes a coin from his pocket and taps crisply on the tin smoke pipe which emerges from the side. In an instant the window is opened and Big Bill Rockefeller crawls through the window. The candle glows again downstairs. Eliza is listening to her strange husband's account of his wanderings.

Since the family appeared at Owego Bill has not been seen by the neighbors. They know nothing of him or his whereabouts or his habits. People talk about him in whispers. The charge still stands against him in Auburn and so whenever he visits his family it is at night and by stealth, entering through the upper window in order not to excite attention.

In the morning there is a great pother among the children over the arrival of their father. He is full of jokes and stories and he always comes home with his pockets full. He gives each child a five-dollar gold piece. What the other children did with theirs is not known but John's always went into the blue bowl.

The family seemed rich when William Rockefeller was home and when he left he gave his wife what perhaps seemed ample funds to last until his next visit, to pay the bills, provide for the house and pay the charges at Owego Academy. But ofttimes his absences were longer than the supply of money he left behind. And Eliza knew this. And so she watched the pennies with a jealous eye. As for John, he hoarded his small fortune. He grew more attentive to his savings as he advanced in years. He was able to see the grim processes of economy at work. He might lack a good enough suit to get into the school picture, but he held fast to his gold pieces at home.

Big Bill is older now—past forty, and a little sobered. But he is no solemn-visaged puritan. There is a wild, lawless streak in the man's make-up. He will never sit down to a life of revolving daily duties. Where has he been? What has he been doing? This remained a mystery to his family, at least to the younger ones, who had learned, somehow, not to talk about their father's affairs. It is doubtful if Eliza knew fully how her husband was occupied. It is probable he had shifted his operations—his medicine selling—further West for he talked about Ohio and the great movement over the mountains.

It is also probable that he is doing somewhat better—enough to provide for his family to which he was devoted in his rough way and to see whom he risked the return to Owego and made long and arduous journeys through the forests. But the family is still poor. They are not without food or shelter or clothes, but their house is humble and poorly furnished, most of their food is such as they produce themselves and their clothes are made from cloth purchased in the village and put together by Eliza herself. Many of the old inhabitants who were acquainted with the family seem to be agreed about this.

Thus the family lived until 1853. The older children had two years at Owego Academy. John himself was fourteen years old, though he was far older than this in gravity and intelligence. Then one night Eliza was aroused by the tapping of the coin on the stovepipe. A few days later the neighbors saw the Rockefeller belongings being loaded on a wagon—boxes, baskets, furniture. Mrs.

Rockefeller went among them and with tears in her eyes said "Good-by." The Rockefeller family were on the move once more —this time for a long journey, up past Richford and over the plank road around Lake Owasco and on to Lake Erie and then, over the Alleghenies into the Western Reserve, into New Connecticut as Ohio was then called. Thus the family brought to a close its troubled life in New York.

PART TWO

BUSINESS AND RELIGION

CHAPTER I. NEW CONNECTICUT

THE ROCKEFELLER caravan did not stop at Cleveland. It moved on to a small village a little to the southwest called Strongville. There Bill Rockefeller established his family in a good house—the best it had yet lived in. Apparently Big Bill was doing fairly well, though he was certainly not a man of means. He was lavish enough with his money when he had it, but like all knights of the grip there were seasons when he had to pinch a little. He still spent most of his time away from home and he kept pretty quiet about what he did, save that he sold medicines.

II

JOHN did not remain long in Strongville. He was old enough now for high school and his father arranged for him to live in Cleveland and become a pupil at the Central High.

In 1854 this youth, then fourteen years of age, but well able to take care of himself and with a tidy sum saved over many years, bade good-by to his mother and made his first entry into the great world alone.

Cleveland at this time was a sprawling little town huddled around the flats on the Cuyahoga River running out to Lake Erie. The first railroad had entered Cleveland just two years before when the first train on the Cleveland, Columbus, and Cincinnati Railroad, bearing the governor and almost the entire legislature, made its inaugural run amid a general holiday. The population had now grown beyond 17,000. A Board of Trade was busy pushing

NEW CONNECTICUT

the name of the town far and wide. The first iron ore destined to add so much to the city's wealth was brought in that year. There was already a medical school and two hospitals. The Lake fleet was becoming famous and prosperous. The stagecoaches were busy bringing in new settlers, visitors, and traveling men. Little Cleveland was getting to be known for its manufactures. But as yet it depended chiefly on two industries—the receipt of produce from the many small farms all around and its shipment to the East and the handling of the stream of travelers which flowed incessantly from all parts of the Northeast, converged on Cleveland and then moved West. Many stopped. Ohio was filled with former newcomers from Connecticut and eastern and southern New York. That is why it was called New Connecticut and the American New England Association in Cleveland was as important and active as the Iowa Association in Los Angeles today.

Young John Rockefeller took a room in a boarding house in Erie Street and began at once attendance at the Central High School.

III

HE WAS not there long before he made two acquaintances who were to play important parts in his life. One of these was a round, hardy boy named Mark Hanna. Rockefeller had come almost directly from the Owego Academy where he was a fellow student of Tom Platt to the Central High School of Cleveland where he found himself a class below Mark Hanna. One of these would become the boss of New York State, the other the boss of Ohio and both occupy commanding positions of leadership in the nation at a time when Rockefeller was to find himself in frequent collision not only with the national government but with the governments of New York and Ohio.

Another friendship even more important than these was established at this time. There was an old gardener living in Cleveland at this time named Alexander Sked, known for years as Deacon Sked. Sked was a deacon in the newly formed Erie Street Baptist Church Chapel at the corner of Erie and Ohio streets, not far from where Rockefeller lived. The church itself, destined to fame because of Rockefeller's membership in it and known later as the Euclid Avenue Baptist Church, had been set up only about three years before with Rev. J. Hyatt Smith as pastor. Rockefeller met

Sked and the old deacon brought him into the church. He was baptized in 1854 and immediately became a regular and faithful attendant at Sunday School. The church was just beginning to flourish in a small way. It had a library and three hundred students in the Sunday School. And it was in this Sunday School rather than at the Central High that Rockefeller was to make most of his friends.

IV

ONE FRIEND he was to find at the High School in the class preceding his. This was Laura Celestia Spelman. She was the daughter of a gentleman of some means and of some importance in Cleveland at the time. Though the same age as himself she was yet a full year more advanced. There were some differences between them. She was a good student. He was an indifferent one, though there is no doubt about his earnest attention to his studies. She was interested in books and music. He was not. She was an Episcopalian and went to the fashionable church of the city. He worshiped in the humble little chapel of one of the poorest churches. He lived in a cheap boarding house on Erie Street and was a simple, unpolished, grave, and a little awkward country boy, whose clothes and manner marked him as such. She lived in a fine house and counted her friends among the best people in Cleveland. Some of the old students have said they were friends. Others insist they were merely acquaintances and that the friendship which ripened into their marriage began later. At least one very intimate friend of Laura Spelman was very much astonished in later years when she heard the two were engaged.

In Central High School Rockefeller was known as a serious boy who had no girl friends and went in very little for fun. He was known as a plodding student in mathematics but in nothing else. There are three brief essays on Education, Freedom, and St. Patrick still extant written by him as exercises at this time which reveal that composed, orderly, deliberate habit of thought which shone out in his very few statements and letters in after years. Rockefeller has always possessed the faculty for expressing himself with great clearness and accuracy and with a certain quaint, homely, yet rounded and formal conciseness and this method of mind is already apparent in these essays which are marked by an intelligent simplicity a little unusual in so young a person.

At school all the students were required to recite—that ancient Friday afternoon practice of all the old schoolhouses. John's usual contribution when called upon was a lugubrious piece which began "I'm pleased although I'm sad." The line fitted him well and many of the pupils, particularly the girls, quick to spot the weakness in another's armor, used to speak of him as Old Pleased-Although-I'm-Sad.

CHAPTER II. TWO MEDICINE MEN

IN STRONGVILLE, as everywhere, the neighbors asked each other what Bill Rockefeller did for a living. Then one day Uncle Joe Webster, one of them, went on a trip and his journey brought him at evening into the village of Richfield, Summit County, Ohio. Inside the hotel and on the wall his eye was fixed by a small sign reading: "Dr. William A. Rockefeller, the Celebrated Cancer Specialist, Here for One Day Only. All cases of Cancer Cured unless too far gone and then they can be greatly benefited."

Could this be Big Bill Rockefeller from Strongville? Uncle Webster did not have to wait long. For a little later a crowd gathered outside the hotel around the buggy of a big man in a long black coat and with a big dark red beard. Going outside Webster found Bill Rockefeller beginning to talk—his high pitch, as it was called then and still is. So this is what Bill Rockefeller did for a living. He was a pitch man. And he called himself Dr. Rockefeller! Uncle Joe called him Doc. And thereafter he was called Doc Rockefeller. Apparently he was doing well too, for he charged twenty-five dollars for a cancer treatment, though he sold his medicine in bottles for a smaller sum.

Here doubtless was the explanation of his move to Strongville. As the immigrant wagons passed through Cleveland and then continued the long journey over the plains Westward their road lay directly past Strongville. Here was a rich territory for the medicine man. Traveling in primitive ways, ailments were plentiful and the travelers always had some funds with which to buy remedies. And so Doc Rockefeller must have found it profitable to keep close to that incessant stream of pioneers as they headed for the new country. His attention was probably called to Strongville by the presence there of the Humistan family—distant relatives.

Webster talked with him after his show that night and the Doctor grew expansive about his operations. He said he had been traveling in ever-widening circles and had carried his doctoring into Iowa. He was spending more and more time in that state. He told Webster how he was buying up new land there. And he boasted of the devious ways in which he was getting it. He loaned money to farmers at twelve per cent. But he tried to lend farmers who couldn't pay so he could foreclose on them and take the farms. This may be taken with a grain of salt. The good Doctor was a boastful man and he loved to tell tales about his own shrewdness. Living by his wits, in daily contact with skeptical crowds on whose minds he had to play with his old-fashioned, high-flown "med" oratory, it was natural he should come to put smartness among the cardinal virtues.

The case of Bill Rockefeller is not dismissed by calling him a quack. That word has an unpleasant connotation for us today. There was nothing so unholy about selling medicines in those days nor in peddling them. This was in the day before medical schools began grinding out doctors. There was not a doctor in every neighborhood. Moreover people did not have the fullest faith in the Doctor. There was a great fondness for nostrums. Home remedies were highly regarded and old Indian herb concoctions were looked upon with great favor. A man going about the country peddling medicines would not have been so lightly and unfavorably considered as now. It is probable that the Rockefellers kept the matter quiet because Bill had added to the sale of medicine the trade-stimulating methods of the high-pitch med man.

Of course Uncle Joe Webster carried the news back to Strongville. And after that the elder Rockefeller's calling ceased to be a mystery.

II

But there was another medicine man abroad in those days. Young John D. Rockefeller in Cleveland is on his way home from school. He must pass the Public Square not far from where the Van Sweringen's amazing terminal tower rises today. At one well-traveled spot a crowd is gathered around a gaudy red and gold

TWO MEDICINE MEN

chariot from which a man with a large voice is dilating upon the magical curative powers of a medicine which he sells in half-pint bottles. He passes out little circulars to those who do not buy. The bottles contain a "marvelous oil brought up from many hundreds of feet under the rocks. It can banish almost every form of disease. Even blind persons have been made to see by it." On the circulars there is a bit of verse:

"The healthful balm from Nature's secret spring,
The bloom of health and life to man will bring;
As from her depths the magic liquid flows
To calm our sufferings and assuage our woes."

The passing youth may have felt a boy's interest in a free show, but he had no thought of what things he himself was to do with the magic liquid in those bottles, for it was petroleum. The chariot was advertising Kier's American Oil. This sovereign remedy for almost everything was put up by a man named Samuel Kier. Kier occupies a place of first importance in the history of petroleum. At the time he was almost the only man who was making a commercial use of petroleum, which he put up in half-pint bottles and sold as a medicine "celebrated for its curative powers," "a natural remedy," "procured from a well in Allegheny County Four Hundred Feet below the Earth's Surface. Put up and sold by Samuel Kier, 363 Liberty Street, Pittsburgh, Pa."

There was nothing new about petroleum in America. It was known as petroleum, fossil oil, rock oil, and Seneca oil. The last name came from the fact that it was supposed to have originated on the lands belonging to the Seneca Indians. As early as 1627 the French missionary, Joseph Delarock Daillon, found "a good kind of oil which the Indians called Antonontons," drawn doubtless from Cuba, New York, the site of the first-known oil spring in America.

At first the oil was found floating on the surface of the creeks in New York and Pennsylvania. A man named Ruffner was boring one day in 1806 for salt in Virginia, near the Great Kanawha River, a short distance from what is now Charleston, West Virginia. The Ruffners bored several salt wells successfully but nearly all of them yielded a certain amount of petroleum, some, it is said, as much as 25 barrels a day. This became a common nuisance of salt wells. Oil would sometimes come up with the brine and if it continued or the oil was too abundant the salt well had to be abandoned. The salt men cursed the oil.

KIER'S PETROLEUM, OR ROCK OIL

Celebrated for its Wonderful Curative Powers.

A NATURAL REMEDY!

Procured from a Well in Allegheny County, Penn'a.

FOUR HUNDRED FEET BELOW THE EARTH'S SURFACE.

PUT UP AND SOLD BY

SAMUEL M. KIER,

No. 389 LIBERTY STREET, PITTSBURGH, PA.

The healthful balm, from Nature's secret spring,
The bloom of health, and life, to man will bring;
As from her depths the magic liquid flows,
To calm our sufferings, and assuage our woes.

FACSIMILE REPRODUCTION OF CIRCULAR ISSUED BY SAMUEL M. KIER IN 1850, WHO SOLD PETROLEUM IN HALF-PINT BOTTLES AS A MEDICINE, FOR 50 CENTS A BOTTLE.

Samuel Kier's father, Thomas Kier, was a druggist in Pittsburgh. He was a man of substance. President Buchanan was at one time his partner in a boat line on the old Pennsylvania Canal from Pittsburgh to Philadelphia. Thomas Kier and his two sons,

Samuel and James, looking for a new enterprise, purchased a piece of land near Tarentum, Pennsylvania, in 1847 and put down some salt wells. One of the wells was bored by the spring-pole process. And from this well poured large quantities of oil mixed with the salt. Thomas Kier could use a little in his drug store but most of it was utter waste. About 1849 Samuel Kier conceived the idea of capitalizing the Indians' faith in the oil and putting it up in bottles as an ointment. This Kier was an extraordinary man whose services to the oil industry have been a little obscured. He had energy, dash, imagination. He evinced at once a robust and lively faith in advertising. He got drug stores to display his bottles and he provided them with all sorts of literature and novelties. Among them was a little hand-bill in the form of a $400 bank note on which was printed some facts about his oil. He proclaimed his discovery as heralding a "new era in medicine." He printed countless testimonials. He fitted out several gilded chariots which traveled all over the country, holding street corner meetings, selling half-pint bottles of oil and distributing hand-bills. It was Kier's chariot which young John D. Rockefeller heedlessly passed on the Public Square in Cleveland.

CHAPTER III. THE CHAIN COLLEGE

THE FAMILY plan was for John to go to college. This idea doubtless originated with his mother. But his father began to mutter about it on the score of expense. Doc Rockefeller felt that a man needed to be smart. In a world where one had to get along by his wits it was well to be shrewd. What could college do for you on this head?

John was now fifteen years old. In a sense he was a man, certainly in practical matters. He had seen and understood a little at least the strange situation which existed in his family, the mysterious comings and goings of his father. He was aware of the secretiveness about the Doctor's business. In later life he said that he owed a great debt to his father. "He trained me in practical ways. *He was engaged in different enterprises* and he used to tell me about these things and he taught me the principles and methods of business."

It is doubtful if Bill told his son of all his different enterprises. He was fond of boasting of his own smartness and how he bested people. The man had practically no moral code. He would descant on his own cunning performances for any one's entertainment and it was undoubtedly due to his wife's incessant caution that he did not talk more freely about his calling, about which he felt no sense of shame. He was what was later called a "slicker" and he was fond of doing what he could to be sure his sons would be "slickers" like himself. "I cheat my boys every chance I get," he told Uncle Joe Webster. "I want to make 'em sharp. I trade with the boys and skin 'em and I just beat 'em every time I can. I want to make 'em sharp."

Young John, however, had his own ideas about the matter of going to college, though he looked upon it chiefly as a means toward the practical end of getting along. His failure to go disappointed him a little. More than fifty years later he said:

"I think a college education is a splendid thing. I hadn't the advantage of a college education; but I had a good mother and an excellent father and I like to feel that whatever I may have lost through failure to secure a college education I made up in my home training. . . . The home training gives him [the young man] something he cannot get in college."

This singular statement affords some peep into Rockefeller's idea of education. His mother's precepts in religion and her discipline and his father's teaching in business made up to him what he lost in college. What college can do for you is to train you in the practical problems of business. If there is any doubt about his meaning it is found in the following sentence used in his autobiography: "Better than a college education is the training that he gets in the technical schools that have sprung up all over the country."

But at this time college seemed to him to be the place where he would get that training which would enable him to get along in the world. That very year he had written down his views on the subject in his essay on Education at Central High School:

"When we look around us and see the continual progress education is making, and also the great changes which have been constantly taking place since it began to rise, we cannot but think every one ought to endeavor to improve the great opportunities which are now offered them.

"Had Isaac Newton been an unlearned man, on seeing the apple fall to the ground, would he not rather have eaten it than inquired why it fell?"

But old Bill Rockefeller objected to his son going to college. It cost too much. Something in this sober youth recoiled from pressing the matter. "The mere thought," he said later in a singular explanation, "of support by my father gave me a cold chill—it gives me one now to think of it." Instead he went to B. S. Folsom's Commercial College which was merged with Bryant and Stratton's Business College. It has been already observed that there is little in our complex business structure today the germ of which cannot be found in an earlier era. One observes with interest then that this prophet of the modern era in business should have, long before the Civil War, gone to a college which, in the old Cleveland *Leader*, proudly proclaimed that it was a "Chain College," with branches in seven cities. The school was in the Rouse Block where Marshall's Building now stands at Superior Avenue and the Public Square. Here the youth's chief study was the one he continued to love all his life—bookkeeping. He graduated in 1855. In the Summer of that year this prematurely matured boy, armed with his business college certificate, the practical instructions of his father, the piety and discipline of his mother, and a settled resolve to get rich set out to find his first job.

II

FOR PERHAPS a month John went home for a brief vacation. But once again the home had shifted. Doc Rockefeller had moved his family to its fifth home, from Strongville to Parma, a small village somewhat closer to Cleveland. In August the boy returned to his Erie Street boarding house and launched his hunt for work.

They had been having hard times in the West. Conditions had really improved, but as is always the case the improvement goes far before people begin to realize it. It was a sweltering Summer. The business section of Cleveland was down in the flats along the Cuyahoga River where the hot, humid air was almost stifling. As he started, this boy had a plan. He passed all retail stores and small shops. He went only to banks, railroad offices, wholesale merchandising offices. He called only on the head men. The hot Summer wore on and he kept up his rounds from morning until night getting refusals everywhere. He broke the day by walking to his Erie Street room for dinner. Then he continued his search until the last place had closed. When he was discouraged the vision of his father arose. "I didn't think of discouragement," he told friends afterwards. "What I thought of was getting that job. I simply had to get work for father said if I could not find anything to do I might go back to the country."

By the end of September he had visited every place in the small business section of Cleveland. But he decided to make one more try along the docks. He went to the office of Hewitt and Tuttle, produce commission merchants in Merwin Street. He saw Hewitt and told him he understood bookkeeping. The junior partner, Tuttle, acted as bookkeeper but needed help. Hewitt told him they thought they might give him a chance and to report back after dinner. Curiously he did not ask what the pay would be and Hewitt did not name it. It is possible they did not have a regular place open; that they yielded to a little persuasion; that he went to work very much on trial, for he was working for three full months before anything was said about money.

As he left the office all that Hewitt saw was the serious-faced boy as he walked out with an almost measured slow step. He walked to the corner, without a smile and with calm deliberateness as long as he might be in view of the Hewitt establishment. As he turned the corner he started skipping down the street without further restraint.

The calendar of the Rockefeller family is marked by certain festal days—days observed by the family with formal celebration—days when the flag is sent up to the top of the estate flag-pole. Of course, the first of these days is July 8th, the feast of John D.'s birth. Next in order is September 26th, 1855, the date of his first job. It may be questioned if there is any day quite so important as this one. As the years passed Rockefeller himself kindled a kind of religious and sentimental glamor about it. One day in 1905 a large delegation from the Chamber of Commerce of Cleveland called at the beautiful Forest Hill home of the millionaire John D.

THE CHAIN COLLEGE

Rockefeller to welcome him on his return to Cleveland. In replying to the chairman's speech Rockefeller said:

"This is a great day in our family. You have noticed the flag flying from the staff. The flag is in honor of a day away back that will always be remembered by me and my family." It was the twenty-sixth day of September. One evening in 1908 he was driving over the new viaduct in Cleveland with a companion. Suddenly Rockefeller rose in the open carriage. "Look! Look!" he cried in a surge of emotion. "Look at that rectangular building! I commenced my career there at four dollars a week."

III

IN THE afternoon on September 26th after dinner the newly hired clerk started out to work. The streets were hot with dust after a long dry spell, the thermometer stood at eighty-two and the warm mist, like spent steam, drifted up from the lake and the river. The boy hurried on, not heeding the heat. He gave not a glance as he passed the Cleveland Theatre to the alluring poster which announced that Miss Kimberly would appear that night in "Camille." Nor did he give a thought to the poster in front of the Athenaeum which promised at that more popular playhouse "The Robber's Wife and Woman's Rights One Hundred Years Hence." The stage had no lure for the pious Baptist youth, nor has it had since. When he reached the docks every one was excited over the gale of the night before. Captain Wilkins had come in a little way down from Hewitt's with the steamer *Queen City* minus her rudder. There were ominous stories about the *Baltimore*, sunk in the storm that night. Her passengers had been brought in, some by Captain Wilkins, some in the *Steamer Sun*.

The new clerk was waiting at Hewitt and Tuttle's when his employers got back from dinner. The building faced on Merwin Street, its rear gave on the river wharf. Merwin Street is still there, but the great river bridge passes over the spot where the building stood.

Young Rockefeller, in his job-hunting, had been hearing much of hard times. On the high desk of the office he saw a copy of the morning's issue of the old Cleveland *Leader*. There he read the produce report of the day. It furnished an auspicious note for the beginning of this business career. He read:

"Compared with last year we are even now rich and getting richer. Business of all kinds is brisk; enterprise has received a healthy impetus all over the country. Gold is flowing in from California and but little is flowing out. With this state of things and with an immense surplus of produce to export at good prices how can we do otherwise than look the future in the face with a smiling countenance and be thankful for the rich blessings of the year."

How indeed! That night before he went to bed he read from his Bible with more than his wonted devoutness. Surely God was in His heaven. He had begun His great experiment with this useful servant. The boy could not see then what vast plans God had for him. But he was sure then, as always he has been sure since, that the hand of God was in it. He put out his candle and turned to bed. He was weary with the excitement of the day. He muttered to himself. "Fine! Fine! Everything is coming on. John. But be careful now! Careful!" And thus he fell asleep.

IV

ALL OVER the country at this moment the cast of characters for the coming gaudy drama of American business was forming. Close by in Ohio was Mark Hanna, eighteen years old, a student in Western Reserve College. Andrew Carnegie, barely twenty, was getting thirty-five dollars a month as secretary to Tom Scott, then in the telegraph department of the Pennsylvania Road in Pittsburgh. Thomas Edison, a boy of eight, was getting his lessons in the village school of Port Huron, Mich. Two politicians who were to play a leading rôle in the drama, were in Ohio—William McKinley, just twelve years old, a student at Union Seminary in Poland, and John Sherman, whose law was to smite Rockefeller's great trust, was a Whig Congressman at thirty-two from an Ohio district. John D. Archbold, a boy of six, was at school in Leesburg, Ohio.

Armour, the packer king, was working as a miner in California. Havemeyer was a clerk in a sugar house. Theodore N. Vail, ten years old, was in school at Morristown, New Jersey. The great railroad chieftains were struggling through various kinds of boyhoods. Jay Gould, just twenty-one, was making surveys, Collis P.

Huntington was in the hardware business in Sacramento, George Pullman, twenty-four, was moving warehouses on the Erie Canal, E. H. Harriman was getting ready to go to Trinity School and James J. Hill, about Rockefeller's age, was in school in Rockwood Academy. John Pierpont Morgan, a youth of eighteen, was at school in Germany. The land was filled with obscure boys who were soon to come crowding upon the stage in the hectic and disorderly comedy of America's amazing industrial rise.

CHAPTER IV. A BOY WHOLESALER

ISAAC HEWITT was a prosperous man. The chief business of his firm was produce, but Hewitt himself was a large owner of real estate. He had a business block, a number of dwelling houses and some small warehouses and stores. Tuttle, the junior partner, worked for a salary of $2,000 a year and looked after the books. Young Rockefeller worked under him and gradually took over the handling of the books. Moreover the new clerk began to assume one small job after another, collecting rents, attending to repairs, dealing with plumbers, carpenters, making good bargains and scrutinizing the bills. A shipment of marble came from Vermont by railroad, canal boat, and lake boat. The way-bills were complicated. There seemed to be errors—but too small to bother Mr. Hewitt. But the young bookkeeper pointed them all out to Mr. Hewitt and also found some damage to the shipment. He set about adjusting them and succeeded in settling all in favor of the firm.

One day, while Rockefeller was in a neighboring office on business, the merchant glanced hastily at a newly presented bill and bade the clerk pay it. Rockefeller looked at him in astonishment.

"Do you pay your bills without going over every item?"

The old merchant laughed.

"In our office I look at every single item," said Rockefeller, "and it must be right before our bills are paid."

It is not to be wondered at that ere a year this tall, gangling, solemn youth already had a reputation for great reliability, prudence, and thrift in the little business world around the docks.

The winter came on. The boy still boarded at Erie Street with the same pious, talkative, Baptist landlady. And as yet nothing was said at Hewitt's about his pay. Boys, in those good old days, frequently worked for many months or longer without pay "while learning the business," their pious employers meantime gathering in their services for nothing. This boy's money was scant. He lived on his own savings, scrupulously refraining from asking help from his father. But he did not bring up the subject of salary with his employers.

Meantime he did something which has always been treasured as one of the chief events of his life. He opened a bookkeeping account of his own. He bought a little book for ten cents and wrote across it "Ledger A." He has preached a dozen sermons at Sunday School from Ledger A. Not all the money in the world could buy this little volume, he has many times declared. Carefully, religiously, every day he set down in this small ledger every penny paid out. This book is full of meaning for those who search for secrets in the minds and hearts of rich men. The first entry in Ledger A is a gift of ten cents to the "Missionary Cause." One wonders if John D. Rockefeller's dime gifts today are dictated by a sentimental reverence for this first ten-cent philanthropy. Very quickly follow other sums—ten cents to "Mr. Downe, our young minister," slip rent (which means pew rent), one dollar. Then come the following in December:

Sabbath School	.05
Present for Mr. Farrar (Superintendent)	.25
Five Points Mission, N. Y.	.12
Macedonian (religious paper)	.10
Present to Teacher, Deacon Sked	.25

Here was a total of sixty-two cents in one month. In November, from the twenty-fifth, when he began the book, the entries totaled $1.20. In five weeks the donations equaled $1.82. This boy had as yet received no pay. It was a bitter winter and he did not feel he could buy a good overcoat for himself. When he went to work after New Year's Day, Mr. Tuttle called him aside and handed him $50—his pay for fourteen weeks—$3.50 a week. It will be seen his actual earnings from November 25th to the end of the year turned out to be $17.50. Thus he had given more than a

A BOY WHOLESALER

tithe of his earnings though they were not yet collected, though he says he had no thought of tithes.

But Mr. Tuttle, in addition to giving him $50, also told him that henceforward his salary would be $25 a month. And so his benevolence continued. January 16th he gave six cents to the missionary cause and ten cents to the poor of the parish—"all in one Sunday" as he later commented. February 3rd he gave ten cents to the foreign missions and ten cents to some charitable cause. March 3rd the foreign missions got another ten cents; ten cents went to the poor of the parish, a dollar for pew rent and before the week was out another ten cents to the missions. Later in the month he gave a dollar to the Young Men's Christian Association.

In the four months from November 25th to the end of March he earned $67.50. Of this he gave $5.58 to various religious and charitable purposes. In the same month he spent $9.09 for clothing.

"I could not secure the most fashionable cut of clothing," he told his Sunday School class later. "I remember I bought mine then from a cheap clothier. He sold me clothing cheap such as I could pay for and it was a great deal better than buying clothing I could not pay for."

He could have gotten a good coat from Mr. Isaac Isaacs, who kept a good store and advertised coats for $4. We do not know what Rockefeller paid, but we know he indulged in one extravagance. He paid $2.50 for a pair of gloves. This item puzzled him in later years for he had always worn mittens. And yet it was blizzardy on those Cuyahoga flats. And bookkeeper's fingers must be kept nimble.

This boy was only sixteen years old. He was not then the great oil ogre, with a country howling at his heels and angry ministers declaring that he gave his millions to ease a troubled conscience—that his religion was a cloak for his malefactions. There must have been something sincere about this religion. He was very young, intensely practical and embarked with a terrible earnestness upon the business of getting along in the world. Yet the record reveals that he gave almost a tenth of what he earned. Certainly it is rare for so young a boy to be concerned at all about systematic giving.

II

THE YEAR 1857 brought trouble to Cleveland and to all the country. It was the year of one of those panics which at intervals shake the nation. The town had grown rapidly. People poured in from New England and all the East. All around the Cuyahoga River the factories were making their appearance. Cleveland had twenty-one flour mills, twenty-seven clothing factories, seventeen boot and shoe plants, thirteen furniture factories, seventeen machine factories, fifty lumber mills. The factory age was upon the nation. But save in a few industries, they were still small affairs and each community had its collection of plants which had sprung up to take the place of the numerous little handcrafts and mills which the factories supplanted. Thus Cleveland had its own furniture and clothing and shoe factories and almost every other community the same thing.

The Rockefeller family, which had been in Parma for two years, once again shifted its headquarters to Cleveland. The elder Rockefeller was doing very much better now. He was older, wiser, and better schooled in the strange business he had adopted. He moved his family into a house at Number 33 Cedar Street, and the character of this house indicates the improved circumstances of the Rockefellers. It still stands and is in every respect a good house. In those days it must have been looked upon as a very good one with its twelve rooms, including a bathroom, which has the appearance of having been built into the house originally.

This year the name of Rockefeller's father appears in the Cleveland directory and strangely enough his occupation is given as "Physician." This designation is explained partly in the classified section of the directory where William Rockefeller's name appears among the physicians. But after it in parentheses is inscribed the illuminating word "Botanic." Big Bill was now openly a herb doctor. But he did not practice his herb medicine in Cleveland. He was still on the go, still known for his long absences and sudden re-appearances.

John D.'s name appears this year in the directory at 33 Cedar Street. He was still at Hewitt and Tuttle's, rolling up a reputation for thrift and sagacity. William, Jr., was also at work; Frank was at school.

III

NEITHER as a boy nor man was Rockefeller a reader. At Hewitt and Tuttle's however he found and read a book—"The Life and Letters of Amos Lawrence" by his son. Lawrence was the great founder of the New England textile industry, one of our first millionaires and perhaps our first millionaire philanthropist. The youthful bookkeeper liked that book. He read how the rich Lawrence wrote to his secretary to bring him several hundred dollars, admonishing him to have it in nice new crisp one and five and ten dollar bills, for, he observed, "though I cannot go out I will doubtless have some visits from my friends." The soberfaced boy thought "how nice that was" and how, when he was rich, he would like to be able to give out nice crisp new bills. He remembered this book and this portion in after life and spoke of it.

Cleveland newspapers printed daily reports of produce prices and movements. A reporter visited Hewitt's office daily for news. One day the reporter came in almost dragging behind him another. He introduced his shuffling, stuttering companion to Mr. Hewitt and announced he was to be the new man on that beat. His name was Charles Browne. After that young Rockefeller came to know Charles Browne. Later still the world came to know him under the name of Artemus Ward. And Rockefeller became a reader of Artemus Ward's books and liked them.

IV

JOHN's salary at Hewitt and Tuttle's was $400 during 1856 and very little more in the following year. He was eighteen years old, but he had not been a boy for years. Tuttle had left the firm and this youth was doing all and more than Tuttle had done. He thought he was worth more than he was getting and told Mr. Hewitt so. Hewitt agreed his clerk should have more and offered him $700 a year. But John thought he ought to have $800. He said so. Hewitt replied he would consider the matter. The weeks went by and Hewitt, like an old-fashioned business man, put off the decision. He probably was not thinking about the subject at all. But John was. He was thinking about that and a good many other things besides.

A little way down the street, working for Otis and Company,

was a young Englishman named Maurice B. Clark. Clark had left England ten years before and landed friendless and penniless in Boston amidst the Bunker Hill celebration. He had moved about a good deal—a farm hand in Massachusetts, chopping wood and teaming in Lorain County and then to Cleveland and a job with Hussy and Sinclair. Though well in his twenties he had gone to Folsom's Business College and there doubtless had met Rockefeller. In 1857 he was with Otis and Company, produce merchants. He had saved $2,000 and he had been looking at the merchants in Merwin Street and River Street and had concluded he was as able as they to manage his own business. All he lacked was capital. He was twenty-eight years old and he went to eighteen-year-old John D. Rockefeller and proposed that they form a partnership and go into business for themselves. Clark's proposition was that each one put up $2,000. The plan appealed to Rockefeller. But he had only $800, which he had saved over the course of many years, beginning with that little blue bowl back in Moravia. He could scrape together another $200. And so he went to his father and asked for a loan of $1,000.

The Doctor had often boasted that he would give each of his children $1,000 on coming of age.

"Yes," said the expansive, bearded Botanic Physician. "I will let you have the thousand. As you know, John, when you are twenty-one you are to get $1,000. I will advance the $1,000 now and you can pay me interest on it until you are twenty-one when the debt will be wiped out."

This piece of generosity pleased the son greatly. Then the doctor added with a sly smile: "But, John, the interest will be ten per cent."

On April 1, 1858, the firm of Clark and Rockefeller, Produce and Commission, opened its doors at 32 River Street. Another feast day in the Rockefeller saga had been established.

That night the young eighteen-year-old wholesale merchant went to his room to kneel and pray for guidance and success. His mind was aflame with the golden prospect which stretched out before him. He went to bed but could not sleep. He talked to himself about all this. In his Bible he had read the counsel of the Psalmist—"Commune with your own heart upon your bed and be still. Selah." "Now a little success," he murmured. "But soon you will fall down. Soon you will be overthrown. Because you have got a start you think you are quite a merchant. Look out! Look out or you will lose your head! Go steady!"

V

THE NEW firm prospered from the start. But at the very outset the young partners realized they needed money. Times were hard and bills were seldom paid when due. Before many months the firm had reached a crisis. Rockefeller had met his first crisis by borrowing from his father. Now it was the young partner who had to take the lead. He went to Truman P. Handy, the firm's banker. Handy was a fine old character—a grave, dignified gentleman of the old school, who had been watching this serious, methodical boy coming into the bank every day with the firm's deposits. Without any shuffling Rockefeller asked the old banker for a loan of $2,000.

"All right, Mr. Rockefeller," Handy replied, without hesitation. "Just give me your warehouse receipts. They're good enough for me."

The readiness with which the loan was made astonished the young merchant and taught him one of the great lessons of his life. He was to be, for many years, an inveterate borrower and Handy was destined to hand over many thousands to his young depositor. Rockefeller always remembered this with gratitude. Years afterwards he urged Handy to buy Standard Oil certificates. Handy didn't have the money so Rockefeller loaned it to him.

Rockefeller didn't limit himself to the finances. His whole soul was in every detail of the business. He went out of town on little trips to solicit business. He went to many places in Ohio and soon extended his operations to Indiana. He began to learn another lesson—that business conducted on a large scale can be operated more cheaply. So the firm began buying in carload lots, getting better prices and lower railroad rates.

One day the largest consignor of produce sent a big shipment to the firm. He followed it into the office and asked Clark to let him have an advance against the shipment before the bill of lading was received. Clark agreed to send it. When Rockefeller returned later he objected firmly. An angry argument arose between the partners. Clark was incensed at Rockefeller's excessive caution. Rockefeller agreed to accept full responsibility and to go to the consignor and reason with him. But the consignor refused to reason. He stormed. But the quiet youth who addressed him did not storm. He talked quietly. The more unreasonable the other fellow, the more need he had to retain possession of his reasoning faculties. He explained that the request was unbusiness-like and he stuck to his guns. The advance was not made, but that consignor continued to do business with Clark and Rockefeller. Later the firm learned that an old country banker they had had occasion to ask for an accommodation had been watching the transaction and they concluded he had inspired it to make a test of them.

At the end of the first year the new firm had done a gross business of $450,000 with a net return of $4,400.

VI

THE NEED for money was a continuous thorn in the young merchant's side. He borrowed everywhere. One source which he had to tap occasionally was his father. The loans were not large but they were essential. They were indefinite loans for no specified time. And they cost the son many a frown.

Down in River Street everything is in motion. Business is brisk, but money is tight. John is bending over his ledgers studying deeply their meaning. Suddenly he is aware of a huge bulk of a man standing in the doorway. He looks up to see his father. The Doctor's face is solemn, his mouth set firmly over the thick bush of whiskers on his chin.

"John," he says in almost sepulchral tones, "I've got to have that money."

John tries to look unconcerned but a shadow sweeps over his face. He suppresses the stir of irritation which he feels, for he believes that his father is acting his gravity.

"Of course you shall have it," he replies.

The demand comes at a most inopportune moment. But the next day when the Doctor calls, John hands him a roll of bills. The Doctor puts them in his wallet and goes out. John follows his father's figure with a scowl. The old man walks solemnly to the corner, turns it and then stops to have a bit of a laugh.

"That's the way to make him sharp," he snickers. "That's the way to make him hustle." Then he adds with a touch of pride, "And he got it too."

That pleased the old man—that his shrewd, up and coming young son John could go out and get the money.

VII

IT WAS 1859. The air was full of ugly talk. Another presidential election was coming on. There was plenty of violence in the minds of the people. There was even talk of war. There were arguments of great violence and ill-feeling along River Street. Business was being forever interrupted with discussions of the fugitive slave law. Cleveland, the largest city on the Lakes, was the opening of the underground railroad through which runaway slaves were hustled into Canada. The Lake piers where they were smuggled aboard the boats were just a few blocks from Rockefeller's place of business. All through the Summer of 1859 Cleveland was a kind of Mecca for abolitionist pilgrims and the county jail was the temple. There some thirty-seven residents of Oberlin and Wellington—all prominent citizens—were walled up awaiting trial. John Price, an escaped slave from Kentucky, had made his way to Oberlin. The college town was full of hot-blooded youths who harbored many runaways from Kentucky. Price was decoyed from Oberlin by a slave catcher from Kentucky and taken to Wellington. The whole town of Oberlin—professors, students, residents—rose en masse in pursuit. At Wellington they battered down the doors of the hotel, captured Price, rushed him to Cleveland and shipped him across Lake Erie. All of the leaders were indicted and, refusing to give bail, preferring the rôle of martyrs, were awaiting trial in the Cleveland jail. A great convention was held in Cleveland, outside the jail walls. Speakers talked from a raised platform so that the martyrs inside the walls might be a part of the meeting. The aroused people poured into Cleveland by trainload and wagon-load. Business in River Street was at a stand-still. Every one had gone to the great meeting outside the county jail. But Rockefeller remained at his work. He had one interest—his business. He had a secondary interest—his church. Outside of these he wasted no time. He joined no societies. He was a member of no clubs. He played no games. He went to no plays. He attended no concerts or lectures. All this fury in River Street irked him.

His path lay between the house in Cedar Street, the office in River Street and the Sunday School in Erie Street. Occasional forays into the country on business were his only departure from this triangle.

A little later that year Cleveland was first shocked and then thrilled by the news that a certain John Brown had captured the arsenal at Harpers Ferry. Then came the news of the hanging of John Brown. Buildings were hung with white paper bordered with black mourning strips. Bells were tolled. Business houses were closed the day old John Brown hanged. But the firm of Clark and Rockefeller went about its affairs and there twenty-year-old John D. Rockefeller, produce merchant, was industriously minding his own business.

VIII

THE ROCKEFELLER family was moving forward now. The good Doctor had attained a kind of prosperity. John was perhaps the most prosperous young man in business. William Rockefeller, Jr., had a good job and Frank was working now. There was an excellent revenue flowing into the family. Mrs. Rockefeller began to enjoy a kind of ease on the score of money. But there were still the Doctor's long and uncertain absences. There was, too, the Doctor's talk. He had a loose kind of ethics and he liked to tell of the smart things he had done, the people he had fooled, and the slick tricks he had played. Mrs. Rockefeller was now a regular and faithful attendant of the Baptist Church and the bad example of the adventurous and mysterious wanderer who was her husband troubled her deeply. Then there was not too much sweetness in the relations of the boys, or at least between the calm, superior John and the rather wild and passionate and undisciplined Frank.

The house in Cedar Street was considered no longer adequate for the rising young merchant. So the family built a new house in Cheshire Street. Whether this house was financed by young John or old Bill is not possible to say. Certainly the construction was superintended by the son entirely. He said in later years his father had always advised him to build a house and so he had put up this one—which leads one to suppose it was his house. The building still stands in Cheshire Street near Prospect—a substantial, large, strongly built home beyond doubt such as would be occupied only by people in very good circumstances.

A story has been told that a little before this time John became a trustee of the Erie Street Baptist Church, though his name does not appear in any of the old directories among the trustees at this time. It is certain, however, that he saved the institution from ruin. It was attended almost wholly by a very humble group of Christians. A mortgage of $2,000 was long past due and foreclosure was threatened. One day the pastor preached in a tone of great disconsolation and wound up with the distressing announcement that the little church was about to be sold over their heads. The message fell upon every soul there as a kind of doom. But upon one soul it produced a very different result. That was the very practical soul of young John D. Rockefeller. To him, nineteen years old then, perhaps more than to any other member of the congregation, that little building had been a true spiritual refuge. More than any other he found there his chief distraction from the world, the flesh, and River Street. The thought of its loss appalled him.

When the service was ended and the congregation was filing out the members found young Rockefeller at the door. He stopped the flow of the unhappy worshipers. He demanded from each man a pledge for some part of that $2,000. He buttonholed, expostulated, with every one. When all had left he felt reasonably sure of averting the disaster. Then he called at the homes of every member until he had gotten a pledge from each. In a few months he had collected the entire $2,000 and paid off the debt. For this, it is said, he was made a trustee of the church.

IX

Thus this youth of twenty moved toward mature manhood, already matured far beyond his years. It was dawning on everybody that this young man was well able to take care of himself, that he had a cool head on his shoulders. That was it—his head was cool. Other men got angry, stormed, argued. He remained cool and smiled. He was a good-looking young man, with a calm, serious, dignified air. The eyes were small and a little close together. But they were unwavering and brilliant and the whole face had the open, frank, pleasant appearance we are accustomed to see in young ministers. The forehead was high and the face long, but with wide, rolling jaws, broad chin, and full mouth. Everywhere, in his home, in his store, things had a way of being as he wished them. Thus he rose to be looked upon already as one of the most successful merchants of the town, deepening his hold upon his religious membership at the Baptist Church, the family growing in prosperity and respectability save for the old cancer doctor who came and went mysteriously, while the country itself moved with the stride of Fate toward war. But young Rockefeller paid no heed to all the strange, mighty forces which were moving around him.

Meantime, in another part of the country, Fate was preparing an event which was to have a profound influence upon the fortunes of the whole world but chiefly upon the fortunes of the young produce merchant in River Street.

PART THREE
OIL DORADO

CHAPTER I. DRAKE HITS OIL

EARLY in the Fall of 1859, John G. Hussy, a banker and one of the leading produce merchants of Cleveland, went away on a trip. Hussy's establishment was not far from Clark and Rockefeller's. Clark had worked for Hussy for six years and there was a good deal of visiting between the offices of the two firms. And so, while there was much secrecy about Hussy's trip, Clark and Rockefeller knew where he had gone. He had gone to Venango County, Pennsylvania, where there was great local excitement about some new means of getting petroleum.

Some weeks later—November 18th—the *Morning Leader* in Cleveland carried a brief item with an inconspicuous heading. It recited that "the oil springs of northern Pennsylvania were attracting considerable speculation," and that there was "quite a rush to the oleaginous locations." It also noted that Drake's well "yielded 25 barrels of oil a day at 10 cents a barrel."

This was the first printed notice of the event in Cleveland almost three months after it occurred. Hussy was one of those who had "rushed to the oleaginous locations." Apparently he was the first Clevelander to rush and the only one for some time.

II

SOMETIME in 1854, when John D. Rockefeller was still a student in the Central High School, Mr. George H. Bissell walked into the rooms of his old friend and teacher, Professor Crosby at Dartmouth College. Bissell, a graduate of Dartmouth, had first taught school in New Orleans and later became a lawyer in New York. He had just gone back for a visit to his old school. During their chat Professor Crosby picked up a small bottle filled with a thick, dark fluid.

"That is petroleum," said Professor Crosby.

"And what is petroleum?" inquired his former pupil.

"Well, it is a mineral oil found in a good many places which some people use for medicine. In a few places it is used as an

BRINE WELLS IN TARENTUM, PENNSYLVANIA, WHICH YIELDED SOME PETROLEUM AS A NUISANCE BY-PRODUCT.
(From *Romance of Petroleum* by J. D. Henry)

illuminant. This bottle was sent to me by an old friend of mine, Dr. F. B. Brewer, who once studied here. Brewer says this is found floating on the surface of most of the creeks in his part of Pennsylvania. He believes it can be refined and used as kerosene is used."

Crosby then explained that he had refined some of it and that it made a very good illuminant and he believed that it might be possible to collect enough of it on these Pennsylvania creeks to make it pay. Crosby's seed fell upon fertile ground. Bissell thought a good deal about it and finally decided to go to Pennsylvania and investigate. He reached the oil creek regions in the fall of 1854 and spent much time wandering around the little settlement of Titusville examining the greasy coating of the little stream called Oil Creek. Without disclosing his plans Bissell bought 103 acres of land on Oil Creek in Cherrytree Township from Brewer and

Watson, who owned a sawmill close by. This Brewer was the brother of the doctor who had sent the bottle to Professor Crosby. In November Bissell paid $5,000 for the land. But the deed, with an eye to future corporate operations, proclaimed the price to be $25,000.

Back in New York, Bissell, with his partner, Jonathan G. Eveleth, organized the Pennsylvania Rock Oil Company. This was the first oil company. Very fittingly it had plenty of water in its capitalization. This was fixed at $250,000. The land was turned in at $25,000. All this was completed by December 30th, 1854.

The Pennsylvania Rock Oil Company, however, did not travel very far. The promoters soon found that it was impossible to gather enough oil by known methods to make the business profitable. Skimming the oil from the surface of the creeks, soaking it up by spreading blankets on them or collecting a few barrels here and there from the salt wells in which petroleum was a by-product, were the only means known of recovering petroleum. The promoters spent all their available money and the enterprise came to a standstill. The stage was perfectly set for a great oil industry if the oil could be obtained. The coal-oil business had been enormously expanded. Everybody who could afford it used kerosene lamps with coal oil made from coal shale. The difficulty with coal oil was its cost, which went as high as a dollar a gallon. Refining a good illuminant from petroleum was far less expensive. But there was no petroleum.

III

THERE was, of course, nothing new about petroleum, as a possible illuminant. Away back in 1833 Professor Benjamin Silliman wrote about the oil he had studied from the famous Cuba Spring in New York—"a fountain of petroleum near the line which divides Allegany County from Cattaraugus." He had also studied Seneca Oil, which he said came from Oil Creek. "I have frequently distilled it in a glass retort and the naphtha which collects in the receiver is of a light straw color and much lighter, more odorous and inflammable than petroleum."

We have seen how Samuel Kier put petroleum up in little medicine bottles and sold it as Kier's American Oil. But Kier had an inquiring and adventurous mind. From his salt wells at Tarentum in Pennsylvania he got far more petroleum than he could use for medicine. That required only two barrels a day. He played continually with the idea of finding other uses for the oil. He had seen the people around Tarentum use it as an illuminant, burning a cotton wick dipped in the crude petroleum and emitting a dim, foul-smelling mixture of smoke and flame. Kier took some samples of his oil to Philadelphia and to a chemist named Professor J. C. Booth. Booth suggested refining by distillation and he gave

SAMUEL KIER.

Kier directions for erecting a still. Kier constructed a one-gallon still and produced a good grade of refined oil which he called carbon oil, a name which clung to the business for many years. But it would not burn in the ordinary coal-oil lamp. Kier thereupon invented a lamp suited to the new oil. He then went into the business of refining and selling this oil. And he also manufactured in small quantities the lamp he had invented.

About this time there was in business at 187 Water Street, New York, a man named Colonel A. C. Ferris. There is no doubt he was among the first to see the commercial value of oil as an illuminant. Ferris was in what he called the carbon oil business. He also had perfected a lamp which would burn this carbon oil. In February, 1858, we find him contracting for two-thirds of the oil product of MacKeon and Finley from their wells at Tarentum. The New

ERIE STREET BAPTIST MISSION, ROCKEFELLER'S CHURCH IN CLEVELAND AND PARENT OF THE PRESENT EUCLID AVENUE BAPTIST CHURCH.

DEACON ALEXANDER SKED, WHO RECEIVED ROCKEFELLER INTO THE CHURCH.

Courtesy of Euclid Avenue Baptist Church

ROCKEFELLER FAMILY GROUP ABOUT 1859. SEATED LEFT TO RIGHT, JOHN D. ROCKEFELLER, LUCY ROCKEFELLER, WILLIAM ROCKEFELLER; STANDING, LEFT TO RIGHT, MARY ANN ROCKEFELLER AND FRANK ROCKEFELLER.

Courtesy of Miss Kate Steele Curtis of Chicago

York Kerosene Company, venders of coal oil made from shale, about this time became excited over the possibility of making kerosene from petroleum and in March, 1858, we find them buying nine barrels of carbon oil from Ferris and nineteen barrels in April for $581.47—more than $30 a barrel. The New York company wanted more but Ferris could not give it to them without depriving other customers. Thus we see there was a good market

COLONEL A. C. FERRIS, FIRST NEW YORK CITY OIL MAN.

for petroleum and its use as an illuminant was well established. But all of the pioneers were baffled by the problem of getting crude oil.

IV

On a warm summer's day Bissell, walking along the street, took refuge from the sun under an awning which shaded a druggist's window. He was immediately struck by the window display which was given over wholly to Kier's American Oil. Scattered among the bottles were Kier's famous $400 bank notes. One side of the note simulated a government bill. The other side bore the advertisement for Kier's oil. It was the picture on the advertisement which struck Bissell—a derrick supposed to represent the well—the salt well—from which Kier obtained his oil.

OIL DORADO

That is the way to get petroleum, thought Bissell—drill for it—drill deep. Oil had always come up from the ground in salt wells. The deeper the well the more oil. What if we drill deeper—may we not reach the true and abundant source of oil?

The thing seems so obvious that one wonders why no one thought of it sooner. Kier boasted that he got his oil by drilling. Yet it had not occurred to him to do that very thing. All the time Kier had the secret but did not know it. Bissell, as we have seen,

KIER'S $400 ROCK OIL NOTE WHICH SUGGESTED METHOD OF DRILLING FOR OIL.

was a man of action. Having formed this plausible theory he was ready to act upon it. All this was sometime in 1857, just as young John Rockefeller was setting up as a produce commission merchant in Cleveland.

For three years the Pennsylvania Rock Oil Company was nearly dormant. Bissell had submitted a sample of the oil to Professor Benjamin Silliman of Yale, the son of that Professor Silliman who twenty years before made the first oil studies. Silliman declared the oil excellent as an illuminant after distillation. To this he added: "There is ground for believing that the company has in its possession a raw material from which by simple and not expensive processes they may manufacture very valuable products." On the strength of this Bissell interested several New Haven capitalists, among them a banker named Townsend.

At this time there was in New Haven a tall, solemn man of great dignity who was a conductor on the New Haven Railroad.

DRAKE HITS OIL

His name was Drake. Edwin L. Drake was born March 19, 1819, at Greenville, Greene County, New York. He had wandered about much. His early boyhood was spent in the Catskills. Later, in turn, he worked on a farm in Vermont, on a Lake steamer between Detroit and Buffalo, then in Ann Arbor, Michigan, as a night clerk in a hotel at Tecumseh, back to his old home in the Green Mountains and then to New Haven where he became a clerk in a dry goods store. Later still he turned up as a dry goods clerk on Broadway and after that as express agent on the Boston and Albany Railroad. In 1849 he got a job as a conductor on the New York, New Haven and Hartford Railroad and settled down in New Haven. Drake had a small savings account in Townsend's bank and that gentleman advised the quiet, gentle, amiable conductor to put something into the oil investment. Drake risked $200.

When Bissell conceived his great idea to drill for oil he went, all on fire with the scheme, to his New Haven associates. Infected by Bissell's enthusiasm they organized a new company called the Seneca Oil Company and looked about for a man to command the drilling expedition into Pennsylvania. Townsend thought of Drake. The conductor, who had moved about so much, was ready to try it again. The Seneca Oil Company made a contract with E. E. Bowditch and E. L. Drake to pay them five and one-half cents' royalty on every gallon of oil recovered. This was later raised to twelve cents a gallon for forty-five years.

Thus we see Drake did not originate the idea of commercializing oil. Many men—Kier, Peterson, Ferris, and others—had severally nursed that notion. Neither did Drake invent the plan to drill for oil. The credit for that simple but epochal conception must go to Bissell. But from this point on the credit belongs to Drake.

V

DRAKE made his appearance in Titusville in December, 1857. He was now Colonel Drake. Townsend, the canny old New England banker who had chosen him for this job, had elevated him to the rank of Colonel. This title, Townsend explained, would serve to command attention and respect for "Colonel" Drake amid his new surroundings. Titusville, in the northwestern corner of Pennsylvania, sprawled on the banks of Oil Creek, a diminutive settlement of two hundred and fifty souls—farmers and workmen in the lumber mill. Lumber was being cut all along the Allegheny and rafted down the river to Pittsburgh. Titusville was one of the stopping places for the loggers and there were four hotels to refresh and shelter them. Having looked over the ground Drake went back to New Haven to gather his family and belongings. When he got back to Titusville—May 1, 1858—he got lodging and board for his entire family, including his horse, for six

COL. EDWIN L. DRAKE'S FIRST WELL NEAR TITUSVILLE.

dollars a week. He went to the sawmill of Brewer and Watson and announced his intention of boring an artesian well.

When Drake began he met every kind of difficulty. He engaged two men as drillers successively and each one failed to appear. He could get no driller. Meantime his funds began to dwindle. The Seneca Oil Company seemed to lose interest in his expedition. By the Fall of 1858 he had made practically no progress and his funds were gone. But Drake saw the growing market for kerosene made from coal. Moreover he had visited Ferris on his way through New York and Kier at Tarentum. And he was profoundly impressed with the importance of finding an adequate supply of oil. And so in spite of every obstacle—the failure of his drillers to appear, of his engine to come, of the Seneca Oil Company to send funds and of the coming of the winter—he was undismayed. He found two kindly friends who were impressed with his earnestness and honesty. They were Uncle Peter Wilson and a man named R.

D. Fletcher and they endorsed his note for $500 and enabled him to go on with his plan.

During the Winter Drake sought another driller. He went to Tarentum and called on a Mr. Peterson who had been operating salt wells for years. Peterson put him in touch with Uncle Billy Smith, an old Tarentum blacksmith, who turned out to be the very man for Drake. Uncle Billy was a patriarchal Vulcan with a huge gray beard. Born in the early days of the century, he was a blacksmith of the old school who shoed horses but also turned out all sorts of iron and steel tools—a hinge for the house door, a hammer for the carpenter. Smith had made the salt-drilling tools around Tarentum for years for both Kier and Peterson. Smith agreed to go with Drake for $2.50 a day and pay for his two sons, Sam and James. He made his appearance in May, 1859, with drilling tools forged in his own blacksmith shop. He built a rude frame house for himself near the site of the proposed oil well—the very spot where General Benjamin Lincoln had passed with his troops during the Revolution and where his weary Continentals had bathed their tired feet in the healing oil that floated on Oil Creek.

When Smith and his sons got their drill down eighteen feet the soil caved in. Uncle Billy asked Drake to get a hollow pipe six inches square through which the drilling tool might be sent down. At thirty-six feet the drillers hit rock. And, with the aid of a little six-horse-power engine, they began actual boring through the rock on August 1st. They went down three feet a day. On August 20th, Saturday, the men stopped work. The tools were withdrawn from the soil. They had gone down 69½ feet. Next day—Sunday—Smith and his son Sam went to the well to look around. The boy strayed over to the tubing and looked down.[1] He saw something about a foot from the top. In great excitement he uttered a cry: "Oil! Oil!"—a cry that has stirred the blood of men many times since. The old man saw at a glance that their labors had been rewarded. He rigged up a simple pump and began to pump the dark liquid out. Drake did not arrive until the next day. When he came he found Smith and his son guarding the

---

[1] Sam Smith was living in Titusville in 1929 when the writer visited him. Many of the details of the Drake discovery were supplied by him. He insisted that oil was struck on Saturday, August 20, not Sunday, August 21. However, all the evidence among the records of the regions support the date used in the text.

well. Smith led Drake solemnly to the pump and pointed down. "What's that?" asked Drake.

"That's your fortune," proclaimed Uncle Billy. The old blacksmith then put in a seed bag and pump and in a moment the oil was flowing all over. A new era had been born. A new form of wealth had come into the world. Sam Smith ran to the Brewer and Watson mill with the news. The mill hands ran about collecting barrels of all sorts. Jonathan Watson came and, stroking his long white beard, looked for a while with a critical eye at the flowing oil. Then he ran back to the mill for his horse. Reining up before the mill office for a moment he called to William Kirkpatrick, the head sawyer.

"Bill, I've got to go home on some business right away," he told Kirkpatrick. "You stay here and look after the mill until I get back."

Watson, now thoroughly excited, put spurs to his horse. He was galloping as fast as the animal could carry him to gather up as many leases of the adjoining land as he could get.

Kirkpatrick watched his employer ride away through the forest clearing. It took him just two minutes to decide what was up. So he called to his assistant, Jim Tarr.

"Watson wants me to look after the mill until he gets back," he hurriedly informed Tarr. "He's gone away on important business. But I got important business too. So you look after the mill 'til I get back." Kirkpatrick leaped on his horse and was off at a gallop. Jim Tarr stood watching his disappearing superior and wondering what madness had suddenly seized the mill. Up to now it was Drake and Uncle Billy who were looked upon as a little crazy. Now suddenly everybody had become a bit touched.

As for Drake, he got aboard his horse and lit out in the direction of Meadville to get barrels. He managed to get twenty-eight. At the same time he made a deal with a teamster named Alderman to haul his oil to Meadville. Here then was born in that one day the whole creaky machinery of the new oil business—the wildcat well, the barrel business, the teamster, the lease hunter, whose tribe was to increase until all the valley swarmed with them.

By evening there was a ring of farmers and village folk from Titusville around Drake's derrick. The news that Drake had succeeded swept over the countryside. For days the farmers straggled in and stood around watching the oil being pumped into barrels, tins, anything. The whole valley of Oil Creek slowly rose to a pitch of wild excitement as the value of Drake's achievement seeped into the minds of the landowners.

Off in New York two men shared the excitement. They were Bissell and Eveleth. Bissell's fever in the oil quest had cooled considerably. Now a telegram came from Drake announcing the discovery of oil. Both law partners kept the news to themselves, but, with as little show of excitement as possible, hurried around to all the stockholders of Seneca Oil Company stock and bought it for as little as possible. Then Bissell went with all speed to Titusville.

Today in a little clearing in the forest about three miles from the center of the present city of Titusville, close by the sluggish, greasy water of Oil Creek, there stands a huge bowlder bearing on its face a bronze tablet marking the spot where this historic well was bored. As one stands before it, out of the stillness of the woodland comes the steady muffled pounding of innumerable little oil wells which, seventy-one years after Drake's discovery, are still bringing petroleum to the surface.

VI

THIS was the news which sent J. G. Hussy from his bank and his produce business in River Street, Cleveland. But few others, if any, knew of the event in Cleveland. The popular story has it that the news ran over the country instantly like wild-fire. Hussy and perhaps a few others knew of it in Cleveland, but the news did not begin to spread around the country for three months and it was not until after Christmas that the tide of adventurers began to flow into the regions.

The news reached Pittsburgh before it did Cleveland. And one of the first men on the scene was Samuel Kier. He bought the first oil from Drake. He contracted for two-thirds of the output at fifty-six cents a barrel. The balance was shipped to Schieffelin and Company, wholesale druggists in New York City. Alderman, the teamster Drake had contracted with at Meadville, would fill four barrels and wagon them to Meadville, one load a week over the old road by way of Kerr Hill and another load in some other direction.

Drake's well continued to flow at the rate of about twenty-five barrels a week and Uncle Billy Smith continued to operate it.

VII

JONATHAN WATSON, who had galloped away from his mill as soon as he heard the news, got a lease on the farm of the Widow McClintock and without delay set up a derrick. An Englishman named William Barnsdall formed a partnership—Barnsdall, Mead, and Rouse—and started drilling in Crawford County close to Tidioute. The derricks began to appear all along Oil Creek. Ferris, the New York pioneer kerosene trader, came down to look over the situation. He immediately got leases under the firm name of King and Ferris and began drilling at Tidioute. Before Christmas the derricks were in place on numerous farms between Titusville and Oil City and as far as Franklin. No more oil was brought in before Christmas but the entire valley buzzed. The farmers had just had the most disastrous year in their history. This was the year of the June frost. And while the inhabitants were bewailing the strange mishap which had killed a large part of their crops another frost appeared and completed the work of destruction. And now suddenly from out of the depths of despair they found themselves rising on a tide of prosperity.

Lease hunters were running up and down Oil Creek buying the land if they could, leasing it where they could not buy. Here was born the thing which has been the curse of the oil industry—the royalty owner. The leases provided for cash payments and then a percentage for the landowner of all oil recovered on the land leased. That system has persisted to this day. Between the mouth of Oil Creek and its confluence with the Allegheny River there were forty-three farms and these had suddenly acquired an amazing value. It was believed at the time that all the oil was close to the creek and no drilling was attempted anywhere else. Before Christmas, along this lazy stream could be heard the sounds of numerous little engines pounding away as they raised and lowered their wooden walking beams and sent the pipes down through the rock in search of this new wealth.

VIII

JAMES EVANS, a blacksmith, living on French Creek, a tributary of Oil Creek near Franklin, was boring for salt. He was not looking for oil. And when oil began to show in the flowing brine he was disgusted. On second thought he decided to have a look at Drake's well. What he saw there decided him to proceed with his drilling. He saw what Bissell had guessed and what Drake had proved, that, while salt water came up at a level of about fifteen or twenty feet, the oil lay deeper down below the surface of the rock. Evans went on with his drilling, working by man power without the aid

KICKING DOWN AN EARLY WELL.
(From Frank Leslie's *Illustrated Newspaper*, 1865)

of an engine. After days of toil he saw a black fluid rising in the tube. That news that oil had been struck in Franklin spread like wild-fire. The town dropped its work and rushed hatless to Evans' well. Evans' daughter got the news from a neighbor. She ran out crying: "Dad's struck ile." The town took up the cry. "Dad's struck ile" was shouted by every one in glee. The church bells were rung. The court, which was in session, adjourned and judge, lawyers, litigants, and attendants all went out to see the mighty work of the heroic blacksmith Evans. The oil he pumped out was clear, smooth as silk and free from grit. And soon it came to be known as Franklin Lubricating Oil.

In January, excitement was sent to a higher pitch by the coming in of oil on the Hamilton McClintock farm two miles above Oil City. The petroleum shot out at the rate of sixty gallons a minute. Just before this Mr. Hussy, the Cleveland produce merchant, arrived in Titusville. He became, so far as is known, the first buyer of royalty oil. A farmer named David McElhenny sold the oil rights on his 180-acre farm for $1,500 and one-fourth of all oil recovered. Hussy bought out McElhenny's royalty.

Now the era of quick profits was coming. Barnsdall, Mead, and Rouse had been drilling since September. In February after oil was found on the Hamilton McClintock farm, they sold a one-third interest in their as yet unsuccessful well to William H. Abbott for $10,000. Two days later the well began pumping and in its first six months yielded 56,000 barrels of oil worth $16,700. The next month Jonathan Watson's well on the Widow McClintock's farm came in. And now the excitement rose to great heights and the valley began to fill up with prospectors and adventurers from every part of the country.

IX

ODDLY enough Drake did not realize the extent of his discovery. He believed he had hit the only vein and he smiled indulgently at the men who ran about madly looking for oil land, until the busy walking beams began to drive their pipes into oil pools. Drake loved to play cards and he was a devoted fisherman. He did not permit these distractions to take him from his business, but he looked after his own well and at his leisure put down a line for fish or sat around in a friendly game. One day a little after the coming in of his well he was out fishing with Mr. R. D. Fletcher who had helped finance him. They were joined by a farmer named Gibson and of course the talk turned to oil and the Drake well.

"I'll bet there's oil under my farm," said Gibson, whereupon Drake and Fletcher broke into a hearty laugh. Drake was not the only one who felt that way. There was Dr. Brewer. He was among the first to suspect the petroleum floating on Oil Creek might have a commercial value. He was the man who had sent the sample to Professor Crosby of Dartmouth which had started Bissell on the quest. But at the very moment when Drake's well seemed to prove the whole case Dr. Brewer seemed to lose faith in the value of the oil finds. He was a pleasant, jolly man and one day he handed around some cigars and said: "Have one on me. I traded oil stock for these."

Uncle Billy Smith, an expert driller, who had learned much about oil at Tarentum, was offered large sums to go into drilling with other men at many times the price paid him by Drake. But he stuck with Drake for three years and then left the oil regions.

Drake himself got a commission as a justice of the peace and as such helped to draw up most of the leases of oil lands. Even after other wells proved the richness of the valley Drake failed to see that fortune in oil which Uncle Billy promised him as he looked for the first time on the black liquid in his well. He made no effort to exploit his find in any way. He sold the oil from his own well and made good fees as a justice of the peace. It is said he bought one lease from Jonathan Watson in Titusville for $2,000, but could not keep up the payments and in 1863 sold it for $10,000. Center Street runs through that piece of land now. He made about $3,000 a year as a justice of the peace and in 1863 left the oil regions with about $15,000. He went to another region where men often are lured to drill for riches—Wall Street—and there lost all he had. Then for a long time he dropped out of sight.

Yet he had made a far richer discovery than the man who first turned up a nugget of gold on Sutter's farm in California. Since 1859—the year of Drake's discovery—this country has produced three billion dollars in gold. In 1929—a single year—our wells yielded a billion barrels of crude oil—forty-two billion gallons worth 9.7 cents a gallon in the crude state or over four billion dollars and worth three times that much in refined products. A year of petroleum is worth a cycle of gold.

CHAPTER II. A VISITOR AT THE CREEK

ALONG River Street they talked about oil. The produce trade knew that Hussy had made an investment in Pennsylvania and that he was drilling. But as usual most people said nothing would come of it. Meantime young Mr. John D. Rockefeller kept his mind severely on his produce business.

He was now twenty years old. He had been a merchant for two years and in a small way he was already a successful business man. River Street had come to know his sagacity and gravity. It saw him come to work every morning early. It did not see him go home very often at night. Those who remained late saw him many times at the high bookkeeper's desk poring over the firm's books under the yellow light of a gas jet. The man was marked by a tremendous earnestness and concentration. He belonged to no organizations. He went to no theatres. He attended no dances or

OIL CREEK A FEW YEARS AFTER DRAKE'S DISCOVERY.
(From *Romance of Petroleum* by J. D. Henry)

parties. He had one diversion—the Erie Street Baptist Church. Of course the pastor was one of his very good friends. Old Deacon Sked, now very old and a florist, continued to be a close church companion. Rockefeller was a faithful attendant at Scripture lessons every Wednesday evening.

He was tall, raw-boned, holding his head erect, yet appearing a trifle stooped because of his strong, full, rounded back. He dressed in the best of clothes and with the greatest care. His bearing was dignified and calm and he took care to detract in no particular from this effect. Although but a youth among the seasoned merchants of River Street every one addressed him as "Mr. Rockefeller." The man's countenance had already acquired a maturity far beyond his years. A careful observer might have noted that while his face and head were large, the size was accounted for by the large rounded jawbone and the broad area of the parietal region. The nose seemed inadequate and weak. The eyes were the most unusual feature. They were small and the brow was quite smooth, yet these eyes and this brow gave an appearance of thoughtfulness without any of those wrinkles, furrows, and frowns which artists use to depict this effect. The eyes, in fact, were not so small as they appeared. They were brilliant, but the visible area of these luminous balls was reduced by the drooping lids which hung low over them. At a distance this gave an illusive appearance of languor to the face which was suddenly dissipated on a nearer approach, much to the discomfiture of many a man who advanced on him in argument. He had a way of looking ahead of him—walking along the street, in his office, moving from one spot to another, appearing not to see anything but what lay straight ahead. But he looked with extraordinary intentness at anything on which he fastened his gaze. Even as a young man he had a way of looking straight into the face and eyes of those he addressed with unfaltering steadiness. The whole effect of the young man's appearance was one of quiet, composed, grave preoccupation.

He was beyond a doubt resolved to be rich. He was already on the road to riches. He would have grown wealthy had he never heard of oil. This second year of the produce business had brought to him and his partner a net income of $17,000—which they divided—a large sum for those days. He had, apparently, no grand designs at this time. He met each day's problems as they arose and they were just the ordinary problems of the small business man.

He had learned one important lesson. He had seen that to go along slowly on one's own earnings was a snail's pace. Hussy, who had already plunged into oil, like many business men of the period, prided himself on the fact that he never owed a dollar to any man. His firm paid its bills with promptness, bought everything for cash and never sought a loan from any one. But young Rockefeller saw that by using as much of other people's money as he could borrow he could accumulate in a single year the growth that would take five or six years to attain. He has spoken many times of his prodigious energy as a borrower. His partner, Clark, was fond of telling a story of his youthful associate. One day a wealthy business man stepped into the office of Clark and Rockefeller and after greeting Mr. Clark asked for Rockefeller and said:

"Mr. Clark, you may tell Mr. Rockefeller when he comes in that I think I can use the $10,000 he wants to invest with me for your firm. I have thought it all over."

"Good God!" cried the amazed Clark. "We don't want to invest $10,000. John is out now trying to borrow $5,000."

To prepare his subject for a little loan of $5,000, Rockefeller had told him he was thinking of investing $10,000 in the banker's business. When Clark told Rockefeller of this on his return, the young merchant was shocked at Clark's folly in letting the cat out of the bag.

"And the funny part of it," Clark would say, "is that John got the $5,000 after I had made my blunder. Oh! he was the greatest borrower you ever saw."

The Rockefeller family was now on a rising tide. Frank was at work. William was with the firm of Hughes and Lester and saving his money. In another year he was a partner. A group picture extant taken at this time of the three boys and two girls reveals a group of well-to-do young people. All are in good clothes. The boys all wear large watch-chains, a luxury at that period. The girls have the conventional jewels. John and his elder sister—Lucy—strongly resembled each other and their mother. William and Mary Ann were alike and bore a striking resemblance to their father. Frank seemed a composite of both strains. The father, old Doctor Bill, still roamed the highways vending his pills. But now he remained away for longer periods. His stays in Cleveland were shorter. The family no longer depended wholly on him for support. It must be said of him that he had always borne that obligation well, but now when it pressed upon him less urgently he seemed to let it fall gradually and lightly from his shoulders. He was drifting slowly out of the lives of the family in Cheshire Street.

II

However close Mr. Rockefeller held his nose to the grindstone in River Street he could not fail to hear the talk about oil. The coming of new wells confirmed the discoveries of Drake. Oil began to find its way to Cleveland. Several Cleveland merchants made the trip to the "oleaginous locations" and returned with glowing tales of its coming wealth. The coal-oil refineries in the city were alarmed and there was talk of erecting a refinery or two in Cleveland to handle the local trade.

About this time several Cleveland business men decided the matter ought to be looked into. Young Rockefeller was called into the discussion. Some one, it was agreed, should be sent to Titusville—some one who could be depended upon not to be swept away by the prevailing excitement. The man chosen to make the journey was "Mr. Rockefeller," the young merchant just approaching his twenty-first year. Old newspapers in Cleveland refer to this group of men and to the sums which they agreed to contribute to the enterprise. These accounts fix the date of the investigation sometime in 1859. It is probable, however, that it was sometime in the early Spring of 1860, after the new oil developments had confirmed the value of Drake's discovery. In any case, it came about that Mr. Rockefeller made his first visit to the oil regions of Pennsylvania.

III

To go to Titusville Rockefeller had to go by railroad to Meadville and then by team overland through the forest roads. As he reached the creek the scene which greeted his eye was very different from that which met Drake's as he first entered the region. The first oil rush, with the end of Winter, had begun. Here was the beginning of one of those strange episodes in American history which have been repeated at intervals—such as California saw in the gold rush of forty-nine. The cry of "Oil!" ran around the country as the cry of gold had done ten years earlier. Rockefeller, as he wandered along Oil Creek, saw its banks and those of French Creek and the Allegheny River dotted with tall derricks and dumpy engine houses with tall thin smokestacks, from which the black smoke poured over the once green farms of the creek. There was a steady stream of arrivals into the new towns—Titusville, Oil City, Franklin, Meadville, Tidioute. These tiny settlements were once just clusters of a few small stores and loggers' hotels. Now hastily constructed shacks were going up and rudimentary business streets were taking form, lined by small, rude, unpainted one-story affairs, roughly boarded stores, lawyers' offices, oil drillers, notaries, and traders, and a few saloons. Oil City had been just a hotel, a gristmill, a store and two houses. Now it was a forest of derricks and a huddle of shacks. The trees along the banks of the stream—green and pleasant hemlock and pine—were felled and in their places were dirty mounds of coal and cinders and logs and

TITUSVILLE, THE NEW OIL CENTER, SHORTLY AFTER DISCOVERY OF PETROLEUM.
(From an old print)

charcoal and noisy, chugging engines and ceaselessly swaying walking beams.

A new industry had sprung into life. Everything had to be provided for it. One of the first great needs was barrels. Brewer and Watson, the sawmill men, in addition to drilling, turned their mill into a barrel-making business on a large scale. It is said this firm expended $750,000 on barrel-making before it began to make any money. Bissell, too, set up a barrel factory at Franklin.

Drilling was proceeding feverishly along the lowlands of the creeks and river. Smaller fry were soaking up the waste oil from the streams with blankets. Excitement was rising higher with each new well. Every week dozens of new drills were started. Every now and then the cry ran 'round the region that oil was found in some new location. The engines were pounding at Tidioute. Watson, Tanner and Company brought in a well there yielding 480 barrels a day and another well was opened at the same time yielding 300 barrels a day. There was a rush for Tidioute. Then came news of oil at Henry's Bend. The drillers rushed down to the Bend. In one place men anchored a raft in the river and began boring in the river bed. There was an angry cry against this. At night citizens cut the ropes of the raft. Fights followed. The raft went on with its drilling, its defenders camped at its edge with shotguns.

Rough men were coming in—floaters without money or plans—attracted by the tales of quick and easy wealth. The barrooms were crowded at night with boisterous, noisy adventurers playing cards, drinking whiskey, arguing and brawling. More serious prospectors sat around the hotel lobbies—the American House, the Anthony Hotel, the Eagle House, and dozens of others. The talk was of oil, oil, always oil; and sometimes about this new man Lincoln who had been named by the Republican party to run for President.

IV

WAGONS! Long, incessant lines of wagons! Like a huge snake that endless procession of wagons crawled out of Titusville and Oil City. There were no railroads. The nearest railroad station was at Corry, sixteen miles away. There was another at Union City, twenty-two miles away, another at Meadville, thirty miles away and a fourth at Erie, forty miles distant. Pittsburgh became the first great oil market. It was reached by Allegheny River boats. But Erie became the first important overland market. And oil was sent to Erie and the other railroad connections by wagons. Small refineries went up along Mill Creek there. They were just little stills ranging from a barrel or two to ten or fifteen barrels a day of refined oil. The teams made two trips a week and some men like the Hon. Electra K. Range had as many as twenty hauling his oil. Every stable and barn in the neighborhood of Mill Creek was used for wagons and teams. One might see as many as fifty oil wagons parked around the corner of Eighteenth and State streets in Erie.

A long, low dray, carrying from six to ten barrels, sinking deep into the mud of the dirt roads, the horses straining furiously to drag it forward, urged by a flow of picturesque and vehement profanity from the grimy, burly wagon driver and a crack from his long blacksnake whip—this was the first transportation engine of the oil regions. The teamsters had to be strong, fearless men. The going was hard and when the weather was bad and the roads impassable the teams pulled off the roads and traveled over the harder grounds of the farms. This brought war with the farmers. But the teamsters were resolute, brawling men who found diver-

TEAMING IN THE OIL REGIONS.
(From Frank Leslie's *Illustrated Newspaper*, 1865)

sion in these turbulent encounters. More than one farmer saw the great blacksnake whip uncurl menacingly toward him. Finally the farmers armed themselves. Occasionally a teamster was shot or a farmer beaten up. And so the long, slow procession of wagons lumbered on to Erie through the plowed-up roads and hostile farmsteads, with their teamsters cursing, singing, fighting, exploding their long whips and brandishing their muskets when necessary. They became the masters of the region. They made their own terms for hauling oil. Crude petroleum that cost eight dollars a barrel and later two dollars a barrel, cost five dollars a barrel to haul to Erie. A few of the teamsters hoarded their money and later grew to be rich men as producers and refiners. Most of them spent it in the saloons which now began to appear all over oildom and

A VISITOR AT THE CREEK

with the gamblers who came with their cards and their roulette wheels and other devices of the devil.

There were as yet no turnpikes or prepared roads of any sort. The traffic to Pittsburgh went by river. Oil City became the center for this trade. Oil was carted from the wells to Oil City and then towed along the Allegheny River. Refineries appeared also in New York. The crude oil was put aboard boats at Erie and carried by water to the metropolis. Kier was refining it in Pittsburgh, Ferris and Schieffelin in New York. As yet Cleveland and Philadelphia had not gotten into the trade.

V

Young Rockefeller surveying the situation at Titusville quickly saw that this oil business divided itself into three departments—producing, refining, and transportation. It was plain to be seen there was money in the refining industry. Crude oil cost from two to twelve dollars a barrel and the cost of refining it was but thirty cents. Coal oil made from shale cost one dollar a gallon and it was clear that there would be a shift from shale oil to petroleum. But would the supplies of petroleum hold out? No one could say anything on this point with authority. The refining business was as yet, like almost all business, purely local. In Erie they made oil and sold it to grocery stores in the town and its environs. The same thing was true of Pittsburgh and New York.

As to producing, the disorder of this must have shocked Rockefeller. It would be impossible to imagine a business more harried by uncertainties and wild competition. After Drake hit oil and until January, 1860, crude fetched twenty dollars a barrel at the well. In February it was eighteen dollars a barrel. In April it was twelve. The wells were coming in now in numbers and with abundant production. No man could tell what the price of crude oil would be. As a matter of fact, it went to seven dollars before the Summer was over and by December sold from two to three dollars and a half a barrel. The producing business was worse than the refining business. The latter was subject to the peril of an extinction of oil. The former would of course die if the oil gave out but it was open also to the alternative danger of being ruined by excessive overproduction and price demoralization. Moreover the swindling stock faker had already invaded the oil fields. Several wild-cat oil companies were formed in Erie and stock salesmen were at large reciting luminous tales of golden riches and selling beautifully engraved certificates of stock.

This was the new industry which young Mr. John D. Rockefeller surveyed. He made up his mind definitely that the business of drilling for and producing crude oil was an excellent business to remain away from. As to refining—there were not enough facts available for an intelligent decision. It was a pure gamble. Thus he reported to his associates when he returned to Cleveland. Stay out of the oil business. But keep an eye on it. If the supply of crude petroleum should ever be established as a continuing product, then consider entering the refining business but leave production severely alone. Here was wisdom in good earnest. Seventy years of the oil business have confirmed the soundness of that judgment based on a first inspection of oildom by this twenty-year-old business man.

CHAPTER III. VEGETABLES AND WAR

Now while the countryside swarms to Titusville and Oil City and the Creek regions for oil and riches, the shadows gather over the country. They fall long and dark over Cleveland. In the Summer, while the lease hunters and the derrick men are rushing to Oil Dorado from all parts of Pennsylvania and Ohio, these two states are at fever pitch over the approaching storm. They have formidable candidates in the field for the presidency. Pennsylvania backs Simon Cameron. Ohio puts forth Salmon P. Chase. And in June the Republican Convention nominates Abraham Lincoln! Down in River Street they have hardly heard of him. It is probably certain young Mr. Rockefeller had not. The debates of Lincoln and Douglas had interested him little. He was full of scorn of the politicians who were always stirring up trouble, paying attention to every one's business but their own. As for him, all this was no part of his business and he paid no attention to it. In River Street the talk of politics became almost unbearable. Incessant gabbing about slavery and Kansas and Nebraska and state's rights.

VEGETABLES AND WAR

But as the Winter came on Mr. Rockefeller did notice one thing. This oil business was getting more interesting all the time. Wells were coming in with great frequency. Refineries were going up now—small affairs—along Woolworth Run in Cleveland. Oil had been found in West Virginia and some at Mecca in Ohio. It looked as if the fears of a failure of supplies were unfounded. Take away that fear and the oil business was worth going into. Rockefeller

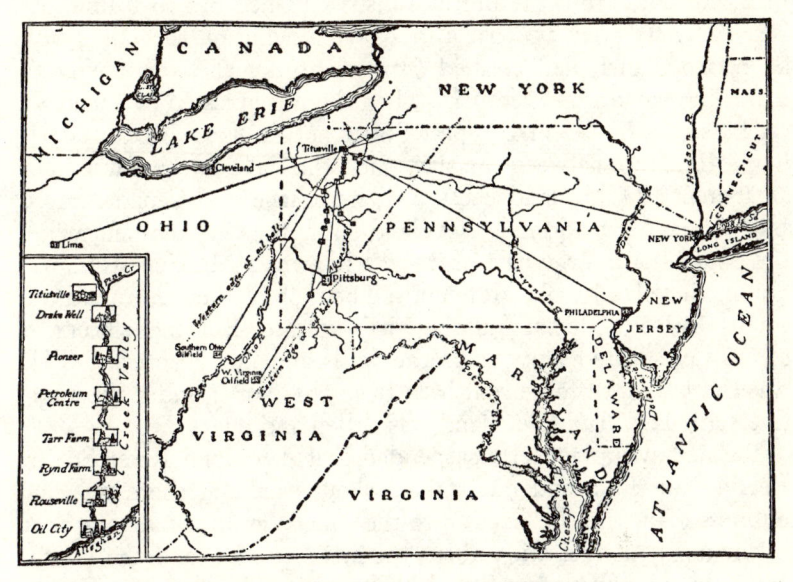

MAP OF EARLY OIL REGIONS IN PENNSYLVANIA.

kept his eyes on it without taking them off his produce business. But now he had them fixed on another thing too. Lincoln had been elected and South Carolina had answered with a broadside of gunpowder at Fort Sumter. The state had formally seceded. By Christmas it was plain the other Southern states would secede. The South was actually setting up a rebel government. All this foreboded trouble and in Cleveland things looked black indeed. For Ohio, which gazed over its northern border across the Lake to Canada, looked over its southern frontiers into the slave states of Virginia and Kentucky. Both were aflame with the war spirit. What about business? What about the produce business? Here was the country climbing out of the panic of 1857 and now war-makers were preparing to imperil business again. It was enough to stir the wrath of any business man.

As for Cleveland—it seemed to have lost its senses—to be scarcely less inflamed than Kentucky. The madness had even invaded River Street and the Flats. One day a low rumble rolled along the river—a muffled roar from the Public Square. The produce district saw crowds running toward the center and soon men and boys from the produce district rushed out to follow the roar. The cry went up that a mob was moving on the jail. Lucy, an octaroon girl, had escaped from Kentucky and was trying to make her way across Lake Erie when she was arrested by the slave catchers in a house on Prospect Street not far from Rockefeller's home. The race between the slaves and the slave catchers was long an irritant to Cleveland because of its nearness to Canada. Here another slave girl was in a Cleveland jail at the very moment when the South—or a large part of it—was in armed rebellion. Indignation in Cleveland broke all bounds. The mob blackened around the county jail and demanded the girl's release. But the officers in some way spirited her out of the walls and into Kentucky. This was the last slave to be sent back from the North under the fugitive slave law. And Cleveland was sullen and angry.

Business was practically suspended that day along River Street. Feeling was high and men talked about war. But there was one business man who did not run to the county jail nor take any part in the angry conversation about the slave catchers and the South. He held close to his books and his business. This was Mr. Rockefeller.

Hardly had the slave girl fury died down when the town was aroused by the passage through it on his way to Washington of Abraham Lincoln, the president-elect. Once again men and women left their offices and shops and homes and thronged to greet the new hero. A mass meeting of 30,000 howled themselves hoarse in Melodeon Hall where the tall, solemn Lincoln spoke to them gravely of the great burden he was on his way to assume. Sentiment in Cleveland was at fever pitch. And so two months later when Lincoln issued his call for 75,000 volunteers the men of Cleveland sprang to arms in great numbers. Fort Sumter fell April 12th. Ten days later the Grays marched away from Cleveland and Camp Taylor was established. In a few weeks another

VEGETABLES AND WAR

regiment—the Seventh—departed and others were organizing. The Lincoln Guards were formed in May. "Are you going?" That was what the young men of Cleveland asked each other. Mr. Rockefeller pondered the question. In 1854, a youth in high school, he had written in his essay on Freedom: "It is a violation of the laws of our country and the laws of our God that man should hold his fellow man in bondage. Yet how many thousands there are at this present time even in our own country who are bowed down by cruel masters to toil beneath the scorching suns of the South. How under such circumstances can America call herself free? It is a freedom which if not speedily checked will end in the ruin of the country."

The youthful essayist was a good prophet. Here was the chance as Lincoln had said as a young man "to hit this thing hard." Here too was the threat of the country's ruin at its door. But Mr. Rockefeller did not rush to arms. Here he was with a growing business on his hands, moving toward that wealth he so much coveted, and here were politicians and cranks pushing the country into war. Still the situation was difficult. All the young men were going. Young clerks and some little more than office boys, truck drivers, and messengers and a good many merchants were going from River Street. It was a hard problem.

Apparently William was not going either. Then in September the youngest brother—Frank—not yet eighteen, enlisted and marched away. This made the situation more difficult. It was troubling young Mr. Rockefeller very much, particularly as some twenty-two men went from the Erie Street church. Lucy, his older sister, wrote to her friend Mary Curtis—John D.'s old school-teacher—back in Owego and told her all the news of the family. All the young men were going to war, she wrote. But John is considering the matter. He has not yet made up his mind. But he finally settled the matter. He decided he would not go. There were plenty of men to do all the fighting necessary. He needed to stay at home and look after his business. And so Mr. Rockefeller never went to war.

Many years later, in 1903, John D. Rockefeller, retired, was playing golf with Levi T. Scofield, a retired architect from Cleveland who was a Civil War veteran. A newspaper reporter went to Rockefeller one day as he finished his golf game and informed him that Mr. Scofield had just given on his own authority some details of Rockefeller's war record. Scofield said that young Rockefeller, while he did not enlist, more than made up for it. He had only $10,000 in cash at the time, all tucked away in a strong box. Nevertheless he gave Scofield $300 out of his strong box to enable him to go and then guaranteed to give the families of twelve soldiers each $300 a year until the war ended. The reporter asked Mr. Rockefeller if this was true.

"I guess it is a fact," he answered, "if Scofield says it is, although I had forgotten all about it until now. There were few banks then that were reliable and we kept our money in our safes. I had but $10,000 then."

This incident is reported for what it is worth as Rockefeller's own version of the war episode. In later years Mr. Rockefeller claimed to intimates that he contributed to twelve soldiers' families in order to enable the men to go to war.

II

BUT YOUNG Mr. Rockefeller was not the only business man who kept away from war. Henry H. Rogers was twenty-one when the call to arms came and Flagler was thirty. Andrew Carnegie, an ardent patriot, went into the military railway service. John Wanamaker, too, was an extraordinarily patriotic man, keeping his place in his Bible marked with a little American flag, but he went not to the wars save as a man with goods to sell the government. J. P. Morgan, who said, "Don't be a bear on the United States," as a young man made his first big money during the war "selling the United States short" in the Gold Room and devoted the remaining years of the war to building up his new banking business. Armour, Clark, Gould, and scores of others each attended to their own special business interests, leaving the fighting to be done by others.

The business men of the country did not appear to very great advantage during the Civil War. That is a chapter which has not yet been written. There was much profiteering among merchants and manufacturers and shameful extravagance among the newly rich. Congress had to investigate charges of corruption. Contractors made exorbitant profits and swindled in the most orthodox fashion. Shoddy was delivered to the soldiers. Lincoln had to remove his Secretary of War. Professor Charles Beard says that from one-fourth to one-fifth of the money paid out of the Federal Treasury was tainted by the tricks of swindlers.

As for Rockefeller, his firm made a great deal of money during the war so that when it was over he was a rich man. But there is no evidence that he engaged in any questionable transactions or dealt in any improper way with the government.

III

THE WAR brought the curtain down upon the first act in that hectic tragi-comedy of the oil rush. It fell upon a scene which made a fitting finale for the wild performance which had been in progress along those turbulent Creeks.

On April 17th, 1861, a group of men were sitting around the lobby of Anthony's Hotel in Titusville. News had just come of the fall of Fort Sumter—five days after that momentous event. What did this mean to the oil industry? The more sanguine thought the fight would soon be over. But the oil industry itself was moving into troublous days. Oil was down to a dollar a barrel. The great ogre overproduction was devouring it. The wells had been coming in so fast the excessive supplies of oil were getting out of hand. But there would soon be an end of that. While they talked the gods were even then making ready to open their hands and let disaster drop upon the regions. A man red with excitement rushed in.

"Oil!" he cried. "Millions of gallons! A regular fountain of oil! Shootin' up in the air like a fountain!"

"Where! where!" cried every one, jumping up.

"At Rouseville," the frantic man answered. "Little and Merrick's well on the Buchanan place. Come quick! Nothin' like it ever seen!"

He rushed out and behind him every man in the hotel. The word had gotten around and all Titusville had rushed into the streets. It was five o'clock, just growing dark. One of the men in that lobby was Mr. Rouse, after whom Rouseville was called, a large producer. He ran with the rest. As the crowd neared the Buchanan farm they beheld a stream of oil flowing heavenward sixty feet high—a huge, black eruption of petroleum—the first great oil gusher. The crowd stood in a ring around the amazing geyser which made a black lake of foaming grease. Suddenly a blinding flash of red flame leaped heavenward with a roar as of a thousand cannon. In some mysterious way the first gusher had caught fire almost in the moment of its birth. The blazing oil was thrown in a shower of fire over the spectators and in a moment scores of persons were running about like so many living torches. A wide column of flame rose heavenward as from a giant jet and disappeared into a rolling mass of black smoke shot with streaks of flame overhead. The cries of the victims as they leaped about in a death panic added to the horror of the scene. Suddenly the crowd saw Mr. Rouse making his way across the sea of grease. Fire shot from his clothing. Twice he stumbled but rose, laboring, ablaze, through the burning oil. The crowd saw him put his hands in his pockets, take out his wallet, his papers, and hurl them with all his strength outside the rim of fire where they were picked up. He pushed on out of the flaming lake and collapsed on its shore. Portions of his body were burned to a cinder. Yet he remained calm and when carried to a place of safety, as attendants gave him after every word spoonfuls of water, he dictated his will leaving large gifts to various public purposes, among them a sum to build a good road in the oil regions. Then he expired. Ten persons were killed and eleven others were seriously burned. The scene of this tragedy is still pointed out in the oil regions and may be reached along that road which the heroic oil man provided for in his will as he died.

The righteous lifted their eyes to heaven and shook their heads as if they understood. The wicked oil cities had felt the hand of Divine vengeance. "For behold, the Lord will come with fire and with his chariots like a whirlwind to render his anger with fury and his rebuke with flames of fire."

Thus the news of the war came to the oil regions. This catastrophe spread a cloud of gloom over the whole countryside. It was the first great fire in a country which was destined to live for years under the dread of fire day and night. The fire burned for three days, by which time it was smothered with earth and manure. Then Little and Merrick began to barrel the oil it yielded. The full extent of the disaster was not the fire. As this well gave off thirty barrels an hour oil fell to fifty cents a barrel. Then came Lincoln's call to arms. Many who had begun to find petroleum was not so generous a mistress as she promised to be forsook her for the field. Many, however, remained to continue their drilling. In June there were sixty-one wells on Oil Creek, nine at Franklin, six on French Creek—135 wells producing 1,300 barrels a day. And new wells came in every week. Then in September came the great Phillips well flowing 4,000 barrels a day. Soon followed the Empire well with 2,000 barrels a day. The nation could not have supplied barrels for this flood any more than the world could buyers. Thousands of barrels of oil were flowing into the streams. Wells were plugged. By the end of the year oil had dropped to ten cents a barrel. The war was under way. The adventurers who had flocked into Titusville and Oil City were now flocking away. It looked as if the great Oil Bubble had burst.

CHAPTER IV. ROCKEFELLER GOES INTO OIL

CLEVELAND was beginning in 1862 to be aware of a nuisance along Walworth Run. Little refineries had appeared there for distilling petroleum into kerosene. From his store young Mr. Rockefeller could see the unpleasant scum which trickled down from the Run into the Cuyahoga River. Citizens complained about this, but there were some men who said that the industry which produced that scum would some day make Cleveland rich. Occasionally a young fellow named Samuel Andrews would come over to Rockefeller's store. Andrews had a little refinery—a small affair of ten barrels' capacity. He was essentially a mechanical man and among the first in Cleveland to see that kerosene would supplant coal oil as an illuminant. He was desperately poor and really lacked business ability. He had gone into oil refining from candle making—a natural drift. He devised methods for getting a higher yield of kerosene from crude oil than his neighbors and was the first, or among the first, to find a use for the residuum as a fuel for his still. Andrews' wife took in sewing to help him. He saw the need of more capital and he kept pressing Rockefeller and his partner to back him in a larger refinery. Andrews' attention to details and economy in his little refinery commended him to Rockefeller. But this cautious young merchant weighed other considerations as well. The produce business was prosperous. The war was bringing plenty of business and high prices. Though but twenty-two years of age Rockefeller found himself among the well-to-do men of Cleveland. Moreover he was committed to the idea of fixing his attention upon one business. Yet this oil industry fascinated him. He had been watching

"POMEROY'S EXPRESS"—PROSPECTORS ARRIVING BY BARGE.

it for two years. He had been listening to Andrews for almost that long. Now in 1862 the oil industry seemed to have reached its lowest estate.

When this year opened crude oil was selling for ten cents a barrel. The price began to improve as the months wore on, but a new difficulty had revealed itself. The oil regions began to assert themselves as the natural refining center. There were plenty of refineries at Erie, Pittsburgh, Philadelphia, New York, Cleveland, and other places. But refiners began to ask themselves how they could compete with the region refiners who had the crude oil at their doors. Several Cleveland refiners answered the question by taking their refineries to the Creek—as the oil country was then called. One was Lowry, Fawcett and Company. Another was a firm of which Alexander Scofield was a member—one of the ablest business men in Cleveland. Great refineries were arising in the oil cities. On the whole, in this year 1862 the oil industry in Cleveland did not offer a very rosy promise to the business men along River Street. Yet it was in this year that young Mr. Rockefeller made his decision after two years of cautious examination to yield to the persuasions of Samuel Andrews. With his partner, M. A. Clark, he invested several thousand dollars in a new firm which was called Clark and Andrews. His own name was kept out of it. But John D. Rockefeller was now in oil.

II

THIS year a husky, aggressive, yet genial young Scotchman named Andrew Carnegie made a journey from Pittsburgh to the Creek. There he saw with amusement and surprise the signs of a feeble attempt to stage a second oil rush. He saw men knocking up a shanty in a few hours, teams of two men working the treadles of the oil drills, a few new adventurers arriving at Oil City by barge with their carpet bags and their chests on their shoulders. On one drill with its puffy little engine chugging away was a sign announcing the destination of the drill—"Hell or China." It all looked good to the shrewd Andy Carnegie for he and his partners this year bought a farm and backed a company to drill for oil. The farm later yielded a million dollars' cash dividends in a year and later came to be worth five million dollars.

III

THIS year a new word came to be pronounced frequently in the Pennsylvania oil regions. It stood for something new in American business. Combination. In January a group of oil-well owners along the Creek met to discuss their affairs. The flood of oil threatened to destroy them. And so these individualists who really believed that men should be left alone to pursue their own interests— the doctrine of Adam Smith that the world will run along best by itself which all men cherished—these individualists met to see if something could not be done to assist the world in its way of running. Let us combine, they said, to hold the price of oil up to two dollars a barrel. Oil cannot be produced profitably for less.

Apparently there was something wrong somewhere with this theory of *laissez faire*. Here was a little heresy though the heretics did not realize it.

IV

SURELY great changes had swept over the face of the land in the twenty-three years since the baby John Rockefeller was born at Richford. Chief among these was that the infant manufactures of 1839 had now grown to robust manhood. Already the value of manufactured products exceeded the value of agricultural products. There were what men called big factories.

Matthew Baldwin was building one hundred locomotives a year and employing eight hundred men. Robert Hoe was making rotary presses for Europe as well as America. Up in Hartford the Colt Arms Factory was doing things which set men to talking as they now talk about Ford. Indeed E. K. Root, the Colt superintendent, was the Henry Ford of his day. He did audacious things. He did away with handwork. He tooled up his machines, and put everything on platforms and jigs and cranes. Business men said he was crazy. Social workers said he was an enemy of mankind. But Colt paid him the staggering sum of $25,000 a year. The sewing machine makers were rising to be the magnates of the day—like the automobile makers of this decade. Isaac Singer and Elias Howe and Wheeler and Wilson had formed a patent pool. They maintained gaudy salesrooms glistening with mirrors and gilded furniture in the big cities. Sewing machine row with its shiny showrooms was the precursor of automobile row.

The age of iron and the age of invention was dawning. The telegraph, the cylinder printing press, the penny newspaper, the Atlantic cable, the sleeping car, the shoe-sewing machine, the passenger elevator, the Great Western, above all the Bessemer process for making steel—these marvels astounded the people. Great factories were rising everywhere. McCormick was making reapers, Case was making threshing machines. Studebaker wagons were known everywhere. Deer was making plows. The foundations of huge enterprises were being laid. Epoch-making first steps were being taken in the great American field of machine tools. The English already had sent a commission to study American methods. At Chicopee Falls Ames Brothers employed a thousand men. Most important of all, the railroads had now established their dominance.

ROCKEFELLER GOES INTO OIL

They were no longer just feeders of the canals and rivers and lakes. In 1850 there were no lines connecting East and West. A traveler from New York to St. Louis before this would have had to use fourteen different railroads, several canal boats and two or three stages. Now—by 1860—a vast net-work of rails spread over the whole East from the seaboard to the Mississippi and on into Iowa and Missouri.

Motion—powerful, irresistible, surging motion—agitated the nation, almost unperceived amidst the smoke and clouds and fogs of political discussion and then of war. Waves of new peoples flowed in from Europe, the immigrant trains moved endlessly westward, filling the middle-western prairies and crossing the mountains. Above all the vast natural resources of the continent were being uncovered—copper and silver and iron and coal and gold—the vast grain fields of the West and Northwest—the seemingly limitless timber riches now available because of the railroads—petroleum and salt and sulphur and zinc. America became a land teeming with riches, with a busy, new, hungry, undisciplined horde of workers from every corner of the world feverishly digging and hunting and struggling in a wild scramble called competition to find the treasures and rush them into the markets of the world.

And while the armies drove at each other upon the battlefields of the South, the Morgans and the Carnegies and the Rockefellers and the Havemeyers and the Goulds and the Vanderbilts and their fellows looked calmly over all this chaotic scramble and searched for the road to order. Slowly, in little spots here and there, the germs of organization were incubated. Many men, while they still talked about individualism, saw there was something wrong. Some force had to step in somewhere to restrain the savage elements of competition which seemed to devour the weak and the strong. And so here and there—while social reformers cried out against the machine and the rich—and the rising labor leaders denounced the capitalists—other men were pronouncing that word which was to bring upon itself the execration and hatred of the nation for the next fifty years—the word which a few Creek oil producers in the year 1862 used in Oil City and which, perhaps, John D. Rockefeller had never yet even heard of—Combination.

V

JOHN D. ROCKEFELLER was now twenty-two years old. It is an age at which young men think of many things besides business. Mr. Rockefeller was thinking of something else. But not much else.

He was thinking, for instance, of the Erie Street Baptist Church. This was his one diversion. He taught a Bible class there on Wednesday nights. He never missed a Sunday service. He attended faithfully the meetings of the trustees. His was the last word in counsel about the financial affairs of the congregation. In all things he conformed to the model he had seen set forth by St. Paul in his Bible—"Not slothful in business; fervent in spirit; serving the Lord."

He thought of one other matter. His mother noted that he made visits to a young lady he had known in his high-school days. This was Laura Celestia Spelman. He had had his nose buried deep in his business since those old days. But she had moved about a bit. She was born in Massachusetts and then went to Akron, Ohio, to live. Then her father moved to Cleveland where she went to high school and came to know John Rockefeller. After graduation she was sent to a boarding school in Worcester. She returned to Cleveland the year Colonel Drake struck oil.

She was a serious, but pretty, little black-haired girl, amiable, but knowing well her own mind. Her graduation essay was entitled "I Can Paddle My Own Canoe." And that she was now doing as a teacher in the Cleveland public schools. She lived in an atmosphere of severe religious devotion. Like her young friend Mr. Rockefeller she was brought up from her childhood to hate liquor with all her soul. Her mother was an active member of the W.C.T.U. Her father established a seminary at Atlanta in later years for negro girls. Religion was therefore an obvious tie between this young teacher and the youthful produce merchant who had just invested in oil. They went to different churches, but after a while people began to notice that Cetty Spelman was going to the Erie Street Baptist Church with John Rockefeller. That dominating young gentleman, who has always ruled everything he has touched, and who as a boy required all games to be played

Right, "COLONEL" EDWIN L. DRAKE, WHO DRILLED THE FIRST OIL WELL. *Left*, BILLY SMITH, HIS DRILLER

Upper left, HENRY M. FLAGLER. *Upper right,* S. V. HARKNESS.
Lower left, HENRY H. ROGERS. *Lower right,* JOHN D. ARCHBOLD

his own way, had brought the pious young lady from her aristocratic Episcopal parish to the humble Baptist mission.

However, the courting was neither energetic nor conspicuous. It did not take the young business man away from his business many nights a week. Indeed many friends of Cetty Spelman failed to observe that usually conspicuous phenomenon—the growing friendship which leads to the altar.

VI

THE TIDE of war was rolling close to the oil creeks of Pennsylvania. Lee's victorious and apparently invincible army was marching northward. May 2nd and 3rd, 1864, the Battle of Chancellorsville was fought and Lee was driving further north into Pennsylvania. The news of this movement sent a shudder of alarm through the oil regions. There was an almost total suspension of business. The price of oil shot upward. Men were asking $3.50 a barrel at the wells. But workers were leaving for the army. The draft officers were moving around the country gobbling up the slackers. By the end of June notices were posted in the oil towns that the draft officers would be in the oil country Monday and Tuesday, July 9th and 10th. The government wanted seven hundred men from that district. It would be a blow to the business. "But," said the Oil City *Derrick*, "unless we are mistaken, every one is ready to face the music." Then came the belated news of the defeat of Lee at Gettysburg and Fort Hudson. And a wave of relief swept over the regions.

VII

IN CLEVELAND, Mr. Rockefeller, busy with his produce business, was becoming more and more interested in his oil investment. The oil firm of Clark and Andrews was prospering. The demand for kerosene was growing. The old coal-oil business was swept away. The trade to Europe was growing. In 1862 Europe took eleven million gallons. In 1864 it took twenty-seven million. Moreover the business was becoming organized. The railroads were extending their lines into the regions. The Atlantic and Great Western had a line as far as Meadville and now it was pushing a branch from Meadville into the regions as far as Franklin. Then it ran its line on to Oil City. Other railroad schemes were afoot. While the state was aflame with excitement over Lee's invasion, Dr. Samuel Kier was busy incorporating a road to be known as the Mahoning and French Creek Railroad. At the same time work was being rushed on a new division of the Philadelphia and Erie that promised a new outlet to the lakes and the seaboard. Thus the oil regions at first bottled in the mountains from their natural markets, reached only by barges and teamsters, was opening

STREET SCENE IN TITUSVILLE—HER FAMOUS STREETS OF MUD.

its doors. Up to this point the teamsters carried the oil to the distant railroad connections. Now the teamsters were required merely to carry oil from the wells to the oil region railroad depots.

VIII

ONE DAY in March, 1863, the Widow McClintock thought she would hurry along the kitchen fire. So she poured some kerosene from a small can of oil into the stove. It was an historic act. The oil caught fire, leaped to her clothing, spilled in flames over the floor, set fire to the house and burned the unhappy woman's body to a cinder. The Widow McClintock was a pioneer, for thereafter the same happy thought was to occur to thousands of servant girls and housewives with almost the same tragic results. But this was but the beginning of the story.

Mrs. McClintock had an adopted son named John Steele. He

was twenty, handsome, married, and a teamster. He had a local reputation for the vigor and richness of his profane vocabulary. But he was a thrifty and likeable chap. When the McClintock farmhouse fire was extinguished, neighbors went in search of John Steele. When they found him with his team he hurried back to the farm. He was genuinely grieved at the tragic end of his foster-mother. But he remembered that she had always hidden her royalties from the farm oil leases around the house. Before

ADVENTURERS RUSHING TO THE CARS STARTING FOR OIL CREEK.

Johnny Steele ended his search of the house that day he unearthed several hundred thousand dollars. At least so runs the legend, though Steele always insisted it was not nearly so much. Also he found a will leaving all to him. Thus began one of the most picturesque and widely-advertised careers of the time—the adventurous performances of Coal Oil Johnny—the first gift of the oil regions to the entertainment and amusement of the nation.

By this time the oil cities had blossomed like the gold towns of California, with their crops of saloonmen, gamblers, prostitutes, idlers, and thugs. The dance halls lined the main streets of all the towns. Coal Oil Johnny, through with his wagon and his team, went at once to the man he had commissioned to watch them and presented him with the outfit. Then, accompanied by an agreeable companion, he arrayed himself in conspicuously modish clothes and set out to see the world, beginning in the gambling hells and dance halls of Titusville. Of course, he fell at once into the hands of sharpers. He made his progress to New York and then through all the cities of the East, followed by newspaper reporters and schemers of all sorts. For a while his royalties amounted to hundreds of dollars a day and these, along with his principal, he flung about him with a lavish hand. He stopped at the most fashionable hotels, appeared at the race tracks and the smartest restaurants attended by sycophants and parasites of both sexes. He would build a monument to soldier heroes anywhere on request. He handed out gifts to charities with magnificent gestures. He gave the reporters interviews about the millions he had inherited and the daily thousands that flowed into his hands. Whatever the actual sum of his fortune was he did not take long to spend it. Very suddenly the wells on the McClintock farm became sluggish and stopped. And quickly thereafter Coal Oil Johnny was broke. His brilliantly arrayed figure disappeared from the bright places and the legendary name of Coal Oil Johnny faded from the papers. He returned to the oil regions where he was soon found slinging baggage at the depot in Franklin. Later he moved to Nebraska where he settled down as a hard-working, substantial family man who tried to forget the hectic year of fabled riches through which he had passed as through a fire. Another generation so far forgot all about him save his name that it supposed the title of Coal Oil Johnny belonged to John D. Rockefeller.

CHAPTER V. TWO DECISIONS

THE WAR was now drawing rapidly to a close. John D. Rockefeller had done well. He thought he could see ahead now clearly. And so he made the two most important decisions of his life.

One was to ask Cetty Spelman to be his wife. Her decision could hardly have been difficult. John Rockefeller was twenty-five years old. He was tall, strong though lean, handsome, with well-rounded strong jaws and a large firm mouth. He carried himself with dignity very unusual in so young a man. In the church he was looked up to as a successful man. He was already regarded as rich. His income was considerable. He was moving with long strides toward his goal of the large riches he so much coveted. He was quiet, kindly in his bearing. Above all he was strong.

But he was immersed in business. And so when Miss Spelman accepted him, he surrounded his approaching marriage with the secrecy in which he enveloped all the other important events of his life. And when he was married, it was very quietly. There used to be a story among his old Standard Oil companions that he spent the afternoon at the circus and at night put in several hours' work at his office. Though this story is vouched for by one of the oldest of his former associates it must be repeated with caution.

He certainly did spend some time that day at work in his office and he visited the small cooperage plant of his oil business. Before he left he treated the workmen there to a good dinner. And as he was leaving he said to the foreman: "Treat them well, but see that they work."

He was married September 8th, 1864. The young couple moved into a house next door to his father's home which still was at 27 Cheshire Street. The Cleveland directory gives his own residence as Number 29.

II

THE SECOND decision had to do with oil. As the end of the war came into view with its promise of a great revival in the oil industry, Rockefeller began to make plans to abandon the produce business altogether and devote himself wholly to oil. In January, 1865, an event occurred which hastened that step. This was the discovery of oil at Pithole and the rise of another oil fever which ran over the country like a madness.

Andrews and Rockefeller had hit it off well together and had decided to make a go of it without Clark, the other partner. This meant that Rockefeller must sell his interest in the produce business to Clark and buy out Clark's interest in the oil firm. There was no difficulty about selling his produce interests. But Clark had his own ideas about oil. He wished to remain in the oil industry and proposed to buy out Rockefeller. We have Rockefeller's own account of how the matter was settled. The partners met to discuss it. Clark appeared with his lawyer. Rockefeller went alone. It was decided to collect all the cash assets of the oil business, pay the debts and sell the plant and good will to the highest bidder. Some one said: "Let us sell them now and let the lawyer act as auctioneer." This suited all parties and the auction began. Clark said $500. Rockefeller promptly raised the bid to $1,000. The bidding went back and forth a little breathlessly. Rockefeller was surprised at the price Clark was willing to pay. But he had formed his own opinion of the value of this business and he continued to top Clark's bid each time. Finally Clark said $72,000. Rockefeller, without a moment's hesitation, said $75,000.

"I'll go no higher, John," said Clark. "The business is yours."

"Shall I give you a check for it now?" purred Mr. Rockefeller.

"No, settle at your convenience."

This twenty-five-year-old business man had done well indeed. He could make his check for $75,000. More than this his credit was so soundly established that his partner, who knew his affairs better than any one else, was willing to refuse the check and permit Rockefeller to pay in his own time.

Thus John D. Rockefeller committed his fortunes wholly to the oil business which for the next thirty years was to feel the influence of his dominating genius and for the next sixty years was to be more or less under the shadow of his reign, long after he had withdrawn from actual rule.

PART FOUR
WAR AT THE CREEK

CHAPTER I. THE MAGIC CITY

A FARMER named Thomas Brown thought there might be oil under the farm of Thomas Holmden, about four miles from Plumer and six from the Allegheny River. So he proceeded to look for it with a hazel twig. Professor Silliman of Yale had just lectured all those foolish persons who resorted to the spirits and divining rods to find oil. But Thomas Brown had never heard of Professor Silliman. If he had he would have known better than to look for oil with a hazel twig. As it was he sauntered forth on the Holmden farm along Pithole Creek with his mystic twig and where it dipped he put down his drill. On January 8th, 1865, a few days later, Brown hit oil. And the well at once brought in two hundred barrels a day. The news ran over the region like a prairie fire and immediately prospectors began flocking to the spot. In January, when Brown started to drill, there was in the forest an old farmhouse or two and some unprofitable farms. By May the countryside was sprouting derricks. In another month a town had been laid off; two entire streets were built, lined on both sides with shops, offices, dance halls, and saloons. Pithole, the magic city of Petrolia, had sprung almost full blown out of the forest.

Wells were coming in almost daily. Farms were being bought and sold and leased and split up and, while huge sums of money were passing, still more amazing figures adorned the tales that were spread throughout the country. The simple truth might have served to stir the cupidity of the country's adventurers. A farmer named Rooker sold his farm for $280,000. The purchasers within two months had leased out ninety sites on it on the usual royalty basis and cash bonuses of $315,000. The United States well on the Holmden farm where the oil was discovered was producing eight hundred barrels a day and the farm was estimated to be worth three million dollars. By October the oil regions as a whole were producing about 10,000 barrels of crude a day and Pithole was supplying 6,000 of them. The new city had a population of 15,000. Ten months before it was a clearing in an unpeopled wilderness.

The name of Pithole flew over the country. It was on every tongue. The oil regions gained a kind of fabled notoriety exceeding that which followed Drake's discovery. The war was over. The energies of the nation were released for new pursuits and new excitements. Newspapers sent correspondents to make word pictures of it. Oil companies sprang up everywhere. Over 1,000 blue sky oil stock concerns were formed in Philadelphia. The actual capital in use in the regions was estimated at from one to three hundred and fifty millions, but twice as many millions in worthless stock certificates were hidden away in the strong boxes and mattresses and mantel clocks of people all over the country. Stock salesmen swarmed over the land with their beautifully engraved certificates and almost every one with a few spare dollars owned a few shares in some wild-cat adventure.

Towns sprang up everywhere. And the names suggested a picturesqueness which appealed to the imagination and recalled the brave days of '49. There were Stand-Off City and Short Stop, Red Hot, Alamagoozlum, Tip-Top, Two Thieves, Dead Beat, Strychnine, Chance Shot, Calaboose Run. But the two towns whose reputations for wild and riotous living rose to the most dubious fame were Pithole and Petroleum Center. To these suddenly transformed wheat farms flowed the adventurers of a continent. By train, by stage and wagon, on horseback and afoot they flooded in. Men fought to get on the trains. The hotels were crowded. The guests were glad to sleep on the chairs in the lobbies. Hundreds of men worked almost madly felling trees to make lumber for houses, hotels, shops, and derricks. The Astor Hotel got hammered up somehow. One might see there a huge room with fifty or sixty cots hired to lucky sleepers at a dollar apiece a night, each man slumbering with one hand under his pillow on his revolver. The city grew faster than order and government could be fitted to it. Before it was ten months old, however, it had fifty hotels, three of them palatial buildings according to the standards of the time. Its streets were lined with buildings—some of them very good ones, schools, churches, banks, and stores. But in all of these new towns were those sinks of iniquity, the dance halls. In Petroleum Center were several blocks given over to saloons, gambling joints, and dance halls. The Union army was being de-

NIGHT SCENES IN OIL REGION HOTEL LOBBY.

mobilized. Soldiers were streaming home and thousands of them flocked to Pithole and other oil towns. Creek settlements were filled with lieutenants, captains, colonels, and even a few generals. As for the rank and file, released suddenly from the iron discipline of the army and with their pay in their pockets, they reveled in the licentious merriment of Pithole's free-and-easies.

Chief among these frolickers were the teamsters. They were the blades who were making the money from the boom. Little was needed to enter this rough calling. A good spring wagon, a pair of horses and a resolute soul. The oil poured from Pithole so fast that there were hardly wagons enough in the land to handle it. Fifteen hundred teamsters were busy hauling oil from Pithole to the refinery at Miller's Farm. They also carted the crude in barrels to the dump boats and the dump tanks by the river. At times these ravenous profiteers demanded as high as three dollars a barrel to haul oil from the well to the refinery. Twenty and even thirty dollars a day was not excessive for the teamster to make.

And as the money was easily made it went quickly when the shadows gathered over the little red-light districts of Petroleum Center and Pithole.

II

ONE STRANGE visitor well-lodged at the United States Hotel watched the opening scenes of this turbulent and colorful drama. For weeks he remained there playing billiards with some of the young dandies, visiting the cafés, attending the prize fights, and generally amusing himself but giving no evidence of the amazing tragedy he was composing. Early in April, just as the throng of prospectors and speculators was moving toward Pithole, this faultlessly dressed sojourner left Oil City and went to Washington. On the night of April 14th, 1865, he murdered Abraham Lincoln.

III

WHILE Pithole and the mushroom towns that lined the Creeks wallowed in their disorder and wickedness, the more antique cities of Oil Dorado—Titusville and Oil City and Franklin—fell slowly under the dominion of the policeman, the Chamber of Commerce, the preacher, and the "better element." They ceased to be sinks of iniquity, but, as one traveler put it, they did not cease to be "sinks of mud."

The hills and banks of the streams were greasy with the pitch of petroleum and crowded with its derricks, its shacks, its little engine houses. Piles of barrels, pools of crude oil, smoke, charred trees, and blackened hillsides, cinder heaps that marked the many fires—the whole valley presented an appearance of indescribable blackness and bleakness. The towns were for the most part hastily assembled rows of plain board shanties, an ill-defined street where the business was done, the rude homes standing in the open fields. But even in Oil City and Titusville and Franklin, where brick buildings and good homes were making their appearance, the pervasive smell of the oil, the streets, churned up channels of slush, lit at night by smoking oil lamps and natural gas flares, presented a dismal appearance.

But the two mighty Amazonian twins of the times—Culture and Righteousness—had invaded these cities. Gentlemen with high hats and long coats and elaborate whiskers and their ladies, reveling in the luxury of their newly acquired wealth, began to form themselves into clubs and literary societies and social organizations of all sorts. The hotel dining rooms could be converted into ball rooms and Titusville soon became noted for its balls—from the teamsters and the drillers up to the lawyers and traders and brokers. Oil City had Bliss' Opera House and Corinthian Hall, the Academy of Music and Crittenden Hall. Dramatic troupes from New York made their appearance and singers, piano and violin soloists, lecturers, came through in a steady procession.

OIL SEEKERS—ONE SEEKS AND FINDS; THE OTHER SEEKS AND DOESN'T FIND.
(Frank Leslie's *Illustrated Newspaper*, 1866)

Even Pithole—wicked, vulgar Pithole, the Upstart of the Creeks, began to take on airs. The Swordsmen's Club was the rendezvous of the Pithole aristocracy. It had a clubhouse which pretended to elegance where the elect of the town could repair for drinks and cards and convivial society. Its balls and promenades were the last word in the gay social life of Petrolia— Alas, too gay! the ladies and the ministers in Oil City and Titusville sighed. For there in Titusville and Oil City the Devil had been having a hard time of it. At least the Sabbath had been rescued—no amusements, no trains running from Oil City to Franklin on Sunday, no Sunday barber—a barber had just been fined ten dollars for shaving a man on the Sabbath—even the famous Sunday well, which ran six days a week and rested automatically for one, closed down every Sunday. The hand of God was in that, to be sure, said the pious wild-catters and speculators.

IV

SAMUEL VAN SYCKEL found himself in a violent quarrel with the teamsters over the hauling of his oil from Pithole. The teamsters quarreled with every one—the producers, the railroads, the refiners, the farmers. But the quarrel with Van Syckel was one they had reason to regret forever. For it ended their days in the regions. Van Syckel determined to be rid of these troublesome tyrants. So he built a pipe line four miles long from Pithole to Miller's Farm. In the gin mills and dance halls the teamsters roared with laughter at this crazy experiment. But on October 1st, 1865, Van Syckel drove oil at the rate of eighty barrels an hour to the refinery at Miller's Farm. Working ten hours a day it could do the work of three hundred teams. And it could work twenty-four hours a day. Van Syckel's experiment proved the pipe line to be feasible and began a new era in the oil industry. Immediately other lines were built. The Pennsylvania Transportation Company built one paralleling Van Syckel's. Henry Harley built another from Benninghoff Run to the Schaeffer Farm.

The Oil City *Register* hailed Van Syckel's pipe as "a wonder of wonders." But the teamsters saw it first with sullen, then with violent anger. The pipes ran along the ground and the oil was forced through by means of three engines stationed at intervals. The teamsters cut the pipes and the line had to be guarded. Of course, they were still required in places but as the pipes grew in length and number, the teamsters ceased to be the tyrants and chief human problem of the region. The great Amazons, Culture and Righteousness, smiled as they departed.

Van Syckel sold his pipe line to Abbott and Harley who consolidated it with their own into the Allegheny Transportation Company. As for Van Syckel himself, he was another picturesque pioneer with whom Fate dealt cruelly. He introduced many innovations into the oil regions but finally got involved in expensive and ruinous litigation with the Standard Oil Company over patents and processes and died in Buffalo with but little material reward for his services.

V

In February, 1866, the Widow Rickerts, a washerwoman who owned a lot in Pithole, went out to her well to pump some water. She brought up a bucket of petroleum. The news of Mrs. Rickerts' good fortune ran around the neighborhood and there was a hurried lowering of buckets into wells. Other neighbors brought up petroleum. The excitement ran all along the Creek. Thousands rushed to Pithole to see the wonders. Have the water wells of Pithole turned to Oil? Is the whole valley dissolving into petroleum? The sky is red with the flames of the Tremont Hotel, which, like so many of the new buildings of Pithole, is being fed to the Fire-God and, by the red light, Pithole people exhibit to their neighbors the miracle of the water wells. Soon the story gets around that it is all due to the leakage from some of the pipe lines. In the midst of the fever that fills the atmosphere on Pithole Creek a strange foreboding fills the air. At the very moment when the town is being organized, a government provided, and a new police chief is summoning the populace to order, some of the bigger wells seem to halt their flood. Disasters hang upon the town. The ice in the Creek breaks up as Pithole's first winter melts and rushes down upon the town, causing the waters to rush over the city. Boats ply along Center Street. The ice hurls itself against the bridges, rushes over the banks, and crushes down buildings. The fires come almost weekly. The Franklin Hotel burns. The Mead House and fourteen buildings burn. Next month half the town is swept away. The wells pause. A kind of panic runs over the place. People who two months before choked with emotion as they cheered for Pithole as if it had been their childhood home tore down their dwellings and moved away the lumber to some fresh oil farm. The Pithole *Register* implores them to remain. But the blight is on the town. The cry of oil goes up from Olean and Pleasantville. The evacuation of Pithole has begun. Buildings are coming down. The roads are full of teams hauling lumber and pipes and engines and derricks to Pleasantville. The Oil City and Pithole Railroad becomes bankrupt. Fires sweep the remaining unguarded buildings. Every day oil wells gasp and falter and quit. Men are rushing away from the doomed city. The Postmaster says his office, which six months ago ranked third in Pennsylvania, is now choked with uncalled-for letters. Pithole, that rose from the forest like the rabbit from the magician's hat, is ready to give itself back to the wilderness. In another year it will be just a huddle of rotting, falling, or charred ruins. In a year or two more, with a church and two dwellings and a population of six people, it will be only a memory.

CHAPTER II. THE HOSTILE CAMPS

There swims into this story now a dashing figure destined to play a part of the first importance in the destiny of John D. Rockefeller. About the time Rockefeller launched out into the oil business a young man appeared in Cleveland with an invention—nothing less than the perfect horseshoe. He was seeking financial backing and took desk room in an office in the same building with Clark and Rockefeller. This man was Henry M. Flagler.

Flagler was born in 1830 in a little village just south of Rochester, New York, the son of a Presbyterian minister. He got some education up to the time he was fourteen, when he tumbled his small belongings into a carpet bag and struck out to hunt his fortune. He landed in the little town of Republic, Ohio, with a five franc piece, a five cent piece, and four coppers. This was a small capital, but apparently it was more than enough, for Flagler never spent the five cent piece. He owned it the day of his death. He wandered about, working as a clerk in a store selling candles, shoes, and soap, a boat hand on the Erie Canal, a general store helper in Orleans, New York. Here he saved a modest stake and went to Saginaw, Michigan, and into the salt business.

The importance of this step can hardly be exaggerated, as will appear later. In Saginaw Flagler married the daughter of Dr. Harkness, of Bellevue, Ohio, who was interested in the Saginaw salt wells. Many tales of his adventures here are told. One is that he amassed a fortune of $50,000 and lost it. If he made a fortune he certainly lost it for he then went to Bellevue, his wife's home, and into the grain business. Through his shipments of grain to Cleveland to the firm of Rockefeller and Clark, he became

THE HOSTILE CAMPS

acquainted with John D. Rockefeller. And when he took himself out of the grain trade and decided to stake his fortune upon his invention of a perfect horseshoe, he went to Rockefeller's offices and settled down with a desk in the same building.

At this time Flagler was thirty-five years old, a man of extraordinary virility and good looks. He was the very glass of fashion. He possessed a mass of luxuriant wavy hair, which he combed with the most scrupulous care, and affected a flowing mustache artfully curled at the ends. He was saved from being a dandy by his distinguished appearance and the brilliant and commanding glance of his eyes—eyes which exercised an extraordinary spell over women and which never failed to perceive the near approach of beauty. The lure of riches was always alive in the strong, restless mind of Flagler. He was bold, fearless, unscrupulous. Rockefeller was not slow to perceive that the new tenant in the Case Building had a mind of rare clarity and vigor. Rockefeller was exceedingly cautious in his friendships. But very soon these two men were drawn together. Flagler would drop in to talk about the business, about oil and the times. And the busy Mr. Rockefeller would pause to talk with him. Ofttimes they walked home together.

II

When Rockefeller bought the interest of his partner, Clark, in the oil firm he immediately formed a new partnership which he called Rockefeller and Andrews. Its office was located in the Sexton Block. The refinery, located across the river, had a capacity of one hundred and fifty barrels of crude a day.

Rockefeller immediately proceeded to organize his new business. As he looked over the oil industry of that day he saw nothing but disorder, chaos, waste, incompetence. The system which men worshiped with a kind of religious reverence—free competition—had now gotten complicated by some new factors which the average business man did not understand. But Rockefeller did understand them. The man who, when a boy, would not do any little task without sitting down and thinking out the easiest way, would not now attack a new career without examining with a minute scrutiny all the factors in the picture. Rockefeller saw that competition was complicated now by two powerful forces. One of these was this new flood of raw materials which was pouring out upon the nation. The other was the widening of the markets. The country was producing with ease far more materials than it could use and hence the wild scramble of producers to sell and the utter demoralization of price. Moreover, the railroads now made almost the whole country a possible market. A man was now in competition not only with his rivals in the town, but with innumerable other rivals in other towns and states. All this Rockefeller saw but the method of dealing with it in a large way had not yet dawned on him. But he did two things which mark the beginning of his complete design.

First of all he inaugurated a policy of ruthless economy in all operations—what he called "attention to little details." Andrews was a good mechanical man. Rockefeller prodded him ceaselessly for more tightly organized production, improved processes, more kerosene from crude. He began to make his own barrels. He cut away from the draymen who had that branch of the business in their hands and did his own hauling. Refiners in Cleveland bought their oil from jobbers who bought it from the wells. Rockefeller went to Titusville and made arrangements to purchase his oil direct from the wells. John D. Rockefeller was turning out his kerosene at a lower cost than any other refiner in Cleveland. He was selling it in Cleveland and the adjacent territory but was slowly building up the Western and Southern trade, selling his oil at wholesale to the jobbers there.

Now he saw that the export side of the oil business was growing rapidly. American refiners sent 30,000,000 gallons abroad the year Rockefeller and Andrews began business. This more than doubled the next year. The next year—1867—it was 97,000,000 gallons. Very little oil had been exported from Cleveland. Rockefeller saw that this would be the most important part of the industry. Hence in 1867 he induced his brother William, then a young produce merchant, member of the firm of Hughes, Davis, and Rockefeller, to abandon his produce and go into oil. He formed a separate firm called William Rockefeller and Company and sent William to New York, where he opened an office at 181 Pearl Street. This year—1867—William's and John's names appear for the first time in the New York directory. But William alone settled there. He became a selling agent for Rockefeller and Andrews in the export trade. He was a pleasant, smiling,

THE HOSTILE CAMPS

genial young man, with much of his father's jovial and friendly nature, and a good salesman. He soon became a familiar and well-liked figure along the docks, trading with the exporters of kerosene. Thus in 1867 Rockefeller had already split his business into two firms—one a refining firm in Cleveland, the other a selling firm in New York.

III

THERE now emerged what might be called the battle of the cities. There were, perhaps, 250 refiners of oil scattered in various places, all in violent competition with each other. But this competition was not merely a contest between individuals. It was also a contest between cities. At first each city's refineries manufactured kerosene to market in its own immediate neighborhood. But now the use of kerosene was general throughout the United States and the world. And so each city found itself contending for a share of those markets. The chief refining centers were New York, Erie, Philadelphia, Pittsburgh, Cleveland, and the little cities of the oil regions usually grouped together. Baltimore and Boston and Buffalo refined only small quantities, but they were important shipping points.

The refiners in the oil regions—at Titusville, Oil City, Franklin, and neighboring points—enjoyed the greatest advantage. The oil was produced at their door. They needed to make but a single shipment—refined oil to the seaboard. New York refiners, too, had to pay freight on but one shipment, but that was crude oil, and hence it was bulkier and more costly than refined. Besides New York was closest to the most populous markets and strategically located to negotiate foreign sales. The same thing was true of Philadelphia, whose refiners had to pay but a single freight charge on crude. Pittsburgh and Cleveland were at a distinct disadvantage. The refiners in Cleveland, for instance, had to bring crude oil from the regions, a long haul, and then ship the refined oil over a much longer distance back to the seaboard. They enjoyed a favorable position for capturing the Western and Southern trade, but they were seriously handicapped in the race for the richest trade of all—the oil markets of Europe. Pittsburgh was in a better position than Cleveland. It had better railroad connections and besides enjoyed the advantage of cheaper river transportation rates on crude oil from the regions by way of the Allegheny River.

It is obvious that the oil region refiners possessed such natural advantages that it is easy to see that many Cleveland refiners thought the regions would ultimately have the whole business. The largest refineries in the world were there. Downer Brothers had developed an immense plant making not only kerosene but pure white paraffin and some lubricating oils. There was also the refinery of the Ludovici Brothers. The Ludovici Brothers were two Germans who came to the regions in 1862. They built a refinery which cost half a million dollars—a forerunner of the elaborate modern business plant. There were beautiful offices, hardwood floors, marble mantels, fine furniture, rich carpets, mirrors, pictures, and statues. William Wright, who visited the regions in 1865, writing in *Harper's*, reported twenty refineries between Oil City and Titusville. They were making kerosene, naphtha, benzine, and gasoline. But of course kerosene was the chief product—kerosene for illuminating purposes.

In spite of its handicaps, however, Cleveland had thirty refineries along Walworth Run and the Kingsbury River. And in 1866 these refiners made three times as much kerosene as they did in the preceding year.

IV

OIL, FROM its birth, has been at once the child and mother of wars! Refiners battled with each other; producers and refiners quarreled over prices; cities fought for markets and advantages. But to understand the events upon which we are about to enter we must keep in mind that there was a war between railroads as well.

When oil was discovered there were no rail lines entering the oil regions. They could be reached only by boats and wagons. Three railroads, however, approached the oil creeks. And as soon as the industry developed these roads built branches into the oil cities. In the end the railroad map was about as follows: The Pennsylvania tapped the producing country two ways—the Oil Creek Railroad to Corry, connecting with the Philadelphia and Erie (a branch of the Pennsylvania) running to Erie; and the Allegheny Valley Railroad from Franklin to Pittsburgh.

The New York Central had one outlet. A branch of the Lake

THE HOSTILE CAMPS

Shore and Michigan Southern ran from Franklin to Ashtabula on Lake Erie connecting with the main line of the Lake Shore which ran between Cleveland and New York.

The Erie had one outlet. It had a branch running from Titusville to Corry and Meadville connecting with the Atlantic and Great Western, a subsidiary of the Erie.

The railroad wars which followed then were between the Pennsylvania, the Erie, and the New York Central. Later the Baltimore and Ohio entered the fight and each of these roads was presided over by men who have since been admitted to a kind of legendary gianthood.

Commodore Cornelius Vanderbilt had just assumed the mastery of the New York Central. Jay Gould by 1868 had got control of the Erie, after the long and costly battles between Vanderbilt and that brazen and pious old scoundrel, Daniel Drew, for possession of the road. J. Edgar Thompson, a great railroad builder, ruled the Pennsylvania, but he was assisted by the handsome, dashing, powerful Tom Scott, through whom, as vice-president, the Pennsylvania effected its control over the politics of the state. The legislature was called Tom Scott's legislature. Later Scott became president of the road and Cassatt vice-president. These two men were to play a leading rôle in the battles which were to agitate all the oil regions.

Scott was the son of a tavern keeper on the old turnpike from Philadelphia to Pittsburgh. He began life with little education and as a toll collector on the state road. He entered railroading as a station agent at Altoona. He rose rapidly and was a vice-president of the Pennsylvania when the war broke out. He directed the transportation of the first troops rushed from the North to the defense of Washington and he did this with such ability that he was brought to Washington, made a Colonel of Volunteers and later assistant secretary of war and given command of the transportation of troops throughout the remainder of the war. His assistant earlier in life when a train dispatcher was Andy Carnegie. Now Carnegie worked with him on his wartime job. After the war he took command of the railroad's machinery for riveting its hold upon the state, directing its elections, managing its lawmakers and executive officials and even dominating its courts.

These were the men who were to direct the armies of the railroads in the swiftly oncoming war of oil. In the battle between the cities the roads had their favorites. The Pennsylvania threw its power on the side of Pittsburgh and Philadelphia. The New York Central was disposed to favor Cleveland. The Erie gave its support to Buffalo and New York. The oil regions seemed to have no railroad friends. The interest of the roads was in hauling oil out of the regions, not in developing refineries there. Thus stood the oil scene—refiners everywhere looking at each other with suspicion and distrust, formed into loose groups of unfriendly local rivals, each group arrayed against every other group and supported by a friendly railroad—all save the cities of the oil regions which had only nature on their side.

V

AT THIS time, John D. Rockefeller was, as he himself later said, "all business." He was literally engulfed in the ceaseless labor of developing his oil firm. As a result he had grown serious to a degree which amounted to almost complete isolation from all other impressions save business. His mind was on his plans morning, noon, and night.

He was but twenty-eight years of age, but he was already one of the moderately rich men of Cleveland. He moved this year to a new home on Euclid Avenue, an imposing house, roomy, sitting in the back of a large corner lot, such a house as only a man of means could afford to occupy. The house still stands in Cleveland and still remains the property of the Rockefeller family. From this house he would walk every morning to his office. Frequently he went home to lunch and very often walked home after office hours. It was a long walk but his only exercise. But even these moments were not lost for they were spent in conferences with employees or associates or in turning over in his mind his plans. Incessant planning—this was the key to his progress. For every occasion as it arose Rockefeller had a plan. He left, so far as he could control it, nothing to the whimsical forces of Chance. Chance is made up of those unforeseen elements which the planner leaves out of his calculations. To defeat chance is to look closely and see ahead all those possible combinations which others overlook. To plan minutely, to see more than any one else, is to reduce the control of chance over one's fortunes. This is what Rockefeller did. But he was far from the modern efficiency man making elaborate charts and tables and laying out precise schemes on paper. In later years he said: "I have small faith in the man who plans elaborately on paper. I once asked a landscape gardener to undertake the improvement of 2,000 acres of land. He set to work on an elaborate scheme which I saw at a glance was impossible. He was not practical. He planned too much on paper."

Rockefeller planned in his mind. His mind was a living plan. He made everything show up for some use or else he rejected it. "It has always been my rule in business to make everything count," he told an old friend in Owego. "To make everything count something. I never go into an enterprise unless I feel sure it is coming out all right. For instance, a promising scheme may be proposed to me. It may not altogether satisfy and is rejected. My brother Will would probably go into it and make $10,000. Another equally promising scheme comes along. He goes into that and loses $10,000. The result is he hasn't made any advancement in these two ventures and is actually losing time. Meantime in some surer enterprise I have made, say, $5,000 in the same time the other fellow has lost twice as much. But mine counts and his doesn't. I believe the only way to succeed is to keep getting ahead all the time."

This is why Rockefeller was often accused of being timid. It is why it has seemed difficult for some critics to reconcile his timidity in some things with his apparent audacity in others. He was not timid. He refused to enter upon operations where he could not see the project all the way through. But having satisfied his mind and gone in he hesitated at no sacrifice, no cost, no measures, however vast and even cruel, to drive through to his objective.

At this time he had literally no amusements. He dressed himself with scrupulous care. He went to his office with a high silk hat, frock coat, and striped trousers. He had by now hung upon his pale and bony cheeks a thin drapery of side whiskers, reddish and straight. It was an age when men made up elaborately for their parts. Whiskers trained into the most fanciful cuts and shapes and elegantly barbered were employed to add dignity and éclat to the countenance of the rising sons of the soil as they moved toward riches. Rockefeller's appearance has always been as carefully planned as any other feature of his life. He began with the side whiskers resembling Piccadilly weepers. Later these were trimmed and finally the cheeks were swept clean altogether, the subject committing his dignity to a long mustache which rolled over his lips. Little by little this mustache was edited and limited, the ends were shortened, the hairs more closely cropped until finally it was banished altogether. At the time at which we are arrived the sideboards were in bloom and along with them went all the haberdashery required by the imposing codes of the day.

He had literally no intimate friends. There were no spare nights save Wednesday when he went to his Bible class. Here he had already become a figure of importance. He was the model of the Christian business man. Profound, almost funereal seriousness, fervent attention to prayers and the hymns and the lessons—outside that a deep and solemn composure. In the Bible lessons he read to his class he found many points he was able to apply to himself and incorporate in his own policy. "Study to be quiet and do your own business." This he did. "Seest thou a man diligent in his business, he shall stand before kings." He was the most diligent Christian in Cleveland. "Who can find a virtuous woman? For her price is far above rubies. The heart of her husband doth safely trust in her, so he shall have no need of spoil. She will do him good all the days of his life." Beside him sat his faithful wife, almost his only friend. This was all an excellent religion, thought Mr. Rockefeller. Indeed, at this time his religion took a new hold on him for his first child—Bessie—was born (August 23, 1866). Mrs. Rockefeller was not able to go to church with him so he went faithfully, made notes of the sermons, and was able to repeat to her the wisdom he had gathered from the Euclid Avenue pulpit.

Ida Tarbell talked with many men in Cleveland who knew Mr. Rockefeller at this time. They told her that he rarely smiled and almost never laughed. The only sign of hilarity he ever gave was when he struck a good bargain. This would make him clap his hands. Let it be a very good bargain and he would throw up his hat, kick his heels, and hug his informant. This was written long ago before he took up golf and countless witnesses had beheld him repeat this performance over an exceptionally good putt. One time, Miss Tarbell recounts, he was so overjoyed he kicked his heels and hugged himself and said: "I'm bound to be rich! *Bound to be rich!* BOUND TO BE RICH!"

Instructing his Bible class he warned them over and over against the perils of drink and the dangers that lurked in good-fellowship. He repeated this lecture many times as he grew older.

"Don't be a good fellow," he would say. "I love my fellow man and I take great interest in him. But don't be convivial, always ready to pitch in and be one of the crowd. Be moderate. Be very moderate. Don't let good fellowship get the least hold on you. If you do, you are lost, not only you but your progeny, your family for generations to come.

"Now I can't be a good fellow. I haven't taken my first drink yet. Some of my friends think that I take a too decided stand but I don't. . . . It is my firm conviction that every downfall is traceable directly or indirectly to the victim's good fellowship, his good cheer among his friends, who come as quickly as they go. We have to apologize every day for this class of man who fills our hospitals, our asylums, our poorhouses and the very gutters of our streets. Look on him and don't be a good fellow."

Rockefeller's mother still lived at Cheshire Street, a grave, strong, kindly woman, deeply religious and now a little mellowed as she found herself drifting into easier circumstances. Her husband, the old Doctor, had taken to such very long absences that it was the exception when he was at home. He preserved the deepest mystery about his operations during these absences, though he would tell with elaborate embroidery the most extraordinary tales of how he had gotten the best of all who crossed him. These absences now far from troubling the family were a source of relief. William was in New York. John had moved to his imposing home on Euclid Avenue. Frank was still at home and working in a small produce business of his own in Merwin Street.

VI

THE NEED of money—that was the problem which perpetually haunted Rockefeller in these days. Competition in Cleveland was growing at a furious pace. The oil business there was growing, but Rockefeller and Andrews were moving forward faster than any of their rivals. Rockefeller continually saw his pace halted by the lack of capital. Looking back later, he mused to a friend that often at night he went to bed wondering how he would ever pay the large sum he had borrowed that day and woke up next morning wondering how he might borrow more. He had been for some time meditating a step which promised a solution of this and now in 1867 he was ready, after his usual long, cautious examination of the plan, to put it into execution.

Rockefeller had been watching Flagler, his neighbor in the Case Block. He had shrewdly appraised the talents of that gentleman. But he had also perceived something else. Flagler had married the niece of a man who had lately made a great fortune. This man was Stephen V. Harkness. Harkness owned a distillery near Monroeville, Ohio. Toward the end of the war when the government was raking the land with a fine-tooth comb for values to tax, it fell naturally upon whiskey. John Sherman knew the government was going to put a heavy excise upon whiskey and he mentioned the fact to his friend, S. V. Harkness. Harkness needed nothing more than this tip. He proceeded to buy up with all the funds he could collect every barrel of whiskey he could lay hold of. When the tax was levied, Harkness found himself with an enormous amount of untaxed whiskeys which he could sell at the high prices exacted because of the tax. He promptly turned his investment into cash. This provided him with one of the amplest fortunes in Cleveland. Rockefeller knew of this adventure. And here was Flagler, Harkness' nephew by marriage, at Rockefeller's very door. Here was an entrée to Harkness' treasure chest.

In his many talks with Rockefeller, Flagler's mind had been prepared by well-wrought tales of the fortune in petroleum. Flagler had seen this. The man's mind was so formed that the very difficulties which beset the business attracted him. Finally, at the proper moment, Rockefeller proposed that Flagler should become a partner in his firm and that Harkness should put a lot of money into it as a silent partner. Flagler proved an eloquent advocate with Harkness and the old whiskey baron put $70,000 into Rockefeller's oil business and Flagler entered as a partner to protect the investment. The firm was promptly reorganized under the title of Rockefeller, Flagler, and Andrews. And with its new capital, reënforced by the dynamic and imaginative mind of Flagler, the new oil concern set out upon that extraordinary career in which it made vast fortunes for all its managers and allies, but moreover, organized and built up an amazing industry, brought into vogue a new method of doing business, created a whole brace of social and political issues and—in short—inaugurated an era.

CHAPTER III. A NEW WEAPON

As soon as the new combination of partners got under way two important moves were made. A second refinery was built and operated under the name of William Rockefeller and Company. William remained in New York as selling agent for Rockefeller, Flagler, and Andrews. The new refinery was merely labeled with his name.

The other move was of more far-reaching consequences. Rockefeller and Flagler went to Amasa Stone, vice-president of the Lake Shore and Michigan Central Railroad, and asked for a rebate. There were about thirty refiners in Cleveland in violent competition. But they had made an arrangement with Stone to pay one cent a gallon on shipments of crude oil from the regions to Cleveland. This amounted to forty-two cents a barrel. The rate on the shipment of refined to New York was of course higher. Rockefeller saw he could not compete with the refiners in New York, Philadelphia, and the oil cities unless he could even up the conditions by freight concessions. So he demanded a lower rate. He was in a position to do this. Cleveland was growing as a refining center. Rockefeller was the largest of these Cleveland refiners. The feeling in the oil regions was already bitter toward Cleveland because of its rising importance. The oil towns felt that the refining business belonged to them. Rockefeller laid all this before Stone. He complained that other railroads were favoring Pittsburgh, New York, and Philadelphia. And he probably dropped a hint that his firm might have to remove its refineries to the Creek. Stone agreed to give him a rebate—how much has never been disclosed. But it was at least 15 cents. He probably got a rebate on refined oil shipments to New York, but there is no direct evidence that he did. There was nothing unusual in this procedure. Though he denied it many times, Rockefeller admitted later that he received rebates up to 1880. But "the reason for rebates," he averred, "was that such was the railroad's method of business. A public rate was made and collected by the railroad companies, but so far as my knowledge extends, was seldom retained in full; a portion of it was repaid to the shipper as a rebate. By this method the real rate of freight which any shipper paid was not known by his competitors, nor by other railroads, the amount being a matter of bargain with the carrying companies."

It was common enough, but not so general as Mr. Rockefeller claimed. It was an advantage open to those strong enough to force it. The smaller shippers paid the published rate. But in every case the rebate was secret. In any case men in Cleveland began to be suspicious about the progress of the firm of Rockefeller, Flagler, and Andrews. They wondered at it. By 1869 Cleveland had passed Pittsburgh and become the largest refining center. Rockefeller's refineries had a capacity of 1,500 barrels a day—the largest in the world. He had his own warehouses in New York. By this time the wooden tank car had arrived and he owned his own tank cars. He employed about a hundred men in his refineries in Cleveland and some seven or eight hundred were occupied in making barrels for him. He owned about twenty teams and in this year spent $60,000 on improvements. The firm loaded and unloaded its own tank cars and employed several chemical and mechanical experts to improve its processes of manufacture and make a greater use of the crude by-products.

What could account for this amazing success? His competitors could explain it on no grounds save that he must enjoy some advantages which they did not have. They did in fact overlook his extraordinary sagacity and his slavery to the management of his business. But, as it turned out, they were right in suspecting there was some other explanation.

Among those who suspected this was his brother Frank Rockefeller, who had now gone into the firm of Alexander, Scofield and Company. It was the beginning of the lifelong enmity which grew up between these two brothers. Alexander promptly went to the agent of the railroad, charged him with favoring Rockefeller and demanded an equal rebate. Stone allowed him fifteen cents. W. H. Doane, another refiner, moved by his suspicions, made a similar demand and got ten cents. But both these men declared that though they tried they were never able to get a rebate on their refined oil to New York. Rockefeller did not invent this system, declared Samuel C. T. Dodd, the famous lawyer of the Standard Oil in after years. There is no doubt that Rockefeller did not invent the rebate. But he did introduce it into the oil business. He demanded and got rebates at a time when no one else was getting them.

All this must be looked at in the light of the conditions which existed at that time. Today we understand that the railroads are not strictly private concerns. They enjoy monopolistic franchises from the government. They carry on functions which belong to the people. They have no more right to make discriminatory rates than the post office has. But this idea had practically no public support in the sixties. The roads were in the possession of men who believed they had a right to run them to suit themselves. They charged as much as they could get and surrendered on price when they had to. The policy of the day was for each man to look out for himself. The railroads were in a state of perpetual warfare with each other. The managers were attempting to build their roads and the territory through which they ran. In this competition they made all sorts of concessions to large shippers. And it is quite certain that when Rockefeller and Flagler went to Stone for a rebate they believed they were acting not only within their rights but in accordance with the permissible stratagems of the game.

II

THE BUSINESS of Rockefeller, Flagler, and Andrews had now grown to imposing proportions. The partners therefore decided to incorporate. This was in 1870. Men had been playing with this instrument for some time. As early as 1823 eight states had incorporated 557 manufacturing concerns with authorized capital of $72,000,000. Most of them were in New York and Massachusetts. Oddly enough, Pennsylvania, the great industrial state, lagged behind. By 1837 it had but twenty-two corporations. As late as 1845 we find a Pennsylvania company—the Gloucester Print Works—going to New Jersey for a charter. However, it is worth noting that in this year 1870, when John D. Rockefeller was incorporating the Standard Oil Company, J. Edgar Thompson, president of the Pennsylvania Railroad, was forming the Pennsylvania Company, a holding company, to collect into one owning and controlling agency the various railroads and other holdings of the Pennsylvania Railroad.

By 1870 there were innumerable corporations all over the country. In some states you could incorporate a half million dollar company for fifty cents. But the greater number of these organizations were blue sky ventures brought into being to sell gold, silver, and oil stock to the unwary. Practically all business enterprises were owned by individuals or partnerships. And, aside from the railroad companies, most of the industrial corporations were what the Rockefeller corporation now proposed to be—a partnership, a union of a very limited number of owners employing the corporate form for greater convenience. Real corporations were so rare at the time that in the city directory of Cleveland there was a classification in the back of the volume listing the incorporated companies, and they numbered thirty-two.

The size of Rockefeller's business about this time may be seen from a letter written September 20, 1869, by Dan P. Eels, president of the Commercial National Bank of Cleveland, to Henry F. Vail of the National Bank of Commerce in New York, commending as clients Rockefeller, Flagler, and Andrews.

The letter reads in part: "I have never known him to equivocate or in any particular to misrepresent the facts about his business. . . . His transactions with us have been at times very large, amounting in the aggregate to a number of millions and we have sometimes had his paper to the amount of $250,000 at one time. The present firm employs in its business about $1,000,000 of which $360,000 has been invested in their refinery and real estate and the balance, say, $600,000, is used by them in carrying on their business. . . . They have a manufacturing capacity of nearly 3,000 barrels of crude oil a day, requiring to produce it a daily expenditure of $15,000 to $20,000 a day."

Their actual output, however, was from 1,200 to 1,500 barrels a day. The New York bank, however, did not accept the account of Mr. Rockefeller's firm. Oil was still looked upon as too risky a business.

The Rockefeller company was incorporated January 10th, 1870, in Cleveland. The whole act of incorporation did not exceed two

A NEW WEAPON

hundred words. It stated the name of the concern—THE STANDARD OIL COMPANY OF OHIO. It declared its purpose to "manufacture petroleum and to deal in petroleum and its products." The stock was put at one million dollars, divided into shares of one hundred dollars each. The signers and incorporators and the shares subscribed for were: John D. Rockefeller, 2,667 shares; Henry M. Flagler, Samuel Andrews and William Rockefeller, 1,333 shares each; S. V. Harkness, 1,334 shares; O. B. Jennings, 1,000 shares. The firm of Rockefeller, Flagler, and Andrews took an additional 1,000 shares. They turned their plant and business in at $400,000.

There was another Standard Oil Company at the time—the Standard Oil Company of Pittsburgh which was incorporated by Lockhart, Frew and Company in Pittsburgh, capitalized at $300,000, the year before. That perhaps suggested the name for the Ohio company.

This has been spoken of as a combination—Rockefeller combining all his companies into one. Of course, it had none of the characteristics of a combination. There were no other Rockefeller companies than the firms of Rockefeller, Flagler, and Andrews and William Rockefeller and Company. And these were just two sets of names for two departments.

Of this new venture Rockefeller was easily the master. And this he remained to the end. He was the master then, as he was later, of strong men. Flagler was a man of extraordinary talent. He had more imagination than Rockefeller. He was more restless, more impatient. He was, as Rockefeller said, "on the active side of every question." He was a driving force. He "always wanted to go ahead and accomplish great projects of all kinds," Rockefeller said of him. He had an orderly, analytical mind. He was the "lawyer" of the group. He could grasp the essentials of any transactions and reduce them to a simple statement. He was the oldest of the group and though he spoke in a soft, velvety, pleasant voice, he was a man of resoluteness. He ranked easily next to Rockefeller in the power and influence he exercised over the company. Rockefeller leaned on his advice more than on that of any other partner. Harkness was merely a monied man. His financial position in the community gave weight to the company's credit. And many times he was called on to advance cash. Andrews was merely the mechanical man. He was superintendent of the plants and as the business grew he began to manifest a hesitancy, a timidity, which irked Rockefeller at times. William Rockefeller was the strong reliance of his brother for personal contacts in hostile places. His pleasant ways disarmed hostility. He was always under the domination of his strong, silent, older brother. In later years Frank Rockefeller, who liked William as much as he hated John, said William was always under John's orders.

As for John D. himself the town was beginning to talk about him. He had become a figure. Men turned to look after him as he passed along the street—this man of thirty years—who had built a million-dollar corporation. Yet much as he was talked about it was noted that few people knew him. He was a member of no clubs. He took no part in politics. He was seen on no civic committees. He appeared at no public places or social affairs. A local historian writing about him at this time said: "Although quite a young man he occupies a place in our business circles second to few. Mr. Rockefeller never retrogrades. He has always advanced from the commencement. Close application to one kind of business, an avoidance of all positions of an honorary character, that cost time, and strict business habits have resulted in his success, the fruits of which he now enjoys. He has worked himself and kept everything pertaining to his business in so methodical a manner that he knows every night how he stands with the world."

This was the group of men which started out upon their conquests under their newly unfurled banner—that of the Standard Oil Company.

III

JUST about this time Colonel Zebulun Martin, the genial, prosperous host of one of oildom's best hotels, was visiting New York City. He saw, shuffling along Broad Street, a tall, emaciated, broken man, holding the hand of a boy of twelve. Martin was shocked when he recognized in the shabby and bent form Colonel Edwin L. Drake, the discoverer of oil. After losing his small savings in Wall Street, Drake, in failing health, had moved to a farm in Vermont. Later he appeared at Neversink, near Long Branch, New Jersey, where he hoped the sea air might improve his health. He grew steadily weaker, supported by his wife who took in sewing. He had now scratched together a few dollars to take him and his little twelve-year-old son to New York hoping some old friends might find work for the boy. But he was meeting with no luck. Martin, who met him as he trudged around half leading, half leaning on the child, was touched at the poverty of a man who had opened up such a mine of wealth for the world. He gave Drake twenty dollars—all the change in his pockets. When he returned to Titusville he immediately raised a fund for Drake's relief which amounted to $4,833.50. This money was turned over to Mrs. Drake. That faithful partner of the broken pioneer moved her rapidly failing husband and family to Bethlehem, Pennsylvania, and in 1873 the Pennsylvania legislature granted Drake a pension of $1,500 a year for life.

He died November 8th, 1880, and sometime later a handsome monument was erected over his grave in the cemetery at Titusville. On its base is carved a lengthy epitaph ending with these touching lines:

> "His last days, oppressed by ills,
> To Want no Stranger,
> He died in comparative obscurity."

Many years later three additional lines were carved under these. They ran:

> "This monument erected by
> Henry Huddleston Rogers
> In grateful recognition and remembrance."

Then it was known for the first time that the monument, costing $60,000, had been erected by Henry H. Rogers, one of the most extraordinary characters thrown up by the oil business. It also came out then that Rogers had contributed a liberal addition to the monthly allowance paid Drake by the state and had kept up the payments to his wife after Drake's death. Among all the millionaires of the Standard Oil who amassed fabulous fortunes as the result of Drake's discovery Rogers was the one who cherished for him a warm and grateful remembrance.

Like Drake, old Uncle Billy Smith, who actually drilled the well, never made a dollar out of oil. It is indeed strange that these men, Drake the commander and Smith and his two sons, profited not at all out of their historic achievement. Smith worked for Drake for three years and then went back to his Tarentum farm.

His wife died and in a few years he re-married. But he was a widower again in three weeks. However, this robust son of Vulcan was not destined to celibacy. He married again in less than three months and his third lady, as he put it, "fetched him three children"—General Grant Smith, General Willoughby Smith, and General Worthington Smith. Alas! Smith was not fashioned to

THE DRAKE MONUMENT ON THE SITE OF THE OLD WELL.

make money. Back around his farm in Butler County oil was discovered later and wells drilled on every farm around his save his own. He died suddenly July 29th, 1890.

Oddly enough these men shared the fate of others like them. Shaw, who discovered oil in Canada and who was voted a medal by the Dominion government, died at Titusville where he was working for two dollars a day, a stranger and forgotten. General Sutter, on whose ranch the first gold was found in California, died penniless, a half-crazy old man on the steps of the Capitol in Washington.

CHAPTER IV. THE DREAM OF MONOPOLY

UP TO this year, 1870, the progress of Rockefeller had been that of a shrewd business man—shrewder than his fellows. There is no evidence that he entertained any other idea than that he would make his business as big as he could, be the largest figure in the oil industry and make as much money as possible. He has said as much. "None of us ever dreamed of the magnitude of what proved to be the later expansion. We did our day's work as we met it, looking forward to what we could see in the distance and keeping well up to our opportunities, but laying our foundations firmly." It is probable that few of the millionaires of the succeeding decades "could see in the distance" the lengths they would travel. Just about this time Andrew Carnegie, living in the St. Nicholas Hotel in New York, wrote in his diary: "Thirty-three and an income of $50,000 per annum. Beyond this never earn. Make no effort to increase fortune but spend the surplus each year for benevolent purposes."

But in this year Rockefeller began to see more imposing things in the distance. He saw the desirability of getting his rivals in Cleveland out of the way. Very quickly he saw the possibility of such an objective. He made up his mind to bring about a monopoly of the oil-refining interests in Cleveland and proceeded to lay his plans.

Up to this time politicians had played with this word "Monopoly." The cry against monopoly is almost as old as Anglo-Saxon civilization. But men were never more set against it than now. America, the land of individual opportunity! This was one of the favorite themes of the orator. There had not been much of anything that could be called monopoly in America, yet it was frequently and feelingly denounced as if it existed. So profoundly was it hated that mere bigness was mistaken for monopoly. There was a deep-rooted notion that the safety of the state lay in widespread free competition. The ambitious man could look forward to being the biggest of his trade. But the idea of getting control of an industry hardly occurred to him. But now free competition began to work strange and destructive phenomena. That destructive giant

Over-production began to lay about him. There was something new altogether. Back in 1828 we find the President in his message referring to the tariff and saying, "Domestic competition under an illusive excitement has increased the production [of textiles] much beyond the demand for home consumption." And Clark, in his "History of Manufactures," refers to "Occasional periods of over-production which continued to embarrass American manufactures after 1832." But these were chiefly textile manufactures and over-production was merely occasional and affected only a small section of the population. Now over-production was appearing everywhere—in iron, salt, sugar, tobacco, whiskey, oil, chiefly as a result of the discovery of our natural riches.

John D. Rockefeller and Henry M. Flagler now looked this problem squarely in the face. Other men talked about it, bemoaned it, wondered what could be done about it, whimpered that there were too many in the business. It was characteristic of Rockefeller that he faced it, not as a problem to be wept over, but to be dealt with. He decided to deal with it in Cleveland. And this he now resolutely proceeded to do.

II

AT THE time he formed this resolution there were about thirty refiners in Cleveland. The refining capacity of the town was about 12,000 barrels a day, perhaps more. This was enough to handle nearly all the oil produced in the oil regions, if New York, Pittsburgh, Philadelphia, Erie, Buffalo, and the oil regions refiners did not distill a gallon. It was certainly more than enough to supply the needs of the world. Of this the Standard Oil refineries had a capacity of 1,500 barrels. It will be seen, therefore, that the refining industry was in a very bad way as a result of this over-production. The price of refined oil had been falling since 1865. That year it ranged from 51 to 70 cents a gallon. It was 31½ cents as 1870 opened. In the Fall it was 23 cents. And now to complicate matters Europe, which had hitherto imported only refined oil, began to build refineries and import crude.

Rockefeller's chief competitors in Cleveland were Clarke, Payne and Company, Alexander, Scofield and Company, Clark, Shurman and Company, Hanna, Baslington and Company, Westlake Hutchins and Company, the Cleveland Petroleum Refining Com-

THE DREAM OF MONOPOLY

pany, Critchley, Fawcett and Company. There were a number of smaller plants. Many of them refined just a barrel or two. And most of them used inefficient and wasteful methods. About this time, General James H. Devereaux became vice-president of the Lake Shore and Michigan Railroad and he said that these Cleveland refiners "without exception" had come to him and declared they could no longer compete from Cleveland and that they must either abandon their business or move to the oil country. The open rate on crude from the regions to Cleveland was forty cents; on refined from Cleveland to New York it was two dollars. Had it not been for a water rate in the summer months by lake and canal of one dollar these refiners would have died of their own weakness.

Rockefeller had been getting a rebate on his crude oil and some concessions on his refined shipments to New York. But at this period he determined to better his position with the roads. He sent Henry M. Flagler to General Devereaux with a proposition. The Lake Shore should give him a rate of thirty-five cents a barrel on crude from the wells and $1.30 on refined from Cleveland to New York. In return for this Rockefeller would guarantee to ship sixty carloads a day and assume all risk of fire and load and unload his own oil. Devereaux admitted these rates on the witness stand later. But it is probable that the rate from the regions was twenty-five instead of thirty-five cents and as for the rate to New York, refiners insisted at the time that it was ninety cents and not $1.30. General Devereaux accepted the proposition and this immediately put Rockefeller in a position to out-distance his rivals without any difficulty.

It was not such a secret either. Many competitors knew of it as they did of the earlier rebate. The larger ones tried to compel the Lake Shore to give them the same rate. General Devereaux told George O. Baslington of Hanna, Baslington and Company (Hanna was the uncle of the famous Mark Hanna) that he would give any shipper the same rate who would make the same guarantee. Of course, no one could make such large shipments. Hence no one else got the rates.

This rebate became the subject of violent and unmeasured denunciation as an outrage upon the other refiners in Cleveland. Yet if we leave out the fact that the railroads are public carriers, there is not much difference between what Rockefeller got and what at the time and since large concerns get in the way of what are called quantity discounts. It is still a trade custom to quote one price for a small order and a lower price for a large one. There is scarcely a housewife who pays ten cents for a can of milk who doesn't think she should get three for twenty-five cents. And there is a sound defense of this too. If we believe that the seller ought to make a charge for his service in proportion to the cost of that service and it can be shown that the larger order costs less to fill, there seems no reason why the larger order should not be favored with a lower price because of the economies it permits. This is what the chain store does today and it bases its right to existence on the economies which result from mass buying. Wholesalers know that they actually lose money on orders under a certain amount. This is what happened in the case of the Rockefeller deal with the Lake Shore. When Flagler made the proposal to ship sixty carloads a day Devereaux made a calculation—or perhaps it had already been made for him by Rockefeller. He figured that the amount of business Rockefeller guaranteed, handled in the ordinary way, would require an investment of $900,000 in cars because it would take thirty days to route cars to New York and back and this would use up eighteen hundred cars. But with a guaranteed shipment of sixty cars a day the business could be handled with only six hundred cars and an investment of $300,000. Devereaux claimed he could make more money for his road under this plan at $1.30 a barrel than he could at $2 a barrel handling oil for numerous shippers in the old haphazard way. And Rockefeller could not see why he was not entitled to get the benefit of the savings in operation he was able to assure the road. However, if we introduce the fact that the railroads are public carriers and ought not to make discriminations between shippers then a new face is put upon the matter. But at this time the public character of the roads was not recognized and there was no law prohibiting the managers from fixing their own charges.

With this advantage the business of the Standard went forward at a rapid rate. Within a year there were only twenty-six refiners left in Cleveland. Four went under.

THE DREAM OF MONOPOLY

III

At this time Rockefeller and Flagler were inseparable. Their desks were near each other in the same small private office. They lived not far apart. They walked to the office in the morning frequently. They walked out to lunch together and often went home together walking the whole way. They were together at Rockefeller's home frequently at night. They talked of business—nothing but business. The planning went on endlessly, interrupted by nothing.

But just at this point the planning and the absorption in business was broken for just a brief day by an event at the Rockefeller home. Another baby arrived in April, 1871—another girl—and John D. wanted a son. This child was called Alta Rockefeller. Mr. Rockefeller now had a growing family as well as a growing business and a growing fortune.

IV

In the early Fall of 1871 the plans were all fairly well laid. From this point on a series of moves were pushed with remorseless persistence—plans which were to make an immense noise in the world.

Things were looking up for the producers of crude oil. They brought up too much petroleum but the output was less in 1871 than in the preceding year. Then it was over 18,000 barrels a day. But the Fall of 1871 it was under 14,000 barrels. Pictures have been made of the pitiable plight of the well owners. Yet at the end of 1870 they got three dollars a barrel for oil and by the following Summer the price had gone to five dollars. The growing demand for oil helped this. Also the regions were storing oil. Running through the old newspaper files one sees frequent notes of producers building storage tanks. Also the pipe lines had developed greatly and they provided a large storage while the speculators gambled in pipe line certificates. Thus the price of crude oil went up while the price of refined oil went down. The smaller refiners were threatened with ruin. Even a large concern like Alexander, Scofield and Company shut down their refinery at Columbia Farm in September announcing that they "declined to run it at a pecuniary loss." The Oil City *Derrick* printed a report that unless the price of crude oil declined many refineries would suspend. There were too many refineries. For every barrel of demand there were three of refining capacity.

Rockefeller's plan was to buy up all his competitors in Cleveland. But how could he force them to sell? Now, however, it was becoming plain that something more than this must be done. There was still the excessive production of the other cities. Cleveland led all other cities—it could turn out 12,732 barrels a day. New York and the oil regions were next with 10,000 barrels' capacity each. Pittsburgh was third with 6,000 barrels. Boston had half that. Philadelphia, Erie, Baltimore, and other points ranked in the order named. As long as other cities were producing too much a monopoly in Cleveland would not be a complete solution.

Besides, as long as the railroads fought among themselves each trying to build up its favorite locality with freight preferences the position of the Standard of Cleveland would be imperiled. Then there was this growing shipment of crude, instead of refined, oil to Europe. If Europe got to making her own refined oil five-sixths of the refining industry in America would be lost. The industry would be ruined. The remedy for all these weaknesses was plain.

First, Rockefeller must end competition in Cleveland.

Second, the big refiners in other cities must end competition in their respective cities by getting control of the smaller concerns.

Third, to make this possible the railroads must end their rate wars, enter an agreement for the parceling out of the oil trade and make a decisive rebate agreement with Rockefeller and his allies.

Fourth, these allies would be the large-scale refiners in the other cities with whom, after their small competitors were crushed, he could enter into an agreement covering production.

Fifth, the railroads must then refuse to accept crude oil for shipment to Europe.

Here was a bold and revolutionary scheme, fraught with difficulties, but promising much. Many accounts of this daring plan have since been written but all of them suffer from the temptation to picture Rockefeller and the big refiners as wicked, greedy, unscrupulous brigands, and the producers and smaller refiners of oil in the oil regions as helpless, amiable, kindly, generous souls trampled under the cruel heel of the mighty combination Moloch. The telling of this story has been much affected by adherence to the hero-villain theory of history—in which all the dramas of industry consist of a cast of characters made up of powerful scoundrels and kind-hearted small competitors. Of course, history does not get made according to this pattern. Hence to understand the impending conflict one must understand the character of the oil regions.

V

No ONE can read the records of the oil regions without gathering the impression that the men there had come to think that they had a right—some kind of God-given right—to exploit the oil industry for their own advantage. Cleveland and Pittsburgh and New York and other refining centers they looked upon as invaders of their natural right. Of course, these Oil Creek gentlemen were themselves all outsiders. The drillers, the wild-catters, the producers, and refiners in the oil country were all newcomers who had flocked into the regions when the cry of oil went up. The original owners of the farms fared very well. They supplied nothing but the land on which they happened to be settled when oil was found. Few of them engaged in drilling or developing. They gave leases from which they collected royalties and accumulated fortunes.

As for the producers and refiners, some of them were good business men according to the standards of the time, but most of them were not. They knew little of the oil business and had not an inkling of the changing forces which were pressing on society at the time. They were inefficient even according to the tests of that day. More than one traveler commented on the obsolete machinery they used. They wanted nothing better than to be left alone to pump their wells as fast as they could and sell their oil at the highest price. And as they pumped they had no conception of the problems which their flood of oil was creating. The fire god hovered over the regions sweeping away some well, some tank, some building, often whole blocks of buildings every day and chiefly because of the wanton carelessness of the people. They blamed their troubles on every passing event, never pausing to accuse themselves. Thus they blamed the Franco-Prussian war or the Fenian rebellion or the finding of oil in the East. They often got ridiculously high prices for their oil and they wanted nothing else.

They made the air red with their denunciations of Rockefeller's attempts to combine the refiners. But they were always attempting combinations of their own. In November, 1866, the producers were discussing a "combine for the purpose of attempting to make better terms with the refiners in the price of the crude product." Before the year was out the Oil City *Register* said, "Producers at Titusville and other places are clamoring for a convention of interested persons to take some action looking toward better prices

PRIMITIVE METHOD OF FILLING BARRELS.
(From Frank Leslie's *Illustrated Newspaper*)

for oil." These were the men who were such ardent devotees of the law of supply and demand and the institution of free competition when Rockefeller proposed a combination and when production was less than consumption and when they could get four and five dollars for their oil. But as soon as the supply became excessive and prices fell they lost some of their love for the laws of trade and the principle of competition, as it related to themselves. Then they wanted to combine.

The teamsters had resented the coming of the pipe lines as an invasion of a business which they thought belonged to them. They hitched their teams to the pipes and pulled them apart until the pipe owners protected their property with armed guards. The jobbers felt the same way. They were discussing a combination and

THE DREAM OF MONOPOLY

association with a capital of a million dollars to build tanks and store oil to regulate the price. The refiners of the region had done well—those with intelligence and industry. Their natural advantages more than offset Rockefeller's rebates. One of the largest refineries was that of the Columbia Oil Company which in seven and a half years had paid its stockholders $3,017,600 in dividends. But these refiners had decided their Cleveland and Pittsburgh competitors had no right to exist. They formed into a league with their producing allies and openly boasted in the streets of Oil City that they were "determined to wipe Cleveland out as with a sponge." In 1870 the producers met in Library Hall, Oil City, and adopted a resolution to stop the drill for three months in order to raise the price of oil to the public. It got nowhere because they failed to live up to their resolution, for the papers were filled in the next three months with stories of unrestrained wild-catting. In other words, the men in the oil regions were determined to build for themselves a monopoly of the oil business. The rights of the public to the benefit of improved methods of producing and refining were not within their vision. If they did not succeed in their plans it was because they were too inefficient, too ignorant. And all this was before Rockefeller made any attempt at combination.

These were the men who raised a cry heard " 'round the world" when they learned the refiners had succeeded in doing what they had tried but failed in. A recognition of this fact is essential to an understanding of events which are to follow.

VI

IT WOULD be interesting to know with whom the scheme of the South Improvement Company originated. It is almost certain it did not originate with Rockefeller. Henry M. Flagler testified before the House Committee investigating trusts that it originated with Peter H. Watson and W. G. Warden, who came to him and Rockefeller with the plan full-blown. "We did not believe in it," he swore, "but the view presented by other gentlemen was pressed upon us to such an extent that we acquiesced in it to the extent of subscribing our names to a certain amount of stock which we never paid for." As it happens, however, Mr. Flagler's assertions, on or off the Bible, are of no value. The scheme adopted has all the earmarks of Flagler's mind and experience. Mr. Rockefeller has always insisted the plan originated with Tom Scott of the Pennsylvania and that Logan and Warden were the instruments; that he and Flagler did not like the scheme but went into it because they did not like to break with the powerful Tom Scott; that his plan was to enlarge the Standard Oil Company and take the refining interest into partnership with them; that they felt the South Improvement Company scheme would fail and that then he could say to the others—"Now try our plan." Later, telling of this to a confidant, he said, "I had our plan clearly in mind. It was right. I knew it as a matter of conscience. It was right between me and my God. If I had to do it tomorrow I would do it again in the same way—do it a hundred times." It may seem far afield, but the facts which follow, interesting in themselves, become doubly interesting when connected with the course of events in Cleveland and the oil regions.

This forgotten chapter in American industrial history took place along the course of the Saginaw River in Michigan. In 1859, the year Drake discovered oil, the Saginaw Salt Manufacturing Company drilled for salt in East Saginaw. The first year it produced 4,000 barrels. As soon as this venture proved successful, lumbermen along the river also drilled for salt and got it. In a short time there were sixty-six different manufacturers producing salt. At the same time salt was being produced on the Ohio River and in Onondago, New York. In a short time the market was glutted. These salt men, almost all Saginaw River lumbermen, saw that their problem was a matter of orderly marketing. The Saginaw Salt Company was organized to act as a sales agency. Before long almost all of the salt men in Saginaw one by one had turned their salt over to the Saginaw Company to sell for them. In April, 1868, they formally organized a central coöperative selling agency—the Saginaw and Bay Salt Company. Its stock was owned by the various producers. It effected a virtual monopoly of Saginaw salt, but felt the competition of the Ohio River and Onondago producers. Hence in March, 1871, after much negotiation, the three districts formed themselves into a pool to sell their product, the whole project being committed to the management of a board made up of one member from each district. Each district was allotted a fixed percentage of sales and prices were fixed for salt at various points.

It is interesting to note that Henry M. Flagler had been among

THE DREAM OF MONOPOLY

the first to engage in the salt industry at Saginaw. His father-in-law was a lumber manufacturer and salt producer along the Saginaw River. He had kept in constant touch with the affairs of the salt producers and knew all about this experiment. The completed arrangement governing the salt pool was effected March, 1871, and immediately thereafter we find Rockefeller, Flagler, Watson, and Warden formulating plans for a similar deal in the oil regions.

VII

WHOEVER originated this scheme, Watson, Warden, and Lockhart undertook the business of handling the organization in the oil towns outside of Cleveland. And when the plan was launched Watson became its president and got much of the odium which was heaped upon it. Watson was a man of great force and energy. He was a patent lawyer. He had been assistant secretary of war under Stanton and had a great flowing beard with a clean upper lip like Stanton whom he much resembled. After the war he was made general freight agent of the Lake Shore Railroad and president of the branch running from Cleveland to the oil regions. He owned some oil property himself and had some storage tanks at Franklin. Watson's chief interest, however, was in the railroad rate war. He was alarmed lest the threat of the regions be made good and Cleveland be destroyed as a refining point. This would have wrecked the branch of the Lake Shore of which he was president. And, of course, because the Standard Oil was the largest shipper he was on terms of business intimacy with Rockefeller.

The plan worked out was as follows: Rockefeller in Cleveland, Logan and Frew in Philadelphia, Lockhart, Waring, and Warden in Pittsburgh, and Jabez A. Bostwick in New York agreed to organize a central corporation or association which would comprise the most powerful refiners in the business. Each one in his respective territory was to buy up, with the aid of the pressure the central organization would supply, their competitors in their own districts. They would demand from the railroads a contract which would give them a large rebate on their own shipments and an equally large drawback on other people's. They would aid the railroads by guaranteeing to them some equitable distribution of the freight business. Their advantage would be so great that they could force all competitors to come in while those they did not want would be driven out of business. With the control of the refining business in their hands they could dictate to producers the price of crude oil and they could destroy the competition of refiners in the oil regions whom they all feared.

Through the Fall and Winter of 1871 the business of perfecting this scheme went forward but with such absolute secrecy that not a word of it got around the oil regions. Charters were not so easy to get then as now and so, having decided on forming a new corporation, the promoters had to get hold of a charter. They were able to buy one—an old charter of a company which had been incorporated years before and which was now practically defunct. It was called the South Improvement Company and it was an excellent vehicle for their designs, since it authorized the company to engage in almost any kind of business. In each refining territory the promoters decided on such refiners as they wished to bring in. These they approached but before disclosing their plans they compelled them to sign a written pledge of secrecy. The pledge, which bears upon its face the flavor of Rockefeller's methods, ran as follows:

"I, —— do solemnly promise upon my honor and faith as a gentleman that I will keep secret all transactions which I may have with the corporation known as the South Improvement Company; that, should I fail to complete any bargains with the said company, all the preliminary conversations shall be kept strictly private; and finally that I will not disclose the price for which I dispose of my product or any other facts which may in any way bring to light the internal workings or organization of the company. All this I do freely promise."

While the refiners were being rounded up, Peter H. Watson went to the railroads. He dealt with Vanderbilt of the Central and H. F. Clark, president of its subsidiary, the Lake Shore, who was also Watson's own chief; Jay Gould of the Erie and General George B. McClellan, president of the Erie's subsidiary, the Atlantic and Great Western, and Tom Scott of the Pennsylvania. Here Watson struck a snag which the promoters had not counted on. The roads insisted all refiners should be taken in and Tom Scott insisted that the producers also should be included. This was no part of the plan. As to the refiners, Watson did a little

THE DREAM OF MONOPOLY

lying. He said the promoters already represented the refining interest of the country. As a matter of fact, they represented about one-tenth of the refining interest. As to the producers, Watson demurred about inviting them in. He argued that their interest was antagonistic and they could look out for themselves. But Scott insisted and finally Watson drew up a penciled draft of a proposed contract with producers. Nothing, however, came of this for reasons we shall see.

On January 2nd, 1872, the promoters met in Philadelphia and formally organized the South Improvement Company. And shortly thereafter that company signed written contracts with the railroad companies. These were remarkable documents—perhaps nothing like them had yet appeared in the course of business in this country. The substance of these contracts was as follows:

First, it was agreed that shipments of petroleum products to the seaboard should be allotted to the three railroads, 45 per cent to the Pennsylvania, 27½ per cent to the Erie, and 27½ per cent to the New York Central. Shipments westward were to be divided one-third to each of the roads.

Second, the railroads agreed to allow rebates to the South Improvement Company on all shipments by its members. The contract fixed certain open, gross rates on crude shipments from any point in the oil regions to all refining cities. These rates were 80 cents to Cleveland and to Pittsburgh, $2.41 to Philadelphia or Baltimore, $2.56 to New York and $2.71 to Boston. These figures meant that existing rates were doubled. A similar table of open rates on refined oil between various points was fixed. Then the South Improvement Company was granted rebates on all such shipments ranging from forty to fifty per cent on crude and from twenty-five to fifty per cent on refined. Thus all the refiners in Cleveland would have to pay eighty cents a barrel on crude oil brought in from the regions. Rockefeller would pay this price too but he would get back a rebate of forty cents. The open rate on refined oil to New York was fixed at $2. Rockefeller's rebate was fixed at fifty cents. Refiners in the region would have to pay $2.92 to ship refined to New York, though it was closer to New York than Cleveland from which Rockefeller had to pay only $1.50.

There was nothing new in all this save that it was made between the roads and a combination of leaders of the industry on a large scale to concentrate the business in their hands. But to all this was added another scheme which, so far as I can trace, was quite new and put into the hands of the combination a weapon so deadly that no opposition could stand up against it. This was the drawback. Under this plan Rockefeller in Cleveland, for instance, would pay 80 cents but would get back from the railroad 40 cents on every barrel of oil he brought from the wells. His competitors too would have to pay eighty cents. Forty cents of this eighty cents would be returned, but not to the competitor. It would be returned to Rockefeller. Thus he got a rebate of forty cents on every barrel he shipped and a drawback of forty cents on every barrel his competitors shipped. A more deadly arrangement for the destruction of rivals could hardly be invented. All this was put down in writing, in minutest detail and signed by the railroads and the South Improvement Company.

One other mortal device was introduced. The railroads agreed "to make manifests or way-bills of all petroleum or its products transported over any portion of its lines," which manifests "shall state the name of the consignor, the place of shipment, the kind and actual quantity of the article shipped, the name of the consignee and the place of destination," and this copy the roads agreed to send to the South Improvement Company. In other words every sale made by an independent competitor, together with the name of the customer and all facts about the transaction, was to be reported to the combination. Thus all the details of a rival's business were to be completely exposed to the combination by the roads which were supposed to serve those rivals.

By the middle of January this curious engine for crushing competition was ready to begin its work and Watson was made president.

VIII

ROCKEFELLER now gave an example of the swiftness in action of which he was capable. Perhaps no man in business history has been given to more deliberate meditation upon his plans. He did nothing without long and careful reflection upon every side of a proposed course of action. However, having satisfied himself, he could amaze and confound his opponent with the suddenness of his thrusts. The moment the South Improvement plans were sufficiently advanced to permit safe action he went to work. He

THE DREAM OF MONOPOLY

watched for the right moment and then one day, he put on his high silk hat and walked across the Public Square to the office of a leading banker.

"I want you to have Oliver H. Payne here for a conference," Rockefeller announced. The banker was a little surprised for he knew there was little love lost between these two men. However, he assured Rockefeller that Payne would be there at three.

The firm of Clarke, Payne, and Company was Rockefeller's chief competitor. Payne was the Standard's strongest foe. He was a man of great importance in Cleveland, a grandson of old Nathan Perry who had left a fortune made in the wholesale liquor and grocery business. His father, Hon. Henry B. Payne, was a lawyer of the highest standing at the Ohio bar who was later elected to the United States Senate and was once mentioned prominently for the Presidency. Payne had what Rockefeller did not have—abundant capital, high social standing, powerful political and financial connections. He was a proud, haughty man, who bore himself with such an air that one of Rockefeller's associates spoke of him as the "kin of God." He looked with disdain on the energetic and resolute young man who was challenging him in the oil business and doing it successfully. He had an additional reason for hating Rockefeller. When Payne's father ran for Congress Rockefeller and his associates put up money to defeat him. Payne was proud of his father and deeply resented this. When Rockefeller, therefore, decided to deal with Payne he took the risk of being snubbed. But he did not send an emissary. At three o'clock he strode across the square to the bank where he found Payne waiting for him. He told Payne that he had come to the conclusion that the oil business of Cleveland was doomed unless the leading refiners got together—the interests of all were being impaired by the unintelligent competition of a large number of small, poorly equipped and under-financed refiners who were moving themselves to ruin and involving all in the mess. The leading refiners should put aside their enmities and combine. If they did they could all get preferential rebates and drawbacks from the railroads; they could buy out the weak ones, utilize the good plants and close the poor ones, operate more economically on a large scale, unite with the leaders in other cities, defeat the threat from the oil regions and bring the whole industry under the control of a few powerful leaders.

Rockefeller was never a popular man even before his great moves made him hated. But he had about him a power which few men could resist in argument. It must have dawned on the mind of the haughty Payne that he stood in the presence of a master, an enemy who had the audacity to propose that he turn his business over to his keeping. The interview was brief, curt, but decisive. Payne listened and said little. Rockefeller concluded:

"If we can agree upon values and terms do you want to come in?"

"Yes," Payne replied, put on his hat and walked out. Later that day Payne sent his clerk over to complete the terms with Rockefeller. He did not go himself. When the clerk saw Rockefeller's books and the profits he had made he was astonished.

In later years Rockefeller, recalling this interview, spoke with a little asperity of Colonel Payne's pompous manner. However, at the time he knew that with Payne in his camp in Cleveland, his plans were safe. Payne turned his business over to Rockefeller and took stock for it in the Standard Oil Company. Also he became a member of the Board and later treasurer of the company.

IX

THE DAY the South Improvement Company was formally organized Rockefeller increased the capital stock of the Standard Oil Company from one to two and a half million dollars. The additional stock was provided to issue to such Cleveland refiners as the Standard should absorb. Immediately Rockefeller and Flagler began to call on all their twenty-five rivals in the city. They proposed simply that the refiners should sell out to the Standard. In increasing the stock of the company Rockefeller brought in several new stockholders—O. B. Jennings, Benjamin Brewster—both oil men, Truman P. Handy, Amasa Stone, and Stillman Witt, officers of railroads entering Cleveland. If anything was needed to convince oil men that the railroads were on Rockefeller's side these railroad stockholders were sufficient. When Rockefeller approached a competitor he laid the whole case before him, the hopelessness of the business, his utter lack of any chance of success outside of Rockefeller's combination, Rockefeller's freight arrangements, which gave him a complete and final advantage. "I will send my appraisers to your plant and fix its value. You turn it over

THE DREAM OF MONOPOLY 159

to us and we will pay you in cash or in stock of the Standard Oil Company. You will then own, instead of a refinery that is doomed to failure, stock in a company which is progressing." Then he would add in a tone of friendly and confidential assurance: "Take Standard Oil stock and your family will never know want." No guarantee was ever sounder. What is more, Rockefeller believed in it profoundly. He had absolute confidence in the oil business and in himself. But most of those who heard this promise had no faith in it or in the oil business, which they believed was heading for doom.

The partners in Alexander, Hewitt, and Company, which included Isaac L. Hewitt, Rockefeller's first employer, talked it over. They had received an offer and they called on Vanderbilt. Vanderbilt refused to be drawn out. They went to Peter H. Watson, whom they knew well. Watson equivocated. Then he said ominously: "You had better sell—better get clear." The partners were plainly frightened. They decided to seek a further conference with Rockefeller. Alexander refused to talk to Rockefeller—he hated him. Hewitt, for whom Rockefeller professed a strong friendship, said he would go. He called at the Euclid Avenue home in the morning and walked into town with his old office boy —now tall, immaculate, imposing in his high silk hat and long coat and garmented in the aura of success and power. Rockefeller assured his old employer that if they did not come in his firm would be crushed: "I have ways of making money you know nothing about," he added. "We felt a pressure brought to bear on our minds," Alexander explained later. The firm decided to surrender.

All the refiners approached were sworn to secrecy, but of course, talk got around. Hanna, Baslington, and Company were a strong firm. The Hannas were powerful in Cleveland. They refused to sell. They had made big profits the preceding year and saw no reason to sell. They made up their minds to refuse before Rockefeller got around to them. When he did, Hanna refused point-blank. Rockefeller raised his eyebrows and shrugged his shoulders as if all were up with Hanna's firm. Then he revealed that he had gotten possession of most of the other refiners. Hanna was amazed. So secretly had Rockefeller worked that these men knew nothing of his progress. Then he pressed the point of his advantage from railroad rates.

"You will stand alone," he warned them. "Your firm can never make any more money in Cleveland. No use trying to do business in competition with the Standard Oil Company. If you do it will end in your being wiped out."

This firm decided to sell out too. A few demurred more stoutly. One of these was Frank Rockefeller, John D.'s brother, a partner now in the firm of Scofield, Shurmer, and Teagle. Rockefeller was somewhat shorter with his brother.

"Very well," he said. "We have a combination with the railroads. We are going to buy out all the refiners in Cleveland. We will give every one a chance to come in. We will give you a chance. Those who refuse will be crushed. If you don't sell your property to us it will be valueless."

Frank was indignant, furious in fact. But the firm decided Mr. Rockefeller was in earnest. So they too sold.

The two oil men—Rockefeller and Flagler—kept at it until every refinery in Cleveland, save two or three, sold out. A kind of terror got abroad among the refiners as they talked among themselves almost in whispers about the thing that was wiping them out of business. They had a feeling of despair that odds utterly beyond their strength were being raised against them. In less than a month, twenty of the twenty-five refiners in Cleveland were in Rockefeller's hands.

When Rockefeller was done he had practically the entire refining capacity of Cleveland in his hands—capacity for refining 15,000 barrels a day—the largest by far of any refining point in the country. He had succeeded completely in his part of the great plan and with amazing swiftness. He had a monopoly in Cleveland.

When it was accomplished it was said that Rockefeller had "crushed" his rivals and that he had forced them to sell at sums far below the true value of their plants. Alexander said he had to sell a plant worth $150,000 for $65,000. Robert Hanna insisted he was forced to accept $45,000 for a plant worth $75,000.

There are, of course, two sides of this story. It is quite certain that of the 26 refiners in Cleveland almost all of them were heading for ruin. It is also quite certain that almost all had lost faith in the oil business. They did not believe that even John D. Rockefeller could succeed in it. Mark Hanna was in the oil refining business when he married. His wife's father, Mrs. Hanna has

THE DREAM OF MONOPOLY

said, objected to her marrying him because "he said the oil business was not a legitimate business; it was speculation." Mr. Rockefeller contradicts the statement of Isaac L. Hewitt already reported. Hewitt, he declares, told him his combination could never succeed. "John," he argued, "it can't be done. We've tried it on the Lake Erie shipping companies. They didn't hold together. Yours won't. You'll find it is a rope of sand." Another leading business man in Cleveland objected that Rockefeller's scheme was "too scopey." Even Colonel Oliver H. Payne's partners were skeptical. One of them, James Clarke, who hated Rockefeller and was always berating him, sold his share of the Standard stock—1,000 shares—to Colonel Payne for $113,500. Another, John Huntington, got 500 shares as his part of the sale of Clarke, Payne and Company. He was prevented from selling by Colonel Payne, who guaranteed him against loss. The stock he held later made him a man of great wealth.

Those who were glad to sell and get out but who thought they ought to get a fancy price for their plants abused Rockefeller for not meeting their own appraisals. There were others who welcomed the opportunity to sell at any price. One of these, Frank A. Arter, had a refinery which had cost him $12,000. "It was a hard blow," he said, "when Rockefeller's appraiser valued my plant at $3,000. I had a debt outstanding of $25,000. But what could I do? When conditions were so bad in the oil business that a small refiner could not make money, his plant was worth only what it would fetch as material. So I sold out for $3,000. I had my choice of cash or Standard Oil stock. I asked Rockefeller and Flagler which I ought to take. They both spoke at once. 'If you will take the stock and hold it some day you will get back the full price you asked for your refinery.' I had a hard pull carrying the $25,000 indebtedness for the next four years in order to hold that stock. Sometimes I got worried. One day I met Mr. Rockefeller and asked him: 'How are things going?' He asked: 'Are you still holding your stock?' I said that I did in a way, that I had it what you now would call 'in hock' and was trying to follow his and Mr. Flagler's advice. Rockefeller leaned over and in an undertone said: 'Sell everything you've got, even the shirt on your back—but hold on to that stock.'"

Mr. Rockefeller has persistently denied that any coercion was used in this episode. Yet he was a member of the South Improvement Company. That concern did have a contract with the railroads —all of them—for heavy rebates and enormous drawbacks against which no rival could compete. It would have been simply necessary to show this advantage to Cleveland refiners—already discouraged —to make it plain to them that their lot was hopeless and several refiners have testified that this was done either directly or by innuendo. In any case they understood. It was all done in a pleasant and friendly voice. But it was none the less effective.[1]

Meantime, Logan and Frew were busy in Philadelphia, Lockhart, Warren, and Warden in Pittsburgh, Bostwick and Brewster in New York. But they were moving slowly. These were all able men, but they lacked that resistless power and that furious drive which marked the operations of Rockefeller.

X

SEVERAL times in the midst of this campaign Rockefeller had to make quick trips to Titusville. There oildom worried on its perplexed, half-busy way, utterly oblivious of the blow which hung suspended over it. The visitor from Cleveland walked into a hotel. The lobby was filled with gossiping men and tobacco smoke. "Gentlemen will please keep out of the office and off the counter," read a sign on the wall. Loud talk and boisterous laughter came from the adjoining bar. Rockefeller signed his name on the

[1] Mr. Rockefeller's own explanation, as made to Mr. William O. Inglis, later, is as follows:

"The procedure was without precedent. We find here the strongest and most prosperous concern in the business, which had made money in each year of its existence, turning to its less fortunate competitors, who, it well knew, had been losing money and become discouraged and saying to them, practically: 'We will stand in for the risks and the hazards of the refining business. You need not contribute any money unless you desire to do so.' And I believe in only one instance was any concern willing to do so, and that was in the case of Warden, Frew and Company and Lockhart and Frew.

"The Standard Oil Company assumed all the risks and at a time when it was evident that the larger number of its competitors could not continue to compete with it in the struggle for existence. What did it do? It turned to these men with whom it had been in sharp competition and said to each: 'Come with us, and we will do you good. We will undertake to save you from the wrecks of this refining business and give you a return on the capital which you have in the plant and land; or, if you prefer, we will take the business off your hands.'"

THE DREAM OF MONOPOLY

register and looked it over to see who was in Titusville. Just a few lines above his own he read:

John D. Archbold, $4.00 a bbl.

The inscription struck Rockefeller's fancy. He supposed it then and years later to be a kind of bold announcement of what the signer wanted oil to cost. As a matter of fact, it was Archbold's method of advertising free that he was there prepared to pay four dollars a barrel for oil—that was his bid and his way of making it. Rockefeller had heard of him. He was a very young man, born nine years after Rockefeller (July 26th, 1848). He was but twenty-four years old, the son of a preacher who had shuffled off when the lad was only ten. Two years' clerking in a country store, then to a job in Titusville with William Abbott in the oil business, then a member of the firm while still in his teens, then part of a refining firm in Titusville and then a representative in New York of the refining firm of Porter, Moreland, and Company, of which he was a member—this was the brief but successful career of Archbold. He was a strong, ardent, pugnacious, daring operator and the signature with its flourish about four-dollar oil made Rockefeller feel that he wanted Archbold in the new combine. So he took care to have that gentleman approached. In New York later the promoters there got him to sign the pledge of secrecy and then unfolded this plan. Archbold rejected it indignantly. But he kept his counsel.

XI

ON FEBRUARY 21st, Rockefeller read in the Cleveland *Plain Dealer* the following:

"A gigantic 'little game' has been going on in oil circles in Cleveland to the effect that a single firm has bought up or got control of all the refineries in the city and proposes to monopolize the business, having allied itself with the oil-carrying railroads as well as a similar monopolizing firm in Pittsburgh. Rockefeller and Andrews of the Standard Oil Works are credited with being the shrewd operators in Cleveland."

The paragraph is interesting because, with its critical tone, it was the first bit of criticism to appear in print of John D. Rockefeller upon whose head was to descend such floods of abuse for the next thirty years. What alarmed Rockefeller was not the criticism but the leak. Some weeks before the Titusville *Herald* had spoken of a rumored agreement between the railroads to abolish rebates and equalize freight rates. But this was wide of the mark.

The day following the Cleveland story came a copy of the *Petroleum Centre Record* referring to a "rumored scheme of gigantic combination among certain railroads and refiners to control the purchase and shipment of crude and refined oil from this region." It spoke of "robbing and swindling" and hinted at dire reprisals. Next day the *Derrick* said "a torpedo is filling for the scheme." A kind of fear filtered through the regions. The rumor went around in angry murmurs. Cleveland buzzed with the story. In February a *Plain Dealer* reporter went to the Standard Oil office and tried to draw out Flagler.

"Do you suppose any one firm exists which can obtain control of all refineries here? In this country a man wants to look after his own money and no man or set of men can buy up all the refineries." Yet at this moment the Standard had in its breeches' pockets all the refineries in Cleveland.

"What is this South Improvement Company?" asked the reporter.

"I don't know," said Mr. Flagler.

"I didn't know but what the Cleveland combination might have some connection with it and you could tell."

Flagler laughed. "Do you suppose I would be fool enough to tell you?" he asked and walked away.

February 26th the news was out. After all the planning an error of a subordinate railroad official caused the proposed new schedule of open rates doubling the old ones to be put in force on the oil branch of the Lake Shore Railroad. The meaning of this flashed upon the oil men along the Creek in an instant. Like a blaze of hot anger the news rolled over the Creek. It meant the combination would seize the whole refining industry and would have the Creek refiners by the throat. Business stopped. Producers, refiners, shop-keepers, shippers, drillers, rushed out into the streets of Titusville and Oil City.

In Cleveland reporters went to the Standard Oil office. Rockefeller refused to see them. But they told Flagler the news. Three thousand men had gathered in Parshall's Opera House in Titusville "to defy the 'Anaconda.'"

THE DREAM OF MONOPOLY

"Just a few soreheads who have been preying on the oil regions," Flagler assured them. "This agitation will soon cease."

Nevertheless disturbing reports continued to come in from Titusville. Watson and Warden and other allies were sent for. Rockefeller and Flagler were plainly surprised at the extent of the outburst against them. They had thought little of this in advance. Mr. Rockefeller really had as yet not learned much of how the human mass mind works. He had supposed that the whole thing could be carried out quite secretly. But now it was plain that he faced a fight—the first battle in a long career of warfare, war upon him by courts, by district attorneys, by independent traders, by newspapers, by legislators, Congress, by society itself, war in which he was to be lampooned and excoriated, called by every bitter name the inventive fury of man's anger could conceive, until in the end he was the worst-hated man in America.

XII

IN THE oil regions the wrath of the producers and refiners swept up and down the oil creeks like a flame. Men talked of mob action, said the Oil City *Derrick*. At the head of that paper appeared a figure now destined while his brief editorial reign lasted, to be a voice of thunder among the revolting oil men. He was C. E. Bishop. He had come to Oil City in 1871 from Jamestown, New York, and, with the early partisan journalist's flare for adopting warlike causes, he summoned his extraordinary talents for invective and scorn to castigate Rockefeller and his associates. He perhaps invented the terms "Anaconda," "monster," and "Octopus" which for a generation served orators well in flaying the trusts. At once Bishop printed at the masthead of the *Derrick* an ominous black box and in it the names of the "conspirators" headed by Rockefeller. This black list he published daily until the war was ended. The streets of all Titusville were black with angry men. On the night of the twenty-seventh men poured in from all the towns in the region to a great mass meeting in Parshall's Opera House, Titusville. Speeches were made denouncing the monster. Resolutions were passed condemning the railroads, the combination, the legislature for "putting chains on the people" by creating such charters as the South Improvement Company. Then the meeting adjourned to meet at Oil City two days later. These men were angry. They talked of violence, of burning refineries, of tapping tanks, lynching the leaders. Two days later the producers met at Love's Opera House in Oil City. Orators lashed them to fresh fury. "The South Improvement Company is well named," one said. "In the South they enslave blacks. And this is an improvement on the South for it is intended to enslave whites. John S. Rich de-

THE BLACK LIST.

P. H. WATSON, PRES. S. I. CO.
Charles Lockhart,
W. P. Logan,
R. S. Waring,
A. W. Bostwick,
W. G. Warden,
John Rockefeller,
Amasa Stone.

These seven are given as the Directors of the Southern Improvement Company. They are refiners or merchants of petroleum

Atlantic & Gt. Western Railway.
L. S. & M. S. Railway.
Philadelphia & Erie Railway.
Pennsylvania Central Railway
New York Central Railway.
Erie Railway.

THE BLACK LIST PUBLISHED BY THE OIL CITY "DERRICK."

clares he will burn every barrel of oil he owns before he will sell it to the South Improvement Company." Then a young man arose—small, thin, pale-faced, looking like a young divinity student. He was John D. Archbold. He told in tones full of scorn how he had been approached by the conspirators and sworn to secrecy. He denounced the "conspiracy" and called on producers and refiners in the regions to "unite against the common enemy." It was the region producers who made the most noise. But the refiners came in with a resolution saying they might have made money by going into the combination but preferred to remain out and cast their lot with their neighbors in the regions. Again the meeting adjourned

THE DREAM OF MONOPOLY

to meet in Franklin. Everywhere similar meetings were in eruption, orating, resolving, reporting, exhorting, sizzling with hatred and threats. A 3,000-gallon tank belonging to Peter H. Watson was tapped and 500 gallons of oil run out. A secret society was formed—the Oil Men's League—with fiery oaths, rituals, passwords and slogans about "saving the resources of Pennsylvania." When the full force and meaning of the proposed drawback was understood the fury of their anger knew no bounds. A petition to the legislature for relief was hastily dispatched and 1,000 men were held in readiness to march on the State Capitol to compel the lawmakers to grant that relief. New figures arose to add to the volume of abuse directed against Rockefeller and Watson and Warden—figures which look strange to us now in these rôles. From New York came a delegation headed by Henry H. Rogers of Charles Pratt and Company. In the state constitutional convention a young lawyer rose to call attention to the dangers of monopoly threatening the liberties of the people as exemplified in the South Improvement Company. This was Samuel C. T. Dodd, later to become John D. Rockefeller's counsel and the inventor of the trust. Captain J. J. Vandergrift, one of the leading refiners, signed the resolutions of the Creek refiners—Captain Vandergrift, who was to be a Standard Oil director and head of its pipe lines. Baltimore refiners wired they were ready to join in the fight. At Buffalo citizens met and proposed an independent railroad to the regions and bound the city to raise a million dollars for this purpose and some days later a delegation of Buffalo oil men marched into Oil City headed by the mayor. Delegations arrived from Philadelphia and Erie. Suddenly the newspapers of the country bristled with this exciting story.

XIII

IN CLEVELAND Rockefeller, amazed at the outburst, retired to the silence of his office and refused to see any one, most of all the reporters who clamored for news. He had not counted on anything like this. He and his allies were plainly puzzled. A leading Cleveland railroad man, interviewed, said: "Oil producers will do nothing as they have not the brains, backbone or means to organize resistance." Apparently they thought the tempest would blow over. They tried to induce the New York refiners to come into the combine, offering them a place on the directorate. Watson wired the region urging them to send a committee to confer. But they indignantly repelled his emissary. Gradually news arrived at the Standard office which was indeed disturbing.

In the midst of all the confusion in the oil country it began to look as if something was being gotten done. The oil men had organized the Producers' Protective Association. Captain William Hasson, known to be an able and resolute man, was named president. It mapped out a program—to shut down all work on Sunday, to start no new wells for ninety days, to cease using torpedoes to increase the flow of wells. A joint committee of regions refiners was named to control the whole situation. Creek refiners pledged themselves to rush their operations while producers slowed up theirs. Above all, producers pledged that no crude oil was to be sold to John D. Rockefeller and his associates and to insure this that all oil be delivered to the committee. A million dollars to finance home refiners was pledged and the region divided into sixteen districts to raise the capital and handle the oil. A bill was introduced in Harrisburg to repeal the charter of the South Improvement Company and a bill to authorize the building of pipe lines was offered. Congress was urged to investigate the oil industry, a committee started to Washington to demand action and another bill was offered forbidding all rail discriminations as between localities. To back all this a petition ninety-three feet long was sent to the national capital.

Rockefeller saw that the railroads were plainly frightened. Cornelius Vanderbilt wired the oil men to suspend judgment and action until his agent could treat with them. Rates on the Jamestown and Franklin road were changed four times in as many days. The Atlantic and Great Western restored its old rates.

Rockefeller quickly learned that the resolution not to sell him oil was serious. Word came from his buyers along the Creek that no one would sell them a drop of oil. Brokers suspected of dealing with Rockefeller's agents were watched. Half a dozen were summoned before the Oil Exchange and threatened with expulsion if they sold oil in Cleveland. One man charged with procuring oil for the Standard was Daniel O'Day. He was a big, fearless, resourceful Irishman. He denied the charge, but was tried along with some others, found guilty and ordered to resign from the Exchange. O'Day didn't know he was representing the Standard. His principal was Bostwick in New York who had secretly sold out to Rockefeller. At Tidioute, Rockefeller agents offered an advance of thirty cents for oil but could get none. In the *Derrick* of March 21st we read that a contract was offered to a producer for his year's output at $4.50 a barrel. His name was F. S. Tarbell—a name later to become famous in the oil regions. Tarbell refused the offer.

What Rockefeller saw at this stage of the war must have perplexed him. Here was every refinery he had just purchased and his own in Cleveland completely shut down because he could not get oil. Meantime the oil regions had now done what men said never could be done—they had organized, were raising funds, had a strong, a resolute leader. Was the threat that they would wipe out Cleveland as with a sponge to be carried out? The Oil City *Derrick* of March 21st said feeling against the combination in Cleveland was strong, that "a special detail of police is necessary to guard the property of the ring, sixty men in all being thus employed. A half dozen are stationed around the residences of the officers of the South Improvement Company, the balance of the detail is placed over the Standard Oil works and copper shop." However, no Cleveland paper mentions this and it is probably exaggerated.

No one was more alarmed than Tom Scott. The free pipe line bill disturbed him. But his agent in Harrisburg attended to that threat in the usual way. He got slipped into the bill a little joker to the effect that oil could not be piped out of the state. But Scott arranged a conference with the committee of the oil men in New York. Rockefeller heard of this—that the railroad chiefs were trying to back out of the scheme. He and Watson hurried to New York. There they learned that Tom Scott, Commodore Vanderbilt, and other railroad men were meeting with the oil men. Among the representatives of the oil men were John D. Archbold and Henry H. Rogers. Rockefeller and Watson went boldly to the meeting, knocked on the door, and demanded admittance. The man who opened the door promptly closed it and reported that Watson and Rockefeller wanted to be admitted to the meeting. Henry H. Rogers, using strong language as was his wont, objected to their entering. However, the chairman—an old friend of Watson's—insisted on his coming in. The great bearded railroad man was allowed to come in. A blast of angry protests greeted his entry. Rockefeller remained outside in the hall pacing up and down.

In a few moments the door opened and Watson came out red-faced and flustered. Reporters there at the time wrote that as the pair turned to go away, Mr. Rockefeller seemed "very blue indeed."

The game was going against them now. That day the railroads signed a contract with the producers to end the South Improvement Company contract and to equalize rates. From every quarter now the blows came. In a few days the bill repealing the charter of the South Improvement Company was passed and signed by the governor. The "Anaconda" was slain by law. Rockefeller went back to Cleveland. But in the oil regions men danced for joy. The great beast had been conquered. All over the country news of the defeat of the South Improvement Company was printed. It was indeed defeated. What the oil men did not see for some time was that John D. Rockefeller was not. When the smoke of the battle cleared away it was seen that he had in his hands as a result of the campaign the complete oil industry of Cleveland. In less than a month almost every refinery there had fallen into his hands. He had not won his whole design. But he had won much. He was the only gainer. He had had his first touch of war. He was not to know peace for a generation.

PART FIVE
THE GREAT CONSUMMATION

CHAPTER I. MR. ROCKEFELLER LOOKS ABOUT

A TALL gentleman, in frock coat and silk hat, leaves his bulky, mansard-roofed home in Euclid Avenue in the morning. Almost before he reaches the sidewalk Mr. Rockefeller is joined by another silk-hatted, frock-coated companion who greets him familiarly. The two, with canes swinging, walk briskly down Euclid Avenue. This other is Henry M. Flagler, Rockefeller's most intimate partner. They walk to work very frequently. Rockefeller has a little stoop in his strong shoulders and a shamble in his gate. Flagler is more erect, more handsome, older, more distinguished looking.

They are noticed as they stride down fashionable Euclid Avenue, with its massive brownstone and brick mansions squatting back from the sidewalk amid gardens still bare and gray in the late Winter. Smart rigs stand in front of some of these homes of Cleveland's new gentry of iron and oil and ships. Some of the barons are already on their way downtown behind spanking teams, their own luxuriant whiskers pressed back by the breeze. Rockefeller's fortune has just broken into Cleveland gossip. The aura of worldly success shines around him. People look back at him as he passes.

Rockefeller walks with a measured pace listening. Flagler talks vehemently, gesticulates decisively. He is a man of bold schemes, always for action, for daring stratagems. These two men are in the first stages of a revolution in business. They are preparing without realizing it one step at a time the movement of American life in a new direction.

Rockefeller sensed his unpopularity. The shafts of the relentless *Derrick* stung him a little. The stories circulating in Cleveland about how he had squeezed his former rivals hurt him more. Flagler cared not at all. But Rockefeller was a righteous man. He leaned heavily upon the Baptist Church and its gospel and his Bible. He was a great figure in the church now and all heads turned when he appeared in the aisle on Sunday with Mrs. Rockefeller. He had done nothing for which his conscience reproached him. In a world which at this period was reeking with dishonesty Rockefeller knew he was an honest man. He dealt fairly with his partners; with his customers; with his bankers. Against his rivals he committed the sin of being more intelligent and industrious. There was no law of God against combinations or mergers or rebates. One finds in all this Rockefeller's profound need of the lawless Flagler. The two men were admirably suited to each other. Rockefeller needed about him the odor of sanctity. Yet in the more or less cruel world of business it must have seemed often that certain Christian practices fitted hardly at all. Thus Flagler, a bold, unscrupulous self-seeker, made no bones about conscience. He did whatever was necessary to success. He could be relied upon to propose the needful course, however dishonest or ruthless. Thus he could do a great deal of thinking for Rockefeller untrammeled by the limitations of a Christian conscience. When he produced a workable scheme Rockefeller could be depended upon to find the permissible Christian factors in it. Indeed this dilution of the Christian's soft code with the hard realities of Flagler's rude pragmatism accounts, perhaps, for the refuge which Rockefeller early sought in the conviction that in some way God was concerned in the production of his success —that he was working for God and towards God's ends.

In the late evening Rockefeller—a grave figure—might be seen walking home alone. He saw little as he passed. On these walks it was his custom to review the day, fixing events, dates, faces, names, figures, in his tenacious memory. Also he pondered his situation. The advantages lay all with his rivals could they have known it. But they clung to an outworn system that was unworkable and Rockefeller was one of the few living men who realized this fully. The old day of men working by simple processes from limited supplies and for purchasers near by whose wants were known had passed. The oil regions tinkered with vast mineral supplies, and for a worldwide market. The demand was limited; the supplies were not. Rockefeller knew that this producing machine had to be controlled. He had gotten hold of it in Cleveland, but everywhere else it was untamed. A way must be found to tame it. Thus he began the long fight on competition. It was not inspired wholly by his appetite for wealth. Competition was wasteful, disordered, lawless. The man's mind craved order as the drunkard's blood craves alcohol. Moreover competition had now become war —not a maze of countless little wars between countless little warriors—but a war between powerful antagonists with each other, between great warriors and little ones, war to the death. Rockefeller must crush the oil regions or they would crush him. He knew the almost unanimous judgment of the business world would be against him. He had braved public opinion in its most furious mood and he knew he could stand it. That this thing Public Opinion was something he could and ought to deal with did not enter his mind. He took shelter from it in his scorn.

II

IN THE business offices of Cleveland men began to analyze Rockefeller's success. One general verdict, as Mark Hanna is supposed to have said later, was that "the man was mad about money."[1] He himself said he "was *all* business." He divided his time with nothing, neither boards, nor committees nor politics. He focused his attention on his objectives with a concentration never surpassed and cultivated a mental composure which permitted nothing to ruffle it—neither anger, nor hatred, nor jealousy, nor pride.

There were other elements in his success. Business had complete confidence in his honesty and judgment. A man like Col. Payne, who hated him, could turn his business over to him. Fire almost wiped out his plants. Rockefeller went to Harkness, a stockholder, and asked him for a loan. "All right, John," said Harkness, "I'll

[1] Senator Hanna's wife, after his death, referring to this remark said: "My husband was such an admirer of Mr. Rockefeller that I cannot believe he ever thought such a thing, much less said it. If he had thought it, I am sure he would have said something to me about it."

give you all I've got." He was a borrower in every bank. He moved so fast some directors asked questions about him. After his great fire one director said at a meeting: "Rockefeller will probably be around for money. Is he sound?" Stillman Witt sent for his bank box. "These young men are all right. If they want money and you want more security, here it is. Take what you want."

He saw to it that he had friends planted wherever they might be needed. When his credit was discussed in one bank there was Harkness, a stockholder, to vouch for him. If it was brought up in another bank, another stockholder, Stillman Witt, was there to aid him. When he wanted railroad favors, there was Amasa Stone and Watson, also stockholders, to stand by him. By this time he had tied to his enterprise, one way or another, most of the men of wealth and power in Cleveland.

Rockefeller in his soul was a bookkeeper. He watched his books with loving care. He prided himself on knowing each day how he stood with the world. But he neglected no phase of his business. He visited all plants and talked with the superintendents. They called him the Sponge because he would soak from them whatever information they possessed about everything.

He kept himself away from the public. During the recent oil war, though reviled and haunted by reporters, he remained silent. He was the most difficult man in Cleveland to see. One day he found a subordinate talking in his outer office to a stranger. The clerk later said the man was a friend.

"Well, be very careful what you say. What does he want here? Don't let him find out anything."

"But he is just a friend. He doesn't want to know anything. He has just come to see me."

"Quite so, but you never can tell," warned the cautious oil man. "Be careful, be very careful."

After a while he began to grow secretive even with his partners. When they asked questions, he would sometimes say:

"You'd better not know. If you don't know anything you can't tell anything."

The man was always careful of the art of make-up. He nurtured his dignity. Just thirty-three, yet he was laying down the law to some of the foremost business oldsters of Cleveland. He had grown upon his cheeks a set of side whiskers—red ones. These were gone now. Instead he retained an ample reddish mustache rolling over his thin, compressed lips. His skin was clear and clean. He was tall, strong, a trifle stooped, but big enough to produce an impression.

III

IN NOVEMBER, 1872, a congressional election came on. R. C. Parsons, who had been charged with being a professional lobbyist, was a candidate. In the midst of the acrimonious campaign, there went out to all Standard Oil employees a circular letter which for some reason was called Order No. 1. "We deem the election of R. C. Parsons vital to our interests as well as yours," read Order No. 1. To it was signed the names of Amasa Stone, Stillman Witt, Truman Handy, all Standard directors.

"Why," asked the *Plain Dealer*, "does the Standard Oil want Parsons elected? Has the company any lobbying to do at Washington? It is somewhat strange this corporation should take such an active interest in the election of a man so notorious as a lobbyist."

This order had gone to men who had suffered from the shutdown and who had been helped by public subscription when the Standard did nothing for them. A blast of denunciation greeted the order. But Parsons was elected. Thereafter the Standard Oil was looked upon as a force to be watched in politics.

CHAPTER II. THE COMBINATION OF BRAINS

IN MAY, after the fall of the South Improvement Company, a congressional committee made its report and declared that concern to be one of the "most gigantic and dangerous conspiracies ever attempted." Titusville oil men had just read this in their papers when they were amazed at the appearance of John D. Rockefeller on the streets of Titusville. What could he be doing there? What was worse he was seen on the streets walking with Henry M. Flagler and Jacob J. Vandergrift. Vandergrift! One of the leaders of the region refiners! The three were calling on the Creek refiners and their plan soon became known. Rockefeller proposed that the refiners everywhere join in an association to control production. He had convinced not only Vandergrift but John D. Archbold of this. Finally a meeting was called May 15th and 16th to consider the plan. Flagler was the spokesman. He proposed that all refiners form a Central Association. Each refiner would continue to operate his own refinery, but all purchases of crude oil and all transportation agreements would be made by a central board, which would also allocate to each refiner the amount he was to refine.

At the same time a meeting of producers was in progress in Petroleum Center to consider an offer from "Cleveland capitalists," said to have $20,000,000 capital, headed by a Mr. H. Wayne, to buy all their crude for five years at $5 a barrel for seven-eighths of their output. But the producers were afraid of this proposal and rejected it. In Titusville, where Rockefeller sat silent, listening to Flagler's plea, men jumped to their feet and cried "traitors! deserters!" to Vandergrift and Archbold and those refiners who supported Rockefeller's plan. They refused indignantly to join with the "Cleveland conspirators." So Rockefeller and Flagler went back to their offices. They were convinced that action through the organization of all refiners was impossible. They were now ready for their next step.

II

JOHN D. ROCKEFELLER now began to put into motion that extraordinary series of moves which culminated in 1877 and which led with the inevitableness of Fate to his complete mastery of the oil business. First of all he saw clearly that united action among refiners was impracticable. Next he saw that the oil regions must always remain a threat to him. The interests of the refiners and producers in the regions were antagonistic, yet they had always acted together under the spell of community spirit. The producers he cared nothing about, but he was afraid of the refiners. Their crude oil was at their door. He had to haul his to Cleveland at a cost of 50 cents a barrel. Moreover they had a shorter haul for their refined to the seaboard. He did not fear the small refiners. But suppose a powerful combination like his own should be formed in the regions? There were men of brains there. Pondering this, his plans took form. He made up his mind to bring all the able

THE COMBINATION OF BRAINS

refiners to his side, not only those in the regions, but in all refining centers—Lockhart and Frew in Pittsburgh, Warden in Philadelphia, Pratt and Rogers in New York, Vandergrift and Archbold in the oil cities. What he sought above all was a combination of brains.

"I wanted able men with me," he said later. "I tried to make friends with these men. I admitted their ability and the value of their enterprise. I worked to convince them that it would be better for both to coöperate . . . and if I had not succeeded in getting their friendship the whole plan of the Standard Oil Company would have fallen to the ground. I admit I tried to attract only the able men; and I have always had as little as possible to do with dull business men."

His first step, therefore, was a combination of the strong refiners in a coöperative association. This was the prologue to the swelling theme of his final plan. This was necessary to prove to him the futility of mere association; the necessity of absolute central control. "It is not always the easiest of tasks to induce strong forceful men to agree," he commented afterwards. But he set to work.

III

IN THE first days of August newspapers in the regions carried the report that refiners throughout the country had organized a new association. Rockefeller had moved and the news was out. It leaked out through a letter to the *Derrick* signed "Petroleum" and revealed the startling fact that while John D. Rockefeller was president, Jacob J. Vandergrift was vice-president and Charles Pratt, of Reynolds, Devoe and Pratt of New York City, treasurer. Here was a blow. Captain Jacob J. Vandergrift, the foremost refiner and business man of Petrolia, had gone over bag and baggage to the hated Rockefeller! Captain Vandergrift had gone into oil from the Susquehanna River. When oil was discovered he was the first to tow barges loaded with barrels of oil to Pittsburgh. Later he built the first bulk boat—the precursor of the tanker. After the war he moved to Oil City, drilled for oil, and built a refinery. He was a pipe line pioneer, building a four-mile carrier —the Star Pipe Line—from West Pithole to Pithole—the small germ which by additions and extensions was one day to expand into that far-flung tangle of pipes owned by the Standard. He had varied interests. With his partner, George V. Forman, he owned the Oil City Trust Company. His United Pipe Lines were the largest in the regions. He was a large producer and refiner. Rockefeller had scrutinized closely that patriarchal countenance —the close-cropped chin whiskers covering the strong jaw. He was a man of wealth and a man of God. He hated liquor. In short he was a man who could talk Rockefeller's own language.

Pratt of New York, the most important refiner there, who had been with the regions in their fight on the South Improvement Company, was also in the deal, and Henry H. Rogers, Pratt's partner. The oil men remembered Rogers, handsome, erect, dashing, with flashing eye, as he marched at the head of the New York rebels when the regions mobilized against Rockefeller. What had this indomitable man in Cleveland that he could get hold of such strong men?

The new combination proposed to put the buying of crude and the selling of refined oil in the hands of a committee headed by Rockefeller. The country was divided into districts and each district permitted to refine a certain amount. The *Derrick* said Cleveland was to have 25 per cent, Pittsburgh 25 per cent, New York and Philadelphia 32 per cent and the Oil Regions 18 per cent. It included almost every refiner of importance and was called the National Refiners' Association. Rockefeller went resolutely to work to perfect it. But it took him just six months to convince himself that even an association of the leaders was as impracticable as a general association of all refiners; that they would not obey orders or listen to reason. Accordingly on June 23rd, 1873, Rockefeller summoned a meeting and the refiners' association was disbanded. The experiment, however, was useful for it convinced him definitely that he must do in the country as a whole what he had done in Cleveland. He recalled now how swiftly the whole industry in Cleveland had collapsed into his hands. His appetite now was whetted for greater and more ambitious results. He began to contemplate the world upon a larger scale. The young bookkeeper had grown and he began to see himself the central figure of vaster schemes. Here was born the dream of world-wide monopoly. That then was his next move.

IV

HERE we may take a glance at the oil regions of 1873 as John D. Rockefeller looked them over and made his great resolution. The legend of the oil regions runs thus—a ruthless monster devouring the kindly, amiable, petroleum producers of the Creek. The story is hardly a fair one. The interests of the Creek towns were many —hundreds of crude oil producers with thousands of wells, many brokers and shippers and about thirty-three refiners. In all the tales of Creek warfare, producers and refiners are successfully confused. But they were in fact antagonistic. The Creek refiners justly feared Rockefeller. But he had never engaged in oil production and had never sought to injure the crude producers. He was concerned about them only to the extent that they could be organized on the side of the Creek refiners and thus cut off his supply of crude. The producers had one great enemy. That was not Rockefeller but over-production. They had indeed another which was the parent of the first—their own inability and blindness to the changed world about them. They have been dramatized as innocent victims of Rockefeller. They were foolish enough to suppose they had some sort of God-given right to the oil because they were located at the spot where it flowed. But they were for the most part newcomers in the oil country—adventurers who had flooded in when oil was found, who never dreamed this magnificent treasure was a gift from nature to the nation and that the public had rights superior to their own.

These oil producers were of two sorts. There were the land owners, the old settlers, chiefly ignorant Dutch farmers. The oil had oozed around the farms for ages. It meant nothing to them until an outsider, amid their sneers, proved its value and volume and gave to their worthless farms an almost fabulous value. They still did nothing—merely rented their land out under royalty leases and sat in idleness while other men worked the drills and paid them rich profits. Coal Oil Johnny was one of these. Old Benninghoff, whose murder was the crime classic of the regions for years, was another. Benninghoff demanded his royalties in cash and hid them in all the corners of his dilapidated farmhouse, and went on living in squalor. One night an assassin bashed in his skull and made off with most of his worthless fortune. These were the

180 THE GREAT CONSUMMATION

original royalty owners whose successors have been the curse of petroleum. When the producers sought to save themselves at this time by stopping the drill it was these illiterate farmers who made trouble and demanded that the flood of oil should go on.

STAGES IN THE VARYING FORTUNES OF THE OIL PRODUCERS.
(From McLauren's *Sketches in Crude Oil*)

As for the oil well owners and operators, they were inefficient and wasteful, ignorant, and utterly oblivious of the problems in industry produced by a wholly new set of conditions. They wanted five dollars a barrel for their oil, a price based on the production costs of the most inefficient operator by the most antiquated and wasteful methods plus an indefensible profit. "The profit which men in trade all over the country were glad to get," said Ida Tarbell, who had a profound sympathy for them, "the oil producer despised." They clamored for all sorts of help save self-help. They despised Rockefeller because he appeared on the scene with a perfect respect for all the little things of the business, the little wastes and leaks which they ignored and because he had brought into industry a machine for doing his part of the business which was the most perfect yet produced in the annals of business. They called for laws, more laws. At St. Petersburg they met and resolved "that to give a wider market throughout the world to petroleum, to enhance its price" a committee be appointed "to ask foreign governments to put a proper tariff on refined oil and to admit crude oil free." This is the only instance known of American business men actually petitioning foreign governments to erect a tariff wall against American goods.

To keep the price of crude oil up to American consumers these producers who denounced monopoly now proposed to organize a producers' monopoly, a step which under the laws of today would get them all indicted. The leading spirit in this organization of the Producers' Association was Captain William Hasson, who represented in his character the strength and weakness of the old school as Mr. Rockefeller represented the strength and weakness of the new. In their aims and principles these two men were as far apart as the poles. Captain Hasson was one of the few old Creek settlers who rose to the new opportunities. He was born on a farm at the mouth of Oil Creek which had once belonged to the great Indian Chief Cornplanter. When Drake struck oil Hasson's father sold 300 acres of this land for $750,000. There the son saw Oil City rise. He had headed the Producers' Association which had defeated the "Anaconda." Now he revived it to fight the new "Anaconda"—Overproduction. The price of oil sank steadily. In December, 1872, it was $4.55 a barrel. By February, 1873, it was $2.12. Tanks in the regions overflowed. Hasson's association got an agreement among producers and drillers to sink no new wells for six months. They formed a vigilance committee to enforce the agreement. Groups of men patrolled the country at night to punish offenders. Despite all this production increased. Then they decided on a thirty-day shutdown of all flowing wells. In ten days not a barrel of oil was being pumped. Silence fell over the regions. Then Hasson formed the Petroleum Producers' Association with a million dollars authorized capital. Stock at $100 a share was limited to oil men and their friends. It proposed to buy all oil produced at $5 a barrel, to pay cash if possible, if not to pay $3 cash and the balance when the oil was marketed. This move was noted away from the regions. "It is an attempt," said the New York *Herald*, September 9th, 1873, "to force oil to high prices for the public; the consumers are likely to take a hand in the matter and use their effort to frustrate the design and intent of the shutdown movement by refusing to pay the advanced price." Rockefeller was building a monopoly based on efficient and economical operation, the only excuse for monopoly. Hasson was attempting a monopoly built upon a continuance of waste and extravagance. The public seemed to have a choice between the monopoly of Rockefeller and a few dozen refiners on the one hand and Hasson and a few hundred producers on the other. Hasson's combination was not a defensive one against Rockefeller, as has been supposed. It was an offensive one against the public.

At this point Rockefeller came forward representing his National Refiners' Association and signed a contract with Hasson to buy 200,000 barrels of oil from the Producers' Association. A sliding price scale was fixed. When refined oil sold for 26 cents a gallon Rockefeller was to pay $4 a barrel for crude. For every cent refined rose the price of crude was to be advanced 25 cents until it reached $5. The refiners pledged themselves to admit every *existing* refiner to their combination. The producers pledged themselves to admit all producers, existing or newcomers. The *Derrick* called this an "unholy alliance." It called attention to the limitation in the refiners' agreement to admit only *existing* refiners. It opposed the treaty. So did Captain Hasson. They predicted it would fail. And it did fail. Before Rockefeller had gotten 50,000 of his first 200,000 barrels he notified the Producers' Association that he would exercise his right to cancel the treaty. Again the producers denounced him. Yet what he did was perfectly proper. He would have been a madman to have acted otherwise. The producers had agreed to stop the drill and limit the output to 15,000 barrels a day. Instead the regions proceeded immediately to produce 5,000 barrels a day more than was required by the market. The guaranteed price stimulated production. Independent refiners were buying oil for $2.50. Why should Rockefeller go on paying

$4? He had reserved the right to cancel and he used that right. The Producers' Association blew up. A few months later, as already pointed out, Rockefeller dissolved the National Refiners' Association and took his stand upon the historic conclusion that henceforth he would consolidate the refining interest by absorbing it rather than by entering into a voluntary association with it.

CHAPTER III. BUILDING STANDARD OIL

FOR THE next year Rockefeller devoted himself to building and strengthening his own organization from within. The times were troublous. The nation had been racing through one of the most feverish orgies of financial and public corruption and social extravagance in its history. Suddenly on September 18th, 1873, the great banking house of Jay Cooke and Company in Philadelphia closed its doors. It had been caught in the wreckage of the Northern Pacific scandal. A wave of fright ran through the whole business world. The New York Stock Exchange, for the first time in its history, closed its doors. The great panic of 1873 was on. All over the country business men talked in excited gestures of the great disaster. Stocks and bonds fell to ridiculous figures. Banking houses, brokerage houses, like Henry Clews and Company, manufactures went into bankruptcy.

Grain rotted at the sides of railroad tracks. Ships laden with wheat stood idle in New York harbor. Banks quit paying in currency. Scores of thousands were thrown out of work. Rumors of railroad wrecks filled the air. The oil towns read with a mixture of pleasure and fear that Thomas Scott, master of the Pennsylvania Railroad and of Pennsylvania, had had his notes go to protest. Bread lines formed in all cities. Collections were taken in the churches for the needy. In Cleveland every day brought news of new failures. Some 200 business houses closed their doors there in a short time. Rockefeller, with notes for great sums in every bank, kept close to his books.

Into the small three-room office of the Standard his tall figure appears noiselessly. Silence falls on the whole shop as his silk hat and frock coat are framed in the doorway.

"Good morning, gentlemen," he greets his office with the most meticulous formality. The bookkeeper slides from his high stool and pretends to work at a desk. Rockefeller mounts the stool, looks diligently over the ledgers, turning pages with a grave scrutiny. Then he lapses into thought and gazes out the window without seeing for fifteen minutes, before he slides down from his stool and goes into his private office.

Out of the fever of the depression rose all sort of agitations —labor leaders, socialists, anarchists, apostles of new cults, prophets of doom and of judgment. Among them Cleveland saw the most violent crusade the country had ever known against liquor. It was backed by the church people, though Rockefeller's Euclid Avenue Baptist Church took no part. But the movement swirled all around him and his office. A clergyman and a group of women assembled in front of the old Star Church and marched to Richards and Company, a saloon near Rockefeller's office in the Public Square. The women knelt on the sidewalk, prayed, and sang, "Nearer, My God, to Thee," entered the saloon, knelt on the floor, and read from the Scriptures. They went from saloon to saloon, calling on the proprietors to sign the pledge. Crowds growing in disorder followed them. One saloonkeeper followed with a buggy and beer kegs, passing out free beer. The women attacked their tormentors who returned the attack. For thirty days Cleveland was in a turmoil over this crusade. Rockefeller saw it rise with disapproval. He hated liquor, hoped to see the day when it would be extinguished. But he hated disorder too. And this was disorder.

The oil industry fell amid the depths. The Creek producers who had plotted for five-dollar crude saw it decline to two dollars and then to eighty-two cents a barrel. Refined oil which had sold for 22 to 26 cents in 1872 sagged to around 13 to 16 cents a gallon. The whole nation had sunk down exhausted at the end of its orgy.

II

STRONG men feed on depressions. Rockefeller now nailed down two important advantages for himself. He had been shipping his oil in tank cars over the New York Central to Hunter's Point, Long Island. There it was put into barrels for shipment to eastern points. The barrels were made there in his own cooperage.

BUILDING STANDARD OIL

The Erie Road had a similar plant at Weehawken, New Jersey. They called on Rockefeller to get some of his Eastern shipments.

"Why," said the plausible Mr. Rockefeller, "should I ship oil to your plant at Weehawken when I have my own plant at Hunter's Point? However, we will give you a portion of our oil if you will turn over your Weehawken plant to us so we can handle our own barreling and shipping."

"But," said the railroad, "what will we do about the oil of our other shippers which we now handle at that plant?"

"That will be quite simple," Mr. Rockefeller explained. "We will do the work for all other shippers. We will make the same charge you now make and out of the profit pay you a profit of ten cents on each barrel."

The Erie agreed and the Standard took over the Weehawken plant, thus controlling the terminal facilities of two railroads in New York. Now see the profound shrewdness of this move. Every barrel of oil shipped east by his rivals passed into his hands at Weehawken. Thus he came into possession of full information about the volume, character, and destination of their sales.

This led to the second advantage which he now obtained. The Erie deal produced irritation among the Central and Pennsylvania chiefs. A new rate war threatened. Col. Joseph Potts of the Empire Transportation Company, a Pennsylvania subsidiary, now interposed a friendly voice. We shall hear more of this Col. Potts. Now he warned the roads against another costly war and induced them to hold a conference to agree on some partition of the oil business among them. Rockefeller knew everything that went on behind the scenes and at once saw his chance.

We have seen how he feared the oil regions. He had to haul crude oil to Cleveland and then ship refined oil over a longer haul to New York. Now he saw his opportunity to wipe out this geographical advantage. While they were pondering Col. Potts' suggestion, Rockefeller appeared with the very same proposal. But he had another tucked away in it. He proposed that freight on refined oil to the east be the same no matter where the shipment started from. The suggestion was well baited. The rate on kerosene from Cleveland to New York was $2. From the regions it was $1.50. He urged that the rate on the regions be raised to

$2, which suited the roads. It was no more than just, he argued, as that would put all shipping points upon a just equality. But there was another little item in the plan. Before he could ship kerosene to New York he had to haul crude oil from the oil wells to Cleveland. That cost 50 cents a barrel and was a heavy handicap against him. He now proposed, to perfect this equality he talked of, that the railroads should practically haul crude oil from the regions to any refining point free. That is, he suggested that on every barrel of refined oil he shipped east he should have returned to him the freight he had paid on the crude needed to make that much refined oil. It took seven barrels of crude to make five barrels of kerosene. On every five barrels of kerosene shipped to New York he would have returned to him the freight he had paid on seven barrels of crude to Cleveland. The principle was to apply to every refining point. Thus the whole advantage enjoyed by the oil regions was wiped out at a blow. He was able to apply pressure to the roads at two points. First he threatened to move his oil industry away from Cleveland to the Creek. This forced the Central into line. Next he proposed that he would divide his shipment among all roads. Without Rockefeller it would not be possible to carry out an agreement for division of freight.

The new rate was announced for September, 1874. It was received in the oil towns with a growl of indignation. What strikes the observer, however, is the mildness of this outburst compared with former blasts. There was no public meeting—just a general grumbling. A group of twenty-eight producers met at Parker's Landing and protested. But, after all, the rates applied to the refiners, not the producers, and the refiners seemed too languid to act. There was no leadership and the rank and file were discouraged by their many "victories" from which this indomitable defeated man seemed always to rise with the prize.

III

WITH these new parts added to his machine, Rockefeller was now ready for his grand design. At the same time an event occurred which moved him mightily. To his house, with its three daughters, a son was born. "Always a John in the Rockefeller family," his father had said as he walked through the night with his own mother when the great oil man lay in his cradle on Michigan Hill. Now the next generation of Rockefellers was provided with its John—John Davison Rockefeller, Jr.

CHAPTER IV. THE GRAND DESIGN

ROCKEFELLER had an almost absolute monopoly of the oil business in his territory—Cleveland and the West. His business was in perfect order, almost completely integrated. He had wiped out the geographical advantage of the oil regions. He owned the eastern terminal facilities of two railroads and thus had an eye to the keyhole of his competitors. He had Flagler, Andrews, Payne, William Rockefeller, and Jabez Bostwick. But there remained outside a group of men of great ability—Charles H. Pratt and Henry H. Rogers of New York, John D. Archbold and Jacob J. Vandergrift of the regions, W. G. Warden of Philadelphia, Charles Lockhart of Pittsburgh. Now if he could bring all these men into a combination with himself at the head, a single, unified extension of the Standard Oil Company, which would do in New York, the regions, Philadelphia, and Pittsburgh what he had done in Cleveland, the oil industry of the nation would be in his hands. As organized at the time the refining interest of the country was distributed about as follows: New York, 15 refiners; Philadelphia, 12; Pittsburgh, 22; the oil regions, 27. There were some others in Baltimore, Erie, Boston, and a few other places. In Cleveland, of course, Rockefeller was supreme. He determined to bring all these into the Standard.

He began with Warden of Philadelphia and Lockhart of Pittsburgh. Lockhart, a Scotchman, was one of the foremost men in the industry. A successful merchant in Pittsburgh, he had seen a commercial use for oil as early as 1852. He was perhaps the first Pittsburgher, after Dr. Samuel Kier, to buy oil when Drake made his strike. He organized one of the first Pittsburgh refineries—Phillips, Frew & Company. He was the first American to sell oil in Europe. He went abroad with samples in 1860 and set in motion the vast export trade which was the chief support of his business. In 1865 he established a Philadelphia branch—Warden, Frew and Company, and this firm built the Atlantic Refinery, the beginning of the Atlantic Refining Company, the great Standard Oil concern of Pennsylvania. Thus Warden was Lockhart's partner and together they were the most powerful figures in Philadelphia and Pittsburgh. Rockefeller and Flagler pressed the plan on Lockhart and Warden. Rockefeller proposed first that Warden and Lockhart should come into the Standard—turn over their plants, take Standard stock in payment, and become Standard directors. He would induce Vandergrift, Pratt and Rogers, and Archbold to join on the same terms. Next he proposed that in each city these leaders would begin the acquisition of their smaller rivals as he had done in Cleveland. They would go frankly to those with whom they felt they could make an open offer to buy. In addition he suggested that an association be formed to be known as the Central, of which he would be president. Where caution was necessary this association should invite independent refiners to join as members. This would be a blind for ultimate absorption into the Standard. Lockhart was reluctant as was Warden. Warden, as an officer of the South Improvement Company, had borne the brunt of the heckling and probing at that time. Both were in the Refiners' Association. They were weary of the turmoil and brawling and struggle and wanted to go along in peace. The long beards which hung beneath their shaven lips were growing white. But Rockefeller was relentless. He pressed the argument with all the power of his shrewd and canny mind. During this period it was Rockefeller whose persuasive and overmastering plausibility in face-to-face argument was always used in great moments. But Warden and Lockhart were cautious. They visited Cleveland. They had their accountant go over the records of the Standard Oil Company. Both men had doubted Rockefeller's claims as to the price at which he could make kerosene. They asserted they were making it as cheaply as it could be done. But after weeks of examination and comparisons they learned to their amazement that Rockefeller was making kerosene so cheap that he could sell it to them at a profit at a price below their own costs. Rockefeller was making money. They were not. So they decided to go in with him.

Rockefeller and Flagler then went to New York where they got Pratt and Rogers and Archbold and Vandergrift to come into the plan. This was in the summer of 1874.

THE GRAND DESIGN

No time was lost reorganizing the Standard Oil Company, increasing its capital stock to absorb its new members and adding to its board that extraordinary group of men who were henceforth to direct its destinies. All the leadership in the oil industry was in that group—outside there was no leadership. Rockefeller had literally raided the oil business and confiscated all its brains.

The Standard Oil Company has always been spoken of as a combination of capital. It was that, but, far more important, it was a combination of brains. That was Rockefeller's great design. It was not an accident that a board of directors should have included so many brilliant business men. They did not just happen to come together. They were deliberately handpicked by a master assayist of human ability and put together cunningly, and in accordance with a plan. Moreover as fast as the Standard or its new leaders bought up an independent plant, the personnel of that plant was picked over for its best men to be retained in the combination.

Of course, all this was carried on behind the most profound secrecy. The public learned nothing of it all until the Spring of 1875. Then the New York *Tribune*, which always kept a sharp eye on the oil business, reported that an attempt to reorganize the refiners' association was being made through the Central Association with New York men as prime movers. A month later it warned of an attempt to "rehabilitate the South Improvement Company." It sent reporters to the oil men in Broad Street. Most of them thought the new plan would fail—the oil business was too big for any one man or group to control. What was actually being done was not yet suspected.

Meantime, in Pittsburgh Lockhart had been at work. He formed the Standard Oil Company of Pittsburgh with himself, Frew, Warden, Bushnell, and Flagler as directors. Thus his alliance with Rockefeller became known. He began buying and leasing his rivals. As in Cleveland the weak sisters quit with surprising facility. Some held out, but pressure was applied through railroads and pipe lines. Independent refiners could not get cars. Rates were rigged against them. They tried carrying oil by barges, but the pipe lines refused to run oil to the barges. Railroads refused to accept oil brought by barges. Lockhart bought his first competitor in 1875. By 1877 he had acquired his last. Two years later there was but one refiner in Pittsburgh who held out, of all the twenty-two in existence when Lockhart began. The Standard now had Cleveland and Pittsburgh.

In Titusville, John D. Archbold, the fiery young crusader against Rockefeller, appeared one day. He organized a new company—the Acme. Its ownership by the Standard was secret. But it began buying rivals. Archbold, destined to become one of the most ruthless of the Standard chiefs, used the well-tried Standard methods of persuasion. In three years the Acme had all the region plants. Two refineries remained—the Acme and the Imperial —and the Standard owned them both.

In New York, Henry H. Rogers was at work buying up the competitors of Charles Pratt and Company. He got many. But many held out. Here a real battle of the independents was threatened. When suddenly in the midst of these operations a new battle was precipitated—one of the most spectacular and dangerous ever waged by Rockefeller—the battle which was to put upon him for all time the mark of unconquerability.

CHAPTER V. THE BATTLE WITH THE EMPIRE

Rockefeller's battles hitherto had been against smaller rivals and disorganized producers. He was now to lock horns with an antagonist worthy of his steel, more powerful even than he, backed by money, political influence, and the moral support of a whole industry. This was the powerful Pennsylvania Railroad under the leadership of the resourceful Tom Scott. To understand this contest, however, one must know the story of the pipes.

I

The first carriers of oil were the teamsters, to be succeeded quite early by the pipe lines. The two pioneers in this field were Van Syckle and Harley. Van Syckle early ran into the tyranny of the teamsters and built his first pipe line to defy them. Armed guards had to be used to protect the pipes from the infuriated teamsters. But by the industry as a whole the innovation was hailed as the greatest thing since Drake's well. It was not long before Henry Harley was running oil seven miles from Pithole Creek to the Island well through the pipes of his Pennsylvania Transportation Company. Others began to operate—chiefly Col. Joseph Potts and Captain J. J. Vandergrift. And so the earliest pipe line promoters were Van Syckle, Harley, Vandergrift, and Potts. At first they merely piped oil from the wells to the railroads and Creek refineries, making one of the first great cuts in the cost of producing oil. They were in incessant war with the teamsters. In 1866 we find Harley calling on the governor to protect his pipes. The lines were cut, railroad cars burned, tanks set on fire, and an occasional teamster shot by the guards. Here was the perennial fight of the older order against the new.

By 1872 the Empire Transportation Company of Col. Potts and the Pennsylvania Transportation Company of Henry Harley began taking over the smaller lines. Thus the process of absorption which Rockefeller was carrying on among the refiners of Cleveland was going on among the pipe line companies of the oil regions. By this time the pipes were the one great gatherer of the regions and they had come pretty much under control of the railroads. Jay Gould had seen Harley, who was a civil engineer, a graduate of Troy Polytechnique Institute, had picked him as an able manager, and had bought a controlling interest in his Pennsylvania Transportation Company in 1868, making him general oil agent for the Erie. Joseph D. Potts was engaged in the early sixties to unify the freight services of the Pennsylvania Railroad and this led him to the pipe lines as the natural auxiliaries of the roads. He induced the Pennsylvania to buy Van Syckle's pipe line to Pithole. Potts was the first to issue pipe line certificates for credit balances of oil, a form of paper which was to become almost the same as currency in the regions. Thus his Empire Transportation Company and his lines were owned by the Pennsylvania.

Vandergrift got into the pipe line business when his partner became the receiver of the Oil City and Pithole Railroad. He laid pipes from West Pithole to Pithole to get his oil to the road. This he called the Star Pipe Line. He built other pipe lines until they became so numerous that he combined them all under the name of the United Pipe Lines. These three men therefore—Harley, Potts, and Vandergrift—dominated the situation in 1872.

There was still another figure. He was Daniel O'Day, a Clare County Irishman, who had been raised on a New York farm, had begun work as a freight handler and later was employed by Bostwick and Tilford as an oil buyer. This firm in reality belonged to the Standard and because of his Standard Oil connections, O'Day was almost mobbed during the 1872 oil war. After that war, Rockefeller decided he would have to have pipe lines of his own. Accordingly Bostwick commissioned O'Day to build a small line as a starter which was called the American Pipe Line. O'Day soon extended this to some 80 miles and then in 1875 ran his pipes into Bradford County. In 1874 Rockefeller bought a third interest in Vandergrift's United Pipe Lines and in two years, with the development of O'Day's lines, the Standard owned 40 per cent of the pipes of the regions.

Around 1874 there appeared another picturesque character, Dr. David Hostetter, the maker of Hostetter Bitters. He believed he could pipe oil to Pittsburgh, connect there with the Baltimore and Ohio Railroad and ship it to Baltimore. The B. & O. decided to make Baltimore the chief refining center, and cut its rates. In 1874 Philadelphia exported over 94,000 barrels of oil, Baltimore, 3,315. In a year Philadelphia exported 33,550, Baltimore 35,331. Hostetter, thus encouraged, formed the Columbia Conduit Company. He laid his pipes to within a few miles of the B. & O. tracks when he came to a point where he had to put his pipes under the Pennsylvania tracks. The Pennsylvania ran over a bridge at that point spanning a creek. Hostetter claimed he had bought the bed of the creek and put his pipes down. Next day Tom Scott sent a crew of men, tore up the pipes, and fortified their position. Oil producers, rallying to Hostetter's aid, marched in a body on the creek and drove off the defenders. The Pennsylvania force then returned with a sheriff and an armed posse and arrested thirty of the oil men for riot. None of the arrested men was tried. But a long litigation followed which disgusted Hostetter. He leased his line to three young men—B. D. Benson, David McKelvey, and Major Robert E. Hopkins of Titusville. They ran their oil to the bridge, pumped it into tank wagons, drove it over the tracks, and repiped it to Pittsburgh.

Thus the matter stood in 1876 when Rockefeller's great combination was moving toward completion. As already pointed out

THE BATTLE WITH THE EMPIRE

all the refineries of Cleveland and Pittsburgh and most of those in other places had been bought by Rockefeller. The last stand of the independents was in New York. At this point came the battle to which we have already alluded—the greatest of Rockefeller's career, the one which was to test his mettle as a militant general and which was to establish him finally at the goal he had set for himself—to be the absolute master of the oil industry of the world.

II

ONE MAN who looked upon the swift extinction of these independents with growing dismay was Col. Joseph D. Potts, of the Empire Transportation Company. If Rockefeller should succeed in getting all refineries in his grasp, the Pennsylvania Railroad Company and the Empire would be at his mercy. He could dictate rates and even drive the Empire out of business by merely withholding oil. With these fears in his heart Col. Potts went to Tom Scott, president, and Benjamin Cassatt, vice-president, of the Pennsylvania with a proposal that was to have far-reaching results. The only hope, argued Potts, for the Empire was to establish its own refineries as a guarantee of business for its pipes.

One day in New York Henry H. Rogers, busy gathering up his enfeebled rivals, learned with surprise that a New York refinery had sold out to Potts. Almost at the same time Lockhart in Philadelphia discovered that Potts had bought a refinery there. The two together had a capacity of 4,000 barrels a day. What did this mean? Rogers and Lockhart got in touch with Rockefeller. Was the Empire Transportation Company about to go into the refining business? Was the Pennsylvania Railroad to become a refiner of oil? Could it be that at the very moment when their grandiose plans were flowering so beautifully that so powerful and rich a corporation, backed by the puissant Tom Scott, who carried the Pennsylvania legislature in his pocket, was preparing to throw down the gage of battle to them?

In the presence of such a threat Rockefeller acted with that swiftness and resoluteness which characterized all his moves in a crisis. As he had hurried across the public square to Col. Payne four years before, he now went directly to Tom Scott and Cassatt. He protested. This was unfair. The Pennsylvania Railroad was a carrier. It had no business in the refining field. The Empire was a transportation company. It had no business manufacturing kerosene. Mr. Scott might have answered very pat that the Standard Oil Company was a refiner and had no business in the pipe line field. If he had Mr. Rockefeller would have been ready with his answer—the Standard owned no pipe lines. He always protested as much. Scott and Cassatt, however, stood their ground. Very well, said Rockefeller, it was most unfortunate, but the Standard Oil Company must take its own measures. Here was the threat of war—a threat with iron in it concealed under the air of sanctimonious regret with which it was uttered. The news leaked out among rail leaders. Vanderbilt of the Central, Jewett of the Erie, hurried to Scott. They urged Scott to recede. After all, this was not a fair form of railroad war. Rockefeller again urged Scott to reconsider his decision. A war would be so costly to every one and yet there seemed no other way unless Mr. Scott decided to take his railroad out of the refining business. This time Rockefeller, a persuasive negotiator, made an impression on Cassatt. Cassatt went to Potts. He pictured to Potts the alternative to surrender. It meant war—war with an antagonist who had hitherto proved himself indomitable, war that would cost millions. He urged Potts to sell the refineries or at least lease them to Rockefeller. But Potts was adamant. The man was one of those who hated with all the fury of his Presbyterian soul the new era of corporate industry for which Rockefeller stood. He could grow eloquent as a preacher talking of it. And so Scott had to tell Rockefeller that they had decided not to yield.

That settled the matter. It was war and Rockefeller immediately summoned around him all those brilliant and resourceful men he had been so patiently recruiting. Almost at the same time he sent word to the New York Central and the Erie that he expected them to stand with him in the coming battle. Then he struck his first blow immediately. He cut the price of kerosene in every market where Potts' refineries sold their kerosene.

But Potts too was a resolute and resourceful foe. He was also a man of imagination, inflamed now by what seemed a kind of providential commission to strike the thing he hated so much. He went out at once to organize the independent oil refiners. He moved also to bring the oil producers to his side. He began to build a large refining interest. Before long he had more refineries, tank cars, ships, wharves, and barges—the whole paraphernalia of a vast manufacturing and distributing machine. Here was the foe Rockefeller feared. Here was the man of imagination and brains who was *not* brought into his combination—the man of brains backed by great wealth, a great railroad, the sentiment of the unconquered portion of the industry, and the political power of the state. Here was a threat which must be met without ruth and without quarter or all his great dreams would crumble like a house of cards.

In reply to the cutting of rates on the Central and the Erie the Pennsylvania also cut its rates and it did so with a vengeance. Cassatt admitted later that the road paid back in rebates in some cases more than it received in freight. In one case it carried oil to New York at eight cents a barrel less than nothing. In other words, it actually paid men for the privilege of hauling their oil.

Potts was busy everywhere. At some stations his famous green cars were cheered. Men looked at them roll by as they would army trucks going into action. He himself worked feverishly to unite all independents in a powerful defensive combination. It was not easy. They were weak sisters and Rockefeller's ruthless price cutting wherever they had a footing produced consternation among them. The refiners lost vast sums. Scott and Cassatt became a little alarmed when they saw the huge losses inflicted on their road. Then a heavy blow fell on them.

The element of luck cannot be said to have played a very decisive and controlling part in the achievements of John D. Rockefeller. But now Fate struck a blow on his side. In July the Baltimore and Ohio Railroad ordered a ten per cent wage cut and its engineers and firemen walked out. At Martinsburg they drove strike breakers from their locomotives. Governor Carroll called out the militia and rioting followed in which thirty or forty persons were wounded and about nine killed. Four years before the Pennsylvania had cut wages ten per cent. In June Scott ordered another ten per cent reduction. In spite of much grumbling the reduction was accepted. Then in July, while disorder paralyzed the B. and O., the Pennsylvania increased the length of its freight trains from eighteen to thirty-six cars without increasing its crews. The trainmen walked out and in a few days there was a general railroad strike throughout the East. Mobs attacked and destroyed Pennsylvania Railroad property in Pittsburgh. Governor Hartranft sent troops from Philadelphia and a pitched battle was fought at the roundhouse, soldiers killing twenty, wounding thirty (three children) on the first volley. A wave of anger and horror swept over the country. The soldiers were driven into the roundhouse and the strikers sent in after them cars of blazing whiskey and oil. The roundhouse was burned and with it the union depot, grain elevators, Adams Express, and other buildings. Governor Hartranft personally led 3,000 troops to Pittsburgh to compel peace. He succeeded but not until twenty-five people were killed and 1,383 cars, 104 locomotives, and 66 passenger coaches burned.

The losses to the Pennsylvania Railroad were appalling. Scott and Cassatt were almost crushed. For the first time in its history the road had to pass its dividend. Its stock fell to 27. Scott, Cassatt, and Potts looked at their powerful enemy and saw him prospering in spite of the battle. The Standard made money everywhere. Potts' independents were facing bankruptcy. Everywhere they pressed for business there was a Standard agent and as fast as Potts cut the price of kerosene, the Standard cut lower.

In August Scott and Cassatt called on Rockefeller. They had decided to sue for peace and they had to go to Mr. Rockefeller with their hats in their hands. They went to Cleveland and to Rockefeller, Flagler, and Warden and declared they were ready to give up the fight. Rockefeller made his terms. The Empire Company must give up its refineries to the Standard Oil Company. Scott and Cassatt returned to Philadelphia to break the news to Potts. That heroic warrior was almost frantic with disappointment and rage. He refused to surrender. Thereupon Scott informed him mournfully that the Pennsylvania Railroad had a contract under which it could buy the entire Empire plant at any time. The road, he now announced, formally exercised that option. The blow fell on Potts with crushing force. News of these negotiations got out and financial, oil, and business circles buzzed with rumors. Later Rockefeller and Flagler went to Philadelphia for Scott's answer. It was ready. The Pennsylvania would exercise its option to buy the Empire. It would turn the refineries over to the Standard. The railroad did not want the pipe lines. So Mr. Rockefeller replied that he would take the pipe lines too and the railroad might have the cars.

THE BATTLE WITH THE EMPIRE

The final agreement was reached in October and on the seventeenth of that month the entire business which Potts had reared—refineries, pipe lines, tanks, wharves, ships, everything—were handed over to Mr. John D. Rockefeller. That victorious gentleman was not present in person to receive them. But in Potts' office in Girard Street, at midnight, William Rockefeller, Flagler, Lockhart, Pratt, Bostwick, Daniel O'Day, and J. J. Vandergrift and their counsel received the sword of the defeated Potts. The purchase price was $3,400,000 and the Standard envoys handed over to Col. Potts a check for $2,500,000 as the cash payment. As John D.'s victorious plenipotentiaries filed out into the night Col. Potts found himself in his office alone. The strong jaw muscles under his close-cropped beard tightened, the shaven upper lip pressed down, his arms spread out before him on his desk, his head sank on his arms and he wept. In Cleveland at his Euclid Avenue home, Mr. Rockefeller got a wire announcing completion of the surrender. His prayer of thanksgiving that night must have been more than usually fervent. Had not the Lord God of Abraham, who had divided the Red Sea to drown the Egyptians and covered the land with locusts and sent a murrain upon the horses of Pharaoh, now sent a general strike to confound his enemies?

"I have pursued mine enemies and overtaken them; neither did I turn until they were consumed."

III

When the news of this disaster to the powerful Pennsylvania Railroad reached the oil trade a tremor of despair ran through it. Men talked as if all were over. The Empire pipe lines were added to the others in Vandergrift's system and all combined into one great system, called the United Pipe Lines. As soon as Dr. Hostetter heard the news he hurried to Rockefeller with an offer to sell. Rockefeller took the Columbia Conduit Company and so by the end of the year 1878 he had the entire pipe line business in his hands.

At the same time he brought the railroads together in a new oil freight pool. This time the Baltimore and Ohio came in with the Pennsylvania, the Erie, and the Central. The Pennsylvania got a guarantee of 21 per cent of the traffic to New York and 26 per cent to Philadelphia.

THE GREAT CONSUMMATION

Rebates and drawbacks were not overlooked in this new deal. A rebate of 10 cents a barrel was reserved for all Rockefeller oil. On the side he forced from the Erie an agreement for a drawback of 20 cents a barrel on all oil shipped by competitors. There were still a few scattered operators and this provision was for the purpose of keeping the opposition weak and helpless. In February, 1879, Rockefeller demanded the same drawback from the Pennsylvania. The demand was made by O'Day upon Cassatt in a letter. Cassatt at first demurred. But O'Day exhibited receipted bills from the Erie proving his claim. O'Day did not request. He demanded. And Cassatt agreed.

The refiners, chiefly in New York, who had held out on the hope of Potts' success, now collapsed. In New York they went directly into Rockefeller's bag. In Baltimore they were gathered into a new company called the Baltimore United Oil Company of which J. N. Camden was made president. He had been the head of the Camden Consolidated Company of Parkersburg, West Virginia, a Standard ally.

As 1878 dawned Rockefeller's ambition was realized. The entire oil business of America—refining and gathering—was in his hands, the most complete monopoly that had yet been built in American industry.

PART SIX
GATHERING STORMS

CHAPTER I. THE VOICE OF SCANDAL

AT THE end of six years of incessant and relentless war, with rivals and enemies on all sides, Mr. Rockefeller found himself at 39, the master of the nation's greatest industry, but also the target for its bitterest shafts of criticism. Since 1872 he had been a mark for criticism, but it was such as a man hears little of, that goes from mouth to mouth, and was directed chiefly at his business battles. Now he was to see gather around him those clouds of personal abuse—endless denunciations, attacks upon his character and his integrity, his religious sincerity, his family; attacks by courts, criminal and civil, legislatures, congress, grand juries, and the press, which now began to recognize him as one of our performing celebrities.

To these attacks he opposed one weapon only—silence. There is little doubt that John D. Rockefeller looked with complete approval upon his whole plan up to this point. He had done nothing for which his conscience irked him. If he had sinned it was to be ruthless in carrying out his plans. Like every great commander in history he had not shrunk from his purposes because here and there they involved human suffering on the part of those who lagged behind in the march of progress. Mr. Rockefeller, who found no time for reading books, was an industrious reader of his Bible. There he found plenty to comfort him. Was not Jehovah himself ruthless in pursuing his righteous plans? Did not the Lord turn a river into blood and cover the land with frogs? Did not Moses turn the dust into lice and flies, and cover men and beasts with boils? Did he shrink from these necessary stratagems because weak men suffered? Rockefeller's soul was more shocked and appalled by the inefficiency and waste of business than by the plight of the occasional struggler who fell by the wayside as his juggernaut moved forward.

As he read his Bible one wonders if he ever paused on the story of Moses, whose wisdom was lost upon the Pharaoh because he was slow of speech and slow of tongue. And the Lord sent him Aaron and said, "Thus shalt thou put words into his mouth; and I will be with thy mouth . . . and will teach you what you shall do. And he shall be thy spokesman unto the people; and he shall be unto thee instead of a mouth" (Exodus 4:15).

The subject of public relations hardly occurred to Rockefeller at all. He had marched forward in the mechanics of business. But he lagged hopelessly behind many other men in his understanding of the new human elements which entered the problem. Public Opinion and its might he understood not at all. He went on believing that the oil business, even though he should get it all in his grasp, was his own private business and was none of the public's business at all. He withdrew behind his righteousness and let his enemies howl. The mistake he made was in failing to see the importance of selling, not merely his oil to the public, but his company as well as himself in the bargain.

This was not because publicity was unknown. It must not be supposed that publicity and propaganda is the invention of the last score of years. The art was well understood at that time and there were business men, too, who knew well enough the importance and power of Public Opinion. The great banker, Jay Cooke, knew it and kept a score of newspaper men and editors on his pay roll. Politicians had already understood its importance. Boss Tweed knew it well enough and when he fell some eighty newspapers in New York collapsed. The newspapers, in fact, were for the most part like their European contemporaries, subsidized by politicians. Business interests did the same thing. The method was crude. They handed out money to editors and reporters and in some cases bought newspapers or actually financed them. Tom Scott owned the New York *World* and when he unloaded it, it passed into the hands of Jay Gould. Tilden's advisers recommended distributing from $3,000 to $10,000 a month among thirty newspaper men in New York. The United States Bank at an earlier day had dispensed its thousands among countless editors. The Standard itself was charged with the use of money to defeat the pipe line scheme of Henry Harley and General Haupt. In this case, however, it was not so much Public Opinion Rockefeller dealt with. He used the papers as the readiest means of reaching a definite group of people whose lands were sought by General Haupt and Henry Harley. Rockefeller sought to block their plan of securing rights of way over these lands by throwing suspicion on the credit of Haupt and Harley.

What Rockefeller did not know anything at all about was the modern art of ballyhoo. That art too was already understood. J. Cooke in selling the stock and bonds of the Northern Pacific did things little different from the real estate boosters of California and Florida. Newspapers, lecturers, pamphlets, books, exhibitions, told the story of the gay and tropic luxuriance of what came to be called his Banana Belt in the Northwest and J. Proctor Knott rendered himself famous by his satirical speech in Congress on Duluth, "The Zenith City of the Unsalted Seas."

If he remained silent it was not, however, because he did not often wince under the lashings of public denunciation and scorn. Many years later, speaking to William Hoster, an American reporter in France, of these early troubles, Mrs. Rockefeller sighed: "Those were days of worry."

"I don't know how we came through them," said Rockefeller. "You know how often I had not an unbroken night's sleep, worrying about how it was all coming out. All the fortune I have made has not served to compensate for the anxiety of that period. Work by day and worry by night, week in and week out, month after month. If I had foreseen the future I doubt whether I would have had the courage to go on. . . . I had no ambition to make a fortune. Mere money making has never been my goal. I saw a marvelous future for our country, and I wanted to participate in the work of making our country great. I had an ambition to build."

Very little has happened in Rockefeller's life save by plan, certainly none of the important events. We may be reasonably sure that the amassing of the great fortune was something more than a mere incident.

II

Thus while scandal and gossip loaded Rockefeller's name with infamy he did nothing. Every man who failed in the oil business had a tale to tell of how John D. Rockefeller had crushed him. Men who sold out to him whispered around how they had been squeezed; how the screws had been turned; how Rockefeller had forced them to sell their plants at a mere fraction of what they had put into them.

One such story which poured over his name a peculiarly bitter sauce was the tale of Mrs. Backus, "the lone widow of fatherless children," who, the story ran, was duped by Rockefeller into selling a business worth $200,000 for $79,000. Twenty years later Lloyd told it and thirty years later Ida Tarbell repeated it in her brilliant indictment of Standard Oil.

The story as told made an ugly one. F. M. Backus, a lubricating oil pioneer of Cleveland, died in 1874. After his death his widow for four years operated the business, making profits of more than $25,000 a year. After 1877, when the Standard Oil went into the lubricating business, Mrs. Backus saw that continuance of her company was hopeless. She wished to sell but refused to treat with any one save Rockefeller personally. She appealed to him "as the mother of fatherless children" to deal fairly with her. "He promised," she said, "with tears in his eyes, that he would stand by me," and added that "all he wanted was a controlling interest in the stock of her company." She asked $200,000, "much below what the stock was worth." The Standard offered her $79,000 and at this figure she sold. She asked to retain $15,000 worth of the stock. The answer was a rude "no!" Later, when she threatened to make the whole transaction public, Rockefeller wrote offering to return the plant or give what stock she wanted. The circumstances made a strong appeal to public sympathy—the defenseless widow, the helpless orphans, the command to "get out or be crushed," the confiscation of her property at a third of its value.

The chief gravamen of the charge against Rockefeller was that he took a valuable business at a third of its value and duped the helpless victim into submission. Looking over all the evidence now it is clear that there is not one iota of evidence to support Mrs. Backus' valuation of $200,000. Two years before, when the business was prosperous, she was willing to sell to a Mr. Rose for "considerably less." Rockefeller declared he could duplicate the entire plant for $20,000. Miss Ida Tarbell, pressing this charge against Rockefeller, conceded that the physical reconstruction of the plant might well have been possible at one-third the price at which it sold. But what, she asks, of the good will of a business that was yielding $25,000 to $35,000 a year? One may ask what is the good will of business which is threatened with ruin? If the physical plant was worth only $20,000, then the good will must have been valued at $40,000. This is nothing less than defending a capitalization at three times the actual value and this is precisely what Jay Gould and Daniel Drew and other freebooters were doing with the railroads and what other predatory promoters did later with industry. This became infamous under the picturesque name of "watering stock." Among the charges brought against Rockefeller this one has never been included. When the Steel Corporation was formed men got three and four times the value of their plants in watered stock. Rockefeller always refused to engage in this indefensible policy.

Mrs. Backus was represented in her negotiations by Charles H. Marr, her attorney, and Mr. Maloney, her superintendent. Marr swore later that Mrs. Backus furnished the Standard an itemized estimate of her assets; that the whole statement amounted to $150,000, not $200,000. The item "works, good will and successorship" was put down at $71,000. The rest was made up of oil on hand, cash, accrued dividends, and bills receivable. Rockefeller bought from her only three things—the works and good will and the oil. The former, which she put down at $71,000, he offered $60,000 for. The oil he bought separately for $19,000. The rest Mrs. Backus retained. The real difference between what she asked and what Mr. Rockefeller paid was the difference between $71,000 and $60,000—not so great a discrepancy.

As to duping her, Mr. Marr declared he conferred with her throughout the negotiations and she seemed well pleased with the price. She pictured herself as forced to sell to Rockefeller, yet she was hunting a purchaser for two years. Indeed all the evidence is against the story as told. There is not a shred of support for it save the "re-iterated statements of an embittered woman who feeds her children on the story three times a day," as her brother-in-law described it. Yet this tale was used with immense effect to tarnish Rockefeller's name.

III

PATIENCE and ruthlessness and remorseless logic—these were Rockefeller's resistless weapons in all the negotiations carried on at this time. He made no secret of his intention to monopolize the business. He told more than one man that the Standard Oil Company alone could remain in the refining business. Having set this mark, he was relentless in moving on to it. His method was always the same. He told his competitor he must sell—always in tones of simplicity, directness, and sympathetic benevolence. He looked the man squarely in the eye, with an intentness that was disconcerting, coldly boring into him like steel. But he used words of courteous and gentle kindness. The situation was desperate, he explained. The business could no longer go on as it had. Ruin faced every man in it. No one could carry on successfully but the Standard. He had shown that. He had ways of making the business go. The man had a chance to get out now. He could sell. Mr. Rockefeller would send around appraisers and give him cash or Standard Oil stock for the amount. Take Standard Oil stock, he would urge. If you do the day will come when you will be independent. Take Standard stock and "your family will never know want." He believed this. But his rivals didn't. He had boundless confidence in the oil industry. They had none. Most of them took cash. Those who took Standard stock became wealthy. But most of them took cash. They believed the oil business doomed. Yet they insisted on putting enormous valuations on their profitless plants in a doomed business for "good will." When Rockefeller refused to pay more than the actual value of their refineries they denounced him for his squeeze. But he gave them all their chance to come in with him. When they refused to sell he was adamant. He never permitted circumstances to soften him. He had a plan—he was almost the only man of his day who had. And he had the courage of the great commander who does not shrink back from the sometimes cruel need incident to carrying a great plan forward.

CHAPTER II. SIGNS OF REVOLT

In the midst of Rockefeller's grandiose plans James H. Hopkins, a representative from Pittsburgh, introduced into the House of Representatives in April, 1876, a bill "to regulate Commerce and prohibit unjust discriminations by Common Carriers." America, committed whole-heartedly to the principle of individualism and its hand-maiden *laissez faire* and the efficacy of the "laws of trade" as regulators of business, found something had gone wrong with those laws. Large scale business had made its appearance everywhere. Men had begun to collect together in corporations. The individualistic public seemed powerless against them. The laws of trade, too, seemed to be impotent to hinder them. Little business men as well as the public demanded protection. Leaders continued to mouth about individualism and to cry out for collectivism.

Thirty years before this New Hampshire had named a railroad commission (1844). Between 1853 and 1858, Connecticut, Vermont, and Maine established commissions. They were merely to protect the public against accidents, fires, and the killing of cows on the track. But in 1867 the National Grange of Husbandry pressed its program and got laws for state regulation passed in Illinois, Iowa, Wisconsin, Missouri, Kansas, Nebraska, and Minnesota. Massachusetts in 1869 named a commission to supervise roads in their relations with shippers. But its only weapon was publicity at a time when the methods of publicity were little known.

Meantime railroad abuses multiplied and shocked the country. The roads were in the hands of crooked promoters. The Erie with assets of $65,000,000 had outstanding $155,000,000 of stocks and $25,000,000 of bonds. Vanderbilt, Drew, Gould, Fiske, and others pressed their audacious and picaresque promotions amid the bribery of lawmakers and editors. One reads a harrowing account of these villainies in an address delivered by John Livingston entitled "The Perils of a Nation." Curiously enough, it was delivered at Owego, New York, John D. Rockefeller's old home, September 22nd, 1871. Every public official carried a free pass.

Pennsylvania and New York prohibited passes but the Pennsylvania Railroad ignored the law. Tom Scott, when some of his shareholders opposed the further use of these petty bribes, replied, "With passes I could carry out desirable purposes." Bribery was general. Jay Gould spent a million dollars on the New York legislature to get through a single bill. Railroad barons discriminated in favor of localities in which they were interested. Unfair rates, rebates, price wars, robbed shippers and stockholders. And while the roads lost countless millions their managers grew wealthy. They used the roads as if they owned them outright and without any thought of the public's right in their services. Slowly the public which had been schooled to believe that government should not attempt to do anything about such matters began to feel that in some way something must be done. In 1872 the Windom Committee was named to investigate railroad abuses. It recommended a limited form of railroad ownership, which merely alarmed the railroad barons a little.

Then in 1876 Hopkins introduced his bill to regulate the roads and added a resolution for an investigating committee. All during April petitions poured into Congress from business men in Pittsburgh for relief. The Pittsburgh Chamber of Commerce added its appeal. Hopkins presented supporting petitions from business men bearing nearly 1,800 signatures. In May Hopkins asked unanimous consent to have his resolution considered. A congressman arose and objected. He was the Honorable Henry B. Payne, father of Col. Oliver Hazzard Payne, treasurer of the Standard Oil Company. Then Payne went to Hopkins and suggested that if he would alter his resolution to have the probe made by the Committee on Commerce instead of a "select committee of five" he would not object. Hopkins agreed, but again his resolution was blocked. Some days later Representative James Wilson, of Iowa, later to become famous as Secretary of Agriculture, offered the resolution. This time it was passed by a substantial majority. Why did Standard Oil want the change made?

The Committee on Commerce met. There at the side of the chairman, Hon. Frank Hereford of West Virginia, sat Mr. J. N. Camden, also of West Virginia, as his adviser. Camden was head of the Camden Oil Company, then owned by Rockefeller. The Committee summoned railroad chiefs and Standard Oil heads.

All save two, Benjamin Cassatt and Col. Oliver H. Payne, ignored the Committee's summons. And they refused to produce their papers. Representative Wilson denounced the Committee for its surrender to this defiance. E. G. Patterson, president of the Producers' Union, told the shippers his side of the story. And there was one other witness. He was Frank Rockefeller, John D.'s youngest brother, interested at the time in the Pioneer Oil Company. This was the first public act in the feud of these brothers which lasted practically their whole lives. Frank Rockefeller charged there was a pool of rates and a system of discriminatory rebates. He was on solid ground here. But he went further and charged that the rebates were split between the railroad officials and Standard Oil. Tom Scott indignantly denied this in Pittsburgh and Frank was forced to admit that he was expressing just a suspicion. In the end Payne and Camden routed the Hopkins bill into the committee's pigeonhole.

About the same time a free pipe line bill and anti-discrimination bill was being smothered in the Pennsylvania legislature. But the subject was too urgent to be kept down. Two years later a bill prepared by E. G. Patterson, president of the Producers' Union, and introduced by Louis F. Watson, of Warren County, came finally out of committee, named after Representative John F. Reagan of Texas. The Reagan bill prohibited rebates, drawbacks, discriminations, required publication of rates and equality in rates between localities. "States rights," cried a few unthinking enemies. But the railroad and the oil lobby remained away. The bill passed November 11th, 1878. The oil regions rejoiced. But Mr. Rockefeller and Mr. Scott were not worried. The bill never reached the floor of the Senate. The Producers' Committee reported sadly that "our present lawmakers are ignorant, corrupt, and unprincipled and under control of monopolies"—a verdict which history was to vindicate.

CHAPTER III. THE STORM SPREADS

OILDOM read in the *Derrick* September 19th that Rockefeller had whipped the Pennsylvania and gobbled the Empire. Five days later a call went out from the Grand Organizer of the Producers' Protective Association—"Call a meeting of the unions early next week. Get your canvassers to work. The last crowning infamy of the monopoly has roused up all producers to strike for free trade and equal rights in oil transportation." The organization of secret lodges was pressed and the *Derrick*, boldly telling the producers they were themselves to blame, declared their salvation lay in these lodges. But somehow B. D. Armstrong, the Grand Organizer, had to admit a kind of languor hung upon the oil men. However, by November 21st, delegates from the lodges met at Titusville in what they called the Parliament of Petroleum. There were, they proclaimed, 172 delegates of 2,000 producers representing an invested capital of $75,000,000.

They sat in secrecy for three days. Reporters came from many Eastern cities, but were kept out. December 11th they assembled again behind closed doors. Then the editor of the *Derrick* summarized their plans. They were to form a strong organization; restrict the drill, lease all oil land possible; make an arrangement between refiners and producers. Other plans soon developed. Benson, McKelvey, and Hopkins proposed a pipe line to the sea. Louis J. Emery, Jr., was organizing a new pipe line to Buffalo. The Parliament resolved to support both these plans.

The pipe line to the sea was an old dream. Benson, McKelvey, and Hopkins, who directed Dr. Hostetter's Columbia Conduit Company, now worked to revive it, and they engaged General Haupt to survey the route from Brady's Bend to Baltimore. Their organization was complete in January and the Grand Council adopted the project and named B. B. Campbell and C. V. Culver, chiefly famous for his hectic chain bank failure, to represent it on the directorate. To carry it out a free pipe line law was necessary and a bill was introduced into the Pennsylvania legislature supported by a petition with 8,000 signatures. Immediately opposition broke out which was cleverly exploited by the Rockefeller interests. The New York *Tribune* said the bill and the seaboard pipe line was backed by Belgian and German refiners. Philadelphia was against it. A seaboard pipe line would mean a loss of two million a year to the Pennsylvania Railroad and Philadelphia had millions invested in that road. The Philadelphia Commercial Exchange adopted resolutions opposing the bill. The Pittsburgh Chamber of Commerce adopted a memorial to the legislature to defeat the bill. Region producers instantly countered with a threat to boycott Pittsburgh merchants. Those gentlemen promptly published cards in the oil region papers repudiating the Chamber's action and then the perplexed Chamber rescinded its resolution. April 17th the free pipe line bill passed the House by a big majority and the oil regions cheered. But too soon. The Standard Oil was busy. Its agents circulated petitions against the bill. The oil industry, they said, employs 260,000 men in Pennsylvania. This project will ruin Pennsylvania's oil business and hand it over to Europe. May 9th the Pennsylvania Senate killed the bill.

Meantime the seaboard pipe line promoters were busy everywhere. We find Benson in Philadelphia seeking funds and reporting progress. Baltimore papers record the presence of General Haupt buying 300 acres on Curtis Creek for refineries and tanks and announcing that he has secured right of way over 230 miles from Butler to Curtis Creek.

The other project backed by the Parliament of Petroleum was the Equitable Petroleum Company, a pipe line from the Bradford Field to Buffalo, promoted by Louis J. Emery, Jr. The oil piped to Buffalo would then be run to New York by the Erie Canal. Emery was a resourceful organizer and on August 7th, 1878, he sent his first shipment by canal into New York City—nearly 2,000,000 gallons—five boat loads, piped 80 miles from Bradford to Frisbie Station on the Buffalo and McKeon Railroad, then to Larabie on the Buffalo, New York, and Philadelphia. There it was pumped from tanks on flat cars to canal boats. In the *Tribune* we read that New York City refineries have a fleet of twenty boats and expect to bring in about 1,500 barrels a day. Emery hoped soon to be carrying 6,000 barrels a day. One wonders, if the Standard had such a monopoly, where the refineries were to take this oil? The simple truth is that producers were very much in the dark about the refineries. Rockefeller had far more in his hands than they dreamed.

A few months later the seaboard pipe line organization was completed. It was called the Tidewater Pipe Line Company, Ltd., with B. D. Benson as president and R. E. Hopkins as treasurer and in the first week of 1879 the first construction contracts were let.

II

WHILE these plans were maturing the Producers' Association, after months of secret meetings, launched the American Petroleum Company on Christmas Eve, 1878. This was a corporation with 200,000 shares at $10 each. They were to be sold twice a week in lots of 100. The managers put one amazing feature into that corporation. It put one-half of the capital "in trust" for the purpose "to secure control of the company and the maintenance of its agreed policy." This was four years before the Standard Oil Trust was formed. Sales of this American Petroleum Company stock went forward with a good prospect of success.

Here, then, were three definite plans under way. But despite the optimism of many, a rift appeared in the Producers' Union. In June, 1878, B. D. Armstrong, Grand Organizer, had told the *Derrick* the outlook was far from bright; that the union had not met its expectations; that the seaboard pipe line had divided the sentiment of the producers; that there were 5,000,000 barrels' surplus oil and that the time was not far when Chinamen would be working in the regions at fifty cents a day and, above all, if the producers succeeded in driving Rockefeller out, oil would go to fifty cents a barrel. For this exhibition of treasonable pessimism the Grand Council abolished the job of Grand Organizer and detached the gloomy Mr. Armstrong from the service.

But Armstrong was not the only pessimist. The oil towns were full of weak sisters. In middle November the New York *Sun* reported that the producers were actually in conference with Rockefeller in New York about a compromise. Mr. G. H. Nesbit, of Petrolia, one of the conferees, said to the *Tribune:* "The persons in conference are large producers but do not pretend to represent the union, though several are members of the general council." They discussed restraining production, fixing prices, ending freight discriminations. Rates were still the chief grievance, the independents paying $1.40 from Parker's Landing, the Standard Oil 20 cents. Immediately the Grand Council repudiated the conferees. But the conferring producers went on and after Christmas published a card in the *Derrick* that they proposed a joint commission of producers and refiners to deal with their troubles and called on producers to instruct their delegates to the Grand Council how to act.

Then it was learned that all the conferences had been begun at the instigation of Rockefeller. The rift between the compromisors and the die-hards widened. In March, 1879, when things seemed rosiest for the new pipe lines, Oil City producers proposed a conference with the refiners. The Grand Council voted it down, whereupon the Oil City crowd went to New York to the offices of the Standard Oil. Rockefeller asked for time to prepare a plan. Meantime the American Petroleum Company was opening offices all over the oil regions. But the price of crude oil sank lower—a dollar in January; 95 cents in March; 75 cents in May. In June the implacable *Derrick* called attention to the fact that when the P. P. A. came into existence oil was selling at $2.25 a barrel and is now selling at 70 cents. It intimated that "the producers should take hold of their organization and run it in their interests and not in the interests of pipe lines, oil storers and lawyers." This was the last blast of the heroic little paper on the side of the independents. Its story must come later.

III

"NEVER since the good times of Pithole and the Creek has there been such activity and life," said the *Derrick* in 1876. Oil stocks were being reduced and oil went to four dollars a barrel. Now in 1878 it was down to 70 cents. The higher prices had resulted in furious wild-catting. New fields were opened in McKean County, Pennsylvania, and Cattaraugus, New York. Just as the wheat was ripening in Summit City a wild cat hit oil. The magic cry of "Oil!" sounded as it had at Pithole. In a year a busy wicked city of 12,000 defaced the trampled wheat fields. In two weeks a pasture lane was a street in a town lined with buildings. Land was held at five dollars a front foot and every other door led to a gin mill selling tanglefoot whiskey with dancing partners for the unregenerate. A young man with $25 bought a farm; $20 down, $5,000 in thirty days, $5,000 in six months. Five days later a well came in on the adjoining land. The young speculator refused $20,000 for the farm. Three weeks later another big well spouted on the other side. The youth sold the farm for $110,000. In a year the oil languished, the walking beams slowed down and quit, the adventurers drifted away and soon Summit City joined Pithole and the other ghost towns of Oildom.

But it was the outpouring in the Bradford Field which wrecked four-dollar oil. Early in 1877 northern McKean County became the center of attention. Drillers flocked there as they did into Venango in '59. Rockefeller in New York saw his plans menaced. Just as he had completed his capture of the old oil regions, here was a new oil region, where, perhaps, he would have to repeat all over his laborious conquest of the last few years. With what Ida Tarbell called "surpassing intelligence, energy and courage," Rockefeller rushed the construction of pipes into Bradford. Oil gushed forth in an uncontrolled flood. Producers met at Oil City to consider "a plan to retire oil from the market with a view to keeping up the price"—a plan to circumvent those laws of trade they worshiped so devoutly when they were lashing out at Rockefeller. The *Derrick* implored the producers to cease drilling. It pointed to one farm which had a single lease and a single derrick, being split into 17 leases and 17 derricks. By December, 1878, the Rockefeller pipe line warned that daily runs of oil exceeded shipments by 22,000 barrels in the oil regions. This seems an exaggeration, yet so I find it recorded. The pipe line managers warned the producers. They met to devise some plan for storing oil. Failures multiplied. That month $50,000 of oil paper went to protest. Oil flowed on the ground. Whose fault was this? The only remedy open to the producers was to restrict production. But this they resolutely refused to do. Sixteen hundred wells pumped petroleum into the mounting deluge and while friends urged curtailment, 500 new wells were being drilled. Pledges for a six months' shutdown were distributed but never signed. The region papers hammered away. Producers put $21,787 a day into the ground more than they were taking out, cried the *Derrick*. "Oil covers the ground," it said two weeks later, "yet the drill bounces merrily on." "While a writ of Quo Warranto against the pipe lines

THE STORM SPREADS

may do some good," said a Parker's Landing daily, "a writ of Quo Shut Down Drilling against every sea-cook in the business would be an act to be commended." A meeting of producers in June refused to agree to a shutdown. But the leaders railroaded through this resolution:

"Whereas, the shortest way to $2 oil is through 25-cent oil, therefore be it

RESOLVED that we favor pushing the drill as rapidly and diligently as possible until the goal of 25-cent oil is reached."

In the midst of all this we hear the lash of the landowner's whip—the royalty owner who, when drillers were willing to curtail, demanded that they go on under the terms of their leases.

Yet the producers had the notion that as long as they chose to go on with this stupid and destructive course the Standard Oil Company ought to go on paying them the best prices for their oil, as if there were no "sacred laws of trade" and, what is more, providing pipe lines in which they might store their worse than useless flood. From this futile illusion they were rudely awakened in July when Jabez Bostwick issued an order that no more oil would be accepted in Bradford pipe lines for storage. Oil would be accepted only for immediate shipment. A kind of demoniacal rage greeted this announcement. The very words "immediate shipment" by which the order was known came to have an evil and sinister significance. It worked a hardship on the producers, to be sure, but this was the fruit of their own fatuous folly. Obviously they had to sell the oil they ran into the pipes at the prevailing distress prices or let it run on the ground or cease production. Of course, the Standard buyers were there in the offices of the United Pipe Lines taking oil at the lowest rates.

The producers evidently believed this order was coldly designed to destroy them. "Why," they cried, as reported by Miss Tarbell, "*force us to compete with each other?*" This extraordinary exclamation is worth pondering. These were the men who wanted to strangle monopoly, yet who asked why they should be made to compete with each other. They rushed into the public square at Bradford and denounced the United Pipe Lines. Two days later they met in the square again. Inflammatory speeches lashed them to fury. "Drive this monopoly from the country," cried one fiery orator and he called on his audience to smash the lines and stations. But they did nothing. They just went on pumping oil and drilling new wells. The newspapers of the day record what looks like the most depressing evidences of human folly. Oil at 69 cents in July—output 11,000 barrels a day higher than in January. In August, oil down to 64 cents—output increased another 5,000 barrels a day—20,000 barrels a day more than the preceding August—7,000,000 barrels surplus in the pipes, 2,000,000 more than in January. Yet the newspapers record the melancholy story—"Cole Creek comes to the front with more big wells." "Drilling more active in Byron Center development." "Bradford Field brings in 18 new wells."

Disastrous fires added to the losses. But nothing could stop these blinded men from pumping oil that nobody wanted or from denouncing Rockefeller for refusing to take care of it for them. In New York a *Tribune* reporter asked wise old Charles Pratt what it was all about. "The whole thing is very simple," he answered. "There has been an overproduction and producers are suffering from the natural consequences. We have large refineries under which fires have not been built for months. We have urged the producers to diminish production, but in vain. A pooling arrangement will force up the price for a time. They will sell what is demanded; the rest they will store. This retired stock will increase until it is as cumbersome as they are willing to stand. Then they will stop or diminish production—simply postpone until next month or next year what had better be done now." Pratt showed a clipping from an oil region paper urging investment in oil land as a sure road to wealth. He wrote on the margin: "Read this again in 1880."

In spite of all the storming the "immediate shipment" order remained in force until the situation cleared, which was in December.

CHAPTER IV. AT THE BAR

About this time the wrath of the oil men broke out in a series of attacks which were to bring home to Rockefeller the bitterness of the feeling against him. As soon as the Equitable Pipe Line began carrying oil to Buffalo, Rockefeller called on the railroads to carry out their agreement with him to protect him against competitors. The representatives of the trunk lines met at Saratoga and reduced the rates on his oil eastward to 80 cents. The spectacle of the railroads in a conspiracy with Rockefeller to crush his rivals aroused the righteous indignation of the regions. The Producers' Protective Union sent a committee of twenty-five to Governor Hartranft of Pennsylvania to demand action against the conspirators. The Governor directed the Attorney-General to make an investigation and to institute Quo Warranto proceedings against the Pennsylvania and other railroads to compel them to perform their duties as common carriers.

The Attorney-General directed William McCandless, Commissioner of Internal Affairs, to make the investigation, and that gentleman's representative, James Atwell, appeared in Titusville in September to conduct hearings. After listening to detailed testimony of the union officials reciting a long list of discriminations, McCandless made his report on October 14th, 1878. The report staggered the regions. McCandless found that the complaint filed had not been substantiated "in a way that demands action," and believed that the facts did not warrant him in reporting a case "that is beyond the ordinary province of individual redress."

It would be impossible to exaggerate the violence of the anger which this report produced. Crowds gathered in the streets of all the oil towns. In Bradford they gathered outside the United Pipe Line offices. They jeered and threatened violence. The charge ran around that McCandless had gotten $20,000 from the Standard Oil Company to be used in his campaign for Congress. At Parker's Landing the stuffed figure of a man was found on the morning of the 19th hanging in front of the oil exchange. On one sleeve was a placard reading, "I am Buck. Who are you?" One on the breast read, "The Very Honorable Secretary of State for

Internal Affairs of the Empire State of Pennsylvania." On the forehead was another: "The complaint has not been substantiated in any way that demands action." Around this figure all day swirled men, shaking angry fists at the hanging effigy. As night came they cut it down, tramped on it, and finally burned it. Another effigy hung in the streets of Bradford and another in the new town of Tarpot. Sticking from the pocket of the Bradford effigy was a huge check for $20,000 signed John D. Rockefeller.

A letter printed in the New York *Sun* said: "Send a reporter to the oil regions if you have one who cannot be bought like Buck McC." The *Sun* did. He found the regions in an uproar. A mysterious secret organization had sprung up. Men marched through the streets at night. Chalked on buildings were curious symbols—the letter K with a numeral surrounded by a coffin. It was whispered about that 4,000 men were under arms and ready to attack or seize the railroads. In Bradford there were 8,000 idle men, mostly vagabonds, lawless fellows who would have jumped at the first spark as a signal for turbulence and riot. The Governor hurried to the regions. The remembrance of the Pittsburgh strike riots were fresh in his mind. He declared that to his dying day he would remember with regret those unhappy events and that while he was governor he would not compromise with any form of violence. But at this critical moment the Producers' Union took a hand, the leaders moving among the infuriated oil men and counseling peace. Their influence in the end averted an outbreak.

II

THE HOPE of the oil men was now in the legal proceedings started by the Attorney-General. He made an application for a writ of Quo Warranto in Venango County charging the Standard Oil Company with repeated violations of the law. The writ was served on Samuel C. T. Dodd, attorney for the Standard. The redoubtable *Derrick* cried out: "The Standard is stabbed." Later the Attorney-General filed a bill against the Pennsylvania Railroad in Pittsburgh praying that it be compelled to do its duty as a common carrier and asking for an injunction. The Standard lawyers, of course, attempted to block these proceedings with demurrers. But in the midst of the McCandless excitement the courts decided to take jurisdiction. In January a commission arrived in Titusville to take testimony in the injunction proceedings against the railroad. The oil leaders in reach—Archbold, Frew, Lockhart, and Vandergrift—were summoned. Benjamin Cassatt, then vice-president of the Pennsylvania Railroad, also testified. For the first time the people began to get direct, uncontrovertible evidence of the truth of the charges of railroad discrimination. And feeling ran high.

III

WHILE the regions rang with denunciations of the railroads and the Standard, B. B. Campbell, president of the Petroleum Producers' Association, summoned the Union and launched a move to have Rockefeller and his associates indicted for criminal conspiracy. Some members thought this would be an ill-advised move, but the majority favored a strenuous prosecution. A formal complaint was sworn to by B. B. Campbell and the Grand Jury of Clarion County met to consider the charges. The whole proceeding was carried on very secretly. On April 29th, 1879, while the Producers' Association was in session, news came that the Grand Jury of Clarion County had indicted John D. Rockefeller for criminal conspiracy and along with him Jabez A. Bostwick, William Rockefeller, Daniel O'Day, William G. Warden, Charles Lockhart, Henry M. Flagler, Jacob J. Vandergrift, and George W. Girty, cashier of the Standard. There were eight counts: conspiracy to secure a monopoly of the oil industry, to oppress other refiners, to injure the carrying trade of the Allegheny Valley and the Pennsylvania Railroad, to extort unreasonable rates from the roads and to fraudulently control the prices of crude and refined oil, and several others.

John D. Rockefeller was in New York at this time. Most of his associates were either there or in Cleveland. O'Day, Warden, Lockhart, and Vandergrift were in Pennsylvania. They immediately surrendered and gave bail. But the others, headed by Rockefeller, evaded arrest. In June an application was made to Governor Hartranft to issue a requisition upon the Governor of New York for Rockefeller. But he refused to honor it.

CHAPTER V. THE HEPBURN INVESTIGATION

IN THE first months of 1879, while all this was going on in the oil regions, the Chamber of Commerce of New York City was presenting to the railroad committee of the state legislature evidence of discriminations by the Erie and Central against shippers and localities, of abuses of trust and frauds on stockholders. Among those who sat listening with attention was a young man of stern Presbyterian forebears, able, deeply interested in finance, full of ambition. He lived on his legislator's salary of $1,500 a year in a small fourth-floor room in a house in Albany. This youth was named Alonzo Barton Hepburn. He was destined to play a great part in succeeding years. When he died, John D. Rockefeller, Jr., pronounced a fulsome eulogy, and among his numerous titles was that of "Trustee of the Rockefeller Foundation." But now the tale of railroad abuses he heard stirred him to demand an investigation by a special committee of five. The legislature yielded and that committee, with the young reformer at its head, known as the Hepburn Committee, began its investigations in July. It sat at Albany, Rochester, Utica, New York, Saratoga, and other cities until December. For the first time in the history of the new era an authentic light was thrown on the outrageous system of discriminations, graft, and corruption in railroad and industrial affairs. The nation was shocked. For the first time the name of John D. Rockefeller came to have a national currency as the symbol of the new order and its evils.

The railroads were represented by an array of distinguished counsel headed by Chauncey Depew, then in the full flight of his sparkling oratorical powers. Hepburn declared later that the roads had interposed every obstacle to the success of the inquiry, had refused to produce their books and to answer questions. As for Rockefeller and his Standard Oil comrades, they made a spectacle on the witness stand which produced a great deal of amusement mingled with ridicule and indignation. For the first time they hid behind the phrase which was to become famous in court and committee rooms—"I refuse to answer on the advice of counsel." It seemed impossible to get direct answers to the simplest questions. Here is a sample from the examination of Henry H. Rogers:

Q. You are a member of the firm of Charles Pratt and Company, are you not? *A.* Yes, sir.

Q. That firm is one of the Standard Oil's affiliated firms, is it not? *A.* I don't know that I understand your question.

Q. You ship under the Standard Oil's rates, do you not? *A.* I really don't know whether we do or not.

Q. Are you a member of the Standard Oil Company? *A.* If I was, I think that is a personal question.

Archbold denied the Acme was controlled by the Standard or was affiliated with it (which was a cold-blooded falsehood). He was president of the Acme; a director of the Standard. William Rockefeller and Henry H. Rogers were among the organizers of the Acme but Archbold didn't know if Standard Oil stockholders owned a controlling interest in his company. He didn't know if the Standard controlled the United Pipe Lines. He refused to answer about rates. Finally Simon Sterne, counsel of the committee, asked him in astonishment:

"Well, Mr. Archbold, what function do you play in the Standard Oil now as a director?"

"I am a clamorer for dividends. That is the only function I have in connection with the Standard Oil Company." John D. Rockefeller chuckled when he read that answer in the papers.

When Jabez Bostwick went on the stand and was asked his name he refused to answer on the ground that it might tend to incriminate him. This refusal was based on the Clarion County indictment. This indictment now operated as a most convenient trench for the Standard leaders and seriously hampered Hepburn's inquiry. But the shrewd investigator did succeed in bringing out facts which shocked the country. For instance, he showed that just a month before the inquiry opened representatives of the four trunk roads met at Niagara with Rockefeller's agents. The latter said: "These independents have now got a new pipe line started—the Tidewater. And we are bound to crush it and we want a rate that will do it." Whereupon, while the published rate was one dollar, the Standard was given a rate of twenty cents, which was later reduced to fifteen cents. When this got out the public rate was reduced to thirty cents. It was also shown that while the Standard had a nominal capital of only $3,500,000, it was actually worth $80,000,000. These were new and impressive figures in the America of that day.

The Standard was not the only concern getting rebates. For instance, it was shown that the New York Central had an agreement with Schoelkopf and Matthews to carry the product of their mill 47 per cent under the published rate. During 1877 two firms—Jesse Hoyt and Company and David Dow and Company, had control of the grain market through their rates. Chauncey Depew, the mouthpiece and handy man of the Vanderbilts, defending the roads and turning in anger on the manufacturers, exploded: "Every manufacturer in the state of New York existed by violence and lived by discrimination," and it was "secret rates and by deceiving their competitors as to what their rates were and by evading all laws of trade these manufacturers exist."

Hepburn, future Rockefeller Foundation trustee, denounced the Standard. He called it "a mysterious organization whose business and transactions are of such a character that its members decline giving its history lest their testimony be used to convict them of crime."

He recommended to the legislature a group of acts creating a railroad commission, regulation of railway rates and accounts, all of which ultimately became law.

CHAPTER VI. ROCKEFELLER TRIUMPHS

TRAPPED in his New York office in Pearl Street by the Pennsylvania indictment—he dared not go to Pennsylvania, where the authorities clamored for him—Mr. Rockefeller looked out upon a troubled world. There was the indictment in Pennsylvania, the two civil proceedings in that state, the New York investigation. More important, there were the Tidewater Pipe Line and the Equitable pushing on to success, and finally the nation-wide agitation against him and his system.

This latter he understood very little. He had not yet learned that he was making a change in anything more than the method of business operation. That he was compelling profound social changes he never dreamed. He supposed that he was substituting one form of individual action for another; highly organized, concentrated, private, individual operation for widespread, scattered, individual action. That the business had a social element, that the public had any rights in the matter did not occur to him. The public was important as a buyer of his products. It could refuse to buy from him. Therefore he proceeded from the very outset to recognize the customer character of the public and to cater to it. There was in his nature a sense of order and proportion which amounted to a kind of justness, a form of honesty. It was important to give the customer the best oil and the best service. But how he accomplished this and what other rights of the public as members of society and as citizens he might violate in this was something he did not consider. He had regard for his competitor not at all. This was not wholly selfishness or ruthlessness. It was the result of a definite philosophy of business. Rockefeller was definitely convinced that the competitive system under which the world had operated was a mistake. It was a crime against order, efficiency, economy. It could be eliminated only by abolishing all rivals. His plan therefore took a solid form. He would bring all his rivals in with him. The strong ones he would bring in as partners. The others would come in as stockholders. His primary aim was to eliminate them. He would eliminate them by bringing them in. Those who would not come in would be crushed. He would bring them in by making it impossible to remain outside his organization. Hence he got from railroads, legislatures, producers, every advantage he could. Those who joined him would get the benefit of these advantages. Those who remained outside would be crushed by them. That the men he crushed had any rights did not seem to enter his mind. Therefore when legislatures and politicians rose against him he looked upon it as an insolent truckling to the inefficient and moss-backs. His plan of dealing with these attacks was to withdraw deeper into his silence. Tell nobody anything. Ignore summonses and subpoenas and warrants if possible. That there was a powerful public opinion behind all this which he would one day have to deal with never entered the head of John

D. Rockefeller. The only thing he was genuinely afraid of was the oil regions.

And now the regions had two powerful attacks—one in the courts through an indictment and civil suits, the other through the formation of the Tidewater Pipe Line. The latter he knew how to fight. It was competition. And his lines of battle for that were already laid. But to push them successfully it was necessary that the Pennsylvania court proceedings should be gotten out of the way.

Rockefeller decided to get rid of these suits rather than try them. His lawyers had informed him that there was no chance of conviction. But lawyers might make mistakes. Besides, he had no intention of treating his enemies in the oil regions to the spectacle of John D. Rockefeller led into Clarion County in chains. They were hot on his trail. They kept up a ceaseless clamor upon the Governor for the bodies of Rockefeller and Rogers. But Governor Hoyt evaded and backed water until the state began to be aware of his shifting. Newspapers criticized him. B. B. Campbell asked for a requisition in June. State officials agreed but managed to make postponement after postponement. July 29th Campbell wrote the Governor that unless he acted at once, he, Campbell, would call on him publicly through the papers. Hoyt shillyshallied again. He said the Attorney-General was sick. Campbell carried out his threat of a public demand. But Hoyt still held back. The producers said Rockefeller had killed the Interstate Commerce bill in Congress with Payne and Camden, that he killed the free pipe line bill with purchased legislators, that he had bribed McCandless and now he must have reached Hoyt.

In the midst of this the indomitable man, patiently making his plans in Pearl Street, acted. The trial of Archbold, Vandergrift, and those arrested was fixed for August. He got an adjournment and sent word to Roger Sherman, attorney for the producers. One morning Sherman, ponderous, able, looking like Grover Cleveland, looked up to see a Standard Oil emissary. Mr. Rockefeller would like to talk with him in New York. Sherman was troubled. He sent for Campbell. Campbell suggested that they go. "We will see how badly scared he is." Thereupon Sherman and Campbell went to New York and went into conference with Rockefeller, Flagler, and their counsel.

ROCKEFELLER TRIUMPHS

These conferences, begun November 29th, lasted six weeks. At the time the Standard offices were near the end of Wall Street and reporters for the *Tribune, Herald,* and *Sun* were numerous in the section. Hence the meetings were held at the Fifth Avenue Hotel. Why Campbell and Sherman were not recognized there is not known. But the meetings proceeded in absolute secrecy. No mention was made of them until February 20th, when Campbell and Sherman had secured an agreement and called a meeting of the Producers' Association to consider it.

Rockefeller proposed that all the suits be withdrawn. In return, as finally worked out, he made the following concessions:

The Standard agreed to make no opposition to the "entire abrogation of the system of rebates, drawbacks and secret rates of freight in the transportation of petroleum" on the railroads.

Second, it agreed to full publication of all rates.

Third, the Standard agreed that there would be no discriminations by pipe lines in rates and storage; that rates would not be advanced save on thirty days' notice; that the price of crude would be the same in all districts for the same grade; that the pipes would store all oil offered as long as the production did not exceed 65,000 barrels a day during 15 consecutive days and in any case any immediate shipment oil would be purchased at the going price for certificate oil, provided owners did not sell immediate shipment oil cheaper to other persons.

This agreement, actually reached January 9th, was signed by Campbell and Sherman and the Standard officials. It looked like a perfectly sound arrangement for the producers. But it contained one fatal flaw. The Standard stipulated it would not accept any rate that the roads were not at liberty to give to other shippers. The Agreement with the Pennsylvania Railroad, signed at the same time, provided: "The Pennsylvania Railroad will not pay any shipper of petroleum or its product any rebate, drawback or commission upon shipments different from or greater than that which shall be paid *to any other person shipping or offering to ship like quantity;* and that any discrimination which shall be made in favor of shippers of large quantities shall be reasonable and shall, upon demand, be communicated to all persons shipping."

Here was the old device—rates that would be the same to all persons shipping *the same quantity*. Of course no one could ship as much as the Standard. There had been a bitter debate on this clause. But Rockefeller insisted on it and out of the negotiations he came with an excellent bargain in spite of the fact that he agreed to pay $40,000 to cover the costs of the Producers' Union in its fight.

The Producers' Union which met to consider this agreement was a much humbled affair. In spite of what seemed like progress made against Rockefeller, four-fifths of the lodges organized two years before were dead. Only forty members attended. The Grand Council was not very grand. The report was received in sullen anger. Sherman and Campbell were bitterly denounced. Campbell, big, patriarchal, generous-souled man, sat listening to these reproaches with tears streaming down his cheeks. He had been warned. "I fear," a fellow producer had written, "you will say I am discouraged. No, not discouraged, but disgusted with the poor, spiritless, and faint-hearted people whom you are laboring so hard to liberate from bondage. . . . Are the producers as a class (nothing but a damned cowardly, disorganized mob as they are) worth the efforts you are putting forth to save them?"

The dying Grand Council, in a kind of expiring gasp, approved the agreement with sullen resignation and passed resolutions denouncing the national government, the state government, the Governor for refusing to grant the requisition for "criminals," the judges of the Supreme Court, and everybody in general. Then they passed a resolution dissolving the Producers' Union.

Mr. Rockefeller—organized intelligence against unorganized stupidity—had won again.

CHAPTER VII. CRUSHING THE TIDEWATER

ROCKEFELLER could now turn to crush the Tidewater. This company involved a serious threat. He had spent years perfecting his control over railroad rates. A pipe line to the sea for crude oil would destroy at a blow all these dearly won advantages. He did not believe the project practicable. But oil was now flowing at Williamstown through the Tidewater's pipes. It was no longer a matter of speculation.

Back in the fall of 1878, when the project was started, he had first fought the free pipe line bill in the Pennsylvania legislature. He had also moved to battle the Tidewater's pipes in Pennsylvania. He sent his agents scurrying to buy up exclusive rights for a pipe line from the northern to the southern boundary of the state. If he succeeded in this the right of way would constitute a wall across the state which no other pipe line could cross. Money for this purpose was provided without stint. But in spite of his foresight, the Tidewater managers succeeded in crossing his wall and by April, 1879, the new line was almost ready. The pipe was laid almost the whole way along the ground from Coryville to Williamstown. At Coryville a huge specially built pump was installed to force the oil 28 miles to a level 700 feet higher. A second pump was to drive the oil to the top of the Alleghenies, an additional 1,900-foot level. From that point the oil would run by gravity to Williamsport, where huge tanks were constructed to receive it and where the Reading Railroad had provided 200 tank cars to transport it to New York. The opening of the line was set for May 28th and the occasion was made a festal one. The officers of the line and hundreds of spectators were present. Rockefeller had agents there to observe all that went on. He was quite skeptical of the experiment's success. Byron D. Benson turned the valve which let the first oil into the pipes. The crowd could hear it as it moved forward and up with a clinking, thumping noise. The crowd moved along with it. Soon only the company representatives, workmen, and Standard observers were left to follow the noisy flow of oil as it moved up over the foothills. In New York, Rockefeller, held there by indictments, got a wire saying the first grade had been made successfully. Later another dispatch announced the second had been reached. June 4th, seven days after the first oil was pumped into the pipes at Coryville, the greenish-black stream poured into the tanks at Williamstown. When Rockefeller got this news, he knew the Tidewater was a success, that a new era in oil transportation had arrived, that he had a new and serious fight on his hands, and that everywhere independent refiners would make their appearance unless he could crush this foe at once. He at once compelled the railroads to grant him new and special rates, as we have seen, and got in touch with Roger Sherman to end the Pennsylvania suits and clear the decks for a determined assault upon the Tidewater.

First he began building a seaboard pipe line of his own from Bradford to Bayonne and others from the oil regions to Philadelphia, Cleveland, Pittsburgh, and Buffalo. Then he went to the Tidewater with a proposition. He would buy from it all the crude oil it could run. "We will guarantee to take 10,000 barrels a day. This will mean 10,000 barrels' traffic for your pipes—capacity business—and 10,000 barrels a day freight for the Reading." He also proposed that railroad rates should be advanced, thus giving the Reading a better deal. The proposition was a tempting one. But it was turned down. It would have defeated the prime purpose of the new line, namely, the encouragement of new independent refineries, if Rockefeller got the whole run of the new pipes.

Then he made another drive on the few remaining independent refiners. He offered them such high prices for their plants that they could not resist. All capitulated save one—Ayres, Lombard and Company in New York. Thus deprived of customers for oil, the Tidewater proceeded to build refineries. All through 1879 this battle went on until Rockefeller completed his new treaty with Roger Sherman and B. B. Campbell which quashed the indictments and civil suits and put the Producers' Union out of business. Then he began his offensive against the Tidewater in sober earnest. And now we find him using methods somewhat more questionable, somewhat less Christianlike and somewhat more difficult to defend. But they were swift, intense, secret, and in the end completely effective.

II

THE STANDARD OIL COMPANY had huge refineries at Communipaw and Constable Hook, New Jersey. Crude for these plants was carried to Bayonne by the Pennsylvania and from there to the refineries by the New Jersey Central. Rockefeller decided to take this business from the Jersey Central and to send the crude across Bayonne and to the refineries through pipes. The Standard induced the Common Council of Bayonne to grant a franchise to build its pipes. But the Mayor vetoed it. Rockefeller had the Council, but the Jersey Central had the Mayor. The matter rested until September. By that time the Standard had the Mayor, as well as

CRUSHING THE TIDEWATER

the Council. However, Rockefeller knew that if the franchise were granted the Jersey Central would block the building of the pipes at once by an injunction. He made his plans accordingly. By September 22nd he was ready to strike. The route of the line was surveyed and marked off. All the material for the job—pipes, joints, tools, materials for repairing the streets—all was assembled in the company's yards. All this material was loaded into carts. But not a word of this got out to any one. As night fell 300 workmen, marshaled like an army under command of engineers, were mobilized in the yards. Each cart had its instructions as to the precise spot at which its materials would be unloaded. Each squad of men were told off with specific orders where to march. They were armed with picks and shovels. Every detail of the approaching attack was worked out with infinite care. While all this was in progress, the Common Council, in answer to a sudden call, assembled in its chamber. The Mayor, like the shovelmen, engineers, and aldermen, sat at his desk. An ordinance was introduced. A series of hastily carried motions dispensed with various formalities and in a few minutes the ordinance, passed by the Council, was rushed to the Mayor's desk. The instant that trusted official signed it, word was dispatched to the officer in command at the yards. The gates swung open and the pipe-line army marched out with its wagons, its picks, its shovels, and other impedimenta. In a few hours the necessary trench across the entire city was dug, the pipes lowered and jointed, the trench refilled and the streets repaired. The army worked through the night and when morning dawned and Bayonne citizens went to their work and before the Jersey Central had any inkling of what had been done, oil was flowing under the streets of the city through a pipe line built and completed in a single night. Those who faced John D. Rockefeller in battle soon learned that while he could wait with infinite patience and move unruffled through wise delays, he could strike with the swiftness of a Napoleon.

III

IN APRIL, 1881, W. P. Shell, Auditor General of Pennsylvania, gave Mr. John D. Rockefeller something of a shock by assessing the company with $3,200,000 in unpaid taxes. Pennsylvania was trying to collect taxes on the entire assets of the company, whether in Pennsylvania or not. The Court of Common Pleas sustained the Standard's pleas in part by holding it could be taxed only on that portion of its capital which it brings into the state. It fixed the tax at $33,277 with penalties. But the Supreme Court cut off the penalties. This suit had a strange and pitiable sequel and it is that sequel which concerns us here. Since 1872, E. G. Patterson had been a bitter opponent of railroad rebates and an implacable enemy of the Standard. When the Auditor General began to harass the Standard for taxes, he employed Patterson to collect evidence about the Standard's capitalization and assets and profits. However, William Rockefeller supplied this information, and the Auditor declared he owed Patterson nothing. Patterson, angry at the producers for the manner in which they had failed Potts and quit on the indictment, and now embittered by the Auditor's refusal to pay his fees, fell into a state of misanthropy and poured out the vials of his wrath on his former comrades. Then he sent word to John D. Rockefeller through Archbold that he proposed to attack the Standard further unless he was given the equivalent of his fee in the tax matter. In John D. Archbold Patterson found a ready customer for this sort of business. Whatever arrangement this pair made can only be guessed at. But very soon we find Patterson subscribing to 50 shares of Tidewater stock, and the money for this—$5,000—was supplied by Archbold. With this stock in his possession Patterson then applied to the courts for a receivership for the Tidewater. He alleged gross mismanagement. The Standard Oil Company failed to stand behind him in this fight and the suit was dismissed, Judge Pierson Church strongly intimating that the proceeding looked like blackmail. In this, however, he was wrong. Patterson was consumed with hatred of his old friends and wanted vengeance. And he was a ready tool in the hands of those who wished to destroy the Tidewater.

There is something pathetic in this complicity of Patterson in the Standard intrigues. Indeed, it is strange how, one by one, Rockefeller's enemies find their way into his camp—first Payne, then Vandergrift, next Archbold, Pratt, Rogers, Warden, Frew, Lockhart, and now poor Patterson and—strangest of all—Roger Sherman, the lawyer who had so heroically carried on the attacks which led to the indictment and civil suits. There were bitter murmurs when Sherman surrendered to Rockefeller in 1880. He was

CRUSHING THE TIDEWATER

a big man, an able one, and he had fought valiantly without other recompense than abuse at the hands of the producers. But when he surrendered he turned up immediately thereafter as an attorney for the Standard Oil Company, a post he occupied until 1886, when he again attacked them. Now, in 1882, he appeared in a far from lovely rôle, bringing the distraught and maddened Patterson to the Standard for his questionable business.

IV

STILL bolder attacks were to be made on the Tidewater. In January, 1882, the company applied to the First National Bank of New York for a loan of $2,000,000. A group of Tidewater stockholders, owning a third of the stock, called on the bank and warned it that the company was insolvent. The bank ignored the warning and made the loan.

The next election of directors was fixed for January 17th, 1883, but was postponed by the board. However, on that day the gentlemen who had warned the bank put in an appearance at the company's offices and announced they were ready to vote. These gentlemen were known as the Taylor-Satterfield crowd. And over the protests of the officials, they proceeded to hold an election, to throw out the proxies for two-thirds of the stock held by the protesting officials, and elected themselves directors. Benson, the president, and the old managers barricaded themselves in the office, held on to the books, and instituted injunction proceedings against the rebels. Judge Pierson Church at Meadville, who had dismissed Patterson's receivership suit, ruled against the Taylor-Satterfield insurgents and branded the whole proceeding as "farcical, fraudulent and void." Thus another attempt to seize the Tidewater was frustrated. Was Rockefeller behind this attempt? John D. Archbold issued an affidavit denying this. But who, then, did these revolutionists represent? What interest could they, as stockholders, have in wrecking a company in which they held so much stock? However, a little later Mr. John D. Rockefeller appeared with this Taylor-Satterfield stock in his possession and proposed to the Tidewater an agreement to divide the business. The company was weary of the struggle and so it signed a contract with the Standard to divide the pipe line business in its territory—88½ per cent to the Standard and 11½ per cent to the Tidewater. Two agreements were made, one with the Tidewater Pipe Lines and one with the Tidewater refineries. They were signed October 9th, to be effective from October 1st. In effect these contracts ended the independent life of the Tidewater. It became an ally of the Standard, with that company actually owning a third of its stock. And thus this ambitious enterprise, like all others of the independents, came to an end.

V

WHEN this victory was consummated Rockefeller was in possession of a complete system of pipe lines reaching to every section of his refining empire and from his western plants to the sea. Almost all opposition—transportation and refining—was crushed. John D. Rockefeller was the country's first supreme monopolist.

Immediately he assembled all his pipe lines under the control of one great company—the National Transit Company, of which Henry H. Rogers became the head. But now his relation to the railroad was greatly altered. Instead of being a customer, he was a competitor. But the Pennsylvania Railroad had an ace in its sleeve. To get his pipe line to the seaboard he had to cross the Pennsylvania tracks. To accomplish this he made a traffic agreement with them. He laid his pipes and carried oil to the sea that way. But the Pennsylvania was to get 26 per cent of all the oil traffic. The open rate on this was 40 cents a barrel. But in fact the railroad would carry no oil. Even its 26 per cent of the crude would go in Rockefeller's pipes. But the road would collect 40 cents on it and pay Rockefeller up to eight cents for carrying it, according to the rise and fall in the open rate. Thus Rockefeller now found himself transporting all the oil—his own three-quarters as well as the Pennsylvania's one-quarter. The Pennsylvania practically went out of the oil business.

At this moment John D. Rockefeller, forty-four years of age, had accomplished his ambition—he was supreme in the oil industry and the country knew it. He was and continued to be for many years the symbol of the American monopolist.

PART SEVEN
THE FINAL FLIGHT

CHAPTER I. MOMENTS AT HOME

THERE were many men in America richer than John D. Rockefeller. But as he stood now, at forty, master of the greatest industrial institution in the country, he was certainly among the richest. The properties of the Standard Oil group were valued at $70,000,000. Rockefeller owned 191,700 trust certificates worth $70 each. Thus he was worth in Standard Oil holdings alone something more than thirteen million dollars. He must have had as much again invested in other properties. Almost all of this had been accumulated in ten years.

Though now a man of vast wealth, Rockefeller had given little thought to the question of philanthropy. His wife was greatly interested in the missionary work of the Euclid Avenue Baptist Church and practically all his benefactions, except occasional help to individual needy cases, were to the missionary work of this church. His mind was at this time wholly on the problem of building his fortune.

While retaining the old residence in Euclid Avenue, he acquired about this time the beautiful Forest Hill estate further out on the same boulevard, at that time a suburban site. He had always wanted an extensive country estate where he might build roads, lay out the grounds, and play with trees and landscapes. Forest Hill was acquired as a country home. About this time, however, the growth of his interests on the Atlantic seaboard made it necessary that he spend most of his time in New York, which had now become the oil capital. For several years the family lived at the old Euclid Avenue home in the Winter and at Forest Hill in the Summer, while Mr. Rockefeller stayed for the most part through the Winter months at the Buckingham Hotel in New York. In a few years, however, the supremacy of New York was so complete that Rockefeller decided to move his family to the East and he then acquired the home at No. 4 West Fifty-fourth Street, which he has continued to own to this day. Here then the family took up its Winter quarters, but for many years made Forest Hill in Cleveland its Summer home. Thus, he now possessed three homes —all fine places but nothing gaudy or ostentatious about them.

The made millionaires of the day ran to the most extravagant exhibitions of their wealth. For the Rockefellers it must be said that they behaved with decency and dignity in their new wealth. They were from the start fearful of the effect their wealth might have upon their children. They employed the most elaborate care to protect them from that. When they moved to New York young John D. went to a preparatory school and walked to and from class, while his classmates passed him on Fifth Avenue in their handsome rigs, many accompanied by grooms. The children, so far as possible, were kept from knowing the wealth of their father lest they take an air of superiority with their companions. Edith was at a girls' college and with some classmates went to buy a desk for some common purpose. They wanted to have a bill sent, but the merchant wanted some identification and asked if any of the girls would give the name of their fathers who might be in business. Several girls immediately named their fathers, whereupon Edith said: "My father is in business, too." "And what's his name?" asked the merchant. "Rockefeller, John D. Rockefeller. He is in business in New York." The girl had no idea of the magnitude of her father's affairs nor of the importance of his name. But the merchant did.

Some years before the children wanted a tricycle. Rockefeller suggested to his wife that they buy one for each.

"No," she said, "we will buy just one for all of them."

"But, my dear," he urged, "tricycles do not cost much."

"That is true," she explained. "It is not the cost. But if they have just one they will learn to give up to one another."

Rockefeller himself had always had a strong strain of old-fashioned sentiment. He found his chief pleasures in the companion-

MOMENTS AT HOME

ship of his family and the acquaintances of the Baptist Church. The pleasures of intellectual conversation have never meant anything to him. The small affairs, the trivial chatter of people who talked about their neighbors and their Sunday School completely satisfied his social and intellectual appetites. He attended church with unfailing regularity and when, occasionally, Mrs. Rockefeller could not attend, he would make careful notes of the sermon and then repeat to her the wisdom which fell from the lips of the preacher.

He never missed prayer meetings or trustees' meetings when in Cleveland. In the old days of the Erie Street Mission he had always rung the bell on Sundays and, when he was Sunday School Superintendent, went over regularly before meeting and kindled the fire. He was already one of the leaders of Cleveland business at this time. But since 1871 the congregation had been installed in its new church building at the corner of Euclid Avenue and Huntington (now 18th Street). The simple ways of the old church were no longer in vogue. Mr. Rockefeller was rich. There were several other rich men in the congregation now. The name of the church was changed to the Second Baptist Church and then in 1877 to the Euclid Avenue Baptist Church, a name under which it was destined to attain fame as Rockefeller's place of worship.

He continued to act as Sunday School Superintendent and to deliver instruction to his classes. Rockefeller's presence was an attraction to young men. Acquaintance with the wealthy man and large employer was a thing to be cultivated. After Sunday School pupils would manage to talk to the teacher, to let him know they were candidates for jobs. Rockefeller on his side, when boys seemed a bit unruly, would say: "I keep my eye on the boys in Sunday School. You know we hire a great many people and some of you apply for positions. I watch your conduct in the Sunday School and judge from that when you come to get positions, whether you would be the right sort of boys to work for me." A great many employees of the Standard Oil Company in Cleveland were recruited from those Bible classes.

Rockefeller himself always felt it incumbent on him to give an example in carefulness and economy. As soon as the last Amen was pronounced in his class he made ready to turn out the gas light and when the last pupil went out he turned it off.

About this time he wrote to the pastor pledging certain weekly sums: "Mrs. Rockefeller, $10 each week; self, $30 each week; each of our children, 20 cents each week." He added: "The 20 cents from each child will be earned by the sweat of their brows, pulling weeds, etc."

These, of course, were merely his regular contributions. He came forward in a larger way whenever the church needed money. And he distributed to members of the congregation many and frequent beneficences. There were several old people in the congregation who were entirely dependent on his bounty. During the service he would look around to see who was present. Then he would take envelopes from his pocket and put certain sums in each envelope and write the names of the intended beneficiaries on them. After service as he was shaking hands he would manage to leave the envelopes, well folded, in the palms of those for whom they were intended.

Rockefeller went out hardly at all to social affairs. But there were plenty of family gatherings at home and the Euclid Avenue Church picnics and entertainments were almost always attended by the family. The Rockefeller children all played different instruments and all were members of the church orchestra.

He was devoted to his children. Unlike Morgan, whose children fled from him in terror, Rockefeller fraternized with his. The Forest Hill estate had a fine lake. Many days when, outside that pleasantly wooded park home, his enemies raged in war against his plans and reporters and process servers harried the old Irish guard at his gate, a sturdy swimmer might have been seen, with a straw hat on his head, moving slowly, with a strong, leisurely breast stroke, around the lake. Behind the oil king his children, who were his pupils, struggled industriously in their swimming lessons. Rockefeller would swim sometimes a mile without stopping. In the Winter the frozen surface of the lake afforded a place to skate when Rockefeller made his occasional visits to his family.

"Father was always an enthusiastic skater," John D. Rockefeller, Jr., has said, telling of these early days. "I recall going with him to test the thickness of the ice to see whether it was safe for our sport. The lake was deep, so father deliberately chose a means of saving ourselves in case the ice gave way. We took under our arms long narrow boards, which would hold us up in case we broke through. I didn't realize it at the time, but later I came to realize that this was characteristic of him.

"Well do I recall that one Winter evening when I was staying at Forest Hill and father was there on a visit, his enthusiasm for skating led him to get up shortly after midnight on a Monday morning to go with some of the workmen to our little lake to flood the surface of the ice so as to make it smoother for skating that day. He went at this unusual hour because he would not have the work done on Sunday.

"I have heard father say that he regretted he did not have more time for his family during those early years; and had to leave so much of our training to our mother. Nevertheless, he was always the companion and friend of my sisters and myself, and we learned much from him; but this was not so much by precept as by example."

The Rockefeller children were systematically made to want for things instead of having their wants immediately gratified. Other children they knew had far more than they did. This was particularly true of their cousins, with whom they were always comparing themselves. "We felt we were in a terrible plight compared with them," said John D., Jr. All the children were assigned tasks and were made to work. And for this work they were paid. Indeed, they got no money save what they earned. They were also taught to save. That lesson was incessantly enforced. When one of the children saved ten dollars, the father would then put another ten to it for encouragement. At church they were taught by their mother to put something in the collection plate out of their own earnings. They were rewarded for all attention to duty, but the rewards were nickels and dimes. Young John D. was taught the violin. When he practiced he got five cents an hour. Later, when he was old enough to work around the Cleveland estate, he was paid the same wages as the laborers.

II

WILLIAM ROCKEFELLER lived altogether in New York. Frank was still in the oil business as secretary of the Pioneer Oil Company. Old Doctor William Rockefeller had been drifting more and more out of the family picture. He had always continued at his old trade, spending little time in Cleveland. Gradually his absences became more and more prolonged until about this time, when he disappeared altogether. His name went out of the Cleveland directory. The elder Mrs. Rockefeller continued to live at 33 Cheshire Street, the home from which John D. went to be married. She was a devout member of the Euclid Avenue Baptist Church, at which, in fact, all the Rockefellers, including Frank's family, worshiped. But she was rapidly becoming an invalid. She watched with great pride, of course, but with some dismay, the meteoric rise of her extraordinary son. His picture hung in the place of honor over the parlor mantel. After he moved to New York she made occasional visits to his home and as the years wore on divided her time among the homes of her various sons and daughters.

CHAPTER II. THE GREAT STRUCTURE

THE COUNTRY was now well aware of the industrial giant who appeared in their midst. Congress, legislatures, political parties, newspapers, and publicists began to give Mr. Rockefeller and his company their attention. And well they might, for he had not only reared the most powerful business structure yet seen in the world but had created for them a whole series of bewildering problems.

What was known as the Standard Oil consisted of forty corporations. Mr. Rockefeller and his associates owned fourteen of these completely and controlled a majority of the stock in twenty-six others. In 1870 he had incorporated his company with a million dollars' capital. Now the capital was seventy million. Those two original partners—Rockefeller and Andrews—had increased to thirty-seven stockholders. But Andrews was gone. The rapid growth of the company, the swift pace of his ambitious partner, kept him in a state of nervous terror from the beginning. He was the mechanical director of the concern in Cleveland and each time he learned of the latest adventurous extensions of his more audacious partners, Rockefeller and Flagler, he suffered a shock. The tremendous acquisitions preceding 1879 were too much for him, and Rockefeller became annoyed at his older partner's incessant apprehensions. Finally one day in 1880 Andrews said: "I wish I was out of this business." "What will you take for your interest?" asked Rockefeller calmly. "One million," said Andrews, never dreaming he would get it. A few days later Rockefeller appeared with the million in cash and Andrews went out of the company, breathing a sigh of relief, the first of that extraordinary group to break away. Very soon after the stock went up much higher in value. Andrews complained to friends that he had been pushed out of the company. These murmurings came to Rockefeller's ears. He asked Warden, a fellow-director, to go to Andrews and say that he might have his stock back at the price he sold it for. Andrews, however, said he was through with the oil business. Had he held on he would have ranked next to Rockefeller in wealth. Thereafter he drifted wholly out of the scene. In Cleveland he had built a gaudy and ostentatious mansion which was called "Andrews' Folly." He left little other claim to fame.

It was indeed an industrial empire which was ruled from that small old-fashioned building at 140 Pearl Street. There were refineries at Buffalo, Philadelphia, Cleveland, Baltimore, New York, Portland, Maine, Pittsburgh, Hunter's Point, Bayonne, Rochester, and in all the cities of the oil regions. Practically all the company's leaders were now in New York. Over these men Rockefeller presided as absolute master. His preëminence was never questioned. In spite of this, however, he made it a rule never to act without consulting his colleagues and never to take an important step without unanimous agreement of all the directors. There probably has never been another such board of directors. They met daily. A majority could be assembled at a moment's notice for any important action. They operated behind closed doors. They denied everything and talked outside about nothing. As early as 1876 they formed the habit of lunching together each day, at 140 Pearl Street. William Rockefeller perhaps established and developed the custom. Oddly enough, it was not John D. Rockefeller who sat at the head of the long table, but Charles H. Pratt. On Pratt's right sat Flagler, on his left Rogers. Along the right next to Flagler sat, in order, John D. himself, Archbold, J. A. Bostwick, E. J. Pouch, John Bushnell, and Paul Babcock. Along the left after Rogers sat William Rockefeller, Thomas Bushnell, Benjamin Brewster, F. Q. Barstow, J. Crowell, and J.

H. Alexander. At the foot of the table sat James McGee. These were the rulers of the great corporation. Of course, as the years passed other men took their places at this board. They are all dead now save the undisputed master himself who modestly sat third from the head.

Flagler continued to be the closest man to Rockefeller. All directors had separate offices but Rockefeller and Flagler continued to have their desks together. Flagler was attached to no department. He was the "lawyer" of the crowd. He was the cold, remorseless analyst. He had a flare for sensing the legal values in a plan; was the wizard in contract making. He doubtless conceived the combination idea and invented the drawback scheme. J. J. Vandergrift and Daniel O'Day continued to rule the pipe lines. Jabez Bostwick was the buyer. Henry H. Rogers was in charge of manufacturing. Pratt was the great merchant of the group. Warden and Lockhart looked after their own plants. O. H. Payne was the treasurer. But William Rockefeller, who had confined his attention to exports, was slowly moving over into the financial department over which John D. himself exercised the closest supervision.

Rockefeller expected these leaders to divest themselves of details. Each plant, each corporation, was organized as a unit. Its managers were given wide discretion and held accountable for successful operation. These divisional chiefs were expected not to trouble the minds of the leaders with small details. Rockefeller set up a system of sifting committees, which were empowered to handle all ordinary problems. Only the major question reached the general staff. There was a committee on marketing, a crude oil committee, a manufacturing committee, with departments dealing with making refined products, developing new products. Committees covered all the functions of the vast business.

Rockefeller's hatred of waste ran through the whole enterprise. For the first time a business had been organized on the principle of assembling the best brains in the industry and putting them to work on all of its countless problems. The problem of waste was one of these. Rockefeller saw that the waste of a few pounds which would not be noted in a small business, when multiplied many times in a huge concern, would amount to a large sum yearly.

THE GREAT STRUCTURE

Thus we find the purchasing department sending to the barrel factory this note:

"Last month you reported on hand 1,119 bungs. 10,000 were sent you beginning this month. You have used 9,527 this month. You report 1,012 on hand. What has become of the other 500?"

It is a favorite criticism of Rockefeller that he initiated nothing; that he seized other men's ideas—pipe lines, tank cars, by-products —and used them for himself. The complaint ignores the character of Rockefeller's mind. One might say of Napoleon that he invented neither explosive nor gun. Rockefeller was a commander, not an inventor. The time when a single small business man might attempt to supply all the talents needed to conduct a business was passed. It was Rockefeller's genius to perceive that business on a great scale would need to assemble the differing talents of many men. He did not invent tank cars or pipe lines or paraffin or refining processes. But he organized and used them intelligently. He was among the first to see the changing conditions in our economic world and the need of applying scientific knowledge to industry. He could not be a chemist and physicist and engineer and financier. But he could see the need of chemists and engineers and physicists to improve methods and processes. But he saw also what men have been talking glibly about these last twenty years as if it were just discovered—the principle of integration in industry. He saw men getting rich making barrels, glue, hoops, and lending money to refiners and producers. Much has been written about Rockefeller's predatory competition, but little about the drove of little business men who preyed on producers and refiners, particularly the bankers and money lenders who squeezed them with heavy bonuses. Rockefeller saw barrels made by the most wasteful and expensive processes. The industry paid an oppressive toll for this inefficiency. So he began making his own barrels, his own glue, and hoops, and material of every sort. He used only the best wagons. Horses were bought young and used for three or four years only. Their feed was watched, their stables kept scrupulously clean. In 1872 barrels cost $2.35 each. In 1888 they cost $1.25 each. As the company used 3,500,000 barrels a year this meant a saving of $4,000,000. In 1874 cans cost 30 cents each. In 1888 they cost less than 15 cents and on 36,000,000 a year

Rockefeller effected a saving of $5,400,000. The same thing was true of tanks, stills, pumps, everything used in the business. Experts were at work constantly studying better methods of manufacturing the by-products of oil. It is a fair statement that when Rockefeller's battle with the Tidewater was ended he had brought into being the most efficient large scale industrial manufacturing business

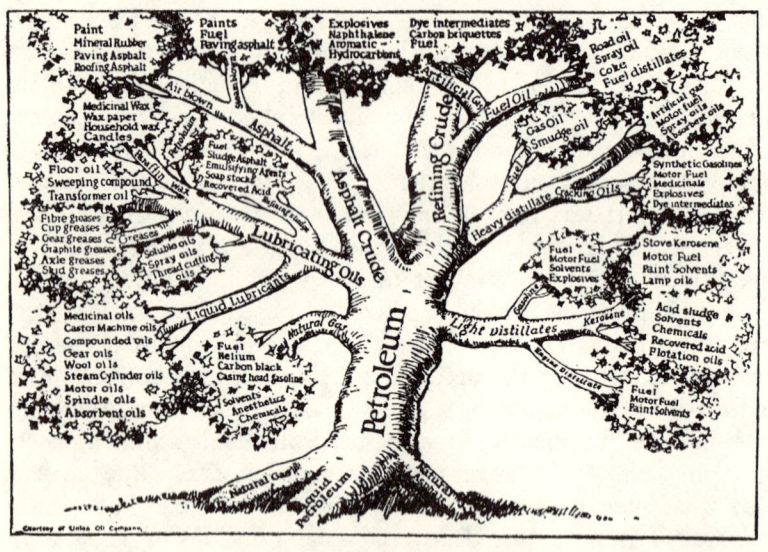

THE BY-PRODUCTS OF PETROLEUM.
(Courtesy Union Oil Co. of Cal.)

in the world, in which every detail was watched with care, in which every saving was made and in which the products were the best that human ingenuity could produce and in which the integrity of the company's brand was guarded as a priceless possession, as indeed it was. For people might curse John D. Rockefeller; but they preferred his kerosene.

II

IN 1870, Henry Clay Pierce, another one of the infant prodigies of the oil business, at the age of nineteen was in possession of a wife and the entire kerosene business of St. Louis. In this year the youthful magnate kissed his still more youthful wife good-by

THE GREAT STRUCTURE

and set out upon an exploration of the then wild and woolly plains of the Southwest. He toured Arkansas and Texas on a pony, with his lamp in one hand and his kerosene samples in the other, astonishing the natives of those primitive provinces with the new illuminant and appointing agents of H. C. Pierce and Company as he traveled. Later he took a partner to supply cash to push his adventurous progress and his firm became known as the Waters-Pierce Company. By 1875, Mr. Pierce, aged 25, was the oil marketing king of Missouri and the great Southwest. Then he looked up one fine morning to find a challenge to battle at his doorstep.

Over in Louisville was another enterprising firm, Chess, Carley, and Company. They had a small refinery or two, but in reality they were marketers, their territory being Kentucky, Tennessee, and certain contiguous states. Chess, Carley, and Company wanted to expand and so they had sent agents into Missouri to contest that profitable market with young Pierce. Pierce, aggressive, warlike, swift in action, replied by throwing an advance army of agents into Kentucky and before Chess, Carley, and Company realized it they were losing more business in Kentucky than they were gaining in Missouri. The war was brief. Chess, Carley, and Company ran up the white flag, they sat down and talked it over with Pierce and wound up with an agreement under which the combatants were to remain thereafter in their own provinces.

But each party carried away something from that conference. Chess, Carley, and Company made a very considerable appraisal of young Mr. Pierce's abilities. And Mr. Pierce found he had been doing battle with the great John D. Rockefeller, disguised as Chess, Carley, and Company. The territory lying west of Cleveland had always been his especial ground. Pierce was not a refiner. He had been buying most of his refined oil from the Standard. The established method of marketing kerosene was from the refiner to the wholesaler, from the wholesaler to the retailer—mostly grocers—and then to the consumer. The Waters-Pierce Company was a wholesaler. So was Chess, Carley, and Company. But the latter was in reality a subsidiary of the Standard Oil which meant that the Standard was actually engaged in wholesaling its own products. After 1875 Rockefeller had decided to wipe out the wholesaler entirely and to market his own oil directly to the retailers and even to retail it to the larger buyers. Accordingly he established other subsidiaries all over the country like Chess, Carley, and Company. And within a few years he was in almost complete possession of the marketing machine. This, as we shall see, was a fateful decision. It produced two results. One was that it became the most powerful weapon in his kit for riveting his monopoly on the oil business. The other was that it became also the most violent irritant on public opinion and resulted in more angry denunciation of the monopolist than anything else he did.

In any case he worked in this with the same swiftness he employed in everything else. In 1878 Mr. Pierce needed money. His business spread out mightily. So he reorganized his company. Forty per cent of the stock was taken by Chess, Carley, and Company, forty per cent by H. A. Hutchins and W. P. Thompson, Standard Oil dummies, of Cleveland. Mr. Pierce and Mr. Waters held only twenty per cent. Shortly after Rockefeller took over the eighty per cent not held by Pierce and Waters. Pierce later proclaimed that he had been tricked and that he immediately bought out Waters and then declared the Standard, which owned 80 per cent of his stock, should never rule him. Twenty years later he was still reciting this brave piece, though Mr. William Randolph Hearst was just sharpening up his big saber to smite the pretense. Gentlemen like Henry Clay Pierce, submerged in preoccupation with money-making, find little use for their sense of humor. The idea of a minority stockholder defying John D. Rockefeller in a corporation in which the latter holds 80 per cent of the stock is a little bit funny, to say the least. We shall see more of all this and of Mr. Pierce.

Mr. Rockefeller had parceled the whole country out into marketing regions. Chess, Carley, and Company had Kentucky, Tennessee, Mississippi. The Waters-Pierce Company had Texas, Arkansas, Louisiana, Kansas, and Missouri. Other subsidiaries handled the marketing in other regions. The whole business centered in New York.

The logic of Rockefeller's great design carried him inevitably into marketing his own products. The old wholesaler was as inefficient as the small manufacturer. He was careless, wasteful, costly. Where there was one competent merchant there were a

THE GREAT STRUCTURE

dozen incompetents. The hard-won savings in the cost of making kerosene were quickly squandered in the costly system of distributing it. Furthermore the job of pushing the uses of kerosene was in the hands of the wholesaler. Only by having possession of the machinery of distribution could Rockefeller exploit the use of his product. There was a still more powerful reason, the importance of which we may see more vividly in its actual operation. This phase of the business Rockefeller had seen in the operation of the Chess, Carley, and Company suit. If he could hold in his hands the instruments of wholesale distribution of the whole country his rivals would be powerless to oppose him.

Of course, Rockefeller's new marketing machine worked with the same meticulous efficiency as his refineries and pipe lines. The old disorder of the coal oil jobbing station was quickly eliminated. Scrupulous cleanliness, constant inspection of implements, buckets, tanks, pumps, and pipes, and wagons and horses, precautions against fire, perfect delivery service, scrupulously just measure—all these things made retailers, whatever they thought of Rockefeller, prefer to buy from him. But in a very short time, as they began to perceive, they had hardly any choice in the matter.

The manner in which this new step made monopoly possible and secure is worth pondering. It illustrates a profound truth in all forms of business and that is that the greater part of all business is transportation. By controlling pipes and railroads Rockefeller had whipped his manufacturing rivals up to the point of getting kerosene to the neighborhood where it must be used. Once at that point there was still a problem of transportation—getting the oil to the retailers. Refined oil was run from the refinery by a pipe into a tank car on a railroad siding. The tank car delivered it to the town where it would be used and emptied it into a storage tank. From there it went to the storage tank of the wholesaler. From this point it must be delivered to the storekeeper. There were several methods. One was to put it in a barrel which was delivered by a truck. The other was in cans protected by a wooden frame. The other was by means of tank wagons. At this time America was a country of small towns. And in a little town a single tank wagon was sufficient to deliver all the oil it needed. Let a wholesaler get possession of the oil trade of a town and a newcomer who introduced a second tank wagon would merely duplicate delivery facilities. The cheapest method of delivery was by tank wagon. But unless the wholesaler had enough customers to keep the wagon busy it was not so cheap. He had to deliver in barrels and cans which was far more expensive. Now in most communities the wholesaler used the barrel and can method. If he did Rockefeller had no difficulty dislodging him by installing his tank wagon delivery. If the wholesaler had a tank wagon service Rockefeller could buy him out or put a wagon into competition with him. The moment he did he cut prices. In this game, which came to be known by the name of predatory price cutting, the individual wholesaler was no match for the Standard. If he attempted to match Rockefeller's drastic cut, his entire business was affected by it. It led to swift and inevitable ruin. Rockefeller could easily cut prices in a single community and assess the losses against business in other places. In this he was ruthless. And in a short time the wholesale business of the country fell into his hands. He controlled the production and course of his product from the refinery to the grocer's door and in many cases to the actual consumer. Smaller refiners who could not hope to own their own marketing machine could not invade most of the communities of the country because there was no jobber left to handle their product.

The country began to be filled with stories of men everywhere being put out of business by the heartless monopoly. Before this the operators who were crushed were limited to a few spots—the few refining cities—and they were not so numerous. Now the men squeezed out were numerous and they were to be found in every city, in every town. Their lamentations were loud, their stories vivid, their characterizations of the monster sulphurous.

III

EVEN at this early day Rockefeller began to encourage office employees to own a little Standard stock. The pompous Col. Payne summoned the office boy one day. "Mr. Rockefeller thinks you should have a little stock in the company," he informed the boy. The lad went to the president of the savings bank across the street and told him he had a chance to get some Standard Oil stock at $25 a share. The banker nearly jumped from his seat. "Get all you can. Get some for me too and I will finance you on your purchase." The boy got 25 shares and the banker took ten of them. The banker's investment was $250. When that gentleman died years later the Standard stock still in his estate was sold at $330,000.

IV

To the reader of today it is difficult to think of the oil industry without gasoline. At the time of which we write the chief business of the Standard Oil Company was the manufacture of kerosene for illuminating purposes. Candles were still widely used in remote places and gas in the better class homes in the larger cities. But for the most part it was the coal oil lamp which supplied the world's chief barrier against the darkness. And as Europe was the most populous and richest part of the world it was the chief market for Rockefeller's kerosene.

This export trade was from the beginning handled by exporters —jobbers who bought the refined oil from the Standard or other refiners and shipped it abroad to wholesale dealers in various countries who in turn sold it to the small retail outlets. It goes without saying that these small wholesale outlets were for the most part inefficient and that they also controlled, subject to competition, the price and service of kerosene to the consumer. They could, of course, shift their business from one refiner to another at will. The whole system of distribution was sloppy, inefficient, wasteful, and costly. All Rockefeller's laboriously wrought economies were thrown away when the oil passed into the hands of the jobber. It was natural, therefore, that Rockefeller should seriously ponder the wisdom of eliminating the exporter and distributing his own product abroad.

Meantime, various incidents began to press upon his attention. Back in 1876, for instance, after he had gotten control of a large section of the refining interest and just as the Empire fight was brewing the exporters in New York began to balk at the price of kerosene. The complaint went up that Rockefeller was destroying the whole industry by raising the price of refined oil. Apparently there was an organized boycott by exporters to bring down the price. But Rockefeller stood his ground, threatened to close refineries and finally in the Fall the exporters yielded.

But there was another consideration. Reports reached Rockefeller continually of oil being found in other parts of the world.

The chief point of competition was Russia. On the shores of the Caspian Sea had burned for centuries the Sacred Fires of Baku. This was nothing but a flame of petroleum bursting up through the rocks. Long before Drake had bored for oil or even before Kier had sold his rubbing ointment crude petroleum was an article of commerce in Russia. But in 1872, the year of Rockefeller's first consolidation, the oil fields of Baku passed into private hands and exploitation began in earnest. By 1879 there were 195 refineries in the Baku district and 1,400,000 barrels were being produced annually. Here was a threat to the markets of Europe and the Orient. Then the experience of America with combination found its way into Russian oil. Nobel Brothers put in $2,500,000. They put down pipe lines, built docks, and tank ships, bought 2,500 tank cars, modernized refineries, built case and can factories, warehouses, tanks, and all the paraphernalia of large scale business. And Russian oil began to find its way into the Orient, to Germany, Austria, and even England as well as Russia. This was a severe threat.

Rockefeller saw all this with growing alarm. He faced the spectacle of his greatest market in the hands of a distribution system which was disorganized, unintelligent, grasping, and ineffective. He decided to become his own distributor. Starting out as a refiner he had gone into the pipe line business, then into the business of manufacturing the by-products of the residuum. Now he believed himself compelled in defense of his markets to enter the distributing business. He was reaching now for every department of oil save production. Out of this he kept religiously. But going into distribution abroad meant also that he would take the step at home too. And this he proceeded to do in 1879.

His first step was to begin the organization of the home markets as we have already seen. His next was to send experts to Europe to study the problem there. Here again he did nothing precipitately. And for five years his agents abroad collected facts, surveyed routes, studied local customs, methods of distribution. Nothing was done until these reports were in hand.

All this may seem elaborate and unnecessary caution. It was not. Rockefeller planned to end the day of the commission man and the jobber. The commission man was or might be an American. The jobber was a native of the country to which he planned to go.

THE GREAT STRUCTURE

He knew that an immense outcry against his new plan might defeat its own end. He had seen much of that at home. Moreover Europe and the Orient were infested with difficulties—tariffs, trade barriers of all sorts, excessive taxes. In China in some small communities the mandarins made it a capital offense to use petroleum; the native priests made anathema any person who used it. There were many in China in influence and power who were interested in the sale of vegetable oils and so in places the great commercial guilds boycotted those dealers who handled kerosene. Many of the same difficulties were met in Japan, India, Siam, Soudan, Liberia, Morocco, Congo, and other places. They had to be overcome or at all events studied. By 1885 the Standard was ready for the inauguration of its foreign merchandising service.

New companies were incorporated in Europe. Rockefeller formed alliances with companies there. He built refineries, put tank cars on the railroads, set up bulk stations, planted small stations. There was an outcry against all this but it did make refined oil cheaper in Europe. Up to this time the Standard sold cargoes of oil of 2,000 to 10,000 barrels to commission men who sent it over in barrels. But in 1885 the company ran its first oil tank steamer carrying a million gallons of oil. In the old days the freight was from $7 to $14 a ton. This was lowered until by 1906 it was $2.50. This business grew amazingly. In about ten years the company had 70 large importing stations abroad, 4,000 interior stations, 16 manufacturing plants, 2,000 tank cars, 4,000 tank wagons, 150 coasting vessels, and barges. It had more wagons retailing oil in Europe than it had in the United States.

The name of the Standard became a household word in every quarter of the globe. The Standard tank was a familiar object in every village of Europe, Asia, and Africa. The Standard delivery service was as familiar along the Nile and the Ganges and the Danube as it was in America—donkey trains in Tunis and Morocco, the camel caravan crossing the desert of the Sahara, with Pratt's Astral Oil, elephants in India bearing the ubiquitous Standard White.

CHAPTER III. THE TRUST IS BORN

THERE were forty corporations in Mr. Rockefeller's group. People spoke of them as part of the Standard Oil Company. But Rockefeller and his comrades denied that this was so. Rockefeller swore in 1880:

"The Standard Oil Company owns its own refineries at Bayonne; it has no other refineries nor any interest in any other refineries. . . . The Standard Oil Company is not now nor has it ever been a stockholder in any railroad, pipe line or other common carrier."

The verdict of the country on this was that Rockefeller lied. John D. Archbold, a Standard director, swore that the Acme Oil Company, of which he was president, was not owned or controlled by the Standard or its directors or affiliated with it. He swore he didn't know the United Pipe Lines were controlled by the Standard. Henry H. Rogers swore that Pratt and Company was not owned by the Standard. After much fishing he admitted Pratt and Company was "in harmony with it." Rockefeller swore that "the Standard Oil Company never had any contract with any lines of transportation in which it was stipulated that it should have a lower rate of freight than other shippers undertaking the same obligations and furnishing the same facilities."

These were categorical denials of everything which the country believed to be well known and the whole batch of Standard leaders were put down as liars and perjurers. One must know something of the set up of the whole Rockefeller group to understand precisely the elaborate details they arranged to enable them to swear to these things or at least most of them, without actually committing legal perjury. And this introduces us to one of the most remarkable figures in that group of remarkable men—Samuel C. T. Dodd, the lawyer of the Standard.

Dodd, like petroleum, was a native son of Venango County, just three years older than John D. After working at the printers' case, he graduated from Jefferson College at Canonsburg, Pennsylvania, studied law, and was admitted to the bar the year Drake struck oil. He tasted his first fame as a member of the constitutional convention of the state by his denouncement of Rockefeller's first at-

THE TRUST IS BORN

tempts at monopoly. He was attorney for Captain J. J. Vandergrift and when that gentleman joined the Standard, Dodd was adopted by Rockefeller as his attorney. Dodd was an eccentric genius. He was a lover of classic literature, had a weakness for exercising his literary powers, wrote occasional magazine articles and at intervals even broke into verse. He wrote the first poem on petroleum to appear in print:

> "The Land of Grease! The Land of Grease
>   Where burning oil is loved and sung;
>   Where flourish arts of sale and lease
>   Where Rouseville rose and Tarville sprung;
>   Eternal Summer gilds them not
>   But oil wells render dear each spot."

Thus sung the barrister who was to achieve fame as the inventor of the trust. After Dodd hit upon this device he became a man of one idea and busied his mind inventing fictions for Standard managers to hide behind. His mind, which at times seemed expansive and humane, was at other times busy treading the narrow mazes of legalistic subterfuge. He affords an instructive example of the curious phenomenon which advocacy works in an honest mind. For himself he always insisted on receiving a very modest retainer for his services to the company. Rockefeller, a little troubled at Dodd's small salary, had an associate urge him to buy some Standard Oil stock, from the increment of which Rockefeller knew he could reap a rich reward. Dodd refused. He insisted that ownership of the company's stock would deprive him of that perfect detachment essential to sound legal service to his client. He might find his interest at war with his judgment and hence obscuring it. Yet this able and upright lawyer could invent with perfect spiritual composure the scheme which helped to explain Rockefeller's alleged falsehood; which enabled Standard leaders, while violating laws in fact to tread with legal safety upon the edges of perjury.

The name Standard Oil was used even at this time to describe a refining corporation—the Standard Oil Company of Ohio (and of Pittsburgh)—and to describe a group of interests. As a matter of fact those interests comprised many corporations—forty of them—of which the Standard Oil of Ohio was just one. The stocks of all these corporations belonged, not to the Standard Oil Company, but to some thirty-seven stockholders, all of whom were stockholders of the Standard. Apparently from 1874 on when corporations were acquired, the stocks were transferred to various Standard men. This is what happened in the case of the Acme Oil Company, the United Pipe Lines, Chess, Carley, and Company and others. And so Mr. Rockefeller and Rogers and Flagler could truthfully say these companies did not belong to the Standard Oil Company. They belonged to the stockholders of the Standard. Here was the forerunner of the present bank-affiliate. However, it was not so easy to swear truthfully that Standard Oil did not own them or control them or *have any interest* in them "directly or indirectly." And so in 1879 when investigations began and prying eyes peeped at them through every chink in their wall, Samuel Dodd cooked up a little scheme which to his legalistic mind added enough to the indirection to make it invisible. On April 8th, 1879, the stockholders of the Standard and of all the other corporations conveyed their stocks to three trustees, George H. Vilas, M. R. Keith, and George F. Chester. These men were employees. Vilas was the head bookkeeper and traveling auditor (the first of the breed). These stocks, valued at $55,000,000, they held until 1882. These three men now owned the companies. This was just a fiction and a legal fiction at that. But it was enough to enable Rockefeller and his associates to deny all sorts of connection with their various holdings.

The public used the term Standard Oil to refer to a very definite group of interests controlled by Rockefeller and his associates. Those gentlemen always refused to understand this perfectly simple and obvious use of English. The Standard Oil had no interest in the United Pipe Lines, they would gravely assert in one breath. But in the next, when they wished to boast of the achievements of the Standard Oil they would tell of the magnificent system of the pipe lines the great company had endowed the oil industry with. Archbold could say the Standard did not own the Acme, that the Standard stockholders did not own it. The Acme stock they owned had been conveyed to Messrs. Vilas, Chester, and Keith. With such thin and watery fictions Dodd's special pleading mind could be satisfied. When Rockefeller was asked in 1888 if he owned any stock in the Southern Improvement Company, he looked gravely at his questioner and replied: "No." The name of the company was the South Improvement Company. The committee was investigating that. Men spoke of it interchangeably as the South and the Southern Improvement Company. On this count he was roundly denounced as a perjurer. But Lawyer Dodd ransacked the old Pennsylvania statutes and actually found a company called the Southern Improvement Company. Rockefeller was quite right, he argued, and later Starr J. Murphy, Mr. Rockefeller's personal attorney, wrote a little article in support of it, in denying he was a member of the "Southern." He would have been untruthful if he had answered otherwise.

Thus these gentlemen escaped the legal definition of perjury. What their moral responsibility was will vary with the philosophy of their critics.

II

OUT OF this fictitious trust of Vilas, Chester, and Keith was born in the mind of Samuel Dodd his great trust idea. And in 1882 he completed for Rockefeller that epoch-making scheme, which was to be so widely copied and was to give a name to the modern big business enterprise. This was the Standard Oil Trust.

By this famous agreement all of the stockholders in all the corporations conveyed their stocks to nine trustees. These trustees were John D. Rockefeller, O. H. Payne, William Rockefeller, J. A. Bostwick, H. M. Flagler, W. G. Warden, Charles Pratt Benjamin Brewster, and John D. Archbold.

These trustees then became the stockholders of all the corporations. They exercised all the duties of stockholders, to elect directors; to have custody of the stocks and bonds, to collect the interest and dividends paid by all the corporations and distribute those earnings to the proper parties.

The trustees were empowered to name themselves as directors on the various corporations thus brought together and of course, this they did, so that they held in their hands the immediate control and direction of the whole fabric.

The various stockholders who thus delivered their stocks received in return trust certificates in denominations of $100. The trustees were then directed to dissolve any of the corporations they wished and to organize others in each state to take over the business of the existing corporations. And these corporations were to be known by the names of the states in which they might be formed.

It was in pursuance of this plan that very soon the trustees began forming the Standard Oil Company of New Jersey, the Standard Oil Company of New York, and others.

Such was the first great trust. Its capital was fixed at $70,000,000. And of this amount the nine trustees controlled 466,280 shares out of 700,000. Thus they owned two-thirds of the stocks in all the companies. It did not change their control which they already enjoyed. But it unified it and effectually prevented any of the rapidly increasing number of stockholders from having any finger whatever in the various corporations.

Dodd, the maker of screens, was much impressed with this invention. He wrote of it in 1888:

"Stockholders of the various corporations referred to became mutually interested in the stocks of all. It was a union, not of corporations, but of stockholders. The companies continue to conduct their business as before. They ceased to be competitive in the sense of trying to undersell each other. They continued to be competitive and are to this day competitive in the sense that each company strives to show the best results in making the best products, at the lowest prices."

With such a definition of competition could this ingenious solicitor be satisfied. Like most lawyers he had a way of mixing up the economic and legal meaning of words.

Of course this trust agreement, like the preceding one to Vilas, Chester, and Keith, was kept a profound secret. It was several years before its general form became known to certain leading business men. It was not until 1888 that the general public became acquainted with its terms.

III

WHILE Rockefeller, under the guidance of Dodd, thus consciously shaped his course, Fate spun its threads for the larger fabric of his destiny at many points remote from him. George B. Selden filed a few years before (1879) papers for a patent on a device for driving a vehicle by an internal combustion engine. Three years before that a German named Otto had invented the four-cycle internal combustion engine and a few years after Selden filed his patent, another German, Gottlieb Daimler, of Manheim, perfected a sys-

THE TRUST IS BORN

tem of ignition for the combustion engine which added enormously to its utility and in another two years Carl Benz was to build a car driven by gasoline which would actually go. And by this time all over America and Europe, in little shops, in kitchens, in woodsheds, skilled and unskilled visionaries worked to perfect that long-dreamed of monstrosity, the horseless carriage which, when it came, was to add to John D. Rockefeller's fortune, after he retired, a greater heap of gold than he was able to earn through all the years of his active business career.

IV

BUT OTHER forces were at work, some favorable, others hardly so good. For one, it was this year, 1882, when Dodd was fashioning his precious trust, that Theodore Roosevelt, twenty-three years old, was making his entry into public life as a member of the New York legislature. He would bring many a pang to the heart of the good Mr. Rockefeller, who as the agent of the Lord (as he was now coming to think himself) was heaping up riches to advance the works of the Kingdom.

And the year before (1881) the first magazine article to reveal an insight into the true significance of what Rockefeller was doing was printed in the *Atlantic Monthly*. The author was Henry Demarest Lloyd, whom we will meet again, and who was destined to perform a historic service some years later. His article—"The Story of a Great Monopoly"—was almost the first to reveal expressly that Rockefeller's progress was an attack on the very fundamental economic religion of the time. Hitherto most of the cries which went up against Rockefeller and the trusts were from his direct victims—refiners and dealers. Here was a warning from a disinterested journalist and student who had become fascinated by Rockefeller's operations in 1876 and had been making notes about them since that time. Lloyd noted that among a large section of our people, immersed in the pursuit of riches, there was a profound admiration for our growing industrial giants. His article produced a good deal of a stir among thoughtful people. Charles Edward Russell stumbled upon it in a library and was deeply moved by it. "It marked a turning point in our history," he said later. The *Atlantic Monthly* ran through seven editions because of that article.

And in 1880 occurred another event of more than passing note.

An old schoolmate of Rockefeller's, Marcus Alonzo Hanna, organized the Cleveland Business Men's Marching Club and thus made his entry into politics. Some students have put this down as the beginning of the definite alliance between politics and business. Before this business men kept aloof from politics. Certain large-scale gentlemen who wanted franchises and political favors went into the market—the legislature or the aldermanic chamber—and bought them outright. Hanna now tried a different way. He was, unlike Rockefeller, a man of many interests. Starting as a wholesale grocer, he found himself in many ventures. He was interested in iron and coal and ships. He was deeply interested in street railways and became later one of Cleveland's street railway magnates. He bought a theatre and produced a few plays. Later he became president of a bank. Now in 1880 he went formally into politics and took with him a train of marching sheep called business men. His move was to produce far-reaching results.

There was to be plenty of business mixed in the politics of the coming years. Rockefeller himself took no active part in political life, though he, as well as Flagler and Archbold and Payne, contributed liberally to campaign funds. Rockefeller gave to the Republicans. Payne made his checks to the Democrats. But there was little or no intimate party affiliation. In 1880, Garfield was a candidate for the presidency—Garfield, whose son, twenty-five years later, would deal Rockefeller and his friends such a crippling blow. Garfield wrote Amos Townsend of Cleveland to know "if Mr. Rockefeller would be willing to assist?" He added: "Do you know his state of feeling toward me? Is it such that I might safely invite him for consultation and talk freely with him about Indiana and ask his coöperation?" But already Mr. Rockefeller's name was a dangerous one to utter during a campaign. "It would not be safe for him to visit you as it would be reported and cut like a knife in Pennsylvania. He is, however, all right and will do what he can." Then the cautious Townsend advised Garfield "to keep your hand off paper." What did Garfield want? Not "raising of means." Mr. Rockefeller can "do what is more important than that." Indiana is the pivotal state, thinks Garfield. McGregor, the Standard agent in Indiana, is anxious to help Garfield. He has charge of the Standard forces in Ohio. Will Mr. Rockefeller back him up in this?

"He could use 500 more of the right sort if sent." Is the presidential candidate suggesting that the Standard send 500 men into Indiana?

V

ONE MEMBER of the Standard Oil group, Col. Oliver H. Payne, looked upon himself as infinitely superior to his able but humble associates. Some of them occasionally referred to him as "God." He was full of exalted ambitions. One of them was to make his father, Henry B. Payne, president of the United States. Henry B. Payne was a distinguished member of the Ohio bar. He had served in Congress. His most distinguished service had been as chairman of the committee of the House which united with the Senate to arrange the Hayes-Tilden inquiry. To the oil trust his chief service had been to defeat the Hopkins and Reagan interstate commerce bills. Now Ohio had named a legislature with a commission to deal with the monopoly evil. Before that legislature ended its life it came to be known as the "Coal Oil Legislature." It defeated the free pipe line bill. The agent of the corrupt interests, himself a member, appeared one day upon the floor drunk. This outraged the dignity of the House. It instituted proceedings against him. He loudly threatened to make public the names of members he had purchased and the proceedings were dropped.

The Democrats had the majority. Who would be United States Senator would be settled at the Democratic caucus. The chief candidates were Pendleton, Booth, and Ward. Pendleton declared he had a majority of the Democrats definitely pledged to him. The Democratic caucus was delayed until the night before the day on which the legislature was to ballot on the election of a Senator. Suddenly there appeared in Columbus Col. Oliver H. Payne, Treasurer of the Standard Oil Company, and various associates. The candidacy of Henry B. Payne for Senator was suddenly sprung. Money made its appearance. It was charged that Col. Payne brought $65,000 to Columbus. Witnesses declared afterward that in the hotel room which was Payne's headquarters Payne sat behind a desk on which the currency was arranged in denominations. The air was full of rumors, charges, denunciations of bribery, and corruption. The Democratic caucus met. The Payne managers moved that the ballot be secret, which was an innovation. When the votes were counted, to the amazement of every one Payne had

46 votes, Ward 17, and Pendleton only 15. Under a cloud of suspicion Henry B. Payne took his seat as a United States Senator.

Later, when the Cincinnati *Commercial Gazette* charged that Payne's election had been bought the House of Representatives of Ohio ordered an investigation, produced a mass of testimony, and then sent a memorial to the United States Senate demanding an investigation. When the charges were first made Payne wrote, "I challenge the most thorough and rigid scrutiny." But when the matter was referred to the Senate Committee on Privileges and Elections, he held his peace and his friends fought any attempt to investigate. He asked that the petition of the Ohio House be referred to the proper committee and characterized the testimony accompanying it as "hundreds of pages of gossip." Thereafter he refused to utter another word in his defense. The Republican Central Committee of Ohio filed a bitter denunciation of his election as procured by fraud and corruption. A convention of Republican editors presented a similar petition. Various Democrats added their criticism. Senator Sherman, Payne's colleague, said: "I believe from my own knowledge of the history of events in Ohio, as well as from papers sent to us, there is a profound conviction in the minds of the body of the people of Ohio of all political parties that in the election of my colleague there was gross corruption." Senator Hoar vigorously denounced Payne's election and led the fight for an investigation. The testimony submitted by the Ohio House is still extant. It is indeed filled with gossip and rumor. But it is also filled with a mass of statements which warrant an inescapable suspicion that that election was tainted by fraud and justified an inquiry. Nevertheless the Senate refused to make it. Sometime later, provoked by a remark of Senator Hoar, Payne broke his silence briefly to defend himself and praise the Standard Oil Company. The venerable Senator Hoar arose and said:

"A Senator who, when the governor of his state, when both branches of the legislature complained to us that a seat in the United States Senate had been bought; when the other Senator from the state arose and told us that that was the belief of a large majority of the people of Ohio, without distinction of party, failed to rise in his place and ask for the investigation which would have put an end to the charges, sheltering himself behind the technicalities which were found by gentlemen on both sides of the chamber . . . I should think forever after would hold his peace."

By the time this statement was made Grover Cleveland was President of the United States. Payne, father of the Standard treasurer, was Senator from Ohio. J. N. Camden, president of a Standard subsidiary, was Senator from West Virginia, William C. Whitney, allied to the Payne family, was Secretary of the Navy. And Grover Cleveland said more than once to friends that he owed his nomination to Whitney. The alliance between business and politics was proceeding merrily.

CHAPTER IV. THE STORY OF RICE

THERE now appeared in the public notice one of the most troublous of the many thorns which pricked the cuticle of John D. Rockefeller. George Rice, a virile and resolute warrior from the Green Mountains of Vermont, began his adventures in oil in the lost town of Pithole. Before that greasy bubble sank back into the jungle Rice went to Macksburg, Ohio, and built a refinery there. He had built it to a capacity of 2,000 barrels a week. He operated at a very low cost, acting himself as chief of staff, while one of his daughters was bookkeeper, another secretary, and his son-in-law general manager.

Rice sold his oil throughout the South in competition with Chess, Carley, and Company and later with the Waters-Pierce outfit. Of course, he soon found himself at war with these ruthless merchants. Everywhere his agents ran into the cruel competition of these powerful and unscrupulous organizations. Rice's agents made a sale to a man named Armstrong in Louisville. But at the last moment Armstrong notified Rice's man that he could not go through with it. He was afraid. Chess, Carley, and Company had told him point-blank that if he bought oil from anybody but them they would break him, that they would spend $10,000 to do this, that they would sell groceries cheaper than he could and thus put him out of business. In Nashville, Chess, Carley, and Company wrote over their signature to Wilkerson and Company that they regretted to learn of the latter's refusal to make proper arrangements. "It is with great reluctance that we undertake serious com-

> Chess Carley
> LOUISVILLE
>
> [GENERAL FREIGHT OFFICE L&N. PM JUN 17 1881 R.R. LOUISVILLE, KY.]
>
> J. M. Culp E
> G.F.A.
>
> Dear Sir:
>
> Wilkinson & Co Nashville received Car of oil Monday 13 — 70 Bbl. which we suspect slipped thro on the usual 5ᵗʰ class rate — in fact we might say "we know" it did — paying only $41.50 freight from here. Charges $59.40. Please turn another screw.
>
> Yours truly,
> Chess Carley
>
> June 16/81

FACSIMILE OF LETTER FROM CHESS, CARLEY & CO. TO RAILROAD FREIGHT AGENT.
(Reproduced from S. O. Company, First Decade by Geo. Rice)

petition with any one. And certainly this competition will not be confined to coal oil or any one article and will not be limited to any one year."

To H. R. S. Duck, of Atlanta, they wrote: "We learned with

regret of your receipt of oil from a competing interest. . . . For you to unite with the enemy and turn against the oil position in Atlanta, will of course bring a competition on other goods and general loss to us and probably to you."

What was meant by "competition on other goods"? These dealers in oil were primarily grocers. If they bought oil from a competitor of Chess, Carley, and Company they were threatened with competition on their groceries. In one town a grocer bought from a Standard competitor. So we find Chess, Carley, and Company writing to its agent, W. C. Chase, there: "The rust proof oats will go today. You had better put your sign out—Rust proof oats to arrive at 98 cents to a dollar a bushel. This will kill him. The same sign should be used for meats, sugar, coffee, etc." In Columbus, Mississippi, the grocers bought their oil from Rice. Chess, Carley, and Company, as was their right, sought to sell these grocers but without success. Then they threatened: "If you do not buy our oil we will start a grocery store and sell goods at cost and put you all out of business." They made good on the threat, at least to the extent of setting up a grocery at which everything was sold at cost and below. But the local grocers met and issued a statement to the public exposing the cruel stratagem. Not a customer crossed the threshold of the Standard store. Rice shipped oil to Wilkerson and Company in Louisville, at the customary fifth class rate. A few days later (June 16th) Mr. J. M. Culp, General Freight Agent of the Louisville and Nashville Railroad, got this letter from Chess, Carley, and Company:

"Wilkerson and Company received car of oil Monday 13th—70 barrels which we suspect slipped through at the usual fifth class rate—in fact we might say we know it did—paying only $41.50 freight from here. Charges $57.40. Please turn another screw."

Five days later freight rates on Rice's oil were advanced fifty per cent. The Standard shipped in tanks. Rice shipped in barrels. On oil in tanks the Standard paid twenty-five cents a barrel. In barrels the rate to Rice was fifty cents. Rice tried to get an arrangement with the railroad to use tanks but could never bring them to the point. What was worse, the Standard companies operated 3,000 tank cars. On these they paid freight on the basis of 20,000 gallons to each car. Of the 3,000 cars only two held 20,000 gallons. Most of them held over 30,000 and many as high as 44,000 gallons. These are but a few of the countless instances of this kind of warfare which Rice met everywhere. It is not to be wondered at that the man became bitter.

II

OIL BEGAN to appear in quantity in the Macksburg field and immediately Rice started production there. At the same time the Standard Oil sent its pipe lines there. The field was served by a small railroad called the Cincinnati and Marietta Railroad. It was in the hands of a receiver—a queer old fellow named Phineas Pease, destined to play a most embarrassing rôle. Daniel O'Day, representing the Standard, demanded that Pease post an open rate of 35 cents a barrel on oil and that he turn 25 cents of this over to the Standard. Pease was troubled by the demand but was afraid of Rockefeller. He wrote his attorney, Edward S. Rapallo of New York, asking how it might be done without involving himself in personal responsibility. Rapallo advised that it could be done and outlined one of those merry little legal fictions so popular then and now. The rate was made thirty-five cents. All shippers paid it but not to the road. It was paid to an agent who represented the Standard and the receiver. This agent turned over 10 cents to the road and 25 cents to the Standard on every barrel shipped. And so between March 20th and April 26th, 1885, the Standard collected $340 in drawbacks on the oil shipped by Rice, while the road got only $136.

When Rice learned this he stopped shipments, built his own small pipe line and quietly started to collect evidence of the outrage. Then in October he filed suit against Pease and got an order directing the terrified old receiver to report on all rates, rebates, etc. Pease sent his freight agent posthaste to O'Day and in twelve days Mr. Rice found in his mail one morning a check from the Standard Oil Company for the $340 of which he had been deprived. But Rice wanted more than the check. He wanted Pease to confess. And so the court compelled Pease to produce all the correspondence. In the end Judge John Baxter, of the United States Circuit Court of Ohio, removed Pease as receiver. "The discrimination complained of in this case," said Judge Baxter, "is so wanton and oppressive it could hardly have been accepted by an honest man, having due regard for the rights of others or conceded by a just and competent receiver . . . and a judge who would tolerate such a wrong or retain such a receiver capable of perpetrating it ought to be impeached and degraded from his position."

The judge named George K. Nash, former governor of Ohio, master to take testimony. To him Pease swore he never paid the Standard any part of the money. Of course he had not. Pease stuck to the fiction invented by Rapallo. But Nash laboriously untangled the skein and resolved the fiction. He also brought out that the Standard had been paid $614 on another man's oil and $639 on still another. And so the Standard returned both these sums.

These revelations raised a storm of abuse and deepened the hatred in which Rockefeller's name was being held by the country. It was a black piece of injustice and it gave a blacker hue to the character of many acts which were not so unjust. O'Day explained that the 25 cents was a charge for carrying the oil in the Standard pipes to the railroad. But this was untrue as Rice's oil was not carried that way. Rockefeller was ultimately compelled to notice this charge. "We repudiated the contract," he told a New York *World* reporter March 29, 1890, "before it was passed on by the courts. It was not agreed to by the officers of the company because our counsel declared it illegal." Then he added a defense which was to be heard many times later. "In a business as large as ours, conducted by so many agents, some things are likely to be done which we cannot approve. We correct them as soon as they come to our knowledge. The public hears the wrong—it never hears the correction."

Rockefeller liked this explanation so much he made it in substance the first sentence of his defense of his company in his book of reminiscences. "It would be surprising if in an organization like ours which included a great number of men there should not be an occasional employee here and there who acted in connection with the business in a way which might be criticized."

Daniel O'Day could not be included under the classification of an occasional employee. Neither could Carley, of Chess, Carley, and Company, who wrote so many of the letters referred to at the beginning of this chapter. Moreover, the same terms, including the drawback, which was undoubtedly the invention of the fertile and unscrupulous mind of Flagler—were levied on many other roads.

The money was not returned until eight months after it was squeezed out of Rice and then only when an exposure was threatened in the court.

III

IT is not true, as has been so many times asserted, that the progress of John D. Rockefeller was due wholly to the rebate and the drawback. His immense efficiency was perhaps the most important force back of his progress. But it would be equally untrue to say that these unjust discriminations did not contribute enormously to his success by helping to cripple his rivals as well as by adding to his profits. Mr. Lewis Emery, Jr., for the Industrial Commission, estimated that between October 11th and March 31, 1879, the Standard Oil Company shipped 18,556,277 barrels of oil. This was the period of the contract with the four trunk roads under which carrying percentages of the freight rate were rebated to the Standard. These rebates ran from 11 per cent on the Baltimore and Ohio to 47 per cent on the Pennsylvania. They averaged about 55 cents a barrel. On that basis the total rebates paid the company were $10,151,218. John D. Archbold, testifying before the same Commission, denied the truth of these figures and offered some evidence in rebuttal. But at best Archbold's defense, in part wholly false, would call for only some modification of Emery's computation. Even after allowing for some reductions such an advantage would hardly be called an unimportant one.

For years since the first appearance of Rockefeller the odor of rebates filled the air. But certainly there was nothing new in rebates when John D. Rockefeller began to use them. "The Standard Oil Company of Ohio did receive rebates prior to 1880," he admitted in later years. "But it received no advantages for which it did not give full compensation. The reason for rebates was that such was the railroads' methods of doing business. A public rate was made and collected by the railroad companies, but, so far as my knowledge extends, was seldom retained in full. A portion of it was repaid to the shippers as a rebate."

That was the truth. But as to never being retained, it *was* retained against the "innocent and the weak" as one commentator phrases it. And Mr. Rockefeller was not playing long with this unfair and vicious weapon before he found new uses for it and

THE STORY OF RICE

began to see that the number who enjoyed it was constantly diminished.

Rebattre, to beat down, that is the origin of the word. It involves the suggestion of bargaining. And that is what it was. The rebate went back to the earliest days of the roads, who were its first victims. The wielder of the weapon then was the canals. For when the railroads came the canals saw their day threatened. And the canals, like the roads later, were in the hands of men who had learned how to play politics and use the lobby. They were able to compel the roads by law to pay to them rebates on every ton of freight they carried. Indeed many of those roads which were in competition with the canals were thus prevented from carrying freight at all and were limited to passengers. Some of these laws were not repealed until the late fifties. Thus in turn each mechanical contrivance fights the coming of its successor. The horse cars held off the trolleys. The trolley lines fight the bus, the little grocer fights the chain, the candle maker fights the kerosene lamp, and the gas company fights the electric light company.

When the railroads got under way they slid into the habit of discriminatory rates so easily and smoothly that they must have been hardly aware of it. At first, of course, they knew little of the modern cult of cost accounting. What the cost was to haul things was a mystery. To complicate this larger shippers at first frequently supplied their own wagons for freight and in certain cases their own locomotives. Hence there were differences in rates depending on what the shipper supplied, and the service he asked. And so in an age of bargaining, every shipper bargained with the railroad company and each shipper, as Rockefeller said, "made the best bargain he could, but whether he was doing better than his competitor was only a matter of conjecture."

Andrew Carnegie was a railroad man before he was a steel master. He was assistant to that master manipulator of rails and men, Tom Scott, of the Pennsylvania, when Scott was the superintendent of the Pittsburgh division and Pittsburgh was just a small city rising on the hills. The railroads wanted traffic; hence they were keen to develop new industries. The man who walked into the superintendent's office and said he was going to start a factory that would have goods to ship could be sure of getting a rate from the road that amounted to a kind of subsidy. In later years Carnegie told how eager Scott was to develop local freight. A man came in and declared his intention of cutting bark to ship to a tannery, hoping later to start a tannery of his own, provided the road would give him a low rate and encourage him. He was sure to get it. A quarryman came to say he was going to open a quarry and wanted a low rate. He got it. When another man came and said that he too proposed to start a quarry, then, as the canny Andy put it, "the plot thickened." Coal mines, iron works, all sorts of plants came one after the other, each asking at first a kind of fostering rate. They got these rates. There was no rule. But by this means the road built up the most extraordinary region of local traffic ever known in railroad history. Moreover the traffic then was from east to west. The freight trains came back to Pittsburgh empty and this led to the road's offering any kind of rate to get freight into those cars on the return trip east. In the end the situation was one in which almost every shipper was paying a different rate, and in which every locality had a different place in the preferences of the schedules. The most ridiculous discriminations arose.

Carnegie laughed over some of these results. Pittsburgh shippers would often send their cargo west on the Ohio River to Cincinnati, a distance of 500 miles, where it would be loaded on the Pennsylvania and would then start back east for New York. It would travel back over those 500 miles by rail and go through the streets of Pittsburgh and on to New York for a cheaper rate than if it had been sent direct from Pittsburgh. "The Pennsylvania Railroad was regarded as a monopoly strangling local interests," said Carnegie, "and so indeed it was."

But he knew how these strange rates had originated and he withheld his criticism.

When, therefore, the railroads sent their branches into the oil regions the scramble for rates began at once. Everybody went to the freight agents and bargained for rates. Who was getting the best rates nobody could tell. We may assume, however, that John D. Rockefeller was not behindhand. Much depended, he explained, upon whether the shipper had the advantage of competition among the carriers.

"The Standard Oil Company," he said, "being situated at Cleveland, had the advantage of different carrying lines, as well as water transportation in the summer; taking advantage of those facilities it made the best bargains possible for its freights. Other companies sought to do the same."

That was true. At the time when the oil men were bitterly denouncing Rockefeller, we find a member of their committee, W. T. Scheide, collecting $7,000 in two months on rebates for the oil shipped by his principal, Neyhart, of New York. This same Neyhart is down in a list of rebates and returned overcharges paid by the New York and Lake Erie Railroad for $188,127 in 1879 and two other shippers, Gust. Heye and S. D. Karns, are credited with over $7,000 apiece. This list was furnished to the Hepburn Committee. Not only in the oil fields but everywhere it was the same.

There is another phase of the rebate which must be conceded in Rockefeller's defense. The simple truth is that in the end the matter resolved itself more or less into a case of quantity discount. There is much to be said for the quantity discount. After all the cost of anything we buy, commodity or service, in an ideal system might well be put down as a figure made up of the cost of rendering the service plus a reasonable profit. If we buy a single article of anything we pay one price. If we buy a dozen or a case we expect to pay proportionately less. And justly. For after all it costs a merchant less per article to sell a number of articles than one. There is one operation instead of a dozen, one package instead of a dozen packages and a quick turnover of money. So it costs a railroad less to stop and pick up fifty barrels of oil at one station than to stop and pick up five barrels of oil at each of ten stations. Particularly is this true when the quantities handled become large. There is no doubt, therefore, that the Standard Oil Company was in a position to ask with some show of reason for a lower rate on 2,000 barrels of oil a day than the man who shipped 50 one day and none the next.

On the question of rebates, therefore, it must at this day be conceded that Rockefeller in asking them was doing nothing more than every other shipper who had enough business to make the demand. Moreover there was on the side of the practice itself— outside its abuses—the defense that it was based on cost of handling and the theory underlying the quantity discount.

If the quantity discount had been recognized as an established principle and rates had been definitely graded based on costs of handling in different quantities and these rates had been open to all a good defense could be made for them. They were, however, a practice which had grown up. And criticism for using them must rest on almost all. Criticism may well be directed at the system but not at Rockefeller for using it.

While this much must be said for Rockefeller, he was not on such solid grounds when he demanded them for himself and insisted that they be refused to others. Rockefeller has always found complete shelter for his conscience in legal and business fictions which he has set up to cover the real character of his acts. For instance, he has always insisted that the railroads reserved the right to grant the same rates to any other shipper handling *as much as he did*. That is true. But there was no such shipper and could not be any other. After a certain development was passed the reservation would be meaningless. But there was an agreement that no other shipper should be permitted to get as big. There was an agreement to protect the Standard Oil against competitors and whenever competitors threatened to grow big enough to match shipments as in the case of the Equitable Pipe Line and the Tidewater, Rockefeller called on the railroads to protect him by lowering rates.

When Mr. Ohlen and others went to Cassatt to demand the same rebates as Rockefeller got and Cassatt refused, Ohlen asked if he would grant them if they shipped as much as Rockefeller. Cassatt bluntly and frankly said No. One asks why the railroads should go so far to protect Rockefeller. Cassatt gave that answer. Rockefeller was the only one who could keep peace among the roads. And how did Rockefeller do this? The roads had made a pool to divide the traffic between them. They could not possibly carry out such an agreement if the traffic was coming from hundred of small refiners and shippers. If it came from one shipper who was in the agreement with them it could be done. Here was the method. Each road was entitled to a specified percentage of shipments from various refining points to others. At the end of the month it was inevitable that these percentages would not work out perfectly. The Standard Oil Company could then rectify these differences the following month by shifting its shipments. This is what Cassatt meant by keeping peace among the roads. This, however, did not mitigate the injustice done to other shippers who

THE STORY OF RICE

were prevented by this means from bargaining for advantageous rates. No one was allowed to bargain but Rockefeller.

But there was one practice which the Standard Oil exacted and which apparently these oil men invented for which no excuse can be found; a practice which perpetuated an injustice so grave, so cruel, so indefensible, that its exposure put a stain upon Rockefeller's name which he has never been able to efface. This was the drawback. Some searcher in our economic history may find a prior use of this deadly and ruthless weapon. I have not been able to find it. It was one thing to go, like every other shipper, to a railroad and demand a rebate of ten or twenty or fifty cents on his own shipments of oil. It was another thing to demand that no other shipper should get a rebate and that, furthermore, Rockefeller should receive a drawback of ten or twenty or fifty cents a barrel on every barrel of oil his rival shipped. By this system Rockefeller in one instance paid $1.20 a barrel for the shipment of his own oil. The railroad gave him back twenty cents as a discount. His rival also paid $1.20. But the railroad gave the twenty cents on his oil to Rockefeller. It was of course secret. Without knowing why, his competitor was being bled white by Rockefeller. The Standard Oil Company always denied this. Rockefeller has never admitted it. But that this was done is attested by evidence so overwhelming that at this day it is fatuous to deny it.

In February and March of 1878, Mr. H. C. Ohlen shipped 29,876 barrels of oil over the Pennsylvania Railroad to New York. On these shipments the Standard Oil Company, which performed no service for Ohlen—which contributed not one cent to the production, transportation, or handling of his oil—collected from the Pennsylvania Railroad 20 cents on every barrel shipped. The road paid the Standard in these two months $5,975.20 profits thus secretly squeezed out of Ohlen.

One cannot help wondering how any business man would have the audacity to approach a railroad with a proposal for such a favor. One wonders why the roads granted it.

It is not easy to trace the genesis of the drawback. Its first appearance is in the South Improvement Company contract with the railroads. There it is all set out in black and white in a contract which bears the signature of the company's officials. The South Improvement Company was to get a set of rebates for itself. In addition to this it was to get $1.06 a barrel on all oil shipped by its rivals to New York. An attempt has been made to explain the reasonableness of the drawback and the inevitable professor is found to do it. The theory advanced is that at the time and for years later it was common for men to hire whole trains. A well-known instance is the excursion train which associations often engaged to run privately-managed excursions. They would then have the right to sell tickets at any rate they chose. Rockefeller made an agreement with the railroads to run a daily train, guaranteeing enough oil to justify a full train. He supplied the cars, the handling, and terminals and was, therefore, entitled to a low rate. Before this an oil train would go along every day, stopping at numerous depots. The oil men would deliver their oil in marked barrels to these depots—one, two or fifty to be picked up by the train, just as milk cans are now. There was never any guarantee as to how many barrels there would be at any station. When a daily train cargo was guaranteed by Rockefeller, the train became in effect his. And as the train continued to pick up barrels for others, Rockefeller was entitled to a part of the profit of that traffic. This is another one of those numerous fictions which strew the path of Mr. Rockefeller. This one is a pure fiction from beginning to end. First of all in 1872 when the South Improvement Company contract was made there was no such train, no such arrangement, no Rockefeller-owned terminals, or handling arrangements. It was not until after this that Rockefeller's shipments justified a train. But it was never regarded as Rockefeller's train. Moreover his train loads ran only from certain places and other trains between other points had to be run just the same; yet he got his drawbacks on these other train shipments. The whole thing is a fiction invented after the fact by an over-zealous apologist. Rockefeller himself never made any such defense. He and all his aids always denied the drawbacks. It was possible to get them because Rockefeller had convinced the railroad presidents that it was to their interest to stop fighting and that the only way to do this was to have one big oil shipper. When he became so powerful he was able to demand it.

CHAPTER V. AN EXPLOSION IN BUFFALO

IT is Winter in New York. The great oil man is ready to go to his office. His home is at No. 4 West Fifty-fourth Street. He himself is arrayed as becomes the great figure he is. Serious, grave, particularly during these days when many oppressive problems weigh upon him, his large frame clad in its unvarying frock coat and striped trousers and high silk hat—there is nothing in the man's bearing which suggests playfulness. He goes to the rear of his home where there is one of those small square yards common to downtown Manhattan homes. The yard is paved solidly, rounded at the edges to form a small basin and is flooded with water which, on this cold winter's day, is frozen hard. Mr. Rockefeller has had this small skating rink built for his children and himself. A servant adjusts the skates to his patent leather boots and then, with his arms folded on his chest, his frock coat flying out behind him, the silk-hatted monopolist proceeds to skate smoothly and solemnly around the yard, doing the "outer edge" until he has gotten the exercise he has prescribed for himself. Then the skates are removed and he drives to his office downtown.

II

BY THIS time the Rockefeller family was definitely established in New York. Mr. Rockefeller himself was fond of returning to Cleveland as much as possible in the Summer. He was drawn there by his growing interest in his fine estate at Forest Hill. He began to steal time in the warm months for playing with the grounds around his new home. Chiefly he laid out walks and drives and, as far as he was able, superintended the laying out of them himself. He tried to get in four or five afternoons a week on his estate. Messenger boys on bicycles would carry messages and papers to him from the Cleveland office. Then he had a telegraph instrument installed and an operator remained on duty at the house every business day.

His friends in Cleveland, as in New York, were almost wholly his business associates—Mark Hanna, Norton Dalton, and G. M. Rudd, and his physician, Dr. Biggar. He made an occasional call on some old friends associated with him in the Standard and had them call. On Saturdays Mrs. Rockefeller frequently had associates in the Sunday School at the Forest Hill home. In New York Flagler lived close by on Fifth Avenue. John D. Archbold, who was rising in power in the company and in Rockefeller's confidence, also had a home on Fifth Avenue.

III

When Mr. Rockefeller went to his office now it was to the new quarters of the Standard Oil Company—26 Broadway, that famous spot which was to become known as the citadel of wealth and power. In 1882 the company had moved from Pearl Street to 44 Broadway. Then in 1885 the Standard Oil Company of New York, a newly-formed corporation, bought the old building at 26 Broadway. One of its tenants was the Standard Oil Trust. Oddly enough, though the nature of that mysterious thing, the trust, was unknown, its existence was quite public, the name "Standard Oil Trust, 26 Broadway," appearing in the city directory.

IV

About this time Rockefeller made one of his first known welfare gifts. His daughter, Alta Rockefeller, was born deaf. The affliction endeared the girl very strongly to her powerful and self-sufficient father. She had a strong religious streak, spending a good deal of her time in the company of her Sunday School companions in both New York and Cleveland. Moreover, Rockefeller's wealth and his Euclid Avenue Baptist Church affiliations drew to him all sorts of clerical gentlemen with worthy causes. In 1885 the Rev. A. B. Christy, pastor of the Lakeview Congregational Church, interested Miss Alta and through her Mr. Rockefeller in the Day Nursery and Free Kindergarten Association and Rockefeller made one of his first, if not his first, gifts for the establishment of a welfare institution to this group. He contributed the funds for putting up a building which was to be known as Alta House.

It must not be supposed, however, that this was by any means his first piece of philanthropy. As soon as he began to make money he began also to increase the scale of his giving. As early as 1881 he gave $3,500 to the Baptist Union Theological Seminary, the forerunner of the University of Chicago. His old letter files at this time abound in records of gifts. February, 1882, he writes Dr. Duncan, pastor of his church: "I will give $1,000 to this object and hope you can get through with it. . . . If, however, you cannot get through with this I will lift again." Later in the year he sends the last installment on a $20,000 pledge to Denison University at Dayton. A letter to some one asking for help advises: "I have already exceeded my appropriation for benevolences for the whole year of 1884 by some $30,000 or $40,000 and have three months with many pledges yet to meet."

There are many purely personal benefactions. One letter is to Pastor Bickel in Germany "to take a long rest and travel at my expense." Another in 1884 runs: "I have been thinking I ought personally to do something for Dr. Clough. The more I see and know about him the more favorably I am impressed with him. He is a great and good man. Before receipt of the letter I had thought to hand Dr. Clough $500; but I have got it up to $1,000 this morning and think it will reach $2,000 by night."

His gifts were scattered around on no special pattern. But even at this early day one notes a sense of dissatisfaction in this more or less disorganized mode of giving. He writes Mrs. Laura M. Irvine that he doesn't like fairs and other devices for raising church funds. He pledges $1,000 a year to a missionary chapel but "I am not willing to be a party to a failure in this undertaking" hence he wants "all who pledge to pay as they are called on." He doesn't like giving a meal a year to "all the tramps that come" to the Five Points Mission in New York. He would do it oftener and "would give them work and make them earn their food." He refuses another appeal forwarded by his mother. "I want to know surely in giving that I am putting money where it will do most good."

V

THIS year a picturesque gentleman appeared upon the stage. He was a vigorous, voluble, bellicose Irishman, named Patrick Boyle. Boyle was a product of Donegal, who, with scant education, joined up for a fight in the Union army when he was only 16 years old and from the battlefields of the Civil War went to the battlefields of Pithole in 1866. After working at various odd jobs he set up a small paper with the pretentious name of *The Laborer's Voice*. Next he turned up with another paper making war on the nitro-glycerine monopoly and still later as a scout for oil locations. In 1885 he was superintendent of the Union Oil Company in the Southern Ohio district. From there he went to Oil City to become the owner and editor of that once fiery tribune of the oil producers —the Oil City *Derrick*.

But the fire of the *Derrick* had been quenched long before this. It hurled its last thunderbolt in 1879. Then, as its owners trembled with rage and disappointment at the spectacle of the mighty Standard gobbling up all the refineries of the regions, the omnivorous octopus wound one of its tentacles around the *Derrick* itself. Did this mark a change in Rockefeller's attitude toward publicity? It is altogether probable that this acquisition was the work of that active and sinister intelligence, John D. Archbold. About this time, Archbold had completed through the Acme Oil Company the absorption of the region refiners. At the same time the Standard Oil, in another region, bought a controlling interest in the Vacuum Oil Company in Buffalo. John D. Archbold, along with Henry H. Rogers, was the instrument of this conquest. In both places we find the Standard making its first steps in news control. In Buffalo Charles Matthews, employed by the Vacuum, founded a newspaper financed by that company called the *People's Journal*. The *People's Journal* did not last very long. And the *Derrick* did not do so very well either. And so in 1885, Boyle, who had experience both as newspaper editor and oil man, bought the *Derrick*, financed by the Standard. Boyle was an aggressive and capable editor, according to the standards of the time, and he soon not only revived the languishing *Derrick* but began to wield the cudgel for his patrons with an unsparing hand, laying about him all the enemies of the Standard as vigorously as the old *Derrick* had thwacked the "Anaconda."

What part Rockefeller had in inspiring these purchases is not known. He of course knew of them. However, he did begin to display some sensitiveness to the incessant criticism which was showered on him. He said to a friend: "You can abuse me, you can strike me, if you will only let me have my own way." But the abuse and the blows were rising in frequency and violence. And occasionally he expressed a sense of hurt.

VI

AT THIS time the great man perceived certain signals from within. Rockefeller had always been supersensitive about his health. Had he had the leisure for brooding he might have become a hypochondriac. He always looked with disgust at the bad eating habits of other men. He often spoke of how others bolted down their food. At an earlier period when he traveled often on the old lines of the West where the trains stopped twenty minutes for meals, Rockefeller took good care not to be hurried. "I noticed," he said, "how in the brief time allowed others gobbled down their food, particularly at the last moment when the train was about to leave, as it so often did, before the full time was up. If I could not finish eating properly I filled my mouth with as much as it would hold, then went leisurely to the train and chewed it slowly before swallowing it."

He was still careful about his food. But in these last dozen years the demands on his time and energy were enormous. He tried to neutralize the drain by taking a brief nap in the afternoon. But in spite of his deliberate and patient methods, his nerves began to exhibit some signs of wear and his stomach began to announce some of the symptoms of indigestion.

He tried to take a little leisure to work on his beautiful estate, but his vast interests, his incessant wars, his relentless critics and enemies, as well as his own insatiable ambition left him no rest, and the disorder continued to express itself at intervals.

VII

IN THE meantime the country was kept continually aware of the so-called depredations of Rockefeller through the stories of threats on little grocers everywhere and the measures used to crush competitors in marketing. So many stories got currency that it was no longer necessary to furnish proof to have them believed. Tales of weird and savage forms of persecution of rivals were circulated, most of which, of course, were without any foundation. However, in July, 1886, Rockefeller received a shock and along with him the whole country when the Grand Jury of Erie County, Buffalo, New York, indicted John D. Archbold, Henry H. Rogers, Ambrose McGregor, and Hiram B. and Charles M. Everest for conspiracy to blow up the works of the Buffalo Lubricating Oil Company, Ltd. Stories that the Standard had set fire to the plants of its competitors had been told before. Now here was a grand jury actually indicting Standard Oil officers for such a crime.

The Standard had bought in 1879 three-fourths of the stock of the Vacuum Oil Company from Hiram B. and his son, Charles M., Everest, who had organized it in 1866. The Everests were retained as managers and they, with Rogers, Archbold, and McGregor, constituted the Board of Directors. The Vacuum had a special process for refining oil which was protected by patents.

In 1881 Charles B. Matthews, J. Scott Wilson, and Albert Miller started the Buffalo Lubricating Oil Company, Ltd. All had worked for the Vacuum company. Matthews was the manager, Miller a practical refiner, Wilson a good salesman. Miller made castings of the Vacuum company machinery to use in the new works. Wilson, the salesman, proposed to go around to Vacuum customers, of which he had a list, and offer them "Acme Harness Oil made by the Vacuum process." This was not a pretty start and Everest was with some reason indignant at what he called their disloyalty. Everest proceeded to block them and he started by going to Miller, the refiner, and inducing him to betray his partners by wrecking their machinery. This was done by building a very hot fire under the oil the first day the new refinery opened and shutting off the safety appliances. This blew out the machinery the very first morning.

The defendants were charged with this as part of a conspiracy to destroy their new rivals. The indictment contained eleven counts charging other oppressive measures, chiefly the bringing of numerous harassing lawsuits which were designed to harry and embarrass the defendants and consume their resources.

The indictment produced a sensation and was eagerly seized upon by Rockefeller's enemies as evidence of his violent methods. Before this Matthews had brought a civil suit for damages against the Vacuum Oil Company on the same grounds and gotten a judgment for $20,000, which was set aside because the damages were not proved. He thereupon instituted another suit for $250,000 and this was pending.

The case was called for trial May 3rd. It made something of a

AN EXPLOSION IN BUFFALO

show in Buffalo, for the sanctuary of the court was crowded, not only with many distinguished counsel, but the even more distinguished prisoners. Mr. Rockefeller and his brother William were there as witnesses. The evidence of the blowing up of the stills was quite complete. The fireman testified he had been ordered by Miller to force the fires and Miller testified he had been hired to desert his partners by Everest. Everest before this had taken Miller to his (Miller's) lawyer to learn if he could break his contract with the new company. The lawyer advised it could not be done. Then Everest said to the lawyer: "Suppose we were to arrange the machinery so that it would bust or smash; what would be the consequences?" The lawyer advised it might involve criminal guilt. "Well," said Everest, "such things would have to be found out before that could happen." No doubt was left in the judge or jury's minds that the Everests were guilty of this atrocity. But there was no evidence directly connecting the Standard leaders, Rogers, Archbold, and McGregor, with the deed and so before the case was given to the jury the indictment was quashed by the trial judge as to these three men.

The evidence of the other acts of oppression was hardly less convincing. Matthews told of threats of suits in the presence of Rogers. Three suits were brought against his company for infringement of patent and all thrown out, the court holding that the Vacuum had no legal patent. Matthews testified he met Everest. Everest said: "I shall do all I can to injure you. How are you going to get your crude?" "From the Atlas," said Matthews, to which Everest replied: "You will wake up some day and find there will be no Atlas or it will be in the Standard." And so it turned out. The Atlas was bought by the Standard.

Great interest was felt in the appearance of Mr. Rockefeller. The court room was crowded to have a look at him. On the stand he was asked:

"What is your business?"
"Engaged in oil refining in Cleveland."
"Where besides Cleveland?"
"I am engaged in it nowhere else."
"Nor ever have been?"
"Never."

These seemed to be extraordinary answers for the man who was then drawing $30,000 as head of the trust with its refineries in a dozen places. Mr. Rockefeller did admit that he knew Rogers and McGregor and Archbold. Archbold had some connection with the Standard but Mr. Rogers was vice-president of the Pratt Refining Company. He knew that these gentlemen had contemplated buying the Vacuum Oil Company but the Standard had no interest in the sale. At the very moment the stocks of Rogers and Archbold and Everest and McGregor in the Vacuum Company were in John D. Rockefeller's possession as one of the Standard Oil Trust trustees and its president.

The jury convicted the two Everests. On the day of the conviction a New York *Tribune* reporter called on Mr. Rockefeller at his home in Fifty-fourth Street. "As far as the Standard Oil is concerned it is completely vindicated by the exoneration of Messrs. Archbold, McGregor, and Rogers." The fact that the managers of a Standard Oil Company, two of its directors in fact, had just been convicted of an outrageous criminal conspiracy to destroy a rival, including an attempt to blow up the works, did not seem to Mr. Rockefeller to in any way dim the radiance of the Standard's exoneration.

"What will be the effect on the Vacuum Company?"

"Oh, it will go on the same as ever . . . so far from the Vacuum wishing to crush out rivals, when it began it had fifty-seven competitors. Now it has ninety-seven. That does not look like a desire to crush out rivals, does it? No, the whole purpose behind this prosecution has been to annoy us."

One wonders how Mr. Rockefeller, who testified under oath that the Standard had nothing to do with the Vacuum, could assume to say what the future course of the Vacuum would be. Even so cautious a man as Mr. Rockefeller could not always remember Mr. Dodd's little fictions.

The sequel to this comedy is worth recording. The Everests, who were convicted of conspiring to destroy a rival's business and of procuring an explosion in their plant, were fined $250 each. But they continued to manage Mr. Rockefeller's Vacuum Oil Company. The connection did not affect their standing. As for Matthews, their victim, the conspiracy to destroy him by harassing suits was successful. Before his damage suit for $250,000 could be tried he went into the hands of a receiver. A few months later the defendants—including the Standard Oil directors—settled for $85,000. Then the receiver filed an accounting. The whole amount was consumed by debts and lawyers' fees. Matthews collected nothing. Thus justice triumphed.

But the incident left its mark upon at least one of the participants—Henry H. Rogers. Rogers was deeply humiliated by the experience of sitting at a trial table charged with a felony. Thereafter he harped upon the incident. He collected papers, statements, documents, to prove his innocence. He was horrified lest his children should ever think he had taken part in such a crime. When Ida Tarbell was writing her book on Standard Oil Rogers brought out his papers to her. Thus fifteen years later he spoke with deep emotion of the experience.

CHAPTER VI. WAR ON THE TRUSTS

ROCKEFELLER had dealt with a new problem—the problem of using the new tools, the management of bigness and the control of production. These same problems faced every industry. The country was definitely committed to the process of assembling business into immense units. Numerous forces were driving it in that direction. It was nobody's coldly conceived plan. It was not the result of a conspiracy. It was the inevitable result of all the new conditions.

In whiskey as in oil wild over-production bedeviled the industry. During the war the government made four successive increases in the tax on whiskey. Each time it did distillers rushed to manufacture as much spirits as possible before the tax went into effect. When the tax became effective there was a let-down in production. But in this curious situation new distilleries were always established during each period of production and speculation in whiskey became as wild as speculation in oil—teachers, ministers, as well as business men, engaging in it. As early as 1871 the whiskey men attempted a pool to limit production, but nature came to their rescue. It ruined Europe's grain crops and those countries had to buy spirits from America. New distilleries bloomed again. There were four times more distilleries than were needed. A new pool in 1881 proposed to limit production and to dump the surplus on Europe. New pools were formed each year up to 1887. Col. Payne was interested in the whiskey business and doubtless from him the distillers got some information of the details of Mr. Rockefeller's trust and so they organized a whiskey trust patterned after the oil trust.

The same story was repeated in other lines. It is said Henry M. Flagler was interested in the cottonseed oil business along with General Samuel Thomas, who had made millions out of Standard Oil stock. A story went around Wall Street that the cottonseed oil people paid the Standard men $250,000 for a copy of the trust agreement and that this was the first time that famous document was ever seen outside the oil trustees' room. There is no proof that this is true. But the cottonseed oil people did form a trust. There was also the rubber trust, Havemeyer's sugar trust, the butcher trust, the glass trust, the furniture trust, the tobacco trust, and numerous others. Local industries began arming against competition in the same way or by the means of pools and outright monopolies.

The nation suddenly saw its vast natural resources pouring forth in an uncontrolled stream. It was playing with that immense and dangerous tool, machinery. Railroads brought the country together into a few vast regional neighborhoods. Cities saw rivals entering with goods which once belonged only to local manufacturers. Thus refrigerator cars enabled the packers to sell all over the country meat slaughtered in Chicago. The local butchers and slaughterers were violently opposed to this and they sought laws to prohibit the sale of beef more than 100 miles distant from the point of slaughter until the packers began selling their stock to the local butchers. The immigrant flood poured over our frontiers, creating a limitless reservoir of cheap labor and an enormous population of consumers. Gold flowed from our mountains, silver and the baser metals were found in prodigious volume. New inventions amazed the world. The rude yet dazzling, brilliant, and vulgar pageant of rich America in feverish movement amid her treasures, her squalor, her glories, and her greed began to astonish and amuse the world.

For the first time in the country's history an immense population of very poor people were assembled in our growing cities. The labor problem terrified men like Jacob Riis and saddened men like Henry George. Labor leaders saw in the rise of the Octopus the approaching slavery of the working man. At first the outcry was confined to Pennsylvania and the oil fields. But gradually the areas of discontent widened as other towns discovered their rubber trusts and milk trusts and sugar trusts and, most hated of all, the railroad trusts. The severity and fury of competition had driven the roads to set up pools, to fix rates, and shipping terms. Cities were discriminated against, shippers crushed by the favors given their rivals. Loud and fierce were the cries which went up from shippers and towns.

Labor troubles grew more intense. Henry George's "Progress and Poverty," a serious attempt to understand the causes of poverty, made a powerful impression on thoughtful men. Former President Rutherford B. Hayes, visiting New York, was surprised to find men like Bishop Whipple, Chief Justice Waite, and Robert C. Winthrop, the personification of Puritan culture, in sympathy with George's doctrines. Hayes himself was touched with this new radicalism. "What?" he said to William Henry Smith, referring to the trusts, "leave uncontrolled the power that buys your councils, your legislatures, your courts?"

The employer as a rule cared little for his workers. They were only so many tools in the furious drive for profits. The workers became conscious of their wrongs. Leaders sprang up to lead them. The Knights of Labor rose to power. By 1886 they had grown from a membership of 110,000 to 730,000. Grand Master Workman Terrance V. Powderly was their Moses. He preached the gospel that "an injury to one is the concern of all." Labor unions appeared everywhere. Strikes became a matter of almost daily occurrence. The walking delegate was abroad in the land. In 1886 the great Southwestern Railroad strike was called. Powderly sought to make it an orderly frontal attack within the law. But there were other leaders with other plans who wished to fan the flames into a great revolutionary conflagration. In the midst of labor's honest movement for the eight hour day there came a strike at the plant of the McCormick Reaper Company in Chicago. There was a collision with the police and some strikers were injured. Next day a great meeting was called in Haymarket Square to protest against "the atrocious attack of the police in shooting our fellow workmen." An anarchist was addressing the crowd. A police captain decided to arrest him. A shot was fired; a bomb was thrown. Eight policemen were killed; sixty persons wounded. The Haymarket riot set the nation aflame. And while it produced a serious re-action against the labor movement, thoughtful men saw in it the germs of serious trouble unless something were done to heal the widening breach between the workers and their employers.

Two other phenomena outraged public sentiment. One was the spectacle of extravagance and riotous living of the new aristocracy. The other was the growing corruption of public officials by big business concerns. The daughters of rich beef and soap and sausage barons began giving their hands to titled European vagabonds. Gaudy mansions rose on the Fifth Avenues and Michigan Boulevards of the country. Mrs. Astor with her snobbish premier, Ward McAllister, proclaimed the caste of the 400. Railroad, street car, and electrical and gas franchises were in the market places of the legislatures and aldermanic chambers and unscrupulous adventurers bribed lawmakers and city fathers in the most unconscionable manner.

For the family of John D. Rockefeller it must be said that it took no part in the vulgar display of its wealth. The family lived decently, quietly, and unobtrusively, its only extravagance being the fine Forest Hill home, which they were then developing. Mrs. Rockefeller was and remained for years unknown to the fashionable society of New York.

II

This growing economic and social problem was getting into politics. As early as 1872 in the Greeley-Grant campaign a national party was launched at Columbus called the Labor Reformers with one of its leading planks a demand for government control of railroad rates. The Republican and Democratic platforms were silent nor did they mention it until twelve years later. In 1880 the Greenbackers renewed the attack. "It is the duty of Congress," it declared, "to regulate Interstate Commerce." It went further: "We denounce as destructive to prosperity and dangerous to liberty the action of the old parties in fostering and sustaining gigantic money, land, and railroad corporations."

Two facts stand out. The first attacks on big business took the form of demands for regulating railroads. And it was, not from the people as a whole, but from little business men who saw their stores and shops threatened, that the attacks came. Little business men hated the railroads because they looked upon them as the instrument by which competitors in distant cities reached into their towns and took their trade. By 1884 the cry of monopoly had risen to commanding volume. The first political convention to assemble that year was the Anti-Monopoly Party. It denounced pooling, stock watering, and rate discrimination and demanded the immediate enactment of an interstate commerce law. Public opinion was aroused. This year, for the first time, the two major parties noticed the issue. The Republicans, behind Blaine, pledged their support to "such legislation as will fully and efficiently carry out the power of congress" over interstate commerce, and it favored the principle of regulation of railroads. The Democrats who nominated Cleveland were less specific. They were in favor of legislation to "prevent monopoly and to restrict enforcement of individual rights against corporate abuses."

From every side swelled the demand for an interstate commerce law, for which agitation had been kept up since the defeat of the Hopkins and Reagan bills. The National Grange had forced the passage of state laws but the courts had emasculated them. These decisions which held the states could not regulate roads engaged in interstate commerce served to give impetus to the demand for a federal law. Finally in 1887 Senator Shelby Cullom, of Illinois, introduced a bill to regulate commerce between the states and providing for an Interstate Commerce Commission. From all over the country Chambers of Commerce and business organizations showered Congress with petitions demanding the passage of this law. This pioneering act by the federal government to interfere in business was undertaken almost exclusively at the demand of business itself.

President Cleveland was called on to name five members of the first commission. As chairman he appointed Judge Thomas M. Cooley, a lawyer of great ability and universally recognized integrity. Morrison, of Vermont, was a socially-minded man. The others were railroad lawyers. The federal courts promptly sheared the commission of all effective powers. There was a powerful element in the Senate which tried to defeat it. Senator Payne of Ohio, O. H. Payne's father, and Senator Camden of West Virginia, a Standard Oil official, both voted against the bill. And critics insisted later that the bill was artfully contrived to invite nullification by the courts. The following year, Commissioner Prouty, newly appointed, said: "If the Interstate Commerce Commission were worth buying the railroads would try to buy it. The only reason they have not is that the body is valueless in its ability to correct railroad abuses."

III

THE WORD "trust" was now in popular use. The people knew well enough what they meant by a trust. But there was a great deal of curiosity among the well-informed as to the precise character of these mysterious things, particularly the Standard Oil Trust. It was getting that kind of dominance in conversation and public discussion which prohibition and gangdom enjoy today. And so in the early days of the session of 1888, the New York Senate ordered an investigation of the trusts. That inquiry occupied only a few days but it produced a collection of revelations which began to give direction to anti-trust agitation. The Senate Committee, with Col. Bliss as its council, met February 28, 1888, in the rooms of the Superior Court in New York City. And with its assembling came the first instances of the practice of process dodging by trust magnates which was to irritate and divert the country for a generation. Subpoenas had been issued for Mr. Rockefeller, his brother William, Archbold, Havemeyer, and others. At Mr. Rockefeller's office the process server was told he was out of town. At his home the officer was informed his quarry could not be seen. Next morning the process server camped in front of the 54th Street home at an early hour. But Rockefeller did not come out and when the impatient officer rang the bell he was told Mr. Rockefeller had already gone. When the process server went to William's house, he was informed that William had gone to Florida. Other oil magnates were out of town when the officer arrived with subpoenas. Finally John D. Rockefeller appeared. He asserted he was not ducking, that he had been in Ohio and hurried back as soon as he learned he was wanted. This is probably partly true. He wished to choose his own time for appearing. In any case on February 28th, amid a great buzzing in the investigation chamber, which was crowded with newspaper men and with spectators eager to see the great monopolist, the committee assembled and Mr. Rockefeller arrived flanked by Joseph H. Choate and Samuel C. T. Dodd, his counsel.

Mr. Choate, then in the full flower of his great reputation at the bar, entered the hearing that morning full of misgivings about his witness. Henry H. Rogers had told Choate when he was employed that Mr. Rockefeller would be their chief reliance on the stand. Choate insisted on having a preliminary conference with Rockefeller. He was taken to 26 Broadway and there he found Mr. Rockefeller lying languorously on a couch in his office. He greeted the great lawyer and then stretched out again in a state of perfect relaxation. Choate sought to ask him questions to draw out his knowledge of the company's affairs. When he left the office Choate turned to Dodd and said: "I don't like your witness, I must say. He seems indifferent and difficult and moreover I got nothing but questions out of him. I hope he makes a better showing on the witness chair." Incidentally, the habit of lying down during conferences and board meetings was common with Rockefeller. It was with this witness Mr. Choate now appeared.

The high light of the investigation arrived when Rockefeller took the witness stand. The great oil Croesus had been brought to bay at last. He was dressed in his frock coat and striped trousers. His hair was beginning to be sparse. Some spectators thought his face appeared a little bony. His light brown mustache was now very close-cropped. There was a look of intense concentration on his countenance mingled with an expression of dreamy sadness. A reporter thought, "It is only when his face is in profile that it exhibits any indications of shrewdness. When fronting one, these characteristics seem to vanish and are replaced by that aspect of mild benignity which one is expected to look for in the Sunday School and pulpit." The reporter missed that intense, unwavering bearing upon one of those small yet piercing eyes.

Rockefeller was a most accommodating witness. The New York *Tribune* reporter next day said: "He seems the embodiment of sweetness and light. His serenity could not be disturbed. With the same sweet smile he replied to Col. Bliss's sarcasms and General Pryor's scornful adjurations. In tones melodious, clear, and deliberate he gave his testimony. The Standard Oil people did well to select him to bear the brunt of the battle. At times his manner was mildly reproachful, at others tenderly persuasive, but never did he betray any ill temper or vexation."

Reading the report of his testimony today one is struck by the apparent frankness with which he answered every question. There was an occasional polite resistance. But on the whole it cannot be said he held back much.[1]

An intense moment arrived when Col. Bliss asked the distinguished witness to produce the copy of the trust agreement. Mr. Choate made a feeble protest against making the document public but finally consented it should be read. As Col. Bliss rose to read it a tremor of expectancy ran over the crowd. But the document proved singularly disappointing and dull reading, in spite of the sensation it produced after its contents had been printed and digested.

Rockefeller answered all other questions freely. The trust now had a capital of $90,000,000. It controlled about 75 per cent of production. Its dividends averaged 7½ per cent a year; its certificates were worth $165; hundreds of its employees owned certificates of the trust. But "monopoly!" Dear no! the Standard Oil Company had no monopoly. There were eleven companies competing with it in the country as a whole. And as for trouble with its competitors! "We have had, and today have, very pleasant relations with those gentlemen."

The man's vast wealth, his appalling success, shone round him like an aura and compelled the men who were trying to convict him of being a public enemy to treat him with the greatest respect. When he left the stand he graciously bestowed his thanks upon all. But he was a little weary of his own tolerance. "You will furnish the list of questions?" he was asked by Col. Bliss. "With pleasure," he replied with the air of a martyr.

[1] The Rockefeller family account of this hearing is that General Pryor was so much impressed with Rockefeller's testimony that, although he began with a ferocious cross-examination, he ended by shaking Rockefeller's hand and becoming a life-long friend. The General told Rockefeller he would like to see his marvelous system at work. The General's son, I am informed, who was present in court, corroborates this.

"Anything, gentlemen, if you will only make an end of me." Then he was asked for the minute book of the trust. "It seems to me," he murmured, "there could be left some little thing that you did not exact of me."

That committee in its brief few days of probing made up an astonishing story of trust development. It is unnecessary to repeat it here since it brought to public attention for the first time much that has been narrated in this volume. The activities of various other trusts covering sugar, cottonseed oil, elevators, and other commodities were pictured in its report.

IV

WHILE the New York Senate was busy with the affairs of the state's great trust makers, the House of Representatives in Washington, January 25th, directed the Committee on Manufactures to investigate the trusts. And just about the time the New York Committee was making its report the House Committee under its chairman, Henry Bacon, began an inquiry into the history and operations of the Standard Oil Trust and the Sugar Trust. The field seemed so vast that the committee decided to limit its probe to these two greatest of combinations. Once again John D. Rockefeller appeared as a witness, but this time without resistance. His testimony was not very important, was brief and got little attention —only a paragraph—in the newspapers of the day. But from March 8th to July 20th the committee called before it almost all the leading characters in the great drama of oil—most of whom we have met in these pages—Rockefeller and his chief associates, Flagler and Archbold and Dodd and O'Day and Bostwick, and all his old foes, John Teagle with his tale of suits and rebates; George A. Rice with his story of espionage, price cutting, and railroad wrongs; B. B. Campbell and Patterson of the Producers', Emery of the Equitable, and Potts of the Empire. The whole disordered and hectic story of the long war over oil was unfolded before the committee. But unfortunately the meat and meaning of it was buried in nearly 1,000 pages of the printed report.

V

AFTER these investigations it was inevitable that some action must be taken by the general government to curb these business monsters. New York State had attempted to deal with the sugar trust. But that institution comprised eighteen corporations only one of which was in New York and within reach of its courts. And so when the Fifty-first Congress convened December 4th, 1889, the first bill introduced in the Senate was by Senator John Sherman of Ohio—an act to "declare unlawful trusts and combinations in restraint of trade." On July 2nd, 1890—the 115th anniversary of the signing of the Declaration of Independence, as some one observed—the famous Sherman anti-trust law was signed by the President of the United States.

The bill was passed unanimously in the House; in the Senate there was one vote against it—Senator Blodgett of New Jersey—and he never vouchsafed the reasons for his opposition. But for all that the measure had hard sledding in both houses. Senator George Vest, of Missouri, thought it unconstitutional. Senator Teller, of Colorado, feared it would be futile, would hit the Farmer's Alliance and National League (another farm organization) and would be invoked against the Knights of Labor. Senator Sherman was sure neither of these bodies would be affected. Senator Morgan, of Alabama, a great lawyer, rose and uttered these words: "All the big fish will escape. The little fish are the men who will have the trouble."

VI

THIS law came at once to be known as the Sherman law because, as Senator Hoar observed, "John Sherman had absolutely nothing whatever to do with it." Whether this was true or not the authorship of the Sherman law has continued to be a subject of controversy ever since.

In 1903, Senator Joseph B. Foraker, of Ohio, made a speech in which he referred to Sherman's great work in connection with the trust law. Senator William Hoar, of Massachusetts, wrote Foraker correcting him. "If there was any man in the world who did not have anything to do with the Sherman anti-trust law it was John Sherman," he said. He elaborated his position in a second letter in which he said: "I wrote every syllable myself." Sherman, said Hoar, had a way of introducing a great many bills by request. "I suppose he introduced this one by request. I doubt very much whether he read it. If he did I don't think he understood it." As a matter of fact, the original anti-trust bill introduced by Sherman was not passed. It was referred to the Judiciary Committee, where it was discussed and altered and finally rejected and an entirely new bill written and reported. It was this bill which was passed. Certain it is that when the House disagreed with the Senate over certain provisions and a conference committee was appointed, it was Hoar and Edmunds who were named for the Senate and they were named again when a second conference committee was required. There can be no doubt that it was not Sherman's bill that was passed and that aside from introducing the original measure, he played a minor rôle in the whole episode. But who did write the bill is not so easily settled.

Foraker, when challenged by Hoar, employed M. H. Humphreys to study the whole record and Humphreys wrote a 120-page book about it. About the same time Senators Edmunds and Albert H. Walker made a similar study. Walker also wrote a "History of the Sherman Law." He found that Sections 1, 2, 3, 4, 5, and 6, with the exception of 7 words in Section 1, were written by Senator George, Section 7 by Senator Hoar, Section 8 by Senator Ingalls. Humphreys came to the same conclusion. What is probably true is that these senators supplied the sections attributed to them and that the bill, when finally agreed upon in committee, was re-written by Senator Hoar, a good deal of a scholar and a master of legislative English who was frequently called upon to pour rudely-wrought measures into clear and concise language.

In any case, the new law was hailed by many trusting souls as a settlement of the trust problem.

CHAPTER VII. WAR WEARY

By this time John D. Rockefeller had completely divested himself of every minor job it was possible to discard. He reserved his mind for the more important problems of grand strategy. When he wrote a note on his desk, his negro servant promptly blotted it for him. He had practically ceased to see people save about essential personal matters. All the affairs of the great company requiring contact with strangers he left to his associates.

The habit of his mind was to simplify everything. Unlike many modern executives he took no delight in surrounding himself with extensive and complicated systems of doing things. His treatment of his daily tasks is a sample of this. When he reached his office in the morning he had as a rule several notations on his cuffs. On his desk he found a single pile of papers requiring his attention. He looked them over one at a time. As he examined each paper he made his decision about it, gave his order, and laid the paper on one side of his desk. If the matter required further thought, he put the paper on the other side. When he was through he had two piles of papers—one with which he was done and which was at once removed, the other representing the problems which required further attention. He then proceeded to go through them again, sending for such officials as were necessary to dispose of them. Each paper represented a decision required of him. He never shrank from the decision.

He could not be hurried. And he could never be threatened, even in a small bargain. One day he was considering the purchase of a horse. The man, to hurry him, said: "Unless you buy the animal today at this price another purchaser stands ready to take him." "Very well," said Rockefeller quietly, "let him have the horse by all means. I do not wish to buy." That ended the matter. Another time a business man left papers for Rockefeller's consideration in connection with a business deal. He returned in a few days and expressed disappointment and annoyance that Rockefeller had not yet examined his proposal. "Mr. Rockefeller promised to look over my papers and I want his decision." The message was carried to Rockefeller. He called for the papers, held them under his chin and with a twinkle said: "Tell the gentleman I have looked over his papers and that I do not care to do anything about the matter."

It was said of Alexander Hamilton that the United States government was the product of his bookkeeping. The Standard Oil Company in part at least was certainly the fruit of Rockefeller's bookkeeping. And to the last he continued to exercise a scrutiny over the accounts of the company. He had also a respect for the man who could manage figures and very little for the man who couldn't. One day he walked into his office apparently in a hurry and summoned his young secretary. He spread out on his desk a sheet of paper covered with columns of figures. Then he took out his watch.

"Mr. Rogers," he said, "I want to see how quickly you can add this sum. I am going to time you. Go ahead."

Rogers knew enough of his new chief to realize that this was a test to hurry or fluster him. Very cautiously the young man went up one column and down the other, thinking of accuracy rather than speed. When he put down the final figure, Rockefeller said:

"Well, you have completed it in the required time. It is very good."

The man's vast wealth was piling up now to fabulous proportions. And of course his investments in stocks and bonds necessarily became enormous. He kept his securities in a vault in the Produce Exchange Building. As they increased, it was necessary to take additional boxes and these were spread out throughout the bank's vaults. His secretary felt this was not a very satisfactory system and so proposed to the Safe Deposit Company that they set aside a compartment for Mr. Rockefeller's treasures where they could be kept together. The company promptly complied with this plan and in due time a large compartment, equipped with many boxes separated from the other boxes by a special steel door and with table and chair for comfortable examination of securities was installed. The secretary was so pleased with this that he wanted Rockefeller to have a look at it. But the great man did not seem to have much interest in the household conveniences of his huge fortune. He put off going for many months. One day the secretary met him as he was entering 26 Broadway and suggested that he go to look at his vaults. Rockefeller consented. Once there he chatted a moment with the bowing vice-president, stepped into the vault, behind which his countless millions were stored in neatly polished steel boxes, looked at one or two boxes and said:

"Yes, Mr. Rogers, it's all very nice. Shows a good system. I'm glad to have seen it. Let's go."

Rockefeller respected money. "You will find it the best of friends—if not the best friend—you have," he told this same secretary. But he cared not at all to finger his wealth or to contemplate its mere evidences. One day as he was leaving his office he felt in his pockets to find that he had not even a nickel there. He wanted to borrow a nickel from his secretary. But Rogers insisted on giving it to him. "No, Rogers," he said, "don't forget this transaction. This is a whole year's interest on a dollar."

II

HERE we must stroll from 26 Broadway around the corner to 52 Wall Street to the National City Bank to meet another figure who now begins to bulk large in the Rockefeller empire. This is James Stillman, small, dark, dapper, elegant, silent—the most taciturn man in Wall Street—more silent than John D. Rockefeller himself. Stillman was the new head of the National City Bank—that extraordinary institution which, with the aid of Rockefeller millions, began to spread out about this period.

Stillman, member of a great cotton house, Smith, Woodward, and Stillman, who had inherited a fortune from his father (a brilliant adventurer who called himself Don Carlos Stillman) came into the Rockefeller compound through his friendship with William Rockefeller. They met in 1883 when Stillman was made a director of the Chicago, Milwaukee, and St. Paul Railroad where William Rockefeller and Harkness were already installed. The pair became fast friends. "I like William Rockefeller," said Stillman, "because we don't have to talk. We sit for fifteen minutes sometimes before either breaks the silence."

When Stillman became president of the National City he made a determined campaign to get into his bank the deposits of the great industrial corporations. He clearly foresaw the coming day of big business. A few years later when his bank reached the $100,000,000 mark in deposits, he observed to a friend that he might live to see it with a billion. "Not in half a century," said his friend. "Oh, yes," replied Stillman, "in a quarter of a century." His forecast was good. But at the time of which we write the bank had only $15,000,000 in deposits. Stillman foresaw that the Standard Oil crowd would be their own bankers and he did not rest until he had William on the board of directors and the Rockefeller millions in his vaults. The bank was then in a little building across the street from its present imposing home where indeed it had been since 1812. Upstairs Evarts, Choate, and Beaman had their law offices and John D. Rockefeller had already engaged the brilliant and witty Choate as his counsel in various investigations and suits aimed at the Standard. The Rockefellers themselves and their associates—Rogers, Archbold, Payne, and others—were already reaching out with their growing surpluses to make profitable investments. Standard Oil directors had for some years been investing in railroad stocks. They sat on the boards of directors of roads controlling 33,000 miles of track. Very soon Stillman was soundly entrenched in the confidence of John D. and was placing large sums for him. As in the case of all his major lieutenants, Rockefeller reposed implicit confidence in Stillman. The telephone at Rockefeller's office in 26 Broadway would ring. Stillman would tell Rockefeller to send him five million. He was always on the lookout for good things and "they were coming along." There would be little questioning. In a day or two Rockefeller's check for five million would be on Stillman's desk. The securities in the new vaults in the Produce Exchange Building were growing rapidly.

III

THE ROCKEFELLER circle of hatred continually widened. First oil producers and refiners cursed his name. Then kerosene jobbers and dealers joined the ranks of odium. Now gas users added their voices to the chorus of opprobrium. "Mr. Rockefeller has no interests in either gas or copper," said Samuel Dodd, the screen maker. This meticulous word juggler for once was careless. Rockefeller had two gas interests. For one, gas oil was coming to be the chief material for manufacturing illuminating gas. His interest in selling gas oil to gas companies was very great. What Dodd meant was that John D. had no interest in the various municipal gas companies which Henry H. Rogers and James Stillman and Charles Pratt were getting hold of at this time. But he was very deeply interested in natural gas companies. As head of the trust he had in his possession the stocks of sixteen natural gas companies which were supplying illuminating gas to many cities in the Middle West. But of course all this was secret—secret as all of Mr. Rockefeller's doings.

One of these companies was the Northwestern Ohio Natural Gas Company, another the Eastern Ohio Natural Gas Company. In 1887 these two companies applied to the city authorities of Toledo for franchises to supply gas. The people thought this an excellent thing—two companies competing for their trade. They granted the franchises. Then they discovered that both companies belonged to the oil Octopus and that they had been hoodwinked. Great was their chagrin at the deception. Rows began quickly about rates. Then the people of Toledo decided to erect their own gas works. A battle started at once between the Rockefeller outfit and the people—litigations, political contests, financial struggles over bonds, and what not. The newspapers rallied loyally to Toledo. Suddenly in the midst of the fight one paper went over to the trust gas company. The trust had bought it outright. This was denied but two of the trust lawyers appeared on its board of directors. Then that valorous pen-brandisher, Patrick Boyle, now editor of the once independent Oil City *Derrick*, appeared in Toledo as manager and editor of the trust paper. He came snorting fire and brimstone. He immediately branded the distinguished and highly respectable editor of the Toledo *Blade* as "that hoary old reprobate, senile old liar." This must have pleased Mr. John D. Archbold in New York, who liked that sort of language. Another journalistic opponent Boyle called "that aged, acidulous, addlepated, monkey-eyed, monkey-browed monogram of sarcasm and spider-shanked, pigeon-witted public scold, Major Bilgewater Bickham and his back-biting, blackmailing, patent medicine directory, the *Journal*, etc."

Thus the Standard's early steps in publicity seemed to be in bad hands. It was not long before the scurrilous Boyle was indicted for slander, and convicted. He got a new trial and then pleaded guilty in order to get a fine instead of a jail sentence. Then the paper failed and was sold. But Boyle's furious barrage of vituperation was but part of the "new publicity." There appeared about this time something quite novel—the Jennings Publishing Company—a press bureau. The fruit of this institution began to reveal itself quickly in the press of Ohio, for the Northwestern Ohio Natural Gas Company and the Eastern Ohio Gas Company were having plenty of trouble all over the state. Here is a little morsel of comment from the Xenia *Herald:*

"Whether the Standard Oil Company is in a trust or outside a trust is a question for the courts to decide; but whether the consumers of oil are getting a better grade at less cost and handling with greater safety is a question for the people to decide. . . . Monopoly and Octopus, Combines and Trusts are haughty words. But the best grades at lower prices are beneficial things."

At the same time advertisement of paraffin and other Standard products began to appear in Ohio papers. The Xenia *Herald* had a contract for advertising with the Standard through the Jennings Advertising Agency and in the contract was this clause:

"The publisher agrees to reprint on news or editorial pages of such newspapers such reading notices—and set in the body type of said paper and bearing no marks to indicate advertising—as are furnished from time to time by the Jennings agency at the rate of   per line."

Later Francis S. Monnet, Attorney General of Ohio, declared that his office had found 110 papers in Ohio which had similar contracts. Here then were 110 purveyors of news and opinion where the flooding tide of abuse of Rockefeller was checked. As we watch the rise of the deluge of hate which overwhelmed the name of Rockefeller and reached its height around 1911 and then see the waters recede slowly but surely until the name stands up like the peak of Tabor with the sun shining on it; as we witness the slow redemption of the name of Rockefeller from odium and the resurrection of its owner to a kind of sainthood and wonder a little at this amazing and interesting—and significant—phenomenon, it will be well to remember this episode of the Jennings Publishing Company. Here is the precise point at which the miracle began.

IV

THE SIGHT which met Mr. Rockefeller now as he looked into his mirror filled him with foreboding. There in the candid glass he saw an old man. The ceaseless work, the endless worry, the streams of abuse, the sleepless nights, and the lack of exercise and rest—all these conspired in a man who was always apprehensive about his health to turn the premonitory warnings of his stomach into a profound menace. The sturdy appetite of the hardy farm boy had gone. His skin had a yellowish hue, the hair was graying and thin at the top and sides. The high cheek bones stood out, pressing tightly against the skin smoothed out almost to shining at those points. Wrinkles appeared here and there in a face that looked bony and old. He must have seen in it even then a resemblance to his mother now herself an old lady, sick, troubled by the brooding shadow of the wayward husband whose mysterious life darkened the hearts of the whole family. A kind of sadness fell upon Rockefeller at this point in his life. He had yet to feel the full fury of the nation's scorn. But public censure was sufficiently robust to have penetrated his soul. The man who had said, "You may kick me and abuse me provided you will let me have my own way," now saw powerful and angry forces in arms against him to thwart him, and he saw that the kicks and abuse were a very high price. To a friend and neighbor he confided that he would like to be loved. But wherever he turned he saw the evidences of hate. And now, in spite of all his minute and fatiguing care, he saw his great structure menaced by multiplying attacks, and his own body at fifty-two, prematurely aged and threatened with collapse. The threat was an offense against his pride. It was inconceivable that he, with his strong constitution and his rugged ancestry and his superior attention to all the details of life, should fail in this one while Flagler, ten years his senior, was still pursuing the ladies. He remained secretive about his occasional indispositions. His friends never spoke to him about it. He tried for a while to put it out of his mind. But it was preparing a decisive blow.

V

His mother was now a confirmed invalid. She had been confined to her bed or a chair for some years. In some way stories have gotten printed in later years that Rockefeller neglected his mother and became indifferent to her. He was in fact deeply devoted to her and wrote to her in terms of gentle and tender endearment, begging her to find the strength to spend a little time with him. About old Doctor Bill a complete silence was maintained. Yet about this time he turned up one day in New York to look over his son's empire. The old medicine trader who had found modern Cleveland too tight-fitting and had pushed farther on toward the new frontiers now, past eighty, came to have a look at the great new Babylon. He was a huge, powerful, broad-shouldered old warrior, with bushy chin beard and clean-shaven upper lip, with long-tailed coat, low-cut vest, and high silk hat at a rakish angle, full of boastful tales of his own prowess. Rockefeller's secretary, George D. Rogers, took him for a stroll around New York. The old sharper who had lived by his wits amid the primitive business civilization of the forests and prairies looked with a suspicious eye upon his guide. Then, by way of letting Rogers understand the formidable fellow he had to deal with, he told his guide of another young fellow who had taken him for a walk in Chicago, three times around the same block, calling him by a different name each time, but never the right one and then asking if they hadn't met in such and such a place. The old fellow stopped as he told this story, held the secretary still with his stick and said: "Well, young fellow, I said to him, 'you're right. I also have been trying to place you and your record, and it just comes to me. You see I have been a government detective for many years and have dealt with many criminals. But your name just comes to me. It is—.' But before I could say another word the young rascal took to his heels."

And the old fellow paused to permit Rogers to admire his smartness. Then he laughed heartily at his own fictitious cuteness. When he left New York he was not seen again for many years.

VI

ON THE twenty-eighth day of March, 1889, Mrs. William Rockefeller at the age of 76 breathed her last. She died at the home of her son William, conscious to the last. Around her grave in beautiful Lakeview Cemetery in Cleveland, her famous sons gathered for their farewell to the strong-minded, brave-souled woman who had watched over all their early privations and difficulties in the old Susquehanna country of New York. Old Doctor Bill was not there. On her tombstone the family cut her name "Mrs. Eliza Rockefeller, Widow of William Rockefeller."

All the old days came back to Rockefeller now, swarming over his busy and troubled mind, and touching in him those deep wells of homely sentiment which are part of the man. A little after his mother's death he and his brother William made a visit to the old homes at Richford and Moravia and Owego where they had passed their boyhood. The houses were still standing almost as they were in that distant day when they made their way up to the Lakes and across to Ohio.

VII

THERE was one spot to which Mr. Rockefeller, the man who wanted to be loved, could always turn for a kind word. This was the church. Sometime in 1889, the Reverend Washington Gladden, a Congregationalist minister of some note, criticized the oil trust at a Chautauqua meeting. He was promptly rebuked by a religious leader present. About the same time the *National Baptist*, a small Baptist journal, expressed a severe criticism of the Standard Oil Company. The *Examiner*, official organ of the Baptist Church, flew to the rescue with the assurance that in business many "leaders are Christian men of the highest excellence. The four most prominent men of the oil trust are eminent Baptists, who honor their religious obligations and contribute without stint to the noblest Christian and philanthropic objects."

The Church Edifice Department of the Home Mission Department of the Baptist Church added its word:

"The oil trust was begun and carried on by Christian men. They were Baptists and the objects and methods of the oil trust are praiseworthy."

There are four activities in our society which are financially non-productive yet which require a great deal of money to support. They are the church, the press, the college, and political parties. These are the vehicles for expressing and exploiting ideas. The church with its multitude of social and welfare and propaganda enterprises needs money at every turn. It must appeal for aid to those who have money. No one has yet devised a means of making the newspaper pay. In earlier days editors depended on subsidies. Then they discovered advertising, which is really another business which has fastened itself upon the press. As for parties and schools, their impecuniosity is well known. Mark Hanna was at this time in way of solving the problem of the former. A whole host of highly pragmatical prexies were giving their attention to the latter. The press was finding its way toward support, as witness the Jennings Publishing Company. As for the preachers—they have always been quite shameless. Long begging has made them hard. They swarmed about Rockefeller for gifts—small and great. And those who got their gifts as well as those who prayed for them made up a chorus of praise which washed as a cooling lotion over the hot soul of the abused monopolist. And so as they turned more and more to Rockefeller he turned more and more to them. But he handed out his benefactions only to the Baptists. And in return they stood ready to defend his name against all comers. The daily newspapers pounded away at him. "It will be a sorry spectacle," said the *National Baptist*, "if the secular papers shall be ranged on the side of justice and the human race while the defense of monopoly shall be left to the so-called representatives of the religious press."

CHAPTER VIII. DISSOLVING THE TRUST

THE ANTI-TRUST law having been passed, now found itself in the hands of lawyers and the courts. The law itself directed the Attorney-General "to institute proceedings in equity to restrain" violations under the law. The Attorney-General of the United States was William Henry Harrison Miller, who for fifteen years had been a law partner of President Harrison before his election. And that gentleman functioned for nearly three years after the law was passed. In those years he instituted five proceedings under the law, one against a group of lumber dealers in Minnesota, one against a group of coal dealers in Nashville, one against the Trans-Missouri Freight Association, a fourth against the National Cash Register Company and a fifth against members of the Distillers and Cattle Feeding Company.

Of these prosecutions one was successful—the one against the Nashville coal dealers, which was quite open and shut. Old Senator Morgan of Alabama shook his head gravely in the Senate cloak room and reminded his colleagues of what he had said about the "little fish only getting caught."

Two of these cases made it quite clear that the war on the trusts must face the awful barrier of the bench and the bar. In the case against the lumber dealers of Minnesota, it was charged that the defendants had conspired "among themselves" to restrain trade by an agreement to raise the price of lumber fifty cents a thousand. Judge R. R. Nelson held that the restraint complained of was not a violation of the Sherman law because in their agreement the restraint "operated among themselves"—their agreement, in other words, restrained no one but themselves. This amazing interpretation, which leaves out utterly the restraint upon the consumers who had to buy their lumber, was sufficient to kill the case. In the Trans-Missouri case, some eighteen western railroads were charged with making an agreement to fix rates and conditions of traffic and these roads controlled the traffic of half the surface of the United States. Another distinguished jurist, Judge Riner of Wyoming, but sitting in Kansas, held that the Sherman law did not apply to railroads and that even if it did the agreement was a reasonable one and the Sherman law was directed only at unreasonable restraints. The railroads were represented in that case by John M. Thurston, general counsel for the Union Pacific, who would very soon be sent to the United States Senate from Nebraska.

The case against Patterson and the National Cash Register Company had a notable dénouement. The Attorney-General charged a series of acts committed by Patterson against his competitors to destroy them. After a long legal battle and before a jury trial, Mr. Patterson and the competitors got together; the National Cash Register Company opened its jaws and the competitors floated in.

DISSOLVING THE TRUST

The attack on competition which Patterson had made was thus, in the very midst of the suit, nailed down and completed. In the meantime, President Harrison and General Miller had disappeared from the picture. Cleveland was president and Richard Olney was his Attorney-General. In one of the five cases brought by Miller, that against the Distillers and Cattle Feeding Company, Mr. Olney had appeared with Elihu Root for the defense. Now Mr. Olney was Attorney-General and when Patterson replied to the government's attack by gobbling his competitors, Mr. Olney considered that a perfect defense and dropped the case.

Those who, in their child-like innocence, supposed the Sherman law would end the trusts must have begun to doubt the efficacy of their medicine. The country swarmed with trusts—the beef trust, the sugar trust, the cottonseed oil trust, the barbed wire trust, the cordage trust, the whiskey trust and numerous others. But they pursued their course without obstruction from the federal government.

II

THERE was a statute in Ohio requiring the attorney-general to proceed against any corporation violating the laws of that state, just as there was a clause in the Sherman law directing the Attorney-General of the United States to proceed against offending corporations. But in Ohio there was a very different attorney-general from the gentleman who filled that post in Washington. He was David K. Watson, then a young man under forty.

The Standard Oil Trust agreement had been read in both the New York and the United States trust investigations in 1889. But in spite of that few people ever had seen it in print. The newspapers, particularly in Ohio, gave it little prominence. Even the attorney-general of Ohio had never read it. He came across it accidentally in a little volume on trusts which he picked up one day in 1889 as he rummaged around a book shop. The moment he read that agreement he perceived that the Standard Oil Company of Ohio, an Ohio corporation, had actually surrendered its functions to the Standard Oil Trust. That was an act in violation of its charter and its corporate powers.

Watson saw what was coming to be overlooked and what has since come to be completely obscured, that a corporation is a creature of the law. Those tall gentlemen who today make such a clamor about government interference in business forget that the very existence of their corporations is the result of one of the most far-reaching government interferences in business ever undertaken. The government has actually tried its hand at the business of creation—bringing into being fictitious entities, resembling human beings in all things save their impersonality, having the capacities of human beings without having to assume the unlimited responsibility of real persons. Watson saw that the Standard Oil Company of Ohio had actually abdicated the powers conferred on it by law and permitted another organization, not recognized by Ohio law, to assume its functions.

Some months after this discovery, on May 8th, 1890, Rockefeller was amazed and shocked to learn that the attorney-general of Ohio had instituted proceedings in the Supreme Court of Ohio to declare the charter of the Standard of Ohio revoked. The blow was a serious one and instantly Mr. Joseph H. Choate, Mr. Samuel Dodd, and Virgil Kline, a new addition to the Rockefeller array of counsel, made an appearance for the company.

About the same time Mr. Rockefeller's old schoolmate, Mark Hanna, then a real power in Ohio politics, was in New York. Mr. Rockefeller told him with a long face of the awful thing which had been started by the irresponsible young attorney-general of Ohio. Thereupon Mr. Hanna wrote to Mr. Watson. Mr. Hanna intimated to Mr. Watson that unless the suit was withdrawn Watson would be the subject of the vengeance of the corporations. Then he added a sentence which was to plague the Ohio boss for many a day. "You have been in politics long enough to know that no man in public office owes the public anything." Mr. Hanna concluded: "I understand that Senator Sherman inspired this suit. If this is so I will take occasion to talk to him sharply when I see him."

It is fair to say that the original of this letter was never published and that the excerpts given here were pieced together seven years later for the New York *World* by one of its reporters who was permitted by Watson to read the letter. However he enjoyed the collaboration of several other friends of Watson who had read it. Watson, who had done his duty in the case, shrank from any sensational publicity. A copy of Watson's reply to Hanna, however, which was printed, contained pretty good corroboration of the above rendering.

Neither the interference of Mark Hanna nor the legal subtleties of Messers. Choate, Kline, and Dodd availed. The Supreme Court of Ohio, March 2, 1892, decided that the trust agreement was void, not only because the Standard Oil Company of Ohio was a party to the agreement, but also because the agreement itself was in restraint of trade and amounted to the creation of an unlawful monopoly. The court did not deprive the Standard Oil Company of Ohio of its charter but ordered it to withdraw from the trust.

The dispatch from Columbus which brought the decision was a blow, but one which undoubtedly was expected. A *Tribune* reporter hurried to the home of Samuel C. T. Dodd with the news. "The decision is a most important one for us," commented the Standard lawyer, "but we shall not take the trouble to carry it further in the courts." The course of the company had already been mapped out. Dodd tried to minimize the whole matter. "The agreements were not really necessary. They were simply made as a matter of conscience. The only effect of the decision will be to inconvenience us a little."

A meeting of trust certificate holders was called for March 11th at which it was practically decided not merely to have the Standard of Ohio withdraw from the trust but to dissolve the trust itself. Another meeting was called for March 21st and Virgil P. Kline hurried to Columbus. He explained to the court that when the trust was formed there were but thirty holders of certificates. Now there were several hundred. The trust certificates would have to be recovered and the stocks returned to their respective owners. All this would take time. The court granted the time and on March 21st the trust held a meeting at 26 Broadway with 200 certificate holders present and formally declared the trust dissolved. Mr. Alexander E. Orr made a speech:

"While the Standard Oil has more than met the expectations of its stockholders . . . it has minimized the cost of production and given to the richest and poorest alike a magnificent light at a bagatelle of the cost that comes within the reach of all. I affirm without hesitation that this trust . . . has been during the period of its existence a boon to the people of the United States and indeed, I may add, to the people of the civilized world and uncivilized world."

The "stricken" certificate holders thus assembled in their lugubrious obsequies felt a touch of martyrdom. In 1884 their certificates were worth $70 on the market. Now they were worth $169. It was difficult for them to think other than well of a hunted friend who had done so well for them besides paying fat dividends every year. Mr. Dodd was especially depressed. With a touch of patriotic pathos he spoke of this trust which had saved the petroleum business of America against the Russians.

But even at this meeting it was clear that Mr. Rockefeller and his advisers had no intention of surrendering the substantial qualities of this precious possession. Already the original forty companies had been reduced to thirty and of these thirty many, like the Standard of New York and of New Jersey, were new. It was decided to wipe out ten or twelve of them—Pratt Manufacturing, Stone and Fleming, Archbold's Acme and others. Various smaller companies were to be merged with the Standard of Kentucky and still others with the Buckeye Pipe Line Company. It was decided that the capital of other companies should be greatly increased—the Standard of New York from five to seven million; the Standard of New Jersey from three to ten million; the Atlantic Refining Company in Philadelphia from $500,000 to $5,000,000. Plainly there were great plans afoot. But the Supreme Court of Ohio did not know of them yet. The trust was dissolved. But there was plenty left to the tale.

How much the Standard's monopoly was destroyed may be deduced from the following headline which appeared in the New York *Tribune* about one year later: THE STANDARD OIL'S LAST RIVAL GONE. Beneath this announcement ran the story of the purchase of the Manhattan Oil Company in Findlay, Ohio, by the Standard. It had forced Rockefeller to raise the price of crude oil from fifteen cents to forty-eight cents a barrel. It had immense refineries at Townsend, Walker, and other points. But it lost millions and the property which the Standard acquired was valued at fifteen million.

At top, JOHN D. ROCKEFELLER AT 18 YEARS OF AGE AND IN 1865.
Below, IN 1867 AND 1870

WILLIAM A. ROCKEFELLER, FATHER OF JOHN D., AND ELIZA DAVISON ROCKEFELLER, HIS MOTHER
NOTE THE STRIKING RESEMBLANCE TO JOHN D. AS THE PUBLIC HAS COME TO KNOW HIM

CHAPTER IX. THE GREAT BAPTIST DREAM

THERE now drifted into John D. Rockefeller's life a man who was to have a profound influence upon it and upon his plans and fame. In Minneapolis was a preacher named Frederick Taylor Gates, who was holding there since 1880 his first and only pastorate. The son of a poor Maine preacher, Gates had worked his way through the Rochester Theological College and was now making something of a name for himself in a local way as a very level-headed minister with a strange mixture of practical sense and evangelical zeal. George A. Pillsbury, the flour king, in 1888 wanted to donate $50,000 to Pillsbury College on condition that the people of Minnesota would give the same amount and he approached Gates with a proposal to raise that sum. Gates resigned his pulpit and in six weeks' time had the $50,000 in hand.

About this time the American Education Society was formed in Chicago. The first article in its program was to establish a great Baptist educational institution in Chicago. And Fred T. Gates was made secretary of that body. His capacity as a finder of funds had become known.

John D. Rockefeller, since the early eighties, had been vice-president of the Baptist Theological Union in Chicago. He had made many generous gifts to that body and had also passed over several checks to the Baptist Union Theological Seminary which languished under the auspices of the Union. Gates soon found he had ample opportunities to see and talk with the great multi-millionaire and to inflame him with some of his own passion for the project he had been enlisted to carry forward. At the same time in New York, the New York Baptists were fired with the ambition to have a great Baptist seat of learning there. Dr. R. S. MacArthur, pastor of the Calvary Baptist Church, was interested in the plan which was to raise $20,000,000 and of course John D., New York's richest Baptist, was selected as the patron. It was a race between Dr. MacArthur and the Reverend Gates. But in some way Gates got the inside track. He and Dr. William R. Harper went over the subject with Rockefeller many times. They finally induced him to pledge $600,000 for the founding of an institution which would be known as the University of Chicago. Gates' hand is seen in the proviso that the benefaction would be made on condition that another $400,000 be contributed by subscription. He had

THE LADIES: "HOW SWEET THE DEAR, GOOD MEN ARE, NOT TO FIGHT. THINK HOW DREADFUL THE CONSEQUENCE MIGHT HAVE BEEN TO ONE OR BOTH OF US."
—*The Minneapolis Journal.*

learned that trick from Pillsbury and now taught the lesson to Rockefeller.

There had been an "old University of Chicago" established in 1856 by Stephen A. Douglas but this had died of inanition in 1886.

This was Rockefeller's first great philanthropic gift and the news produced a very considerable stir, coming at a time when he was being roundly denounced all over the country. Gates went to work to raise the required $400,000 and succeeded with astonishing swiftness. Marshall Field gave a tract of land for the site which was valued at $125,000. Rockefeller handed over his $600,000, the University was incorporated September 10, 1890, and the following July, Dr. William Rainey Harper was named president.

THE GREAT BAPTIST DREAM

Meantime Gates had established very cordial relations with Rockefeller. The latter took a very decided fancy to his new-found clerical friend. As a matter of fact, Gates happened along at the most opportune moment. Rockefeller had been contemplating retirement for some time. He was in his fiftieth year and his health was very much impaired. Moreover his fortune had swollen to vast proportions and he wanted to find some means of making a sound use of it which would be pleasing to the Lord. Gates' fiery zeal impressed Rockefeller because it was coupled with a profound strain of very canny business sense. Accordingly the proposed modest institution which was at first planned to grow under the Harper and Gates husbandry at the time of incorporation got an additional million from Rockefeller. A condition of this was to include the Baptist Union Theological Seminary at Morgan Park as part of the University. New buildings were begun and by October, 1892, instruction began in Cobb Hall, the only building ready for occupancy.

II

When the news of Rockefeller's princely gift was made known the National Baptist Educational Society Convention was being held in Boston. The announcement of the gift was received with cheers—which was quite natural. What was interesting to say the least was that when the announcement was being made and before the audience knew its purport, at the mention of Rockefeller's name the audience broke into enthusiastic applause. When the gift was named and the actual sum of money pronounced the audience rose and sang the Doxology. Men burst out into exclamations of praise and joy. "The man who has given this money is a godly man," chanted one leader. Another rose and exclaimed: "The coming to the front of such a princely giver! A man to lead! It is the Lord's doing. God has kept Chicago for us. I wonder at his patience."

On the following Sabbath throughout the country sermons of thanksgiving were preached in almost all Baptist pulpits. "When a crisis came," intoned one minister, "God had a man to meet it." "God," cried out another, "has guided us and provided a leader and a giver and so brought us out into a large place." In scores of pulpits the phrase: "Man of God!" was uttered. A writer to the

Independent said: "No benefaction has ever flowed from a purer Christian source."

Upon the ears of John D. Rockefeller, assailed by the relentless abuse of the profane press, these blessings must have fallen like a benediction. A few years later, speaking to the first graduating class of his New University, he said: "It is the best investment I ever made. . . . I am profoundly thankful that I have had something to do with this great work. The good Lord gave me my money and how could I withhold it from the University of Chicago?"

This brought the first criticism of Rockefeller's benefactions. The Chicago *Chronicle* said: "John D. Rockefeller has fallen in line with Benjamin Harrison and Mark Hanna and modestly announced that Divine Providence is keeping a special watch over him and his monetary affairs. . . . 'The good Lord gave me my money'! Let the ruined refiners, the impoverished producers, the corrupted legislators of the oil belt stand as an answer to the blasphemy."

III

THAT John D. Rockefeller made this gift as a means of influencing the economic education of the young mind is probably far from the truth. He was a man with countless millions looking for a place to continue the habit of giving to worthy religious causes which he began back in the days when he recorded ten-cent benefactions in Ledger A. And he fell by chance into the hands of men who wanted to start a university. He might have begun with a hospital or any other sort of institution if his fortunate pilots at the time were thus interested.

However, while Mr. Rockefeller did not consciously design the University of Chicago as a fortress in the long line of defenses of the economic system under which he flourished, it is not to be denied that such institutions at least tend to take on that character. It is customary for those who resent this view to insist that Mr. Rockefeller and other rich donors like himself "have never interfered in matters of academic freedom" or have never sought to dictate courses of study or the character of personnel. Such interference or dictation is seldom if ever necessary. The gentlemen who accept the commission of these wealthy benefactors may usually be depended upon to possess a sufficient sense of eternal fitness not to permit subversive philosophy to creep into their class rooms. Here two important incidents bearing on this matter may be disposed of.

Before any of the buildings of the new university were fully finished and within a month of the opening, in a still uncompleted building, a *Journal of Political Economy* appeared in print. It may be accepted freely that John D. Rockefeller did not suggest that; that he did not even know of it. It is at least singular that thus early in the life of this new college—in its very first days—almost the very first use to be made of Mr. Rockefeller's generous money gift was to establish a *Journal of Political Economy*.

Thereafter for a number of years this journal was published each month through a period when the subject of industrial combinations and "trusts" occupied almost a first place in the public mind, when newspapers, popular magazines and economic courses in other institutions bristled with controversy over this important subject. Yet one may search through the table of contents of the *Journal of Political Economy* for many years before he finds any reference whatever to this issue. It just simply was never mentioned.

In a letter to the writer Dr. J. Laurence Laughlin, now eighty-two years old and a widely-known economist who specialized in the subject of money and finance, then editor of the *Journal*, says: "I was editor of the *Journal of Political Economy* and know that articles were chosen solely for their economic quality. We could discuss trusts or any economic subject. No one ever tried to use our columns for their private purposes." One may very well acquiesce in this statement. Yet the fact remains that trusts were never discussed. Which seems to afford some ground for recognizing the validity of that principle already referred to, which operates almost with the force of a law, that it is not necessary for generous donors to lay down rules for intelligent practical beneficiaries who know without being told what is the path of security.

The other incident has the same moral. Prof. Edward W. Bemis was an instructor at Vanderbilt University who was brought by Dr. Harper to the University of Chicago in the Extension Department. In addition he devoted a portion of his time to lecturing in the Department of Economics. Bemis, while by no means a radical, was far removed from the extreme conservatism of Dr. Laughlin. Dr. Laughlin objected to him and he was moved to the Department of Sociology under Dr. Small. Later, while he was not precisely dismissed, he was not reappointed. Thus he found himself out of the University.

A good deal of controversy followed his exclusion. It was whispered around that he had been let out because his views were disliked by the University's rich patron. Dr. Harper finally declared he was let out because he was incompetent. Dr. Laughlin says: "While in the Department of Sociology he got into trouble; and some of his pronouncements fell into the hands of a printer who sold them to a reporter who scented notoriety in them. An examination by the trustees followed and he was not reappointed. There was no intention to make the matter public. There was no truth in the story that he was dropped because of his opinions but because he was not of university caliber. He was an agitator, not a scholar."

Bemis's own story is somewhat different. It is fair to say that Bemis, who became widely known later in the field of public utility regulation and attained to some distinction as one of the pioneers in utility control, was a man of indefatigable industry and unquestioned sincerity. He was, perhaps, not a brilliant economist, but he was far abler than most of the economists who calibrate for university work. He was not a radical but rather a believer in the system of regulation which now has become universal in utility control. He had a collection of views on this subject but was hardly any more an agitator than Dr. Laughlin, for instance, has been in the field of banking and currency management. He has been spoken of in the highest terms by such economists as Dr. Richard T. Ely, E. Benjamin Andrews of Princeton, John R. Commons, and many others. An unprejudiced observer of this whole incident will have to conclude that Bemis was not let out because he was incompetent.

Bemis had made some criticism of the railroads in the famous Pullman strike. The president of a railroad complained to the trustees and to President Harper. Harper then wrote Bemis, July 28th, 1894:

"Your speech at the First Presbyterian Church has caused me a great deal of annoyance. It is hardly safe for me to venture into any of the Chicago clubs. I am pounced upon from all sides. I

THE GREAT BAPTIST DREAM

propose that during the remainder of your connection with the university you exercise great care in public utterances about questions that are agitating the minds of the people."

It ought to be observed that Bemis in the criticized speech had condemned the strikers but had merely said—by the way—that the railroads had not shown their employees a very good example and did not come into court with clean hands.

An implied confirmation of this version is found in a letter from President Harper to Bemis even before this incident. It reads in part:

"I hoped that as time passed there would be opportunity for you doing a larger amount of work in the University proper. Instead of the opportunity becoming better for work on your part the doors seem to be closing. . . . I am persuaded that in the long run you can do in another institution, *because of the peculiar circumstances here,* a better and more satisfactory work to yourself. I am personally very much attached to you. . . . You are so well known and your ability so widely recognized that there will surely be no difficulty in securing for you a good position, one in which you will be monarch, and one in which you will be, above all things else, *independent.*"

At the moment when this episode was weaving itself into the history of our schools, colleges and educators everywhere were standing suppliantly with their hands out to the wealthy industrialists and promoters who were pouring out their wealth in endowments to institutions all over the land.

All this refers to a period more than thirty years ago. It must be said in all fairness that for some years the University has assumed a far more liberal policy and that at the present time no obsequious reverence for its founder leads it to undue restriction upon the academic freedom of its teachers.

IV

BEFORE the great Baptist dream flowered in brick and stone upon the new campus, Gates found himself installed as John D. Rockefeller's most intimate adviser. In the Spring of 1891 Rockefeller's indigestion expressed itself in such violent form that he quit work for a while and retired for several months from active work.

He spent a certain amount of time each day in the fields with his laborers, ate simple foods, slept longer hours. Gradually by the end of the Summer, the color came back to his face and he was able to resume his duties. It was during this time that he resolved definitely to retire from business. But the country was moving into trouble and with his far-flung fortune at stake he did not feel at liberty to carry out his plans. The preceding year the great Baring failure had shaken London and the rest of the financial world. America was shielded from its most virulent effects because of a bountiful wheat crop. But the following year all the forces of business disturbance were assembling, though the country as a whole hardly realized it. Gold was leaving the country at an alarming rate.

In this situation Rockefeller became disturbed about certain enterprises in which he had invested a great deal of money. At the time Gates was traveling about North, South, East, and West raising funds for the new university and rousing the Baptists to his new holy war for Baptist learning. One day he was going South when Rockefeller asked him to have a look at an iron mill in which he had a large minority investment. When Gates returned Rockefeller was astonished at the shrewd and wise account of the business Gates was able to give him. "His report," said Rockefeller, "was a model of what such a report should be." It revealed furthermore that the concern was sailing into troubled waters. A little later, as Gates was going West, Rockefeller asked him to make a similar inspection of a large investment he had in that quarter which was supposed to be very prosperous. Gates found it in very deep water and made an elaborate and able report. This so much impressed Rockefeller that he immediately asked Gates to enter his employ as a personal adviser, "to become, like myself, a man of business," as Rockefeller put it, to assist him in unraveling some of his tangled investments and in working out his proposed philanthropic plans. Gates then became the head of what came to be Mr. Rockefeller's personal staff—the force which looked after his interests outside the Standard Oil Company. One of Gates's chief business services at this time was gathering together Rockefeller's scattered investments in iron mines and railroads and organizing them into the profitable group which Rockefeller later transferred to the United States Steel Corporation. When this

THE GREAT BAPTIST DREAM

work was completed and the Lake Superior Iron Ore Company was brought under Rockefeller's dominion, Gates became its head. Nothing could be stranger than the spectacle of this impecunious Baptist preacher setting out to raise funds for a religious college and winding up in a few years as the president of an iron mine and ore railroad company worth twenty millions, and finally the almoner of America's greatest multi-millionaire, with the power of the purse over those vast treasures.

V

THE PLANS for the great university expanded rapidly under the encouragement of Rockefeller's munificence. In 1893 he gave another half million, $175,000 of it to be used for current expenses and another $50,000 in 1894. Then in 1895 he electrified his Baptist wards with a letter proposing an outright gift of $1,000,000 in cash or securities at his option and an additional two million on condition that the University raise another two million. Here was a princely gift—five million if successful. The new students of Chicago University were thrown into a frenzy of delight at this munificence. To the tune of Daisy Bell they marched around the campus and sang:

> John D. Rockefeller
> Wonderful man is he.
> Gives all his spare change
> To the U. of C.
> He keeps the ball a-rolling
> In our great varsity.
> He pays Dr. Harper
> To help us grow sharper
> For the glory of the U. of C.

But the grateful boys were mistaken in one thing. Dear old Chicago University didn't get all his spare change. That same year B. T. Quillan, deacon of the Euclid Avenue Baptist Church, said that Rockefeller had given in different unrevealed gifts to Cleveland over two million dollars.

In any case with these events, the engagement of Gates, the founding of the University of Chicago, Rockefeller's great career of philanthropy had been launched.

VI

THESE were busy years for the Lord—the land swarmed with his self-appointed agents. Moody and Sankey plucked brands from the burning by the thousands and in the wake of their success a wave of evangelism swept over the country. In Rockefeller's state of Ohio the Reverend H. H. Russell of Berea arose and said: "The time will come when the Lord God Almighty will take a spear like a weaver's beam and he will drive the Satanic liquor traffic down to its native hell." The modest Mr. Russell then proceeded to announce himself as that weaver's beam and to describe rather particularly how the Lord went about acquainting him with his appointment. He thereupon suggested the plan for and forged that mighty instrument of the Lord—the Anti-Saloon League.

"The Anti-Saloon League was begun by God Almighty," he said forty years before Scott McBride made the same claim. And very early in the game God's agent No. 2—Brother Russell—began to get aid from God's agent No. 1—Brother John D.—in the shape of modest slices of God's Gold which had been entrusted to the latter agent. At this time there were in the country three million Baptists and three million Methodists and a million and a half Presbyterians and between them they were ruling the land for the Lord. And there were no works of the Lord under the especial care of the Baptist division of this mighty army which Mr. Rockefeller was not willing to help a little. With good reason Baptist ministers occasionally said, referring to him, in a spirit of pious levity: "And there was a man sent from God and his name was John."

CHAPTER X. IRON MEN AND WAXEN LAWS

ALMOST the first major enterprise which the Rev. Mr. Gates supervised for his great patron brought upon Mr. Rockefeller's head one of the most unpleasant attacks he was called upon to suffer since the Backus case—an attack in which he was pictured as the unfeeling Shylock, squeezing his partners out of a vast fortune through the manipulation of a small loan.

Some of the charges in this case were first made in a lawsuit in 1894. The more damaging ones were not heard until 1912 when Alfred and Leonidas Merritt appeared before the Stanley Committee investigating the United States Steel Corporation.

The first charge was that Rockefeller had tricked the Merritts by palming off on them in a consolidation a group of worthless iron mines. The charge made later was that he loaned them $420,000 on a demand note, then in two months called it suddenly, forced them to the wall and took their mines which he sold later to the United States Steel Corporation for $39,000,000.

The Merritts' charge as unfolded before the Stanley Committee was as follows: They were a pair of innocent and, like all Rockefeller's victims, generous, honest, and trusting old lumberjacks who had discovered the iron ores of the Missabe Range in 1890. They had to build a 64-mile railroad from the range to join the nearest trunk line. In the midst of this work the panic fell upon them. They were desperate for money. Whetmore, an agent of Rockefeller, put into their heads the thought that Rockefeller would lend them money. What Rockefeller really wanted was to get their line and their mines to consolidate with his own. The upshot of it all was that they went into a consolidation with Rockefeller, becoming his partners. They put in their mines and railroad for stock; Rockefeller demanded bonds for his properties. They borrowed $420,000 from Rockefeller on a demand note with the understanding he would carry them until they were out of the woods. Instead within two months he called the note. The panic was still on. They couldn't get the money, so Rockefeller took their properties and left them almost penniless. These properties contained 700,000,000 tons of iron ore, as valuable as the mine holdings of the United States Steel Corporation. They subsequently sued Rockefeller and a jury brought in a verdict for them. Rockefeller settled for $525,000 but he kept the mines.

This was the Merritts' story. Here are the facts. They were not innocent souls as pictured. They were promoters; audacious but not wise ones. Their mines belonged to a corporation which they controlled. Their railroad belonged to another corporation. The Merritts organized a third concern—a construction company—which they also controlled and which made a contract with their railroad company to build a 64-mile road. The construction company spent

$660,000 to build this road. In payment they got from their railroad corporation $1,250,000 in stock and $1,250,000 in bonds. An additional $3,500,000—half bonds and half stock—was issued by the company.

Rockefeller did not propose a consolidation to them. They proposed it to him. They made two unsuccessful attempts at consolidation before they approached Rockefeller. Whetmore was not Rockefeller's agent, but a lawyer and independent promoter who teamed up with the Merritts and worked with them. When the 1893 panic swept down on the Merritt enterprises, Whetmore, peddling the Merritt railroad bonds around, sold one-fourth of them to Gates, as Rockefeller's agent. By July the Merritt dream was foundering. Desperate, Whetmore and Leonidas Merritt went to Gates again. They wanted a consolidation and a loan. It was decided to form a consolidation of all Rockefeller's iron holdings and the mines of the Merritts on the Missabe Range and the railroad. Rockefeller financed the road to the tune of $500,000, taking in payment the Lone Jack and Adam mines of the Merritts and these Rockefeller put into the consolidation. Rockefeller took bonds for his own holdings. The Merritts took stock for theirs. Rockefeller took bonds based on the value of his holdings. But the Merritts issued stock for theirs for over $26,000,000, taking $10,000,000 themselves, for all of which they had put in practically nothing save funds they had borrowed from other people. This was an outrageous piece of watering. In addition to all this Rockefeller loaned the Merritts personally $150,000. The Merritts were profoundly grateful to him. Leonidas wrote Gates he wanted to call on John D. and "grasp him by the hand." He wrote a friend in St. Louis he had "been working for months to effect a consolidation of iron interests on the Missabe Range" and had finally connected with Rockefeller. He felt so highly elated he wrote a volume of blank verse on the subject.

But all this did not save the Merritts. The panic deepened and by January, 1894, they were in troubled waters again. They again went to Gates and asked for money. They sold Rockefeller 90,000 shares of their stock for $10 a share. It was stipulated they could buy back 55,000 shares in a year at the same price plus interest. This they never attempted to do. They took a different course instead. They did not give Rockefeller a call note for $420,000 as

IRON MEN AND WAXEN LAWS 315

they swore to the Stanley Committee. Rockefeller had no such note which he could call. He had loaned them $150,000 and only $25,000 of that was due. To this part of the Merritts' story there was not a scintilla of truth and there is no doubt that the whole tale as told to the Stanley Committee wronged Rockefeller.

The other part of the story is more involved. It was that Rockefeller had put in properties which were worthless and he had gotten his bonds for them upon deliberate misrepresentation and fraud. This charge was made by the Merritts a few months after they sold their 90,000 shares to Rockefeller at $10 a share. It was made in a suit filed by the Merritts in which they asked damages against Rockefeller of $1,500,000. The outcome of this suit, simply stated, leaves something to be desired on Rockefeller's side. A jury decided the case against Rockefeller; the higher court reversed it; and then Rockefeller settled with the Merritts for $525,000. Why did he settle for so much money if the Merritt charges were not true? Frederick T. Gates in 1912 made an elaborate argument to prove Rockefeller's innocence of this charge. Beyond doubt he made a powerful case against which nothing stands save the settlement by Rockefeller. Here is Gates's story, pretty well substantiated. A few months after the consolidation the Merritts fell into the hands of Messrs. A. A. Harris and Son, lawyers. These gentlemen called on Gates and insisted that Rockefeller buy the Merritt holdings above the market. When turned down Harris brought suit against Rockefeller for damages of $1,250,000 on the ground that the Wisconsin and Cuban properties of Rockefeller had been sold them under fraudulent misrepresentation. Rockefeller's defense was first that there was no misrepresentation; that the mines were actually valuable mines, that no damage was suffered and that the Merritts knew fully what they were doing. The jury found for the Merritts, but the court of appeals rejected the verdict and ordered a new trial. Thus the matter stood when Rockefeller settled for $525,000. The settlement would be very much against Rockefeller but for one or two facts. Gates declared the settlement was made to avoid further litigation, to get a retraction of the charges, to end expired option on the 55,000 shares, now worth $20 a share and to quiet a number of other Merritts, twenty-three of them, members of the family holding various nebulous claims. Mr. Rockefeller's surrender under a charge of fraud gave rise to much unfriendly comment. However, two facts conspired to aid Rockefeller's position. For one, Merritts' lawyer, Henry E. Harris, called on Gates during the litigation and tried to sell telegrams and other valuable evidence belonging to his clients. And later the Merritts themselves brought suit against Harris and his son revealing a good many disreputable activities of Mr. Harris in his relations with the Merritts. Also the Merritts signed a statement in which they retracted all the charges made against Rockefeller, declaring they were satisfied from recent independent investigation made by them that no misrepresentation was made nor fraud committed by Mr. Rockefeller. The so-called worthless properties put in by Rockefeller turned out to be very valuable and the whole property, under Rockefeller's wise management and the very canny business judgment of the one-time Baptist minister, became a magnificent property. Not, however, until Rockefeller had put into it many millions for development and eight years of Rockefeller management.

II

It was easy now to get things believed about John D. Rockefeller. The tide of hate which later rose against him was now in flow. Old enemies found the time propitious to call up old scores. Years before old George W. Girty had been cashier of the Standard of Ohio. He was among the first employees. When prosperity came he drew a salary of $10,000 a year. He made money and had a home in Cleveland worth $100,000. Then he defaulted to the extent of more than $275,000. He came home one day with threats of suicide and, without telling his wife the reason, got her to sign a paper transferring their Cleveland home. In spite of the trouble he remained in the employ of the Standard and when he died was given a "state funeral," the Standard spending $1,000 for a special car to carry his remains. He had told his wife his old losses were due to speculation in Standard stocks in which the Standard officials, led by William Rockefeller, had tricked him. Now in 1894 Girty's widow sued the Standard Oil Company for damages in a perfectly hopeless suit.

George Rice roamed up and down the land hurling shafts at the head of Rockefeller. The Central Labor Council of New York, inspired by Rice's attacks, made an application to have the Standard Oil charter of New York revoked. Ladenburgh, Thalman, and Company, refiners, brought suit against the Standard to recover $300,000 damages suffered as a result of freight discriminations—one of the earliest civil suits under the Sherman act—and the court had commanded the Standard to bring its books into court. "Ah!" people said, wagging their heads, "Mr. Rockefeller's chickens are coming home to roost."

III

IN TEXAS was a huge man, weighing 300 pounds, whose name was Hogg. He was governor of the state. Moreover he was a resourceful, popular, and resolute fighter. The wild and woolly Texas kerosene customer found himself in the grip of the Waters-Pierce Company and this, Texans said, is just a wolf in the clothing of a bigger wolf, the Standard Oil Company. This was true, but at the time Texas had no proof of it. Then in the midst of all these other attacks, the grand inquisitors of McLennan County, sitting at Waco, brought in an indictment for criminal conspiracy against John D. Rockefeller, Henry Clay Pierce, Flagler, Archbold, Brewster, and various other lesser fish including a very small fish named E. T. Hathaway, division agent. Governor Hogg immediately made a requisition on Governor Flower of New York for the bodies of Rockefeller, Rogers, Flagler, and others. Governor Flower's secretary informed reporters that a protest was made against honoring the requisition as it was not shown that the culprits were ever in Texas and hence could not be fugitives. But Waco hungered for her prey. Sheriff W. L. Burke was all packed ready to come to New York to bring the villains back. He wrote the sheriff of New York to wire him the moment he had the gang in custody, and that he would hurry on. Governor Hogg fulminated but at 26 Broadway they only laughed at the Waco comedy. Samuel Dodd said it was all done under the new Texas anti-trust law, "one of those crazy socialistic laws which are unconstitutional." And then Mr. Dodd, still slumbering amid his fictions, said the Standard Oil had no interest in the Waters-Pierce Company. Hogg sent a requisition to Florida for Flagler who was a citizen of that state, and it was said Governor Mitchell would honor it. In the end, however, none of the great sinners was caught. The dénouement gave old Senator Morgan of Alabama another good laugh. Mr. E. T. Hathaway, the division agent, was convicted and fined $50. The little fish was caught. He refused to pay his fine, went to jail pending further litigation, remained there for a year handsomely compensated by his powerful patrons, and was released in a year when the conviction was reversed.

IV

WHILST all this was in progress, the American people, sullen in the midst of the depression of 1893, languishing in widespread unemployment and growing poverty of the masses, indignant at the blatant and vulgar displays of a host of rich rogues wallowing in the fruits of dishonesty and graft, shocked by exposures of corruption in public and private life, were treated to one of the darkest chapters in the history of its judiciary.

The Sherman law had been passed, wisely or unwisely, to curb the activities of trusts and monopolies in business. It was aimed at nothing else. During Harrison's administration practically nothing was done under the law. We saw how Mr. Richard Olney, a great New York lawyer, appeared as the counsel for the distillers in the first important suit against the law. When Mr. Cleveland became president he named this same Richard Olney as his Attorney-General, a man notoriously unfriendly to the act. During the next four years—1892 to 1896—there were ten cases either begun or prosecuted under the act. Only one against a large trust was successful—the suit against the Trans-Missouri Freight Association, decided in favor of the Association in Harrison's administration in the lower court. The Supreme Court reversed that decision and held the agreement to fix freights unlawful. There were three other cases against large trusts, one against the pipe trust, one against the sugar trust, and a third against a railroad trust in New York. In the sugar case, the American Sugar Refining Company, making 65 per cent of our domestic production, bought four refineries in Pennsylvania, making the remaining 35 per cent. Here was a complete monopoly. The trust lawyers contended that the Sherman law did not apply to such a combination. These refineries were factories—producers of sugar. The Sherman law applied to combinations in restraint of trade in interstate commerce. These refineries were not in commerce. They made sugar. The sugar did not get into commerce until after they made it. But the

IRON MEN AND WAXEN LAWS

court could not presume they made it with the intent of having it flow into commerce in violation of the law. So strained, so grotesque, so fantastic a construction of the law could hardly be born anywhere save in the brain of a very hard-pressed special pleader. Yet, difficult as it is to believe, the Supreme Court adopted this view, Chief Justice Fuller writing the opinion in the cases. In the third suit—against 32 railroads in the East, which made an agreement to fix rates—the Supreme Court held that transportation was not commerce and that the law did not apply to the railroads. Against these incredible decisions, which could have come only from minds utterly steeped in the worship of the rights of property and money, was heard in dissent the strident voice of old Justice Harlan, who was shocked at the decision and wrote vigorous dissents.

One victory for the law was registered. A man named Moore, in Salt Lake City, refused to sell coal to anybody who was not a member of the Salt Lake Coal Exchange. Moore was convicted and fined $200 but even this conviction was reversed because the court did not have jurisdiction. Truly old Senator Morgan seemed to have been right. Indeed if this were all it would be bad enough. But there were five other cases prosecuted—all against striking workingmen, one in New Orleans against the Workingman's Amalgamated to restrain it from promoting a strike, the other four against various labor leaders, including Eugene V. Debs, to restrain them from or punish them for carrying on the famous railroad strike of 1892-94. Singularly enough all these prosecutions were successful save one, which was dismissed because the indictment was improperly drawn. In the others, in Missouri, Illinois, and California, the courts held that the law applied to striking laborers. Eugene Debs and others were thrown into jail for three to six months. At the end of six years, therefore, the slate of the government's war on trusts was to see almost every trust prosecuted escape through fantastic interpretations by the courts, save in one case, the New York railroad agreement, and one labor man in jail. Against the great trusts whose subjugation the law was especially framed to achieve, no finger was raised. The net that was contrived to catch the Rockefellers, the Havemeyers, the Archbolds, and their like had landed Eugene V. Debs in jail. It was a discouraging phenomenon and afforded endless ammunition to the radical orator and agitator who was then industriously fomenting the elements of discontent in the country.

CHAPTER XI. OLD ENEMIES ON THE MARCH

WE MUST go back now a few years to see what Rockefeller's old enemies, the oil men of the regions, were doing. The oil men had tried to get a bill through the Pennsylvania legislature prohibiting railroad rate discriminations. On the night of April 28th, when that bill was defeated, through the machinations of the Standard, wrath ran high in Harrisburg. The producers called a meeting in Oil City and organized another Producers' Protective Association "to defend the industry against monopolies by selling its own oil."

The first proposal was to stop the drill and limit production. Thomas W. Phillips rose. He was the largest oil producer. "There are 30,000,000 barrels of oil in storage now," he said. "It all belongs to John D. Rockefeller. He bought it at low prices. Stop drilling and the only one you will help will be Rockefeller. His 30,000,000 barrels of oil will immediately become more valuable." He then proposed that a committee call on the Standard and suggest an arrangement; that the Standard sell them 5,000,000 of those 30,000,000 barrels at 62 cents. They would then limit their production to 17,500 barrels a day. Any rise in price would then add to the value of their 5,000,000 barrels. The producers thought this an excellent suggestion. The fact that a shut-down would throw several thousand laborers out of work did not trouble them at all. The regions were made for the producers. However, Phillips thought of the workers and insisted that a million barrels be dedicated to them. Mr. Phillips pointed out also that the drill could not be stopped without the coöperation of the drillers. So the profits of a million barrels were dedicated in trust for them on condition that they refuse to drill wells. The committee called on John D. Archbold in New York and that gentleman promptly agreed to the plan. The drill was stopped, the output limited, and oil rose at once twenty cents a barrel. A few prospectors,

OLD ENEMIES ON THE MARCH

who still believed in the old doctrine of *laissez faire*, individual liberty, which the producers preached, refused to quit drilling. A little nitro-glycerine in their works, put there by the kindly producers in the sacred name of individualism, soon fixed them. Oil went to 96 cents a barrel by the end of the year 1888, but this was very far from the three dollar oil or even two dollar oil they dreamed of. What was worse, in spite of all these elaborate schemes, the output continued to be excessive.

II

By this time the Producers' Protective Association decided to pin its faith on a scheme known as the United Oil Company, a corporation to be owned by the producers to engage in refining. They selected H. L. Taylor as chairman of the committee to organize the project. The reader may remember the name—H. L. Taylor who, with Satterfield, five years before, tried to throw the Tidewater Oil Company into a receivership for the Standard. Why was Taylor selected?

Taylor had a producing company, called the Union Oil Company. Rockefeller at this time had decided to go into the production of oil. He sent an agent to Taylor and arranged to buy out his Union Oil Company. All was profoundly secret and Taylor went on representing the Producers until a rumor of his treachery got out. The Producers summoned him and accused him of selling out to Rockefeller. He admitted it, and was compelled to resign from the Producers' committee.

This year Rockefeller bought substantial interests in three other producing companies—Forrest Oil Company, North Pennsylvania Oil Company, and the Midland Oil Company. This entry of Rockefeller into production cast another shadow over the regions. As for Taylor he continued to prosper and died in 1894 in Buffalo, well-known as a multi-millionaire.

III

When news of Taylor's treachery got about the producers decided to attempt to cut off crude supplies from Rockefeller. They organized the Producers Oil Company owned by 1,000 producers and planned to sell their crude oil abroad. But they failed to find a market and decided they must build up an independent refining

THE FINAL FLIGHT

interest to buy their oil. They gathered together a number of small independent refiners and organized them into the Producers and Refiners Company with $250,000 capital. The Producers Oil Company took $160,000 of this. They laid pipes and pumped crude from the fields to the refiners cheaper than the Standard would carry it. But they still had to get the crude and refined oil to the seaboard.

IV

ROCKEFELLER now met a foe worthy of his steel. This was Louis J. Emery, who in 1892 undertook to meet the need of the new refining interest to pipe oil to the seaboard. He organized the United States Pipe Line Company. He planned to pipe oil from Bradford to Hancock in New York. From there the oil would go by rail to the Hudson River and then down the Hudson to the sea. When Emery got his pipes as far as the Erie tracks seventy railroad workers attacked him. They captured the territory around the tracks and camped there. Emery made preparations for a counter attack, massed men, provisions, muskets, and food. But the battle never came. While he was making this demonstration he secretly got another right of way seventy miles nearer Wilkes-Barre and before Rockefeller realized it had his line completed to the New York, Ontario, and Western Railroad at Hancock. He completed another line from the regions to the sea for piping refined oil—a new idea. Here was a serious threat now for Mr. Rockefeller—a new refining interest with capital, adequate independent pipes from the wells to the refineries and pipe lines to the seaboard to carry both crude and refined oil. The new interests now had crude and refined oil at the seaboard independent of the railroads and of the Rockefeller pipe lines. But they still had to find customers for it. This Rockefeller now proceeded to make almost impossible by cutting prices.

The going was hard for the independents. It would have been impossible but that the United States Pipe Line carried oil for them at cost. As usual the weak spirited were for yielding. A committee went to New York and literally begged Mr. Rockefeller for mercy. He told them in his soft, benevolent tones there was no hope for them but to sell. And this they proposed to do. But a few hardy souls counseled a further effort. They called a mass meeting in January, 1895, at Butler, Pennsylvania, to organize a new company. A great crowd appeared. They came in special trains. There was the usual stirring oratory and excitement. In a few minutes $75,000 capital had been subscribed; in a few days $200,000. The new company was to be called the Pure Oil Company. It was not to supersede the Producers Oil Company or the United States Pipe Line and the latter's subsidiary the Producers and Refiners Company. Its object was to provide funds for refiners who might be hard-pressed.

The organizers were determined that Rockefeller should not get control of this company. To prevent it they created a voting trust and put one half of all the stocks into the hands of "five champions of independence" who were bound to vote the shares only in the interest of the independent interests. Heartened by this new movement the battle was renewed. But hardly had the cheers subsided when a new blow descended. A man named Herman Roth was the agent of the independents in Europe. When the committee called on Rockefeller with a plea for mercy, his agents in Europe called on Roth, informed him the independents were about to sell out to Rockefeller and that he would soon be left in the lurch. Roth believed them and sold his business to the Deutsche-Americanische, the Standard subsidiary in Germany. Emery had to hurry to Europe for the Pure Oil Company and immediately organized another selling subsidiary.

V

The structure of the independent battle was now as follows: The Producers Oil Company organized to find a market for the producers' oil; the Producers and Refiners Oil Company, controlled by the Producers Oil Company to pipe oil from the fields to the refineries; the United States Pipe Line Company, with pipes for both crude and refined to the seaboard.

It was now proposed to unite the United States Pipe Lines which operated trunk pipes and the Producers and Refiners Company which operated pipes to gather oil from the fields. A meeting was called to consider it. Col. John J. Carter, supposed to be an independent producer, was a member of the Producers Oil Company. He owned 300 shares of stock. He went into court to obtain an injunction against this merger. In the hearings it came out that the Standard Oil Company owned 60 per cent of the stock of Col. Carter's oil company. A storm of anger broke out at this. Would the independents never be rid of the perils of traitors and spies? Patterson had turned on them; Taylor had sold them out twice. Now Carter had sneaked into their company. Another meeting was called. Col. Carter appeared. To the amazement of everybody he had not only his original 300 shares but 13,013 more and these belonged to the Standard Oil Company. He had other shares besides—21,848 in all. The leaders were astonished, but they mustered over 30,000 shares and controlled the meeting. The incident shocked and frightened them however. Later they denounced Carter as a traitor and expelled him from the Producers' Association. But the Standard went on buying shares. By January, 1896, they had 29,764, enough with Carter's 300 to control the company. But they laid low. In 1896 Col. Carter bought out the Standard shares and went to the next meeting of the Producers Oil Company with a clear majority. The directors refused to let him vote them without authority of a majority of the stockholders. The company was a limited partnership and stock could not be transferred without the approval of the company. Carter took the fight to court but lost and sold his stock below par.

VI

MICHAEL MURPHY was an active leader in the United States Pipe Lines. One day in August, 1895, the stockholders were meeting when a Mr. J. C. McDowell appeared at the door with 2,613 shares. Murphy stopped him and told him that he believed him to be a Standard Oil spy and that if he attempted to cross the threshold he would throw him out. Mr. McDowell departed. But McDowell brought suit and won. The United States Pipe Lines was not a limited partnership. It was a corporation and the Standard interest was entitled to appear at stockholders' meetings and ultimately gained a director on the board. Assuredly Mr. Rockefeller was an incorrigible man.

VII

THUS this ambitious movement of the independents stood in 1896. One other incident discouraged them. In 1895 Emery decided to extend the pipe line from Wilkes-Barre all the way to Bayonne.

He had to cross the Pennsylvania tracks. So he bought an acre over which the Pennsylvania tracks ran, believing this would entitle him to run his pipes under the ground beneath the tracks. But long litigation held him up. He then bought a farm at the tracks of the Delaware, Lackawanna, and Western road. The farm was low and the tracks ran over a trestle 17 feet high. Emery with fifty armed men went at night, laid his pipes along the level under the road and four feet under the ground, fastened them with heavy timbers and anchored them, set up a camp and prepared for war. Railroad men with picks and bars attacked them and were driven off. Next day two wrecking cars with 250 men renewed the attack. They were again repulsed. There was a truce and an arrangement to refer the matter to the courts. While this was pending two locomotives descended on the camp and attacked it with hot water and coals. The countryside rose to aid Emery. The local G.A.R. loaned 48 muskets. Emery bought some Springfield rifles and held his ground in a state of siege for seven months. In the end the court decided against Emery and the pipes were torn up.

Thus the battle raged when John D. Rockefeller carried out a resolution he had been considering a long time and which will be recorded in the next chapter.

CHAPTER XII. LEAVING THE STAGE

As the year 1893 dawned the world was in so disturbed a state that Rockefeller found it necessary in spite of his seriously impaired health to remain close to his interests. Under the incessant urgings of Dr. Biggar, however, he had made up his mind to retire from active business. Therefore, from 1893 on he was keeping his eye open for the moment when business would be out of its difficulties so that he might carry out this intention to retire.

II

The times were indeed troubled. Two hundred thousand coal miners were on strike in the Middle Atlantic states. In the Summer of 1894 came the disastrous Chicago Railway strike under the leadership of Eugene V. Debs, the calling of the United States troops by Grover Cleveland and Deb's arrest. Coxey's Army was marching on Washington. The hot sirocco devastated the corn belt. Wheat went to 49 cents, its lowest price. Gold was flowing out of the country. When Cleveland entered the White House in 1892 we were very much in the condition of England in 1931. We had five dollars in paper money outstanding for each dollar in our gold reserve. The government was almost bankrupt. The Secretary of the Treasury under Harrison had stood in Wall Street with his hat in his hand almost begging for gold from the bankers there. In the midst of this in 1894 Cleveland's Secretary of the Treasury, John G. Carlisle, went to J. P. Morgan to ask for $50,000,000 in gold. Morgan replied gruffly that the thing was impossible. The great Bull was for the moment at least terrorized. James Stillman was called on. He went across the street to Morgan's office. Morgan was in a state of awe-inspiring disintegration. As Stillman entered Morgan held up his hands. "They expect the impossible of me," he cried. Stillman thought he was on the verge of tears. Stillman, small, calm beside the bulky and turbulent Morgan, calmed the great banker and suggested that he, Stillman, be given an hour to see what he could do. Stillman went at once to Rockefeller who immediately authorized a draft of $10,000,000 on Standard Oil European funds. Stillman, with this beginning, got in touch with a few other capitalists and gathered up another ten million. Then he went to Morgan.

"I have twenty million," he said when he entered Morgan's office. "Where did you get them?" cried Morgan, leaping up and throwing off his despair like a cloak. "He became perfectly bombastic and triumphant," said Stillman, relating the incident later to a Parisian friend. "He took the pose of savior of his country and assumed all the credit." And then Stillman added: "Of course; but then you see he is a poet. Morgan is a poet."

Rockefeller's funds were in demand through these troubled days. The Reverend Frederick T. Gates, who sat at Mr. Rockefeller's cash window, was a busy man. "I have today on my desk," wrote Gates to Andrew R. Merritt October 2nd, 1893, "urgent imperative appeals to save old friends [of Mr. Rockefeller's] amounting to many hundreds of thousands of dollars. I have incurred the enmity of many important business enterprises because I have had to decline to assist them in the last few days."

On that day, Gates said, Rockefeller had loans outstanding to fifty-eight men and companies amounting to $5,969,422—men who could not have gotten money anywhere else. And to do this Rockefeller had borrowed from the banks over $3,000,000, his bank account that day being overdrawn $30,000.

Rockefeller spent a great deal of his time in the seclusion of his Forest Hill home. But he had private wires to his New York offices, his bankers, and other places. Telephones and wires throughout the estate kept him in touch with affairs no matter where he might be. Messages poured in every day keeping him informed of affairs. He was heavily involved in the market and changes in quotations and in the conditions of business were so rapid that his messages were telegraphed direct from the stenographers' notes and were transcribed afterwards.

Rockefeller was deeply interested in the Northern Pacific Railroad. It was in desperate straits and its president, George Baxter, was making heroic efforts to save it from bankruptcy. The day arrived when there was but another twenty-four hours to meet the interest on its bonds. Rockefeller carefully canvassed all his resources to see what he could spare in cash to meet the situation. Throughout the night he arranged to have central offices and stations and branches all along the line of the road report by wire to him the amount of cash in every drawer of the company in the hope that enough might be thus scraped together to save it, supplemented by his own resources. By midnight it was clear when all returns were in that the Northern Pacific did not have enough and so he had to let it sink into bankruptcy.

III

IN THE midst of all this, in 1894 there appeared a book which produced a greater impression than any which had appeared in America since Henry George's "Progress and Poverty." Edward Everett Hale said it was the most important book which had appeared in America since "Uncle Tom's Cabin." It was called "Wealth Against Commonwealth," by Henry Demarest Lloyd. This was the same Lloyd who had in 1881 made the first serious economic analysis of Standard Oil in an *Atlantic Monthly* article. "Wealth Against Commonwealth," which was rejected by a number of publishers, was brought out by Harper Brothers. It contained a vivid, dramatic, highly colorful, yet thoroughly faithful and authentic account of the whole course of Rockefeller's great monopoly from its inception. It was indeed the first connected history of Standard Oil up to that time. There was portrayed the story of the South Improvement Company, the numerous efforts of Rockefeller to form air-tight trade agreements and the final perfection of Rockefeller's monopoly through rebates and various unjust discriminations. The book was unsparing in its denunciations, and revealed a mind on fire with indignation at the attack which Rockefeller's whole course had made upon the system of individualism which Lloyd accepted as proved and established.

Lloyd himself was a man of no small attainments. Born in 1847, the son of a Dutch Reformed minister, he studied for the bar and became after his admission in 1869 secretary to Chief Justice Salmon P. Chase. After that he followed the profession of journalism rather than law, wrote editorials for the New York *Tribune* and contributed to various magazines. He spent several years preparing his book and, as a matter of fact, though its accuracy of statement was questioned, went to great pains to verify all its statements. When it was published William Dean Howells wrote him:

"To think that the monstrous iniquity whose story you tell so powerfully, accomplished itself in our time, is so astounding, so infuriating, that I have to stop from chapter to chapter to take breath. It is like a tale of some remote corruption, some ancient oppression far from ourselves."

The book had an immense circulation and perhaps for the first time gave to the thinking element of the country a clear and connected understanding of the phenomenon at work in their midst. But no one connected with the Standard Oil Company made a reply. This made a most unhappy effect on many hitherto undisturbed minds. Lloyd had drawn a specific, an able, a serious, and a disinterested indictment and the accused persons preserved a profound silence. Finally Rev. B. Fay Mills, a well-known clergyman of the day, went directly to 26 Broadway where he was received by Dodd and one he calls "Rockefeller's manager" —perhaps the Rev. Frederick T. Gates. "I told them," he said

LEAVING THE STAGE

later, "I had come to ask them what was Mr. Rockefeller's theory of life by which he seemed in his private life to be so estimable and in his public life so wicked." Dodd declared they would welcome a complete inquiry into their affairs by a committee of clergymen and economists. And Mills undertook to assemble such a committee. He wrote men like Edward Everett Hale and invited Lloyd to be present and present his proofs. This invitation Lloyd quickly accepted. But the Rockefellers refused to permit Lloyd to appear and the other persons invited refused to serve as judges and the whole project fell through.

Still no answer was made to Lloyd. A year later a reply appeared to come from a wholly disinterested source. Professor George Gunton wrote an answer in the *Social Economist*. He wrote as one who was profoundly concerned for the integrity of economic literature because of this irresponsible performance. He quoted a letter from Professor John A. Hobson, noted English economist, corroborating Gunton's views. Lloyd wrote Hobson who promptly replied that he had written Gunton but that he had written exactly the opposite. Lloyd denounced Gunton for this distortion and Brother Gunton remained silent. Later he appeared as the editor of *Gunton's Magazine* which functioned for many years, a persistent defender of almost everything Rockefeller and the oil trust did. In 1908 it came out that he who had trembled for the integrity of "economic literature" had been getting money regularly from John D. Archbold. Henry Demarest Lloyd and Professor George Gunton may be said to be the originals of two widely different birds in our public history. Lloyd was undoubtedly the first of that band of earnest men who grew in number and aroused the conscience of the nation until they suffered somewhat from Theodore Roosevelt's unjust characterization of "muckrakers." Gunton was at least among the first of that merry band of college professors who write "studies" and "surveys" and "books" and what not for wealthy but undisclosed patrons and seek to give to otherwise dishonest and unimportant creeds the respectability which flows from their titles as professors of economics.

At a later day John D. Archbold attacked Lloyd. In 1900 Rev. Hever Newton at the Conference on Trusts in Chicago, expressed surprise that Standard Oil did not bring suit against

Lloyd. Archbold wrote Newton reproving him and adding: "His [Lloyd's] motive was first sensationalism to sell his book, and second, I have personally a strong suspicion which I think is well grounded that there was a motive on his part meaner and more mercenary than this."

What this motive was Archbold revealed three years later when he said before the Industrial Commission that he suspected Lloyd hoped to share in the proceeds of damages which Rice expected to collect from the Standard.

Of course, there was and there could be no evidence of this and it is doubtless true that Archbold spoke from no other grounds than his natural disposition to look upon every man who disagreed with him as a scoundrel. Archbold, exposed as a briber and corrupter of all sorts of men, unfeeling and boisterous in his attacks on others, left behind him a vast number of words in letters, testimony, and public documents of various sorts. One may search them in vain to find a decent or honorable motive attributed to any man. Lloyd was a highly honored member of the writing profession and after a long life spent in fighting for the interests of the masses, the downtrodden, and the poor, he died in 1903 in Chicago with a touch of martyrdom upon his brow in the thick of a battle against the corrupt traction ring of that city.

IV

AGAIN events moved here and there to touch with gold Mr. Rockefeller's course. In the midst of the great panic there appeared on the streets of Chicopee Falls, Massachusetts, a curious-looking vehicle which moved along the streets without a horse. It was driven by George Duryea, its inventor, and was the first American automobile to actually move on its own power. Thus in this simple way dawned the age of gasoline, foreshadowed fourteen years before when George Selden applied for his patent, and which was to pile upon Mr. Rockefeller's hill of gold a mountain of that same metal. When in 1896 John D. Rockefeller retired his entire fortune could not possibly have exceeded $200,000,000, if indeed it was so great. One is wholly in the realm of guesswork when estimating Rockefeller's fortune. Yet in 1882 it is difficult to see how he could have been worth more than $40,000,000. This would be a very liberal estimate. Between

1882 and 1896 the Standard Oil Company paid dividends of $164,490,000 and of this Rockefeller collected at the most $25,000,000. There was an immense increase in the value of his holdings of Standard stock, yet these in 1893 could not have been worth more than $40,000,000. Of course he had great and extensive holdings in railroads, banks, various industrial corporations including iron and steel. The largest were iron ore and these we know he sold in 1902 to the United States Steel Corporation for $32,000,000. But they were worth not one-third that in 1893. It must be understood that Rockefeller himself had not engaged in any of those extravagant and adventurous stock jobbing transactions like Amalgamated Copper which were the work chiefly of Henry H. Rogers and William Rockefeller. On the whole, therefore, an estimate of $200,000,000 on Rockefeller's fortune at the moment when he retired from active business life and became thereafter merely an investor is quite liberal. This being accepted we are able to see one of the most important and significant facts about the fortune of this man. He was the greatest money maker in the history of the world. Yet in a career devoted without distraction to money making he could not accumulate more than $200,000,000 while afterwards without any effort save as an investor he accumulated four times that sum in half the time. With the advent of the gasoline age which was now dawning, his refineries were to become far more profitable. Gasoline was to outdo kerosene as a maker of money for Rockefeller.

V

TWENTY-FIVE years before the oil regions arrogantly announced that it would wipe Cleveland from the oil map as with a sponge. Cleveland bristled at this. Rockefeller, whatever else might be said of him, was in a way the champion of Cleveland in the oil war. Now Cleveland was to be wiped almost, if not completely, from the map. May 13, 1896, Cleveland papers announced that six months after this date Standard Oil would close its immense plant in Cleveland. A small plant for supplying the local trade was all that would remain. Four hundred would be thrown out of work. The oil capital had moved East. Mr. Rockefeller was a citizen of New York State. He had already bought large acreage at Tarrytown and gotten interested in the building of a country home on the Hudson to supplant the one at Forest Hill. His migration, however, was somewhat softened in its effect by his gift two months later of $600,000 to Cleveland on its centennial anniversary for a park.

VI

BUT WHILE all this was in progress, while the country, whipped by a hundred restless forces, worked itself into a lather and plunged on into the hectic Bryan years, Rockefeller, in spite of the commanding dangers to his business, was compelled to halt. Dr. Biggar demanded that he withdraw from business and give himself up to a rigorous régime of exercise, diet, and rest which he prescribed. And this he did.

And as the country plunged on into the troubled and finally prosperous years of McKinley's régime, the busiest man in America quit work and went in for play. While in the East he spent some time every day in the open playing with his new estate at Tarrytown, building roads, laying out walks and gardens. He drove about in his carriage, mingling with his neighbors and playing neighbor to the old ladies and young teachers he met on his carriage drives. He went on a severe diet of milk. He followed regular hours and got plenty of sleep.

He found time again to devote to his family and his home. His daughter Alta was married about this time to Mr. E. Parmalee Prentice and for the first time the Rockefellers found themselves compelled to deal with certain society notables. His son, John D., Jr., was a student at Brown University.

A wave of evangelism was sweeping over the country. Rockefeller threw himself with zest into his Sunday School classes. His talks to his classes began to appear in the newspapers. The Sunday School was invited frequently to Forest Hill for pleasant evenings and occasionally for picnics when they made merry amid the bowers and lawns of the beautiful estate and sang the old hymns and along with them some of the new ones which Sankey made as famous among Middle West evangelical Christians as the latest Irving Berlin hit might be among modern Americans.

The great social drama of American life rose in intensity and tempo. New forces were appearing and new problems usurping the attention of the people. Rockefeller, whose mind had never dwelt on them, who had never pondered abstractions or wandered deeper into the affairs of the spirit than Sunday School Baptist theology might lead one, let them pass by. His gifts to Chicago University under the piloting of his new-found friend, Dr. Gates, and his small benefactions to countless Baptist churches satisfied him that he was the instrument of the Lord and brought him back balm in the shape of adulation from his beneficiaries. Beyond a doubt Rockefeller spent precious little time analyzing the ethical values in his career. And now that he was through with business and was determined to devote the rest of his days to administering his great fortune in the interest of worthy Baptist objects he felt secure of salvation. He read a little—Artemus Ward, a little of Mark Twain, for whose strong meat he found small appetite, and best of all, Ella Wheeler Wilcox. Better still it was to go to Sunday School and better than all to have the classes out to Forest Hill to frolic and picnic and sing hymns. When the merrymaking was done, in the evening with the old and young of the Euclid Avenue Baptist Church he would stand under the trees and sing out lustily: "When the roll is called up yonder, I'll be there." He had no doubt that this was so.

PART EIGHT

MOUNTAINS OF HATE

CHAPTER I. THE NEW LEADERS

As ROCKEFELLER walked out of 26 Broadway he left his great company in the hands of the men who had begun by fighting him. John D. Archbold, vice-president, became the executive head.

Archbold was a little fellow with a large head and in almost all things the faithful imitator of his great chief. He looked like a preacher. He was a good Baptist and a church trustee. Rockefeller had his University of Chicago and his Dr. Harper. Archbold had his Syracuse University and his notorious Chancellor Day. But there were points of difference. He was an extravagant talker, a truculent battler, full of terrible threats, aflame with righteous indignation, a blustering bluffer with a sharp tongue and a willingness to use it. He believed his side was wholly right and his enemies all scoundrels and blackmailers. He liked a good story and could tell one, loved a game of poker, and was a most ingratiating gentleman in the presence of the ladies.

Many supposed Henry H. Rogers to be the new master mind of Standard Oil. He was as different from Archbold as men could well be. The two hated each other. John D. himself leaned towards the pious and willing servitor, Archbold. Rockefeller for years had a direct wire to Archbold's office and kept that functionary on the griddle. But upon the imperious and profane Rogers he looked with a suspicious eye.

Rogers was a gambler. As a newsboy at fourteen he got his batch of papers one morning in Fairhaven and saw that the packet

MR. JOHN D. ROCKEFELLER IN 1888

JOHN D. ROCKEFELLER
From a photograph taken at Chicago University in 1900

boat had gone down out of Boston with 500 barrels of sperm oil consigned to a local dealer. Rogers hurried to the dealer and proposed to sell him all his papers, thus suppressing in Fairhaven news of the disaster and allowing the dealer to hurry around and buy up and corner the limited supplies of sperm oil, provided the dealer would let him in on the deal to the extent of his $200 savings. The shrewd Yankee whale oil man saw the possibilities instantly, bought all the papers, destroyed them, rushed around and cornered all the oil in Fairhaven and in a single day made a profit which more than trebled young Rogers' $200 investment. This exhibition of brains resulted in a recommendation to Charles Pratt in New York, then looking for a smart boy. He got one.

Rogers was a magnificent and commanding figure, with a gaze which all agreed was the most terrifying in Wall Street. He looked with scorn upon lesser men and critics. "We will see Standard Oil in hell," he thundered, "before we will let any set of men tell us how to run our business." His cronies were Tom Reed and the unregenerate Mark Twain. Men said of him that like the moon he had a bright and a dark side. Among his family and friends he was gentle, generous, warm-hearted. When he crossed the threshold of 26 Broadway the iron and acid in his nature took dominion. His hand was always in a dozen daring enterprises. Mystery and intrigue dwelt in his offices—a series of separated rooms where visitors never saw each other.

His philanthropies were utterly unlike Rockefeller's. Individual and present suffering did not interest Rockefeller. He dealt with human weakness in the abstract. Archbold, son of the oil regions, made his gifts to Syracuse University. Rogers, son of New England, pensioned Drake and built a hospital and nursing home for the men of the oil regions. He gave to men and women, not to causes. He read and laughed uproariously at Mark Twain's "Innocents Abroad." "If I ever meet that man I'd like to do something for him," he said. One day in the Murray Hill Hotel Dr. Clarence C. Rice introduced him to Mark Twain, who at the time was crushed under the weight of the Webster failure. Rogers invited him to his home, took over his affairs, and brought him back to solvency. He did it with infinite delicacy. He gave to Clemens not his money but his time, let him go into bankruptcy, attended creditors' meetings, spending hours and days discussing little bills, all of which he could have wiped out with a pen stroke, then managed Clemens' productions until the bedeviled author came through on his own exertions and with his pride intact.

Rogers found himself in communion with William Rockefeller as John D. fraternized with Archbold. William now held the purse strings of Standard Oil. Because he did he held numerous directorships on financial institutions. He too was an audacious and unscrupulous speculator. There was, however, no serious conflict between Rogers and Archbold. The latter managed the vast physical structure of the oil industry. Rogers, supported by William Rockefeller, commanded in the expansion and operation of the funds of the Standard Oil leaders in their numerous and complicated investments outside of oil.

Ida Tarbell, who was to deliver very soon a devastating blow to Rockefeller's trust, liked Henry H. Rogers. She saw much of him when preparing her attack on Standard Oil. "He was a pirate," she said, "but he was not a hypocrite. He flew his black flag." He said to her in 1906, "I am not a favorite here. I am always for fighting. Mr. Rockefeller is always against fighting. I am a gambler. Mr. Rockefeller does not like gambling. He hates the market. I love it. Every now and then John W. Gates will come here and say: 'Henry, don't you think it's time we had a little fun in the market?' I was always for it and we made lots of killings and had plenty of fun. I must have action. And on Saturday afternoons when the market is closed I've got to have a poker game."

Old Charles Pratt was dead. Stephen V. Harkness was dead. Flagler, oldest of them all, had really ceased to take an active part in the company's affairs. As early as 1877 he had visited Florida, fallen in love with it and, afire with virility and energy, set about building it into an American Riviera. Now, his mind was engrossed with that. When he was seventy-one he was named co-respondent in a divorce action in Syracuse, a circumstance which caused his younger partner, nursing at Pocantico a refractory stomach, to shake his head mournfully. A few months later Flagler got a divorce from his wife under a Florida law which he got the subservient legislature to pass and in a week married a young lady and gave her a wedding present of $4,000,000.

II

STANDARD OIL was now a name signifying many things. To many it was synonymous with John D. Rockefeller. Then there was Standard Oil, the great oil company. Then there was what was generally known in Wall Street as the Standard Oil gang—that group of Standard leaders whose funds were used in all sorts of adventure.

As for Rockefeller himself, he was after 1896 very little connected with any of these groups. He remained as president of the Standard Oil Company, but his retirement, like everything else, was kept a secret. He had not retired to a life of idleness. He had three great interests outside of Standard Oil—his health, his charities, and his personal investments.

About this time—in 1897—young John D. Rockefeller appeared at 26 Broadway, fresh from his graduation at Brown. He occupied his father's office and began to move around from one department to another of the Standard Oil learning all its ways. He was, of course, closely watched as a source of Wall Street news. But he emerged in the limelight but little, save as a director of the Delaware, Lackawanna, and Western Railroad, his first important connection, and as the hero of a flier in leather stocks in which he made considerable money. He was, like his father, a methodical, pious young man, whose chief public activity was as leader of a Sunday School class in the Fifth Avenue Baptist Church, as successor to Charles Evans Hughes.

III

MR. ROCKEFELLER's benefactions were now closely watched by the public—a stream of gifts to various Baptist institutions, chiefly on advice of the Baptist Educational Society and Mr. Frederick T. Gates—gifts to Barnard, Dennison, Wellesley, Lincoln Memorial in Kentucky, and other colleges. Columbia got $100,000 for a chair of psychology. These gifts did not fail to excite suspicion. Attorney-General Monnett of Ohio was asked to speak on trusts before the People's Institute in New York. Monnett was firing at Standard Oil in Ohio. About this time a gift of $300,000 from Standard Oil executives to the People's Institute was made and the invitation to Monnett was canceled. Some ministers murmured against Rockefeller. At the New York Missionary Society meeting Rev. F. C. Tyrell of St. Louis declaimed bitterly: "We have come to the day when the commercial brigand stands not at the highway but behind an oil faucet. The smell of Rockefeller's oil will not impregnate the air with one half the stench as do his donations to colleges of the land for the latter are given in the name of religion."

Dr. H. C. Applegarth, pastor of the Euclid Avenue Baptist

MR. CARNEGIE TO MR. ROCKEFELLER: "IT'S YOUR MOVE, JOHN!"
THIS REFERS TO WHAT THE PUBLIC SUPPOSED WAS A CONTEST IN PHILANTHROPY BETWEEN THE TWO MILLIONAIRES.
(From Cleveland *Plain Dealer*)

Church, undertook to defend his mighty parishioner. "People charge Mr. Rockefeller with stealing the money he gave to the church," he said, "but he has laid it on the altar and thus sanctified it." This was a dubious defense and Rockefeller resented it.

But as a rule the preachers and college presidents looked with hungry eyes toward the great giver and kept their mouths shut. Wherever Rockefeller went the preachers approached with their hands out. At Douglas, Arizona, Rockefeller, after the service, slipped a fifty-dollar bill into the pastor's hand. "I wish you could help us pay the debt on our church," the preacher said. "It would be unfortunate for you," said Rockefeller. "You have a congregation of miners who earn $4 and $5 a day. Induce them to pay the debt. It will cement the church as nothing else could." This was his usual reply.

A curious hunger for Rockefeller money infected some of the preachers. The Tabernacle Baptist Church, Tenth Street and Second Avenue, New York, proposed to build a home for young women. Rockefeller contributed $50,000 in Northern Security five per cent bonds. Later the Northern Security Company defaulted on the interest and Dr. Daniel Potter, the fat, nervous, and bellicose pastor, brought suit against Rockefeller to compel him to pay the interest. Potter's lawyers put Rockefeller through a grilling in court but the pastor had to go without his interest.

Of the gift to Columbia the *World* suggested that "we naturally expect important light on this science from the Rockefeller endowment. One of the obscure problems of psychology is the problem of telepathy." Then the editorial pointed out that the magnate at his desk seemed to be able to communicate mysteriously with distant legislatures, and asked if the new department would explain such mysteries. Meantime the redoubtable Professor George Gunton was first in the attack upon all Rockefeller critics. And from the department of literature of Chicago University came the voice of Professor Oscar L. Triggs proclaiming Rockefeller and George M. Pullman "superior in creative genius to Shakespeare, Homer, and Dante."

IV

SECRECY continued to cloak the operations of the Standard. Its leaders resolutely refused to answer the simplest questions about it—ofttimes to the point of making themselves ridiculous. In the Ladenburgh, Thalman, and Company case against the Pennsylvania Railroad to recover discriminatory rates William Rockefeller was a witness. Counsel had great difficulty getting him to admit, even at this late date, who were on the board of directors with him in the eighties. Once when asked a question he replied:

"I decline to answer on advice of counsel."

"On the ground that the answer will incriminate you?"

"I decline to answer on the advice of counsel."

"Or is it that the answer will subject you to some forfeiture?"

"I decline to answer on the advice of counsel."

"Do you decline on the ground that the answer will disgrace you?"

"I decline to answer on the advice of counsel."

"Did your counsel tell you to stick to that one answer?"

"I decline to answer on advice of counsel."

Whereupon the courtroom burst into a general laugh in which William Rockefeller himself joined.

Another sample of a Standard official on the witness stand is the following:

Counsel: "Will you produce a copy of the Standard Oil Trust agreement?"

William Rockefeller: "I cannot."

"Do you know where it is?"

"I do not."

"Where did you last see it?"

"I don't remember."

"When?"

"I couldn't say."

"What is your difficulty?"

"My failure to recollect."

John D. himself was always very adroit on the stand. He had a caustic tongue too, which he could use with mortal amiability.

"Does the draught bother you?" asked counsel, noticing the open door.

"Oh, no! the draught is not from the door. It is here," pointing to the window at which the lawyer stood.

"Oh, it is from the window?" asked the lawyer.

"No," replied Rockefeller, smiling sweetly and placing his finger on the lawyer's breast. "The draught is right here."

"Pretty hot one, isn't it?" countered the lawyer.

"Oh! a perfect cyclone," replied the oil man with mock alarm.

V

Six years had elapsed since the Supreme Court of Ohio had ordered the Standard Oil Company of Ohio to withdraw from the trust. When Rockefeller decided to dissolve the trust it was settled that each trust certificate holder should surrender the certificate to the liquidating trustees. He was to receive in return the equivalent of stocks in the various companies. But after six years

THE NEW LEADERS 341

only half of the trust certificates were turned in to the liquidating trustees. The result was that they went on administering the affairs of the trust precisely the same as if it had never been dissolved. Sam Dodd, the weaver of fictions, had tricked the Ohio courts.

All was running smoothly when, on the motion of Francis S. Monnett, the new Attorney-General of Ohio, the Supreme Court haled the Oil Trust and its rulers on a charge of contempt. These proceedings brought Mr. Archbold to the front, for the first time, though as always, the great Mr. Rockefeller was the central figure. The testimony of the trust heads was taken in the old Hoffman House in New York by a commissioner of the Ohio Court. At first Mr. Archbold swore that the company was absolutely disentangled from the trust—just a bit of old-fashioned perjury. Then he gave the public an exhibition of his nature. At one point, angered, he shot his finger out at one of the State's Prosecutors, W. L. Flagg, and shouted:

"You keep still or I'll expose you right here."

"You expose!" cried Flagg. "You can't expose—"

"You low-lived—" interrupted Archbold.

"Can any one be low-lived in comparison with a Standard Oil magnate? A decent man would be ashamed to walk on the street with you."

"You're a liar and a coward," cried the little oil executive.

"You are a liar," retorted the lawyer, "and a coward too and all your millions won't help you."

"You are a dirty, stinking liar," yelled Archbold, his supply of invective failing him.

Archbold always had an eye peeled for a blackmailer. He put down every man who challenged the course of Standard Oil as trying to get money out of him. Sitting in the room as he testified was old George Rice, sick, weary with much fighting. Archbold saw Rice there and charged that he had attempted to blackmail the company out of $500,000 by threatening to make trouble for it. When Monnett asked him if Rice had ever been forced to pay thirty-five cents a barrel for hauling oil from Macksburg to Marietta while the Standard's oil was hauled for ten cents, Archbold denied absolutely any such agreement, although he knew a court had passed on the matter. Throughout his testimony he flung insults at Rice. Towards the end he said:

"He has been too busily engaged in his attempts to harass us to attend to business. . . . I can say again I consider his case pure cussedness. . . . But his time is coming and he will meet retribution in the courts. He'll get none of our money."

Rice leaped up: "I don't want any of your money. You have got only dirty money obtained by robbing people."

"Oh, dry up!" sneered Archbold. "There is nothing to you but weight and wind."

How different from the quiet and almost papal dignity of Rockefeller on the stand. When Rockefeller testified Rice still sat in the room. As the great oil man left the stand he walked over to Rice, and putting out his hand kindly, said:

"How are you, Mr. Rice? You and I are getting to be old men, are we not?"

Rice rose and stood coldly without extending his hand.

"Don't you think, Mr. Rice, it would have been better for us all if you had taken my advice years ago?"

"Perhaps it would," answered Rice as people gathered around the two old men. "You said you would ruin my business and you have done so."

"Pshaw! Pshaw!" ejaculated Rockefeller.

The old man's anger flared up.

"Don't you pooh-pooh me. I say that by the power of your great wealth you have ruined me."

"Not a word of truth in it," Rockefeller muttered, turning and pushing his way through the crowd. "Not a word of truth in it."

Before this sensational trial was over Monnett charged that the Standard burned its books to escape detection and that an attempt had been made to bribe him with an offer of $400,000 and his predecessor Watson with $100,000.

The company had steadfastly refused to produce books of record ordered by the court. Then, acting on advice in an anonymous letter, Monnett proved that sixteen boxes of books had been burned in the company's furnaces. Monnett challenged the company to produce a single book to refute the charge. However, he failed to establish that the books burned were those wanted, though later he obtained the testimony of a salesman that the latter had been gathering from various branches account books under pressure and that the company said the law "was hot on their trail."

On the bribery charge the record remains incomplete. The bribe charge was first made by the irrepressible Rice. The company's lawyers demanded that Monnett give names and dates. Monnett replied the proposal had come from Charles Squire, who claimed to be acting for F. B. Squire, secretary of the Standard, Frank Rockefeller, and Charles N. Haskell. Archbold claimed that he had demanded Monnett prove this charge. Monnett claimed that he was about to take testimony to do so when Judge Schauch, in the presence of the Standard attorney, ordered him to cease, declaring the court was able to protect itself. The available testimony relating to both these charges is still extant. Apparently Charles Squire made the proposal to Monnett, but he was quite irresponsible and there is nothing to show he acted for Standard Oil. There remains only the fact, later well-established, that always one of Mr. Archbold's first weapons was bribery.

In any case the contempt proceedings were dismissed, the court dividing three to three. The three judges who voted against conviction were the new members elected since the dissolution decree was made. As a by-product of this contempt proceeding Monnett had instituted ouster proceedings against the Buckeye Pipe Line Company, Solar Refining Company, and the Ohio Oil Company, Standard subsidiaries. These cases never came to trial. Monnett was defeated for re-nomination and Joseph M. Sheets was elected Attorney-General by the Hanna-Foraker machine. Sheets' first act was to dismiss all the Standard Oil suits.

VI

THE STANDARD OIL leaders were now playing with the court. They had no idea of surrendering their monopoly. They were merely looking around for another device to substitute for the trust. They found it in New Jersey. There a law had been passed permitting corporations to hold stocks freely in other corporations. The Standard Oil Company of New Jersey increased its capital from $10,000,000 to $110,000,000 and all the stocks of all the constituent companies held by the liquidating trustees were turned over to the Standard Oil Company of New Jersey which became a great holding company. The holding company was merely substituted for the trust, and everything went along precisely as before.

CHAPTER II. THE STANDARD OIL GANG

IN THE late nineties the country began to hear of the "Standard Oil Gang." This was something apart from the Standard group of oil corporations. Its chief figures were Henry H. Rogers, William Rockefeller, and James Stillman. It had its beginnings in the panic of 1893. While these able men were building their great oil empire they were accumulating vast personal fortunes. The panic of 1893 with its collapse of stock values gave them an opportunity to pick up here and there numerous profitable investments and as the prosperous days following the War with Spain and the discovery of gold in the Klondike rolled in on the country they found themselves richer than they had ever dared to dream. And, directed chiefly by the daring speculative genius of Henry H. Rogers, they embarked on that era of feverish and audacious adventure which Thomas W. Lawson immortalized in iniquity as "Frenzied Finance."

One of the most sensational of their performances was Rogers's Amalgamated Copper episode. Rogers arranged with Marcus Daly, a famous old prospector, and his partners, to buy from them the Anaconda Copper Company for $24,000,000. Certain other mines were added for $15,000,000, making a total of $39,000,000. Now watch closely the magician Rogers as he pulls millions from his hat.

First he and William Rockefeller took title to the mine properties, giving to Marcus Daly a check on the National City Bank for $39,000,000, with the understanding that the check was to be deposited in the bank and remain there for a definite time.

At the same time Rogers organized the Amalgamated Copper Company with a lot of clerks as dummy directors. Next he transferred all the mines to this Amalgamated for $75,000,000. The Amalgamated gave him not cash, but all of its capital stock. Then he took this $75,000,000 of stock to the National City Bank and borrowed $39,000,000 on it. This took care of the check to Daly and his friends.

The next step was to have the National City Bank sell the $75,000,000 of stock to the public. When this was completed Mr. Rogers and his pals had enough to liquidate the $39,000,000 loan from the bank and allow a neat little profit of $36,000,000 made, as you will see, out of nothing.

This was only a beginning. The stock soon fell to 33, at which price the gang bought it back, to resell it later to the same gullible public at 100, thus repeating the profit. This is what Lawson called the dollar-making machine.

II

LAWSON credits Rogers with the invention of this system. As a matter of fact, an Englishman named Ernest Terral Hooley in the early nineties combined ten plants in Great Britain. The plants were worth $10,000,000. Hooley bought them for that, turned them over to a new corporation, and issued $10,000,000 of preferred stock and $10,000,000 of common. At the time, in America were various excessively smart gentlemen busy with merger dreams. One of them was John W. Gates, salesman, promoter, and gambler extraordinary. Mr. Gates was very different from John D. Rockefeller. The latter had built the Standard Oil Company purely as an industrial enterprise. He was not a promoter. There was never any watered stock in Standard Oil. Gates, who began as a barbed wire salesman, was a promoter. Rockefeller made his money manufacturing, transporting, and selling oil. The promoters made theirs manufacturing and selling stocks. Rockefeller and his contemporaries built trusts but purely as incidents to their business as producers. Now onto the stage stepped Gates and Reid and Judge More and Morse and Addicks and Flint and Morgan and, of course, Rogers and William Rockefeller, who began to put together industrial combinations of all sorts with no other aim than to make millions from the stocks. Gates heard of the Englishman Hooley's scheme. And when he showed a barbed wire manufacturer that he could sell his plant to the combination for preferred stock up to its full value which could be sold to the public, and still have common stock for as much again, which he could sell or hold, his scheme to organize the American Steel and Wire Company moved fast. And at his elbow in those days was his adviser, Judge Elbert H. Gary. And when these two got Morgan interested in their $90,000,000 promotion, they laid the foundation for steel history.

After this the mergers blossomed everywhere. America became a jungle of promoter-made, stock-jobbing combinations. Then broke into flower that parent of so much controversy and woe—the holding company in the utility field. This year Standard Oil paid dividends of 94 per cent on its $100,000,000 of stock and this made a juicy example to dangle before the eyes of owners and investors. Judge More formed the Tin Plate Trust, put together plants valued at $12,000,000 and issued $50,000,000 in stock, taking $10,000,000 as his share. Flint formed a chewing gum trust—the American Chicle Company—and assembled $500,000 worth of assets against which he issued $3,000,000 of preferred stock and $6,000,000 of common and the common sold as high as 200 before it collapsed. In the case of United States Steel the Bureau of Corporations reported that its entire issue of $508,000,000 of common stock was water and from one to two-fifths of its preferred as well.

Rogers and William Rockefeller went into gas. The Standard Oil supplied illuminating gas oil from which the artificial illuminating gas was made. This gave them an interest first in edging into gas companies which used the oil and later in controlling and exploiting them. They got control of the Consolidated Gas Company of New York and then went with Elkins, Dolan, and Widener into the United Gas Improvement Company in Philadelphia which took hold of, operated, and exploited gas and electric lighting companies in a score of cities. It was all a merry dance. The nation felt a kind of pride in it as it mounted in fury and extent through the golden years of graft and loot under the benign rule of William McKinley and Mark Hanna.

III

IN THE midst of this growing and disordered orgy, two great powers began to manifest themselves, two powerful financial groups sometimes acting more or less together, sometimes in violent collision and even open warfare. These were the Rockefeller and Morgan groups. There were scores of lesser men who

THE STANDARD OIL GANG

pressed forward their separate ambitions, but sooner or later they found themselves crossing the territory of these giants and falling into their arms. This gave rise to what came to be known as the money trust, particularly when these financial monarchs decided the time had come when they must march together.

Between the two groups the connecting link was James Stillman. Stillman belonged to the Rockefeller crowd, but spiritually and socially he was akin to Morgan. Morgan, huge, masterful, bullying, often violent, now the Master of Wall Street, and Stillman, small, elegant, vain of his small feet, dark, handsome, and silent, grew to be fast friends. Both were autocrats and aristocrats. Both inherited their wealth and looked with disdain upon the men of common clay who surrounded them. Morgan hated Rockefeller and his piety. Morgan and Stillman both hated Carnegie. Morgan awed Stillman a little sometimes with his over-powering personality, but the great man always respected Stillman's profound wisdom in money matters and even more the immense reservoirs of cash which he could command.

The center of the Standard Oil group was the Standard Oil itself, the wealth of its leaders and the great banks under Stillman's domination—the Hanover, Second National, United States Trust, Farmers Loan and Trust, the Central Realty Bond and Trust as well as the National City. There was the Amalgamated Copper, Smelter Trust, and Tobacco Trust, and the magnificent iron ore properties of John D. himself. There were railroad lines referred to as the Rockefeller-Gould group, and then such roads as the St. Paul, special pet of William Rockefeller and the Harkness family, and the Western Maryland of John D. Rockefeller. There were vast telephone, telegraph, and utility concerns, such as the Rhode Island Securities Company (Aldrich-Rockefeller-Elkins), Interborough Rapid Transit (Rockefeller and Belmont), Philadelphia Rapid Transit (Rockefeller, Elkins, Widener), United Gas Improvement Company (Rockefeller, Elkins, Widener), Brooklyn Rapid Transit and Metropolitan Securities (Rockefeller-Ryan), and of course many others, including the powerful Public Service Corporation of New Jersey.

The power of these men over railroads is quickly seen in the railroad directorships they held. William Rockefeller was in the Chicago, Milwaukee, and St. Paul, Central New England, Delaware, Lackawanna, and Western, Lake Shore and Michigan Central, Lake Shore and Michigan, and other New York Central lines, the New York, New Haven, and Hartford, and others. Henry H. Rogers was in the Atchison, Topeka, and Santa Fe, Union

MARS: "I SEE; THEY HAVE BEEN TOO BUSY TO NOTICE MY SIGNALS."
—*The Philadelphia North American*

Pacific. Charles M. Pratt was in the Boston and Maine and Long Island Railroad. This is only a partial list. The fifteen directors of the Standard Oil of New Jersey held directorships in innumerable banks, insurance companies, traction companies, electric light and gas, and industrial concerns of every sort.[1]

The Morgan group was made up chiefly of the great railroad

---

[1] Thomas W. Lawson in his "Frenzied Finance" admitted that so far as he knew John D. Rockefeller took no part in the copper and gas adventures which he described.

consolidations he had effected, the various industrial corporations already formed or in the process of formation by him, like the United States Steel Corporation, Rubber Trust, and others, and his group of banks and insurance companies.

IV

JOHN D. ROCKEFELLER himself had never been on any board of directors save that of Standard Oil. And at this time he took no discoverable part in the vast schemes of exploitation directed by the Standard Oil gang, though he did at times invest in them. He was busy with his philanthropies and in a supervisory way with his personal investments, but these were coming more and more under the immediate direction of young John D., now a part of what was called his personal staff, of which Frederick T. Gates was the head.

In 1901 Andrew Carnegie, master of steel, wanted to retire. J. P. Morgan had put together his rival steel merger, Federal Steel. Carnegie had made up his mind to unload his vast holdings on Morgan. He drove Morgan to a consideration of the project by a series of militant threats against the various units of Morgan's new combine. "If I were Czar of the Steel Company [which he was]," he said, "I would pay no more dividends but put every dollar into tube and wire and nail and hoop and ship plants." As an opening gun he planned the construction of a $12,000,000 tube plant at Conneaut—a gun pointed at Morgan's National Tube Company. Wall Street brokers had shelves full of the stock of the eight metal concerns just formed by Morgan and all outrageously over-capitalized. Morgan was alarmed and was an easy prey for the proposal of a great steel combine when, under the cunning Andy's direction, Charles Schwab at a dinner artfully spun the plan out for Morgan's benefit. Morgan began the formation of his great steel trust and after long negotiations had gathered together a great array of competing plants—all save the Rockefeller ore properties in Michigan. Of these Morgan was afraid. He told Gary these must be included or the whole plan must fail.

To do this Gary told Morgan he must see Rockefeller.

"I would not think of it," growled Morgan.

"Why?" asked Gary.

"Because I don't like him."

But he yielded to necessity and sent word to the secluded oil king that he wished to speak to him. Any one else Morgan wished to see he sent for. But Rockefeller was greater even than Morgan. And so Morgan asked to be permitted to call. Rockefeller said he would be glad to have Morgan visit him, but it must be under-

THE MONEY POWER.
(Cartoon by T. E. Power in the *New York Journal*)

stood no business was to be discussed as "Mr. Morgan knew he had retired from business." The reply of the old fox infuriated Morgan. But he took a chance and called. The moment Morgan opened his mouth to state his business, Rockefeller cut him short. Mr. Morgan had evidently misunderstood. He never talked business with any one. Mr. Morgan might take up any matter he had in mind with his son "who would undoubtedly be glad to talk with Mr. Morgan." The old lion left inwardly roaring at the manner in which he had been dismissed by the fox. He risked one more humiliation and asked young John D. to call on him. When that young business man found himself for the first time in the presence of the great Morgan he was a little abashed. Morgan launched his business brusquely:

"I understand your father wants to sell his Minnesota ore properties and has authorized you to act for him. How much do you want for them?"

Young John D. stood up.

"It is true I am authorized to speak for my father in such matters," he replied, "but I have not been informed that he wishes to sell these properties. In fact I am sure he does not."

And the young man bowed respectfully to Mr. Morgan and walked out, leaving the great banker humiliated again and in silence.

Going at once to his father the very much troubled son reported the interview and asked if he had behaved correctly.

"Time alone," answered the even-tempered father, "can tell whether you acted wisely or not. But I may say to you, my son, that had I been in your place I should have done precisely what you did."

Morgan then sent for Henry M. Frick and asked him to go to Rockefeller and to tell him the "outside price" the combine would offer for his properties. Rockefeller liked Frick. He received him kindly. But the moment Frick mentioned an "outside price" he interrupted. He would not deal with a purchaser who attempted to fix an "outside price." That sounded too much like an ultimatum. Mr. Rockefeller had never submitted to ultimatums. Then he astonished Frick with his proposal:

"I am not anxious to sell my ore properties. But I do not want to stand in the way of a worthy enterprise. Now, Mr. Frick, I will tell you what I will do. I want only a just price. You know better than those gentlemen what that is. I know your judgment is good and I believe you to be a square man. I am willing, Mr. Frick, to put my interests in these properties in your hands. You need not hesitate, Mr. Frick. My confidence is complete. You will receive no complaint from me. Now you will wish to be on your way. I thank you for coming to me."

In a few days Frick reported a price from Mr. Rockefeller $5,000,000 more than the outside figure fixed by Morgan at Judge Gary's advice.

"That is prohibitive," said Gary.

"Judge Gary," said Morgan, "in a business proposition as great as this would you let a matter of $5,000,000 stand in the way of success?"

"But I told you, Mr. Morgan, my price was the outside figure."

"Well," said Morgan, "write out an acceptance."

Later Rockefeller said that he doubted that any one but Mr. Frick could have induced him to sell. "And in my opinion," he added, "if these properties had not been included, I doubt if the United States Steel Corporation could have survived the stress of its formative period."

When the United States Steel Corporation was formed the name of John D. Rockefeller appeared among the directors—his first directorship outside of his oil companies.[1]

CHAPTER III. IN THE LABORATORY OF A CORRUPTIONIST

IN MARCH, 1897, William McKinley, under the sponsorship of Mark Hanna, became President of the United States. And the nation, emerging from the long depression, entered upon an era of rising prosperity. It was the beginning almost of a new age in which the new tools of corporate organization and mechanical invention became a kind of delirious vogue. Combination in the national field of railroads, and industries and in the local field of traction, gas, and electric light companies, sent swarms of lobbyists

---

[1] The account given here is that related by Frick and reported by George Harvey in his life of Frick.

The author has been given another account of this from a source close to Mr. Rockefeller. It is that Mr. Rockefeller never met Morgan more than twice—once casually at a railroad station and once at a dinner. Mr. Morgan, according to this account, asked for a conference, but Rockefeller declined and sent his son and Frederick T. Gates to Morgan's office. Morgan began with: "What is your proposition?" and the young man answered: "We have no proposition. You must have been misinformed. Good morning, sir."

However, Ida M. Tarbell in her "Life of Judge Gary" declares Morgan told Judge Gary he had seen Rockefeller.

LABORATORY OF CORRUPTIONIST

to the national and state legislatures and aldermanic boards. Corruption and bribery upon a grand scale became the order of the day. Politics became a profession of rich and juicy profits, bosses arose everywhere to seize and manage the distribution of the swag. Mr. John D. Archbold, corruptionist extraordinary, official bribe-giver of Standard Oil, was exceptionally well placed in the matter of benevolent relations with bosses. Boss Reed, of the House, was the crony of Henry H. Rogers. Boss Hanna, of the Senate, was the old schoolmate and friend of John D. Rockefeller. Tom Platt, Republican boss of New York, was another old schoolmate of John D. at Owego Academy. Boss Croker, of Tammany, had as his guide, philosopher, and friend, William C. Whitney, of the O. H. Payne connection. Boss Aldrich, of the United States Senate, was a financial ally but, better still, was in the way of becoming the father-in-law of young John D.

But Mr. Archbold did not rely on old memories and pleasant friendships. He talked to his political hireling with bribes, and his guilty cash found its way into some of the most exalted pockets. Of course, the Republican campaign managers were around him continually with their hands out. Letters went back and forth between Archbold and Hanna. In 1900 Hanna writes for money. "There are many important interests in this fight. Should Johnson [Tom L.] carry the legislature the corporations will catch it, *as I am their representative so-called.*" Hanna comes back frequently for money and Archbold writes Hanna whenever there is legislation which Standard Oil fears.

Archbold's chief secret agent in Washington was Congressman Joseph Sibley, of Pennsylvania, destined to achieve upon his exposure, a unique infamy in our congressional history as Archbold's jackal. Sibley was a man of some wealth, president of the Signal Oil Company in Venango County. He had a taste for politics and entered Congress in 1892 as a Democratic reformer representing the oil regions. He was an ardent bi-metallist and a more or less blatant tribune of the people. In the Democratic convention of 1896 which nominated Bryan he received a considerable vote for vice-president. Around 1898, however, if not sooner, Mr. Sibley began to exhibit marked symptoms of friendship for the much harried trusts. Around 1900 we find Mr. Archbold writing

Mr. Benjamin Cassatt, of the Pennsylvania Railroad, that they "hope he will do everything possible in Mr. Sibley's favor on the sure ground that all corporate and vested interests will have at least fair consideration at his hands."

"Fair consideration" were hardly the words. Sibley bombards Archbold with letters, tells him of Senators and Congressmen in need of financial help. He even visits Roosevelt and tells him:

My Dear Mr A.

+ If you think of anything for me to do, let me know +

Sincerely yours,

Joseph C. Sibley

PART OF LETTER TO ARCHBOLD, WHILE SIBLEY WAS A MEMBER OF CONGRESS FROM THE OIL REGIONS.
(Reproduced from *Hearst's Magazine*)

"No man should win or deserve to win who depended upon the rabble rather than the conservative men of affairs." He reports this triumphantly to Archbold. Sibley writes Archbold: "Had long talk with Mr. B. a friend in the Senate, a Democrat. . . . Had you not ought to have a consultation with him . . . if you want to see him I think I could arrange a call in New York." September 23rd, 1903, he writes: "A Republican United States Senator came to me today to make a loan of $1,000. I told him I did not have it but would try and get it for him in a day or two. Do you want to make the investment?" Sibley's letters ranged over the whole field of business and politics. "If at any time my long scribbles annoy you," he humbly bleats to his patron, "chuck them into the waste basket." And again: "If you think of anything for me to do, let me know." Archbold finds plenty for the busy jackal. Some

Senator is to speak against the Standard. Archbold is weary of the "old round of lies" and wonders "if you can find out who it is and guard against the explosion." The chairman of the Republican Congressional Campaign wants $25,000 and turns up later for $5,000 more. Sibley, congressman, paid servant of the people, carried around with him the Standard Oil code—the "Devil's Lexicon" as one critic called it—and used it in some of his reports to Archbold.

Matthew Stanley Quay's admission to the Senate was contested on the ground of fraud—Quay, whose career of bribery and corruption in Pennsylvania reached epic proportions. Archbold writes Deboe, Depew, Fairbanks, Foraker, Spooner, Platt, Scott, Sewell, McLaurin, to support Quay. Archbold has a big money interest in Quay. That voracious grafter delivers only for big pay. Archbold sends him plenty, but he wants more. "My dear Senator," writes the Standard bribe-giver, "not because I think we should, but because of your enticing ways, I enclose you Certificate of Deposit for $10,000." Another time—"My dear Senator: I will do as you say, provided you finally say you need so much. Please ask for payments as needed from time to time, not all at once." Even Standard Oil must resort to installment payments to the imperious and hungry Quay. Then later, after death has cut down the Master Quay, a Certificate of Deposit goes to the pupil, Boise Penrose.

In 1898 Monnett brought his contempt action against the Standard in Ohio. Immediately Archbold gets in touch with Joseph B. Foraker, just elected Senator from Ohio. Foraker sees Monnett in Washington and warns that he will be driven out of politics if he persists in his tactics. Foraker declares he, United States Senator, has been employed by Standard Oil. When Monnett expresses surprise at this peculiar employment the haughty Senator replies tartly that he can form his own professional ethics. But a little later a report reaches Akron that Foraker has been retained by the Standard. The Associated Press asks the Senator about it. "It is impertinent," he replies. "You might as well ask me how much money I have in my pocket. The report is untrue." If the reporter had asked the Senator how much he had in his pocket twelve days later he might have answered $15,000 of Standard Oil money. A certificate of deposit was sent him that day by Archbold. Senator Foraker never appeared on record in the extensive and numerous hearings of the famous case. Why was he employed?

His employer writes him about the Meigs bill in the Ohio legislature amending the so-called anti-trust law, also about a "malicious resolution" for an investigation of Standard Oil and intimating

> June 28, 1898.
>
> Daniel H. Hastings, Governor,
> Harrisburg, Pa.
>
> My dear Sir:-
>
> If it is consistent for you to appoint Judge Henderson of Crawford County, to fill the vacancy in the Superior Court, caused by the death of Judge Wickham, of Beaver County, I will appreciate it greatly.
>
> It is not necessary for me to dwell on Judge Henderson's capabilities. They are undoubtedly well known to you.
>
> Very truly yours,
>
> Jno D Archbold

that the hated Monnett might be engaged to conduct it. A few weeks later another letter goes to the Senator asking about "another objectionable bill" which "needs to be looked after." Later a bill by Senator Price in Ohio needed looking after. Archbold notified Foraker; Foraker sent Archbold's letter to Governor North, who sent for Price and told him Senators Hanna and Foraker both opposed these bills and feared they might damage President McKinley in the approaching campaign. Thereupon Price withdrew them. Senator Jones of Arkansas introduced a bill to strengthen the Sherman anti-trust law. Archbold writes to "my dear Senator" Foraker to look after it.

All this Senator Foraker did not do for nothing. March 26th, Mr. Archbold sent him $15,000, three weeks later $14,500 more; six months later $10,000 and soon after another $5,000—$44,000 in all. About the same time a friend of Foraker's wanted to buy a newspaper and needed $50,000. Foraker got the loan from Archbold, though the paper enterprise fell through and the loan was repaid. All this was in profound secrecy of course, no hint of the Senator's employment reaching the people.

When Judge Jacob Burkett of Findlay, Ohio, was a candidate

New York, August 3rd, 1899.

Hon. Thos. A. Morrison,
    Smethport, Pa.

My dear Sir:—

I am duly in receipt of your favor of August 1st, and it has given me great pleasure to write Senators Quay and Penrose, expressing my earnest desire that it may prove possible and consistent for them to support you for the Supreme Judgeship. I do not know that these letters will have any weight, but I earnestly hope they will.

I hardly feel justified in writing Governor Stone on the subject. I need hardly say that I feel that the position could not be better filled than by your promotion to it.

Very truly yours,

Jno D Archbold

---

for reëlection to the Supreme Court, Archbold became very active. We find him writing to Foraker to be sure of that gentleman's support and urging the judge's great qualifications and integrity and ability. He was one of the three judges who had voted against holding Standard Oil guilty of contempt in the Monnett case. The judge is to be rewarded. But Monnett and Bennett are to be punished by the imperious trust. "We hear with surprise," writes Archbold to Foraker, "that Smith W. Bennett, Monnett's brother-in-law, is to be candidate for Attorney-General" and suggests as a conclusive reason against Bennett's ambition that "he was active against our interests."

Mr. Archbold's allies in Washington were many and we may

form some notion of the persuasiveness of the arguments which Mr. Archbold used from the case of old General Grosvenor of Ohio. Grosvenor around 1897, like Sereno E. Payne and some other Old Guard leaders, was very much for dealing with the trusts. Grosvenor proposed a measure to make the Sherman law more drastic. After 1900 we find him among Archbold's correspondents seeking at one time a thousand dollars for his campaign, which he gets and at another time help, the precise amount of which is not disclosed, and also trying through Sibley to get in touch with Archbold personally.

II

THESE years saw the United States Senate at its lowest level. Standard Oil had plenty of friends. So had other trusts. "We get a great deal of protection for our contributions," said Havemeyer of the Sugar Trust who told the Industrial Commission his trust gave to both parties. The rôle of dishonor was a long one. There was the aged Tom Platt. When news of Platt's death was brought to Roosevelt years later he said: "Dead or alive he's still a damned scoundrel." Platt's partner from New York was Chauncey M. Depew, a member of seventy or more boards of directors and window-dressing president of the New York Central, who began life as a lobbyist for Vanderbilt, and got smeared with some of the muck in the Equitable Insurance scandal. Nobody needed to bribe Depew. He had been the lifelong messenger boy of the money crowd.

The shipping subsidy bill bobbed up continuously and mysteriously through these years. The *Review of Reviews* observed that apparently no one seemed to be interested in this measure. But we find Mr. Archbold writing Sibley and his chief lobbyist, Col. Manley, once presidential campaign manager of Tom Reed, about it. Mark Hanna becomes suddenly interested in the bill and takes charge of it in the Senate. Senator Depew decides to make a speech in favor of it—a great effort. He sends an advance copy of the speech to Archbold before delivering it and that gentleman writes back, "Thanks for your efforts in our behalf." Standard Oil has been interested in subsidies a long time. In 1892 a bill was passed to exempt two ships, the *City of Paris* and the *City of New*

York from the law permitting only home built and manned ships to fly the American flag and collect mail subsidies. The Secretary of the Treasury who first urged this measure was that same Governor Foster who was head and front of the Standard Oil gas fight in Toledo already described. Why did he urge it? The two ships

```
                                     New York, December 18, 1902.

My dear Senator:-

          You, of course, know of Judge Burket's candidacy
for re-election to the Supreme Court bench in Ohio. We under-
stand that his re-election to the position would be in the line
of usage as followed in such cases in Ohio, and we feel very
strongly that his eminent qualifications and great integrity
entitle him to this further recognition.
          We most earnestly hope that you will agree with
this view, and will favor and aid his re-election. Mr. Rogers
joins me most heartily in this expression to you.
          With kind regards, I am,
                              Very sincerely yours,

                              Jno D Archbold
```

LETTER FROM ARCHBOLD TO SENATOR JOSEPH B. FORAKER IN SUPPORT OF ONE OF THE THREE JUDGES WHO HAD VOTED AGAINST HOLDING STANDARD OIL GUILTY OF CONTEMPT.

(From *Hearst's Magazine*)

favored belonged to the Inman Line, later the International. And of this line Henry H. Rogers was president.

The right arm of the interests in the Senate was Nelson W. Aldrich, of Rhode Island, soon to become young John D.'s father-in-law. Aldrich, like Mark Hanna, began life as a wholesale grocer and ended by being a utility magnate tied up with the Elkins and Rockefeller interests. Arthur Pugh Gorman, multi-millionaire, after a lifetime in politics, Democratic leader, was called the left arm of the interests. Senator John W. McLaurin of South Carolina was also one of Mr. Archbold's pensioners. There was John W. Spooner, a fiery protagonist of the people, the flag, and the old soldiers, but in reality a true soldier of the interests until Bob LaFollette ousted him from the Senate.

There was John Kean of New Jersey, who made millions in gas and coal-carrying roads, himself an unscrupulous competitor in the utility field. There was of course the notorious Matt Quay and his dark and silent lieutenant, Boise Penrose. When Quay died Pennsylvania sent the attorney for the Carnegie Steel Company, Philander C. Knox, who turned out better than his antecedents warranted.

There was Stephen B. Elkins of West Virginia, who made millions in a land-grabbing ring in New Mexico before he settled in West Virginia to make more in coal, railroads, and utilities and then turned up as Chairman of the Interstate Commerce Committee of the Senate. Elkins was close to Standard Oil in utility investments and we find Archbold writing his representative in West Virginia at Elkins' request to work for the Senator's election. On election night we behold the other West Virginia Senator, Nathan B. Scott, sending bulletins at intervals to Archbold keeping him posted on the count. "Thanks to you and other friends," he wires, "we now have West Virginia by 25,000."

Presiding over all was the mighty Mark Hanna. When McKinley was elected, he wanted Hanna in his cabinet. Hanna wanted to go to the Senate. But there was no Ohio vacancy, so old Senator John Sherman, on the brink of the grave, was lifted by McKinley to the important office of Secretary of State to make a vacancy in the Senate for Hanna by appointment. Later he was elected by the Ohio legislature. But the election was contested and one representative swore that he was given $1,750 cash to vote for Hanna, and produced the cash. Hanna denied knowledge of it. And the United States Senate refused to exhibit any curiosity as to where the money came from. Later the figure of Mark Hanna was to rise ominously in what looked like a drive by the dark and sinister forces behind all this corruption to seize the very presidency itself. That we shall come to later. For the moment the new Moloch—Big Business—sprawled at its ease in Washington particularly in the Senate, corrupt, contemptuous, greedy, certain of its power. Meantime a half-crazed boy, hanging around anarchist meetings, brooding over the wrongs of the world, was preparing a blow which would give a new turn to all this soon.

CHAPTER IV. LIGHTING THE WORLD

FOR YEARS the cry of "Oil!" had continued to circle the world, first Pennsylvania, Ohio, West Virginia, Indiana, California, Texas, Kansas, Oklahoma, and Louisiana and abroad, Baku, the Dutch East Indies, Galicia. Wherever the cry arose the Standard Oil man with his pipes was there among the first. No matter how remote the well the Standard pipe line was immediately installed. The driller had but to produce his oil and instantly there was a market for it. He ran it into the Standard pipe line, got a certificate for the oil and this certificate he could sell anywhere at any time as good as a government bond. The pipes thus became the real tentacles of the Octopus.

But another grim figure stalked the newly drilled well—War. For oil meant struggle; at first among the oil men of America, then among the great oil men of the world—the Rockefellers, the Nobels, Rothschilds, and between governments—Russia, Roumania, Austria, England, America, and Mexico.

Early in 1888 a Mr. Frank E. Bliss arrived, wholly unnoticed, in London. A few days later the *Gazette* recorded the formation of the Anglo-American Oil Company, capital £500,000. Among the directors were Henry H. Rogers, John D. Archbold. But these names were not so well known then in England. This was the Standard Oil's first great corporate subsidiary abroad. Before long the Anglo-American Oil Company had a monopoly of England's oil trade and held it for years. After that Rockefeller spread his incorporated subsidiaries all over the globe.

In 1898 for the first time production of oil in Russia exceeded that in America. This continued until 1901 when oil began to gush forth in various American fields. The fact, however, reveals the extent of the competition abroad. And that competition was incessant, bitter, and attended with recurrent rate wars, financial stratagems, and international intrigue.

In Manchuria Rockefeller had to fight first Russian and then Dutch East Indies petroleum. He tried to buy a Dutch company in Sumatra, the Moera Enim Company, and the shareholders were about to ratify the sale when the Dutch government intervened and announced: "No Standard Oil in Dutch possessions!" The companies fell into the bag of the Royal Dutch Company. In 1902 the Standard attempted to buy out the Shell Transportation Company of Sir Marcus Samuel. Almost at the moment of success the deal fell through. This was one of the Standard's major set-backs, for a few years later the Shell combined with the Royal Dutch under the domination of the then young Henry Deterding, who was one day to capture the world's oil premiership once held by John D. Rockefeller.

In Russia the Standard was in bitter competition with the Nobels, the Rothschilds, and many smaller interests. The Standard induced the Nobels to form the Russian Refiners Union under which Russian output was limited and the Nobels became the sole distributors. Three years later when the union was dissolved the Nobels had the only marketing machine and the Standard made a working agreement with them. The Rothschilds were indignant and ready for alliance with the Royal Dutch Shell.

In the Galician fields the Austrian government discriminated against the Standard not only by imposing a tariff, but by prohibiting the company from selling to Austrian railways. In Roumania the Standard was permitted to build a refinery but no pipe lines. In Mexico Lord Cowdray held concessions from the Mexican government and the Waters-Pierce Company, which carried the war there, found itself hampered by a $4.50 tariff.

But despite all these handicaps and harassments the corporation prospered everywhere. The great company covered the earth with its stations and its wagons. Carried in tins on men's backs up the mountains of Tibet, on the backs of elephants through the forests of the Upper Ganges, everywhere in a hundred languages the words "Standard Oil" were household words. It had 162 import stations in the foreign service, 5,000 foreign distributing stations, 4,000 foreign tank wagons, and 30 manufacturing plants abroad. In it and behind it everywhere there seemed to be a power no force could withstand.[1]

CHAPTER V. SENATORS IN HARNESS

DURING the years following Rockefeller's attempt at retirement the fruits of his planting were to be offered to him in a singularly bitter mixture. From all sides—from men who believed themselves wronged—an outraged public, politicians, and rivals, came attacks of every sort. The country was ready to believe anything of Rockefeller.

Among the first was one of those three or four cases which put him in the posture of fleecing his friends. In the seventies John and James Corrigan sold their Cleveland refinery for 2,500 shares of Standard Oil stock. James Corrigan then went into iron. In 1883, with Frank Rockefeller as a partner, he bought the Franklin Iron Mining Company. When the panic of 1893 came

[1] The following is a list of the foreign corporations which the company controlled:
Anglo-American Oil Co.
American Petroleum Co.—Holland.
Americanisch Petroleum Co.—Germany.
Deutsche-Amerikanische Co.—Germany.
Danish Petroleum Co.
Königsberger Handels Co.—Germany.
Mannheim Bremen Co.
Korft Refining Co.
Stettin-Amerikanische Co.—Germany.
Roumanian-American Petroleum Co.
Societé ci-denant H. Reith et Cie—Belgium.
Italian American Petroleum Co.
Vacuum Oil Co.—Austria.
International Oil Co.—Japan.
Colonial Oil Co.—Africa and Australia.
Devoe Manufacturing Co. (makes tin cans).
Oswego Manufacturing Co. (wooden cases).
American Wick Manufacturing Co.
Thompson, Bedford and Co.—European trade in lubricating oils.
Many Vacuum Oil Companies in Copenhagen, Genoa, Hamburg, Moscow, Stockholm, Bombay, Kobe, Capetown.

MOUNTAINS OF HATE

Corrigan and Frank Rockefeller found themselves in trouble. Corrigan went to his old friend John D. and borrowed $171,000 at 7 per cent, putting up his 2,500 shares of Standard stock as collateral, a perfectly good business transaction. Later Frank borrowed from John D. and Corrigan endorsed the note putting up his Franklin Iron Mine stock. The pair now owed $402,000. By 1894 the panic deepened and Corrigan and Frank could not meet their

"NOW, JOHN D., LET ME INTRODUCE MY FRIEND."
(*The Rocky Mountain News*, Denver)

notes. They scuttled around frantically and got the Iron Range Company to agree to take the loans but John D., according to Corrigan, frightened the Iron Range people off. To satisfy the loan Rockefeller took the Standard Oil stock, allowing 168 for it. Corrigan protested it was worth 300 but John D. told how the depression had injured the Standard's assets. In their plight Corrigan and Frank, as the story went, were compelled to sell the Franklin Iron Mine Company, worth nearly $2,000,000, for $500,000. Corrigan now brought suit to compel John D. to return the Standard stock on the ground that being in a position to know its value, as president of the company, he had lied about it to Corrigan. The papers aired the story freely and Rockefeller got a good deal of unsavory advertisement. The Backus case and

Merritt case were recalled. Rockefeller was the man who swindled his partners. Yet after all the facts as outlined above do not hang together very well. Corrigan claimed he had paid his $171,000 and that the amount due was Frank's share of the loan, something over $200,000. The 2,500 shares of Standard Oil stock at 168 would amount to $420,000, double the amount said to be due. There would therefore be no need to sell the Franklin Company unless other causes intervened. The story that Corrigan had paid his loan and was sacrificed for Frank's is wholly refuted by the allegation that Rockefeller demanded the sale of the collateral when Corrigan defaulted on a $46,000 note, which was the amount of Corrigan's first note. Why did Rockefeller demand payment? He certainly had a right to do so and there is good reason to believe that when he looked into the state of the investment he found that Frank, a notoriously careless business man, and Corrigan, no business wizard, had got the whole investment into a hopeless snarl.

In any case Corrigan's suit was submitted to arbitrators—William D. Guthrie, William A. Lynch, and William G. Choate, eminent lawyers—and they decided it in Rockefeller's favor.

II

THROUGHOUT the country the irritation produced by the Standard's methods and the whole trust issue grew in intensity. The Standard's war on small dealers brought the subject to the very doors of the people. Monnett's suit in Ohio kept the name of the company and Rockefeller in the public notice and in a dozen states people clamored for some kind of action against the oil Octopus. In Nebraska Attorney-General Smythe began proceedings in August, 1899, under the state anti-trust act, and asked that the company be enjoined from doing business in Nebraska.

Smythe appeared in New York with a commission to examine the Standard leaders. But they laughed at him. "He is just seeking notoriety," said Samuel C. T. Dodd. As for Rockefeller, Smythe's attempts to subpoena him were utterly futile. Out in Ohio too and in Texas the legislatures and attorney-generals stormed against the "oil monster." But Mr. Rockefeller, the retired country gentleman, was more interested in his great and growing Pocantico Hills estate, in his petty wars with the tax assessors, and his battles with the town authorities to build roads. While the great war against the trusts raged over the land, rising to boisterous volume under the lashings of Bryan and the perfect inactivity of McKinley, the hero or rather the archvillain of the piece amused himself in a series of opéra bouffe struggles with village statesmen.

Rockefeller wanted a road to his brother's home. The road had to run under the Croton reservoir, property of New York City, and a private individual could not build such a road. Rockefeller asked the Tarrytown officials to build it, he supplying the money. The officials, however, replied that to build such a road they would have to condemn several private homes. And after some quarreling the project was dropped. A mere matter of taking away from people the small homes they owned in order to make a road from his own to his brother's property did not seem at all unusual to the man who always had his way. John Weber, president of the village, tried to stop Rockefeller's workmen, who in building a road were encroaching on his property. He ordered the arrest of the foreman. The chief of police refused. Weber attempted the arrest himself with his sons. A signal went up and over the hill came charging another crew of Rockefeller workmen armed with picks and shovels to drive the village president off.

The great estate grew amazingly. The farms all around began to come within Rockefeller's fences. He owned practically all of Sleepy Hollow. Each year he added more ground—fine estates like that of Rufus A. Weeks for $50,000 and little plots and houses for as little as $1,700. By 1899 over 1,600 acres surrounded the old house on Kijkuit. The Rockefeller legend of simple living began to suffer a little. New stables were built costing $100,000, three stories high, with two electric elevators, grooms' quarters, and stalls for 22 horses, and young John D. began to scour England for the choicest cobs for the great stables. Carloads of shrubs and trees for fall planting were arriving. "I intend to have a nice house," he told a friend, "even though I have to live on a crust." He had several nice houses now—the town house on Euclid Avenue, Cleveland, beautiful Forest Hill, an estate fine enough for a monarch; the New York town house in Fifty-fourth Street, and Pocantico Hills which, with ducal generosity, he now threw open to the public on certain days as a park. On a sunny day, when the

Nebraska attorney-general was storming about his subpoena, a group of citizens of Pocantico called at the great home to thank the squire for all he had done for the town.

Attorney-General Smythe finally gave up his effort, the referees, on his own testimony, finding in favor of Standard Oil and that attack collapsed.

III

Down in Texas the law was hot on the trail of Mr. Rockefeller's trust, which operated there under the name of the Waters-Pierce Oil Company. Rockefeller and others had been indicted, as we have seen, and the law had got hold of an underling, Hathaway, who served a year in jail before the sentence against him was reversed. Shortly thereafter the state began proceedings against the Waters-Pierce Company to oust it from Texas and on March 19th, 1900, the United States Supreme Court affirmed the ouster decree.

It may be remembered that Mr. Sibley, Archbold's procurer in Congress, wrote his master about a certain Mr. B. in the Senate. This was no less a person than the brilliant and colorful Joseph Bailey of Texas, who had been Democratic leader in the House and was now a candidate for the Senate. Bailey was a glamorous creature, tall, statuesque, handsome, distinguished, the greatest constitutional lawyer and one of the great orators and debaters of his time. He was almost the last of the old order of statesmen, acting and dressing up to the part. At the moment he was the idol of Texas. But Bailey had a fondness for luxury and show, a weakness which requires money.

The keen eye of the wily Sibley saw all this. The two had known each other in the House. About this time Sibley introduced Bailey to ex-Governor Francis of Missouri, a man of great wealth and then spoken of as a possible candidate for the presidency. Francis and Henry Clay Pierce were friends. Pierce was looking for aid and Francis suggested Bailey. Francis wired Bailey to come to St. Louis and Bailey went. There Francis introduced him to Pierce. Pierce explained that he wanted to get back into Texas.

"Very well," said Bailey, "I will do what I can for you."

"And what will be your fee, Senator?" asked Pierce.

"This is a political matter," returned Bailey, assuming the tones and posture he knew so well. "I practice law, not influence. There will be no fee."

This was very beautiful. But the great Senator a little later in the day unlimbered his dignity long enough to ask Pierce for a loan of $3,300. For this he gave his note. But Mr. Pierce immediately charged it off. It was never intended to be paid.

Bailey then had Pierce re-incorporate as a new company—the Waters-Pierce Company of Missouri. He then called on the secretary of state and attorney-general of Texas and assured them that this was an entirely new company, that Standard Oil had no

```
$8000                Washington, D.C. March 1st 1901.
Four months ———— after date I promise to pay to
the order of  H. C. Pierce
              Eight Thousand ————————  Dollars
at his office in St. Louis Mo.
Value received
No._____  Due July 1/1901                J. W. Bailey.
```

NOTE MADE BY SENATOR BAILEY TO HENRY CLAY PIERCE AND WHICH WAS NEVER PAID.
(From *Hearst's Magazine*)

interest in the Waters-Pierce Company whatever and that Mr. Pierce would make an affidavit to that effect. The Attorney-General showed Bailey a copy of the original Standard Oil trust agreement with the name of the Waters-Pierce Company on it. Bailey said he preferred to believe Pierce. Pierce made the affidavit and the company was re-admitted to Texas.

Bailey got charged with acting for the Standard in the senatorial canvass which followed. The legislature even investigated it. But it heard nothing of Mr. Bailey's $3,300 loan. He was elected to the Senate. The day after his election he went to Pierce and borrowed another $8,000. A few weeks later he asked for $1,750 more for Attorney-General Henry, who, of course, never got any of it.

Thus began the downfall of a fine figure. Not long afterward Bailey was in New York. Pierce was there and they met on the street downtown. Pierce took Bailey by the wrist and led him into 26 Broadway and up to the office of the Great Corruptionist himself. The Senator's feet were in the trough now. And he kept them there until he was discovered.

IV

ONE BLOW was aimed at the trusts during the administration of William McKinley—the creation of the Industrial Commission—and this was done on the eve of the approaching congressional

```
                                        February 13, 1900.
Personal

My dear Senator:-
            Referring to your note regarding the new California
Senator - Senator Penrose had already written me on the subject, and
I have asked our people to do everything they can through the Santa Fe.
We have no direct relations of any kind with the new Senator, and I am
dubious about the efficacy of our effort through the Santa Fe.
                                Very truly yours,
                                    Jno. D. Archbold.
Hon. M. S. Quay,
    Beaver, Pa.
```

(From *Hearst's Magazine*)

campaign. The men of the oil regions had never wholly rested. The Pure Oil Company kept up its rivalry with the trust. Toward the end of Grover Cleveland's administration Thomas W. Phillips, one of the organizers of the Pure Oil Company and then in Congress from the oil regions, got Congress to pass a resolution providing an industrial commission to investigate the trusts. But Grover Cleveland vetoed it. Now in 1898 the measure was again brought forward, passed, and signed by the President. The Commission included five Senators, five Representatives, and nine members appointed by the president. McKinley named Thomas W. Phillips as one of his appointees. Senator Kyle was made chairman and Phillips vice-chairman of the Commission. Senator Boise Penrose was a member.

The Commission began with the best intentions in the world. It named a group of economists who have since achieved distinction to make its various studies, Prof. Emery R. Johnson of Princeton, W. Z. Ripley, then of the Massachusetts Institute of Technology, Samuel McCune Lindsey, Prof. John R. Commons, and Prof. Jeremiah K. Jenks of Cornell. The more important studies were made by Dr. Jenks. It is perhaps true that but for Jenks' knowledge of the subject and his persistence in searching out the facts, backed by the vice-chairman of the Commission, Mr.

> Personal   July 18, 1898.
>
> My dear Senator:
>
> I have your favor of the 15th, and will do as you request, provided you finally say that you need so much. Please ask for it in instalments, as needed, from time to time, not all at once.
>
> I have your kind note about Walter, and will do as you suggest.
>
> Very truly yours,
> *Jno D Archbold*
>
> Hon. M. S. Quay,
>   Mountville,
>   Lancaster Co., Pa.

(From *Hearst's Magazine*)

Phillips, very little would have been achieved by the Commission. It investigated the Standard Oil Company, National Steel Company, American Steel and Hoop, Federal Steel, American Steel and Wire, American Tin Plate, National Shear, and International Silver Company, the sugar, and whiskey trusts. And it later went into the affairs of the tobacco, salt, wall paper, cordage, thread, baking powder, coal, and other combinations. It examined 63 witnesses including John D. Archbold, Gary, Schwab, Havemeyer, Flint, and Gunton. It worked through 1899 to 1901, brought in a preliminary report in 1900 and other reports later, filling, in all, fourteen large volumes which today form an immense reservoir of information for the student of our economic history.

Some very damaging evidence of the operations of the sugar and whiskey and other trusts was brought out. Some more or less troublesome facts about the Standard got into the testimony. When the report was made, however, it dealt with singular gentleness with the Oil Company. For the first time an official body recognized the permanency and usefulness of the combination idea. "Industrial combinations have become a fixture in our national life," its preliminary report announced. "Their power for evil should be destroyed and their means of good preserved."

When the Commission was formed, that busy gentleman at 26 Broadway, Mr. Archbold, did not, we may be sure, relax his vigilance. The appointment of Senator Kyle as Chairman pleased him. When the Senator died, just after the first report, Archbold

```
Personal.                                    October 13, 1904.
My dear Senator:-
              In fulfilment of our understanding, it gives me
pleasure to hand you herewith certificate of deposit to your favor
for $25,000.and with good wishes, I am,
                              Yours Truly,
To
Hon Boies Penrose,
          1331  Spruce St.,  (Sgnd) Jno. D. Archbold
                Phila., Pa.
```

(From *Hearst's Magazine*)

wrote to a congressional confidant of "the lamentable death of Senator Kyle." During the investigation Mr. Archbold became disturbed "about some questions antagonistic to our interests." On the Commission was Representative Gardiner of Atlantic City. So Mr. Archbold wrote to Senator Sewell of New Jersey: "We understand that for some reason his [Gardiner's] feelings toward us are not very friendly. We would greatly like to have him set right and are sure if we could have an opportunity of personal contact with him we could set him right, etc. . . . Can you pave the way for us to see him?"

Senator Sewell was the official pass-dispenser of the Pennsylvania Railroad and of course the good senator arranged matters and Mr. Archbold wrote him acknowledging his goodness and, for some reason, put on the letter: "William Rockefeller present."

Two months later the Commission was preparing its report. Archbold wrote Sewell again: "It seems very important that this report should be wisely and conservatively shaped. Representative John J. Gardiner of New Jersey is a member of the Commission and we think it very desirable that you have a word with him on the subject. We have no doubt from what we know of him and coming from the locality he does, that he will treat the subject judicially and sensibly."

When the report was ready Senator Penrose in January sent secretly an advance copy of it to Archbold. Archbold objected to one portion of it. That objection in the light of subsequent corporate history is interesting:

"Corporations should not be required to make public the names of all stockholders. It is an unjust and unnecessary inquisition into the private affairs of stockholders and serves no public good. . . . Private corporations should not be required to make public items of receipts and expenditures, profits and losses. A statement of assets and liabilities is all that can benefit the public. Items of receipts and expenditures, profits, and losses can only benefit the competitors."

A month later Senator Penrose sent Archbold another copy of the report which had been toned down. Archbold replied:

"I have your kind note of yesterday with enclosures, which latter I beg to return herewith. We think the report is so fair that we will not undertake to suggest any change."

It was only a little while before this that Archbold had written Penrose that "I am making a further special effort today to reach Senator Fairbanks on the Quay case." Thus the favors went back and forth.

When Senator Kyle died the Commission needed a new chairman. Archbold had a bright idea of his own. He wrote Senator Penrose:

My dear Senator:

Following the lamentable death of Senator Kyle, we are very strongly of the opinion that you should take the Chairmanship of the Industrial Commission. This seems eminently fitting from every point of view. Your name as chairman would give the report exceptional assurance of integrity and intelligence. You are the ranking senatorial member of the Commission; the interests of your state are preëminent in the matter, and last, and we hope not unfairly, *we make it a strong personal request.*"

This was Boise Penrose, notorious as Quay's fellow corruptionist in Pennsylvania. Mr. Archbold seemed to think he could manage the matter. For he added to his letter a request for "an affirmative answer by wire," so that "we may do what seems possible to aid in the matter." Archbold then wrote a similar letter to Matt Quay urging Penrose's appointment.

A little later Senator Mantle of Montana resigned from the

February 21, 1900.

Hon. Boies Penrose,
    Senate Chamber,
        Washington, D. C.

My dear Senator:

I have your kind note of yesterday with enclosures, which latter I beg to return you herewith. We think the report is so fair that we will not undertake to suggest any changes.

With many thanks, I am

Very truly yours,

Jno. D. Archbold.

LETTER FROM ARCHBOLD TO PENROSE, MEMBER OF INDUSTRIAL COMMISSION, APPROVING COMMISSION'S REPORT EIGHT DAYS BEFORE IT WAS FILED.

Commission and Senator Thomas R. Baird of California was named. Immediately Archbold got in touch with Penrose:

"I have further information that a determined effort will be made at the meeting early in September by the Democrats and disgruntled Republican members to make political capital against the so-called trusts. If Senator Baird can be counted on for sensible action in regard to this question, an effort should be made to have him present at the meetings. It is very desirable also to have him favor Col. Clark for the chairmanship. Can you reach him and will you try?"

Apparently Senator Penrose was coy about the chairmanship. But the Standard had another candidate, Albert Clarke, and Clarke was named.

Before this Commission John D. Rockefeller did not appear. But he filed a series of answers to questions propounded to him. He was asked what are the dangers of combination. He answered:

"The dangers are that power conferred by combination may be abused; that combinations may be formed for speculating in stocks rather than for conducting business; and that for this purpose prices may be temporarily raised instead of lowered. But this fact is no more an argument against combination than the fact that steam may explode is an argument against steam. Steam is necessary and can be made comparatively safe. Combination is necessary and its abuses can be minimized; otherwise our legislators must acknowledge their incapacity to deal with the most important instrument of industry. Hitherto most legislative attempts have been not to control but to destroy; hence their futility."

In answer to the question what legislation he would suggest he replied that he favored a Federal Incorporation act and uniform legislation encouraging corporations and supervision not to hamper business but to prevent fraud.

CHAPTER VI. MICE AND MEN

IT WAS about the middle of August, 1901, that Archbold was writing Boise Penrose about rigging the Industrial Commission. For the next few weeks the "Political Purchasing Agent" of Standard Oil was a busy man, pulling his wires. While he was doing this Theodore Roosevelt, vice-president of the United States, was at the Minneapolis State Fair, where he made a speech. "More and more it is evident that the State and if necessary the nation has got to have the right of supervision and control as regards the great corporations which are its creatures particularly as regards the great business combinations which derive a portion of their importance from a monopolistic tendency." And he used in this same speech the phrase which was to become famous, a reference to the old axiom, "Speak softly but carry a big stick." But his was a distant voice. Roosevelt was futile as vice-president, into which helpless job he had been pushed by Matt Quay and

Tom Platt. William McKinley was preparing to go to the Buffalo Fair. And at the moment there is no doubt that the nation was utterly in the hands of the great combinations of capital, which everywhere, in cities, states, and nation, had corrupted the government.

Hanna, who had called himself the "representative of the corporations," was in control. Morgan was putting over unhindered all his famous consolidations. Harriman bought the Southern Pacific and was building ahead in his adventurous career. Speculation in railroad shares rose to dizzy heights. The trust makers were at work everywhere. In New York Morgan built his steel trust. In Salt Lake City the American Cattle Growers Association, in Florida the Pineapple Growers, in New England the brick-makers made their lesser trusts. Corrupt utility gangs were seizing railroad franchises for nothing. The conscience of the people seemed to have been completely paralyzed under the pressure of the dazzling power of the new Captains of Industry as they were more or less affectionately called. "In not one of the forty-eight states is anything being done to prevent the formation of colossal corporations or interfere with those which already exist," said the *Review of Reviews*. The old individualists seemed weary of the struggle. Moreover popular wrath was quenched in the rising tide of prosperity. Dr. Albert Shaw assured them "in an age of constructive genius" these great combinations like the Steel Corporation, the Standard Oil, and others "would be able to avert violent panics." The fights between the Harrimans, Hills, Rogers, Addicks, and others made a heroic spectacle. The munificence of the great barons touched the imaginations of the people. Carnegie in three months promised libraries to a hundred cities, and proposed to New York City to build sixty-five branches. Even some of the old anti-trust warriors had dropped their weapons and joined in the mad pursuit of wealth. Ex-Governor Hogg found oil on his own paternal acres in Texas and was now marching on riches. Former Governor McMillen of Tennessee was busy building oil interests in Texas. Even the misanthropic Senator Pettigrew was found in Wall Street hunting for the pot of gold.

As August came to an end young John D. was in England looking, it was reported, for a castle in Devonshire for his parents to spend a Summer. John D. himself kept close to the heart of his vast estate which was well supplied with guards because of threats made during the pending steel strike. Senator and Mrs. Aldrich announced the engagement of their daughter Abby to Mr. John D. Rockefeller, Jr., and the two houses were busy with preparations for the happy event. Then in the first week of September, Theodore Roosevelt went into the Adirondacks to hunt, William McKinley went to Buffalo to make a speech and young Czolgosz left Cleveland with a revolver in his pocket. On September 6th McKinley made his speech and when he finished, Czolgosz shot him.

At 26 Broadway the Standard's first thought was of Roosevelt. The man they had shelved was about to be President. In a hundred offices of trust magnates a kind of fear fell on the great captains—fear of uncertainty. They whispered among themselves. The nation went a little mad. A traveling salesman got his name in the papers because he said he overheard a conversation near the Illinois Central depot in Chicago outlining a conspiracy to murder McKinley, Morgan, and Rockefeller. The guards around the Rockefeller estate were doubled and John D. remained indoors. The newspapers poured upon the head of the maddened boy who had assassinated the President the vials of its wrath and hatred. "Futile fool," said a dozen journals. "Not merely the cruelty of it, but the madness and futility of the act." Cruel? Yes. But it had many far-reaching consequences though not those intended by the assassin. All the millions of rounds of ammunition fired in the Spanish-American War never wrought greater and profounder changes than that single pistol shot.

For the moment, however, the nation was thoroughly poisoned by its pursuit of wealth. The death of McKinley left behind a pall under which was tolerance for all the things he stood for —the figure of Mark Hanna standing in tears beside his bier, a hatred of the so-called radicalism which was blamed for unbalancing the mind of his slayer. At this moment Conservatism, fat, rotten, lawless, was at its flood.

II

Mr. Rockefeller himself was all this time as busy with the rebuilding of his health as he had ever been with the building of his fortune. He played golf every day, using a bicycle to ride from one shot to another, a fact which amused some of the ancient and honorable in Scotland who had a good laugh at this device as some of the few American golfers smiled at the pictures of Arthur Balfour playing the game in spats.

He was still a sick man, limited to a diet of milk and graham crackers, watching his temperature to keep from getting overheated. In Winter when golf was denied him he went for long walks and sometimes when stopping in New York City could be seen even in the stormiest weather heavily wrapped walking near his town house.

Life was a mixture of rewards and punishments. He was overjoyed when his daughter Alta, who had been deaf from childhood, returned from Vienna late in 1901 able to hear. A little later she was married to E. Parmalee Prentice at a quiet wedding to which only 150 guests were invited. But a kind of shadow fell over the occasion by the death, a little while before, of Jackie McCormick, Rockefeller's only grandchild, to whom he was tenderly devoted. Then came the marriage of John D., Jr., to Senator Nelson W. Aldrich's daughter Abby. But this was not a quiet affair. The rich Senator provided a spectacle worthy of the union of the two powerful houses. The great gray tea house in which the wedding took place was built especially for the occasion at the Aldrich Summer home at Warwick Neck, overlooking Narragansett Bay. The couple were married before a huge fireplace in the immense chamber, sixty by one hundred feet, provided for the purpose. A thousand guests graced the ceremony and a fortune in rich gifts greeted the bride. There was no wine, for the groom had asked that this be omitted. John D. himself looked with a little disapproval on the elaborate preparations. His wishes, however, were not consulted by the haughty Senator save in one sentimental incident. The wedding was performed by an aged minister, the Rev. J. G. Colby, a superannuated Congregationalist minister, who, thirty-five years before, had married the groom's parents. The pious Baptist youth was married according to the Episcopal service by a Congregationalist minister.

Here again the joy of this highly approved union of his son was diluted by the stormy and truculent Frank Rockefeller, who broke out into one of his frequent quarrels with his older brother.

Pulitzer, the editor of the *World*, had watched these quarrels with growing curiosity for a long time. He kept his busy newspaper on Rockefeller's trail. Of all the journals which at the time heaped almost daily coals upon the head of the harried oil man the one he hated most was the *World*. Only a little before this Pulitzer had touched a tender nerve when he announced that he would give a reward of $8,000 for any information of the whereabouts of Rockefeller's father. He had made several attempts to locate the wayward old doctor. Suddenly a few months before young John's wedding Frank amazed Cleveland by removing the bodies of his two children from the family plot in Lakeview Cemetery. The newspapers published varying explanations of this. In Cleveland newspaper circles it was believed the two men had quarreled about their father. It is probable that the quarrel had to do with the Corrigan suit and nothing more. It made a succulent morsel for the newspapers and the reporters flocked to Frank. He talked volubly but incoherently. He talked about the Corrigan case. "That treacherous act was but a detail in my brother's long record of heartless villainy." He stormed about many things. "When I make all the facts public as I shall, the world will be amazed." The breach between the two men was now irreparable. Later he again startled Cleveland by resigning from the Euclid Avenue Baptist Church and announcing dramatically that he and his family could not worship in a church that harbored John D.

The incident was a source of pain and humiliation to Rockefeller. But now past sixty, this resolute man, who had planned his life and lived all its parts with a cold and reasoning deliberation, permitted neither his family quarrel, the incessant beating of the drums of detractors and critics, the hammering of old business rivals and new enemies nor the still more formidable disorder in his body to ruffle the surface of that illimitable patience with which he looked out on life.

III

IN JUNE, 1901, five men sat down at the Arlington Hotel to discuss a proposal which came from Mr. Rockefeller. They included Dr. R. Emmett Holt, Dr. William H. Welch, Simon Flexner, T. Mitchell Prudden, and Christian A. Herter. Mr. Rockefeller's proposal was that he would contribute $200,000, or $20,000 a year for ten years, toward establishing an institute for medical research.

Rockefeller had been thinking much about the art of giving. Dr. Gates had already organized a bureau of research for studying gifts and the idea of the benevolent trust was taking shape in Rockefeller's mind, fed doubtless by the active mind of Gates, now largely concerned with Rockefeller's investments. About this time Dr. Gates, who had read at the recommendation of a young physician Dr. Osler's book "The Principles and Practice of Medicine," was impressed by the elaborate attention of the medical fraternity to the cure of disease and the neglect of preventive measures. Gates thought much of this and was surprised at the almost complete lack of medical research work in America. Gates discussed it with Rockefeller and the germ once planted in the latter's mind found itself in hospitable soil. His offices and home were deluged daily with letters asking aid and the utter futility of most giving was borne in on his mind. Letters and reports from those institutions which he had helped came in abundance. These he made a practice of reading at his family table and discussing in order to interest his children in this work and the transient character of most of the help given filled his practical mind with a sense of dissatisfaction. When the proposal for a medical research institute was made to a group of leading American physicians they plunged into the plan with eagerness and enthusiasm. The institute was incorporated June 14th, 1901. It began by supporting scholarships and fellowships and made grants to eighteen laboratories for research studies in existing institutions. At the end of the first year the Board decided it ought to have its own laboratory and so in June, 1902, Mr. Rockefeller gave $1,000,000 to acquire land and erect the necessary buildings. Dr. Simon Flexner, Professor of Pathology in the University of Pennsylvania, was chosen to head the work. A site was bought on the East River at East Sixty-sixth Street and work began on the building. But Dr. Flexner organized his laboratory immediately in temporary quarters in July, 1903, with four assistants. This was the beginning of the Rockefeller Institute for Medical Research.

It is not difficult to trace in the plans of the older Rockefeller the influences of his boyhood—the solitary lad of the Finger Lake Regions and its lovely landscapes spending his days producing around his Pocantico and Forest Hill homes a vast demesne of beautiful parks and endless roads; the solemn-visaged Sunday School boy who gave away dimes to church and mission and Y.M.C.A. and Deacon Sked, giving dimes to all he meets; the son of the old quack doctor who roamed the countryside with his futile pills, now creating a great institution for the scientific study of disease.

IV

THE FIRST days of Roosevelt's régime were quiet. The trust makers proceeded upon their hectic course. Mr. Hanna pushed through the ship-subsidy bill. A great anthracite strike got under way with the reactionary and haughty railroad chieftains defying the unions. Even Richard Olney called them unblushing law breakers. Morgan formed the International Harvester trust. That contemptuous banker assumed a kind of majesty. The Census announced there were 185 combinations of capital controlling over 2,000 plants. When Aldrich wanted advice about the tariff on steel he wrote to Frick for "some one in your concern who would make suggestions as to the proper relative rate on products." Hill and Harriman fought for the control of the Burlington and Northern Pacific. The Rockefeller interests backed Harriman. The country enjoyed the great show of these giants battling in Wall Street for Northern Pacific stock, resulting in the disastrous Northern Pacific corner. Then Morgan, Hill, Harriman, got together and patched up the quarrel by forming the Northern Securities Company to hold the stock of the Great Northern and Northern Pacific and the Burlington. Some cautious men in Wall Street shook their heads. The new President might make trouble. But the leaders felt there was a grain of security in the presence of Philander Knox in the cabinet, who could steer the President safely.

Governor Van Zandt of Minnesota had his attorney-general apply to the state courts for an order against the Northern Securities Company. But the order was denied. Then the Illinois anti-trust law was declared unconstitutional. All seemed serene. Suddenly, like a bolt out of the blue, Attorney-General Knox announced that the President had asked him whether he considered the Northern Securities Company a violation of the anti-trust law and that he had answered that it was, and that at the President's order he was about to begin proceedings against the company.

Stocks fell in Wall Street. Soon another blow fell. The beef trust had raised the price of meat. Hordes of women on New York's East Side assaulted their butcher shops. Knox filed a suit in Chicago asking for an injunction against the unlawful price-fixing agreements of the trust.

Many obese and plethoric gentlemen in Wall Street cursed the President and said, "I told you so." Then Congressman Littlefield of Maine introduced a bill to compel corporations to file yearly statements, revealing certain essential facts about their operations. Knox collaborated with Littlefield and suggested a Bureau of Corporations with unlimited power of investigation. "The fellow is a renegade," said the barons. Senator Knute Nelson offered a bill creating a new Department of Commerce comprising a Bureau of Corporations. Roosevelt got Nelson to offer an amendment authorizing the President to make public the information of this bureau any way he pleased. The matter was before the Senate. Standard Oil was in arms. Archbold was busy writing letters. Suddenly Roosevelt called in two newspaper reporters and informed them that he had seen telegrams to nine Senators—Hale, Spooner, Elkins, Kean, and others—from Rockefeller. They read: "We are opposed to the anti-trust legislation. Our counsel will see you. It must be stopped. (Signed) John D. Rockefeller." Most of the Senators named denied they had received such wires. When the bills were passed Roosevelt admitted that he had released the information to help the passage of his bills. This was the first taste of that peculiar way of fighting which Roosevelt was to use many times thereafter.

Another measure was the Elkins rate bill providing penalties for rebates and rate discriminations. Still another measure made it possible to expedite the trial of anti-trust cases. Under this the Northern Securities case was hurried to trial and decided in favor of the government. This was the first great anti-trust law victory. It shocked and angered the bewildered industrialists. For the new Department of Commerce Roosevelt named as Secretary George L. Cortelyou, his secretary, and to the Bureau of Corporations he appointed James R. Garfield, son of the former President, a young man of energy, enthusiasm, and lofty civic consciousness. It was now clear that the man in the White House was in earnest about his trust policy.

V

THERE was but one safe course for the confessed industrialists—to get rid of Roosevelt. And so an impetus was given to one of the most extraordinary presidential campaign booms in our history. Hanna and Roosevelt drifted farther apart. Hanna, who had shrunk from a cabinet post, had now become so completely the embodiment of all the troubled yet powerful forces of finance and corruption in the Republican party that he came to be looked upon as their logical candidate for the presidency. The former wholesale grocer, traction magnate, political boss, and slush-fund dispenser actually came within hailing distance of the White House. The time for the conventions was approaching. Hanna's strategy was to have all delegations go uninstructed. The forces of money and of the organization were on his side. Roosevelt's position was precarious. But now Hanna was afraid of Matt Quay. When Quay's seat in the Senate was being contested Hanna had fled from Washington to avoid voting. Now Quay was showing a strange friendliness for Roosevelt. Hanna wanted to bring him into line. He wrote Archbold to handle that commission. Archbold wrote Quay and asked him to call. But the old Pennsylvania fox found excuses to remain away. Archbold kept after him and kept his secretary busy sending letters and wires wherever his influence would help Hanna.

Meantime Hanna became ill and Roosevelt began to make love to Archbold. Sibley wrote Archbold in February, 1904, that the President was anxious to have him for lunch. "He urged strongly that you come over to meet him." But Archbold thought it best to remain away. Sibley wrote again that the President was delighted to hear of the friendly attitude of Standard Oil and said Senator Aldrich had given him the same assurance. Were the wily Standard chieftains playing a double game with Roosevelt? All this time they were working industriously for Hanna. But the Ohio boss was a very sick man. What if he should die on them? And so the oily Sibley kept in touch with Roosevelt. The game came to a head quickly enough for in a few weeks Hanna died in Washington. The whole opposition to Roosevelt collapsed. The Supreme Court affirmed the Northern Securities decision. Old Matt Quay died. Prosecutions of trusts were popping up everywhere.

At a gridiron dinner Roosevelt shook his finger under the nose of the great J. P. Morgan. Surely the drift was away from the captains. Doom seemed to stalk their plans. They turned to Judge Alton B. Parker for a Democratic candidate, sponsored by Thomas F. Ryan and August Belmont, associates of the Rockefellers in the New York utility field. Parker said: "The common law as developed affords a complete legal remedy against monopoly." What more could a trust magnate want? But the Parker hope turned to ashes in their hands. After all, there is plenty to government besides the president and there was more danger in a congress of Southern Democrats and Western radicals than in Roosevelt. And as election approached the business leaders drifted back into the camp of their old love, the Grand Old Party. The Standard contributed $25,000 to the Republican congressional campaign fund, another $25,000 to the Roosevelt fund through Senator Penrose and handed a check for $100,000 to Bliss, the Republican treasurer, the same gentleman who collected for Hanna and another $30,000 from Archbold, Rogers, and William Rockefeller to Harriman's fund. In the end all the forces which had stood behind McKinley lined up behind Roosevelt. The Bryan wing of the Democrats remained cold to Parker and the mis-cast Democratic candidate was ingloriously defeated.

VI

WHILE all this was in progress Rockefeller remained studiously away from the spotlight and the stage. What part he took behind the wings must be a subject of guess. We find Archbold in 1902 writing the industrious Sibley, who for some reason wanted to see Mr. Rockefeller, that "Mr. Rockefeller never comes to business and I see him infrequently." He had quite ceased to visit his office. He did, however, have a direct wire to Archbold's office and was in frequent communication. Did he discuss Mr. Archbold's contributions to the sly art of "setting statesmen right"? We may well guess that he did not. Rockefeller did not require the discussion of details like this—indeed preferred not to have them. It was the settled policy of the company to use its money everywhere and anywhere, in state and national councils, to produce results. The policy settled, Rockefeller never concerned himself with the details of carrying it out. William Rockefeller, always very close to his brother, knew all about such matters. And undoubtedly John D. knew in general, if not in detail, what was being done. He took no part in the campaign, however, as indeed was his custom. He looked with growing distrust upon Roosevelt but for the time being kept his counsel.

He had during these years, for the first time in his life, leisure for meditation. And he began to talk to men who looked out upon a larger world of thought than he had ever explored. We begin to see evidences of his moving beyond the bounds of the little Baptist universe in which he had done his very meager thinking. He begins to talk about higher education and its importance and finally betrays an interest in extending his educational gifts beyond the Baptist corral.

In 1898 an educational movement got started in the South at the First Capon Springs Conference for Christian Education in the South. The next year appeared Mr. Robert C. Ogden, John Wanamaker's partner, as a participant and very soon he was the head and ruler of what came to be called the Ogden movement. Meantime Rockefeller had been managing his gifts to Baptist institutions through the Baptist Educational Society still dominated by Dr. Gates. And out of these two movements grew the plan for the General Education Board. Early in January, 1902, acting as counsel for Rockefeller in this matter, Edward M. Shepard submitted to a small group the plan for the General Educational Association. The group was interesting. It included young John D. Rockefeller, Frederick T. Gates, and Dr. Wallace Butterick, who was responsible in a measure for the plan, Robert C. Ogden, and a few others. But it is significant to note the presence of Dr. Albert Shaw, editor of the *Review of Reviews* and Mr. Walter H. Page, editor of *World's Work*. The Ogden movement found itself merged into the Rockefeller Board. After a while Mr. Ogden became president of the Board with Dr. Wallace Butterick as secretary. The founder's gift this year was a million dollars. The charter set forth the objects of the Board as "the promotion of education within the United States without distinction of race, sex, or creed." But the first million gift was specifically limited to education in the South, the principal to be expended over a period of ten years. It was not until June, 1905, that Rockefeller gave to the

Board its first permanent endowment of $10,000,000 to be used for higher education in the United States.

Meantime a stream of princely gifts to various causes were made—seven million to the Post-Graduate Medical College and hospital in Chicago, a half million to Johns Hopkins Hospital, $350,000 to Teachers College in New York, a thank offering for the escape of his family without injury when his Pocantico Hills house burned in 1904. Besides he had begun the custom of giving each year a Christmas gift of a million dollars to the University of Chicago.

He nursed with unending care his precarious health. And while he seemed to be somewhat better, a strange affliction came upon him, which induced him to remain in seclusion for some months. This new disease was called alopecia. It caused his hair—on his head, his mustache, his eyebrows—to fall out with startling rapidity so that he remained utterly bald. When he got back to Pocantico the villagers hardly recognized him. Thereafter when he appeared in public it was in the little dark skull cap which became familiar in his pictures.

CHAPTER VII. THE MUCKRAKERS

IN APRIL, 1906, while fighting to put through his railroad bill, Roosevelt in a speech dedicating the new House of Representatives Office Building, made a reference to the Man with the Muckrake in Bunyan's "Pilgrim's Progress," "the man who could look no way but downward with the muckrake in his hand," who could not see the celestial crown offered him because he continued to "rake to himself the filth of the floor." He was repeating a phrase which he had used a few weeks before at the gridiron dinner.

Roosevelt was referring to that extraordinary group of journalists who, in magazines and books and newspapers, were uncovering the amazing graft of business and politics and were producing what the *Atlantic Monthly* called the "literature of exposure." This eruption of denunciatory writing constituted a phenomenon in the life of the time and exercised a powerful effect upon the public mind. As in all movements, the dramatic narratives of dishonesty in high places came from the pens of a mixture of serious and able men and from pure sensation mongers. Roosevelt's unlucky phrase grouped them all together and furnished his own enemies with an odious label which they proceeded to make powerful use of. Every critic thereafter was called a muckraker. Every unfriendly discussion of the vast, undisciplined pestilence of knavery in big business and public life was refuted by being branded as muckraking. No historian of the times now pretends to deny not merely that grave abuses grew up, but that the public conscience seemed to have become inert. That the revelations of the so-called muckrakers, which turned the light upon these dark places, were the most potent agent in awakening that languid conscience, cannot be denied. Roosevelt's phrase did an injustice to the earnest writers and editors who not only furnished for him the most effective support he got but made a contribution of lasting benefit to the developments of the times.

Roosevelt had a way of turning upon his own friends to square himself with powerful enemies. He was a very practical politician. The great trust buster and political reformer, he still knew how to cultivate the trust barons and the bosses. He invited Morgan to dinner when he was elected vice-president. He tried to make friends with Mark Hanna. George W. Perkins was one of his staunch friends. Roosevelt always liked and fraternized with old Matt Quay. When he thought he might have gone too far in any policy of attack he would turn upon those in the same pack with himself to mollify the pursuers. This he did when he made his "muckrake" speech.

The movement had been gathering strength for some time. Its beginnings must be traced to about 1894 when Henry Demarest Lloyd published his "Wealth Against Commonwealth." Lloyd might perhaps be called the Father of the Muckrakers. After that the next impetus came from the newspapers. Joseph Pulitzer and William Randolph Hearst were publishing in almost savage rivalry the *World* and the *Journal*. Both put themselves on the side of what came to be referred to with varying affection or scorn as the "masses." Exposures of corrupt politicians, franchise-grabbing traction magnates, ice trust managers, "malefactors" of all sorts filled the pages of these papers, which the more conservative publishers referred to as "yellow journals." For some years a magazine known as the *Arena*, ably edited, took the popular side and monthly produced articles of exposure of various political and economic abuses. In 1902 there began to appear in *McClure's Magazine* a "History of Standard Oil," by Ida M. Tarbell.[1] Ida M. Tarbell had already made a considerable impression with a "Life of Lincoln" which was printed serially in *McClure's* and increased the circulation of that magazine in an amazing way. She was a woman of exceptional ability as an editor and writer who had had a special training at the Sorbonne in Paris in the technique of historical research. She was born in the oil regions, grew up there, as a child had heard the incessant discussion and agitation following the great battles between the producers and Rockefeller. Her family had been engaged in the oil industry and her brother was at this time an official of the Pure Oil Company, the indomitable independent group which alone had been able to successfully hold its place against the Standard.

Oil and its battles, however, had receded from her interests. It was far from Titusville—in Paris—that her attention was redirected to the Standard. Wickham Steed had read Lloyd's book and the two talked of it. This interest remained academic until after the success of her "Life of Lincoln" in *McClure's* when the magazine was looking for another big story. While the story was in preparation Mark Twain called on S. S. McClure to inquire what kind of story was being prepared and to suggest that his friend Henry H. Rogers would like to talk to McClure. McClure suggested that Miss Tarbell see him and she jumped at the chance to try out some of her findings on some one representing the Standard Oil side.

When she called on Rogers at 26 Broadway he received her cordially and inquired: "Is there any way we can stop this?" She answered: "No, there is no way on earth in which you can prevent the publication of this story." He did not press the point

[1] Lincoln Steffens in his Autobiography (Harcourt, Brace and Company, 1931) assigns to his article in *McClure's Magazine*, October, 1902, the honor of being the "first muckraking article." It was called "Tweed Days in St. Louis" and told of Joseph W. Folk's battle against the St. Louis boodlers. However, when Steffens went to *McClure's*, Ida Tarbell had already begun work on her history of Standard Oil. And long before Steffens' articles magazines like the *Arena* had been pressing the work for exposure.

but asked her to promise that before she printed any charges she would bring them to him and give him an opportunity to explain. To this she agreed and thereafter, while preparing her story, called at 26 Broadway at least twenty times and had as many conferences with Rogers. Rogers made a profound impression on Miss Tarbell. She liked him, found herself admiring his frankness, his lack of pretension and cant. Once when she outlined to him a particularly bad performance at Titusville, he shook his head gravely and said: "You know, that was the worst thing we ever did."

Miss Tarbell spent two years following the course of Rockefeller's company, visiting the oil regions, Rockefeller's early homes in New York, Cleveland, and other oil centers. And in 1902 *McClure's Magazine* began publication of her story. The serial ran for two years and was read with hungry interest by people everywhere. Miss Tarbell retold again much of the early history and many of the incidents which had been first narrated by Lloyd. But she had the benefit of a fuller understanding of those events and the accumulation of a great mass of data which were not open to Lloyd. Besides she carried the story further along—to the formation of the Pure Oil Company in the late nineties. She talked with Lloyd at the outset of her labors and while her story was being published Lloyd followed it and expressed the greatest satisfaction and delight at her fine performance.

Miss Tarbell's story was not, of course, a life of Rockefeller, but a record of the abuses of the Standard Oil Company from 1872 to 1898. It was a mixture of historical narrative and indictment. No critic could complain that she had not examined the facts, for the evidences of minute and painstaking investigation were stamped upon every part of the work. Less dramatic in its style than Lloyd's book, it was nevertheless far more dramatic through the skillful management of its incidents. An analysis of a great economic episode pushed forward serially through two years (later in two volumes) with remorseless logic, it was at the same time a story of absorbing interest. Of this remarkable book it is just to say that it remains to this day the ablest document of its kind ever produced by an American writer.

The success of this monumental work was so great that before it had been completely published as a serial critics of the current vogue of graft in business and politics sprang up everywhere and

THE MUCKRAKERS

the age of the muckrakers was in full career. Burton J. Kendrick told the story of the Astor Fortune and writers like David Graham Phillips, with his "Treason of the Senate," Lincoln Steffens with his "Shame of the Cities," and dozens of others dealt crippling blows at the respectability of some of our commercial and political nobility. The movement for Pure Food laws, for honesty in advertising and against the patent medicine fakirs which got its impetus from Dr. Harvey Wiley and his "Poison Squad" in the Department of Agriculture was pushed with dramatic fervor by magazines like *Collier's*. Thomas W. Lawson electrified the country for a while with his "Frenzied Finance," published as a serial in *Everybody's*. This was a lurid, highly fevered account of the operations of Henry H. Rogers and William Rockefeller and James Stillman in Amalgamated Copper, Boston Gas, and other hectic financial stock manipulations. The whole subject of the grasping, unscrupulous, domineering business man and his corrupt political ally got into fiction and on the stage. And by a kind of fatality each offense fastened on other rich men and each blast of invective hurled at others, left another coating of infamy upon the name of Rockefeller. "There are worse men than John D. Rockefeller," said the *Arena*. "There is probably not one, however, who in the public mind so typifies the grave and startling menace to the social order." He had indeed taken on the character of a symbol. He was the victim of another circumstance. The same writer expressed it. "John D. has one vulnerable point, his religious instinct. Dissimulator and hypocrite by nature, the so-called development of veneration is nevertheless plainly marked." People felt less repugnance for the heretical Carnegie or the unregenerate John W. Gates or the worldly Rogers or the magnificent Morgan than they did for the pious John D. who was put down as a hypocrite, giving with one hand to countless charities and with the other collecting back the sum of his bounty from the poor by raising the price of kerosene.

As in the case of Lloyd, so Rockefeller kept his peace in the face of the Tarbell articles. In the South a friend undertook to suggest that he would reply on some points to Miss Tarbell. "Not a word!" Rockefeller interrupted. "Not a word about that misguided woman." Gaylord Wilshire met Rockefeller at a banquet in Santa Barbara and asked him about the Tarbell articles. "All without foundation," Rockefeller replied. "The idea of the Standard forcing any one to sell his refinery is absurd. The refiners wanted to sell to us and nobody that has sold and worked with us but has made money and is glad he did so. I thought once of having an answer made to the *McClure* articles, but you know it has always been the policy of the Standard to keep silent under attack and let our acts speak for themselves."

II

THE ORGY of denunciation and exposure got a lively and sensational turn from an attack on Rockefeller from within the church which loaded his name with more odium and gave him more pain perhaps than any other which he suffered. In April, 1905, he gave very secretly $100,000 to the American Board of Commissioners of Foreign Missions, a Congregational body. A body of Congregational ministers meeting in Boston engaged in a hectic debate over a resolution that "the acceptance of such a gift involves the constituents of the board in a relation implying honor to the donor and subjects the board to the charge of ignoring . . . the repeated and formidable indictments in specific terms for methods which are morally iniquitous and socially destructive." Immediately the newspapers broke out into a violent discussion of "tainted money," a phrase which was to share with "muckrakers" the popularity of the papers for some years. Every editor, educator, and preacher in the country contributed his view to the propriety of accepting Rockefeller's money. Precious few said a word for Rockefeller himself. There were many, however, who, while condemning the manner in which Rockefeller made his money, defended the gift. Of course, the clerical and pedagogical beneficiaries of his gifts came bravely to his defense. "Why let the devil have all the good tunes?" said the New York *World*. Letters poured in to the New York *Tribune* which made much of the matter. One of these urged that the money "be taken out of its evil path," and used the phrase "the tainted money of Judas," from which, perhaps, the term "tainted money" sprang. "Take it from the unspeakable Turk; take it from the devil himself. Above all take it from a bad man, a gambler, a thief, if with his wickedness he has a weakness for doing good. Let the taint in some of his money be cleansed. Let the gold as well as the wroth of a bad man prove the good," suggested the *Independent*.

The Memphis *Commercial Appeal* expressed most graphically the essence of the attacks. "Captain Kidd was a pirate. If he had quietly dropped into a New England town some night and left a lot of stolen goods with a fence he would be liable under the law. If on the other hand he had made his way to a parsonage, told the minister who he was and that he wanted to make a present of 10,000 Spanish doubloons to build a new chapel, what would be thought of the preacher who could accept that which it would be a crime for a fence to receive?"

The most redoubtable of all Rockefeller's assailants was the Rev. Washington Gladden, of Ohio, a widely known preacher of the day and a moderator of the Congregational Church. Gladden indeed moved merrily to the attack. Gladden was a product of the Finger Lake Region, like Rockefeller, and actually went to the old Owego Academy where Rockefeller got his early education. He had been belaboring Rockefeller for many years. Now he raked over Rockefeller's past to prove the charge of the Boston ministers that Rockefeller's money had been obtained by "methods morally iniquitous and socially destructive." He filed a written protest with the Prudential Committee of the Congregational Church. "The good that is done," he protested, "by lowering our ethical standards might best be left undone. Shall the young men and women of the missionary colleges be taught to regard Mr. Rockefeller as a great benefactor? The colleges might better be closed."

At first the Prudential Committee declared the gift had come "voluntarily and unsolicited," giving an impression that to refuse it would be an ungracious and unChristian act. They spoke of it as a "surprise." They maintained this attitude until Frederick T. Gates threatened to expose their importunities if they did not reveal frankly the conditions under which Rockefeller made the gift. As a matter of fact, the gift had been made reluctantly by Rockefeller only after he had been pestered by the Rev. James Barton, of the Committee. Both young John D. and Frederick T. Gates had written Barton refusing the interviews he asked with the old man. But Barton kept up his importunities and finally Gates sent $100,000 saying very significantly, "There is no reason known to me on Mr. Rockefeller's part why you should make any distinction in acknowledging this contribution than if it had been made by any one else."

The religious journals flew to Rockefeller's defense, approved the gift and the man who made it. Dr. Lyman Abbott in the *Outlook* thought the Boston protest showed the church could not be bought. Certainly it proved no such thing for the church officials approved and accepted the gift. Those who denounced it were rebels in a small minority.

Rockefeller himself, throughout, though deeply pained and chagrined, remained silent. He went to prayer meeting at Euclid Avenue Baptist Church where he was received with acclaim and asked to speak. He talked a little and then said: "I have talked too long, I am afraid. There are others here who want to talk. I don't want you to think I am a selfish monopolist." The congregation caught the meaning and laughed and applauded him heartily.

Gladden told reporters he was going to start a movement against accepting gifts from rich malefactors but the agitation soon died down. The appetite for gifts from "those rich malefactors" was too extensive and voracious. In the midst of it all Rockefeller made his contribution of $10,000,000 to the General Education Board. The agitation undoubtedly left a deep stain upon his name, but it made some friends for Rockefeller too. "What was intended," said *Current History*, "as an earnest, intelligent protest, took on the character of an uproar, made Rockefeller look like a much abused man and brought him much undeserved sympathy."

The unreasoning distinction made against Rockefeller among rich men was a little puzzling. The same papers which fulminated against the oil man, supported the countless local pleas being made everywhere to Andrew Carnegie for libraries. A candid, unbiased examination of the Rockefeller fortune at this time must have forced any man to admit that of all our great fortunes it was the most honestly acquired. Rockefeller had dealt honestly with his associates, with his workmen, and with his customers. His wealth had been accumulated out of the profits of building a great industrial enterprise. His offenses had been committed almost wholly against his competitors. They consisted in those deceptions, intrigues, and stratagems which had always been employed in business against rivals. They seemed worse perhaps because used upon a larger field. Also they got so much advertisement. But they were employed not as the main engine of his success, but merely as part of a larger design; they were incidents in a grandiose scheme of industrial empire building which had as its fundamental, major objective the development and perfection of a new system of business—a system which was destined very soon to be universally adopted. The cruelty of Rockefeller's own conduct is much magnified by focusing the attention upon the sufferings of the victim, particularly when we overlook altogether the part which stupidity and ignorance of most of the victims played in their own destruction. For years the Rockefeller legend was the story of little men crushed. The tale of a small refiner or dealer brought to ruin always made an appealing story. The constructive work of Rockefeller in building a great business and in pioneering in the field of efficiency and honest administration within the business itself was wholly overlooked. Even the establishment at this time of a pension system for old employees, thirty years in advance of scores of large business concerns today, was almost completely passed over. The distinction between the Rockefeller fortune made by way of accumulated profit in the building not merely of a great business but a great business system and those fortunes made by the group of glorified stock-jobbers like Morgan and Gates and Havemeyer and Moore and Reid and Gould and others was utterly overlooked. You will look in vain in the Standard Oil Company for performances like the organization of United States Steel where plants were bought for double and treble their value in stock and where promoters' fees running to hundreds of millions of dollars were drawn out by the organizers and where the entire half-billion shares of common stock had no physical property whatever back of it. The Standard Oil was never over-capitalized. Indeed, it was always under-capitalized. When Rockefeller acquired a company he paid its actual value in cash or stock. There was no water. And this, oddly, was one of the first causes of his damnation. It came from the sellers who thought they ought to get fancy prices for the "good will" of their business. And even so intelligent a critic as Ida Tarbell joined in this reproof without, it seems, quite understanding its import.

All this was very puzzling to Rockefeller. "Standard Oil," he said later, "has no water in its stock, has never issued bonds or shares through bankers, no underwriting syndicates of selling schemes, has always paid bills, keeps 60,000 men employed, pays well, cares for them when sick, pensions them when old, brought a million dollars a week into the country."

Yet he was loaded with contumely and shame while the Morgans and Carnegies and Garys and others were honored. Carnegie had sold armor plate to the Russians for $249 and exacted from the United States Navy from $520 to $700 a ton. Moreover a congressional committee had said of the steel leaders, Carnegie, Corey, Schwab, "The unblushing character of the frauds to which these men have been parties and the disregard for truth and honesty which they have shown for our committee render them unworthy of credence."

Out of the capitalizations of Morgan countless millions of dollars had been lost by the hapless thousands of investors who had been lured into putting their savings into the outrageously watered stocks. When the panic of 1907 came all the industrialists in steel and copper and cotton cut wages, but Standard Oil not only did not cut wages but increased employment by providing during the recession for extensive construction works, an expedient for depressions which today, more than twenty years later, we are still considering.

Rockefeller could not, therefore, understand what could be the explanation of the odium in which he was held while his fellow capitalists came in merely for a kind of good-natured spoofing, from the people who otherwise admired them.

As for his money and his gifts, he said nothing, though he was stung into submitting to his first interview. This was in the *Woman's Home Companion* in 1915. And in that he made merely an indirect reference to the storm which raged around his gifts. He said: "God gave me my money."

CHAPTER VIII. GOD'S GOLD

Down on his knees in the dim glow of the Wall Street twilight old Daniel Drew prays to the Lord for a blessing on his latest market venture. Uncle Dan'l with his clever pupils, Jay Gould and Jim Fisk, had just completed their most daring raid on Erie stock. In its train came a string of losses, bankruptcies, and suicides which made it a classic in Wall Street villainy. Now secretly old Dan'l had deserted his two confederates and set a snare for them. He had promised sometime before $250,000 to build a theological seminary at Madison, New Jersey. Now the $250,000 was due. And old Uncle Dan'l planned to catch his partners, Gould and Fisk, unawares and squeeze from their unregenerate wallets the $250,000 needed for his divinity school plus a good deal more for the pious founder himself. His bomb was placed. The fuse was lit. The event was in the hands of Heaven. And so now as Wall Street hurried home from its day's labors, the devout old gentleman fell upon his knees amid his ledgers and his market tables and implored the Lord to smile upon his new enterprise for the sake of his divinity school. As it turned out, however, the Lord was on the other side of the market. Gould and Fisk fooled their pious old master, shifted their position, squeezed him mercilessly and wrung a million from his sanctimonious hide.

But the picture of Daniel Drew, as pious an old cutthroat as ever scuttled a pool or squeezed a short, on his marrow bones praying the Lord for the success of a crooked Wall Street deal, so that he might endow his college of divine learning, is one which has provoked no end of mystery, scorn, and derision. For it is but a symbol of a phenomenon very familiar to the last generation and not wholly expunged from this one.

No stranger bedfellows ever lay down together in a man's soul than this oddly assorted pair—religion and thrift—room-mates in the breast of the business man—living together, as many people have believed, in sin.

John D. Rockefeller of course was the outstanding case. But there were many others. Rockefeller's day was signalized by the appearance of three very famous Sunday School superintendents— John D. himself, John Wanamaker, and John E. Searles. They were the rich apostles. Whatever they did, they had their texts ready, particularly John Wanamaker, who was a veritable man of texts, who went about with his Bible and the day's lesson marked with an American flag. Rockefeller, stung by the "tainted money" episode, submitted to his first interview. It was in the *Woman's Home Companion* and in it he declared that "God gave me my money." Searles was a grave, narrow Puritan, with a clean-shaven lip and a long patriarchal beard. At the Methodist conventions he looked more sacerdotal than any preacher. The rising generation does not know him but he was familiar to the last one in the investigations of the Sugar Trust and its unscrupulous financial operations which he directed with a rare genius for intricate antisocial corporation promotion.

But they were not the only ones. In New York City all the multi-millionaires were well-known church members, save perhaps Andrew Carnegie. And Andy was something of a dissenter in the matter of religion, whiskey, and living. But most of the multi-millionaires of the day were well-known members of the various Protestant churches, so that the churches were actually identified by their names. Grace Church was the church of J. P. Morgan and R. Fulton Cutting. St. Bartholomew's was the devotional refuge of the Vanderbilts and their connections. At Trinity Church there were the Astors. Old John Jacob started out as a member of the Dutch Reformed. In the days when he was performing some of his most skillful operations on the trappers of the Northwest the consistory used to meet at his house and he soothed his troubled spirit at eventide reading his Bible and the "Rise and Progress of Religion in the Soul." But now his family had soared upward, as so many good Baptists and Methodists and Lutherans, upon the wings of wealth into the lofty reaches of the Episcopal Church. Of the 75 multi-millionaires of the New York of the 1900's, half were communicants of the Episcopal Church. St. Thomas parish alone had seven multi-millionaires. All the others had their wealthy trustees and vestrymen. The Baptists and Methodists, however, were not so well supplied though the Baptists had in Mr. John D. Rockefeller the prize package of all. In all churches the odor of prosperity mingled with the odor of sanctity. It looked as if one of the greatest tactical blunders in the life of Christ was his unthinking shot at the rich man, the Kingdom of God, the Camel and the Needle's eye. No one can say with certainty that these rich men actually got into Heaven. But certainly they were to be found herded in large numbers in the vestibule.

II

IF THE rich man goes after the church, it must be said in all fairness, that the pursuit has not been a one-sided affair. Mahomet has not had to go far. The Mountain has more than met him halfway.

It is no longer possible to run a church on a shoestring as Christ did. The open-air church is not popular with either apostle or disciple. Even the Salvation Army has moved in out of the weather. Particularly in our modern cities, with high real estate values, excessive costs of raw materials, coal and light, help and religious paraphernalia, and the growing love of the prosperous Christian for luxury and comfort, the plant cost and overhead of religion are appalling.

These great expenditures arise out of the weakness which the modern apostles have for the good things of life and out of the adventitious aids which religion must call to its service to put its messages across.

It is the church's unappeasable appetite for funds to support its vast array of secular activities and its costly ritualistic services which makes it the slave of Mammon. The value of church property in New York as put down by the tax assessors for exemption purposes is $282,659,289, which is far below its actual value. And this does not include, besides, large holdings of taxable real estate stocks, bonds, and cash held for investment purposes. Trinity Church alone has dividend-paying real estate valued at $15,000,000 and an income of nearly $2,000,000 a year from its investments. It takes a lot of money to shelter a Christian soul. St. Paul's Chapel is valued at $5,000,000 with but 334 dues-paying communicants—an average of $15,000 per soul, which is more than three times as much as the investment required to house a whole family in the flesh. The church of Christ at Broadway and 71st Street has a plant valued at $1,200,000 with 400 dues-paying members or about $3,000 per member.

The excessive character of this is evident from the investment of the Roman Catholic Church. In Manhattan the plant of all Protestant communions averages $900 a member. The Catholic establishment averages $66 a member. And the latter includes not merely churches, but hundreds of schools, hospitals, colleges, asylums, convents, and club houses.

In the Protestant churches these sums are raised largely through the munificence of a few wealthy patrons. In the Catholic Church they are collected in small bits from the masses of its devotees.

The effect in each case is somewhat different. In the Protestant churches it has set the preachers to running after rich men. In the Catholic Church it has tended to subordinate piety in the priesthood to the hardier and more indispensable virtues of practical business capacity. No one can blame a poor bishop for preferring a hard-headed business man as a pastor, one who can frisk the congregation extensively and meet the parish bills, to a pious but impractical priest who may save a lot of souls but put the parish into bankruptcy. After all lost souls drop more or less noiselessly into hell, but the parish budget is loud and irrepressible.

In a simpler age St. Francis of Assisi said: "It is my definite wish that the brothers shall avoid the acceptance of churches, dwellings, and all other things that may be offered them on conditions which are unfavorable to the holy poverty we prize as our rule."

But there is no "holy poverty" in the Protestant churches today and not too much of it in the Catholic Church either. Instead we have "holy riches"—God's Gold. The preachers therefore cannot be too squeamish about the texts in the Bible dealing with riches and business. Hence we have seen an incessant appeal to wealthy men to get them inside the church. And as the church has taken on these passengers one by one it has had to keep on dropping text after text which could no longer ride with them. At the time of which we write a well-known Protestant clergyman turned a bit of light on the lay deputies of the Protestant-Episcopal Church of America. Out of four deputies from New York, three were multi-millionaires. From Long Island two of the four were millionaires. Massachusetts sent two multi-millionaires, West Massachusetts sent three, and Pittsburgh two. Of course, the great lay figure of the Episcopal Church of that day was J. Pierpont Morgan. As a New York delegate he appeared surrounded by that magnificence which attended him everywhere. He rented a house in the convention city which was always referred to as Syndicate House. A special train brought him and his guests, bishops, and important divines to Syndicate House where they were entertained upon the most lavish scale. But all the wealth and magnificence was not at Syndicate House. After one of these Triennial conventions the hotel proprietor declared that while he had entertained railroad, fraternal, sporting, and other groups at his hotel he had never seen men spend so much money or women who wore so much jewelry as these Episcopalian leaders who met to set in order the temporal affairs of the religion set up by the wayside preacher of humility and poverty who walked barefoot the hard roads of Galilee.

Practically all of the Standard leaders were godly men and many of them sprang from the loins of preachers. Archbold was a deacon in the church, William Rockefeller worshiped in the church he built in Tarrytown. Old Jacob Vandergrift was a man of exacting piety and a soldier in that division of the Lord's army that warred on the Demon Rum. William Wardell was almost a professional pietist, was the first real angel of the prohibition party and ran first for Mayor and then for Governor of New York on the Prohibition ticket. Charles Pratt was a generous giver to religious work of all sorts in Brooklyn. James Stillman ended the day always with a prayer that God would protect the deposits of the National City Bank. When William McKinley was reëlected in 1900 and marched back into office followed by that picturesque and picaresque crew of the anointed—Quay and Penrose and Foraker and Kean and Elkins and Platt and Depew and Aldrich and the rest to the chantings of the Archbolds and Havemeyers and Harrimans and Rogerses and Addicks and Morgans and the lesser Keepers of the Sacred Gold, Mark Hanna wired the president in congratulation: "God's in His Heaven. All's well with the world."

III

"CALL upon me in the day of trouble and I will deliver *thee* and *thou* shalt glorify *me*." There is a text the business man can understand. He sees himself actually propositioned by the Lord. The Party of the First Part will help the Party of the Second Part when the latter is in trouble. In consideration thereof the party of the second part will *glorify* the party of the first part. There is the coin in which the Lord's dues can be paid. Glorification. What is the Lord after? That's the natural inquiry for a business man, even though he doesn't put it into words. The Lord wants to be glorified. It runs through the whole of the Old Testament. The prophets promulgate many laws, but those decretals which are set forth with the greatest particularity refer to this demand for glorification.

And so old Daniel Drew on his prayer bones in Wall Street and John Wanamaker kneeling in his first store praying for credit and issuing promises of glorification knew what they were doing.

"Jesus is the best friend you have," says a minister of the gospel. "He can pull you out of the worst perplexities. Why, Christ meets the business man in the street and says: 'O Business Man, I know all thy troubles: I will be with thee. I will see thee through.' Look out how you try to corner or trample on a man who is backed by the Lord God Almighty."

This is not an isolated view. The Christian preacher is continually pointing out the advantage of belonging to the Christian church. Our Christian Science friends, though they press the matter further, are not the only ones who promise treasures here as well as in Heaven.

"The wealthy men of our cities as well as of our farms are chiefly religious men," says the Rev. Wilbur F. Crafts. He tells us he got a prominent Chicago business man to make a list of 100 leading business men and the survey showed 70 church members, 24 who attended service frequently, three dissipated, and three Jews. And why not? "The Bible books," he explains, "from Joshua to Job are a series of sermons on success and failure, illustrated by brief biographies of 50 rulers, all enforcing the text which is the keystone of all Old Testament history—As long as he sought the Lord, God made him to prosper."

IV

WHEN in July, 1902, the country was on the verge of a coal famine and the anthracite regions on the verge of civil war, George Baer, the leader and spokesman of the coal barons, was appealed to in the name of religion and humanity to do something for the workers and thus avert the threatened catastrophe.

"I beg you not to be discouraged," he replied. "The rights and interests of the laboring man will be protected and cared for— not by the labor agitators but by the Christian men to whom God in His infinite wisdom has given control of the property interests of the country."

This was a well-settled view. It arose out of the very necessity of bringing all this gathering of gold into conformity with the Christian ideal. It flowed too from that development of Christian philosophy which began with Calvin when the idea of individual development was stressed and social obligation almost completely obscured. Money getting and piling was so inevitable, and the money getters so essential to the church which could count on no other means of support that it was easy to invent the idea of the Divine Trust. The rich men gathered their riches in the vineyard of the Lord. They did so as His servants and agents. The money was not theirs at all, but the Lord's and they held it in trust for Him. "The silver is mine and the gold is mine," saith the Lord. "Is not Gold the sole proprietor of everything?" asked Wesley. "God gave me my money," said Rockefeller. Here is the foundation of Rockefeller's paternalism in employment and in social giving. To William Hoster, he said: "Perhaps I might have succeeded as a preacher, if I had been good enough. I have the most radical, old-fashioned ideas about the duty of every man to contribute to the betterment of his race. I believe the power to make money is a gift from God—just as are the instincts for art, music, literature, the doctor's talent, the nurse's, yours—to de developed and used to the best of our ability for the good of mankind. Having been endowed with the gift I possess, I believe it is my duty to make money and still more money, and to use the money I make for the good of my fellow man according to the dictates of my conscience." This strange phenomenon is explained by John A. Hobson, the English economist, as a kind of partnership between God and Mammon in which God is very decidedly on the big end of the bargain. Mammon presides over the accumulating or gathering department; God, over the giving and spending departments. Mammon makes the money and God spends it.

V

Now it is very easy to poke fun at these hard-headed, profit-sharing, percentage partners of the Deity. The phenomenon, however, is not to be dismissed with a gesture of derision. The soap-box orator is ready, of course, with an explanation of the business man's piety as he is everything else. He writes them down as hypocrites who use religion as a cloak for their own wickedness or as an instrument for supporting established interests, lulling the worker to slumber, to look for his reward in Heaven instead of in his pay envelope. But these explanations have the fault of being too obvious.

Doubtless there is a good deal of hypocrisy among business men as among all sorts of men. But this does not explain their religious leanings. Certainly it does not explain John D. Rockefeller's religion. Rockefeller was a pious boy long before he was a millionaire business man. His loyalty to the Sunday School of the old gardener Deacon Sked when he was in his teens can hardly be set down by the most hardened critic as a plot to blind the workingman with religion or to shield the rascalities of an inoffensive boy. John D. did a good many things later in life when he was struggling against the forces of ignorance, cupidity, and conservatism which could hardly have gotten by the Founder of Modern Business but his religion then, as now, was about the same as it was in his youthful days at the Erie Street Baptist Church mission. John Wanamaker and John E. Searles and John D. Archbold and many other business men flaunted religion a bit ostentatiously in their later years. But Wanamaker, the Y.M.C.A. secretary, preceded Wanamaker the merchant and Archbold the minister's son antedated the munificent benefactor of Chancellor Day's Syracuse University and Archbold the writer of the famous Foraker and Bailey bribe letters. Rockefeller's many declarations of religious belief are marked by simplicity and genuineness. "I have *never* had occasion to doubt," he said. There is every reason to believe this.

A sounder explanation may be that the business man's religion is not the offspring of his business instincts. It is the other way around. His business instincts are the children of his religion. The religious boy is the father of the business man.

The most vital part of our present-day religion comes from the Old Testament. In the early days of Christianity an effort was made to apply the principles of Jesus to life and it resulted in a social order which was almost communistic. This lasted until a Roman Emperor was converted and the Christian religion became a state religion and Christian bishops became interested in state subsidies and rich benefices. After that the Christian religion began slowly to disappear and Europe went back to the Old Testament for its morals and its ethics. And the ethics of the Old Testament are bad ethics. Who has not observed the devotion of the modern

Christian to the Old Testament? The New Testament is infinitely richer in spirituality and in elevated philosophy. But the Old Testament is richer in drama. It is indeed one of the greatest of dramatic narratives, teeming with high adventure, vigorous characters, stirring descriptions, and magnificent imagery, with salacious details, tragic situations, and poetic fervor. It is the Old Testament and its heroes that the modern Christian is in love with. I do not know a worse collection of heroes to hold up for the imitation of the young mind than these gentlemen.

Abraham, afraid of being slain by some monarch who coveted his wife, passed Sarah off on Pharaoh and then on Abimelech as his sister. Sarah herself was not above telling a lie outright directly to God himself. Jacob put over on Laban when dividing the goats a deal as raw as any real estate shark ever practiced on an unsuspecting prospect. He was guilty of an abominable deception on his poor blind father to rob his own brother of his rightful blessing and he was abetted in the swindle by his mother Rebekah. As for Jacob's son Joseph he knew how to turn a pretty trick whenever it served his purpose and he became famous for one of the most complete and ruthless grain corners in history when as Pharaoh's minister he got the Egyptians at his mercy during a famine and stripped them of their cattle, their lands, and their treasure. These men were not the villains of the stories. They were not the black sheep. They were the prophets of the Lord—the holy men of the race who walked and talked with God. Jacob, fresh from his shameless swindle of his brother, was immediately confirmed without reproof by his father in the blessing he had stolen and went forthwith to the famous dream of the ladder of angels where the Lord made him a big grant of land and said to him, "Behold, I am with thee." Indeed God himself was represented as not above a little swindle, for did He not instruct Moses how to advise the Jews on the eve of their deliverance to go about borrowing jewelry from their Egyptian neighbors so that when a few days later they would move out of the house of bondage they would have a nice load of ill-gotten loot to carry off with them?

These are the books, this is the God, these are the tales, and heroes held up to us for generations. It is difficult to see how a business man raised on this pabulum, confronted with the necessity of putting over a little deal like Jacob's goat trick on Laban or

Joseph's grain corner or Moses' big jewelry loan in Egypt, could help feeling, after all, that if these great Prophets of the Lord could get away with it why could not they?

The whole emphasis of the Old Testament is laid on the rituals, as well as on the human passions with which God himself was perpetually tortured. Who can read Leviticus without having a vision of a God in a frenzy of pride and anger and egotism, strutting, swaggering, menacing, denouncing penalties, threatening death, suffering, almost frothing as He punctuates every sentence with a crescendo of boasting that "I am the Lord thy God."

This religion has held up to us a selfish, jealous, pitiless Deity. Is it not hard to believe that one who follows the Old Testament faithfully, believes it, honors it, reverences it, will be implicated almost of a necessity in a low order of ethics and will have all the emphasis of spiritual life transferred from the substance of religion and humanity to its dramatic forms.

It is impossible to read the Old Testament without getting the impression that religion was pretty much a matter of burnt offerings, of killing the bullock properly, separating the fat and washing the inwards according to the law; a religion of hosannas and praise-giving; a religion of glorification. This is the religion which was ladeled out to the young people of the last generation and which the business man received along with the rest of the faithful. And as these business men grew in years and intellectual power, their energies were consumed in their material pursuits. They had neither the time nor the inclination to stand off from their early religious ideas and scrutinize them. When the gnawings of spiritual hunger attacked them at intervals they turned very naturally to the only religious nourishment they knew, the old-fashioned religion. It was a moronic kind of religion seen nowhere in its undiluted form better than among the negroes. "Glory to God!" the ejaculation with which the colored worshiper punctuates the singing of his spirituals and the chant-like exhorting of his preachers, is a perfect expression of this religion—not a religion of thought or a religion of ethics, but a religion of praise-giving and glorification of the Lord God of Hosts.

Thus it is possible for the practical business man, confronted with the hard necessity of "succeeding" each day, to adopt practical measures to that end. That's business. And when he wants religion he puts business behind him, goes to prayer meeting or Sunday School and contributes glorification to the Lord without stint. Or he builds a church or endows a mission for the Glory of God. Perhaps it will be a gain for society when this religion of praise-giving is utterly done for; when the business man who wants to be religious will have to find refuge in a religion with fewer hymns and more ethics.[1]

CHAPTER IX. ENEMIES CLOSE IN

ALL THE opponents of Mr. Rockefeller's great company and the system he had organized were now rising to their full power. The Old Guard won a victory in the final session of Roosevelt's first administration when they defeated in the Senate the Hepburn rate regulation bill which had passed the House. Foraker was among the leaders in opposition. The Depews and Platts and Elkinses and Keans were there to strangle it. Congress adjourned amid the ceremonies of Roosevelt's inauguration. And then began that series of attacks which did not end until Rockefeller's great company was dissolved. During McKinley's administration but six anti-trust suits had been prosecuted, two of those legacies from Cleveland's lethargic régime. One of these suits was an important victory for the Sherman law—the famous Addystone Pipe case in which the early contention that restraint among producers that was mutual and did not apply to non-members was not unlawful. The Supreme Court upset that untenable position. With the advent of Roosevelt, prosecutions were begun by Knox. Knox had done nothing in his year of office under McKinley and in his first year's report did not even mention the Sherman law. Up to this time the law was practically a dead letter. But thereafter he instituted five prosecutions—one of them the Northern Securities case. Now, however, Knox was in the Senate and there began a frontal attack upon the trusts along the whole line. During Roosevelt's second term thirty-nine suits were instituted, most of them major prosecutions of the leading combinations, something which had not been done before.

Rockefeller looked with rising disgust at the whole proceeding.

[1] This chapter originally appeared in *The Forum*, Aug., 1930, and is reprinted by permission.

He remained quiet but when the attack against the packers rose in intensity he could restrain himself no longer. He gave out a statement of protest. He declared:

"If we limit opportunity we will have to put the brakes on our national development. Will the individual strive for success if he knows the hard-won prize is to be snatched from him at last by his government? We must build up, build up for years to come. Is it common sense to tell our young men on whom the future depends that they can hope for no other reward for carrying our commercial flag forward than frenzied attacks at home? And all the handicaps their government can pile on their business to satisfy the violent prejudice against them? Take the attack we made upon our own packing business, for example. I know none of the men in the beef trade. I never dealt with them. . . . But it is safe to assume from the proportions of their industry that they are sound business men. And it is safe to assume too that no business could have been built to such proportions on such false principles or by such unsound methods as they are charged with. We are too young a nation for this tearing down."

Opportunity! The land of opportunity! That was the slogan we liked. Rockefeller was still talking about individualism. The packers were sound because they had built a big business. That was his test.

II

Up from the West welled the voice of unrest. The first revolt against the House rules which would flower later under Taft in the disarming of Cannon was staged then. In Wisconsin appeared a figure which was to assume the proportions of a phenomenon later—LaFollette—"Little Bob"—who had won one campaign for governor on the direct primary issue and a second one in a fight against tax-evading railroads. Now he was demanding railroad regulation in his state. The day of populism was past. The revolt was in the Republican party. Hepburn, Republican leader in the House, sounded a warning to the railroads—"reform or a revolution at the ballot box." Public ownership sentiment was growing everywhere. Chicago elected Mayor Dunne on that issue. And this produced a sobering effect upon the minds of the railroad leaders. Then came the insurance scandals. An interesting sidelight was furnished on the attitude of men toward large scale scoundrels in business. Young James Hazen Hyde had been caught red-handed in shameful conduct of the controlling interest he held in the Equitable Life Insurance Company. Henry C. Frick had made the report which unmasked him. Then Frick went to Roosevelt to suggest that Roosevelt make Hyde ambassador to England to get him out of the Equitable. Roosevelt, oddly, was not shocked at this preposterous proposal, and actually offered to send Hyde to Belgium. But Hyde declined. The anthracite strike under the reactionary Baer in Pennsylvania shocked the country. Everywhere men saw corruption. Senator Mitchell of Oregon was convicted of accepting fees from land grabbers to represent them against the government. Senator Burton of Kansas was indicted and convicted for taking fees to represent other interests. Roosevelt kept up his attacks, undoubtedly arousing the conscience of the better elements among the business men of the nation. Against Rockefeller he directed more than one telling shot. The nation, he warned in one speech, must grapple with the problem of its great fortunes. "Of course no amount of charities," he said, "in spending such fortunes can compensate in any way for misconduct in acquiring them,"—an obvious thrust at Rockefeller. And he suggested the possibility in time of taking them over through progressive inheritance taxes. Roosevelt undoubtedly had the ear and heart of the country. But the whole troupe of Mr. Archbold's performing seals and Mr. Rockefeller's fawning beneficiaries dutifully stood to their guns for their rich patrons. The religious defenders were the most blatant. Rockefeller and Archbold indignantly denied the use of rebates and drawbacks. But in the *Bibliotheca Sacra*, one of the most dignified of religious journals, one writer called rebates quite proper and even defended the ethical character of drawbacks.

III

KANSAS had a little oil in 1899. But in 1903 oil became an industry there—a million barrels that year; five million the next. Wildcatters and adventurers swarmed over the state. Four thousand wells pumped oil and the Standard was there with its pipe lines and its refineries—two huge ones which could handle 10,000 barrels a day. The Standard was the only buyer. There was a market then for 10,000 barrels a day. But the producers insisted on pumping as high as 35,000 barrels a day. The Standard begged them to stop. But they kept on. The price sank from $1.30 to 70 cents a barrel. The producers were in arms. The Standard was robbing them, they cried. The governor proposed to build a state refinery. The Standard replied, very stupidly, with a refusal to buy any more oil in Kansas. The producers organized as they did in Pennsylvania. The legislature replied that under its constitution Kansas could not go into the oil business. But an ingenious oil man found a way. The state could own penitentiaries and could put its convicts to work. So the legislature passed a bill appropriating $100,000 to build a state penitentiary with a kerosene distillery plant attached.

The Standard undoubtedly used its power in Kansas ruthlessly. At Humboldt an independent refiner named Webster bought oil from the producers. The Standard refused to buy any more oil from them because they sold to a competitor. In the Indian Territory the company disconnected its pipes from producers who sold to a competitor. The pipe lines were the weapon which made all this possible. To reach them the legislature passed four laws —one declaring the pipe lines to be common carriers, prescribing uniform rates on railroads or pipes, putting pipes under the jurisdiction of the railroad commission and prohibiting discrimination in rates between localities. And immediately prosecutions were begun under the state anti-trust laws.

The laws did bring some relief at first. The independent refiner at Humboldt resumed shipments. "The old rate," he said, "to Kansas City was 17 cents. Now it is 8½ cents. We can do business now on the same level as the Standard."

At the same time, just as Washington was making ready for Roosevelt's inauguration, Congress passed a resolution calling on the Bureau of Corporations to investigate the Standard Oil in Kansas.

The Standard was clearly wrong in its ruthless policy but the producers were guilty of indefensible selfishness and folly. The Standard had oil in their tanks enough to last it for two years. They had paid $4,719,574 for it. Now the price had sunk to $1,200,000 below that. Yet the producers continued to pump oil and expected the Standard to go on buying.

IV

Bogus independents—this was the charge which now ran current against the Standard. Oil men said that in their fights against the Standard they were always being hampered by companies which appeared to be independent but somehow managed to deal their fellow independents mortal blows at critical moments.

Anthony N. Brady, gas magnate of New York and Chicago, had trouble with the Standard about 1890 about prices on oil for illuminating gas in Chicago. He went into the Lima-Indiana fields, formed his own oil company, and built a refinery and pipe lines. Later, having accomplished his purpose, he sold his business to the Manhattan Oil Company. Later when independents warring with the Standard went to get oil in the Lima-Indiana field they found themselves being balked in various ways by the Manhattan. They began to say the Manhattan Company was not an independent; that it was a bogus independent, which meant that it secretly belonged to the Standard. This Standard officials vigorously denied. Here, however, was what happened.

In 1899 Mr. Horace Maxwell Johnson, barrister, of London, called on Brady and said he and his associates wished to buy a going oil concern in this country. Brady ended by selling to Johnson for $615,000 the Manhattan Oil Company. The stock of the Manhattan Company was then transferred to the name of the General Industrial Development Syndicate. There were some suspicious things about the sale. First, in the contract of sale by Brady to the British interests was a stipulation that the Standard Oil Company of Indiana should supply Brady with oil for his Chicago gas works. How could Johnson or the General Industrial Development Corporation bind the Standard of Indiana to supply oil to Brady? The simple truth was that the money for the General Industrial Development Company, Ltd., had all been supplied by the Anglo-American Oil Company in London, the English subsidiary of the Standard. Thereafter the Manhattan Company operated as an independent pipe line while its officers and the Standard managers protested that there was no connection. Indeed in 1908 Mr. Archbold swore in the government's final dissolution suit that he had never heard of the General Industrial Development Company, although he and Rogers were members of the

Board of the Anglo-American Oil Company which supplied over half a million dollars for financing it.

When these facts were brought out later Rockefeller came in for a good deal of criticism for the extensive maze of intrigue and deception used in these bogus concerns. The Standard of Indiana is fighting independents in Missouri and Illinois. The Standard of Indiana belongs to the Standard of New Jersey.

UNCLE SAM, THE MODERN GIANT KILLER.
(From the *Saturday Globe*, Utica. Referring to Anti-Trust Law)

Among all the independents there is one which seems always to find a way of injuring its fellow independents. When a refiner from Cleveland comes to Lima for oil, he finds all the available oil has been bought up by the Manhattan Company. This company secretly belongs to the Industrial Development Corporation, Ltd., of England. The Industrial Development Company secretly belongs to the Anglo-American Oil Company of England. And this belongs to the Standard Oil Company of New Jersey.

There were other bogus companies. Down in Texas the independents were harassed by the Security Oil Company, a bogus independent. The stock of this company was owned by the London Commercial Trading and Investment Company. Mr. Frank B. Kellogg, government attorney prosecuting the Standard, was surprised to find that this London Commercial Company had the same offices and the same secretary as the Industrial Development Corporation which owned the Manhattan Company. Before Mr. Kellogg got through he showed that this company too in fact belonged to the Anglo-American Oil Company. There was still another mysterious independent—the Republic Oil Company. Scofield, Shurmer, and Teagle had fought John D. Rockefeller from the earliest days right up to the late nineties. Then they quit the field and sold their business to the newly organized Republic Oil Company of New York. This concern began to operate as an independent in Missouri but other independents soon found that it seemed to be on the side of the Standard. Suspicions were murmured. Charges were uttered aloud. From 26 Broadway came an indignant denial. The president of the Republic Company sent out to all its employees and managers a strong statement denying that there was any truth in this. But all the time the reports of the Republic Oil Company were being sent secretly not to 26 Broadway, but to 75 New Street, its back door. Its dummy directors met in the office of Mr. Tilford, a director of the Standard.

These were cases of bogus oil independents on a large scale. The principle was used even to harry and ruin little dealers. At Oneonta, New York, a small concern, the Tiona Oil Company at Binghamton, had gotten the best of the Standard. The dealers there were almost all selling Tiona oil. A Standard Oil tank wagon driver from Albany was sent to Oneonta. He was instructed to buy twenty-five barrels of oil from the Tiona Company at Binghamton and then to take it to Oneonta and to peddle it around from house to house at the price he paid for it. He was to put a sign on his wagon announcing that it was Tiona Oil at eight cents a gallon. The other dealers seeing this cut the price of their Tiona oil and soon there was a price war in Oneonta. It became bitter. One dealer put a sign out saying: "Free Oil—Come and Get Your Cans Filled." Of course the dealers began to blame the Tiona Oil Company, accusing it of selling to others at lower prices than the general rate and thus involving them all in a ruinous rate war. This was what the Standard wanted. A condition like this afforded it an opportunity to go into Oneonta and take a lot of the Tiona's trade. In this particular case the Tiona Oil Company investigated and learned where the rate war started.

They refused to sell any more to the Standard's secret bogus independent. He used Standard oil for a while, but hearing rumors of approaching trouble from the enraged dealers he left Oneonta while his skin was whole.

All these bogus oil independents were now to turn to ashes in Mr. Rockefeller's hands.

V

ON THE wave of a popular uprising in Missouri, Joseph W. Folk, the intrepid prosecuting attorney of St. Louis who had wrecked the ring of boodlers in that city, was elected Governor of Missouri. Into office with him went an ambitious, vigorous, and able young attorney-general, Herbert Hadley. The notorious Henry Clay Pierce, with his Waters-Pierce Company, continued to pose, despite Texas revelations, as an independent defying John D. Rockefeller and fighting the Standard for the oil trade of Missouri.

Herbert Hadley had collected evidence that the Waters-Pierce Company and the Republic Company were both bogus independents and in 1905 he brought suit to forfeit the charter of the Waters-Pierce in Missouri and to prohibit the Republic Oil and the Standard of Indiana from doing business in that state. He alleged that they were all owned by the Standard Oil, constituted a monopoly and divided the oil business of Missouri between them. The young attorney-general wanted the testimony of the Standard officials and armed with a commission to take testimony arrived in New York in January, 1906. He caught Henry H. Rogers with a subpoena, but the others scuttled away. Then began a hunt to find Rockefeller. He seemed to have dropped utterly out of sight and the whole country looked on as the process servers looked everywhere for him. At Tarrytown people said he was safe in the vast Tarrytown estate. There Superintendent Hemingway laughed at this and said he was 400 miles away. Reporters sought him in Cleveland. Friends there said he was on a private yacht cruising along the Atlantic. In February a correspondent in Naples reported that Rockefeller arrived there on the *Deutschland*. William was safe from the process servers in Italy. Dr. Charles Eaton, Rockefeller's pastor, declared he knew nothing of his patron's whereabouts. The good doctor thought it was all a great joke—"the cutest thing Rockefeller ever did. The cunningest process servers, the shrewdest detectives, and smartest reporters in the country can't find him." But soon a letter from a Lakewood resident revealed that the old monopolist was there safe from the subpoena. Hadley's commission was no good in New Jersey. Then the facts came out. When Hadley reached New York, Rockefeller literally fled from his process. With his trunks he drove to the ferry landing at Tarrytown but gave out that he was leaving Tarrytown by railroad. Reporters waited at the station but the old fox fled over the river by ferry. He took refuge in his great estate there with a guard at the gate and guards surrounding the grounds. Searchlights, operated by armed guards, were installed covering all roads. Delivery wagons were searched at the gates. Even members of his family unknown to guards had difficulty getting in. If visitors were expected a full description of them was given at the gates. Then only John received them. This John was a "guard"—a handsome, polished, courteous Irishman, said to be a graduate of Trinity College, Dublin, who spoke several languages and was said to be a very high salaried person.

About this time his son, young John D., was blessed with a new baby and the old gentleman was very anxious to see it. This softened him a little. Moreover his whereabouts had been discovered and Mr. Archbold, who was being examined at the time by Hadley, announced that Mr. Rockefeller's health was not good and that maybe if Hadley paid him a visit he would answer his questions. Hadley replied there was one place to answer questions and that was in the witness chair. But Hadley relented sufficiently to say that if Rockefeller wanted to visit New York to see his new grandchild and would ask immunity from a process server it would be granted. Whether Rockefeller asked or not, the fact is reporters found him one day on a ferryboat bound for New York. "Are you going to see the new baby?" they asked. "Oh, I can't say anything. Whenever I have anything to say I send it to the papers. I can't say anything about my plans really." In the end Hadley gave up for the time being so far as Rockefeller was concerned and went back to Missouri. A few days later Mr. Rockefeller emerged and where, more properly, than at his Sunday School? Is there a plaintive note in the talk of this certain rich man who had gone down from Pocantico to Lakewood to hide from his tormentors?

"It is wrong," he told his class, "to assume that men of immense wealth are always happy. If a man lives his life to himself and has no regard for humanity he will be the most miserable man on earth. All the money he can get will not help him to forget his discontent. To hide one's self from the world and live alone, secluded from one's fellow men like a hermit, will make a man's nature sullen and wretched. The kind of man I like is one that lives for his fellows—the one that lives in the open, contented with his lot and trying to bestow all the good he can on humanity."

Hadley, however, kept at his job and succeeded in getting Mr. Rockefeller and his colleagues on the stand. Every conceivable obstacle was put in the way of the hearing. At the first session Standard attorneys insisted that testimony be taken in long hand. When the responsible executives reached the witness chair they took refuge behind the familiar "I decline to answer on the advice of counsel." They denied that territory was divided between Standard units to prevent competition. Hadley asked:

"Does the Standard Oil of Ohio have a limited territory?"

Rockefeller answered: "It has not."

"Has it not in the last five years?"

"Not to my knowledge. Its field is the world. That is its mission, to light the world with the cheapest and best."

When Rockefeller made this answer Hadley had before him maps showing the territory within which the Standard of Ohio and other Standard units were required to operate, maps which were kept on every executive's desk.

Hadley had difficulty catching Henry Clay Pierce as a witness. When he was finally brought to the stand he unbosomed himself with amazing frankness. For years Rockefeller and his associates had resolutely denied that the Standard had any interest in the Waters-Pierce Company. Pierce himself, to get back into Texas under Bailey's counseling, had sworn that the Standard people owned no stock in his company. Now he testified to the following story: When he reincorporated to get back into Texas in 1901 all the stock was issued in his name. Mr. Charles Pratt went with him to the Mechanics National Bank in New York where Pierce transferred 2,750 shares, representing the Standard interest, to a Mr. Garth, cashier of the bank, retaining 1,250 for himself.

ENEMIES CLOSE IN

Dividends were sent to another person until 1904 when Garth turned the stock over to Mr. M. M. Van Buren and it was then registered in Van Buren's name. Van Buren was John D. Archbold's son-in-law. That settled the question of the Standard interest in the Pierce Company and down in Texas Pierce was promptly indicted for false swearing.

Pierce further swore to Hadley that the Standard dictated his policy and that territory was allotted to him covering Missouri, beginning at Hannibal and extending diagonally across the state to a point south of Fort Scott, thence along the route of the Missouri, Kansas, and Texas Railroad, including Oklahoma, Louisiana, and Texas. North of that line belonged to the Standard of Indiana.

Hadley had established all his charges against the Standard. After denials by Archbold and others the Standard was forced to admit that it owned the Republic Company. The Standard of Indiana then made a remarkable proposal. It suggested to the State of Missouri that it would incorporate a separate company in Missouri and the stock for four years would stand in the name of two trustees, one selected by the state and one by the Indiana corporation, all under the approval of the Supreme Court. The state declined the offer but a more outright invitation to government regulation has never been known in business. Hadley obtained complete judgments against the three defendants and all were affirmed by the higher courts, which also approved a fine of $50,000 against each of the three defendants. This was a disastrous battle for the Standard.

VI

THE ARROGANCE and folly of the Standard Oil management in Kansas were now to bear bitter fruit. As a result of that episode, James R. Garfield, under the Campbell resolution, had been investigating the Standard performances in Kansas as well as upon the larger scale of national operation. Garfield planned a series of reports covering production, transportation, refining, and marketing. When Congress convened in December, 1906, following Roosevelt's election, the Hepburn bill for railroad rate regulation was immediately pressed for passage. The President gave the subject of rate regulation first place in his message and with little or no delay the Hepburn bill was passed by the House by an overwhelming majority—346 to 7. But in the Senate, packed with the representatives of the railroads and the trusts, the Committee couldn't agree on a report. Elkins, coal and railroad and utility magnate, chairman of the Senate Committee, and his colleagues objected to the clause which permitted the Interstate Commerce Commission to fix rates and put those rates into effect immediately. They wanted to reserve to the roads their appeal to the courts and have the new rates suspended pending court action. The bill was finally reported out without recommendation and Washington enjoyed the spectacle of Roosevelt's rate bill committed in the Senate to the direction of his bitterest enemy, the Democratic Tilman of South Carolina, who had been mortally insulted by Roosevelt when the President struck his name from the Senate invitation list of the White House. Foraker, Elkins, and the whole railroad and oil Camorra fought the measure.

In the midst of this battle Roosevelt sent to the Senate a report of the Corporation Bureau made by Garfield dealing with transportation in the oil industry. In transmitting it Roosevelt said: "The Standard Oil has benefited almost up to the present moment by secret rates, many of these secret rates being clearly unlawful." This really summarized Garfield's findings. The report itself contained an impressive array of facts outlining countless discriminations on the New York Central, New York, New Haven, and Hartford, the Illinois Central, Southern, Chicago, and Alton, and the Chicago, Burlington, and Quincy. Archbold, for the Standard, replied to the Garfield report, called it "unjust and unfair," complained that the investigation had been made to study the Kansas case and was now used to influence railroad legislation while Garfield refused to make public the facts in Kansas. He insisted no rebates were found, that the complaints were merely about so-called "secret rates" and he denied that competitors were crushed, insisting that there were 125 independent refineries then doing business. Roosevelt was denounced for making Garfield's report on Transportation public out of its regular order as if there were some sort of infamy in this. But Roosevelt's blow was well-timed and aimed. Garfield's report was released by the President May 2nd and before the month was out the rate bill was passed in the Senate and became a law. The cause of the Standard was hardly helped by the exhibition, throughout the discussions, of Mr. Rockefeller's flight from the processes of the Missouri courts.

VII

THROUGHOUT these events Rockefeller was planning his first trip abroad to visit his daughter, Mrs. Strong. A strange malady had fallen on this young woman. The daughter of the world's richest man, a nervous disorder had brought her down to where she lived in continual fear of dying in poverty. Just after the passage of Roosevelt's rate bill and the departure of Attorney-General Hadley for Missouri, Rockefeller sailed on the *Deutschland* accompanied by his wife, his daughter, Mrs. Parmalee Prentice, and his physician, Dr. M. F. Biggar of Cleveland. About the same time Andrew Carnegie sailed for Europe. Yet how different the setting-out of these two men. Carnegie hard, ruthless, guilty of far more serious breaches of established ethics than Rockefeller, left acclaimed by newspapers and a host of friends to go to a kind of triumphal tour of Europe, received by ministers, writers, and potentates. Rockefeller's departure was cloaked in the usual secrecy, his name not on the passenger list, no one at the steamer to bid good-by save his son. When the cry of "All Ashore!" was sounded young John D. turned and said: "Well, I guess I shall go ashore, father." "All right," replied the elder Rockefeller and without more ado or even a handshake the son walked down the gangplank.

Immediately the newspapers said Rockefeller had gone to avoid appearing as a witness before the Interstate Commerce Commission. This was not true. But he was hardly comfortably established at Compiègne, France, when in July he was indicted in Hancock County, Ohio, along with several directors of the Standard of Ohio for violating the Valentine anti-trust act of Ohio. The warrant out now was for his arrest and at 26 Broadway it was said that he would return July 28th. The sheriff of Hancock County announced he would be at the pier to arrest the harried oil man. When he did return he was an unhappy man who had need of all his fortitude. On the way home, as on the journey to France, he found himself shadowed by two reporters. "That was hard to bear," he said, "but I don't think they liked it either." He left behind, in a state of great exhaustion, his stricken daughter. Stories of the death of his mysterious father had gotten into the papers and it is possible they were true. The country was ablaze with criticism, denunciation, exposure of himself and his career. It was known that Roosevelt was preparing a major blow.

Almost for the first time in public he softened the surface of the soul which he exposed to his enemies. To a reporter he opened his heart. "I never despair," he said a little wistfully. "Sometimes things that are said of me are cruel and they hurt, but I am never a pessimist. I believe in man and the brotherhood of man and I am confident that everything will come out for the good of all in the end." He talked about life and men. "I know you have tried hard to see me," he said. "I admire persistence. It is commendable, especially in young men, and it will win in the end." Then he added a word about the country which was then bristling with hatred and damnation of him. "Europe is a nice place, but I love my country best. Yes, all the hard things that my countrymen say of me can never be cruel enough to offset my love of country and home."

He was not arrested at the dock. His counsel had arranged for his appearance in Ohio and when he landed he went in a few days to Forest Hill in Cleveland. There he expressed the hope that the public suspend judgment until both sides should be heard. He was becoming more and more sensitive to criticism. To some one else he said that he wished he and the public might become better acquainted. He began to think that perhaps his side of the story was not being heard at all. He had made little effort to get it heard save by legislators and courts and Congress and officials and then the talking had been done mainly in that form of utterance which Mr. Archbold specialized in. As for the public, Mr. Rockefeller now perceived that it had some sort of mysterious power in its hands. It got its information chiefly from headlines. "We are leading an awful fast life in this country," he told a reporter in Cleveland. "It is simply rush along all the time. The newspapers for the most part keep pace with the times. They show the life of their readers. Their life is accelerated by the headlines; concentrated excitement all bound up in a few words. People see the big lines, rush to read the paper, rush off again to read some other paper and rush to a fire. It's rush, rush, rush all the time." He entered a plea of "Not Guilty" in the Ohio suit and then settled down in Cleveland for the Winter.

VIII

THIS was not a pleasant Winter for Rockefeller. He was now one of the celebrities of the world. His name was a household word on every continent. Wherever he went crowds gathered to have a peep at him and to a man of John D.'s yearning for privacy in all that he did this was a source of endless annoyance. Through the Spring the papers were filled with the uproar in Washington as Roosevelt and the balky Republican Senators battled over Roosevelt's program. After Garfield's report the public awaited with interest the blow which was expected to fall on the Standard crowd. This heightened the interest in Rockefeller. Every Sunday when he appeared at the Euclid Avenue Baptist Church crowds gathered there for a glimpse. And among them were reporters seeking interviews, photographers hunting pictures, cranks seeking redress, mendicants of every station looking for help and a sprinkling of people who had a grievance against Standard Oil who came for justice. Rockefeller found it necessary to employ a bodyguard who would look out for him, chiefly in navigating these crowds. Dr. Eaton, the pastor, was in a state of frequent apprehension for the safety of his distinguished worshiper. "Keep a sharp look-out for Mr. Rockefeller," said Eaton to Rockefeller's protective companion. "I fear these ugly crowds that gather to see him get in and out of his automobile." Finally Eaton asked for special plain-clothes men to watch the crowds.

A good many of the curious gave cause for apprehension. One day a drunken man stepped out of the crowd and put his hand on Rockefeller's shoulder. Before he could open his mouth, Rockefeller's attendant took the offending hand and shook it warmly while the oil man slipped away. Another Sunday an old lady stepped in front of Rockefeller. She had come all the way from Kentucky and announced she had brought her trunk and expected Rockefeller to care for her while she remained in Cleveland. She had been hit by a Standard Oil wagon and wanted Rockefeller to settle with her. Another Sunday a well-dressed man with a large bundle of letters in his hands blocked Rockefeller's path into the church. He announced dramatically he was a nobleman and an officer and that he wanted justice. Rockefeller, with the pastor, hurried forward into the doorway and up the stairs, the "nobleman" behind him and Rockefeller's attendant in hot pursuit. Upstairs Rockefeller and the clergyman locked themselves in while the attendant got rid of the intruder.

One night a trustee informed Rockefeller that there was a socialist present occupying a pew opposite Rockefeller's. The oil man kept his eye on the man throughout the service, who in turn eyed Rockefeller furtively. Rockefeller intended to speak that night but was so disturbed that he kept his peace. After this incident Rockefeller confided to his attendant that Mrs. Rockefeller thought he ought not to speak at meetings.

Above all he was in mortal fear of reporters. One day a reporter of a Cleveland paper accosted him. Rockefeller looked at him and recognizing him said: "You are the only reporter who ever quoted me correctly." Later he said: "I am not afraid of reporters publishing what I say but what I do not say." Hence he steered clear of them always.

With the coming of Spring Rockefeller went to Pocantico where he resumed the development and expansion of his estate. He began the building of his new home to replace the one destroyed by fire. He planned his house so that the sun would shine in it all day. He looked after every detail of the plan himself and was so busy with it that he did not have time to play golf.

About this time Rockefeller's secrecy about his health manifested itself. There was little doubt that he had retired from active business management because of his health and frequent references were made to it by members of his family. It was a subject in which the public which disliked Rockefeller got a good deal of satisfaction. The spectacle of the richest man on earth unable to eat a square meal was a little too good not to be enjoyed. Endless quips and many grim jests were made about it. About two years before a report from Atlantic City was printed that Rockefeller had offered a standing reward of a million dollars to any one who would restore his stomach. This was later denied but the story persisted and was passed about with evident relish. When Rockefeller arrived from Europe attended by Dr. Biggar, the latter, when asked by reporters about Mr. Rockefeller's health, replied a little crisply: "Mr. Rockefeller is in the best of health. Mr. Rockefeller has enjoyed excellent health for the last eighteen years."

ENEMIES CLOSE IN

As the years have gone by this attitude with reference to the illness episode has been adopted as the settled policy of Rockefeller and his immediate family and entourage. Inquirers are told today that Mr. Rockefeller was not sick when he retired, that as a matter of fact instead of suffering from stomach trouble he was overweight and his first care was to reduce his weight. It is, as a matter of fact, a question whether Rockefeller was ever very seriously ill. In spite of the denials today he did suffer with stomach trouble but there is some ground for suspecting that the ailment was not a very grave one and that it was greatly exaggerated in Rockefeller's own mind, taking on, in fact, for a while the form of an obsession. In any case about this time his health was greatly improved. He was again able to eat freely, though he continued to eat with discretion. Moreover he was now approaching seventy, growing older, and he continued to follow the careful program of rest, exercise, and moderate eating which had brought about his recovery. Secret in all things, he now sought to be secret even about his illness.

He had now adopted that regimen of orderly living which he has kept up to this day and in which his life was coming to be lived in a fixed orbit. He rose at 6, breakfasted at 8, and from 9:30 to noon played golf usually with some visitors. After lunch he rested on a couch. After this he went for an automobile ride which he never failed in no matter what the weather.

All this time the threatened attack from Roosevelt was much on his mind. He got many visits from Samuel C. T. Dodd, chief counsel of the company, and once actually made a visit to his office at 26 Broadway, the first in many years. He visited the luncheon room and was surprised at the number of new faces he saw there. "We old fellows are being pushed aside," he commented.

Roosevelt at least would do something to accelerate the push. The blow he had been preparing was now ready. The first phase of it came in the Fall. It was an indictment of the Standard Oil Company of Indiana for violations of the Elkins Act.

The company was charged with accepting secret rates on shipments over the Chicago and Alton Railroad from Whiting, Indiana, to East St. Louis. The published rate on oil between these points was eighteen cents a barrel. The Standard was charged with getting a secret rate of six cents for three years. Garfield had traced 1903 carload shipments and each carload shipment was set down as a separate offense and made the subject of a separate count.

The other case was instituted in Missouri and was an action under the Sherman anti-trust law to dissolve the Standard Oil monopoly. It was alleged that the Standard Oil Company of New Jersey was a holding company which had merely stepped into the shoes of the old trust, that this holding company held the stocks of all the other subsidiaries and ruled them as a single concern; that it used them to destroy competition and enjoyed a practical monopoly of the business of refining and piping oil. Of all the great suits against the Standard this was to be the most sensational.

Rockefeller was at Forest Hill when the news of this attack was brought to him. The same day news came from France that his daughter Bessie, the wife of Charles A. Strong, had died the preceding day at Cannes.

The same day a Grand Jury in Ohio brought in another indictment. In various places a dozen actions were being pressed against him and his company. The tide seemed now to be running strong against him.

As for the indictments and suits, they made a stir when brought in, but in a little while men said nothing would come of them. Even the grave and conservative Dr. Lyman Abbott in the *Outlook* thought the forces "that make for combination are too strong. . . . Can wealthy and influential law breakers be made to obey the law?" People everywhere answered to themselves "No."

CHAPTER X. THE BIG STICK STRIKES

THE YEAR 1907 opened with major actions pending against Rockefeller and Standard Oil in three spots—in Ohio, Indiana, and Missouri. At this moment, Rockefeller, now within hailing distance of seventy, was for the first time seriously concerned about his fame. The flood of abuse even within the church and the endless attacks made this aging man feel that as he neared the grave he was leaving a very dubious monument.

An interview with an able reporter, Mr. William Hoster, had served to open his eyes a little to this problem of publicity. Hoster had been sent by his paper to cover Rockefeller's European trip. With a good deal of tact, he managed to get acquainted with Rockefeller, through Dr. Biggar, and to reveal frankly his mission. Rockefeller took a fancy to him and on one occasion in Compiègne opened up his heart. When Rockefeller complained of the harshness of the public judgment Hoster surprised him by saying:

"It is your own fault, Mr. Rockefeller. You refuse to see reporters or to make known your side of the case. Here I have had to come all the way to Europe to get you to talk to me and even now you insist nothing shall be printed. It's your own fault."

"So it's all my fault," he returned, eyeing the reporter quizzically. Then he shook his head. "Perhaps it is.

"They will know me better when I'm dead, Mr. Hoster," he continued. "There has been nothing in my life that will not bear the utmost scrutiny. Is it not patent that I have been made into a sort of frightful ogre, to slay which has become a favorite resource of men seeking public favor? It is not from the body of the people whence I sprang that these denunciations come, but from the self-seekers who would be leaders. What advantages had I that every other poor boy did not possess? No one could have begun life with less than I had. Does any fair man accuse me of grinding him down?

"I am talking to you now as man to man. I am not one who wears his heart on his sleeve, and I cannot bring myself to make fit answer to these repeated slanders. But it is a fact that all of this criticism comes from, or is inspired by, men who have been my business competitors—men who would have bested me if I had not bested them—and from public officials seeking favor, agitators and demagogues."

A little later he said: "I believe Mr. Roosevelt is a sincere man. He undoubtedly has the confidence of the people. He is robust, virile, dashing; he appeals to their imagination somewhat as Napoleon appealed. A man so busy cannot be always right. We are all bound to make mistakes at times. I think he does not always grasp every side of a question. Sometimes I wish that he might be more fair. I do not mean that he is consciously unjust. He is often uninformed."

"As a matter of fact, Mr. Rockefeller," Mr. Hoster inquired, "do you really know exactly what you are worth?"

"Of course I do," he replied. "That is simply a matter of looking at the balance sheet which is submitted at the close of the day."

"And you do not possess a billion?"

"Nothing like it—not by one-third of that amount. I want to make clear to you the injury that is done to me by these persistent stories that I am worth a billion dollars. They provoke in the minds of thousands thoughts which lead to great unhappiness. Is any one so foolish as to believe that there is a man in the United States worth a billion dollars? Do you understand how much money that is? That story is a ridiculous fable."

In February then when he made his greatest gift, $32,000,000 to the General Education Board, while many editors hailed it as a magnificent and intelligent endowment, there were many who believed he was moved by a desire to brighten the colors of the cloud in which, of necessity, the judges then considering his cases must view him. He had previously given $11,000,000 to the Board. Now he added $32,000,000 more, the gift being transmitted by his son. By this time Frederick T. Gates was president of the Board.

II

Hardly was the gift published when the irrepressible state of Texas indicted Henry Clay Pierce for false swearing and instituted ouster proceedings against the Waters-Pierce Company based on the revelations in Hadley's Missouri suit. Pierce had sworn that Standard Oil had no interest in his company when under Bailey's advice he applied for reëntry to Texas in 1900. The habit of resting heavily upon fictions can poison the mind in the end. When Pierce was reported to have been indicted for perjury he indignantly replied: "That is not true. I was never indicted for perjury. It was for false swearing." "You lie," cried Jacques in the "Two Orphans" when accused of stealing a coat. "It was a cloak."

Here we may dismiss Pierce from this history. He resisted extradition but Governor Folk turned him over to Texas. He was tried in November, 1909, in a sensational trial but acquitted, since the only evidence of his false swearing was his own statement in the Missouri court. The victory, however, was a dubious one. For before this his company, the Waters-Pierce Company, belonging mainly to the Rockefeller interests, was convicted for violating the Texas anti-trust law and fined $1,623,900. Pierce paid the fine to prevent confiscation of the company's property. But now the state compelled him to sell all the property of his company in Texas and this brought $1,431,741—$200,000 less than the fine. The sale, however, was just one more fiction. In

THE NEW PIPE LINE.
(By Davenport in the *Evening Mail*, New York)

1911 when the Standard Oil dissolution decree was affirmed by the Supreme Court, the company was considering the expulsion of Pierce. It planned to elect the now famous Col. Robert W. Stewart president. The fight came to a head at the annual meeting of the company in 1912 and after a bitter struggle, which went through the courts, the Standard sold out its holdings to Pierce. But this vigorous, unscrupulous, audacious man continued in trouble and in 1923 died leaving less than a million out of a fortune which must have been not less than twenty times that much at one time.

III

ON AUGUST 13, 1907, the country was treated to a genuine sensation when Judge Kenesaw Mountain Landis, in Chicago, fined the Standard Oil Company $29,000,000. Rockefeller was visiting an old friend and distant relative, a farmer named William Humiston, outside of Cleveland, when news of the fine was brought to him. He seemed little disturbed by it but continued to talk of

A FLOOD OF CARTOONS LIKE THIS PLAYED ON THE MANNER IN WHICH ROCKEFELLER WAS CHARGED WITH PAYING FINES AND MAKING GIFTS AND COLLECTING THEM FROM OIL CONSUMERS.
(From *Minneapolis Tribune*)

farming, lunched under the trees in the farmyard and during the meal lectured his host on the evils of over-eating. Later a reporter called on him and he gave out a statement. "A great injustice has been done the company," he said. "It was from ignorance on how the great business was founded. *For all these years no one has known and no one seems to have cared how it came into existence.*"

Judge Landis had held the company guilty on 1,462 counts, calling each carload shipped at the secret rate a separate offense.

When the jury found the company guilty Landis called on its counsel to furnish him with statements of the company's net profits from 1903 to 1905. They complied and showed a profit of $81,336,994 in 1903; $61,570,110 in 1904, and $57,459,356 in 1905. Counsel had urged that the so-called secret rate injured no one as there were no other shippers of oil over the road. "It is novel indeed," replied Landis, "for a convicted defendant to urge the complete triumph of a dishonest course as a reason why such course should go unpunished." He thereupon imposed a fine of $20,000 for each of the 1,462 counts, thus arriving at the figure of $29,240,000.

The fine instantly hoisted Landis into fame. He was then just forty-one years old. He had begun life, after graduating at law, as secretary to Roger Q. Gresham when he was Cleveland's Secretary of State and later practiced law successfully in Chicago, representing many corporations and railroads.

While most papers praised Landis and even lamented that jail sentences were not possible, for the first time in Rockefeller's history a large number of editors were on the other side. It is "yellowism in the judiciary," said the Brooklyn *Eagle*. "No theory of law or justice sustains such a thumping penalty," complained the New York *Times*. The Hartford *Post* swallowed the whole Standard Oil defense and criticized Landis. "Mere futile sensation," "Playing to the galleries," "An imposition on its face," "Claptrap and farce," "Opéra Comique," said papers from Boston to Denver.

The Standard itself, which now had in Mr. Jerome I. Clark a press agent, went into a frenzy of defensive publicity. Men worked through the night sending out huge packing cases full of copies of a statement of the company's side framed for employees but sent to newspapers and schools and others.

IV

A WEEK after this famous fine, there was a severe slump in the stock market. Some stocks, such as Union Pacific, went off as much as seventeen points. Standard Oil stock, oddly enough, resisted longest, but after a few days sank from 500 to 421. Immediately Wall Street and corporation leaders sent up a chorus that Roosevelt was driving the country headlong into ruin. The Landis decision was blamed for shaking confidence in "business." Harriman always claimed this started the 1907 panic. Meantime Roosevelt had directed suits against the Tobacco Trust and the Powder Trust. The Interstate Commerce Commission was investigating Harriman's vast schemes and reported with alarm that Harriman's consolidations had ended railroad competition in one-third the territorial area of the United States. Franklin K. Lane, who wrote the report, recommended that railroads be prohibited from owning shares in other roads. To a reporter Rockefeller said: "The runaway policy of the present administration can have but one result. It means disaster to the country, financial depression, and chaos." Roosevelt was not the man to be deterred. He denounced the "malefactors of great wealth" as the real guilty agents behind the depression. "As far as I am concerned," Roosevelt said, "and for the eighteen months of my administration that remain, there will be no change in the policy we have steadily pursued, no let up in the effort to secure the honest observance of the law, for I regard this contest as one to determine who shall rule the government." Rockefeller confided to a friend later that his statement about the "runaway administration" had been made to a reporter with the understanding that it would not be published. "I could have cried for that young man," he said, referring to the youth who had betrayed him.

As a matter of fact, there had been a serious slump in railroad shares and a slight stock market panic back in March many months before the Landis fine. Then Harriman blamed Roosevelt. The situation had been brewing for some time. It had been created by the irresponsible, selfish, and wild speculations of the large group of railroad, mining, and industrial promoters who had been permitted through two administrations to carry forward their audacious schemes. The guilty hands behind the whole bad business were not those of Roosevelt and Kellogg and Garfield and Landis and the men who sought to check the frenzy, but those of Harriman and Morse and Heintz and Flint and Rogers and William Rockefeller and Morgan, who had pumped the financial structure of the country full of water. The shaky edifice was now springing leaks everywhere. The water was running out at a hundred rotten holes.

When about two months later the crisis was reached with the failure first of the corrupt combinations of Heintz and Morse and then a flood of rumors about banks everywhere, the crumbling of stock market values and finally the crash of the Knickerbocker Trust Company, the only thing which the financial saviors thought of was the stock market. Roosevelt's Secretary of the Treasury George B. Cortelyou was induced to release $25,000,000 of government funds to national banks in New York. J. P. Morgan, who had rushed back from an Episcopal convention to save the situation, became virtual dictator. In his library, with the Stillmans and Garys and lesser figures moving about like so many secretaries, he moved the pieces on the board. The government funds placed by Cortelyou were used to make loans to stock brokers to save the crashing values in stocks, many of them worthless. Roosevelt was bitterly criticized for this, but he knew nothing of it and it is probable that both he and Cortelyou were imposed on by the great bankers who were managing things. Morgan began to assemble funds to steady credit as he did in 1893. Again it was Stillman who brought in large gobs of the necessary cash. They got $10,000,000 from "Uncle John" as Rockefeller referred to himself in describing the incident. "They always come to Uncle John when there is trouble," he commented with ironic relish.

Then came an incident which was to call for an endless amount of explanation later. Colonel Oliver H. Payne, so long treasurer of the Standard, was now busy chiefly managing his great fortune. The firm of Moore and Schley was one of the most important brokerage houses in Wall Street. It handled accounts for the insiders and was looked upon as one of the most solid in America. As a matter of fact, at the time the firm held an immense amount of the stock of the Tennessee Coal and Iron Company as collateral for loans. Payne was not only one of their largest clients but a close friend. The Tennessee Coal and Iron stock was then almost worthless on the market. The brokerage firm was on the verge of bankruptcy. Payne advanced them large sums and exchanged securities with them to save them. His loans were threatened with complete loss if Moore and Schley were not rescued. Payne had his attorney go to J. P. Morgan and lay the matter before the dictator. He explained that there was no hope for Moore and Schley but to have the United States Steel Corporation buy the Tennessee Coal and Iron Company. This would save Moore and Schley's loans and also Payne's. The United States Steel Corporation wanted this company though Judge Gary and Henry C. Frick pretended at the time that they did not. The situation offered them an opportunity to swallow the Tennessee Company if properly managed. Gary and Frick hustled by special train at midnight to Washington and called on Roosevelt in the morning before nine

"WE'VE BOTH HAD A PERFECTLY CORKING GOOD TIME!"
(From the *Daily Eagle*, Brooklyn, N. Y.)

o'clock. They explained to him that the Steel Corporation was urged to take over the Tennessee Company because an "important" company held an immense amount of the stock as collateral and was threatened with ruin. In fact it would collapse unless the Steel Company took over the Tennessee concern before the opening of the Stock Exchange. The collapse of this "company" would be a crushing disaster, they explained. Their only anxiety was their fear that the President would not understand their motives and if they took this iron concern it would result in a prosecution

JOHN D. ROCKEFELLER AND MRS. JOHN D. ROCKEFELLER IN 1904

Upper left, IDA TARBELL. *Upper right*, FRANK S. MONNETT. *Lower left*, GEORGE RICE. *Lower right*, HENRY DEMAREST LLOYD

under the Sherman law, a thing they had been worrying about for some time. The gravity of the situation appealed to Roosevelt. They did not disclose the name of the "company" that was in danger and he supposed it was a trust company. He assured them that he would not consider it any part of his duty to interpose objections. Gary telephoned the Morgan offices a little before ten o'clock that everything was all right and when the Exchange opened almost the first announcement was that the Steel Corporation had taken over the Tennessee Coal and Iron Company. It was not until the Stanley investigation in Taft's administration that it was learned that the whole performance had been staged on one side to save, not a trust company as Roosevelt supposed, but a stock brokerage house and on the other side to enable the Steel Corporation to gobble up another powerful subsidiary without bringing on a collision with the impetuous president.

There is a little more to this story which has to do with the manner in which Payne and Pratt—the two Standard Oil directors—became interested in the Tennessee Coal and Iron Company. The Steel Corporation had really wanted the Tennessee company. Sometime before George Kissler, an able and audacious Wall Street promoter and operator, had gotten control of the Tennessee company. He had bought the stock in the open market at from $22 to $97 a share. Then he decided to unload and through the firm of Moore and Schley organized a pool to push the price of the stock up. Moore and Schley interested Payne and Pratt in this pool—a pure gambling operation. Kissler sold out 225,000 shares of his stock to this pool, at $115 a share. Moore and Schley held all this stock as collateral.

Having sold out to the pool, Kissler went into the open market and quietly accumulated the remaining 110,000 shares of the company, a powerful minority interest. When the pool heard of this its members became worried. A gambler like Kissler in the market with such a block of stock could mean no good for their speculation. Moore and Schley then got in touch with Kissler and entered an agreement that he and the pool would not sell any part of their stock at less than $150.

Then they tried to sell out to the Steel Corporation. Morgan favored buying. But Gary and Frick balked, insisting they could buy, if they held out, at half the price. Meantime the dark clouds of the panic of 1907 gathered over the market. Stock prices sagged. There were no buyers for Tennessee Coal and Iron Company. The Steel Corporation wanted it but held aloof. Hence the price of the company's stock also slumped. It was thus Moore and Schley found themselves trapped holding this huge amount of collateral. Payne and Pratt and the whole pool were involved. Payne advanced securities to Moore and Schley to tide them over. But as the approaching panic gathered force, Payne and his associates faced heavy losses and the brokers, ruin, if they could not unload the Tennessee Coal and Iron Company stock at a good price. It was at this point that Payne's attorney went to J. P. Morgan and appealed to him to save the brokerage house. It was then this famous deal, to save a couple of stock brokers and their rich clients from loss in a gambling pool, was put over on the unsuspecting President.

However, neither of these expedients—the Cortelyou $25,-000,000 government deposits nor the Tennessee Coal and Iron Company purchase—averted the panic. By December the country was in the midst of a serious financial depression.

V

THE LANDIS fine was of course promptly appealed to the United States Circuit Court of Appeals. But the Standard Oil effort did not stop there. Roosevelt got many letters expressing amazement at the destructive character of his crusade against business. Lee Higginson of Boston wrote him begging him to mitigate the vigor of his thrusts. Henry C. Frick, who was close to Roosevelt, felt the fine was the most serious cloud over-hanging the country. He went to Philander C. Knox, then in the Senate, and urged him to intervene with the President. Knox prudently suggested that Frick write Roosevelt. Frick did and urged the President to take some steps to have the Department of Justice settle the matter to which Roosevelt replied that it would be better to have the Standard Oil attorney make some proposal. Nothing came of it all, however, and the case had to take its course through the appellate courts. A year later, in August, 1908, that court repeated the sensation of the original judgment by reversing Landis' decision, revoking the fine, ordering the case back for a new trial and severely criticizing Judge Landis for his decision.

The opinion was read by Judge Grosscup who held that Landis

erred in considering each carload shipment as a separate offense and he stigmatized the big fine as an "abuse of judicial discretion." Judge Grosscup ordered a retrial of the case and Landis promptly let it be known that he would not sit in a second trial. Roosevelt was aroused by the reversal and spoke his mind. "The President would regard it as a gross miscarriage of justice if through any technicalities of any kind the defendants escaped the punishment which would have been meted out to any weaker defendant guilty of an offense. The President will do everything in his power to prevent such a miscarriage of justice." He directed Attorney-General Bonaparte to bring into the case Frank B. Kellogg who had successfully prosecuted the Northern Securities case and was now pressing the Government's dissolution suit against Standard Oil. Judge Grosscup refused to comment on the President's implied strictures in spite of the fact that he came in for a good deal of savage criticism. He had had a very distinguished career as a liberal jurist, had written several vigorous anti-trust decisions, including one in the packers' cases and was a student of the economic conditions of the times. In spite of this there is little doubt that the decision, as pointed out at the time by the San Francisco *Bulletin*, produced a very unpleasant effect upon the minds of the people.

CHAPTER XI. MURDER WILL OUT

MR. JOHN D. ARCHBOLD had a negro valet, named James Wilkins, who for twenty years had been a trusted employee. Wilkins had a son named Willie Winkfield and he, with Charles Stump, worked as messengers and file clerks in the office of the great Mr. Archbold. Willie was well aware of the important spot in which he worked and was more than a little interested in some of the documents which he saw on Mr. Archbold's desk and in the files. There were letters and wires to great statesmen, lordly senators, rulers of men, reaching as high as vice-president of the United States and even to certain presidential aspirants.

Willie found himself in 1904 in need of funds for some reason.

The 1904 election was in full blast and it must have occurred to the wily negro that some of the letters that went across his employer's desk would make mighty ammunition in an election. The thought took root and germinated in his mind. He confided it to Stump, who was a white man, and the two decided to try their hand at a little profitable pilfering. They went to the New York *American,* Hearst's morning paper, informed the managing editor that they were in possession of some very valuable documents and proposed to sell them. Finding him a prospective customer, Winkfield and Stump then hung around Archbold's files as much as possible. They took away at night letters and telegrams which they delivered to one of the editors of the New York *American.* The documents were photostated and returned to Archbold's files. They got $20,500 for their loot. Sometime later for some reason wholly unconnected with their offense they were dismissed from the company. The editor's eyes opened wide as he read these incriminating documents and he took them at once to his chief, William Randolph Hearst. Hearst did not publish the letters then but put them away in his safe to await the day when it would suit his purpose to bring them to light. Mr. Archbold continued to sit at his desk and write to his political allies and employees, little dreaming of the sword which hung over his head. Through 1907 and the early part of 1908 Taft and Foraker jockeyed for the Republican presidential nomination, though as the convention approached it was clear Taft, with Roosevelt's powerful backing, would get the prize. For a while the Standard Oil crowd, bitter in their hatred of Roosevelt, were prepared to raise an immense fund to punish the warlike President. However, Taft was named, with Bryan as Democratic candidate. William Randolph Hearst brought out his Independence League party and nominated Thomas L. Hisgen, of Massachusetts, for President. Hisgen was a manufacturer of axle grease from crude petroleum and had been at war with the Standard Oil for years.

The campaign was moving along rather dully when on September 17th, 1908, Hearst appeared at Memorial Hall in Columbus, Ohio, in Taft's own state, as a speaker with Thomas L. Hisgen. Hisgen droned along in a tedious criticism of the trusts. Then Hearst arose. In the high inadequate voice for which he is noted he began to read some of the letters which had rested for three years in his safe. They were to Senator Foraker and Mark Hanna. The letters directing these powerful gentlemen what to do were interspersed with others remitting certificates of deposit for large sums. The speech was artfully contrived and when it was printed through the country in full the next day with copies of the letters it created a profound sensation.

At 26 Broadway the leaders were thrown into consternation. Archbold of course issued a denial. Foraker, wiser in such matters, admitted the genuineness of the letters but said that they dealt with state affairs in Ohio where he held no official position and hence were quite ethical. He added, "That I was employed as counsel for the Standard Oil Company at the time and presumably compensated for my services was common knowledge. At least I never made any effort to conceal it. On the contrary I was pleased to let people know I had such clients." He had forgotten how he had denied his employment to an Associated Press reporter when asked about it at the time. However, Hearst was ready with a crushing reply in his next speech. He read a letter from Archbold to Foraker about the Jones bill pending in the United States Senate intended to strengthen the Sherman anti-trust law. About the same time he received from Archbold a certificate of deposit for $50,000. Foraker replied that letters and telegrams commending him poured in from all over the country. The eccentric Col. Henry Watterson wrote an editorial denouncing Hearst and calling Foraker's vindication complete. Frank S. Monnett, former attorney-general of Ohio, came forward and told how Foraker had attempted to call him off the Standard Oil prosecution, and repeated the story involving Governor Haskell of Oklahoma, who was now treasurer of the Democratic Campaign Committee. Then followed from Hearst right up to the end of the campaign an almost daily ration of letters to prominent Republican politicians—Quay, Penrose, Platt, Depew, Elkins, Fairbanks, Joe Sibley, in the House, Nathan Scott of West Virginia, and others. And as a counter accompaniment denials and cross charges and denunciations came from the lofty gentlemen who wriggled and squealed in the grasp of Hearst. Hearst was called a scoundrel for buying stolen letters. But this did not in the least dilute the poignancy of the poison which he poured over the Standard and its hirelings in Washington.

Roosevelt, who hated Foraker, flew to a denunciation of him and rang the charges every day upon the wickedness of Haskell, "the Standard Oil hireling," who was now the Democratic treasurer. Haskell resigned as treasurer and T. Coleman DuPont as Chairman of the Speaker's Bureau of the Republican Committee. The exposure in the end drove Foraker from public life and shortly afterward he resigned from the Senate.

Through all this John D. Rockefeller himself said nothing until near the end of the campaign. On October 29th, he appeared suddenly for the second time in 14 years at his office at 26 Broadway. Reporters were sent for and the following statement was given out, as if in answer to a question as to whom he would vote for:

"I will vote for Taft. If for no other reason I support Taft because on comparing him with Bryan, his chief opponent, I find the balance of fitness and temperament entirely on his side. The election of Mr. Taft, will, I believe, make for law and order and stability in business. He is not a man, I judge, to venture with rash experiments or to impede the return of prosperity by advocating measures subversive of industrial progress. . . . I feel the more impelled to answer this question because it cannot be said that the present administration has in anyway whatever favored the special interest in which my life has been devoted."

Roosevelt became furious at this statement. "It is a perfectly palpable and obvious trick on the part of the Standard Oil people to damage Taft," read a statement from the White House. "It is a cheap trick intended to aid Bryan. Rockefeller has everything to gain by his election," said James R. Garfield, Secretary of Commerce. Lodge in Boston cried out it was an eleventh hour trick to defeat Taft. Another statement from the White House charged by implication that Rockefeller's statement was made by agreement with the Democratic party. Norman Mack from the Democratic side charged that Rockefeller had contributed $1,000,000 to Taft's Committee.

The simple truth is that Rockefeller's statement was a perfectly honest one and expressed his genuine opinions. He was not a man to be swept off his feet. He had made his estimate of Taft better than either Roosevelt or the country. And he knew perfectly that Taft as President with a Republican Senate and House was infinitely to be preferred by his interests to Bryan. And he was far too clear-visioned to permit his hatred of Roosevelt to confuse him on such an important decision as this. Here, as in so many other places, history vindicates his wisdom.

II

TAFT's administration was but a few months under way when the case against the Standard in which it had been fined $29,000,000 was retried, this time before Judge Anderson. When the government's testimony was presented, Judge Anderson, without calling on the defendant, directed the jury to bring in a verdict of "Not Guilty." Thus ended the great fine and men everywhere repeated what had been said so many times that nothing could ever be done to Standard Oil. In fact, Wall Street was so highly concentrated on the fine case that it had almost lost sight of the more important dissolution suit which Frank B. Kellogg had been pressing.

Mr. Rockefeller continued to play golf daily. One day he was interrupted in his game to be told that Henry H. Rogers had died. This was May 19, 1909. These grim warriors were wearing out. Rogers had been more or less inactive for about two years. The death of his wife had been a serious blow to him. Mark Twain tells how he found Rogers in his home after that event quite dazed and helpless. "Everything is going away from me," he almost sobbed. "I am being left alone." His own death followed a stroke of apoplexy. Rockefeller a few days later produced a mild sensation by appearing once more at 26 Broadway. Rogers's death necessitated attention to certain matters and this had brought the more or less retired oil man to his old office. It was his last visit to those old haunts.

All through 1908 Frank B. Kellogg had been grilling witnesses and putting together the long history of the Standard Oil monopoly in the dissolution suit. In that suit Kellogg assembled most of the charges against Rockefeller and his company which have been reviewed in this history. He alleged not merely that the Standard Oil Company of New Jersey, controlling 65 corporations, possessed a monopoly over the petroleum industry, but that it employed "rebates, preferences, and other discriminatory practices," "restraint and monopolization by control of pipe lines and unfair practices against competing lines; contracts with competitors in restraint of trade; unfair methods of competition such as local price cutting at the points where necessary to suppress competition; espionage of the business of competitors, the operation of bogus independent companies and payment of rebates on oil, with like intent"; and so on. The case brought before the court the accuracy of the whole indictment of the conduct of the Standard Oil Company and the career of Mr. Rockefeller. Through three years Kellogg put together through the evidence of innumerable witnesses whose testimony filled 20,000 pages, the long story of John D. Rockefeller's war on competition. On November 20, 1909, the court crowned Kellogg's immense effort with a complete judgment and ordered the Standard Oil Company of New Jersey dissolved as a holding company and directing it to divest itself of all its subsidiaries in thirty days. The decision was a double blow to Rockefeller, not merely because it ordered in the most complete way the dissolution of his great monopoly but put the seal of judgment on most of the charges which his enemies and critics had brought against him. The decision of the lower court was unanimous. However, the Supreme Court of the United States remained and people simply shrugged their shoulders and said: "Wait! Nothing will ever come of it."

III

THE MOST relentless of John D. Rockefeller's pursuers was Joseph Pulitzer, publisher of the New York *World*. He was a bitter critic of Rockefeller's methods. Back in 1900 he had offered a reward of $8,000 for information of the whereabouts of Rockefeller's father and at intervals had kept newspaper men on the hunt for the old man whose wayward life was the skeleton in the Rockefeller closet. Pulitzer was a little criticized for this as it had the appearance of an ungenerous personal attack on a phase of Rockefeller's life which seemed not in the domain of permissible criticism. But Pulitzer pursued the search for years and in 1908 published a story of the final end of old Dr. William Rockefeller, which dealt a deep wound to the feelings of the Rockefeller family. Pulitzer's story charged that Dr. William Rockefeller had settled in South Dakota and for 35 years had lived a double life, with a wife in Freeport, Illinois, to whom he had been married shortly after the family moved to Cleveland. The article which was written with a great deal of circumstantial detail set out that the old man had died in 1906 at the age of 96 and was buried in an unmarked grave in Freeport, Illinois.

Rockefeller himself ignored this report, though Frank Rockefeller denied its truth, saying his father was still alive on his ranch in South Dakota.

The publication of the story made an unpleasant impression and perhaps produced a reaction of sympathy for Rockefeller. It was, however, an example of the virulence of the attacks made upon him at the time.

IV

ALL THIS hatred and odium began to sear the souls of these hitherto self-sufficient gentlemen. They began to think about public opinion a little. Mr. Rockefeller had told a reporter when he returned from abroad that he wished he and the public might get a little better acquainted. It would not be true to say that Rockefeller had made his great gifts to buy public favor. But having made them it is not too much to suppose that so astute a man as Rockefeller was blind to the opportunities they offered for reaching the public mind. When a group of men were called together to discuss the General Education Board we find among them Dr. Albert Shaw and Walter H. Page. At that time the three important journals of review were the *Review of Reviews*, the *World's Work* and the *Outlook*. Dr. Shaw edited the *Review*, Mr. Page was editor of *World's Work*. It was within the possibilities of human nature that these men, after sitting down to dispose of Mr. Rockefeller's millions, would feel at least more restrained in their criticisms. As for the *Outlook*, the venerable Dr. Lyman Abbott, who edited that journal, had been the beneficiary of the bounty of James Stillman of the National City Bank who had contributed liberally toward the *Outlook*. In one way or another not only Mr. Rockefeller but other powerful financial leaders were nestling up close to the magazines and newspapers. It would not be true to say that these men were bought. But certainly their minds were affected. Dr. Abbott and Dr. Shaw had both criticized Standard Oil. But one begins to perceive a tendency to what might be called reasonableness. When Rockefeller was indicted in Ohio in 1906 Dr. Abbott, chronicling the fact, hastened to warn readers that an indictment was not a conviction though the indictment was for things which everybody knew the Standard Oil was guilty of.

In 1924 an old friend of this narrative turns up as manager of the Industrial Relations Department of the General Electric Company. It is Dr. Charles A. Eaton, Rockefeller's old pastor, who, like Dr. Gates, ends up by forsaking the cloth for the count-

My dear Professor

Responding to your favor. It gives me pleasure to enclose you herewith certificate of deposit to your favor for $5,000., as an additional contribution to that agreed upon to aid you in your most excellent work. I most earnestly hope that the way will open for the enlarged scope as you anticipate.

Very truly yours,
Jno. D. Archbold.

Prof. George Gunton,
41 Union Sq.

LETTER FROM ARCHBOLD TO PROF. GEORGE GUNTON, EDITOR OF "GUNTON'S MAGAZINE," SENDING AN "ADDITIONAL" $5,000 "CONTRIBUTION" FOR "YOUR EXCELLENT WORK."
(From *Hearst's Magazine*)

ing room. In addition he goes to Congress. At a convention he tells the National Electric Light Association:

"In this country we are supposed to be governed by ideas; we live by the art of thinking. The three institutions that deal in ideas are the school, the church, and the press and those are the three institutions that we persist in starving to death. . . . What I would like to suggest to you gentlemen is that while you are dealing with the pupils, give a thought to the teachers and when their vacation comes, pay them to come into your plants and learn the public utility business at first hand and then they will go back and you needn't fuss—they can teach better than you can."

Dr. Eaton was not the first to discover the three starveling professions. Back in these early days J. P. Morgan had put the redoubtable George Harvey in as editor of Harper's including *Harper's Magazine* and *Harper's Weekly*. Archbold stood ready to lend a helping hand to any underpaid journalist. To Prof. George Gunton, editor of *Gunton's Magazine*, he writes: "My dear Prof.: Responding to your favor it gives me pleasure to enclose you herewith certificate of deposit for $5,000 as an additional contribution, etc." When Ida M. Tarbell's story was published Gunton rushed to the attack. He writes a long diatribe crying down the book. He accuses her of stealing it all from Lloyd and calling it a "history" to mislead. He is full of fear for "honest history and decent literature." This amazing hireling, who, according to Ida M. Tarbell, got $15,000 a year from Archbold for 15 years, includes in the same volume which denounces Miss Tarbell a spicy article flaying Bourke Cockran for "selling his eloquence."

To R. H. Edmonds, of the *Manufacturers' Record*, Archbold writes: "Your own work has been most admirable" and follows this with a certificate of deposit for $3,000 for another year's subscription. The Hearst papers turned up another Archbold letter enclosing $1,250 to Thomas W. Grasty for a year's subscription to the *Southern Farm Magazine*.

We have seen how that other group of the "starveling professions," the pulpit, fared. One of the most notorious was Chancellor Day of Syracuse who is said to have invented the system of shaking down rich men for college endowments. It was impossible to bring any sort of charge against the Standard leaders which Chancellor Day was not willing to defend. One clergyman publicly called upon the church to turn him out. But instead the church offered him a bishopric. He called Roosevelt's denunciations "the ravings of a disordered mind" and playfully sends to Archbold a little ditty which the boys at Syracuse sang:

> We have a Standard Oil pipe running up to John Crouse Hall
> And a gusher in the stadium will be flowing full next Fall.
> We need the money, Mr. Archbold,
> We need it right away.
> It's the biggest "ad" we've had
> Since the bull-dog ran away.

In 1905 Archbold's handy man Sibley in one of his numerous letters writes him:

"An efficient library bureau is needed, not for a day or a crisis but a permanent healthy control of Associated Press and kindred avenues. It will cost money but will be the cheapest in the end."

Apparently something like that was done. An old journalist named J. I. C. Clarke was installed as publicity man. What he was able to do of course is not known. But a most noticeable rift is to be observed in the cloud of criticism. Papers begin to speak a little more kindly of Standard Oil and Mr. Rockefeller. The *Woman's Home Companion* prints a nice little piece about "How the World's Richest Man Spends Christmas." Mr. Archbold turns up in the *Saturday Evening Post* with a defensive article and confesses that the company has made the mistake of not stating its side of the case.

Then in 1908 Mr. F. N. Doubleday of the *World's Work* falls in with Mr. Rockefeller and is charmed at his simplicity, his directness, his lack of secrecy, and so on. It ends by Mr. Rockefeller agreeing to write his memoirs for *World's Work*. Before they are printed, however, Mr. Doubleday writes a very fulsome account of Rockefeller, draws a most alluring portrait and disposes of all the ugly charges made against him. Then Rockefeller's "Random Reminiscences of Men and Events" begins to run serially in the *World's Work* in October, 1908. It is then published as a book and is, of course, not so much a collection of reminiscences as a defense of Mr. Rockefeller's life and deeds.

V

THE DECREE ordering the dissolution of the company was appealed to the Supreme Court. The counsel proceeded with their preparation for its argument there and Mr. Rockefeller went his way to nurse his health and press forward his great philanthropies. The enemy movements of 1908 had doubtless impaired his mood for giving. But in 1909 he again unloosed his bounty. One famous gift of a million dollars to fight hookworm in the South was made and two considerable donations were offered, one to the Anti-Saloon League and another to the Bureau of Municipal Research. Additional sums were handed out to various colleges. He gave perhaps $15,000,000 this year, which the impious sneeringly said was a kind of fifty per cent split with the Lord on the savings in the Landis fine case. And while he waited for the Supreme Court to pass upon the validity of his towering industrial edifice, he had to listen a little to the small voice of murmuring ministers within his own church. "How long will the Baptist Church continue to maintain an attitude of timidity whenever John D. Rockefeller and Standard Oil are mentioned?" asked a young minister at a Boston conference amid an embarrassing silence.

All the time he was meditating his most important philanthropy. He began by giving $10,000,000 to Chicago University. The gift was made from the General Education Board. Then Frederick T. Gates pointed out that Rockefeller had given $50,000,000 to the General Education Board altogether, that $30,000,000 was for the Board and the other $20,000,000 to be used during his lifetime as he and his son might direct. In making this gift Rockefeller required that $1,500,000 of it be used for a chapel "as the spirit of religion should penetrate and control the university."

In 1910 on March 9 the Standard Oil attorneys filed in the Supreme Court their briefs in the dissolution case. Five days before a bill was introduced in Congress to incorporate the Rockefeller Foundation, Rockefeller's latest benevolence. He proposed to give a huge sum to this Foundation which was to carry forward, with the aid of intelligent research, the giving away of his vast fortune. It was a magnificent conception. He had already given away about $150,000,000. The Foundation was designed to distribute his millions for the "acquisition of knowledge, the prevention and relief of suffering, and the promotion of any and all the elements of human progress." It was to be a clearing house for all his benefactions and young John D. had just withdrawn from almost all his directorships in order to devote his whole time to the management of the great benevolent trust. The endowment of the Foundation was to be in perpetuity, its resources were to be $100,000,000, it was to be exempt from taxation and to be under the direction of a self-perpetuating board. As Rockefeller had been the most thoroughly constructive and most honest of all the great captains of industry he now proposed to make the most impressive use of his great fortune in the cause of humanity. Criticism to many features of his proposed Foundation was uttered. But on the whole men began to say that, after all, John D. Rockefeller's millions were coming to the public use at last. Some, however, did not fail to observe that as the $32,000,000 gift to the General Education Board had been timed just before the Landis decision, this $100,000,000 gift was timed just as the Supreme Court faced consideration of the dissolution suit. In any case the spectacle of two arms of the government facing two aspects of the activities of this extraordinary man appealed to the imagination of the time— Congress considering the greatest gift in history for the alleviation of human suffering and the Supreme Court considering whether or not it ought not declare the whole structure by which this money had been made an offense against the laws of his country.

Congress did not immediately act on the Foundation. But before the year was out the Supreme Court pronounced its verdict upon Rockefeller's work. It upheld the decision of the lower court and in one of the most important judicial pronouncements of the great court, ordered the Standard Oil monopoly dissolved within thirty days. The decision was rendered by the late Chief Justice Edward Douglas White in an opinion unhappily clouded by a singularly cumbersome and obscure English style, but weighty and momentous for all that. Reviewing the facts Chief Justice White said:

"We think no disinterested mind can survey the period in question without being irresistibly driven to the conclusion that the very genius for commercial development and organization which it would seem was manifested from the beginning soon begot an intent and purpose to exclude others which was frequently manifested by acts and dealings wholly inconsistent with the theory that they were made with the single conception of advancing the development of business power by usual methods, but which, on the contrary, necessarily involved the intent to drive others from the field and to exclude them from their right to trade, and thus accomplish the mastery which was the end in view. And, considering the period from the date of the trust agreements of 1879 and 1882, up to the time of the expansion of the New Jersey corporation, the gradual extension of the power over the commerce in oil which ensued, the decision of the supreme court of Ohio, the tardiness or reluctance in comforming to the commands of that decision, the methods first adopted and that which finally culminated in the plan of the New Jersey corporation, all additionally serve to make manifest the continued existence of the intent which we have previously indicated, and which, among other things, impelled the expansion of the New Jersey corporation. The exercise of the power which resulted from that organization fortifies the foregoing conclusions, since the development which came, the acquisition here and there which ensued of every efficient means by which competition could have been asserted, the slow but resistless methods which followed by which means of transportation were absorbed and brought under control, the sytem of marketing which was adopted by which the country was divided into districts and the trade in each district in oil was turned over to a designated corporation within the combination, and all others were excluded, all lead the mind up to a conviction of a purpose and intent which we think is so certain as practically to cause the subject not to be within the domain of reasonable contention."

Here was a verdict on the whole history of the great company which was conclusive not only in law but in history, since it was the unanimous affirmation by the highest court of an unanimous finding of the lower court.

The decision was unanimous on the facts and on the question of dissolution. But there was one dissenting opinion to one phase of the law expounded by the Chief Justice. For the first time he gave judicial sanction to what has come to be known as the "rule of reason"; the doctrine that the restraint of trade to constitute a violation of the Sherman anti-trust law must be "an undue restraint," an "unreasonable restraint" to be determined by the court on all the facts. To this the aged old warrior of the court, Justice Harlan of Kentucky, who had stood as the uncompromising champion of the law from the start, filed a protest of unusual vigor. It inserted "words in the anti-trust act which Congress did not put there," he declared, as he pounded his desk. It was "judicial legislation." The court said to business, "You may now restrain commerce, provided you are reasonable about it; only take care that the restraint is not undue." The old justice grew eloquent and predicted that many mischiefs would flow from the court's pronouncement and endless uncertainty. Who can say he was not right in this? The rule of reason proved to be the break in the law through which the United States Steel Corporation and other great combinations were able to crawl. The decision was the beginning of the end of the monopoly of the Standard Oil Company, though no one believed it then and many doubt it today. But it was the beginning of a new phase of trust law development in this country.

The court commented on the delays which Rockefeller had managed to force in dissolving the old Ohio dissolution decree

"PIGS IS PIGS."
(From the *Post-Dispatch*, St. Louis)

of 1892 and gave the company just thirty days to divest itself of its 33 subsidiaries. This presented the directors with a difficult problem. There were 983,383 shares of Standard of New Jersey, valued at $98,338,300. Each holder of one of these shares was to receive for it an equivalent in the shares of each company— thirty-four altogether, the Standard of New Jersey and each of its 33 subsidiaries. John D. Rockefeller owned 249,995 shares of the holding company. He therefore received $\frac{983,383}{983,383}$ of each company. In the case of the small stockholders it was difficult to make this fraction represent an exact unit or block of stock.

The liquidators worked over the problem for the full thirty days allowed by the court without giving out any information as to what they would do. The distribution was made on the last day allowed. The managements of the companies began to move around. When it was all complete there were thirty-four companies, each under the immediate and final management of its Board of Directors, instead of the directors of the New Jersey company. Of course, they remained as they had been—producing companies, manufacturing companies, refining companies, pipe lines companies, marketing companies, without a shadow of competition between them, each with its territory and its functions marked out as definitely as before. Moreover the majority of the stock in all companies belonged to a small group of men. The same men therefore were able to command the obedience of the directors in each company. To 26 Broadway each company looked for its guidance and the final word in all matters of policy. For this reason the country began to laugh a little at the "alleged" dissolution. Four months later a newspaper commentator pointed out that when the company was "dissolved" its shares were valued at $663,793,525 and that March 8th the stock market valuation was $885,044,700. The net result of the dissolution seemed to have been to add $200,000,000 to the company's market value and over $56,000,000 to the market value of Mr. Rockefeller's holdings.

The reason for this was obvious. The public for the first time learned what the real assets of Standard Oil were worth. Unlike every other company, which was bulging with water, the Standard companies were all capitalized at far less than their true value. When that value was learned speculation in Standard Oil stock became a little wild. To the public at large, however, the rise in value seemed to be the unconquerable John D. Rockefeller's answer to the Supreme Court. It was not so. With the details of the dissolution completely worked out, Mr. Rockefeller formally resigned as the executive head of the Standard Oil companies. He had retired in the middle nineties, but had always retained his titular post as president of the Standard of New Jersey. How far after that he exercised any actual authority is not easy to say. When charges were made against the conduct of the company he was always ready with the explanation that he had retired. However, he did not fail to boast several times of reforms like old-age pensions, which were not instituted until after his retirement. Archbold had been the actual director of the company's affairs for many years and now he was named president to succeed Rockefeller. If Rockefeller was in no way responsible for the shameless operations of Archbold in the bribery of public officials, he certainly joined now in a tacit endorsement of that ambitious and extensive episode of political corruption by making Mr. Archbold his successor.

The excuse continually offered that he could not be held responsible for all the offenses charged against all the numerous employees of the company loses much of its force when we remember that there is no record of any of the accused officials ever being dismissed or disciplined—neither Daniel O'Day in the Marietta Railroad rebate scandal, nor the Everests after the convictions in Buffalo nor Archbold after his exposure by Hearst nor any of the innumerable smaller fry caught in the act of oppressing their immediate competitors.

In any case Rockefeller stepped out now and along with him his brother William and several other of the old guard directors. From this point on the forces of our vast economy, more powerful even than John D. Rockefeller, set to work upon the dynasty he had reared and slowly, imperceptibly as the years wore on, developed again in the oil industry the competition against which he had battled and in his own group of companies introduced the elements of final emancipation from his power.

VI

For a little while the name of Rockefeller was to have a brief rest. McCutcheon had made a cartoon in the Chicago *Tribune*, depicting Rockefeller standing before a newsstand covered with magazines bearing his name on the cover and asking the dealer: "Have you got something here to read not about me?"

He busied himself with his vast Pocantico Hills estate, transplanting giant trees twenty inches in diameter. "It is truly interesting what liberties you can take with trees if you once learn how to handle the monsters." He had learned that about society itself. He looked with a distant interest at his vast fortune. The papers occasionally carried stories about Rockefeller dickering with the Gould estate for the Missouri Pacific or Denver and Rio Grande, or changing the management of the Western Maryland or increasing his holdings in Standard Oil stock. But the impression these created that he still gave his time to business was wholly erroneous. He had an office and a staff headed by Gates and his son which looked after such matters. He discussed them with these agents as little as possible.

He saw with satisfaction the "very sensible" manner in which Mr. Taft was managing things and blamed him but little for the outrageous legacies of suits against the trusts which Roosevelt had left him. Taft had become very kindly in his feeling toward Roosevelt's old enemies and Roosevelt looked upon it with growing resentment. He played golf with Frick and dismissed the warnings from some of his intimates about it. It was only Mrs. Taft's influence which prevented him from playing golf with Rockefeller. J. P. Morgan would slip up to Beverly, the President's Summer home, in his motor boat to see Taft without being detected. Taft told his aide that Senator Aldrich had suggested that he would call at the White House and bring John D. along for a conference on some business matters but that Taft had declined the conference. In April, after the Supreme Court decision, dissolving the Standard Oil, Aldrich made an appointment to visit the White House with his daughter and her husband, John D. Rockefeller, Jr., for lunch. Taft didn't want any one to know of the visit. He had the usher telephone Senator Aldrich to drive to the East Entrance where the party was hustled by a side door into the White House. Taft directed that no entry or minute of the visit be made anywhere. "It is strange how public men shudder at the names of Aldrich and Rockefeller," commented Archie Butt who managed the details of the secret visit. The campaign was coming on. The split with Roosevelt had come. In another year, Woodrow Wilson was nominated by the Democrats and Taft went down to the most ignominious defeat ever suffered by a candidate. Woodrow Wilson and a Democratic administration moved into power. Rockefeller shook his head at that and chalked up another bad mark against his old enemy Roosevelt.

VII

WHILE all this was going on Mr. Rockefeller was busy with his health and his plans for his great Foundation. He divided his time between his various estates, spending the Summer at Forest Hill, the Winter in Florida, the Spring in Lakewood, and the Fall and portion of the Winter at Pocantico.

He was now devoted to golf. He had begun this game in February, 1899, at the suggestion of a gentleman named Elias Johnson who had observed to Rockefeller that his long, measured sweep in pitching horseshoes indicated that he had the makings of a good golf swing. For some time he played with just a moderate interest in the game. However by April, 1903, we find him writing from Lakewood to a business associate: "I believe I have recovered my health. I feel better now than I have felt in years, but at my age a man's health is as uncertain as April weather. I believe the improvement in my condition is due to my newly acquired habit of playing golf. During my California stay I became an adept and enjoyed the game immensely. I feel like a new man."

He used a bicycle to ride around the golf course, pedaling from one shot to another. He had the usual difficulty keeping his eye on the ball. Hence his caddy was instructed to stand in front of him as he prepared to swing repeating over and over, "Keep your head down! Keep your head down!" Those who played with him then and since are a unit in saying that Rockefeller is scrupulous in reporting his score. He never fools himself. "If his ball went into the woods," said a well-known publisher who played with him often, "he plays it out no matter how many strokes it takes and counts them all. I have played with Andy Carnegie, also. And I found that Andy would bear watching—he would cheat a little on the score." Rockefeller himself complained to a friend "that he was sorry to say he had met ministers who did not hesitate to cheat a bit on the links." Then he gave a humorous imitation of a well-known minister kicking the ball surreptitiously from behind a stump. In golf Rockefeller followed a principle he adhered to in business. George Harvey once asked him to what one thing more than another he attributed the success of the Standard Oil Company. After pondering a while, Rockefeller replied: "To the fact that we never deceived ourselves."

He had become by 1912 a very proficient golfer. His best score at this time furnished by a man who played over 500 games with Rockefeller, was made October 30, 1912. His score for the nine holes was:

$$4\ 4\ 3\ 4\ 6\ 4\ 6\ 4\ 4 = 39$$

He enjoyed riding around the country in Cleveland or New Jersey or New York, constantly changing the course. He would wear a yellow duster and on cool days a paper vest under that and a straw turtle hat, occasionally tied to his head with a veil, if there were a lady along. And he had already got into the habit of picking up for company on his rides working people or neighbors he might pass on the way—provided, of course, he knew them.

His chief concern at this time was his plan for organizing the Rockefeller Foundation. Mention has already been made of the bill introduced into Congress to charter it. The bill was offered March 2, 1910, in the Senate. After an explanation of its purposes by Starr J. Murphy it was promptly reported favorably.

The announcement of the plan brought out a wave of acclaim. Of course the chorus of preachers lifted up their voices. Men like Dr. Charles F. Aked of the Fifth Avenue Baptist Church called Mr. Rockefeller "the most valuable single asset humanity possesses today," and papers like the Philadelphia *Press* spoke of the "far sighted benefaction which dwarfs all other gifts and sets before the world a world example." More significant were the comments of papers like the New York *Press* which had talked much of tainted money but now said: "A better and broader dissemination of great wealth could scarcely be imagined."

But there was plenty of criticism. The Springfield *Republican* said the gift called for "the greatest scrutiny." The stream of protest swelled and made itself felt until finally the bill was withdrawn and redrafted. It was not introduced again until 1912. Then it was proposed that if at anytime a public institution should be set up by Congress or the states, embodying the same purposes as the Foundation then the remaining assets of the Foundation should be turned over to such public institution. It provided that Congress might at any time limit the activities of the Foundation;

that the gift should be no more than $100,000,000; that the income should be spent and never added to the principal; that any gift to the Foundation might be ordered distributed fifty years after being made upon approval of two-thirds of the trustees and that then it must be distributed within the next fifty years; that objection to self-perpetuating boards might be met by providing that new members must be approved by the President of the United States, Chief Justice, Vice President, and Speaker of the House, and the Presidents of Harvard, Yale, Columbia, Johns Hopkins, and University of Chicago, and that the property of the corporation should be exempt from the federal tax only.

In this form the bill was passed by the House and reported favorably by the Judiciary Committee of the Senate, but in the rush of legislation in the last days of the session in the dying hours of the Taft administration it was not reached for a vote. Thereafter it was never re-introduced. Instead a charter was asked and granted by the State of New York, May 14, 1913. Immediately the incorporators, including John D. and his son, perfected organization and shortly after Dr. Charles Eliot of Harvard and A. Barton Hepburn, who thirty years before had denounced Standard Oil, were added to the board. In three payments Mr. Rockefeller handed over in securities a little more than $100,000,000.

A list of the securities included in this gift must have been interesting to the investor of that day. It included stock in all the thirty-three Standard Oil units valued at $49,503,455.36. There were seventy-two different bond issues and stocks in some forty companies—railroads, ship-building, banks, hotels, development, steel, equipment companies—selected from among the Rockefeller assortment.

Mrs. Rockefeller added her mite, $48,000 in bonds in four separate groups, the income to be used at the Board's discretion to various Baptist ministers' homes. Thus this great work was launched. At the outset the trustees resolved "that the advancement of public health through medical research and education, including the demonstration of known methods of treatment and prevention of disease afforded the surest prospect of such usefulness." The Rockefeller Sanitary Commission set up by the Institute for Medical Research had been grappling with the hookworm disease in the South. That commission had found over 2,000,000 persons afflicted with the disease there and had treated or caused to be treated some half a million of them. The Foundation adopted its cue from that work and set up an international commission to cope with hookworm throughout the world.

In a few months the Foundation was busily at work. Mr. Rockefeller was enjoying the acclaim which he was receiving. He was at Forest Hill and, upon the whole, happy. He was also a little saddened by the death (May 20, 1913) of his oldest partner, Henry M. Flagler, in Florida at the age of eighty-eight. There was one cloud on the horizon. It was the illness of his wife. There was, indeed, another which he could not see and which was preparing at that very moment to shatter very rudely any illusions he may have entertained of the early redemption of his name from its old infamy.

CHAPTER XII. THE LUDLOW MASSACRE

ROCKEFELLER left Forest Hill in August, 1913, the day after tax listing day. The assessors had been after him. Ohio had a new law compelling any one living for more than six months in the state to pay taxes on their real and personal property. The assessors sensed a juicy cut of some $12,000,000 in taxes on Rockefeller's supposed $900,000,000 estate. That battle waged for a year much to Mr. Rockefeller's chagrin. Indeed he soured a little on Cleveland after that. He declared he would spend a fortune rather than pay a cent of the tax, which was finally fixed on an appraisal of $311,000,000. But Rockefeller took the matter to court and won and the two tax assessors who attempted to collect were dismissed by the governor.

As he left Forest Hill for Pocantico an ominous event was taking place in Denver, Colorado—an incident which was to end in putting upon his already deeply tarnished fame its last serious stain. In 1902 Rockefeller became interested in the Colorado Fuel and Iron Company. He owned not a majority interest but a large enough minority interest to have actual control of the company. It had been worked extensively for eleven years and was now a valuable property consisting of twenty-four mines in Colorado.

The actual management of these mines was in the hands of the Board of which John D. Rockefeller, Jr., Frederick T. Gates, and Mr. Jerome D. Greene, all members of what we have seen was Mr. Rockefeller's personal staff. Mr. Gates had now retired, his place being taken by Starr J. Murphy, a lawyer. Mr. Rockefeller himself, it must be said in all fairness, was very far from these properties, knew little or nothing of what went on there, treated them pretty much as just an investment and left all the details of more immediate contact and management to his staff. The immediate management was in the hands of the Chairman of the Board, Mr. L. M. Bowers, and the President, Mr. J. F. Welborn, two thoroughly reactionary figures.

Iron mines, as frequently happens, do not get discovered on the edges of cities. They are apt to turn up in remote and desolate places. That is what happened in the case of the Colorado Fuel and Iron Company mines. When mines are worked, however, they must have workers and these must be housed. All the property in and around the mines belonged to the company and, of necessity, it was compelled to build houses to shelter its workers and their families. The necessary fruit of this, of course, was that a town sprang into being, with houses, streets, stores, and people, who required food, medical attention, religious consolation, and policing. The company proceeded to supply all these things. It owned the houses and the streets, the store and the church and the meeting hall. It hired the doctor, the preacher, and the police. The workers were subject to it therefore, not merely in their actual employment but in their homes, their schools, and in all the intimate matters of their lives.

That abuses should grow up in such a community was inevitable. These abuses, affecting hours, pay, working conditions, however, became intensified when to them was added the additional abuse that the men could not even discuss their grievances among themselves. The company would not suffer them to organize. It would not permit them to even meet to discuss organization. It would not allow United Mine Workers' organizers to even enter the town. And any man who displayed restlessness under these conditions and exhibited symptoms of revolt was promptly packed out of town. To be fired was to be evicted though cases were known where men were driven from the town, though their families re-

THE LUDLOW MASSACRE

mained and they could not even enter it again to visit their own wives and children. The town was the private property of the company. One of the chief grievances of the men was against the criminal guard system, the privately hired and paid deputy sheriffs who ruthlessly enforced the intolerable ordinances of this medieval community.

In August of 1913, as Mr. Rockefeller prepared to move from his Forest Hill estate, the miners made a demand upon the company for certain reforms. They had, of course, met in another town and the demands were sent through Frank Hayes, organizer of the United Mine Workers. They asked for recognition of the union, a ten per cent advance in tonnage rates and the Wyoming day scale, the eight hour day for all, pay for narrow work as well as dear work, and a miner elected checkweighman. Two additional demands might well have commanded at least the attention of employers anywhere in this twentieth century. They demanded the right to choose their own doctor, to trade at any store, and to board anywhere. They demanded the abolition of the infamous criminal guard system and the enforcement of the Colorado mining law. The demands conformed to the conditions in mines in Illinois, Indiana, Ohio, and Pennsylvania. These demands the company did not even answer. Then on September 15th the workers met in a Denver convention and called a strike for September 23rd. The Organizer Hayes made numerous efforts to get the mine officials to talk with him. They refused. He sent letters to the operators urging a conference. They were ignored.

On September 23rd, the miners struck. To strike was not merely to leave their jobs. It was to leave their homes. They took their belongings and went out en masse, men, women, and children, and into the mountains where they set up tents near a place called Ludlow, to which name they were to give a dark and sinister fame. This was beyond the limits of the mine property. Immediately the company had the sheriff, Tarr, whom it had elected and controlled, swear in 326 deputy sheriffs many of them belonging to the Baldwin-Felts detective agency famous for its strike-breaking activities. These guards patrolled the limits of the camp and as was to be expected almost daily clashes occurred. There were three battles in October, the worst being on October 17th near the Forbes mine. These clashes were alternately the fault of the miners and of the guards. Finally on October 29th, the Governor sent the militia to Ludlow to supersede the guards.

This restored order, but sullen and angry order under pressure. The adjutant in command, General Chase, a confirmed miner hater, was a red flag to the strikers. He set up a commission to hear cases; put men into a filthy jail at Trinidad, held prisoners incommunicado, including Mother Jones, and even refused to honor habeas corpus writs of the court on the ground of military necessity. Finally by April of 1914 the striking tent colony at Ludlow had been sufficiently reduced to permit of the withdrawal of a large part of the militia. A detachment of thirty-five men was left to preserve order under Major P. J. Hancock. Hancock had with him Lieut. K. E. Linderfeldt, a soldier of fortune, who had been in endless quarrels with the miners and who had sworn "to get" John Tikas, one of the mine leaders. Linderfeldt commanded one small company. Another company was made up wholly of mine guards who had been enlisted in the militia.

Once again clashes began between the strikers and the militia, chiefly under Linderfeldt. On April 20th a fight started. A bomb was exploded as a signal for help which everybody mistook for the beginning of a fight and in a few minutes a battle was in progress between the militia and the miners. It lasted from morning until night and ended in the capture by the militia under Linderfeldt of the Ludlow tent colony which he promptly proceeded to put to flames. John Tikas was captured and brought before Linderfeldt. While thus in custody Linderfeldt struck him over the head with the butt of his gun, killing him. The next day the strikers found in caves under some of their tents the charred bodies of two women and eleven children.

The news of this grewsome discovery swept through the now dispossessed and desperate miners. Almost crazed with anger and grief they became in an instant a mob of madmen howling for revenge. The cry of the "Massacre of Ludlow" went up through the region. The call to arms swept the mining country and the strikers rushed through the mining district of the Colorado Fuel and Iron Company, burning and destroying whatever they could lay their hands on. The Empire mine was set on fire. Three mine guards were killed in one battle. The battle raged into the Black Hills and was renewed daily. The whole country was shocked.

THE LUDLOW MASSACRE

April 29th the strikers fired the Forbes mine and killed nine employees there. Later in the day they killed Major Lester. The warfare was not ended until the Federal Troops arrived. Linderfeldt was court-martialed and released. But about 163 miners were arrested and charged with murder. One of them was John Lucas, a strike leader, who had lived in the Ludlow tent colony. This briefly is a fair account of the famous Ludlow massacre and the Battle of the Black Hills which shocked the country and resulted in bringing John D. Rockefeller once more and for the last time before the bar of public opinion.

Now for Rockefeller's part in all this. First of all it must be remembered that the closed camp condition in Colorado was a heritage—a legacy from another day. Slowly throughout the country the workers fought relentlessly against these ancient abuses and drove them out. The Colorado mines had resisted this partly through the bad social minds of their immediate managers and partly through the languor of the workers themselves. Perhaps nothing was more remote from John D. Rockefeller's attention than the conditions in this property. Moreover he became interested in these mines after he had ceased to take a very active part in business and when he was disposed to permit his holdings to pass into the condition of mere investments. As a matter of fact Rockefeller had studiously focused his attention even in his days of active business upon the Standard Oil Company. It is not difficult to perceive how many bad conditions could have grown up in Colorado without exciting his attention. In the case of his son, John D. Rockefeller, Jr., and the pious Frederick T. Gates, perhaps, a more serious case might be made out. They were members of the board and were supposed to be familiar with the workings of the company. A condition like the closed camp at Ludlow ought to have made some impression upon the minds of a humanitarian like Dr. Gates who was ranging the world for causes on which to bestow Mr. Rockefeller's benevolence, and Rockefeller, Jr., who was now chief manager of his father's benevolent trust. After all is said that can be said for these two men, there still remains a weight of responsibility which they cannot escape. One must be less than fair, however, if he fails to remember that a man's mind is after all an instrument of limited range; that young Rockefeller's energies had been taken up completely with the management of his father's vast benevolent interests, that he too had looked upon his father's holdings as investments; that the mind can receive only a limited number of impressions; and that, in the multitude of his interests, the conditions at Ludlow simply did not make any impression on his already completely usurped attention. This, it would seem, is but fair, in spite of the fact that attention had been directed to the sore ten years before by a similar, though far less violent strike.

It is not so easy to acquit the Rockefellers for their conduct after the strike broke in all its fury. However, it is easy to see a difference here between the younger Rockefeller, the product of a newer age, and the older Rockefeller, who though he had been a pioneer in the development of the purely material mechanism of big business, lagged behind in a remote age of the mind in reference to its social phases. He was in every sense a very old-fashioned man. He believed in the Bible of John Calvin and Roger Williams. He accepted the view of divine interposition in human affairs and piously admitted, like the haughty George Baer, that God had committed to his own humble hands the administration of the material things he had accumulated. He leaned contentedly to the Pauline doctrine of good masters and obedient servants. He did not in the least perceive that the rise of huge organized groups of men within society put the unorganized part of society a little at their mercy and exerted a strain on the theory of the individualism he worshiped along with all his Victorian contemporaries. The public interest in another man's business— railroad or factory—seemed to him the veriest heresy. The right of private property he surrounded with all the sanctions of his religion. Workmen used *his* property, *his* tools and while they were at liberty to employ those tools or put them aside, they were utterly without right to tell him how the tools ought to be used. They had no right to organize and above all no right to strike. A strike was a use of force. It was violence in itself. The employer had a right to ignore the striker, to hold him off, to resist his force, and, if necessary, to put him down. When Henry C. Frick shocked the country by shooting down ruthlessly the striking iron workers at Homestead, John D. Rockefeller wrote him a letter approving his course and expressing sympathy. Only this very year when Colorado was aflame and his name was bandied about in hatred and fear, he refused to give his own workers on his estates a holiday on Labor Day. "Instead of spending money on amusements my employees will have an opportunity of adding to their savings," he said. "Had they been given a holiday money would have been spent foolishly." Their right to spend it foolishly and their hunger for something besides mere working and saving were something he simply did not consider.

To all this must be added that in the oil business and at his home he was the best of employers. He paid the best wages, ensured continuing and permanent employment to his employees, provided hospital facilities for them when sick, and old age pensions when aged and in all his long career, outside of a little trouble here and there, never had a strike. But all this he accorded to his employees in a spirit of benevolent paternalism. Their right to demand it and to organize to get it he never conceded, in spite of the perfectly obvious fact that there was not very much benevolent paternalism among most employers.

Therefore when the tent colony was burned on April 20th and Colorado was on fire with indignation and horror at the spectacle of maddened workers burning, slaying in desperate and blind vengeance, Congressman Martin D. Foster went to New York to get Rockefeller to intervene in Colorado, he met with a flat refusal. Foster did not see the elder Rockefeller, but appealed through his son. He left New York declaring that Rockefeller's attitude was little short of defiance not only of the government but of civilization itself. Rockefeller's mind had a trick, not an uncommon one, of closing up tight to the logic or appeal in his enemy's argument the moment that enemy rose to assert his own rights by the use of those weapons which Rockefeller himself employed to protect his own. He was for making no concessions whatever to organized labor.

II

IT WAS at this stage that a great white light broke upon the mind of the younger Rockefeller. The chorus of denunciation which came from numerous sources shocked him. The nation had felt the invigorating effect of a dozen years of social reform. The spectacle of this odious survival of labor conditions supposed to be extinct caused not only the older Rockefeller but his son to be bitterly arraigned by men and journals the younger man, at least, was compelled to respect. He saw the rise of the storm with a good deal of horror. It seemed to shake him from the ground on which he had been standing so long without examining it. His first reaction was a determination to put his side of the case before the people. He got plenty of advice. Much of it was the kind which appealed to the old-timers—the kind that led Archbold to subsidize the Guntons and Days and Boyles. He was urged to hire advertising space and tell his story. Some advised him to buy a newspaper and make it ring with his defense. At this point some one suggested that he seek a professional adviser and named Ivy Lee as the most likely one for the job. Lee was acting in the capacity of publicity man for the Pennsylvania Railroad with the title of executive assistant. Young Rockefeller had him call, induced him to undertake the job of straightening out their public relations in the mine strike and got the Pennsylvania to release Lee temporarily for the job. Lee's counsel, Rockefeller said, was the first advice he had had which did not involve deviousness of one kind or another. What Lee proposed was really something new in the Rockefeller system—the study of public opinion. It meant not merely placing the affairs of the corporation before the public in the most favorable light, but "shaping the affairs of the corporation so that when placed before the public they will be approved."

Immediately newspapers and public men began receiving bulletins signed by the president of the iron company giving its side of the events as they developed. This was the publicity part of Lee's campaign. But something else happened. The Rockefeller Foundation named W. MacKenzie King, former labor minister of Canada, a commissioner to study the whole subject of the iron company's labor relations and recommend a plan for reforming it. This was modifying the company's conduct to command public approval. It was the beginning of a wholly new policy on the part of the Rockefellers and the Standard Oil Company. King went to work and very soon made a report recommending an elaborate system of relations which was a little hastily dubbed the plan for industrial democracy. The younger Rockefeller urged this plan upon the coal company officials in October, 1914. Welborn replied that it seemed meritorious but that it would embarrass the company while the strike was pending. The miners, in fact,

THE LUDLOW MASSACRE 461

were now virtually defeated. And in December they capitulated completely. December 10th the strike was declared ended.

Immediately the company took steps to put into effect what came to be called the Rockefeller Plan which had been outlined by King. On January 15th, 1915, delegates of the miners—one for each 250—met with the mine operators in Denver to discuss the plan. That plan provided that employees at each mining camp would have the right to meet once a year, elect by secret ballot their own chairman and secretary and select from among their number representatives to act for them with respect to working and living conditions. The camps were divided into five districts for election purposes. Each district was provided with a conference committee and the miners each year would have the right to elect representatives to a joint conference committee on conciliation, safety and accidents, sanitation, health, housing, education, and recreation. The scheme was criticized by the United Mine Workers and undoubtedly had some defects. It was, however, an immense step in the direction of civilized working conditions and a year later the Industrial Commission expressed the belief that it was adopted in good faith.

But the agreement included some other features which represented a concession to the miners of some of those demands on which they had launched their strike. Employees were conceded the right to hold meetings on company property; to buy in any stores they chose; to select their own doctor; employ their own weighmen, and to carry complaints from district superintendents to superior officers and finally to the president of the company. Two years later John Fitch, who had made a study of the controversy for the *Survey*, returned to Colorado and found a great and favorable change visible there. He found union locals organized in all Colorado Fuel and Iron Company camps and ninety per cent of the miners in them. They held meetings openly, though the unions were not recognized. All of the objectionable political figures had been gotten rid of and there were no company marshals in evidence. Fitch found Welborn actually in conference with a representative of the union. The unions were not officially friendly to the plan and there was some talk of a strike for union recognition and the grievance machinery was not being much used. Yet on the whole the condition of the mine property represented a great advance over the indefensible medievalism which existed before the strike.

To the plans of young John D. for all this the old industrialist at Pocantico Hill was opposed. It is not difficult to imagine what his objections were. Nevertheless he interposed no obstacle to what he must have supposed was his son's chimerical dream. He did come around to approving it later. The reforms inaugurated, however, and the plan for resisting forces which were loading the Rockefeller name with odium were the younger man's. The old man, then seventy-five, was at the end of his business and public career. The years had rolled over his head producing no change in the antiquated social philosophy with which he had started his business life. All that came after 1914 was the work of his son, imbued with the spirit of a new generation. It was to confer upon the fame of the older man an immense cleansing and regenerating boon.

CHAPTER XIII. MRS. ROCKEFELLER'S DEATH

WHILE the miners and operators struggled in Colorado, the I.W.W. made several demonstrations against the Rockefeller home at Tarrytown. Some of the agitators got into the grounds and smashed windows. Later the dairy barn was burned and this was attributed to incendiaries. Guards were thrown around the estate and Rockefeller's going and coming was kept a profound secret. In June, annoyed by the conditions in Tarrytown he and his family made a little trip to Maine heavily guarded. They were back again soon. This was the first Summer they had not gone to Forest Hill. Mrs. Rockefeller was quite ill and her illness, together with the unpleasant agitation about the estate and throughout the country and the feeling about the old home in Cleveland, threw a shade of sadness over the family. Rockefeller felt thrust out from Cleveland. He dared not go there lest he be served with papers in the tax suit involving millions. In spite of all the money he had given Cleveland, in spite of all the countless millions he had bestowed upon the country

JOHN D. ROCKEFELLER, ABOUT 1907, RETURNING FROM CHURCH. TWO OF MR. ROCKEFELLER'S GRANDCHILDREN ARE WALKING JUST BEHIND.

JOHN D. ROCKEFELLER AT THE AGE OF 93
From a photograph taken in June, 1932

MRS. ROCKEFELLER'S DEATH

which persisted in harrying him, now he seemed an exile from the home his wife loved best.

On September 8th, 1914, he and his wife celebrated their golden jubilee. How far they had moved since that far-away day when the young oil refiner and the little black-haired schoolteacher had joined hands in Cleveland. She was wheeled out on the lawn and there enjoyed a quiet celebration with her children and grandchildren. The next day was her seventy-fifth birthday and her husband had a brass band come up from New York as a surprise for her to give a concert and play the tunes she liked best. Slowly all the familiar things in Rockefeller's life were moving away from him. During their last stay in Cleveland one day at the Euclid Avenue Baptist Church he was making a talk. Mrs. Rockefeller sat beside him. He was talking about his own life when suddenly he stopped and looked into the pallid face of his wife.

"People tell me I have done much in my life," he said, then paused. "I know I have worked hard. But the best thing I ever accomplished and the thing that has given me the greatest happiness was to win Cetty Spelman. I have had but one sweetheart and am thankful to say I still have her."

He was not to have her long.

Toward the end of January he left the Calvary Baptist Church where he had gone for some years and returned to the Fifth Avenue Baptist Church. "It is good to be home again," he said. Then he left for Ormond Beach in Florida. Mrs. Rockefeller was too ill to go along.

As March dawned Mrs. Rockefeller became quite ill. A specialist made some blood tests and said she would be better. In about a week she expressed a wish to go out into the gardens and see the flowers. Servants carried her out. On March 12th, she said to her sister, Lucy Spelman, who had lived with her since their father's death and who always kept close to her, that she would like to have a wheel chair so as to go oftener into the garden and see the flowers. Her sister sent a messenger posthaste into the city for the chair. An hour later her nurse handed her a glass of milk. She drank it and said it tasted good. Then she sank back on her pillow. Her nurse and her sister rushed to her but she had already ceased to breathe.

Rockefeller and his son, who was with him, started immediately for New York. Of course, the news of Mrs. Rockefeller's death was immediately known throughout the country. The news came following all the bad temper and hard words of the Ludlow episode. Death, however, has a gentle way with it. As the train moved north from Florida with the aged oil man he was much surprised and deeply touched by the tenderness with which every stranger he met, railroad officials, conductors, brakemen, and strangers who recognized him, spoke softly and looked with sympathy, and even expressed their sorrow at his grief.

The funeral was held at Pocantico Hills March 15th, in the room where Mrs. Rockefeller died. Young John D. and his father stood together. "Mother," said the younger man, "looks so beautiful lying there in bed that we simply cannot take her out of our home today. She looks as if she were just sleeping." The older man remained silent. In the midst of his grief some voice within must have murmured against the strange ways of Fate. The family vault was in Cleveland. Now with his wife dead a hand seemed to be raised against him there. The tax case! If he were to take her there officers would meet him at the train and serve him with papers—those process servers! Would there never be an end of it! And after the funeral service on the fifteenth the body continued to rest in her room until next day. Then it was taken from the Pocantico Hills home and placed in the Archbold mausoleum in Sleepy Hollow. Armed guards remained at the tomb. A few weeks later Governor Willis of Ohio removed the two tax commissioners who began the $311,000,000 tax assessment suit and plans were made to dismiss the suit to collect the taxes. Rockefeller waited for this proceeding to take his wife's body home.

On July 15th, Rockefeller went to Forest Hill to make arrangements for the funeral in Cleveland. He went heavily guarded. On August 11th, in a blinding electrical storm, Mrs. Rockefeller's body was removed from the Archbold tomb and sent to Cleveland where she was buried finally in the family tomb in Lakeview Cemetery, with only members of her immediate family present.

A few months later—November 22, 1915—an attempt was made to assassinate John D. Archbold. A bomb was found in the driveway of his Tarrytown home. The police attributed it to the I.W.W.'s, as a protest against the execution of Joseph Hillstrom in Salt Lake City. This was at best a guess. The bomb was found, before it exploded, by a gardener. The following year, December 5, 1916, in his sixty-eighth year, John D. Archbold ended his turbulent career.

CHAPTER XIV. THE LAIRD OF KIJKUIT

WHILE the miners in Colorado muddled through their squalid war with Rockefeller's thirteenth-century-minded executives, Europe flung herself into a very modern orgy of blood-letting and destruction. And presently America, which had been enjoying the spectacle through the papers, the magazines, and the movies as a fascinating and majestic hippodrome, suddenly found herself, with a little dismay, drifting into the carnage.

Rockefeller looked on the European war with undisguised disfavor. In 1915 America announced a billion-dollar loan to the Allies. Newspapers printed an alleged interview with Rockefeller in which he said he had refused to participate in that loan. Earlier in the war, to companions on the golf links, he had expressed himself freely against the war. But Standard Oil officials quickly gave out that the company would take a portion of the allied loan a little later. Rockefeller, returning from Cleveland and asked if he had any hand in the loan, replied: "Ridiculous! You boys know very well I retired from business twenty-five years ago."

The truth was that Rockefeller's vast business structure was world-wide and under it, like a collection of wholly disconnected foundations, were the nations of the world. He saw those scattered pillars quivering, swaying, some crumbling, all threatened with collapse. He was of course against the war—the chaos and disorder which delivered those shocks.

As the United States stood on the brink of the war, some of Rockefeller's statements were recalled. They were interpreted as being unfriendly to the Allies. However, friends pointed out that he had never made a public statement, that what he had said was merely his private views and that what he deplored was the conflict itself. When America plunged in he found it advisable to make a statement. He handed this to newspaper men:

"We must all stand behind the President regardless of consequences. Party, racial, and religious differences must be sunk into the melting pot of the common cause—harmonious patriotism. A state of war already exists with Germany. German U-boats are sinking ships without regard to cargo, life, nationality, or property values as recklessly as any pirate of the Spanish Main and American vessels are being compelled to arm themselves to stand off this menace."

It was under the hammering of the war, which shook up and beat out so many enduring prejudices among us that the old, hard, refractory hatred of Rockefeller began to crack a little. He made immense purchases of liberty loans. Toward the end of 1917 it was said his contributions to Y.M.C.A., Red Cross, liberty loan, and other drives amounted to seventy million dollars. As drive succeeded drive and patriotic donations were called for at public meetings, in theatres, churches, immense subscriptions by John D. Rockefeller produced thunderous applause. Men were applauding and cheering the name of Rockefeller. He made a gift to the town of Dole in France where Pasteur was born and the town named a street after him—the Avenue John Rockefeller. He gave with a free hand to all sorts of private activities. He contributed generously to Belgian relief and in 1919 when Cardinal Mercier visited America, accompanied by Cardinal Hayes, the venerable prelate went to Pocantico to deliver the gratitude of the Belgian people. The Rockefeller Foundation also not only made numerous excellent gifts but took an important part in all sorts of relief work. In 1917 the Foundation released $10,000,000 of its funds for war work, thus invading its principle funds. In August, 1917, Rockefeller reimbursed the Foundation the sums expended out of its principle to the extent of $5,500,000. He turned his New York City house into a Red Cross workroom and put the now unused Forest Hill estate in Cleveland at the disposal of the city for a war truck garden. His name now became associated weekly, almost daily, with patriotic giving and with works of healing and relief, as it had once been confounded wholly with deeds of ruthless trade war. The inscriber of resolutions who for more than forty years had been busy "whereasing" the name of Rockefeller into infamy and abhorrence, was now no less diligent

THE LAIRD OF KIJKUIT

in engrossing memorials of gratitude from men and officials and associations all over the land. Meantime he now had a brand new and highly intelligent public relations counsel, Mr. Ivy Lee, the heritage of the Ludlow episode. And all the good deeds of Mr. Rockefeller got faithfully recorded. Even when twenty-five men of draft age from his estate went into service the incident was chronicled as if Mr. Rockefeller himself had generously added them to our war machine. Even his hitherto reprobated huge income came in after a fashion for some of the new immunity, for did it not yield to the government, as the rumor went, $38,000,000 in income tax in 1918? This rumor was denied. A tax of $14,000,000, however, was paid by some one. And of course Rockefeller alone seemed capable of yielding so much fruit.

But Mr. Rockefeller had not yet wholly adjusted himself to the technique of personal salesmanship which Mr. Lee had invented for him. He still had a way in certain small matters of irritating the public. In 1918 as the coal shortage loomed, he laid in an immense store for Pocantico, buying direct from the mines. When his bins were filled he had several carloads over. People at Pocantico asked that he let them have the coal at the mine price. But he shipped it back to the mines. His own bins filled, he replied that the country might need the coal on account of the war. He closed his garage and other buildings at Pocantico to save coal. This left him with a surplus which he graciously sold to 98 families at Ossining and charged $8.75 a ton for it. The official distributor at Ossining refused to approve any such price, lopped $1.32 a ton off Mr. Rockefeller's bill and settled for $7.43 a ton. It would take a little more time before Mr. Rockefeller's able and adroit public relations counsel would rid him of all his unpleasant habits. Nevertheless his name came out of the war, as out of an alchemist's crucible, if not pure gold, at least with a first plating, over which time, clever management, and above all the changing world would lay many another coating.

II

ROCKEFELLER was a very old man now. As the war came to an end he stood upon the threshold of fourscore years. For many years his most constant and dearest employment was in the building of his magnificent estate at Pocantico. Now, nearing the age when most men sink wearily into the arms of senility he found himself in endless struggles with his neighbors and with the towns about him as he pushed out relentlessly all over the country around Tarrytown the frontiers of his immense estate. In the breast of the vigorous old monopolist the law of his nature seemed to be as potent as ever—the inordinate appetite to own everything about him. There was, indeed, in his bosom an old, deeply rooted love of land, of trees, of roads, and landscapes, going back to the remote days when as a boy he sat under the apple trees and looked with pleasure upon the richly clothed hills of his own Finger Lakes country. But there was something more than just love of the land in his heart. There was his ceaseless hankering to mold all the things he dealt in to his own plans, to order things as he wished them, to make the roads run his way, to impose his design upon the landscape. Town officials got in his way, as legislators and prosecutors did of old. Men's homes stood in his path as other men's oil plants had stood in his path twenty and thirty years before. In pursuing his plan, however, to devour the whole countryside about him he considered very little the feelings of the small home owners who were his neighbors and whose hearts might be as deeply rooted in their small patches as his was in his expanding acres. He was always willing to pay well for land and doubtless John D. Rockefeller has never been able to understand why any poor man could reasonably stand in the way of one able to buy his way. To those who stood in his way— house owners, railroads, commissioners—he opposed the same ceaseless purpose, the same stubborn patience which wore out the resistance and fortitude of all his old adversaries in oildom.

As Rockefeller bought extensively on both sides of the tracks of the New York Central's Putnam Division he soon found he had a railroad running across his estate. This road was essential to the village of Tarrytown. In 1917 the Central notified the village trustees that the division would remove its tracks and run them around another section of Rockefeller's property. It is said this operation cost Rockefeller $700,000.

Apparently he did not count the cost of anything needed to build this huge toy of his. At one point in his path as his advancing acres flowed over the Tarrytown region, St. Joseph's Normal College, standing on 300 acres, was in his way. He gave the college

THE LAIRD OF KIJKUIT

$500,000 for its land and then handed it over another million to build another college on another site. Then he turned the place into a beautiful woodland.

North Tarrytown wanted to build a stand-pipe near Croton Aqueduct on a piece of Rockefeller's property. It was essential to the town's water supply. But the old watchdog of his acres objected. It would spoil his view. He put up $25,000 and induced the trustees to build elsewhere. Far away on a piece of public property stood a smokestack. As his eye roved over the landscape this distant chimney disfigured the picture. He did not rest until he persuaded the trustees of that village to camouflage the offending object.

Through his estate ran the Longwood road from North Tarrytown to Mount Pleasant. Rockefeller had gradually acquired property on both sides. But the road was still used by many people. However, he wanted it discontinued as a public road and in January, 1926, filed a formal petition. Here he encountered one of those implacable enemies with which his career has been strewn. John J. Foley, a milkman, had inherited his quarrel with Rockefeller. Twenty-five years before Rockefeller had sought to close another road on which Foley's father operated a hotel and bar. The elder Foley had fought but finally Rockefeller had had his way. Now as Rockefeller sought to close the Longwood Road, Foley, the son, appeared with a petition signed by 100 citizens of North Tarrytown protesting against his application. The petition was defeated by a vote of three to two. But the aged battler had long ago learned that almost everything can be accomplished by him who keeps everlastingly at it. Within three weeks the petition was again renewed. Foley and his protestants were absent and the vote went to Rockefeller. He had succeeded in quieting the rebel milkman and his neighbors.

Years before a Swede named John Melin owned a saloon on the edge of Rockefeller's estate. He had a neighbor named Hyman Levy, a merchant, and the two made a solemn compact never to sell their lands to Rockefeller. They resisted the continuous persuasions of Rockefeller's agents. Then one day, several days later, Levy scratched his leg and worried so much about contracting blood-poisoning that he lost his mind, a thing no man can afford to do who has John D. Rockefeller to deal with. In spite of this Melin held to his agreement. But as years passed misfortune dogged his steps; his wife and then his sister died; his business languished; he married again and sank deeper into debt. Finally on July 25th, 1908, his saloon was put on the block. John D.'s agent of course was there and got the property.

Some five years later on a cool November day Hyman Levy suddenly recovered his mind. He looked about and was amazed to find Melin's saloon gone and the land enclosed in the Rockefeller estate. Rockefeller's agent was promptly on the scene. He convinced Levy that Melin had violated his agreement and induced the merchant to sell his own place for a good round sum.

Here in this more than royal demesne, this ancient compound of industrial Croesus and country squire, in a life as inexorably planned and ordered as the solar system, carries on with relentless purpose the design of lengthening out his existence to the last possible minute. But not at all in that perfect simplicity and frugality which good salesmanship has induced the world to imagine characterizes the ways of Rockefeller. No other human being lives in so costly an estate. The estate itself extends northward from North Tarrytown to the very boundaries of Ossining and takes in all the village of Eastview, Briggsville, Pocantico Hills, and Mount Pleasant. Scores of large estates and many hundreds of small homes have given way to make room for this private park, exceeding in extent and beauty any great public park in the world. Hundreds of old houses, renovated and improved, are now occupied by his superintendents, foremen, and workers. The old Foley Inn still stands, repainted, and fitted with modern improvements. The village of Eastview now makes a settlement for some of his employees. He owns it all save the poorhouse! The village of Pocantico is no more. Within his fences are 5,000 acres. Outside them is another 3,000 acres of the costliest suburban land in America. The land alone over which his vast parks and countless buildings are spread can be worth no less than fifty million dollars. And this is but one of his homes. The beautiful estate at Lakewood is still kept up and religiously occupied for a month or two each spring. Rockefeller still owns the fine estate at Forest Hill, though the house has been destroyed by fire and he has not been in Cleveland for sixteen years. He has a fine estate at

THE LAIRD OF KIJKUIT 471

Ormond Beach in Florida where he spends his winters and still owns, or did until two years ago, the Euclid Avenue home in Cleveland and has the town house in Fifty-fourth Street in New York.

But the place he calls home is Kijkuit, the broad house on the hill of that name, the little Olympus where the Jove of Pocantico reposes, though the town house in Fifty-fourth Street is his legal domicile. The summit got its name from the Dutch, who merely translated the Indian name which meant Lookout—an apt name, for from this beautiful home the present Sage of Kijkuit may range with his failing eyes the broad sweep of the Hudson from West Point to New York. This house, of course, is merely one of more than seventy-five buildings on the estate occupied by Rockefeller, his family, and his attendants. More than a hundred families live within his fences. Besides the elder Rockefeller's home, John D., Jr., has a still more beautiful and elaborate ivy-covered palace of brick and stone. And John D.'s married grandchildren live on the estate also in their own homes. Pocantico is an all-Rockefeller settlement. There is a children's playhouse which cost more than a million to build. Mechanical toys of the most elaborate kind, gymnasium apparatus, bowling alleys, a swimming pool—sixty by one hundred and twenty feet—are in this building. Next to it are the tennis courts and near by the house is John D.'s famous golf course.

The costly old stable has been replaced with a huge garage which houses John D. Rockefeller's fleet of fifty cars, including nearly every known make. These, of course, are the cars used for various purposes on the estate. Mr. Rockefeller himself used one car for fifteen years. There are repair shops—like a good-sized factory—dairy houses, and numerous other service buildings.

Seventy miles of private roads wind to every part of the estate, all beautifully paved and laid out to harmonize with the landscape. Many lakes, little streams, and rivulets, and a picturesque little Japanese lake dot the estate. The Japanese lake is enclosed by little walls of red Japanese stone and is surrounded by Japanese Ginkgo trees and strange shrubbery and plants from Japan. Indeed the estate is a veritable exposition ground of trees and plants. There is a grove of so-called dwarf orange trees, each over 300 years old, each standing twenty feet high, planted in huge tubs brought from the estate of the Marquis d'Aux at Le Mans, France. There are bay trees from Italy, ancient box trees and hedges from Holland, jasmine from the south of France, more than 40,000 rhododendrons. There are many other orchards and vegetable gardens which afford John D. and his immense retinue much of their fresh foods. What is needed from the outside is ordered from local dealers. It is ordered by the housekeeper at the main house by telephone. When the delivery truck reaches the road a little distance from the house it is switched off into and through a small tunnel to the delivery entrance and then sent out again without ever getting very close to the house. No one gets near the house without passing inspection. There are many gates and all are guarded. Indeed the whole estate is carefully policed.

The year around this extraordinary menage employs about a thousand people and at times the number is increased to fifteen hundred. The management of so extensive and complicated a domestic establishment becomes a problem not of housekeeping but of government. And upon the model of a city government the estate is organized. It has its own waterworks, with an appropriate department. It has its Department of Safety, which includes a completely organized fire and police department. There is a Department of Public Works which manages the roads and a Department which among other things manages the assessments of the estate, for Rockefeller's property is assessed not as one but as a thousand parcels. Over all is a superintendent, of course, and over him as chief burgomaster, Lord of the Manor or Great Earl, the Aged Laird of Kijkuit himself. As a matter of fact, however, in recent years his son John D. Rockefeller, Jr., has taken over little by little the details of management and may be said to be now in fact the officiating Administrator or Acting Mayor.

Whatever else this amazing barony may be, it is assuredly not true that the man who surrounds himself with such elaborate magnificence and such an extensive establishment lives with typical American simplicity. Here Rockefeller, far in advance of his contemporaries in the invention and organization of means to develop and direct the rushing era of mass production, but with a sixteenth century mind in the realm of social and religious phenomena, is

THE LAIRD OF KIJKUIT

able to play out his final years in the rôle most pleasing to him —that of a benevolent despot.

III

THE WAR interrupted the orderly course of Mr. Rockefeller's benefactions. With the return of peace he was able to turn again to the development of the several great boards which he had founded—the Rockefeller Foundation, the General Education Board, the Institute for Medical Research.

From the first Mr. Rockefeller had reserved to himself and his son the disposal of two million dollars a year of the revenues of the Foundation. In 1917 he relinquished that and two years later —December, 1919—he gave to the Board an additional gift of $50,438,768 in securities. It is not easy to trace all his separate gifts to the Foundation which on the face of the reports seem to have been $155,000,000 by 1919. Dr. George Vincent, President of the Board, however, in the 1922 report credited Mr. Rockefeller with having given the Foundation $182,704,624.

All this time the General Education Board had been handing around great sums—$15,700,000 between 1902 and 1919. This had gone to 120 different colleges. And as a college, to obtain a donation, had to raise an additional sum itself, these colleges were thus enabled to increase their endowments by $50,000,000.

On Christmas Day, 1919—when he announced his grant of fifty million to the Foundation—Rockefeller gave the same amount to the General Education Board to be used in coöperating with institutions of higher learning to increase teachers' salaries.

In the preceding year he had made another princely gift. The Medical Institute concentrated on the laboratory study of disease; the Foundation dealt with a multitude of human welfare problems throughout the world; the General Education Board was devoted to aiding education. This left a large field of philanthropy untouched. Mrs. Rockefeller, during her life, aided many causes which appealed especially to her—missions, hospitals, churches, child and woman welfare activities. Mr. Rockefeller continued to aid these through his personal staff. However, in 1918 he decided to establish these philanthropies upon the same business and organized basis as his others. He therefore set up a new foundation which he called the Laura Spelman Rockefeller Memorial Foundation and endowed it with $73,000,000.

After a time it became apparent that these various boards were crossing into each other's territory, duplicating effort, which was wasteful and, perhaps, getting into jurisdictional quarrels. In 1928 therefore he decided to apply to them the same process he had used on oil refineries. He decided to do a bit of consolidating. The Laura Spelman Rockefeller Memorial and the Rockefeller Foundation were merged into a single new corporation called the Rockefeller Foundation. The General Education Board was left intact. But the frontiers between the two were carefully staked out. The Foundation now has as its major function the advancement of knowledge of the medical sciences, the natural sciences, the social sciences, formerly the special care of the Spelman Memorial and the humanities. The Foundation divides with the General Education Board the field of education. The work of educational research belongs to the Foundation. The work of education belongs to the General Education Board. Where an undertaking embraces both objects then it will belong to the Foundation if research is the principal object; to the General Education Board if education is the principal object.

Thus the giant Rockefeller benevolent trusts stand, though we must make an addition. In recent years he has managed to permit the great bulk of his vast fortune to drift into the hands of his son by some process, we may be sure, which will save it from the ravages of the inheritance tax collector. And there has been a kind of understanding that this mighty fragment which exceeds what he has already given away (or did before 1929) shall be in itself a kind of benevolent trust at the disposal of his son. That son himself has made some very extensive benefactions. The most important is his creation of an International Education Board, incorporated under the laws of Virginia, and provided with a fund of $21,000,000 and chartered "to promote and advance education, whether international or otherwise, throughout the world." This body has also been incorporated in the Foundation. But the younger Rockefeller has made numerous other gifts to universities, libraries, churches, institutions, and various public purposes. By the end of 1928 his gifts had totaled $65,234,606.29.

THE LAIRD OF KIJKUIT

The total Rockefeller gifts, therefore, up to 1928, have been as follows:

By John D. Rockefeller:

Rockefeller Foundation and Laura Spelman Memorial	$256,580,081.87
General Education Board	129,197,900
Medical Institute	59,778,141.14
University of Chicago	45,000,000
Miscellaneous	18,365,000
Total	$508,921,123.01

By John D. Rockefeller, Jr:

Various gifts	65,234,606.29
Total	$574,155,729.30

This, however, is not the total of the sums which the public has received. For many years in addition to grants out of the principal of these endowments, immense sums in interest have been dispersed which would add not less than $175,000,000 to the above, so that it may be reasonably stated that various public philanthropic enterprises have received from the Rockefellers a sum equaling seven hundred and fifty million dollars.[1]

How much of this great fortune then is left? No one not in Rockefeller's confidence can answer. Several extraordinary facts, however, stand out in this connection.

---

[1] An idea of the sums received by the public, as distinguished from the capital sums given by Rockefeller, may be gathered from the following. He gave the Rockefeller Foundation $182,704,624. But that Foundation, up to 1928, gave away the following sums:

Before 1922	$ 76,000,000
1922	9,911,408.78
1923	8,431,075.20
1924	7,288,822.39
1925	9,113,730.43
1926	9,741,473.66
1927	11,223,123.79
1928	9,690,738.52
Total	$141,400,372.77

After which most of the principal was still intact.

First, Rockefeller's gifts have been about three times as great as the fortune with which he retired in 1896.

Second, that fortune could not have been more than two hundred million and an amount at least four times as much was added by sheer investment after retirement.

Third, in 1929, after having given away the immense sums

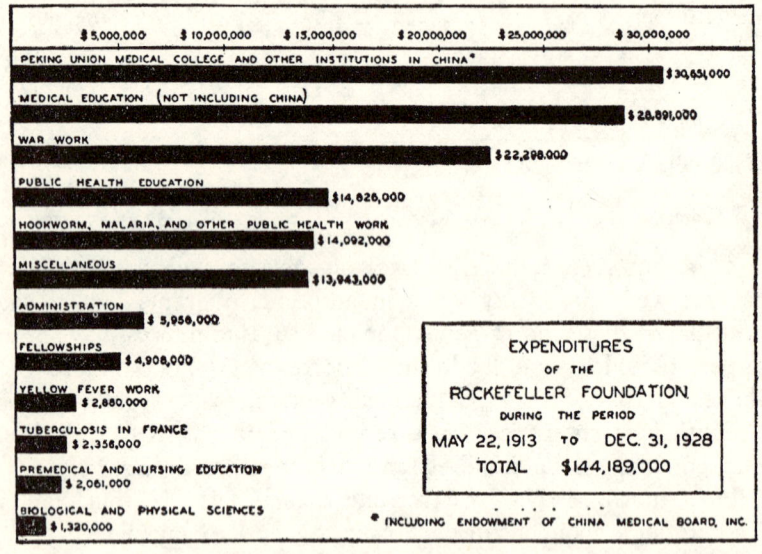

PEKING UNION MEDICAL COLLEGE AND OTHER INSTITUTIONS IN CHINA*	$30,651,000
MEDICAL EDUCATION (NOT INCLUDING CHINA)	$28,891,000
WAR WORK	$22,298,000
PUBLIC HEALTH EDUCATION	$14,626,000
HOOKWORM, MALARIA, AND OTHER PUBLIC HEALTH WORK	$14,092,000
MISCELLANEOUS	$13,943,000
ADMINISTRATION	$5,956,000
FELLOWSHIPS	$4,908,000
YELLOW FEVER WORK	$2,880,000
TUBERCULOSIS IN FRANCE	$2,356,000
PREMEDICAL AND NURSING EDUCATION	$2,061,000
BIOLOGICAL AND PHYSICAL SCIENCES	$1,320,000

EXPENDITURES OF THE ROCKEFELLER FOUNDATION DURING THE PERIOD MAY 22, 1913 TO DEC. 31, 1928 TOTAL $144,189,000

* INCLUDING ENDOWMENT OF CHINA MEDICAL BOARD, INC.

(Courtesy Rockefeller Foundation)

tabulated above, the fortune in the hands of John D. Rockefeller and his son must have been very near a billion dollars. In other words, Rockefeller's fortune has grown through mere increment faster than he could give it away.

Fourth, that fortune must be, at this time (1932) enormously reduced as a result of the widespread and drastic contraction of security values due to the depression.

Some light is thrown on this by the fate of a trust fund set up by Mr. Rockefeller in 1917 for his daughter, Mrs. Parmalee Prentice. Then the father set aside 12,000 shares of the stock of the Standard Oil Company of Indiana in a trust under the control of the Equitable Trust Company and certain trustees. The income was to be paid to Mrs. Prentice along with $30,000 a year to her husband.

At the time these shares had a par value of $100 but were quoted on the curb at $750. The Standard of Indiana thereafter had a phenomenal growth and the stock was split once while several times thereafter stock dividends were declared. When the stock was split it became 48,000 ($25) instead of 12,000 shares of $1,000 each. The 48,000 shares ultimately became 356,350 shares, not counting a few thousand which were disposed of. In 1929 they were worth $63 a share or $22,450,050. Today (May 27, 1932) the trust has shrunk to $6,102,497.

How shall we measure in terms of wisdom, virtue, and social utility these extraordinary gifts, so stupendous in terms of dollars? The answer calls up the whole question of the soundness of private philanthropy. Looked at subjectively the matter involves the intricate and obscure anatomy of human motive. Men have said that Rockefeller gave to create an ambush of good will behind which he might carry forward his schemes of profit or that he was silencing the murmurings of a guilty conscience, or to redeem his damaged fame.

Rockefeller's large-scale philanthropy did not begin until he had retired from active participation in his most cherished great dreams of profit. And as to the murmurings of a guilty conscience, there is no evidence that Rockefeller's conscience has ever troubled him. He has been well content with his course. He has been always committed to that paternal concept of Christian society in which the management of affairs is supposed to be entrusted by Divine wisdom to the efficient and the strong, who, in accumulating riches for themselves, provide employment for their less capable brothers and who, upon the principle of noblesse oblige are charged with the obligation to use their riches for a good purpose. This may be said to be the superficial reason for Rockefeller's philanthropies.

When this has been said it is still to be admitted that men's minds arrive at such convictions by processes not so obvious to themselves. It falls out that such a philosophy fits admirably the purposes of the acquisitive man. And no man who has examined the operations of his own mind or who has read the history of human weakness needs to be told that the mind has an infinite talent for inventing philosophies to support its own desires. It would be folly to deny that vanity plays a large part in the motivation of rich men's public charities. And then there is the pure luxury of giving as a form of personal indulgence; a kind of weakness which leads men to seek the pleasant sensation of witnessing his beneficiaries basking in the warmth of his own generosity; a weakness which leads him to lie down and luxuriate in the gratitude of others as some men do in a warm bath. The element of sacrifice in Mr. Rockefeller's giving can hardly be considered, for after handing out more than half a billion dollars, he still retains at least as much for himself. Nevertheless it ought to be conceded that there is something on the side of the rich man like Rockefeller whose weakness is for giving usefully to a world for which he feels a bond of sympathy rather than one like Morgan, who spent his money chiefly upon himself and who got his delights out of wallowing in his fortune and looking down with scorn upon the men from whom he had squeezed it. Subject to all these considerations, therefore, Rockefeller must be given credit for having used his fortune for a social purpose. He has done something more. He did not merely give. He brought to bear upon his giving the same patient intelligence he employed in his gathering.

He assembled machinery to be sure his gifts were not wasted on unworthy objects. He aimed to put aside the salve box for the knife in reaching the cause of human suffering. He had a horror of giving where the gift was not needed. Some Brooklyn citizens wanted to build a hospital. Through St. John McKelway, they asked Rockefeller to bear half the cost. He asked for time to consider the matter. They thought it a polite refusal. Months later he sent for McKelway. He had an exhaustive report before him and a large map of the neighborhood of the proposed hospital. "If you will examine this map," he said, "you will see there is already a hospital in this neighborhood doing most of the work you propose as well as your hospital could do it. The other part of the work, which is not being done, will, however, require twice as much as you seek to raise. If you will change your plans and double your part, I will give you twice what you ask for. And now how do you propose to support the institution?"

"The Lord will provide," answered McKelway, whose group had really not considered that point.

"Perhaps he will," said Rockefeller. "But the Lord is pretty busy. I think we had better create a little surplus."

"To give is an art," he said. "To give to everybody who asks is

THE LAIRD OF KIJKUIT

an injustice, because it takes from more deserving ones. I am fortunate that there are times when I can say 'No.'"

As time wore on he ceased to be interested in helping people directly. The processes of his giving were focused on the root causes of human suffering. The area of his assistance ranged over a vast territory. It required human agents. It would be strange if these have always answered to the most perfect standards of human behavior. His gifts must be judged by the broadness of the conception, the dignity of the purpose, and the magnificence of the bounty.

The Medical Institute has now organized an extensive plant for the laboratory study of disease. It has an extensively equipped institution in New York and another in Princeton where a staff of some twenty-two able medical scientists and twice as many associates and assistants are enabled to pursue "under favorable conditions and with adequate support for an indefinite period, unhurried and unhindered by the urgency of obviously practical or immediate results" the problems of diseases in men, animals and plants. It has three departments—its laboratories, its hospital and its department of animal and plant pathology. Its whole resources are devoted to research. There is no teaching. Its hospital is purely for experimental and clinical research.

The Institute has studied cerebro-spinal meningitis, infantile paralysis, epidemic influenza and epidemic encephalitis. The public is in some degree familier with the work of such men as Dr. Alexis Carrel in surgery, Dr. Hideyo Nagouchi in Rocky Mountain spotted fever, trachoma and yellow fever; Dr. Rose in the study of hookworm; Drs. Wade Hamptom Brown and Richard Mills Pearce in the study of syphilis. The net dividends of the Institute to society, however, would require an amount and degree of auditing which the present writer feels he has no capacity to make. Its work is in the domain of the physical sciences and there progress must depend upon the patient accumulation of knowledge. At intervals startling discoveries excite the popular imagination. Not infrequently they represent the final reaching and grasping of some rich result in which the long, patient and almost unrewarded climb up the lower stages of the journey are almost obscured. Every such discovery is always just one more piece of knowledge achieved on top of other immense accumulations of knowledge. Mr. Rockefeller has wisely provided a mechanism for slowly, patiently broadening the base of knowledge and piling it up for the benefit of those who may be moved to climb higher. The conception would seem to be an intelligent one. The provision in the way of funds is ample. The care in organizing has been minute. Whether or not the mechanism thus created achieves as much as it might reasonably be expected to achieve, will depend upon the human energy with which it is implemented at different periods in its life.

As to the General Education Board—it has given up to 1929, $81,068,510.73 to more than 200 colleges and innumerable schools. The giving has been done according to a plan which has resulted in the accumulation of twice as much again in endowments. The more substantial result has been the creation of a huge plant for education in America. That is a beginning. Perhaps the education will come later. Up to now the system of which this has been so important a part, has had one unhappy effect. Almost every college president in the land has been hanging with his hat in his hand and his eye on his economics department around the almoners of the Rockefeller boards and other rich men of the country. Putting our system of higher education at the mercy of millionaire industrialists and financial promoters has had upon our colleges the same influence as it has had upon the church and the press. This, we may hope, is a passing phase. It may be that in another generation the schools and the endowments will remain free from the influence of the donors and their economic interests.

As for the Rockefeller Foundation there can be no doubt of the immense value of its assistance to countless worthy and noble human activities. It has aided innumerable medical schools, it has made studies of disease all over the world—tuberculosis in France, yellow fever in Guatemala and other places, malaria in Arkansas and Mississippi, hookworm in the South and throughout the world, infantile paralysis everywhere. It has established scholarships and has supported hundreds of fellowships to assist earnest students to pursue their researches, equipped laboratories, and done a hundred other useful works.

The popular picture of the philanthropist Rockefeller is of a cold and bloodless incarnation of scientific giving. As a matter of fact, he has always had his own little private charities. He maintains a large pension list on which appeared until they passed away the names of many of the old timers of Oildom, not a few those who claimed they had been crushed by the ruthless industrialist of the earlier days.

IV

WHAT of the vast enterprise which Mr. Rockefeller reared and the system of which he was the chief architect? One must concede that it has borne rich fruits for its creators. What have been the dividends of society, of labor, for instance?

Before the Sunday School class of the Fifth Avenue Baptist Church, May 1, 1910, Mr. Rockefeller said:

"I think the most valuable donation is a gift to honest labor. During the forty years I have been in a particular branch of business our company has paid out each working day from $60,000 to $70,000 or $20,000,000 a year to honest laboring men. This in forty years makes a total of from $600,000,000 to $700,000,000. That I regard as the greatest pleasure which may be given to man."

The statement is full of meat. It is fully in harmony with the Wesleyan ethic that from the upper levels of the social structure the benefits of wages descend upon the workers beneath as a kind of gift "to honest labor" from the appointed of the Lord. But this is the least of its implications.

In those forty years the laborers had drawn from the enterprise $600,000,000. But in that same time Mr. Rockefeller and his associates had drawn a sum equally as large in dividends. But there still remained in undistributed assets a sum at least as large again, the accumulated value of the years which had not been withdrawn. This belonged to Mr. Rockefeller and his colleagues. To put the matter differently, Mr. Rockefeller and his few associates took as their share a sum twice as great as the thousands of workers. It is probably true that Rockefeller paid as good if not better wages than most of his contemporaries and that he did not loot his enterprise through the medium of stock jobbing operations as most of his contemporaries did. The Standard Oil may be looked upon, in the matter of administration and treatment of labor, as a capitalistic administration at its best. Yet there seems to be something obviously out of gear in a mechanism which makes so unjust a distribution of the rewards of industry.

What of the public dividend in the way of lower prices for oil? There is but very little evidence that the Standard was ever actuated in Rockefeller's day by any overmastering desire to reduce prices. It was in pursuit of profits all the time. It was in pursuit of monopoly until restrained by law. The price of oil fell over a long course of years under the influence of innumerable developments. The Standard, so far as appears in the records, was never a leader in the reduction of prices. It was a leader in the adoption of modern producing methods as they appeared and in the perfection of large-scale and economic management. But it passed on to the public the benefits of those economies only to the extent that it was pressed by actual or threatened competition.[1]

Mr. Rockefeller's achievement must be classified under the head of organization. He originated practically nothing. He added little or nothing to the innumerable devices by which the price of oil was brought down. But he led the way in the use of almost everything, in the organized employment of all the devices and forces which were available for large scale production. He was also among the first to deal with the new problems of industry. The forces of trade and industry had become wild—no longer amenable to the corrective elements of the old automatic economy. These new forces needed regulation, but society remained blind to this. In a growing and spreading collectivism they continued to talk the language of the old individualism. Government disclaimed the right to regulate. Rockefeller discarded, after experiment, the idea of regulation by association. He committed his fortunes to regulation by private monopoly through the corporate form. Sixty years ago he saw the need of planning against the untamed and destructive forces of an unregulated economy. He set about erecting a mechanism for planning in the industry in which he worked. He left out of the planning authority the public which paid all the bills. His mechanism might be good as long as it was benevolent. But sixty years of such planning have served to demonstrate that it is almost never benevolent and that it will not work. It is now in process of abandonment. It is for this reason we may properly say that we approach the end of the Rockefeller era.

[1] For a full exposition of the course of prices during Rockefeller's régime as head of the Standard see "The Trust Problem" by Jeremiah Jenks and Walter E. Clark, Fifth Edition, pp. 107-114 (Doubleday, Doran).

V

SINCE 1915 we have been witnessing the phenomenon of selling Mr. Rockefeller to the American people, a process carried on under the sales direction of Mr. Ivy Lee, who, as we have seen, joined the Rockefeller staff at the time of the Ludlow troubles. Mr. Lee has done a most excellent job. But he has had the collaboration of forces even more potent than his efficient sales machine.

Mr. Lee introduced something new into this sort of personal salesmanship. He asked Mr. Rockefeller and Standard Oil to look itself over, to mend its manners, to remove "the harmful irritants," from its methods and to consider the public reaction to its acts when making its policies. He went further and induced the great company to take the public more into its confidence, to remove the Chinese wall of secrecy behind which even its most harmless operations took place. The press was supplied continuously with full information about all the good deeds of Standard Oil. So far as I know, however, but little effort has been made, in recent years at any rate, to interfere with the printing of anything. The emphasis has been placed rather upon cultivating good relations with the press.

But something more potent than all this has been at work. Before 1915 Mr. Rockefeller was performing on a wholly different stage. Then he was at war with the existing system. Newspapers and magazines were filled with the stories of his ruthlessness, of attacks by legislators and prosecutors, the flight of witnesses and the pursuit of marshals, the tales of men who had been ruined, stories of bribed lawmakers, of railroad corruption, of unfair discriminations. But for years Rockefeller had no part in such transactions. The old headlines read "Rockefeller Indicted Again," "Standard Oil Before the Bar," "Oil Men Lay Ruin to Rockefeller," "Standard Oil Magnates Dodge Subpoenas." The modern headlines run: "Rockefeller Gives Another Million to Unemployment Fund," "Rockefeller Foundation Fights Pellagra in Georgia," "John D. Gives Dimes to Children." In the old magazine the stories were entitled: "Is the Senate the Corrupt Tool of Standard Oil?" "Tainted Money," "The Church and the Reward of Iniquity," "Rockefeller Faces Justice." Today they are: "How the Rockefellers Give Millions," "When I Caddied for John D.,"

"Employee Representation in Standard Oil," "Rockefeller Now Plays One Hundred Per Cent Golf."

The figure of the striding, ruthless monopolist in high hat and long coat gripping his walking stick and entering a court house has been replaced by pictures of a frail old man, playing golf with his neighbors, handing out dimes to children, distributing inspirational poems, and walking in peace amid his flowers. Another generation has rolled in upon us. He has outlived the men who denounced him and the generation which hated him.

The world has changed. The industrial world has changed to conform to the pattern he set for it. The press has changed. The old press was owned or controlled largely by men interested in politics. It reveled in the denunciation of business men. The modern press belongs to business. It is on the side of business. It is very naturally on the side of the advertiser, particularly the big advertisers. Standard Oil is a very big advertiser. Stories criticizing Rockefeller are not now desired. Stories critical of business are not desired. What is called "constructive" material is what is wanted. We have seen not merely the sale of Mr. Rockefeller to the public but all business and along with it the once-hated master of Standard Oil.

VI

WHAT of the great company? The evidences of its life and ubiquity dot the roadsides of the world. People have a way of thinking of it as a vast empire, operating under scores of different names, but all ruled by a few master minds at 26 Broadway under the dominion of John D. Rockefeller, acting through his son. It is a hardy legend. But it isn't so.

The Standard when dissolved in 1911 split into thirty-three corporations. But all had the same stockholders. The old directors continued to rule the affairs of each company. Under the old order each corporation had a separate region to work in. The Standard of New York operated in New York and New England. The Jersey company had New Jersey, Maryland, Virginia, District of Columbia and the Carolinas. Pennsylvania was served by the Atlantic Refining Company. The Standard of Indiana had as its domain Indiana, Illinois, Iowa, Michigan, Minnesota, Missouri, North and South Dakota. The Standard of California had the Pacific Coast and part of Arizona. Then there were the Standard of Kentucky,

THE LAIRD OF KIJKUIT

of Kansas, of Nebraska, of Ohio, the Continental Oil Company, the Vacuum Oil Company, each with its special sphere of influence marked out. These were refining and marketing companies. Besides there were pipe line, shipping, manufacturing and financial corporations. After the dissolution all these companies continued to operate in their allotted fields. People laughed when they thought of the "dissolution decree."

But now the old regional frontier lines of the great Standard confederacy are being slowly obliterated. Competition, the arch devil of business in Rockefeller's creed, has actually invaded Standard Oil itself. The Rockefellers have actually withdrawn from five Standard units. The various Standard units are becoming wholly independent and competing concerns spreading out over their old boundaries as full-fledged rivals of each other.

VII

AMID the elaborate and ostentatious settings of his various estates the sober-faced boy of the Finger Lakes regions, who wanted to be worth a hundred thousand dollars, moves toward the final scenes in his long and significant life. The country has become familiar with an aged, slightly stooped, amazingly wrinkled old gentleman photographed in a hundred attitudes on the golf course. Rockefeller plays every day when the weather permits and always has a guest or two or more to play with him. To his various homes comes a steady stream of friends, curiosity seekers, old associates, and new ones anxious to have a game of golf with the richest man in the world.

Wherever he may be his daily routine is about the same. He rises at seven, strolls around his house and perhaps the garden giving nickels to each member of his establishment he meets. He glances at the newspaper and then has breakfast. At a quarter to nine he indulges for fifteen minutes in a game of numerica—something like Canfield solitaire. This sort of lubricates and cranks up his mental machinery.

At nine he is in his office, where a secretary and several assistants look after his business affairs. At 26 Broadway under the direction of his son is the more imposing business staff which manages his vast investments. But here at home he keeps a certain amount of business under his own hands. He likes to buy and sell stocks. He always has a collection of shares which he keeps more or less active in the market. This keeps his mind from growing rusty. He gets reports on the progress of all his great philanthropic boards and on the major features of his larger investments. Sometimes he puts his hand deeply into some enterprise that interests him particularly, as when he had Andrew J. Thomas, the famous architect, build for his son a large group of model apartments in Tarrytown. A voluminous mail is delivered to Pocantico every day. Sometimes there will be 2,000 letters, most of them asking for money, many of them telling him what to do with his wealth. He never reads an appeal for help. It goes to his staff at 26 Broadway.

At 10 o'clock business is done and he is on the golf links. He will have the village minister or the priest at Tarrytown, the high school principal, some friends, or some notables anxious to meet him as partners and foes. He used to play nine holes, but now plays no more than eight but stops short of that if he feels fatigued. At noon he is done. Then he bathes, changes his clothes, lies down for a rest, and lunches at 1:15. After lunch he plays two or three games of numerica and at half past three goes for a motor ride. He seeks always new routes and is apt to invite into his car any person of the village he meets whom he knows. This ride may extend from twenty-five to fifty miles. At 5:30 he enjoys a long rest, after which he changes into his dinner jacket and sits down to his table with a group of guests. He never dines alone. At 8:30 dinner is over and then he brings the day to a close with his guests in conversation, perhaps music from his magnificent pipe organ or perhaps a performer or two brought to the house for the purpose, or some games of numerica, or songs. He is in bed by 10 o'clock.

This program is almost unvarying. The names of the guests who will sit down with him to dinner on any day can be given at any time by his household a week or two ahead.

The favorite guests are the simple people who live around his homes. Rockefeller never has felt any hunger for the companionship of the brilliant. He has had few if any friendships among scholars or thoughtful men save such alleged scholars as have been the beneficiaries of his bounty. He has not been a student himself; he has read little; he has pondered very little the abstract and philosophical basis of things. In religion he has been satisfied with the theology of the village preacher. In economics he has been content with such principles as have fallen in with his own interests. In government he has been well pleased with what we have had, save that he would like to see the government remain out of business affairs as thoroughly as it did when he first set to work. In politics he has taken his beliefs from the bookkeeping sections of his mind and always supported the Republican candidates. The test of his own interests has been the basis for adopting views on most subjects and about the fundamental principles of all these things he has reflected hardly at all. His mind is perfectly adapted to weighing and measuring material things. It is formed to proceed with perfect orderliness. His spirit is regulated by an almost boundless patience and a relentless appetite to have its own way. It has been able therefore to move with extraordinary efficiency toward any goal it selected. When it relaxed, however, and sought diversion, the conversation of workmen, clerks, village preachers, and business men like himself afforded him all the variety he needed.

A few years ago after service one Sunday morning at Lakewood he handed around to all, instead of dimes, little slips of paper on which was printed a poem. He had a reporter read it while he listened raptly.

"Lord of all pots and pans and things, since I've no time to be
A saint by doing lovely things for watching late with Thee,
Or dreaming in the twilight, or storming heaven's gates,
Make me a saint by getting meals or washing up the plates."

"Isn't that beautiful?" murmured the aged man, moved by this glorification of lowliness from the soul of a servant girl poet.

It must not be supposed that his life, though rigidly ordered, is merely a wearisome plodding on to the final goal. Rockefeller has said many times that he is happy. "He lives each day with a zest and a satisfaction and happiness given to few men," says a friend who has seen much of him. "From his early morning stroll in the gardens, singing the songs of his youth or the old hymns in a round full baritone voice, to the time when he listens to the last strains of the evening music his daily life is a round of work, play and, above all, of gratitude." There is no reason to doubt this picture. Nor is there any reason to withhold admiration for the man who, by his complete conquest over himself, has exhibited the capacities of the human mind for achievement. His is the outstanding example of a planned life.

For the rest almost any newspaper reader can tell the round of Rockefeller's life—his journeys at stated seasons each year to Florida, to Lakewood, to Pocantico; his giving away of dimes wherever he meets people, his birthdays each year, his golf games and his advice about cheerfulness and health and work and lately his appearances in the sound pictures and, we must not fail to observe—the movie audiences who smile pleasantly at his appearance and applaud as he murmurs, "God bless Standard Oil."

VIII

Mr. Rockefeller once wrote:

"The great majority of my associations were made so many years ago that hardly a month goes by that I am not called upon to send some message of consolation to a family with whom we have been connected and who have met with some fresh bereavement. Only recently I counted up the names of the early associates who have passed away. Before I had finished I found the list numbered some sixty or more."

This was written twenty-four years ago in the *World's Work* when Rockefeller, nearing seventy, thought himself an old man. Since then another quarter century has rolled over his head. It has washed from the scene practically all that was left of the men who worked with him and served him and fought him. As he sits now by the fireside in his room at Pocantico, musing upon all that great company of adventurers and crusaders and counts them over the number must appall him—the serious and authoritative Pratt, the dashing and commanding Harry Rogers, the sly and truculent Archbold, the bold and unscrupulous Henry M. Flagler, and a host of still younger men; the Hannas and Aldriches and Sibleys and Elkinses and Forakers who served him so profitably and the Rices and Lawsons and Pulitzers who harried him and the more powerful antagonists—the Roosevelts and Bryans who laid on such heavy blows—all are gone. Rockefeller himself, who by the force of his patience, his resoluteness, and his irrefragable concentration, became the master of all his associates, has, by aid of those same qualities, hung grimly to life and outlived them all.

SOURCES

To AVOID *the incessant use of reference notes, distracting to the average reader and of interest only to the occasional student, I have attempted to arrange here the sources of the material on which this history is based. As far as practicable I give below, classified according to the parts into which the book is divided, the published works, public records, magazine and newspaper articles, from which I have drawn.*

It is necessary to add here two comments:

First, that much material has been derived from personal interviews with men and women who either had a part in the events narrated in this volume, or were in a position to know something of them;

Second, that an immense amount of the material has been drawn from the newspapers of the period in New York City, Cleveland, and the Oil Regions. These papers have been read, day by day, over many periods and I have prepared for my own convenience an index to some of these papers which is obviously too voluminous to be included here.

PART ONE—THE QUIET YEARS, 1839-1853

ANCESTRY

Records of "Rockefeller Family Association, Transactions," 1910 to 1926, Volumes I, II, III.

EARLY YEARS

Data about John D. Rockefeller's early life in New York is of course meager. The writer visited Owego, county seat of Tioga County, Richford, Moravia, and Auburn, county seat of Cayuga County, all in New York. He talked with many old residents and relatives of the Rockefeller family and went through the files of all available newspapers in those towns, as well as the material in the local libraries and the Historical Society of Auburn. He is greatly indebted to the researches of Mr. Leroy Kingman, an old schoolmate of John D. Rockefeller at Owego Academy and founder of the Owego *Gazette*. Mr. Kingman truly answered to the character of the old-time antiquarian, deeply interested in the early history of Owego and Tioga County. He made it a practice over a great number of years while editing his newspaper to interview all the old residents of the region who possessed recollections of its history; and these interviews, together with notes and elaborations by Mr. Kingman himself, appeared frequently in the columns of the *Gazette*. They constitute to this day an invaluable repository of historical material about Tioga County and incidentally the early days in Tioga of John D. Rockefeller, his family and associates. The writer is indebted to Mr. Harry E. Kingman, the son of Mr. Leroy Kingman, and now editor of the *Gazette*, for making this material available to him.

BRUTCHER, CHARLES, "Joshua, a Man of the Finger Lakes Region." Published by the author, 1927.
KINGMAN, LEROY W., "Our County and Its People—a Memorial History of Tioga County." Elmira, N. Y., W. A. Ferguson Co., 1897.
PIERCE, H. B. and HARD, D. H., "History of Tioga, Chemung, Tompkins and Schuyler Counties, New York." Philadelphia, Everts and Ensign, 1897.

ECONOMIC HISTORY

BEARD, CHARLES A. and MARY R., "The Rise of American Civilization." The Macmillan Co., 1929.
CLARK, VICTOR S., "History of Manufactures in the United States," Vols. I, II, III. McGraw-Hill Book Co., 1929.
KIER, MALCOLM, "Industries in America, Manufacturing." The Ronald Press, 1928.
PUMELLY, J. C., "Historical Data on Pioneer Days." New York, 1892.

PART TWO—BUSINESS AND RELIGION, 1853-1859

Cleveland, Ohio, *Herald*—files, 1859-1880.
Cleveland, Ohio, *Leader*—files, 1859-1880.
AVERY, E. MC., "A History of Cleveland and Its Environs." New York, Lewis Pub. Co., 1918.

SOURCES

"Historical Sketches"—Seventy-five Years of the Euclid Avenue Baptist Church, 1851-1926. Collected and arranged by Historical Committee of the Church, Cleveland, Ohio, 1926.
JOBLIN, MAURICE, "Cleveland Past and Present." Cleveland, 1869.
JOHNSON, CROSFIELD, "History of Cuyahoga County, Ohio." Cleveland, 1879.
KENNEDY, JAMES H., "A History of the City of Cleveland." Imperial Press, Cleveland, 1896.
ORTH, SAMUEL, "History of Cleveland." Cleveland, 1910.
ROBINSON, W. SCOTT, "History of Cleveland." Cleveland, 1887.

PART THREE—OIL DORADO, 1859-1864

Oil City *Derrick*—files
Titusville *Morning Herald*—files
Documents, magazines, pamphlets and exhibits in the Drake Museum in Titusville.
The *Derrick's* "Handbook of Petroleum," Derrick Pub. Co., Oil City, Pa., 1859.
    This is a day-to-day history of the oil regions compiled from the files of the Titusville *Morning Herald*, Oil City *Register*, Oil City *Derrick*, Pithole *Daily Record*, Petroleum Center *Record*, *Petroleum Age*, *Oil Men's Journal*, Bradford *Era* and Venango *Spectator*.
BACON, RAYMOND FOSS and HAMOR, W. A., "The American Petroleum History." McGraw-Hill Book Co., 1916.
CONE, ANDREW and JOHNS, W. R., "Petrolia." D. Appleton & Co., 1870.
CORNELL, WM. M., "The History of Pennsylvania." 1879.
EGLE, WM. H., "Illustrated History of the Commonwealth of Pennsylvania." 1880.
HENRY, J. D., "History and Romance of the Petroleum Industry." Bradbury, Agnew & Co., London, 1914.
HENRY, J. T., "Early and Late History of Petroleum." Philadelphia, 1873.
LIDGETT, ALBERT, "Petroleum." I. Pitman & Son, New York, 1919.
MCLAURIN, J. J. "Sketches in Crude Oil." The author, Harrisburg, Pa., 1896.
"Oil Region Reminiscences of Oil Men's Association of Butler County." 1907.
REDWOOD, SIR BOVERTON, "Romance of Petroleum." Royal Institute of Great Britain, London, 1917-19.

SOURCES

REINHOLT, OSCAR HALVORSEN, "Oildom, Its Treasures and Tragedies." National Petroleum Institute, Washington, D. C., 1927.
STOCKING, G. W., "The Oil Industry and the Competitive System; A Study in Waste." Houghton Mifflin Co., Boston and New York, 1925.

PART FOUR—WAR AT THE CREEK, 1865-1872

Volumes given above and also the following:

"A History of the Rise and Fall of the South Improvement Company." Petroleum Producers Union, Oil City, Pa., 1873.
LLOYD, HENRY DEMAREST, "Wealth Against Commonwealth," New York, 1894.
MONTAGUE, G. H. "The Rise and Progress of the Standard Oil Company." Harper & Bros., New York, 1903.
TARBELL, IDA M. "History of the Standard Oil Company," Vols. I, II. The Macmillan Co., 1904.

PARTS FIVE-EIGHT *INCLUSIVE*, 1873 TO PRESENT

GENERAL HISTORY

ADLER, CYRUS. "Jacob Henry Schiff." American Jewish Committee, 1921.
BURR, MRS. ANNA ROBESON. "Portrait of a Banker" (Stillman). Duffield & Co., 1927.
CARNEGIE, ANDREW, "The Autobiography of Andrew Carnegie." Houghton Mifflin Co., 1920.
CLARKE, GEORGE J. "Jay Gould in His True Light." New York, 1901.
CLEWS, HENRY, "Fifty Years in Wall Street." Irving Pub. Co., New York, 1908.
COREY, LEWIS, "The House of Morgan." G. Howard Watt, 1930.
CROFFUT, W. A. "The Vanderbilts and the Story of Their Fortune." Bedford, Clark & Co., New York, 1886.
HARVEY, GEORGE, "Henry Clay Frick, the Man." Chas. Scribner's Sons, New York, 1928.
HOVEY, CARL, "The Life Story of J. Pierpont Morgan." Sturgis and Walton Co., New York, 1911.
JOHNSON, W. FLETCHER, "Life of Jay Gould." Edgewood Pub. Co., 1892.
FLEMING, W. L., "The Sequel of Appomattox," Chronicle of America Series, Vol. 32. Yale Press.

SOURCES

LLOYD, CARO, "Henry Demarest Lloyd," Vols. I, II. G. P. Putnam's Sons, New York, 1912.
MYERS, GUSTAVUS, "History of Great American Fortunes," 3 vols. Chas. H. Kerr & Co., Chicago.
MUNRO, N. L., "$100,000,000! How Commodore Vanderbilt's Great Fortune Was Made," New York, 187?
OBEHOLZER, ELLIS PAXON, "A History of the United States Since the Civil War," 5 vols. (4 already published). The Macmillan Co., 1926.
OGILVIE, J. S., "Life and Death of Jay Gould." The Author, New York, 1892.
PAYNE, A. B., "Mark Twain." Harper & Bros., 1912.
SULLIVAN, MARK. "Our Times," "The Turn of the Century," "Pre-War America." Chas. Scribner's Sons, 1929, 1930.
TARBELL, IDA M., "The Life of Elbert H. Gary, a Story of Steel." D. Appleton & Co., 1926.
THOMPSON, HOLLAND, "The Age of Invention," Chronicles of America Series, Vol. 37. Yale Press.
WHITE, TRUMBULL, "The Wizard of Wall Street and His Wealth or the Life and Deeds of Jay Gould." Mid-Continental Pub. Co., Chicago, 1892.
WRIGHT, C. D., "Industrial Evolution in the United States." Chas. Scribner's Sons, 1902.

TRUSTS

State of New York, Report of Senate Committee on General Laws on Investigation Relative to Trusts. Sen. Doc., 3rd Sess., Vol. 5, March 6, 1888.
State of New York, Trust Investigating Committee—Report and Proceedings, March 9, 1897.
State of Ohio, Trust Investigation of Senate of State of Ohio, 1898.
United States House of Representatives. Trust Investigation of Committee on Manufactures. Proceedings in Relation to Trust, No. 3112, 1888.
United States Industrial Commission. Industrial Combinations, Vols. 1, 4, 13, 1900.
United States Senate, report of Committee Investigating Money Trust. Known as "Pujo Investigation." Washington, 1912.
ANDERSON, P. LEWIS, "The Rule of Reason." New York, 1911.
COTTER, ARUNDEL, "United States Steel, a Corporation with a Soul." Doubleday, Page & Co., 1921.
DEWING, A. S. "Corporate Promotions and Reorganizations." Harvard Economic Studies, 1914.

DODD, S. C. T., "Combinations: Their Uses and Abuses, with a History of the Standard Oil Trust." G. F. Nesbitt & Co., New York, 1888.
GRAY, W. H., "The Rule of Reason in Texas." The Author, Houston, Tex., 1912.
JENKS, JEREMIAH and CLARK, WALTER E., "The Trust Problem." Doubleday, Doran & Co., 1929.
KEEZER, D. M. and MAY, STACY, "The Public Control of Business." Harper & Bros., 1930.
PETTIGREW, R. F., "Triumphant Plutocracy." The Academy Press, New York, 1922.
"Portrait and Biographical Record of Saginaw." Biographical Pub. Co., Saginaw, Mich., 1892.
STEVENS, W. S., "Industrial Combinations and Trusts." 1913.
SWEET, WILLIAM H., "Brief History of Saginaw County." Michigan Pioneer and Hist. Soc. Collections, Vol. 28, 1900.
RIPLEY, WILLIAM Z., "Trusts, Pools and Corporations." Ginn & Co., 1916.
WALKER, ALBERT H., "History of the Sherman Anti-Trust Law." The Equity Press, 1910.

Magazine Articles

"Tendency of Modern Combination." A. Youngman, Journal of Political Economy, Appendix, 1907.
"Protection Afforded by the Law," Harper's Weekly, Aug. 8, 1908.
"Onward March of Privileged Wealth," Arena, Jan., 1909.
"State Partnership with Business," Independent, Feb. 18, 1909.
"Government Investigation," Current Literature, June, 1909.
"Sherman Law Decisions and Possible Results," Harper's, Dec. 11, 1909.
"Argument for Publicity," Review of Reviews, Oct., 1911.
"Recent Trust Decisions," Political Science Quarterly, Dec., 1911.
"Trust-Busting vs. Regulation," Outlook, Aug. 2, 1913.
"Monopoly," Outlook, Oct. 12, 1912.
"Morgan-Rockefeller-Carnegie, a Digest of Their Testimony Before the Industrial Relations Commission, Harper's Weekly, Feb. 20, 1915.
"Coming to Grips with Monopoly," New Republic, Mar. 28, 1923.
"LaFollette and Standard Oil," by W. Hard, Nation, Sept. 17, 1924.

SOURCES

RAILROAD PROBLEMS AND REBATES

Commonwealth of Pennsylvania vs. Pennsylvania R. R. Co., United Pipe Lines, etc. Testimony, 1879.
State of New York, Report of Special Committee on Railroads, New York State Assembly, 1879.
Interstate Commerce Commission Bill. See Congressional Record, Vol. 17, 1886, 1st Sess., 49th Cong., pp. 3861, 4118, 4344, 4706, 4874, 6815, 7247, 7203, 7250, 7269, 7308, 7350.
FERNON, T. S., "Notes on the Anti-Discrimination Craze in the Pennsylvania Legislature." Philadelphia, 1883.
MOODY, JOHN, "The Railroad Builders." Chronicles of America Series, 1919, Yale Press.
PARSONS, FRANK, "The Heart of the Railroad Problem." Little, Brown, & Co., Boston, 1906.
RIPLEY, WILLIAM Z., "Railway Problems." Ginn & Co., 1913.
RIPLEY, WILLIAM Z., "Railroads; Rates and Regulation." Longmans, Green, 1913.
WALKER, GUY MORRISON, "Railroad Rates and Rebates." New York, 1917.

Magazine Articles

"Railway Discrimination and Industrial Combinations," Annals of American Academy, Jan., 1900.
"Wealth and Secret Discrimination of Freight Rates," Independent, Feb. 20, 1902.
"New Anti-Rebate Law," Independent, Mar. 12, 1903.
"Unjust Discrimination," Independent, Dec. 3, 1903.
"Atchinson Road's Rebates," Independent, Jan. 12, 1905.
"Railway Rebates and Preferences," Outlook, July 1, 1905.
"Railroad Rebates," McClure's, Dec., 1905.
"Foraker, Opponent of Government Rate Making," Harper's Weekly, Mar. 11, 1906.
"Railroad Rate Debate in the Senate," Independent, June 14, 1906.
"Railway Rebates and Earnings," Independent, July 26, 1906.
"Important Rebate Decision," Independent, July 12, 1906.
"Do the Railway Rate Law and the Sherman Anti-Trust Law Need Amendment?" Harper's Weekly, Aug. 18, 1906.
"Secret Rates," Outlook, May 4, 1907.
"Decision as Regards Railway Rebates," Outlook, Mar. 7, 1908.
"No Rebates by Contract," Outlook, Mar. 28, 1908.
"Oil Trust Rebate Case," Independent, Mar. 18, 1909.

SOURCES

"Strengthening the Elkins Act," Journal of Political Economy, April, 1909.
"Railroad Freight Rates in Relation to Industry and Commerce," Nation, October 14, 1909.
"Early Railroad Monopoly and Discriminations in Rhode Island," Yale Review, Nov., 1909.
"Rebate Conspiracy," Cosmopolitan, Dec., 1909.
"Questions About Rebates," Outlook, Dec. 9, 1911.
"Decline in Exports with Drawback Allowance," Iron Age, Jan. 8, 1914.
"Railroads Still Rebating," Literary Digest, Feb. 14, 1914.
"Railway Discriminations," Journal of Political Economy, May, 1912.
"Railroad Rate Situation," Journal of Political Economy, Nov., 1912.

STANDARD OIL COMPANY

State of Pennsylvania. Standard Oil Company Investigation, Report to Governor, Philadelphia, 1884.
State of Ohio. Report of Attorney-General. 1899.
State of Ohio. Attorney-General Monnett vs. Buckeye Pipe Line Co., Solar Refining Co., Standard Oil Company. Decided Jan. 30, 1900—61st Ohio State Reports, 520
State of Missouri. Attorney-General Hadley vs. Standard Oil Co. of Indiana, Waters-Pierce Oil Co. and Republic Oil Co. No. 218 Missouri Reports, Mar. 9, 1908.
Circuit Court of United States, Southern District of Ohio, Eastern Division. Case of Parker Handy & John Paton, Trustees, vs. Cleveland and Marietta Railroad Co., et al. 1885.
United States Supreme Court, Lake Shore and Michigan Central Railway Co. vs. Scofield, Shurmer and Teagle. Transcript of Record, October term 1886, No. 1, 290.
United States Bureau of Corporations, Report of Commissioner of Corporations on Petroleum Industry. Washington, 1907.
United States Bureau of Corporations, Statement of Commissioner in answer to allegations of Standard Oil Company concerning its conviction at Chicago for accepting concessions on shipments over Chicago and Alton Railroad. Washington, Government Printing Office, 1907.
Interstate Commerce Commission, Report on Discriminations and Monopolies in Coal and Oil, 1907.
United States Circuit Court of Appeals—7th Circuit. Opinion Reversing Judgment of United States District Court—United States vs. Standard Oil Co. of Indiana, Chicago, 1908.

SOURCES

United States Circuit Court for Eastern Division of East Judicial District of Missouri. United States of America vs. Standard Oil Co. of New Jersey. Vols 1 and 2, Washington, 1909.
United States Supreme Court, Standard Oil Co. of New Jersey vs. United States of America. Opinion delivered by Mr. Chief Justice White; dissenting opinion by Mr. Justice Harlan, delivered May 15, 1911. (U. S. Senate, 62nd Cong., 1st Sess., Doc. No. 34). Washington, Government Printing Office, 1911.
United States Senate, Industrial Relations Committee Report. Sen. Doc. 415, 64th Cong., 1st Sess.
BUTLER, BENJAMIN F. "Argument Before Committee on Commerce of House of Representatives for an Investigation of the Monopolies of the Standard Oil Co. and its Subsidiaries." Washington, Gibson Bros., 1880.
Four Brothers Independent Oil Co., "Oil War! to the Consumers of Kerosene Oil." Artist Printing Co., Williamsett, Mass., 1909.
General Service Corporation, "Report on Standard Oil Co. and former Subsidiaries." F. S. Smithers & Co., New York, 1912.
History of the Organization, Purposes and Transactions of the General Council of the Petroleum Producers' Unions, and of the Suits and Prosecutions Instituted by it from 1878 to 1880. 1880.
HUBBARD, ELBERT, "H. H. Rogers, Little Journeys to the Homes of Great Business Men." New York, 1909.
HUBBARD, ELBERT, "The Standard Oil Company." The Roycrofters, East Aurora, New York, 1910.
KLEIN, HENRY H., "Standard Oil or the People: The Cause of 'Hard Times' in America." The Author, New York, 1914.
LLOYD, HENRY DEMAREST, "Wealth Against Commonwealth." New York, 1904.
Oil City *Derrick*, "Pure Oil Trust vs. Standard Oil Co., being report of an investigation by United States Industrial Commission compiled from private and official sources, 1899-1900." Derrick Publishing Co., Oil City, Pa., 1901.
Oil and Petroleum Manual, Year Book, 1910-1931.
RICE, GEORGE, "Standard Oil Company and Standard Oil Trust." Marietta, Ohio, 1897.
TARBELL, IDA M., "History of the Standard Oil Company," 2 vols. The Macmillan Co., 1904.
"Truth's" Investigator, "The Great Oil Octopus." T. F. Unwin, London, 1911.
SHERMAN, ROGER, "The Standard Oil Trust: The Gospel of Greed." New York, 1892.

WINSTON, A. P., "Public Opinion and the Standard Oil Company." Nixon-Jones Printing Co., St. Louis, 1908.

Magazine Articles

"Policy, Methods and Aims of Standard Oil Company," by John D. Rockefeller. Engineering Magazine, Jan., 1901.
"Genesis of Standard Oil," by W. M. Clemens. New England Magazine, Mar., 1902.
"Rise and Supremacy of Standard Oil," by G. H. Montague. Quarterly Journal of Economy, Feb., 1902.
"Standard Oil Company," by G. H. Montague. Independent, Sept. 17, 1903.
"New Benefits to Oil and Steel Workingmen," Gunton's, Feb., 1903.
"Later History of the Standard Oil Co.," by G. H. Montague. Quarterly Journal of Economy, Feb., 1902, Feb., 1903.
"Ida Tarbell's Tale of the Standard Oil," Gunton's, Feb., 1904.
"Oil Fields and Pipe Lines of Kansas," Outlook, May 6, 1905.
"Beef and Oil Trusts," Independent, Mar. 2, 1905.
"Study of the Master Trust," Arena, Oct., 1905.
"Kansas State Refinery Bill and Its Significance," Arena, May, 1905.
"Legend of the Standard Oil Company," by G. H. Montague. North American Review, Sept., 1905.
"Defense of Standard Oil," Review of Reviews, Aug., 1905.
"Kansas Conscience," Reader, Oct., 1905.
"President and Standard Oil," World Today, June, 1906.
"Trail of Standard Oil," Living Age, Nov. 17, 1906.
"Kansas Oil Rates Complaints," Outlook, Apr. 14, 1906.
"Ohio Standard Oil Case," Outlook, Nov. 3, 1906.
"Roosevelt's Message and the Garfield Report," Outlook, May 12, 1906.
"Standard Oil Convicted," Outlook, Oct. 27, 1906.
"Standard Oil on Trial," Outlook, Nov. 24, 1906.
"Kansas Oil Producers' Problems," Outlook, Feb. 10, 1906.
"Commissioner Garfield and the Standard Oil Trust," Outlook, Dec. 15, 1906.
"Profits of Standard Oil," Outlook, Dec. 15, 1906.
"Standard Oil on the Defensive," Outlook, May 26, 1906.
"Standard Oil Cases," Independent, Nov. 22, 1906.
"Indictments," Current Literature, Sept., 1906.
"Is the Senate the Corrupt Tool of the Standard Oil Company?" Arena, Jan., 1906.
"At the Bar," Arena, Mar., 1906.

"Standard Oil Report," Outlook, June 1, 1907.
"Standard Oil Decision and the Stock Exchange Collapse," Nation, Aug. 15, 1907.
"Standard Oil Fine," North American Review, Sept., 1907.
"Standard Oil Troubles," Nation, Aug. 8, 1907.
"Judge Landis' Decision," Outlook, Jan. 19, 1907.
"Production of Oil," Outlook, Sept. 28, 1907.
"Oil Prices and Standard Oil Profits," Outlook, Aug. 24, 1907.
"Monopoly Methods," Outlook, Feb. 9, 1907.
"Standard Oil Defense," Outlook, Aug. 31, 1907.
"Transportation Phase of the Oil Industry," Journal of Political Economy, Oct., 1907.
"Standard Oil Company at the Bar," Current Literature, Sept., 1907.
"Oil Trust Fined $29,240,000," Aug. 8, 1907.
"Oil Trust Trial," Independent, Sept. 26, Oct. 17, 1907.
"Oil Trust Suits," Independent, Aug. 15, 1907.
"Interstate Commerce Commission's Report," Arena, Mar., 1907.
"Methods," Independent, Feb. 7, 1907.
"Progress in the Big Fine Case," Outlook, Nov. 21, 1908.
"Standard Oil Case," by G. H. Montague, Outlook, Sept. 19, 1908.
"Rehearing in the Indiana Case," Outlook, Aug. 29, 1908.
"Oil Trust and the Government," Political Science Quarterly, Mar., 1908.
"Reversion of Judge Landis' Judgment," Outlook, Aug., 1908.
"Petroleum, a Great American Industry," Independent, Mar. 5, 1908.
"Oil Trust Judgment Annulled," Independent, July 30, 1908.
"Oil Trust and the Campaign," Independent, Oct. 1, 1908.
"Story of Hisgen and the Octopus," Current Literature, Sept., 1908.
"Escape of the Standard Oil Company," Current Literature, Sept., 1908.
"Standard Oil and the Conscience of the Nation," Arena, Dec., 1908.
"Popular Rule or Standard Oil Supremacy, Which Shall It Be?," Arena, Mar., 1908.
"Methods of Standard Oil Co.," American Magazine, Dec., 1908.
"Standard Oil and the Courts," Nation, July 30, 1908.
"World-Wide Triumphs," by C. M. Keys, World's Work, Aug., 1908.
"Word to the Standard Oil Company," World's Work, Nov., 1908.
"How the Standard Oil Does Its Business," World's Work, Sept., 1908.
"Great Standard Oil Fine," World's Work, Sept., 1908.
"Government vs. Standard Oil Company," World's Work, Sept., 1908.

SOURCES

"Commissioner of Corporations and Standard Oil Co.," Outlook, Jan. 4, 1908.
"Dissolution of Oil Trust Ordered," Independent, Nov. 25, 1909.
"Standard Oil Decision," Nation, Nov. 25, 1909.
"Chapter in High Finance," Nation, May 27, 1909.
"New Trial for the Standard Oil Company," Outlook, Jan. 16, 1909.
"Standard Oil in Missouri and Texas," Outlook, Feb. 13, 1909.
"Unconscious Pirates," Nation, Apr. 22, 1909.
"Standard Oil Case," Outlook, Dec. 4, 1909.
"Standard Oil Acquitted in Big Fine Case," Outlook, Mar. 20, 1909.
"Experiences in the Oil Business," by John D. Rockefeller. World's Work, Mar., 1909.
"Standard Oil and Other Decisions Under the Sherman Anti-Trust Law," World's Work, Jan., 1910.
"Defense of Standard," Outlook, Mar. 26, 1910.
"Trusting Prosperity," Independent, Mar. 17, 1910.
"Standard Oil Decision," by A. D. Noyes, Forum, Jan., 1910.
"Another Blow at Standard Oil," Current Literature, Jan., 1910.
"Supreme Court and Standard Oil," Current Literature, June, 1911.
"Doom of the Monopolizing Trust," World's Work, July, 1911.
"Standard Oil Ex-Subsidiaries," Review of Reviews, Oct., 1911.
"Standard Oil Decision—and After," by Theodore Roosevelt, Outlook, June 3, 1911.
"Standard Oil Decision—an Interpretation," Outlook, May 27, 1911.
"Dissolution of Standard Oil," Outlook, Aug. 12, 1911.
"After the Standard Oil Decision," Nation, May 25, 1911.
"Standard Oil Company—Bankers," by J. Moody and G. K. Turner, McClure's, Mar., 1911.
"Empire of Oil," Living Age, May 20, 1911.
"Condemnation of the Standard Oil Trust," Living Age, June 24, 1911.
"Supreme Court Speaks," by E. G. Lowry, Harper's, June 3, 1911.
"Results of the Standard Oil Decision," by F. B. Kellogg, Review of Reviews, June, 1912.
"In Status Quo," Nation, Sept. 5, 1912.
"Greatest Killing in Wall Street," McClure's, Aug., 1912.
"Standard Oil at 900," Literary Digest, Mar. 30, 1912.
"Dissolved Trusts Under Scrutiny," Literary Digest, June 15, 1912.
"Higher Standard Oil Dividends," Literary Digest, Nov. 30, 1912.
"How a Dissolved Trust Prospers," Literary Digest, Mar. 23, 1912.
"Germany Ousting Standard Oil," Literary Digest, Nov. 23, 1912.

SOURCES

"After Standard Oil in Germany and Asia," Literary Digest, Oct. 26, 1912.
"Standard Oil and the Judiciary," Hearst's Magazine, Sept., 1912.
"What's the Explanation?" Everybody's, June, 1912.
"Steel and Oil Prosperity," Literary Digest, Apr. 4, 1914.
"Standard Oil and China, Partners," Literary Digest, Feb. 28, 1914.
"Employee Representation in Standard Oil," Independent Management, May, 1920.
"Speeches at Standard Oil Meeting of Employees and Company's Representatives," Independent Management, July, 1920.
"Fifty Years of the Standard Oil Company," World's Work, Mar., 1920.
"Standard Oil Melons," Literary Digest, Oct. 28, 1922.
"Rockefeller Money in Oil," Literary Digest, Apr. 21, 1923.
"No One Man Ownership in Standard Oil," Literary Digest, Jan. 13, 1923.
"Vision of Dollar Gasoline," Literary Digest, Mar. 17, 1923.
"Standard Oil Salaries," Literary Digest, Mar. 3, 1923.
"Is the Standard Oil Crumbling?" by Ida M. Tarbell, New Republic, Nov. 14, 1923.
"Sinclair vs. Standard Oil in Russia," Nation, Aug. 6, 1924.
"After Standard Oil Again," Literary Digest, July 12, 1924.
"Standard Oil Greater but Less Dominant," Literary Digest, June 14, 1924.
"Black Golconda, the Evolution of Standard Oil," by I. F. Marcosson, Saturday Evening Post, May 3, 1924.
"Where Workers Are Partners: Standard Oil Company of New Jersey," by W. C. Teagle, World's Work, July, 1924.
"America and Mosul," by L. Fischer, Nation, Dec. 30, 1925.
"Standard's Place in the Oil Business: Recommendations of the Federal Trade Commission," Literary Digest, Mar. 28, 1925.

GOVERNMENT AND BUSINESS

Testimony Before Sub-Committee on Privileges and Elections, United States Senate, 62nd Cong., 3rd Sess. Senate Resolutions 79, 386, 418, Moses E. Clapp, chairman. Government Printing Office, Washington, 1913.
ACHESON, SAM HANNA, "Joe Bailey, the Last Democrat." The Macmillan Co., 1932.
ADAMS, F. B., "The Waters-Pierce Case in Texas." Skinner and Kennedy, St. Louis, Mo., 1908.
BEER, THOMAS, "Hanna." A. A. Knopf, 1929.

SOURCES

BISHOP, JOSEPH B., "Charles Joseph Bonaparte, His Life and Services." Chas. Scribner's Sons, 1922.
BISHOP, JOSEPH B., "Theodore Roosevelt and His Time," 2 vols. Chas. Scribner's Sons, 1920.
BUSBY, L. W., "Uncle Joe Cannon." Henry Holt & Co., 1927.
BUTT, ARCHIBALD W., "Taft and Roosevelt." Doubleday, Doran & Co., 1930.
CRAWFORD, W. L., "The Whole Story of the Unholy Alliance Between Senator Bailey and Standard Oil." Eclectic News Bureau, Dallas, 1907.
CROLY, HERBERT S., "William Howard Taft." Minton, Balch, 1930.
FORAKER, JOSEPH BENSON, "Notes of a Busy Life." Stewart and Kidd Co., Cincinnati, 1916.
LAFOLLETTE, ROBERT, "Autobiography." R. M. LaFollette Publishing Co., Madison, Wis., 1913.
LAWSON, THOMAS W., "Frenzied Finance." Ridgway-Thayer Co., New York, 1904.
KENNAN, GEORGE, "E. H. Harriman." Houghton Mifflin Co., 1922.
MOTT, T. BENTLEY, "Myron T. Herrick, Friend of France." Doubleday, Doran & Co., 1929.
PRINGLE, HENRY F., "Theodore Roosevelt." Harcourt, Brace & Co., 1931.
OLCOTT, CHARLES S., "Life of William McKinley." Houghton Mifflin Co., 1916.
ODEGARD, P. H., "Pressure Politics." Columbia University Press, 1928.
STEFFENS, LINCOLN, "Autobiography of Lincoln Steffens." Harcourt, Brace & Co., 1931.
WINKLER, JOHN K., "W. R. Hearst, an American Phenomenon." Simon and Schuster, 1928.

Magazine Articles

"Treason of the Senate," by David Graham Phillips, Cosmopolitan, Feb., 1906.
"Justice vs. Politics," Harper's Weekly, Sept. 21, 1907.
"Virtues and Vices of the Government," Outlook, Sept. 28, 1907.
"More Archbold Letters," Independent, Oct. 29, Nov. 5, 1908.
"Additional Archbold Letters," Independent, Oct. 8, 1908.
"Archbold and Foraker Letters," World's Work, Nov., 1908.
"Foraker and Standard Oil," Nation, Sept. 24, 1908.
"Hearst's Forgeries," by A. H. Gleason, Collier's, Oct. 5, 1912.

SOURCES

"Roosevelt and Standard Oil," by A. M. Law, Harper's Weekly, Sept. 7, 1912.
"Penrose Accusations," Literary Digest, Aug. 31, 1912.
"Campaign Funds in 1904 and 1912," Literary Digest, Sept. 7, 1912.
"Another Standard Oil Lesson," by W. R. Hearst, Hearst's Magazine, Dec., 1912.
"More Letters Relating to Mr. Roosevelt and Republican Campaign Committees," by W. R. Hearst, Hearst's Magazine, Nov., 1912.
"More Standard Oil Letters," by W. R. Hearst, Hearst's Magazine, Oct., 1912.
"New Standard Oil Letters and Their Lessons," Hearst's Magazine, June, July, Aug., 1912.
"Lesson of the Standard Oil Letters," by W. R. Hearst, Hearst's Magazine, May, 1912.
"History of the Standard Oil Letters," Hearst's Magazine, May, 1912.
"Letters to Standard Oil Faithfuls," Hearst's Magazine, May, 1913.
"Friendly Letters of Standard Oil," Hearst's Magazine, Apr., 1913.
"When Standard Oil Carried West Virginia," Hearst's Magazine, Mar., 1913.
"Standard Oil Spider and the Senatorial Fly," Hearst's Magazine, Jan., 1913.
"Standard Oil Treacheries," Hearst's Magazine, June, 1913.
"Standard Oil and Its Hirelings of the Press," Hearst's Magazine, July, 1913.

JOHN D. ROCKEFELLER

Commonwealth of Pennsylvania vs. John D. Rockefeller, William Rockefeller, J. A. Bostwick, Daniel O'Day, William G. Warden, Charles Lockhart, H. M. Flagler, Jacob J. Vandergrift, Charles Pratt, and George W. Girty. Court of Quarter Sessions of the Peace for the County of Clarion, Pennsylvania, 1879.
Standard Oil Co. vs. William Scofield et al. Court of Common Pleas, Cuyahoga Co., Ohio, 1880.
Case of James Corrigan vs. John D. Rockefeller. Court of Common Pleas, Cuyahoga Co., Ohio, 1897.
Anti-Saloon League Year Book, 1908-present.
CHERRINGTON, E. H., "History of Anti-Saloon League." American Issue Publishing Co., 1913, Westerville, Ohio.
"Famous Living Americans." C. Webb & Co., Greencastle, Ind., 1915.
FORBES, B. C., "Men Who Are Making America." B. C. Forbes Publishing Co., 1916-17.

GATES, FREDERICK T., "The Truth About Mr. Rockefeller and the Merritts." G. P. Putnam's Sons, New York, 1911.
HARDEN, MAXMILIAN, "Monarchs and Men." John C. Winston Co., Philadelphia, 1913.
HOWE, M. A. DEWOLFE, "Causes and Their Champions." Little, Brown, & Co., Boston, 1926.
HUBBARD, SILAS, "John D. Rockefeller and His Career." 1904.
ROCKEFELLER, JOHN D., "Random Reminiscences of Men and Events." Doubleday, Page & Co., New York, 1909.
ROCKEFELLER, JOHN D., JR., "Addresses Delivered at Pueblo, Col., at joint meeting of employees and representatives of Colorado Fuel and Iron Co." W. H. Kistler Stationery Co., Denver, 1915.
SPARGO, JOHN, "A Socialist View of Mr. Rockefeller." C. H. Kerr & Co., Chicago, 1905.
YOUNG, JOSIAH R., "Satan's Reception of John D., a Satirical Poem." The Knapp Press, New York, 1907.

Magazine Articles

"Character Sketch of John D. Rockefeller," by Julian Ralph, Cosmopolitan, June, 1902.
"French Judgment of John D. Rockefeller," Review of Reviews, Apr., 1904.
"Rockefeller's Sermon," Outlook, Oct. 7, 1905.
"Lengthened Shadow of a Man," Current Literature, June, 1905.
"Study of Character, Motive and Duty," by W. G. Joerns, Arena, Aug., 1905.
"Rockefeller as a Truth Teller," by W. Gladden, Independent, June 8, 1905.
"How the Richest Man in the World Observes Christmas," Woman's Home Companion, Dec., 1905.
"Rockefeller and Mob Opinion," World's Work, Sept., 1906.
"Protecting the World's Richest Man," by William R. Stewart, Pearson's Magazine, Oct., 1906.
"Rockefeller's Protest," Independent, Oct. 11, 1906.
"One Kind Word for John D.," by Frederick Palmer, Collier's, 1906.
"Opportunity in America," Cosmopolitan, Aug., 1907.
"Limiting Opportunity," Independent, Aug. 15, 1907.
"Thirty-two Millions," Independent, Feb. 14, 1907.
"Bright Side of Rockefeller," Current Literature, Mar., 1907.
"Roosevelt vs. Rockefeller," by Ida M. Tarbell, American Mercury, Dec. and Jan., 1908.

SOURCES

"Mr. Dooley on a New Literary Light," by F. P. Dunne, American Mercury, Dec., 1908.
"Owners of America," by A. H. Lewis, Cosmopolitan, Nov., 1908.
"Two John D. Rockefellers," Current Literature, Nov., 1908.
"Rockefeller Will Vote for Taft," Independent, Nov. 5, 1908.
"Master Builder of Standard Oil," by S. C. T. Dodd, Review of Reviews, Mar., 1908.
"Impressions of Rockefeller," by F. N. Doubleday, World's Work, Sept., 1908.
"Simplicity of Rockefeller," Current Literature, May, 1909.
"Country Home of Rockefeller," House Beautiful, June, 1909.
"Rockefeller at Play," by W. Hemmingway, Harper's Weekly, Feb. 13, 1909.
"Religion and Conduct," Living Age, July 24, 1909.
"Random Reminiscences of Men and Events," by John D. Rockefeller, World's Work, Oct., 1908 to Apr., 1909.
"Intimate View of Rockefeller," American Magazine, Nov., 1910.
"Uncle Sam's Present to John D. Rockefeller," Current Literature, Sept., 1912.
"Tolstoy and Rockefeller," by M. Harden, Bookman, Dec., 1912.
"American Millionaire's Hobby," House Beautiful, Mar., 1913.
"Rockefeller's Dilemma," by L. Wallis, Harper's Weekly, Nov. 8, 1913.
"Cunning and Dishonest," by Frank P. Walsh, Survey, Nov. 14, 1914.
"Federal Industrials Relations Commission and Rockefeller Bureau," Survey, Oct. 10, 1914.
"John D. Lets the Cat Out of the Bag," Current Opinion, Nov., 1917.
"Sargent's Rockefeller," New Republic, Feb. 9, 1918.
"John D. Now Plays 100 Per Cent Golf," Literary Digest, May 24, 1919.
"Paul Manship's Dramatic Vision of Rockefeller," Current Opinion, July, 1920.
"Mr. Rockefeller in Art," Literary Digest, June 19, 1920.
"Our Biggest Money Maker," Literary Digest, July 9, 1921.
"Recollections of J. D.," by G. D. Rogers, Saturday Evening Post, July 30, 1921.
"More About J. D.," by G. D. Rogers, Saturday Evening Post, Dec. 10, 1921.
"Billionaire Era: The Rockefellers and Ford," by A. Train, Forum, Dec., 1924.

"When I Caddied for John D.," by J. O'Donnel, Collier's, Aug. 1, 1925.
"His Master's Voice," by Henry Pringle, American Mercury, Oct., 1925.
"Ivy Lee, Minnesinger to Millionaires," New Republic, Nov. 20, 1929.
"Black Legend," Atlantic Monthly, May, 1929.

PHILANTHROPIES

General Education Board. An Account of Its Activities, 1902-1914. Yearly Report, 1914 to present.
Laura Spelman Rockefeller Memorial. Annual Report 1922 to 1928. For later years see Rockefeller Foundation with which Memorial was merged in 1929.
Rockefeller Foundation. Annual Report, 1913-1930. New York, Rockefeller Foundation.
Rockefeller Foundation. Information furnished by Rockefeller Foundation in response to questionnaire submitted by United States Industrial Relations Commission. New York, 1915.
Rockefeller Foundation. The Philanthropic Boards Established by John D. Rockefeller, New York, 1916.
Rockefeller Institute for Medical Research. History, Organization and Scope of Scientific Work. New York, 1906, 1911-12, 1914, 1921, 1923-24, 1926-29, 1931.

Magazine Articles

"Gift of $10,000,000 for Colleges," Review of Reviews, Aug., 1905.
"Rockefeller and the American Board of Foreign Missions," Outlook, Apr. 1-22, 1905.
"Report of Prudential Committee of American Board," Outlook, Apr. 22, 1905.
"Scapegoat," Outlook, Apr. 15, 1905.
"Church a Witness Bearer," Outlook, Apr. 22, 1905.
"God's Gold," Missionary Review, May, 1905.
"Reply to Dr. Gladden by Starr J. Murphy," Independent, May 18, 1905.
"Church and the Reward of Iniquity," by W. Gladden, Independent, Apr. 20, 1905.
"Tainted Money," Independent, Apr. 6, 1905.
"Correspondence on the Rockefeller Gift," by J. L. Barton, Independent, Apr. 20, 1905.

SOURCES

"Rockefeller and the American Board of Missions," Current Literature, May, 1905.
"Baptists and Mr. Rockefeller," by J. B. Calvert, Independent, Feb. 1, 1906.
"King's Ransom for American Education," Outlook, Feb. 16, 1907.
"Gift to General Education Board," Science, Feb. 15, 1907.
"Clergyman on Rockefeller's Grip on the Baptist Church," Arena, Feb., 1909.
"Rockefeller's Greatest Gift," by W. H. Allen, Survey, May 15, 1909.
"Founding a Philanthropic Trust," Current Literature, Apr., 1910.
"Universal Benefaction," Harper's, Mar. 12, 1910.
"Looking a Gift Horse in the Mouth," by A. J. Portenar, Independent, June 23, 1910.
"Rockefeller Intends to Establish a Benevolent Corporation," Independent, Mar. 10, 1910.
"Questioned Benefaction," Independent, June 23, 1910.
"Bill to Incorporate the Rockefeller Foundation," Nation, Mar. 10, 1910.
"Philanthropy and Poet," Nation, Mar. 17, 1910.
"Great Endowment," Outlook, Mar. 12, 1910.
"Final Rockefeller Gift to University of Chicago," Outlook, Dec. 31, 1910.
"Congress and the Rockefeller Foundation," Jan. 7, 1910.
"Incorporated Charities," Popular Science, Apr., 1910.
"University of Chicago and Rockefeller," Science, Dec. 30, 1910.
"Should the Rockefeller Foundation Amend Its Charter?" Survey, Mar. 26, 1910.
"Reasons Against Federal Chartering of Rockefeller Foundation," Survey, Mar. 26, 1910.
"Rockefeller Foundation," by S. J. Murphy, Survey, Apr. 2, 1910.
"Rockefeller Foundation Charter," Survey, Dec. 24, 1910.
"Donation for Promotion of Human Welfare," Survey, Mar. 12, 1910.
"Philanthropic Trust," World's Work, May, 1910.
"Economic and Moral Aspect," by W. Babcock, Survey, Mar. 11, 1911.
"Plan of Incorporation," Survey, Jan. 14, 1911.
"Amending the Charter," Survey, Jan. 14, 1911.
"Rockefeller Hundred Million Foundation," Independent, Feb. 8, 1912.
"Charter of the Rockefeller Foundation," Survey, Feb. 24, 1912.

"Rockefeller Foundation and Stricken Europe," Outlook, Nov. 11, 1914.
"Rockefeller Foundation to Study Industrial Unrest," Survey, Oct. 10, 1914.
"$20,000,000 to Improve Our Doctors," Literary Digest, Oct. 18, 1919.
"Gift for Improvement of Medical Education in the United States," Science, Oct. 3, 1919.
"Gift for Medical Education from John D. Rockefeller," School and Science, Oct. 4, 1919.
"Mr. Rockefeller's Gifts," Science, Jan. 2, 1920.
"Mr. Rockefeller's Gift for Increased Salaries of Academic Teachers," School and Science, Feb. 14, 1920.
"Mr. Rockefeller's Gift for Education," School and Science, Jan. 3, 1920.
"How the Rockefellers Give Millions," Ladies' Home Journal, Mar., 1925.
"Responsibility of Wealth," by A. Davis, Saturday Evening Post, May 23, 1925.

INDEX

Abbott, Dr. Lyman, 392, 422
Acme Oil Co., 190, 219, 250, 320
Africa, 247
Albany, N. Y., 218
Alcohol. See Prohibition
Aldrich, Nelson W., 359, 377, 380, 449
Alexander, J. H., 238
Alexander, Hewitt & Co., 159
Alexander, Scofield & Co., 136, 147
Amalgamated Copper Co., 344
American Petroleum Co., 210, 211
American Sugar Refining Company, 318
"Anaconda," origin of term, 165
Andrews, E. Benjamin, 308
Andrews, Samuel, 105, 139
Anthony's Hotel, 103
Anti-Trust Law. See Trusts
Applegarth, Dr. H. C., 338
Appleton, Samuel, 29
Archbold, John D., 62, 187, 217, 237, 285, 292, 317, 361; attempted assassination, 464; Bailey, checks to, 367; bribery letters, 353; bribing Foraker, 353; character, 334; corruptionist extraordinary, 353; early life, 163; forms Acme Company, 190; finances magazines, 272, 441; Gunton, pays, 441; Hanna, aids, 382; Hearst, exposed by, 434; indictment in Buffalo, 273; Industrial Commission, before, 370; influencing, 372; letters stolen, 433; Lloyd, attacks, 329; political contributions, 353; religion, 334; Rockefeller, sides with, 176; Sibley, Joseph, his agent, 353; South Improvement Co., fights, 166; Standard Oil Co.,

elected President of, 448; acting head of, 334; trial of, 222; witness stand, on, 219
Armstrong, B. D., 208
Armour, Philip, 62
Arter, Frank A., 161
Asia, 247
Astor, John Jacob, 29
Astor, William, 29
Atlantic & Great Western R. R., 154
Atlantic Monthly, 253
Atlantic Refining Co., 188
Atlantic Refinery, 188
Atwell, James, 215
Auburn, N. Y., 33, 36
Austria, 246

Babcock, Paul, 237
Backus, Mrs. F. M., accuses Rockefeller, 202
Bailey, Joseph, 367
Baird, Thomas R., 373
Baku, 246
Ballyhoo. See Publicity—Jay Cooke
Baltimore and Ohio R. R., 192
Baltimore United Oil Co., 198
Baptist *Examiner*, 296
Baptist Union Theological Seminary, 270
Barnsdall, Mead & Rouse, 86, 88
Barnsdall, William, 86
Barrels, 84, 94
Barstow, F. Q., 237
Baslington, George O., 145
Baxter, Judge John, 260
Bayonne, N. J., laying pipes through, 226
Beard, Prof. Charles, 102
Belmont, August, 29

INDEX

Bemis, Prof. Edward W., 308
Benninghoff, Old, 179
Benson, B. D., 192, 208, 210, 225
Benzine, 128
Bibliotheca Sacra, 309
Big Island, 40
Biggar, Dr. M. F., 269, 325, 417
Bishop, C. E., 165
Bissell, George H., 75, 85
Bogus Independents, 409, 410, 415
Bohlen, John, 29
Booth, Prof. J. C., 78
Booth, John Wilkes, 120
Boston, 127
Bostwick, Jabez A., 153, 162, 169, 187, 192, 213, 217, 219, 237, 238
Bowers, L. M., 454
Boyle, Patrick, 271, 292
Bradford Field, 212
Brady, Anthony N., 409
Brevoort, Henry, 29
Brewer, Dr. F. B., 76, 88
Brewer & Watson, 76, 94
Brewster, Benjamin, 158, 162, 237, 317
Bronson, Isaac, 29
Brooks, Peter C., 29
Brower, Scott, 35
Brown, Thomas, 117
Bryan, William J., 3
Bryant, John, 29
Buffalo, 127, 144
Buffalo Lubricating Oil Co., Ltd., 274
Burkett, Judge Jacob, 356
Bushnell, John, 237
Bushnell, Thomas, 237
Butterick, Dr. Wallace, 384

Camden, J. N., 198, 206
Cameron, Simon, 98
Campbell, B. B., 208, 217, 222, 285
Carlisle, John G., 326
Carnegie, Andrew, 62, 102, 107, 129, 143, 263, 347, 417
Carter, Col. John J., 323
Cary, first oil man, 22
Cassatt, Benjamin, 193, 198, 207, 217, 266, 354
Catlin, Gen. Isaac C., 45
Cayuga Joint Stock Co., 37
Central High School, 51, 52
Chain College, 57, 59

Charles Pratt and Co., 219, 248
Chase, Salmon P., 98
Chess, Carley & Co., 241, 243, 250, 257, 258
Chicago, University of, 443; Bemis incident, 307; founded—gift from Rockefeller, 305; founding *Journal of Political Economy*, 307; origin of, 304; Rockefellers gift to, 311
Choate, Joseph H., 283, 300
Christy, A. B., 270
Cincinnati *Commercial Gazette*, 256
Cincinnati & Marietta R. R., 260
Civil War, 99, 100, 109, 111, 114, 115; and oil, 98, 103; beginnings in Cleveland, 71; rich men in, 102; Rockefeller in, 101
Clark & Rockefeller, 68
Clark & Andrews, 107
Clark, H. F., 154
Clarke, Payne & Co., 157, 161
Cleveland, 66, 85, 93, 100, 105, 106, 107, 126, 127, 128, 133, 135, 144, 151, 155, 160, 162, 185, 269, 331; in 1854, 50
Cleveland, Grover, 222, 257, 281
Cleveland *Plain Dealer*, 164
Coal oil, 79
Coal Oil Johnny, 112, 113, 114, 179
Colorado Fuel and Iron Co., 453
Combination, 107, 109, 139, 150
Commons, John R., 308
Communipaw, N. J., 226
Competition, 27, 125, 150, 173, 213, 221, 484
Constable Hook, N. J., 226
Corporations, 26, 27; holding company, 138; merger movement, 345; New Jersey laws, 343; rise of, 137; rise of promoters, 345
Corrigan, James and John, 363
Cortelyou, George L., 381, 429
Coryville, Pa., 225
Court Actions against Rockefeller, 216
Cowdray, Lord, 362
Coxey's Army, 326
Crawford County, 22
Crosby, Prof., 75, 88
Crosby, William, 29
Crowell, J., 237
Culp, J. M., Company, 258

INDEX

Culver, C. V., 208
Curtis, Mary, 42, 101
Cushing, John P., 29
Czolgosz, 376

Daillon, Joseph Delarock, 55
Dalton, Norton, 269
David Dow & Co., 220
Davison, John, 7, 14, 38
Day, Chancellor, 334
Debs, Eugene V., 319, 326
Dennen, Mrs. Sarah S., purchase of Rockefeller birthplace, 15
Depew, Chauncey, 218, 220, 358
Depression, of 1855, 61; of 1857, 66; of 1873, 183; of 1892-96, 310, 325; of 1907, 381, 428
Deterding, Henry, 362
Doane, W. H., 136
Dodd, Samuel C. T., 137, 167, 216, 248, 251, 253, 283, 285, 300, 301, 341, 365, 421
Drake, Edwin L., 75, 81, 85, 88, 89, 93, 140
Drake Monument, 141
Drawbacks, 156; from Erie R. R., 198; in Macksburg, 260; instances of, 260, 267; suggested origin of, 267
Drew, Daniel, 129, 395
Duck, H. R. S., 258

Eaton, Dr. C. A., 31, 419
Edison, Thomas, 62
Education, business college, 57, 59
Elkins Fortune, 4
Ely, Richard T., 308
Emery, Lewis J., Jr., 209, 262, 285, 322
Empire Transportation Co., 185, 191; fight with, 190
England, 246
Equitable Petroleum Company, 209
Erie, Pa., 95, 106, 127, 144
Erie Railroad, 129, 154, 185, 191, 218
Erie Street Baptist Church, 51, 90, 101, 110
Euclid Avenue Baptist Church, 51, 184, 233, 270, 338, 419
Europe, 247
Evans, James, 86, 87
Evarts, Choate and Beaman, 290

Everest, Hiram B., 273, 274
Everest, Charles M., 273, 274

Factories, attacks on, 26
Ferris, Col. A. C., 78, 86
Field, Marshall, 304
Fillmore, Millard, 38
Finger Lakes, 32, 35
Fires, 40, 123, 214
Fitch, John, 461
Flagler, Henry M., 102, 124, 125, 134, 144, 145, 147, 151, 152, 160, 165, 171, 175, 187, 217, 236, 238, 278, 285, 317, 336, 453
Fletcher, R. D., 83, 88
Flexner, Dr. Simon, 378
Folk, Joseph, 412
Folsom's, B. S., Commercial College, 59
Foraker, Joseph B., 286, 355, 435
Forest Hill, 269, 366
Forman, George V., 178
Franklin Lubricating Oil, 87
Franklin, Pa., 86, 87, 93, 120, 121, 127, 153, 167
French Creek, 86
Frenzied Finance, 344
Frick, Henry C., 432

Garfield, James A., 254
Garfield, James R., 381, 415
Gardiner, John J., 371
Gas, 21
Gasoline, 128
Gates, Frederick Taylor, 303, 309, 310, 311, 313, 315, 326, 337, 379, 383, 443, 454
Gates, John W., 345
George, Henry, "Progress and Poverty," 279, 327
Germany, 246
Gessner, Dr. Abraham, 37
Girard, Stephen, 29
Girty, George W., 217, 316
Gladden, Rev. Washington, 391, 392
God's Gold, 306, 394
Gold, discovery of, 37
Gould, Jay, 62, 102, 129, 154, 191, 206
Government and Business. See Regulation
Graft in business, 407

Grand Jury of Erie County, 274
Green, Hetty, 33
Greene, Jerome D., 454
Grosscup, Judge, 432
Grosvenor, General, 358
Gunton, Prof. George, 329

Hadley, Herbert, 412
Hale, Edward Everett, 327
Handy, Truman P., 69, 158
Hanna, Baslington & Co., 145, 159
Hanna, Mark, 51, 62, 145, 173, 254, 269, 300, 301, 352, 358, 359, 375, 380, 382
Harkness, Stephen V., 134, 139, 173, 336
Harlan, Justice, 445
Harley, Henry, 122, 191
Harper, Dr. William R., 303, 309, 310
Harriman, E. H., 5, 63
Harrison, Benjamin, 297, 318
Hartranft, Gov., 215
Hasson, Capt. William, 181, 182
Hathaway, E. T., 317
Haupt, General, 208, 209
Havemeyers, 62, 278
Hayes, Rutherford B., 279
Haymarket Riot, 280
Hearst, William Randolph, 286
Henry's Bend, 95
Hepburn, Alonzo Barton, 218, 220
Hepburn Committee, 218, 220, 265
Hereford, Frank, 206
Hewett family, 32
Hewett, Frederick, 45
Hewitt, Isaac L., 63, 159, 161
Hewitt & Tuttle, 360
Hiawatha Island, 40
Heye, Gust., 265
Hill, James J., 63
Hoar, William, 256, 286
Holbrook, Z. Swift, 309
Holding companies, 27, 138
Holmden, Thomas, 117, 118
Hopkins, James H., 205
Hopkins, Mark, 4
Hopkins, Robert E., 192, 208, 210
Hoster, William, 201
Hostetter, Dr. David, 192, 197
House of Rothschild, 33
Hoyt, Governor, 222

Humistan family, 54
Humphreys, M. H., 287
Hunter's Point, L. I., 37, 184
Huntington, Collis P., 4, 62
Huntington, John, 161
Hussy, John G., 75, 85, 88, 89

Independent, 306
"Immediate Shipment" order, 213
Individualism, 23
Industrial Commission, 262, 369
Industry, Competition in, 126; early organization, 24; factory beginnings, 24; growing unrest in, 279; in 1843, 21; in the '80's, 278; integration in, 126; in 1862, 108; textile mills, 26; welfare in, 28
Interstate Commerce Bill, 222
Interstate Commerce Commission, 280; Cullom bill, 281; defeated by Standard Oil, 207; Elkins bill, 416; first commission, 281; fought by Standard Oil, 206, 282; Grange demands, 281; hampered by courts, 282; history, 205; Hopkins bill, 205; Law passed, 281; origin, 205; Rockefeller's attack on, 222
Investigations, first congressional, 175; Hepburn, 218; New York legislature, 1880, 218; New York Senate Investigating, 1888, 282

Jay Cooke & Co. fails, 183
Jenks, Jeremiah K., 370
Jennings, O. B., 139, 158
Jesse Hoyt & Co., 220
Johnson, Horace Maxwell, 409
"Joshua, A Man of the Finger Lakes," 39
Journal of Political Economy, 307

Karns, S. D., 265
Kean, John, 360
Kellogg, Frank B., 433, 437
Kendrick, Burton J., 389
Kerosene. See Petroleum
Kerr Hill, Pa., 85
Kier, Samuel, 55, 57, 77, 85, 112, 187
Kijkuit. See Pocantico Hills
Kirkpatrick, William, 84
Kline, Virgil, 300, 301

INDEX

Knott, J. Proctor, 201
Knox, Philander C., 360, 432
Kyle, Senator, 371

Ladenburgh, Thalman & Co., 317, 339
La Follette, Robert, 3, 360, 406
Laissez-faire, 23, 108
Lake Erie Railroad, 265
Lake Owasco, 32, 33, 35
Lake Shore & Michigan Railroad, 128, 145, 153, 154
La Monte family, 40, 43
La Monte, Susan, 43
Lamps. See Lighting
Landis, Judge Kenesaw Mountain, 425
Laughlin, Dr. J. Laurence, 307, 309
Laura Spelman Rockefeller Memorial Foundation, 474
Lawrence, Amos and Abbott, 29
Lawson, Thomas W., 345; "Frenzied Finance," 348, 389
Leases, oil. See Petroleum
Lee, Ivy, 460, 467, 483
Lennox, James B., 29
Lewis, Aaron R., 11
Lighting, whale oil, candle, 21
Little, Jacob, 29
Little & Merrick's Well, 103
Lincoln, Abraham, 98, 100, 102; assassination, 120
Liquor. See Prohibition
Livingston, John, 205
Lockhart, Charles, 153, 162, 187, 189, 217
Logan & Frew, 153, 162
Louisville, Ky., 241
Lowry, Fawcett & Co., 106
Lloyd, Henry Demarest, 253, 329; "Wealth Against Commonwealth," 327, 386
Lubricating oil, 87

MacArthur, Dr. R. S., 303
Macksburg, Ohio, 257
Mahoning & French Creek R. R., 112
Manhattan Oil Company, 409
Martin, Col. Zebulun, 140
Mason, John, 29
Matthews, Charles B., 274
McAllister, Ward, 280
McCandless, William, attack on, 215
McClellan, George B., 154

McClintock, Hamilton, 87
McClintock, Widow, 86, 88, 112
McGregor, Ambrose, 273
McKelvey, David, 192, 208
McKinley, William, 62, 352; assassination, 375
McLaurin, John W., 360
Meade, G. L., 37
Meadville, Pa., 85, 93
Mergers, 27
Merritts (Alfred & Leonidas), attack on Rockefeller, 313, 314
Michigan Hill, 6, 8, 13
Miller, Albert, 274
Miller's Farm, 119, 122
Miller, William Henry Harrison, 297
Millionaires, 29, 30
Mills, Rev. B. Fay, 328
Money Trust, 346
Monnett, Francis S., 293, 337, 341, 342, 435
Monopoly, 153; early agitation, 23, 26; historic hatred of, 143; in oil—advanced by marketing, 243; kinds of, 182; oil mergers, 188; of producers, 150; of salt, 152; political issue, 281
Montaigne, Buffington, 40
Moravia, N. Y., 31, 35, 38
Morgan, J. P., 5, 63, 102, 326, 350, 380, 383, 394, 429, 449
Morgan, Senator, 286, 298
Morris, Gouverneur, 29
Muckrakers, 385
Murphy, Michael, 324
Murphy, Starr J., 251

Naphtha, 128
Nash, George K., 261
National City Bank, 290, 345
National Refiners' Assn., 178
National Transit Company, 230
Nebraska, attack on Standard Oil in, 365
Nesbit, G. H., 210
New Connecticut, 49
New Jersey Central Railroad, 227
New York, 106, 127, 135, 144, 155, 218
New York Central Railroad, 128, 129, 184, 218
New York *Herald*, 182, 223

INDEX

New York *Sun*, 223
New York *Tribune*, 189, 209, 210, 214, 223
New York *World*, 200, 300
Nobel Brothers, 246, 362
North American Gas Light Co., 37
Northern Pacific Railroad, 327; scandal, 183
Northern Securities Company, 380, 382
Northwestern Ohio Gas Co., 292

"Octopus," origin of term, 165
O'Day, Daniel, 168, 192, 198, 217, 238, 260, 261
Ogden, Robert C., 385
Ohlen, H. C., 266, 267
Oil. *See* Petroleum
Oil cities, contest of, 127
Oil City, 86, 87, 93, 94, 98, 120, 121, 127, 165, 272
Oil City *Derrick*, 111, 164, 165, 169, 172, 177, 208, 211, 272
Oil City *Register*, 122
Oil City Trust Co., 178
Oil Creek, 22, 76, 85, 86
Oil Men's League, 167
Oil Regions, Competition in, 128; Description of, 149, 179; division in, 210; feared by Rockefeller, 176; natural advantages, 128; over-production, 147; producers in, 149, 179; refiners' battles, 128; revival war, 320; war on Cleveland, 151; war weary, 224
Olney, Richard, 299, 318
Orient, markets of, 246, 247
Orr, Alexander E., 301
Over-production, 181, 212, 214; rise of, 144; speculation in whiskey, 277
Owego Academy, 44, 48
Owego, N. Y., 17, 40

Page, Walter H., 384
Parker, Alton B., 383
Parker's Landing, 186
Parsons, R. C., 175
Patterson, E. G., 207, 228, 285
Payne, Henry B., 157, 206, 222, 255, 281
Payne, Oliver H., 157, 161, 173, 187, 206, 207, 255, 281, 429
Pease, Phineas, 260

Pennsylvania Company, 138
Pennsylvania Oil Regions. *See* Oil Regions
Pennsylvania Railroad, 128, 129, 154, 191, 195, 196, 263
Pennsylvania Rock Oil Company, 77, 80
Pennsylvania Transportation Co., 122, 191
Penrose, Boise, 360, 372
Perkins, Thomas H., 29
Petroleum, at Tarentum, 57; barrels, 84; by-products of, 240; Bissell's plan, 75, 80; boom oil towns, 118; carbon oil, 78; competition, 127, 128; Cuba, N. Y.—discovery of Daillon, 55; Cuba spring, 77; Disorder in industry, 125; Drake's drill, 81; Drake hits oil, 75; early markets, 95; exports, 126; first oil man, 22; first prices, 85; first royalty lease, 84; foreign trade, 253; gasoline, 253; Gessner lamp, 37; in Kansas, 407; in Mexico, 362; in Ohio, 260; in Russia, 245; in Virginia, 55; kerosene, 245; Kier's American Oil, 55, 56, 79; Kier's lamp, 78; leases, 86; lubricating oil, 87; Macksburg field, 260; oil found, Aug. 21, 1859, 83; over-production, 144, 173; Parliament of, 208; prices, 106; Prof. Silliman distills oil, 77; refining centers, 127; schemes to raise prices, 181; Seneca oil, 77; stopping drill, 181; used as medicine, 55; world-wide development, 361
Petroleum Center, Pa., 119, 176
Philadelphia, Pa., 106, 127, 135, 144, 155
Philanthropy, 230, 234; Baptist Union Theological Seminary, 270; criticizes, 338; Education Board started, 384; estimate, 476; Foundation approval and criticism, 451; Foundation bill to incorporate, 443; Foundation gets $100,000,000, 452; Foundation incorporated in New York, 452; Foundation and General Education Board, further gifts, 473; Gates joins Rockefeller, 303; General Education Board gets $32,000,000, 424; influence of, 337; Medical In-

INDEX

stitute founded, 378; merging boards, 474; personal charities, 270; Rockefeller's first gift, 64; stream of gifts, 385, 443; to Alta Rockefeller Day Nursery, 270; to colleges, 337; to Dr. Duncan, 270; total gifts, 475; University of Chicago. *See* Chicago, University of; value of, 479; war gifts, 466
Phillips, David Graham, 389
Phillips, Thomas W., 320, 369
Pierce, Henry Clay, 240, 242, 317, 424
Pillsbury, George A., 303
Pioneer Oil Company, 235
Pipe Lines, battle with railroads, 325; combination in, 191; crushing Tidewater, 224, 228, 229; David Hostetter, 192; Equitable Pipe Line, 220; free pipe line bill, 169, 208; Henry Harley, 122, 190; history of, 191; immediate shipment order, 213; in Bradford, 212; Independents' plan, 208; Kansas laws, 408; lines to sea, 225; new pipe line war, 322; origin of, 122; Pennsylvania Transportation Co., 122; railroad control of, 191; rate agreements, 223; Samuel Van Syckel, 122, 190; Standard Oil enters, 192; teamsters attack, 191; Tidewater Pipe Line, 220, 222; formation of, 210; United Pipe Line Co., 178, 248; United States Pipe Line Co., 322; Vandergrift's Star Pipe Line, 177
Pithole, Pa., 117, 118, 119, 120, 121, 123, 124, 177, 211
Pittsburgh, Pa., 85, 106, 127, 135, 144, 155, 189
Platt, Tom, 45
Pocantico Hills, 366
Politics, corruption in, 407; Garfield approaches Rockefeller, 254; Rockefeller's first action in, 175; Standard Oil contributions, 355, 383
Potter, Dr. Daniel, 339
Potts, Col. Joseph D., 185, 191, 193, 285
Pouch, E. J., 237
Pratt's Astral Oil, 247
Pratt, Charles, 177, 178, 187, 214, 335, 336
Pratt Manufacturing Co., 302

Prentice, E. Parmalee, 332
Prices, 482; first, 85, 106; fixing, 182; price-cutting, 244; schemes to raise, 181; slump in, 184; slump of 1879, 211;
Producers. *See* Oil Regions
Producers Oil Company, 322
Producers' Protective Association, 168, 181, 208, 210, 215, 217, 223, 320, 321, 324
Producers and Refiners Co., 322, 323
Producers' Union, 207, 210, 224
Profits, 331
Prohibition, 133, 184; liquor in Richford, 17; Rockefeller's contributions, 312; Rockefeller family and, 30; Washington Society, 38
Publicity and advertising, 484; Boyle's rôle in, 292; bribing reporters, 200; buying Ohio papers, 293; buying papers, 200; changing standards, 483; dependency of press, 297; early uses, 200; favorable, 306, 466; final achievements of, 483; financing Boyle, 271; friendly articles appear, 442; George Harvey, 441; Gunton's defenses, 329, 441; ignored by Rockefeller, 200, 220; in Ohio, 292; Ivy Lee employed, 460, 467; Ivy Lee's work, 473; Jennings Publishing Co., 293, 297; Moses and Aaron, 200; publicity man employed by Standard Oil, 442; purchase of *Derrick*, 271; United States Bank, 201; used by Jay Cooke, 200
Pulitzer, Joseph, 378
Pullman, George, 63
Pure Oil Company, 323, 369

Quay, Matthew S., 355, 382

Railroads, abuses, 205; Allegheny Valley R. R., 128; Andrew Carnegie on rates, 263; blocks inquiry, 218; early rates, 25; enter oil regions, 111; Erie Railroad, 128; Elkins Rate bill, 381; expansion of, 278; favors cities, 129, 130, 135; fought by canals, 263; Hepburn Rate bill, 405; in oil regions, 128; in South Improvement Co., 154; Lake Shore and Michigan R. R., 129; New York

INDEX

Central R. R., 128; Oil Creek R. R., 128; origin of rates, 263; Pennsylvania R. R., 128; rate discriminations, 211, 220; rate wars, 195; rebates. *See* Rebates; regulation of, 281; spread of, by 1860, 109; Standard Oil control of, 347; traffic agreement, 155, 230; uses of passes, 205; war on independent pipe lines, 325

Rapallo, Edward S., 260

Rebates, amount paid, 262; become known, 145; defense of, 265; derivation, 263; denounced by Judge Baxter, 260; discriminations, 185; enjoyed by others, 265; explained by Rockefeller, 261; George Rice's charges, 258; in Macksburg, 260; not only reason for Rockefeller's success, 262; origin of, 263; Rockefeller agrees to abandon, 223; reasons for, 146; Rockefeller defends, 136; Rockefeller first, 135, 137; Rockefeller gets another, 198; wide use of, 220

Refiners, 128

Regions. *See* Oil Regions

Regulation, 205; public interest in business, 221; Hanna organizes business, 254

Religion, 42; church criticism of Rockefeller, 296; church praises Rockefeller, 305; church support of Rockefeller, 296, 305, 338; Erie Street church, 110; God's gold, 312, 394; in Richford, 20; ministers seeking gifts, 339; Rockefeller as Sunday School Superintendent, 332; Rockefeller becomes trustee in church, 73; Rockefeller joins Baptist Church, 51

Republic Oil Co., 411

Reynolds, Devoe and Pratt, 177

Rice, George, 257, 285, 316, 341

Rich, Chauncey, 7, 19, 30

Richford, N. Y., 7, 13, 16, 17, 108

Rich men in war, 129

Rickerts, Widow, 123

Rochester, N. Y., 218

Rockefeller, Alta, 147, 332, 417

Rockefeller and Andrews, 125, 133

Rockefeller, Edith, 232

Rockefeller, Eliza Davison, 19, 20, 21, 30, 31, 34, 35, 36, 40, 42, 47, 48, 72, 133, 236, 295; courtship of, 14; death, 296; liquor and, 17; marriage, 15

Rockefeller Family Association, 10

Rockefeller, Flagler and Andrews, 135, 137, 139

Rockefeller Foundation. *See* Philanthropy

Rockefeller, Francis, 34, 36

Rockefeller, Frank, 34, 35, 92, 101, 133, 136, 140, 160, 207, 235, 362, 377, 378

Rockefeller, Godfrey, 6, 8, 10, 13, 15

Rockefeller Institute of Medical Research, 379, 479; hookworm disease, 452

Rockefeller, Jacob, 30

Rockefeller, John D., ancestry, 9; accused of lying, 248, 250; attacked by Lloyd, 328; attacks by Rice, 257; as witness, 283, 285, 342, 414; attacked by Frank Rockefeller, 207; appearance, 283, 294; attacks on, 294; attacks Rice, 341; attention to details, 239; Backus attack, 202; battle with neighbors, 469; battle with Empire Transportation Co., 193; becomes wholesaler, 68; birth, 6; birth of son, 186; bookkeeper, 63, 174; borrower, 69, 70, 92, 133, 174; boycotted, 321; boyhood ambition, 46; boyhood in Moravia, 35; boyhood in Owego, 40, 46; boyhood in Richford, 20, 30; builds home, 72; buys out partner, 115, 116; buys Pocantico estate, 331; captures all pipe lines, 197; career, estimate of, 481; change in public opinion of, 466; character, 392; church appearances, 419; children, 234; conciliating opinion, 439; contempt proceedings in Ohio, 341; controls terminals, 185; combination of brains, 139, 177; condemns Ida Tarbell, 389; Corrigan case, 363; courtship, 110; court attacks on, 216; criticism of, 218; criticizes Rickford, 31; crushes Empire Transportation Co., 194; daughter married, 332; decides not to go into oil, 98; defends

INDEX

rebates, 136; defends Standard Oil, 393; denies having billion dollars, 424; denies coercion, 161; demanded exclusive rates, 266; description of, 131; developing estate, 467; dodging summons, 282, 412; early poverty, 45; earnings, 331; education, 44; enters oil business, 105; Euclid Ave. Baptist Church, 130; expanding pipe lines, 212; explains rebates, 261; examines Drake discovery, 93; father's favorite, 33; freight advantages, 185; first action in politics, 175; first job, 60, 61; first salary, 67; first sees oil, 89; first trip abroad, 417; fights Tidewater, 228, 229; Flagler, 147; becomes partner, 134; followed by crowds, 419; forms Standard Oil Co., 138; fortune, size of, 330, 427, 476; freight discriminations, 230; Garfield approaches, 254; gasoline, 253; Gates heads staff, 309; Girty, Mrs., charges by, 316; goes into oil production, 321; golf, 377, 437, 450, 451, 486; habits, 90, 288, 485; hated by producers, 181; health impaired, 273; his version of Standard Oil Co., 162; homes burned, 40; homes, Forest Hill, 4 West 54th St., 232; illness, 294, 310, 325, 332, 385, 413, 421; in Central High School, 51, 52; in Civil War, 98, 101, 102; indicted in Pennsylvania, 217; indictments withdrawn, 223; investigated, 282; investments, 290, 291, 292, 327, 347, 449; indicted in Texas, 317; invades England, 361; indicted in Ohio, 417; job, day, 60; joins Baptist church, 51; Landis fine, 426, reversed, 432; launches General Education Board, 384; laying out roads, 269; Ledger A, 64; Lloyd's denunciation of, 328; loans from father, 68; loses hair, 385; luck, 195; marriage, 114, 115; meets Gates, 303; meets John D. Archbold, 162; meets Artemas Ward, 67; memory, 173; Merritt charges, 313; moderate mode of living, 232, 235, 280; money trust, 346; monopoly complete, 198; moves to Cleveland, 50; moves to Moravia, 31; Nebraska suit, 365; on Black List, 165; organizer, 239; organizing foreign markets, 246; organizes marketing, 242; organizes oil business, 126; over-production. *See* Over-production; Owego Academy, 44; perfects combination, 188; personal loans, 326; philanthropy. *See* Philanthropy; philosophy of business, 221; philosophy of giving, 306; planning, 130, 148; plans monopoly in Cleveland, 143; praises wife, 463; pressure on rivals, 204; proposes refiners' association, 176; raises turkeys, 34; reading, 332; Refiners' Association collapses, 178; religion, 20, 42, 65, 90, 132, 173, 199, 389, 443; reporters, fear of, 420; relinquishes wealth to son, 474; requisition for, refused, 217; retirement, 332, 337; Rice attacks, 316; Roosevelt attacks, 381, 407; schooling, 43; sentimental, 232; sets up pension system, 393; skating, 234, 269; social life, 234; son's marriage, 377; South Improvement Co. *See* South Improvement Co.; Strongville home, 50; success not due wholly to rebate, 262; supreme in oil business, 230; supremacy challenged by Dutch, 362; Sunday school, 52; Sunday school superintendent, 233; swiftness in action, 156; Taft announces for, 436, 449; tax fights, 227, in Cleveland, 453; tainted money, 390; trustee in church, saves church, 73; views on combination, 374; views on criticism, 272, 417; views on giving, 271; views on money, 201; views on great war, 465; views on newspapers, 418; views on Roosevelt, 423; views on wealth, 414; visits Titusville, 175; war on competition, 221; war contributions, 466; war on pipe lines, 225; war on rivals, 244, 258, 259; wife dies, 462; wins Archbold, 176; writes book, 442

Rockefeller, John D., Jr., 186, 218, 234, 235, 332, 337, 351, 359, 377, 413, 417, 449, 454, 459, 462, 464

518 INDEX

Rockefeller, Laura Celestia Spelman, 52, 110, 111, 132; death, 462
Rockefeller, Lucy Avery, 12, 13
Rockefeller, Lucy, 92, 101
Rockefeller, Mary Ann, 92
Rockefeller, William Avery, arrival in Richford, 8; as a farmer, 33; birth, 10; builds school, 32; book about, 38; "botanic physician," 67; courtship, 14; disappears, 235; leaving Cleveland, 92; lends money to son, 68; leaves Owego, 47; leaves Moravia, 38; horse-stealing incident, 35; indicted, 38; marriage, 15, 17, 19; moves to Moravia, 31; medicine selling, 32; moves to Owego, 47; moves to Cleveland, 50, 66; moves to Parma, Ohio, 59; prosperous, 72; reappears, 295; reward for finding, 378; story of death, 438; teetotaler, 37
Rockefeller, William, 19, 35, 101, 126, 133, 135, 140, 187, 217, 228, 235, 237, 238, 344, 345, 371, 383, 389
Rogers, George D., 295
Rogers, Henry H., 102, 141, 167, 169, 178, 187, 193, 219, 222, 230, 238, 248, 273, 334, 344, 361, 387, 412, 437
Roosevelt, Theodore, 3, 253, 376, 380, 381, 382, 385, 407, 421, 433
Root, Elihu, 299
Rosekrans family, 32
Rosekrans, Joshua, 39
Rothschilds, 29
Rouse, Mr., 103
Rouseville, Pa., 103
Royalty owners, 86
Rudd, G. M., 269
Russell, Charles Edward, 253
Russia, oil in, 246; Royal Dutch Shell, 362

Sabin, John, 35
Sage, Russell, 4, 34
Saginaw Salt Co., 152
Salt Monopoly, 152
Saratoga, N. Y., 218
Sargent, John Singer, 3
Schermerhorn, Peter, 29
Scheide, W. T., 265
Scofield, Alexander, 107
Scofield, Schurmer and Teagle, 160
Scott, Nathan B., 360
Scott, Tom, 62, 129, 152, 154, 169, 192, 193, 194, 200, 206, 263
Sears, David, 29
Second Baptist Church, 233
Selden, George B., invents automobiles, 252
Seneca Oil Co., 82, 85
Shaw, Dr. Albert, 375
Shaw, Robert G., 29
Shell, W. P., 227
Sherman anti-trust law. See Trusts
Sherman, John, 62, 286
Sherman, Roger, 222
Shipping subsidies, 359, 380
Sibley, Joseph, 353, 354, 358, 367
Silliman, Prof. Benjamin, 77, 80, 117
Sked, Deason Alexander, 51, 90
Smith, Adam, 23, 107
Smith, Rev. J. Hyatt, 51
Smith, Sam, 83
Smith, Uncle Billy, 83, 89, 141
Smythe, Atty.-Gen., 365
Smythe, Dr. William, 44
Southern Improvement Co., 250
South Improvement Co., 251, 267; and Rockefeller, 148; black list, 165; defeated, 170; investigated, 175; fight against, 165; oath, 154; organized, 155; origin of, 148, 151; plan for, 153; revival of, feared, 189; scheme disclosed, 163
Spies, 156
Spooner, John W., 360
Standard Oil Company, 248; absorbs rivals, 188; at 26 Broadway, 270; adopts holding company, 343; abandons Cleveland, 331; buys into Waters-Pierce Co., 242; buying into rivals, 324; becomes a trust, 251; bribery charges, 343; Cleveland office, 164; Chess, Carley & Co., 241; crushing retailers, 411; distribution system, 241; dissolution suit, 422, 437; dissolution suit appealed, 442; dissolved, 1911, 438; earnings, 331; employee stock ownership, 244; export trade, 245, 361; fight Interstate Commerce Commission, 206; fined $29,000,000, 425; fate of, 484; form of organization, 249; gas

INDEX

interests, 292; gets pipe lines, 192; group of interests, 347; indicted, 421; in politics, 175; investigated by N. Y. Senate, 284; investigated by Congress, 285; increases stock, 158; integration, 239; kerosene markets, 245; Kansas attack, 408; luncheon conferences, origin of, 237; liquidating holding company, 447; methods and organization, 238; meaning of term, 250, 337; organized, 138; origin of name, 139; political contributions, 383; reorganized, 1874, 188; reorganizing, 302; Standard Oil gang, 291; size in 1870, 236; size in 1880, 237; takes Pittsburgh refiners, 189; takes Region refiners, 190; takes New York refiners, 190; trust dissolved in Ohio, 299; Supreme Court confirms dissolution, 444; Waters-Pierce fined $1,623,000, 425; indictment, 317
Standard Oil Company of New Jersey, 252
Standard Oil Company of New York, 252
Standard Oil Gang, 344
Standard White, 247
Stanford, Leland, 4
Stanley Committee, 313
Steele, John. See Coal Oil Johnny
Steffens, Lincoln, 389
Sterne, Simon, 219
Stewart, Robert W., 425
Stillman, James, 290, 326, 344, 347, 389
Stone, Amasa, 135, 158
Stone & Fleming, 302
Strongville, Ohio, 50, 53
Stuyvesant, Peter G., 29
Summit City, 211
Sutter, Gen. Johann August, 37

Tabernacle Baptist Church, 339
Tainted money, 390
Tank cars, 136
Tarbell, F. S., 169
Tarbell, Ida M., 40, 132, 212, 213, 277, 336, 387
Tarrytown, N. Y., 331, 462
Taxes, 227
Taylor, H. L., 321

Taylor-Satterfield, 229
Teamsters, 95, 112, 119, 150, 190
Tennessee Coal and Iron Co., 429, 430
Thomas, Gen. Thomas, 278
Thompson, J. Edgar, 129, 137
Tidewater Pipe Line Co., 210, 219, 220, 222, 224, 228, 229
Tidioute, 86, 93, 95, 169
Titusville, Pa., 76, 81, 85, 88, 93, 98, 103, 113, 120, 121, 127, 141, 162, 165, 175, 176, 190, 387
Toledo, Ohio, gas war, 292
Trans-Missouri Freight Association, 298
Tracy, Ben, 45
Trusts, butcher, 278; cotton seed, 278; court decisions on, 298, 318, 405; Dodd invents idea, 251; Distillers and Cattle Feeders' case, 298; forerunner of, 250; first trust and trustees, 251; glass, 278; growth of, 380; Harrison ignores, 298; investigation by Congress, 285; in politics, 383; New York Senate investigation of 1888, 284; National Cash Register case, 298; origin of, 248; pools, 277; rise of, 278; Roosevelt attacks, 428; rule of reason, 445; Standard Oil Trust, suit to dissolve, 422, dissolution decree appealed, 442, Supreme Court dissolves, 444, bared, 284, held illegal, 299, 301, contempt case, 341; Sherman law, 297, 318, 445; authorship of, 286, 287, passed, 286; tobacco, 278; Trans-Missouri Freight Association case, 298
Twain, Mark, 335
Tyrell, Rev. F. C., 338

United Oil Company, 321
United Pipe Lines, 213, 219, 248, 250
United States Bank, 201
United States Bureau of Corporations, 381, 415
United States Department of Commerce, 381; United States Pipe Line Co., 322, 323, 324
United States Senate, 359, 363
United States Steel Corporation, 349, 352
Utica, New York, 218

INDEX

Vacuum Oil Company, 272; indictments, 274
Vail, Theodore N., 62
Vanderbilt, Cornelius, 129, 168, 194, 220
Vandergrift, J. J., 167, 175, 177, 187, 191, 217, 222, 238
Van Rennselaer, Stephen, 29
Van Syckel, Samuel, 122
Vilas, Chester & Keith Trust, 250, 251
Vincent, Dr. George, 473

Walworth Run, 105
Wanamaker, John, 102
Warden, W. G., 151, 153, 162, 165, 187, 217
Washington Society, 38
Water power, 25
Waters-Pierce Oil Co., 242, 257, 367, 412

Watson, David K., 299, 300
Watson, Jonathan, 84, 86, 88, 89
Watson, Louis F., 207
Watson, Peter H., 151, 153, 154, 159, 165, 167, 169
Wayne, H., 176
Webster, Joe, 53
Weehawken (N. J.) terminal, 185
Welborn, J. F., 454
Welch, Dr. William H., 378
Western Reserve, 49
Whale oil, 37
White, Chief Justice, 444
Wilkerson & Company, 259
Williamstown, 225
Wilson, J. Scott, 274
Wilson, Peter, 82
Witt, Stillman, 158, 174
Worthington, George, 45

DISCARDED

AUG 6 2025